# GREEK TRAGEDY AFTER THE FIFTH CENTURY

Did Greek tragedy die along with Euripides? This accessible survey demonstrates that this is far from being the case. In it, thirteen eminent specialists offer, for the first time in English, broad coverage of a little-studied but essential part of the history of Greek tragedy. The book contains in-depth discussions of all available textual evidence (including inscriptions and papyri), but also provides historical perspectives on every aspect of the post-fifth-century history of tragedy. Oft-neglected plays, such as *Rhesus*, *Alexandra*, and *Exagōgē* (the only surviving Biblical tragedy), are studied alongside such topics as the expansion of Greek tragedy beyond Athens, theatre performance, music and dance, society and politics, as well as the reception of Greek tragedy in the Second Sophistic and in Late Antiquity, and the importance of ancient scholarship in the transmission of Greek tragic texts.

VAYOS LIAPIS is Professor of Ancient Theatre and Its Reception at the Open University of Cyprus. His latest book is *A Commentary on the Rhesus Attributed to Euripides* (2012). He is currently coediting *Adapting Greek Tragedy* for Cambridge University Press and writing a new commentary on Aeschylus' *Seven against Thebes*.

ANTONIS K. PETRIDES is Associate Professor of Classics at the Open University of Cyprus. He is the author of *Menander, New Comedy and the Visual* (Cambridge, 2014) and the coeditor of *New Perspectives on Post-Classical Comedy* (2010). He is currently preparing a new critical edition and commentary on Menander's *Dyskolos*.

# GREEK TRAGEDY AFTER THE FIFTH CENTURY

*A Survey from ca. 400 BC to ca. AD 400*

EDITED BY

## VAYOS LIAPIS
Open University of Cyprus

## ANTONIS K. PETRIDES
Open University of Cyprus

CAMBRIDGE
UNIVERSITY PRESS

# CAMBRIDGE
## UNIVERSITY PRESS

University Printing House, Cambridge CB2 8BS, United Kingdom

One Liberty Plaza, 20th Floor, New York, NY 10006, USA

477 Williamstown Road, Port Melbourne, VIC 3207, Australia

314–321, 3rd Floor, Plot 3, Splendor Forum, Jasola District Centre, New Delhi – 110025, India

79 Anson Road, #06–04/06, Singapore 079906

Cambridge University Press is part of the University of Cambridge.

It furthers the University's mission by disseminating knowledge in the pursuit of education, learning, and research at the highest international levels of excellence.

www.cambridge.org
Information on this title: www.cambridge.org/9781107038554
DOI: 10.1017/9781139833936

© Cambridge University Press 2019

This publication is in copyright. Subject to statutory exception and to the provisions of relevant collective licensing agreements, no reproduction of any part may take place without the written permission of Cambridge University Press.

First published 2019

Printed and bound in Great Britain by Clays Ltd, Elcograf S.p.A.

*A catalogue record for this publication is available from the British Library.*

*Library of Congress Cataloging-in-Publication Data*
NAMES: Liapes, Vaios, editor. | Petrides, Antonis K., editor.
TITLE: Greek tragedy after the fifth century : a survey from ca. 400 BC to ca. AD 400 / edited by Vayos Liapis, Antonis K. Petrides.
DESCRIPTION: Cambridge : Cambridge University Press, 2018.
IDENTIFIERS: LCCN 2018020100 | ISBN 9781107038554 (hardback)
SUBJECTS: LCSH: Greek drama (Tragedy)–History and criticism.
CLASSIFICATION: LCC PA3133 .G685 2018 | DDC 882/.0109–dc23
LC record available at https://lccn.loc.gov/2018020100

ISBN 978-1-107-03855-4 Hardback

Cambridge University Press has no responsibility for the persistence or accuracy of URLs for external or third-party internet websites referred to in this publication and does not guarantee that any content on such websites is, or will remain, accurate or appropriate.

# Contents

List of Figures and Tables     *page* vii
List of Contributors     viii
Preface     xi
List of Abbreviations     xii

Introduction     1
*Antonis K. Petrides*

PART I TEXTS     23

1. Greek Tragedy in the Fourth Century: The Fragments     25
*Vayos Liapis and Theodoros K. Stephanopoulos*

2. The *Rhesus*     66
*Almut Fries*

3. Hellenistic Tragedy and Satyr-Drama; Lycophron's *Alexandra*     90
*Simon Hornblower*

4. The *Exagōgē* of Ezekiel the Tragedian     125
*Pierluigi Lanfranchi*

PART II CONTEXTS AND DEVELOPMENTS     147

5. Beyond Athens: The Expansion of Greek Tragedy from the Fourth Century Onwards     149
*Brigitte Le Guen*

6. Theatre Performance After the Fifth Century     180
*Anne Duncan and Vayos Liapis*

7   Music and Dance in Tragedy After the Fifth Century          204
    *Mark Griffith*

8   The Fifth Century and After: (Dis)Continuities
    in Greek Tragedy                                              243
    *Francis Dunn*

9   Society and Politics in Post-Fifth-Century Tragedy           270
    *D. M. Carter*

PART III  RECEPTION AND TRANSMISSION                             295

10  Attitudes Towards Tragedy from the Second Sophistic
    to Late Antiquity                                             297
    *Ruth Webb*

11  Scholars and Scholarship on Tragedy                          324
    *Johanna Hanink*

*Bibliography*                                                    350
*Index Locorum*                                                   392
*General Index*                                                   403

*Figures and Tables*

Figure 1  Red-figure volute-krater attributed to the Darius Painter, ca. 340–330 BC. Princeton University Art Museum, Carl Otto von Kienbusch Jr., Memorial Collection Fund, y1983-13.   *page* 44
Table 1  Aegean and Ionian cities with Dionysia festivals featuring tragic contests.   159
Table 2  Cities in continental Greece and Asia Minor with Dionysia festivals featuring tragic contests.   161
Table 3  Cities with festivals (other than the Dionysia) featuring tragic contests.   162

# Contributors

DAVID CARTER is Associate Professor of Greek at the University of Reading. He is the author of *The Politics of Greek Tragedy* (2007) and editor of *Why Athens? A Reappraisal of Tragic Politics* (2011).

ANNE DUNCAN (BA Swarthmore College, PhD University of Pennsylvania) is Associate Professor, Department of Classics and Religious Studies, University of Nebraska-Lincoln. She specializes in ancient performance history and culture. She is the author of *Performance and Identity in the Classical World* (2006) and numerous articles on Greek and Roman drama and performance issues.

FRANCIS DUNN (BA and PhD Yale) is Professor of Classics at the University of California – Santa Barbara. His research specializes in Greek poetry, especially tragedy, and in fifth-century BC literature and culture. He is the author of three books: *Tragedy's End: Closure and Innovation in Euripidean Drama* (1996), *Present Shock in Late Fifth-century Greece* (2007), and a *Commentary on Sophocles' Electra* (forthcoming). He has also edited three volumes: *Beginnings in Classical Literature* (1992), with Thomas Cole; *Sophocles' Electra in Performance* (1996); and *Classical Closure: Reading the End in Greek and Latin Literature* (1997), with Deborah Roberts and Don Fowler.

ALMUT FRIES is Lecturer in Classics at The Queen's College, Oxford. She obtained her first degree from the University of Göttingen and her doctorate from the University of Oxford. She is the author of an edition, with introduction and commentary, of the pseudo-Euripidean *Rhesus* (2014) and of several articles on Greek epic, drama, Pindar, Indo-European comparative mythology and ancient and Byzantine metrical scholarship.

MARK GRIFFITH is Klio Distinguished Professor of Classical Literature at UC Berkeley, where he also holds an appointment in the Department of

Theater, Dance, and Performance Studies (TDPS). He received his BA (1968) and PhD (1973) from Cambridge University. He is the author of monographs on *The Authenticity of Prometheus Bound* (1977), *Aristophanes' Frogs* (2013), and *Greek Satyr Play: Five Studies* (2015), and has edited Aeschylus' *Prometheus Bound* and Sophocles' *Antigone* for the Cambridge Greek and Latin Classics series. He has written articles on Greek tragedy and satyr-play, Vergil, Hesiod, Greek lyric, mules, early Greek education, music, and performance, and is currently writing an ethnomusicological book on *Music and Difference in Ancient Greece*.

JOHANNA HANINK is Associate Professor of Classics at Brown University. She is author of *Lycurgan Athens and the Making of Classical Tragedy* (2014) and *The Classical Debt: Greek Antiquity in an Era of Austerity* (2017).

SIMON HORNBLOWER held teaching and research posts at Oxford and UCL until retirement in 2016. His *Lykophron* Alexandra: *Greek Text, Translation, Commentary and Introduction* (2015) was reprinted in corrected paperback in 2017. His monograph *Lykophron's* Alexandra, *Rome and the Hellenistic World* was published in 2018.

PIERLUIGI LANFRANCHI is Assistant Professor of Greek Literature at Aix-Marseille University (France). He is the author of *L'Exagoge d'Ezéchiel le tragique* (2006) and coeditor of *Jews and Christians in Antiquity: A Regional Perspective* (forthcoming).

BRIGITTE LE GUEN is Professor Emerita of Ancient Greek History at the University Paris 8. She has published numerous articles and edited several books on Greek theatre. She is the author of *Les Associations de Technites dionysiaques à la période hellénistique* (2001), and is currently preparing a synthesis on the history of the Greek Hellenistic theatre and an edition (with translations and commentaries) of the documentary evidence on Greek and Roman theatre audiences.

VAYOS LIAPIS is Professor of Ancient Theatre and Its Reception at the Open University of Cyprus. His latest book is *A Commentary on the Rhesus Attributed to Euripides* (2012). He is currently coediting *Adapting Greek Tragedy* for Cambridge University Press, and writing a commentary on Aeschylus' *Seven against Thebes*.

ANTONIS K. PETRIDES (BA University of Thessaloniki, MPhil and PhD Trinity College, Cambridge) is Assistant Professor of Classics at the Open University of Cyprus. He is the author of *Menander, New Comedy and the Visual* (2014) and the coeditor of *New Perspectives on*

*Post-Classical Comedy* (2010). He is currently preparing a new critical edition and commentary on Menander's *Dyskolos*.

THEODOROS K. STEPHANOPOULOS is Professor Emeritus (since 2016) at the Department of Theatre Studies, University of Patras. His research interests include forensic rhetoric and Greek tragedy. He has published several articles on tragic fragments (Euripides, minores, adespota). He has also translated, among other texts, a number of Greek forensic speeches and tragedies (published and performed on stage), most recently Euripides' *Medea* (2012).

RUTH WEBB is Professor of Greek at the University of Lille and a member of the research team UMR 8163 'Savoirs, Textes, Langage' (CNRS, University of Lille). She is the author of *Demons and Dancers: Performance in Late Antiquity* (2008) and *Ekphrasis, Imagination and Persuasion in Ancient Rhetorical Theory and Practice* (2009) as well as numerous articles on dance and on rhetoric, particularly the use of appeals to the imagination.

# Preface

Currently, there is no such thing as a single volume providing a thorough and scholarly, yet accessible survey of Greek tragedy after the fifth century. Despite some important recent studies in the field (e.g., Easterling 1997; Csapo 2010; Gildenhard and Revermann 2010; Csapo et al. 2014; Vahtikari 2014; Kotlińska-Tomà 2015; Hornblower 2015; Wright 2016), non-specialist readers still tend to disregard the fact that the genre continued to develop and even thrive in the fourth century and, in many cases, later. As a result, students and scholars interested in the evolution of Greek tragedy after the age of the three great tragedians have nowhere to turn for a comprehensive study discussing and analysing the most important aspects of this complex, variegated and often elusive phenomenon. We hope that this volume goes some of the way towards filling this bibliographic gap, and trust that it will be of interest to students and scholars in Classics, Theatre Studies, and related fields.

The origins of this volume go back to early 2012, when we decided we should channel our common interest in post-fifth-century Greek drama into coordinating a multi-authored work that would both provide comprehensive coverage on a relatively under-researched topic and stimulate further research on it. We were fortunate enough to ensure the collaboration of some of the most distinguished scholars working in this field today, and we wish to extend to all of them our heartfelt thanks. We also wish to thank Dr Michael Sharp, Commissioning Editor at Cambridge University Press, for his unflagging support, valuable advice, and constant interest and assistance. Last but not least, we are grateful to the Cambridge University Press's Syndics for approving this project, and to its anonymous readers for a number of perceptive and immensely helpful comments.

# Abbreviations

Names of ancient authors and works are abbreviated according to LSJ[9] or OCD[4].

| | |
|---|---|
| BNJ | I. Worthington, *Brill's New Jacoby*, online publication (2009). |
| CAH | *The Cambridge Ancient History*. 14 vols. (2nd edn., Cambridge University Press 1961–2005). |
| CID IV | F. Lefèvre, *Corpus des inscriptions de Delphes*. IV, *Documents amphictioniques*, with contributions by D. Laroche and O. Masson. (Paris 2002). |
| Coll. Alex. | J. U. Powell, *Collectanea Alexandrina* (Oxford 1925). |
| DFA[2] | A. W. Pickard-Cambridge, *The Dramatic Festivals of Athens*, 2nd edn. revised by J. Gould and D. M. Lewis (Oxford 1968, reissued with supplement 1988). |
| FGrHist | F. Jacoby, *Die Fragmente der griechischen Historiker* (Berlin 1923–58, reprinted electronically Leiden 2005). |
| FRHist | T. Cornell, *Fragments of the Roman Historians*, 3 vols. (Oxford 2013). |
| GLP | D. L. Page, *Greek Literary Papyri* (Loeb series, Cambridge, Mass. 1942). |
| GP | A. S. F. Gow and D. L. Page, *The Greek Anthology: The Garland of Philip and some contemporary epigrams*, 2 vols. (Cambridge University Press 1968). |
| HE | A. S. F. Gow and D. L. Page, *The Greek Anthology: Hellenistic Epigrams*, 2 vols. (Cambridge University Press 1965). |
| IACP | M. H. Hansen and T. H. Nielsen, *Inventory of Archaic and Classical Poleis* (Oxford 2004). |
| IG | *Inscriptiones Graecae*. |

| | |
|---|---|
| *IGUR* | L. Moretti, *Inscriptiones graecae urbis Romae*, 4 vols. in 5 parts (Rome 1968–90). |
| *I. Iasos* | W. Blümel, *Die Inschriften von Iasos*, 2 vols. (Bonn 1985). |
| *I. Lampsakos* | P. Frisch, *Die Inschriften von Lampsakos* (Bonn 1975). |
| *I. Oropos* | V. Petrakos, Οἱ ἐπιγραφὲς τοῦ Ὠρωποῦ (Athens 1997). |
| *I. Priene* | Fr. H. von Gaertringen, *Die Inschriften von Priene* (Berlin 1906). |
| *I. Samothrace* | P. M. Fraser, *Samothrace, the Inscriptions on Stone* (New York 1960). |
| *IIsolMil* | G. Manganaro, 'Le iscrizioni delle isole Milesie', *Annuario* 41–42 (n.s., 25–6) 1963–4: 293–349. |
| *IMT Kyz Kapu Dag* | M. Barth and J. Stauber, *Inschriften Mysia & Troas* (Munich 1996). |
| K.-A. | R. Kassel and C. F. L. Austin, *Poetae Comici Graeci*. 8 vols. (Berlin 1983–2001). |
| *LGPN* | P. M. Fraser et al., *A Lexicon of Greek Personal Names* (Oxford 1987) |
| *LIMC* | *Lexicon Iconographicum Mythologiae Classicae*, 8 vols. (Zurich and Munich 1981–99). |
| LSJ[9] | H. G. Liddell, R. Scott and H. S. Jones, *A Greek – English lexicon* (9th edn. Oxford 1940), with revised supplement ed. P. G. W. Glare (Oxford 1996). |
| Mertens-Pack[3] | CEDOPAL: Base de données expérimentale Mertens-Pack[3] en ligne (http://cipl93.philo.ulg.ac.be/Cedopal/MP3/dbsearch.aspx). |
| *Milet* I 3 | A. Rehm, *Das Delphinion in Milet* (Berlin 1914). |
| OCD[4] | S. Hornblower, A. Spawforth and E. Eidinow (eds.), *The Oxford Classical Dictionary* (4th edn. Oxford 2012). |
| *OGIS* | W. Dittenberger, *Orientis Graeci Inscriptiones Selectae* (Leipzig 1903–5). |
| *PCG* | R. Kassel and C. F. L. Austin, *Poetae Comici Graeci*, vols 1–8 (Berlin and New York 1983–2001). |
| Perinthos-Herakleia | M. H. Sayar, *Perinthos-Herakleia (Marmara Ereğlisi) und Umgebung: Geschichte, Testimonien, griechische und lateinische Inschriften* (Vienna 1998). |
| *PMG* | D. L. Page, *Poetae Melici Graeci* (Oxford 1962). |

| | |
|---|---|
| P. Oxy | *The Oxyrhynchus Papyri* (Oxford 1898). Now also published online, under the general editorship of N. Gonis, D. Obbink and P. J. Parsons (URL: www.papyrology.ox.ac.uk/POxy/). |
| R.-E. | G. Wissowa et al., *Paulys Realenzyklopädie der klassischen Altertumswissenschaft* (Stuttgart 1893–1980). |
| SEG | *Supplementum Epigraphicum Graecum* (Leiden 1923–). Now also published online under the direction of A. Chaniotis, T. Corsten, N. Papazarkadas and R. A. Tybout (URL: http://referenceworks.brillonline.com/browse/supplementum-epigraphicum-graecum). |
| SIG³ | W. Dittenberger, *Sylloge Inscriptionum Graecarum* (3rd edn. Leipzig 1915–24). |
| Suppl. Hell. | H. Lloyd-Jones and P. Parsons, *Supplementum Hellenisticum*, revised by H.-G. Nesselrath (Berlin 2011). |
| TrGF | B. Snell, S. Radt and R. Kannicht, *Tragicorum Graecorum Fragmenta* (Göttingen 1971–2004). |

# Introduction
## Antonis K. Petrides

### Postclassical Tragedy and the Theories of Decline

Aristophanes' *Frogs*, a comedy produced only months after Euripides' demise (405 BC), famously proclaims that tragedy died along with the great man. Euripides, Dionysus laments, is survived by incompetent youngsters, 'a thousand times more babbling' than him, but in essence good enough to piss once on the hallowed art and take their leave (*Ra.* 89–95). In Dionysus' opinion, the tragic genre could only have a future if Euripides was brought back from the dead.

Aristophanes' construction, to be sure, is laden with irony. Undoubtedly, the lines mentioned previously are 'a feeder for a joke', which has sometimes been taken too seriously.[1] The joke, however, is much more elaborate than a simple jibe at the likes of Iophon; it is integral to the comic poetics of *Frogs* – poetics of generic competition, that is, which aims, always in a humorous vein, to privilege comedy rather than to expostulate about the sorry state of current tragic plays.[2]

*Frogs* 'unexpectedly' ends up valorizing Aeschylus rather than Euripides; still, and this is crucial, the former's victory in the *agōn* ensues only *after* his own tragic mode has been debunked and every aesthetic principle discussed in the contest has been abandoned in favour of a hazy new criterion: Aeschylus prevails because he is presumed to be more beneficial to the polis. The paradox, of course, is crystal clear: how could Aeschylus' kind of tragedy possibly 'save the city' (*Ra.* 1501), if it has already been demystified as obsolete and out of touch with the common man, whom it is supposed to improve morally (*Ra.* 1502–3)?

---

[1] Csapo et al. 2014: 3. For the need to read the critical statements of comic playwrights ironically see Wright 2012.

[2] Sells 2012 makes a similar point regarding the generic poetics of *Frogs* examining the play's pararitual agenda.

In fact, the contest of *Frogs* evokes the first epirrhematic *agōn* of the *Clouds*. In the latter play, Worse Argument and Better Argument are mutually discredited as models of civic education – the former as cynical and immoral, the latter as admirable and reminiscent of better days, but still too archaic to suit modern society. In *Frogs*, Aeschylus and Euripides, two extremes in their own right, cancel each other out to the benefit of an implied middle option. This middle option is not Sophocles, as Aristotle would later suggest; 'serious' drama is dismissed *tout court;* Aristophanes' comedy, and nothing else, emerges as the real *didaskalos* of the body politic. In *Frogs*, as elsewhere, Aristophanes is not deploring the supposed decline of tragedy so much as celebrating yet another triumph of comedy in the contest of genres.[3] After all, in the scales of Aristophanes, tragedy had always been found wanting.

Be that as it may, the *Frogs* discourse was viewed both in ancient and in modern times as a legitimate encapsulation of the history of tragedy after the fifth century – namely, as the first piece of evidence attesting to the formulation of a tragic canon, which distinguished the three great poets of the fifth century (Aeschylus, Sophocles, Euripides) from their lesser contemporaries and degenerate descendants.[4] Nietzsche, too, in *The Birth of Tragedy* (1872), to name but one notable modern case, sides unequivocally with Aristophanes' perceived judgment, speaking of 'wicked Euripides', whose 'sophistical dialectic' killed the spirit of tragedy, and thus he was ultimately deserted by Dionysus.[5] As Csapo et al. note (2014: 1–3), the ultimate modern origin of Nietzsche's thesis, along with practically all other pejorative approaches to postclassical tragedy until the mid-twentieth century, was the 'organic' model for the history of Greek tragedy developed by the Schlegel brothers.[6] This model, which was the result of misunderstanding Aristotle as much as Aristophanes, saw the fifth century, in biological terms, as the 'bloom' and the fourth as the 'decay' of the genre. The Schlegels' approach was firmly rooted in Romanticism and German nationalism; when transplanted to Britain from late nineteenth to mid-twentieth century, it was further enveloped by the nostalgia of an empire lost: for British theatre historians writing at the time of their own

---

[3] On Aristophanic comedy and generic competition, see principally Bakola 2008; Biles 2011; Bakola, Prauscello and Telò 2013.
[4] On classical plays being transformed 'from repertoire to canon', see Easterling 1997, Nervegna 2014, and the chapter by Duncan and Liapis in this volume.
[5] Geuss and Speirs 1999: 54.
[6] For a fresh view of Aristotle's periodization of tragedy, esp. regarding where he put the dividing point between the tragedy of yore and the tragedy of 'today', see Carter this volume.

empire's decay, the loss of Athenian hegemony coincided with the vanishing vitality of tragedy. In the 1950s and 1960s it was the Cold War and (mostly French) structuralism with their binary schemata that determined the critical agenda. The prevailing conviction of this time was that tragic drama was inextricably linked to the Athenian polis and Athenian democratic self-definition. The upshot of such a view was natural enough: as soon as the context of performances was changed (by exporting the plays to other cities), the real 'moment' of tragedy (Vernant and Vidal-Naquet 1990) was gone.[7]

Until as late as the 1990s, serious scholars could still speak of postclassical theatre as plagued by 'crisis'.[8] One had to wait for the new post–Cold War conditions to foster more appreciative perspectives on tragedy after the fifth century:

> The current climate of free trade, the internet, and high levels of personal mobility have made scholarship much more ready to look for and accept evidence for a multicultural, interconnected and networked Mediterranean, where former generations noticed only cultural and economical isolation. We are also equipped with better tools to find evidence of interconnection. Cultural studies have become multidisciplinary, more receptive to complex models of cultural interaction, and far more sensitive to the interactivity of political, economic and cultural production. Indeed, the ancient theatre is a paradigmatic locus of both forms of interactivity, between cultures and within them.[9]

Nevertheless, deep-seated prejudice dies hard. For instance, even the monograph often credited for having redirected attention to postclassical tragedy, namely Xanthakis-Karamanos (1980), still brims with mixed perspectives, and for all its merits, it fails to dispense with the traditional myths. This book's laudable goal is to assess later tragedy more favourably, not as the unworthy heir to the throne, but as embodying a positive 'new direction', in response to the wider transformations of the period. However, despite assurances that 'tragedy was never cultivated with more enthusiasm than during the fourth century', or that 'the poetic value [of the new playwrights] should not be underestimated', the discourses of old still resonate in the author's assertion that the 'new direction' to which fourth-century tragedy turned brought about nothing short of 'the end of serious drama', which was now replaced by a so-called 'anti-tragedy'.

---

[7] Cf. Csapo et al. 2014: 14–15: 'To say that theatre is Athenian in the fifth century but international in the fourth, and that its real function was Athenian self-definition, is effectively to say that in the fourth century it is an empty shell'.
[8] See, for instance, Ghiron-Bistagne 1974; Kuch 1993.  [9] Csapo et al. 2014: 17.

Xanthakis-Karamanos assumes – despite the fact that the remains of fourth-century drama are too scattered to support such sweeping generalizations – that fourth-century playwrights en bloc developed a strong taste for the rhetorical, the pathetic and the sensational, as well as for the carefully crafted romantic plot. In her view, the fourth century substituted 'the highly tragic issues' of fifth-century drama with little more than *pièces bien faites*, which brought about a 'disintegration' of that 'perfect blending' between speech, song and delivery achieved in classical tragedy. In departing 'from the severity and purity of classic style', the fourth century caused a gradual 'withering' of the 'inner power of tragedy'. As it transpires, the 'anti-tragedy' theory, far from being a new, more approving hermeneutic model for understanding Greek tragedy after the fifth century, is practically a masked reformulation of Schlegel's model of organic decline.

One needs to remind oneself constantly that evaluating postclassical tragic drama is ultimately a matter of critical perspectives and priorities,[10] and, furthermore, that the perception of the fifth century as a period of unparalleled and unsurpassable grandeur was nothing if not a construction of fourth-century cultural agents (politicians, orators, philosophers, as well as dramatists):

> It is the fourth century that canonised the fifth, exalted its poets as culture heroes and models [...]. Indeed, it could be said with some justice that fourth-century theatre was the parent of its parent. It selected, shaped and cultivated 'fifth-century theatre' precisely to serve as the greatest cultural bloom of the Classical era, and so we have received it. That it could do so is testimony to the immense power and importance of theatre in the fourth century. The way it did so is testimony to the ideals and values of fourth-century theatre, for fifth-century theatre is in an important sense, an artefact of the fourth century and cannot properly be understood unless we moderns acknowledge that, at least from our perspective, the shadow falls the other way.[11]

Apart from its prejudicial character, the 'decline' narrative rests on inherently problematic historical premises. Proponents of this view refer to the notorious 'death of the polis' and the supposedly concomitant 'decline in the political energy' of theatre, which, as Xanthakis-Karamanos

---

[10] Cf. Csapo et al. 2014: 6 and Easterling 1993: 568f: 'For sensationalism, triviality, affectation and so on we ought perhaps to read elegance, sophistication, refinement, clarity, naturalism, polish, professionalism – a new kind of cosmopolitan sensibility deeply influenced by, and interacting with, the classical repertoire'.

[11] Csapo et al. 2014: 24.

opines, resulted in the ascendancy of 'melodrama' in the fourth century. Melodrama, which Xanthakis-Karamanos equates with the aforementioned 'anti-tragedy', is imagined to have been more attractive to audiences in a period in which people were too weary of war and economic hardship to stomach 'true tragedies',[12] and in which an expanding theatre market demanded more exportable plays with lighter, more universal (i.e., not Athenocentric) themes. As current research has shown, however, this view is simply unhistorical. To start from the obvious, as evidenced by performances of Athenian drama outside Athens as early as the time of Aeschylus,[13] exportability was never a problem in the case of tragedy, whose myths were already Panhellenic and whose specifically Athenian resonances, accentuated by the institutional and civic context rather than by the mythic material itself, could easily be redefined.[14] More importantly, historians have demonstrated that despite the gradual formation of larger commonwealths in the course of the fourth century – especially, after the conquests of Alexander – the polis and its old institutions retained their significance as the fundamental framework of social organization and culture.[15] Furthermore, research into none other than the supposedly 'apolitical' and 'escapist' Menander has shown convincingly that such dominant themes as marriage, procreation, gender or class may have been Panhellenic, and thus transposable to various contexts, but they could all remain pertinent to the Athenian polis itself.[16] In other words, judging by Menander, fourth-century theatre could still be energetically polis-oriented, even if the polis was now increasingly integrated into larger political formations; it could still engage with civic ideology and the issues of polis life, even if the polis itself was no longer democratic; and, of course, it could still be relevant in and to Athens, even if its themes were transferrable to other socio-political milieux. Even Menander's comedy, therefore, which scholars used to regard as mere light entertainment (being itself supposedly a token of decline compared to the Aristophanic political extravaganzas), has been revealed not to eschew the 'serious issues' and to engage dynamically with the hegemonic discourses of the polis. If this is so, then it would be rash to suppose, based on the little evidence we have, that

---

[12] Xanthakis-Karamanos 1980: 41.   [13] See, for example, Dearden 1990, Bosher 2012a.
[14] On exported plays in the postclassical period see Dearden 1999.
[15] On the 'death of the polis' as a historiographical myth see, for example, Ma 2008 and, with especial reference to the theatre, Le Guen 1995. On Athenian civic ideology under the Macedonians and the Ptolemies, which pivoted on an obstinate preservation of the institutional framework of the polis, see Habicht 1998: 1–5.
[16] See, for example, Lape 2004 and 2010.

the audiences of contemporary tragedy had lost their tolerance of and taste for 'true tragedies' or that politically minded (that is to say, polis-oriented) tragic narratives were exclusively reliant upon the supremacy of democratic Athens. The fact that fourth-century tragic theatre was now developing in new socio-political environments need not mean 'the end of serious drama'.

## Continuity and Change in Tragedy After the Fifth Century

The decline theory, and its cognate 'anti-tragedy' theory, both modern perpetuations of an ancient teleological myth and its Schlegelian avatar, are supported neither by the surviving texts nor by the archaeological record. The latter, in fact, categorically attests to the opposite, at least from a quantitative point of view: not only did interest in tragic performances *not* wane after the Peloponnesian War, but, quite the reverse, in the fourth century and increasingly in later periods, both tragedy and comedy knew a period of spectacular growth,[17] which amounted to a veritable 'cultural revolution'.[18]

The process of exporting Athenian theatre beyond the confines of Attica to be performed in the new-fangled religious and secular festivals multiplying everywhere[19] accelerated to such an extent that by the third century BC Athens was merely one of many great hubs of theatrical activity, albeit arguably the most venerable still. The end of Athenocentrism in the fourth century was a universal phenomenon, which did not concern only the new performance venues. Theatre practitioners, too, including playwrights and actors, no longer exclusively (or almost exclusively) originate from Athens. Theatre is now a bona fide international form.

With theatre buildings of increasing grandeur and capacity[20] cropping up in every Hellenistic city aspiring to be considered a *polis* (Pausanias, 9.4.1); with an increasing number of rich and powerful patrons (monarchs no less) willing to finance theatrical activity; and with a buzzing trade of theatrical by-products (vase paintings, mosaics, wall paintings, terracotta figurines, masks, even scripts circulating in book form) echoing the performances, theatre became a staple of life throughout the Hellenistic world. The physical space of the theatre was now a locus of multiform

---

[17] See Le Guen 2007 and this volume. See also Taplin 1999.    [18] See Hall 2007.
[19] On Hellenistic theatre festivals see Le Guen 2010 and this volume.
[20] On the evolution of the Hellenistic theatre building see generally Bieber 1961: 108–28, and Gogos 2008 with special reference to the controversial case of the Theatre of Dionysus in Athens.

civic activity in the context of a new performance culture. From theatrical performances to paratheatrical and theatricalized political events, such as popular assemblies and public displays of magnificence and power by sovereigns,[21] theatricality engulfed every aspect of public life, addressing audiences fully equipped to 'read' what they saw in minute semiotic detail.[22] It even became a metaphor for the vicissitudes of human existence (*theatrum mundi*).[23]

For their part, theatre practitioners were now well trained, specialized professionals,[24] generously rewarded both in financial terms and in the form of honours, privileges and other distinctions. Their histrionic talents were esteemed and sought after for purposes beyond the theatre: it was not uncommon, for example, for actors to be dispatched to serious diplomatic missions as ambassadors. In a remarkable feat, which surpassed even the organization of the Homeridae in the late Archaic and classical periods, by the beginning of the third century BC at the latest, actors became unionized. Their most important guild,[25] the 'Artists of Dionysus' (Διονυσιακοὶ Τεχνῖται), included all theatre practitioners; however, its internal structure was determined by a caste system, which distinguished, for instance, 'protagonists' from 'deuteragonists' (i.e., star actors from sideshows). The Artists were powerful institutions, exerting total control over theatrical activity, both in organizational and in artistic terms.[26] If Aristotle could complain about the power of actors in his own time (*Rhet.* 1403b33), he had seen nothing yet. For the actors' superstardom did not manifest itself only in hefty fees and civic honours; actors also influenced the dramaturgy itself, by demanding or encouraging (or even concocting) parts that showcased their diverse skills in gestural language, emotional expression, vocal delivery, mimicry and singing. The mounting demand for theatrical spectacle also gave rise, alongside the traditional full-scale performances, to novel ways of performing tragedy, most prominently in an 'anthological' manner, that is, by performing extracts rather than the entire play, either

---

[21] Chaniotis 1997 and more extensively 2009: 41–63, 103–40.
[22] The point is elaborated in Petrides 2014: 107–13.   [23] See Kokolakis 1960.
[24] On the specialization of actors in postclassical theatre see Chaniotis 1990.
[25] Other guilds, beyond the Artists of Dionysus, also developed over time, such as τὸ Κοινὸν τῶν περὶ τὴν Ἱλαρὰν Ἀφροδίτην τεχνιτῶν, which probably comprised mimes; on this organization see Fountoulakis 2000, Aneziri 2000–1.
[26] On the actors' unions, the standard reference works are Le Guen 2001 and Aneziri 2003. Cf. also Aneziri 1997, 2001–2; Lightfoot 2002; Le Guen 2004a, 2004b. A complete prosopography of the Technitai is compiled by Stephanis 1988.

in public or in private occasions hosted by the elite.[27] Even the texts of the 'old tragedies' – fifth-century tragedies now enjoying the status of canonical works – did not remain untouched by the force of star actors. As the state of our texts evinces, it was not uncommon for actors, who were now both the protagonists and the producers of 'old tragedies', to boost their roles (e.g., by protracting some *rhēseis* (set speeches) or by introducing more extensive lyric parts that afforded them further opportunities for virtuoso singing).[28]

As for the play scripts, the three major tragic playwrights of the fifth century, especially Euripides,[29] had enjoyed the status of classic authors already since the beginning of the fourth century. The existence of such a canon is evident in Aristotle (e.g., *Poet.* 1449a15–18, 1453a23–30, 1460b33), who may have recognized the odd flash of brilliance in contemporary plays, for example, in Astydamas' *Alcmeon* (*Poet.* 1453b29 = *TrGF* 60 F 1b), which he juxtaposed to the quintessential *Oedipus Tyrannus* of Sophocles. Nonetheless, Aristotle, apparently in the belief that *Oedipus* marks the *telos* (the goal towards which the genre strove) and the perfect *physis* (the definitive nature) of tragedy, could not but regard everyone and everything that came after as stages of a slow decline. Canonization hinged not only on the genuine popular admiration for the commonly acknowledged figureheads of the tragic genre, but also on political and psychological factors. It must be no accident that the Peace of Antalcidas (386 BC), which ended the so-called Corinthian War unfavourably for Athens, coincided with the introduction, albeit *hors concours*, of performances of 'old tragedy' in the Great Dionysia.[30] This and the other grave military setbacks that befell the Athenians in the course of the fourth century – namely, the humiliation at the so-called Social War (357–355 BC), which resulted in the disbandment of the Second Athenian Confederacy,[31] and the crushing defeat at Chaeronea by Philip II of Macedon (338 BC), which signalled the end of Athenian political autonomy[32] – enveloped the cultural and political might of fifth-century Athens with a nostalgic aura.

---

[27] On the different methods of consuming theatre in the Hellenistic period, see Gentili 1979a, Jones 1991, Nervegna 2007.

[28] On actors' interpolations and their detrimental effect on the texts of the plays see Page 1934, Hamilton 1974, Garzya 1981, Mastronarde 1994: 39–49. On the overall process that secured the survival of Greek tragedy see Garland 2004.

[29] Lauriola and Demetriou 2015 set out much of the convoluted story of Euripides' reception in antiquity and in modern times. See also Easterling 1994, Revermann 1999–2000.

[30] On the institution of παλαιὰ τραγῳδία see Katsouris 1974, Hanink 2015.

[31] On the Peace of Antalcidas and the Social War see Cawkwell 2005: 175–97.

[32] On Chaeronea see Cawkwell 1978.

The statesman Eubulus' decision, soon after the Social War, to use the budget surplus in order to enhance public festivals[33] and, much more decisively, the activities of Lycurgus in the 330s BC provide evidence that, just as fast as it was losing its political influence, Athens was reinventing herself as the metropolis of Greek culture. The clear material *presence* of the three great tragedians – of classical grandeur itself – was a big part of this project of Athenian self-reimagining. This presence was impressed upon popular conscience in the 330s, on the initiative of Lycurgus, in two ways: first, by erecting their statues as visual markers of an unsurpassable standard to be revered in the refurbished Theatre of Dionysus (which Lycurgus had remade in stone to increase its audience capacity);[34] and second, by the preparation of an official state edition of the *oeuvres complètes* of 'the Big Three' to be cherished as a communal heirloom.[35]

However, it was not just the old plays that enjoyed the limelight in the postclassical era – far from it: the production of 'new tragedies' (καιναί τραγῳδίαι) swelled like never before, as the market was gradually being globalized. As early as the middle of the fourth century BC, the most successful playwrights of the day, such as Astydamas (*TrGF* 60), are reported to have produced twice, sometimes even three times as many plays as their fifth-century colleagues.[36] The coexistence of new plays alongside the 'classics' in a variety of performance modes, as mentioned previously, but also in book form,[37] created conditions of both osmosis and creative antagonism between fifth- and fourth-century tragedy. The influence of Euripides (and Aeschylus, albeit to a lesser extent) on the new plays was paramount, but the push for innovation in plot, diction and performance never waned.

Consequently, the death of Euripides was not 'the end of an era'[38] at all, in the sense of marking the death of theatre or even of tragedy as we

---

[33] On the statesman Eubulus, who dominated Athenian politics in the years 355–342 BC, see OCD⁴ *s.v.*

[34] On the Lycurgan Theatre of Dionysus see Papastamati-von Moock 2014.

[35] On Lycurgus' edition see Scodel 2007 and also Duncan and Liapis, this volume; on his general contribution to 'the making of classical tragedy' see Hanink 2014.

[36] These numbers may be exaggerated, but the difference is still telling: Astydamas is attributed 240 plays, whereas Sophocles is given 123 and Euripides around 90. See Liapis and Stephanopoulos, this volume.

[37] On literacy, education and the gradual spread of book culture in the classical and early Hellenistic period see Kenyon 1951; W.V. Harris 1989: 65–115, 139–46; Robb 1994: 214–51 (on the fourth century in particular); Yunis 2003 (on the 'emergence of the critical reader').

[38] The myth of Euripides' demise as an 'end of an era' is forcefully debunked by Easterling 1993.

know it. The tragic genre continued to develop and even thrive in the fourth century and, in many cases, later. Theatre continued to be practiced and followed enthusiastically, plays were written and produced with increased vitality, and were even perhaps possessed of comparable quality and staying power: not a few fourth-century plays (e.g., Astydamas' *Hector* and *Parthenopaeus*, Theodectas' *Lynceus*) acquired the status of classics in their own right, alongside the masterworks of the previous, 'golden' era. Periodization, after all, is always a tricky venture, which can obfuscate simple truths:[39] as Francis Dunn's and David Carter's chapters in this volume show, in postclassical times there was significant *continuity* as well as change in the tragic genre, both as an artistic form and as an ideological ('educational') platform of the polis.[40] Continuity in tragedy was perhaps even stronger than in comedy, which reinvented itself much more drastically during its evolutionary course through the fourth century.

Nonetheless, even having done away with misleading paradigms, scholars of Greek tragedy after the fifth century continue to face the serious challenge of trying to determine the value of the evidence at hand. Not the least of their problems is that centuries of bias and bad methodology are encapsulated in the critical terminology itself. Pejorative semantics still insinuate themselves into scholarly discourse, for example, through the use of such terminology as *tragici minores* to refer collectively to any tragedian, from the fifth century or later, beyond the 'Big Three'.[41] The issue, of course, is not one of nomenclature but one of substance. The very term *post*classical is problematic, even if used non-qualitatively, as in this volume and elsewhere in recent years: the negative suggestions of epigonism that the term carries weigh heavily on whatever is 'coming after' the great classical past[42] – be it fourth-century tragedy, comedy, or 'Hellenistic' literature at large.

Among other negative upshots, in such metadiscursive situations, which brand a whole section of the past as an a priori inferior carryover, the tendency to fit everything into prefabricated interpretive moulds is almost reflexive. Let one suggestive example suffice. Discussing the so-called Gyges fragment (*TrGF* 2 F 664 = P. Oxy 2382), which is now commonly

---

[39] On the general questions concerning periodization and ancient culture see Golden and Toohey 1997.
[40] This is emphasized also by Kuch 1993, although he continues to entertain the idea of postclassical tragedy's 'decreased political commitment' due to 'the city-state's relatively limited possibilities at the time' (p. 548).
[41] This time-honoured but misleading practice is followed even in the latest edition of *TrGF*.
[42] On 'coming after' see Hunter 2008: 8–26.

## Introduction

believed to be Hellenistic,[43] Denys Page argued in favour of an early-fifth-century dating, with the following rationale:

> Look again at the language and style ... we shall find the dignity, simplicity and reserve of the early style [*sc.* the style of Aeschylus' time]; where in it shall we find any of those features which we associate with Alexandrian literature of any type?[44]

In other words, for Page the fragment's perceived quality alone was sufficient to militate against a later dating. Such circular logic is not uncommon in these situations: Page presupposes from the start that the fragment is early classical, the implication being that certain qualitative traits can only belong to this period, and then returns to the fragment to magnify whatever virtues it may have, in order for it to conform to his preconceived ideas. The so-called postclassical tragedy at large has been habitually put under similar distorting lenses. This volume will insist that *any* totalizing aesthetic judgments, either derogatory or laudatory, on material that is scattered and heterogeneous, to say the least, should be withheld, or even better, avoided altogether.

### The *Status Quaestionis*

Given the vagaries of periodization and canonization, as well as the regrettable state of our textual evidence, it seems natural enough that postclassical tragedy was slow to grasp the serious attention of scholars. Interest in postclassical tragedy was directed at best towards the edition and philological study of individual fragments and, more rarely, playwrights,[45] with no large-scale commentary (apart from the short yet illuminating notes in the successive editions of the *Tragicorum Graecorum Fragmenta*) or a synthetic monograph available until the early 1980s.

The remains of the vast postclassical tragic production are indeed not particularly fascinating. For the most part, what we possess are deplorably short and uninformative book fragments reflecting the specific interests of the authors that quote them: for example, gnomic utterances suiting the *Anthologium* of Stobaeus, trifling curiosities reflecting the eccentricities of

---

[43] Lesky 1953; Kotlińska-Toma 2015: 178–85; Hornblower, this volume.
[44] Quoted by Hunter 2008: 11 from Page's Inaugural Lecture at Cambridge; see further Page 1952.
[45] Bartsch 1843 (on Chaeremon), Ravenna 1903 (on Theodectas and Moschion), and Webster 1954 and 1956 (the former on the value of Aristotle's *Poetics* for reconstructing the plots of fourth-century tragedies, the latter more generally on fourth-century Athenian art and literature) are, for all the questionable speculations included in them, rare examples of monographs or extensive studies dedicated to postclassical playwrights in the nineteenth and the first half of the twentieth century.

Athenaeus' dining aesthetes, and other sporadic survivals. The small number of papyri that have resurfaced over the years have certainly contributed to our understanding of the period but have not changed the general picture a great deal.[46]

Even more disappointingly, the few substantial texts that do survive are either singular, perhaps experimental, phenomena or they are likely to be otherwise untypical of the structure, style or even quality of most postclassical tragedy. The *Alexandra* of Lycophron, a unique text in every way, is in essence an extended messenger speech, too idiosyncratic to be considered representative of any norm.[47] We also cannot be certain whether the *Exagōgē* of Ezekiel, a third-century BC Jewish 'epic' drama[48] of which around 269 lines survive (*TrGF* 128), was an isolated phenomenon catering to the needs of a particular community, the Hellenized Jews of Egypt, or whether such was the kind of tragic drama generally written in that period. Finally, in a cruel twist of fate, the one example of a postclassical tragic play that survives intact and that would fit comfortably into any formal definition of Greek tragedy is at the same time the most misleading. The *Rhesus* was inserted into Euripides' corpus, probably by an error of attribution, displacing a genuinely Euripidean namesake.[49] Scholars, most importantly Liapis (2012), have pinpointed an astonishing number of faults undermining both the dramaturgy and the language of the play. There have also been more charitable readings,[50] and the discussion on the play's merits will probably remain open. The crux of the matter is the following: even if the *Rhesus* is indeed to be regarded as a major disappointment, it is still ill-advised to use it as the basis for all-encompassing conclusions such as Kuch's (1993: 548, 550) on the quality of postclassical tragic drama:

> The tendency to bring suspense and distractions into tragic drama including the production of show effects [*sc.* as opposed to writing tragedies of serious political commitment] predominated as is apparent in *Rhesus.* [. . .] To judge by *Rhesus*, fourth-century tragedy had obviously more the intention to entertain and to offer interest and excitement rather than to promote

---

[46] For a useful overview of the most important papyri pertaining to fourth-century tragedy see Xanthakis-Karamanos 1997.
[47] The very status of the *Alexandra* as a tragedy, even an experimental one, is contested. The text is omitted in the first comprehensive monograph on Hellenistic tragedy to appear in eighty years (Kotlińska-Toma 2015). On the play see now Hornblower 2015, and this volume.
[48] 'Epic' in the sense of comprising, apparently, not a unified *mythos* around a single *praxis*, but a long string of episodes stretching over an extended period of time.
[49] On this scenario see Liapis 2009.   [50] Burnett 1985; Fries 2014; and this volume.

self-understanding according to the standards of fifth-century polis democracy.

Quite simply, one should *not* judge by the dubious standard of *Rhesus*.[51] Condemning, as Kuch does, five centuries' worth of 'postclassical' tragic production on the shaky foundation of one arguably mediocre play would be the same as belittling the whole of fifth-century tragedy based on the shortcomings of, say, Euripides' *Andromache*. The faults of the *Rhesus*, such as they may be, must remain the faults of the *Rhesus*, not of the entire tragic production after the fifth century. After all, the *Alexandra* is a Hellenistic *tour de force*, and the *Exagōgē*, although often scorned for not complying with the Aristotelian doctrines on tragic structure, is not without its charms. At the very least, these two texts, untypical as they may be, attest to the undoubtedly positive fact that, in the Hellenistic period, 'tragedy' was a diverse phenomenon that could take a plethora of forms and guises.

Scholars started looking more closely at the postclassical tragic fragments from the 1970s onwards. Interest was bolstered by the gradual accretion of relevant papyri and the constant enrichment of the *TrGF*, but also by the appearance of groundbreaking scholarship on a number of issues pertaining to the subject. Sifakis (1967) was the first to highlight the diversity and ebullience of Hellenistic theatre life, which the dearth of texts often obscures. Webster ([2]1967) collected all archaeological data illustrating tragedy and satyr-play. Pickard-Cambridge (1968, second augmented edition 1988) offered the most thorough exposition of Greek theatre practice going much further than the fifth century. Mette (1977) made the epigraphic material concerning theatrical performances in Athens and beyond readily available to the theatre-oriented classicist (recently, Millis and Olson 2012 masterfully reedited the two most important inscriptions relating to Athenian production). Finally, Ghiron-Bistagne (1976) systematized the information on actors mainly in the Hellenistic period. Her pathbreaking work was continued by Stephanis (1988), an exhaustive prosopographical lexicon of all theatre practitioners of antiquity. Le Guen (2001) and Aneziri (2003) focused more closely on the Hellenistic actors' guilds, while Easterling and Hall (2002), and Hugoniot et al. (2004) contributed valuable collections of articles on the art of acting, most of which concern the postclassical period. Csapo (2010) is the most

---

[51] Cf. Liapis (2012: lxxii), commenting on Thum 2005, who contrary to Kuch 1993 denies that *Rhesus* is a fourth-century play, because it does not share the supposed general tendencies of that period.

comprehensive study to-date of the ancient actor's art in relation to the shifting ideological discourses on theatre. More general works have laid the groundwork for the volume at hand and, one hopes, for future studies: these include Kannicht et al. (1991), a survey of Greek tragedy from the origins to Ezekiel; Green (1994) on the interaction between theatre and society from classical to Imperial times; Csapo and Slater (1995), a judicious selection of sources on classical and postclassical theatre in English translation; and Wilson (2000) on the institution of *khorēgia* and (2007) on Greek theatre festivals.[52] Interest in postclassical theatre is mounting: in the last couple of years as many as four books on the topic have seen the light of day: Csapo et al. (2014) offers a wide-ranging overview of Greek theatre in the fourth century; Vahtikari (2014) studies the proliferation of theatre performance outside Athens in the late fifth and fourth centuries (expanding the scope of Bosher 2012a); the authors in Lamari (2015) examine the pivotal phenomenon of tragic reperformances in Athens and beyond; and Kotlińska-Tomà (2015) contributes a useful exposition of Hellenistic tragedy (on this book, though, see Petrides 2015).[53] Most recently Wright (2016) published the first of two volumes on 'the lost plays of Greek tragedy'. Significantly, Volume 1, which deals with every known fifth- and fourth-century name but the Big Three, labels these playwrights 'neglected authors' rather than *tragici minores*. The paradigm is certainly shifting.

Nonetheless, excluding the *Alexandra*, the *Exagōgē* and of course the *Rhesus*, which have been studied at length in monographs and commentaries, scholarly output on postclassical tragedy still consists mostly of individual case studies and disquisitions on specific issues.[54] The aforesaid book by Xanthakis-Karamanos (1980) deserves credit as the first attempt to examine the material comprehensively and synthetically, but for the reasons stated previously it should now be regarded as out of date.[55] Postclassical satyr-play has been more fortunate: the 'poetae minores' of

[52] See also Le Guen 2010 on money as a factor in Greek dramatic contexts.
[53] Cf. also Martina 2003. Roman tragedy seems to have modelled itself occasionally on postclassical Greek plays but more importantly to have utilized some of the techniques established by fourth- and third-century Greek tragic playwrights: see, for example, Tarrant 1978 and Boyle 1997 on Seneca; and Erasmo 2004: 52–80 on the *fabula praetexta*, which may have been influenced by the reappearance of historical drama in such Hellenistic playwrights as Moschion (possibly early third century). Researches on Menander and postclassical comedy (e.g., Wiles 1991, Lape 2004, Petrides and Papaioannou 2010, and Petrides 2014), which focus on the interaction between performance semiotics and civic ideology in an era of alleged 'apoliticism', can also provide insights applicable to contemporary tragic drama.
[54] For example: Collard 1970, Stephanopoulos 1988, 1995–6, 1997, etc.
[55] For a review of Xanthakis-Karamanos 1980 see Stephanopoulos 1984.

this genre (once again the term is used in reference to all satyr-play authors other than Aeschylus, Sophocles and Euripides) have been competently commented upon by Cipolla (2003). Most volumes dealing with 'tragedy after the fifth century', such as Gildenhard and Revermann (2010), concern themselves with the reception of classical drama rather than with the continuing evolution of the genre after Euripides, or (as in the case of Csapo et al. 2014) with the broader socio-economic aspects of theatre primarily in the fourth century. Currently, there is no such thing as a *vue d'ensemble*, a comprehensive study discussing from a variety of viewpoints the most important aspects of this complex, variegated and often elusive phenomenon that is Greek tragic dramaturgy after the fifth century, avoiding the pitfalls described in the previous pages and applying the many advances of recent years in the theory and methodology of working with fragmentary literature, dramatic or otherwise.[56] The volume at hand aspires to fill this bibliographic gap.

## The Contents of This Volume

The volume consists of three parts. Part I ('Texts'), comprises four chapters, which focus on the textual evidence for postclassical Greek tragedy, and provide analysis, discussion and doxography on key texts or fragments of texts.

Chapter 1, 'Greek Tragedy in the Fourth Century: The Fragments', by Vayos Liapis and Theodoros K. Stephanopoulos, provides an exhaustive survey of all major fragments of fourth-century tragedy. While it naturally focuses on the most celebrated playwrights of the era (Astydamas, Carcinus Junior, Chaeremon and Theodectas), it does not exclude other, less distinguished figures (Diogenes, Dicaeogenes, Antiphon, Patrocles, Dionysius of Syracuse, Diogenes of Sinope, Sosiphanes of Syracuse). The chapter scrutinizes the material at our disposal with a fundamental call for caution: what survives from the tragic production of this period does evince a theatrical culture that is still flourishing and vibrant, spreading all over the Greek world; the fourth-century playwrights do attempt bold experiments with all the essential components of tragedy, such as myth, music, stagecraft, acting, etc., often in rivalry with the fifth-century dramatists; however, the remains are too scattered and heterogeneous to justify the sweeping conclusions and schematic inferences of earlier scholars. In fact, we cannot even be certain whether 'fourth-century

---

[56] See, for example, Most 1997, Arnott 2000, Dover 2000, McHardy et al. 2005.

tragedy' constitutes an actual generic turn or simply a convenient periodization tag – possibly even a misleading one.

The tragedy of Rhesus is the subject of Chapter 2 by Almut Fries. Fries reexamines the fundamental questions affecting the play's interpretation and takes issue with critics who condemn it as lacking deeper significance. She begins with the play's scene and setting, cast of characters, distribution of roles and relationship with its most immediate sources (*Iliad* 10, the Epic Cycle, and, as regards the character of Rhesus in particular, stories preserved in the Homeric scholia and perhaps in local Thracian lore). The play's structure and meaning are scrutinized in an extended section, which attempts to make the case for a play of much better quality than otherwise believed. The 'eclectic' dramaturgy and stagecraft of the *Rhesus*, with its unique mixture of archaizing and unprecedented elements, is also afforded attention, whereas the play's language and style are connected with the issue of its authenticity and date. The chapter concludes with an overview of *Rhesus*' reception in antiquity.

Hellenistic tragedy is the focus of Simon Hornblower's Chapter 3, entitled 'Hellenistic Tragedy and Satyr-Drama: Lycophron's *Alexandra*'. The abundant inscriptional record preserves more than sixty names of tragedians from this period, all of whom were highly prolific. Several thousand tragic plays were written in the centuries after Alexander's death, and tragedy permeated intellectual and public life on an unprecedented scale. That these texts did not pass the test of time was not necessarily due to their lack of quality or popularity. The general image of Hellenistic tragedy, as gleaned from indirect sources and the few fragments that survive, is of a genre which continued mainly to dramatize traditional mythological episodes, but did not shy away from historical subjects (contemporary or older) and even political themes. Hellenistic tragedies probably also displayed a greater proneness to melodrama and other excesses of violence, spectacle and pathos compared to the fifth and fourth centuries, whereas in terms of poetic style they are set apart by their metrical conservativeness (tendency to avoid resolution in the iambic trimetre). Hornblower's chapter eventually concentrates on the *Alexandra*, and discusses the possibility of extensive interpolation (which is discarded), as well as questions of content, genre, authorship, date and politics. Hornblower's central thesis is that the Lycophron credited with *Alexandra* is *not* Lycophron of Chalcis, the poet of the Pleiad, but a namesake (or grandson or pseudonymous author) writing in the time of Flamininus and in the aftermath of the battle at Cynoscephalae, a whole century later. The second-century dating is also consistent with what Hornblower understands to be the play's political thesis: *Alexandra*, he suggests, goes against much Greek and foreign feeling in celebrating Roman military and political ascendancy. Hornblower's chapter concludes with a brief overview of what remains of Hellenistic satyr-drama with special emphasis on Lycophron of Chalcis, Sositheus and Python's *Agēn*.

Chapter 4 'The *Exagōgē* of Ezekiel the Tragedian', by Pierluigi Lanfranchi, looks at the seventeen extant fragments of Ezekiel's *Exagōgē*, the most substantial piece of Hellenistic tragic drama at our disposal barring the *Alexandra*. The identity of the author, the date of the play, the place and the occasion on which it was produced are hotly debated issues; however, the vibrant community of Hellenized Jews living in Alexandria provides the likeliest context for a tragedy actively attempting to recast the Jewish tradition in the language and conceptual frameworks of the Greeks. The *Exagōgē* tells the story of Moses and the great exodus of the Jews from Egypt. It dramatizes the first fifteen chapters of the Book of Exodus, although in certain cases material is drawn from different sources. The most impressive surviving fragment is a messenger speech recounting the miraculous crossing of the Red Sea. The vexed issue whether the *Exagōgē* even deserves to be labelled a 'tragedy' highlights the narrow limits of definition and prescription in this new, wide and diverse cultural environment. For sure, if Aristotle is any measure, the play violates some of the fundamental conventions of classical Greek tragedy (primarily the propensity to uphold the unities of time and place) and lacks some of Aristotelian tragedy's principal constitutive elements (for instance, *hamartia* and *peripeteia*). Nevertheless, in many other aspects, primarily in metrical form and dramatic structure, the *Exagōgē* conforms to the norms of the tragic genre and is heavily influenced by fifth-century tragedy (the aforementioned messenger speech in particular bears a palpable relation to those of Aeschylus' *Persians* and of Euripides). Ancient audiences, Lanfranchi concludes, would have no trouble categorizing the *Exagōgē* as a tragic play.

Part II ('Contexts and Developments') analyses aspects of the sociopolitical, cultural, literary-historical and performative frameworks that circumscribe the development of Greek tragedy after the death of Euripides.

Chapter 5, 'Beyond Athens: The Expansion of Greek Tragedy from the Fourth Century Onwards', by Brigitte Le Guen, reviews all the documentary evidence (literary, inscriptional, archaeological) attesting to the dissemination of tragedy after the fifth century, first to the Western Mediterranean and Macedonia, and then, through the conquests of Alexander the Great, to the four corners of the Greek-speaking world. Le Guen shows that this phenomenon, together with the diversification of the venues and occasions of performance, had obvious repercussions on the meaning and function of tragedy in the Hellenistic era. Still, she warns that it would be a misconception to believe that the diffusion of tragedy either severed the ties of theatre with its patron god, Dionysus, or that it signified the end of the symbiosis between polis (not necessarily the Athenian polis) and tragedy.

Chapter 6 ('Theatre Performance After the Fifth Century'), coauthored by Anne Duncan and Vayos Liapis, begins by looking into the process of canonizing fifth-century tragedy, especially the works of the three great tragedians. Among other things, it explores the theatrical environment, equipment and performance mode of postclassical tragedy, expounding on the main innovations in terms of the performance medium and focusing especially on what was undoubtedly the most spectacular device of postclassical drama, the actor itself. The chapter concludes by setting the record straight regarding the vexed issue of the chorus in postclassical tragedy, by insisting once again that the evidence does not support the traditional straightforward narrative of decline, but makes for a much more variegated picture.

One of the common misconceptions concerning tragedy after the fifth century is that the amount of sung and danced scenes included in the plays was significantly reduced. It is Mark Griffith's first goal in Chapter 7 ('Music and Dance in Tragedy After the Fifth Century') to show that, even if there was reduction in the chorus' active involvement in the action (this is still better evidenced in comedy rather than in tragedy), and even if the practice of inserting *passe-partout* choral parts (*embolima*), whose librettos had nothing to do with the action, was indeed widespread, tragic drama remained a highly musical event. The second major question Griffith addresses is whether the postclassical period saw significant changes in the actual music played, that is, in the melodies, tunings and musical styles. Evidence from the musically notated papyri and other sources suggests that the wider changes in the music of the period carried over into the performances of tragedy. Not least because Athens had no distinctive musical tradition of its own, Griffith notes, theatre music had always been, and continued to be, a melting pot of different music styles from around the Greek (or even Asian) world as well as a ready receptacle of innovation and change.

Chapter 8, 'The Fifth Century and After: (Dis)continuities in Greek Tragedy', by Francis Dunn, calls for a more nuanced understanding of fourth-century tragic drama, away from the tendency to over- or misinterpret the evidence at hand. Dunn cautions against the assumption that fourth-century tragedy was any less diverse than the tragedy of the preceding era and advises that any attempt to (re)construct universal trends runs the risk of being unfounded and reductive. The data at hand paint a much more complicated picture than commonly acknowledged: fourth-century tragedians adopt some of the innovations of the late fifth century, but also move in their own, different directions in other respects. Dunn explores this dual tendency first by focusing on aspects of song and plot, and then by discussing broader developments in naturalism, theatrical self-reflexivity and what he calls 'ethical contingency', that is, the uncertainty of living in the present without reliance on the past or the future. Dunn also reassesses a number of sweeping generalizations about fourth-century tragedy, such as that it saw a decline in choral song; that it follows late Euripides in constructing exclusively melodramatic plots; or that it exhibits increased literary/theatrical self-consciousness compared to fifth-century tragedy. Breaking with the past is just as common in this period as continuing on established and proven trajectories.

Chapter 9, 'Society and Politics in Post-Fifth-Century Tragedy', by David Carter, further contributes to the understanding of the continuities that bind fifth- and fourth-century tragedy closely together. Carter's special focus is the political, intellectual and ethical emphases within the plays, which appear to have remained unaffected by the changing social and political conditions, for example, by the loss of empire. Carter debunks the myth that tragedy in the fourth century was more rhetorical than political (*Po.* 1450b4–8), in the sense that the plot stopped having specifically Athenian resonances and developed a tendency towards mere rhetorical embellishment. He identifies clear connections between the fifth and the fourth centuries in matters relating to the values and the discourses of the democratic polis; such connections are strong enough to suggest that at least in terms of its political concerns, as well as in its use of rhetoric as a structural device rather than as an end in itself, Greek tragedy after the fifth century was quite similar to the tragedy of Sophocles and Euripides.

The third and final part of the volume, entitled 'Transmission and Reception' explores aspects of the tragic dramas' *Nachleben* in the Imperial period. It concludes with a view of tragedy at large from the postclassical scholar's standpoint.

In Chapter 10, 'Attitudes Towards Tragedy from the Second Sophistic to Late Antiquity', Ruth Webb focuses on the multifarious attitudes towards tragedy in the first centuries AD, which emanated from the double survival of the genre as both a living performance art and an authoritative text. Tragedy survived the spread of Christianity, despite the opposition of the Church: a range of different forms of the genre (new and old plays, sung extracts, performances with chorus or without a chorus, etc.) were still performed in a variety of venues until the sixth century AD. Beyond the stage, tragedy in this period could be consumed in three further ways: in schools, as an instrument of linguistic, rhetorical and moral instruction; at home, in silent, private perusal; and in social events, in the form of dramatized readings. Tragic plays were now studied extensively, not always as unified wholes but also in order to be mined for examples of Attic usage, as sources of maxims useful for moral edification and rhetorical exploitation, and as compendia of information on questions of mythology, topography, etc. Rhetoricians employed tragic plots – especially Euripidean ones, on account of their being more 'plausible' – as raw material for exercises in argumentation, *ēthopoiia* (rhetorical presentation of character), etc. Readers of tragedies in this period never lose sight of the fact that the scripts are but the bare bones of a multisensory phenomenon. The scholia and other written sources on tragedy show readers fully active in imaginative reconstructions of the original performances, aided of course by their familiarity with a continued performance tradition. However, the old Aristotelian idea that the spectacle as imagined in the act of reading is complete, hence one can dispense with the performance and the performer, had now taken root.

Finally, if one seeks to reconstruct the fragmented image of tragedy after the fifth century, one cannot afford to disregard the significant tradition of scholarship *on* tragedy, which thrived alongside the production of old and new tragic dramas throughout the Hellenistic and Imperial periods. In Chapter 11, 'Scholars and Scholarship on Tragedy', the last in the volume, Johanna Hanink speaks of the importance of this tradition, and contributes a succinct overview of its evolution and general trends, from its tentative beginnings in classical Athens to its peak in Alexandria, Pergamum and Rome. As regards the beginnings of tragic scholarship, Hanink underscores the archival diligence of the Athenian state, and the catalytic influence of Lycurgus and his 'official edition' of the three canonical tragedians on the transmission of tragedy to the later generations. The birth of scholarship as we know it occurred thanks to the researches of Aristotle and his school, whose activities ranged from yet deeper archival research to literary history, theory and criticism. The great scholars working under the patronage of the Ptolemies in the Mouseion of Alexandria achieved the next great leap. They were especially preoccupied with issues of authenticity, and produced 'corrections' (*diorthōseis*) of texts (practically, critical editions) with a good mind for locating spurious attributions of titles, lines and passages. Alexandrian scholars usually accompanied their editions with extensive commentaries (*hypomnēmata*) and various treatises providing all sorts of elucidation on the texts. Hanink concludes her chapter with an examination of tragic scholia and the 'Lives' (biographies) of the tragic poets. Although their reliability may vary, modern researchers can still profit immensely from ancient scholia not only as a source of *realia*, variant readings or other practical information, but also as a monument of shifting scholarly perceptions regarding major issues of theatre interpretation, such as poetic style, dramaturgy and performance practice.

PART I

*Texts*

# PART I

## Texts

CHAPTER I

# Greek Tragedy in the Fourth Century: The Fragments

*Vayos Liapis and Theodoros K. Stephanopoulos**

Is it meaningful to speak of 'fourth-century tragedy' as anything other than a convenient periodization tag? The question is treated extensively by Dunn, Duncan/Liapis and Carter in their respective chapters in this volume, but the fact of the matter is that firm evidence is comparatively limited, and allows us to identify only in general terms whatever specific trends might allow us to think of fourth-century tragedies and tragic performances as being distinct from those of the fifth century. One fourth-century development we *can* be certain about is the crystallization of a tragic canon, in which the three great tragedians of the fifth century have pride of place. The creation of a tragic canon was institutionalized with the establishment, in 386 BC, of revivals of 'old tragedy', i.e., of a tragedy by one of the fifth-century masters, in the context of the Great Dionysia; to all intents and purposes, this may be treated as a watershed moment, which created an ipso facto distinction between the fifth century and what came after (see further Duncan and Liapis, this volume). What came after often adopts an agonistic attitude with respect to the canonical tragedians of the previous century, especially Euripides: as far as we can judge by the scant remains, fourth-century tragedians seem eager to emulate their illustrious predecessors, whether by revisiting the same or similar tragic myths or by offering new and sometimes remarkably innovative treatments of traditional material. Tragedy in the fourth century should by no means be seen as derivative or as operating invariably under

---

* The sections on Carcinus Junior and on Chaeremon have been authored by Theodoros Stephanopoulos and translated by Vayos Liapis; the rest of the chapter is the work of Vayos Liapis. Both authors have read and commented on each other's sections but remain responsible only for their respective contributions. Stephanopoulos wishes to thank Liapis for his translation and comments. Liapis records his gratitude to Christine Mauduit, to the École Normale Supérieure (Paris) and to Labex TransferS for a visiting professorship in 2015, which gave him the opportunity to air before an expert audience some of the ideas presented in this chapter. Liapis is also grateful to Paul Demont, Pierre Judet de La Combe, Christine Mauduit, Anne-Sophie Noel, Antonis Petrides and Theodoros Stephanopoulos for comments and criticisms which improved much of this chapter.

the shadow of the fifth-century canon: there is sufficient evidence, mainly from Aristotle's *Poetics* but also from the textual remains themselves, to suggest that innovation was never far from the thoughts of fourth-century tragedians (see Dunn, Griffith, and again Duncan/Liapis, this volume). During that same period, tragedy spread beyond the confines of Attica to other parts of the world, to become a truly international medium of high prestige. Although the expansion of theatre beyond Attica had begun already in the fifth century, it reached new heights in the fourth century (and later): non-Athenian actors and playwrights now rose to unprecedented fame, and theatre productions and buildings proliferated throughout the Greek (and later non-Greek) world. This tendency was, of course, encouraged decisively by Alexander the Great's energetic promotion of theatre and the stupendous expansion of Macedonian power from the Balkans to the Indus River (see Le Guen, this volume).

In what follows, we shall proceed to examine the evidence for fourth-century tragic texts. This survey will include principally the remains of four major figures, which are, however, little more than mere names to us – namely, Astydamas, Carcinus (Junior), Chaeremon and Theodectas – but also those of less prominent tragic playwrights, such as Diogenes of Athens, with whom we begin our overview.[1]

## Diogenes of Athens

A rather shadowy figure, Diogenes of Athens (*TrGF* I, 45) is often confused in the ancient sources with his namesake, the Cynic Diogenes of Sinopē (*TrGF* I, 88), on whom see later in this chapter. According to the Byzantine lexicon known as the *Suda*,[2] he was active (γέγονεν) at the time of the fall of the Thirty Tyrants, i.e., 403 BC – which may be the date of his first dramatic victory.[3] The *Suda* credits Diogenes with eight titles, but seven of them are attributed by Diogenes Laertius (6.80) to Diogenes of Sinopē – although even the latter's authorship of the plays was questioned by Satyrus (fr. 1 Schorn), who attributed them rather to Philiscus of Aegina.[4]

Among the tragedies attributed to Diogenes of Athens by the *Suda*, only *Semelē* is likely to be genuinely his, as it overlaps with none of the titles

---

[1] Fourth-century playwrights are examined in the order in which they have been arranged in *TrGF* I.
[2] δ 1142 (II.101.23–4 Adler).
[3] For γέγονεν = *floruit* see Rohde 1888 (esp. 219 with n. 1); Schramm 1929: 9; Hoffmann 1951: 146–7; Arnott 1996: 4.
[4] Cf. *TrGF* 88 T 1, 3; 89 T 2. See further the extensive commentary by Schorn 2002: 152–61.

attributed by Laertius to Diogenes of Sinopē. The only surviving fragment of *Semelē* is rife with exotic details concerning the Asiatic cults of Cybele and Artemis, especially in connection with the musical instruments used in them (percussions and the stringed instruments *magadis* and *pēktis*).[5] The orgiastic context and the use of such instruments as the drum (*typanon*) and the bull-roarer (*rhombos*) suggest a syncretism between the cults of Cybele and Dionysus, already evidenced in Euripides' *Bacchae* (58–9, 78–82, 123–34)[6] – after all, Dionysus will have been central to a play named after his mother Semelē. To judge by the speaker's repeated 'I hear' (1, 6 κλύω μέν ... κλύω δέ), the play will have taken place away from the Asiatic locations described, and its setting may well have been Thebes. The fragment's style is elaborate and long-winded, with rare words (χαλκόκτυπος) or unusual meanings (ἀντίχερσι = 'responsive to the touch'), and seems consistent with the anecdotal judgment of Diogenes' style by his elder contemporary, the tragic poet Melanthius, who said mischievously that he could not watch Diogenes' tragedies because 'the words obstructed his view' (Plut. *Mor.* 41D).

## Dicaeogenes

There is very little we can be certain about with regard to Dicaeogenes (*TrGF* I, 52). A fourth-century BC (360s?) inscription found in Athens[7] mentions a performance (perhaps also a victory) by Dicaeogenes in the context of, no doubt, the Rural Dionysia of Acharnae: there were two joint *chorēgoi* for that performance, both of them Acharnians, and Acharnae is one of the demes for which the practice of *synchorēgia* – the sharing of the expenses for a theatrical performance by more than one *chorēgos* – is securely attested.[8] But it is uncertain whether what Dicaeogenes composed was a tragedy or a dithyramb, for he is also mentioned in ancient sources as

---

[5] On the *magadis* and the *pēktis* (the latter assuredly a harp) see West 1994: 70–5; on these instruments, and on the possibility that Diogenes' κρεκούσας μάγαδιν (l. 10) means 'thrumming an octave concord' rather than referring to *magadis* as a specific instrument, see West 1997: 49.
[6] Further on the syncretism see W. Allan 2004: 131, 141–2; Munn 2006: 163–9. For castanets and drums in the cult of the Great Mother cf. *TrGF* II, F 629 (although not assuredly from a tragedy).
[7] *IG* ii² 3092 = *TrGF* I, DID B 6.
[8] See Wilson 2000: 265, 306–7, 379 n. 1. On the archaeological and epigraphic evidence for the Rural Dionysia at Acharnae see Goette 2014: 84–5 and esp. 100 (no. 1). *Synchorēgiai* were more common at deme level than in the city.

an author of dithyrambs (T 1), and he was apparently praised by ancient critics for his musical compositions in tragedy.[9]

From the handful of Dicaeogenes' fragments that survive, F 1b is a reflection on the power of erotic desire to turn people away from their own kin in their zeal to please the beloved person. It is impossible to ascertain the context of this fragment, though one might be tempted to speculate – though not with confidence, given the paucity of our information – that it could come from *Medea* (cf. F 1a), a play which may conceivably have featured Medea's murder of her brother (called Metapontios in this play instead of the more common Apsyrtos) as part of her scheme to facilitate her and her lover Jason's escape from Colchis.

Of Dicaeogenes' *Cyprians* we know only that it featured the third kind of *anagnōrisis* in Aristotle's classification, namely recognition by memory (διὰ μνήμης):[10] its hero 'wept upon seeing the painting'. If the play concerned Teucer's arrival at his new home in Cypriot Salamis, then the hero may have betrayed his identity by weeping at the sight of, e.g., a painting of Ajax's suicide or of the Trojan War – just as Aeneas weeps on seeing a depiction of the Trojan War in Juno's temple, or as Odysseus gives himself away when he hears Demodocus sing of the Trojan Horse.[11] Alternatively, *Cyprians* may have dealt, as conjectured by Wilamowitz,[12] with the unfortunate love of Thracian Phyllis for one of Theseus' sons, who deserted her after their wedding to settle in Cyprus, where he met his death.[13]

## Antiphon

Antiphon the tragic poet (*TrGF* I, 55) is undoubtedly to be distinguished from the late-fifth-century orator and intellectual Antiphon, son of Sophilus, from Rhamnous.[14] Unlike his oligarchic namesake, the tragedian Antiphon held anti-tyrannical convictions, as a result of which he was

[9] This assessment, however, is forcefully opposed by Philodemus, *On Poems* 4, col. x (Sbordone 1969: 335).
[10] Ar. *Poet.* 1454b 37–55a2.
[11] Verg. *Aen.* 1. 453–93; *Od.* 8.521–9.20; Webster 1954: 298. For an alternative conjecture see Lucas 1968: 170 (on Ar. *Poet.* 1455a1).
[12] See app. crit. on *TrGF* I, 52 F 1.
[13] For the myth's ancient testimonies (esp. Apollod. *Epit.* 6.16) see Pfeiffer 1949: 395, *ad* Call. fr. 556.
[14] As Gagarin (2002: 43 with n. 19) remarks, Aristotle makes a point of distinguishing the orator from the tragedian by always calling the latter either 'the poet' or the author of a named tragedy. The question whether Antiphon the orator is to be identified with Antiphon the sophist is of no concern to us here; see e.g., Gagarin 2002: 37–52 (unitarian); Pendrick 1987, 1993, 2002 (separatist).

put to death by Dionysius I, the tyrant of Syracuse, where he visited as an ambassador,[15] although a late source (Plut. *Mor.* 833C) implies that he may also have produced some of his tragedies there, or at least helped Dionysius in his own dramatic writing.

Of Antiphon's tragedies we have only meagre remains. From Aristotle's passing comments, it appears that the heroine of his *Andromache* (F 1), after the fall of Troy, tried to save her son by giving him to someone else to bring up as her or his own child. The play may perhaps have included a speech or a debate in which Andromache stated that she could bear to live away from her son, so long as this guaranteed his prosperity, and that she would be content to love him without being loved back by him, as he would be ignorant of his true mother.[16] A papyrus fragment, which has been tentatively attributed to this play, preserves the remains of a lament, surely by Andromache, for the death of Hector. In lines 24–6 the speaker addresses her child, asking him to follow her – perhaps to be smuggled away into someone else's care?[17]

Antiphon is also credited with a *Meleager*,[18] which included (like Euripides' *Meleager*, fr. 530–1a Kannicht) a description of the Calydonian boar hunt. From Aristotle's condensed remarks on the play, one gathers that it will also have included the quarrel between Meleager and his maternal uncle Plexippus over the hide of the Calydonian boar – a quarrel that resulted in the latter's murder by the former.[19] The play will surely have included Althaea's subsequent curses against Meleager and her quenching of the burning brand that magically kept her son in life.[20] In F 2 the speaker specifies that the Aetolians gathered at the behest of Oeneus, Meleager's father, 'not in order to slay the beast but so that they might bear witness to Meleager's excellence for the rest of Greece'. This may have acquired an ironic hue later in the play, when Meleager

---

[15] For the ancient sources see *TrGF* I, 55 T 1–7.
[16] Cf. Arist. *EE* 1239a 35–8; *EN* 1159a 27–33; Webster 1954: 299–300 with further remarks on Antiphon's *Andromache* as a possible model for Accius' *Astyanax* and Ennius' *Andromacha Aechmalotis*.
[17] See Lobel 1936; for the tentative attribution to Antiphon see Morel 1937 and cf. Webster 1954: 299–300. See also now Wright 2016: 144.
[18] Presumably, *Meleager* was sufficiently well known to attract the commentary of the second-century AD Peripatetic philosopher Adrastus of Aphrodisias: Ath. 15.673f; Wright 2016: 145.
[19] Arist. *Rhet.* 1379b 11–5; cf. Ov. *Met.* 8. 425–45. Wright (2016: 145) argues that 'the clash of wills between Meleager and his uncle seems to have been at the centre of Antiphon's tragedy'.
[20] Cf. *Il.* 9. 529–99; Bacch. 5. 97–126; see further Gantz 1993: 328–35.

succumbed to Atalanta's charms,[21] to whom he handed the prize of the boar's hide, and subsequently killed his uncle.

## Patrocles

Patrocles (*TrGF* I, 57), a native of Athens who may have moved on to the Greek colony of Thurii, unless Patrocles of Thurii is a different poet (*TrGF* I, 58), will have been active by the first decade of the fourth century, assuming that he is the Patrocles satirized in Aristophanes' *Wealth* (83–5), which was produced in 388 BC. In his only surviving fragment, from an unidentified play, someone gloats over an urn containing an enemy's ashes, and reflects on the futility of hurling threats against one another and making bold plans for the future when death is so close at hand. The first two lines in particular – 'and now fortune has put together all those dread words into such a small container' – are reminiscent of Electra's lament over the urn supposedly containing Orestes' ashes in Sophocles' *Electra* (1126–70); cf. esp. 1142, 'you have come to me as a small mass in a small container'.[22] But the obvious Schadenfreude with which the words are uttered in Patrocles' fragment suggests that it comes not from a lament but from a speech of gleeful relief.

## Astydamas

Astydamas (*TrGF* I, 60) enjoyed unparalleled popularity in his time. His tragedy *Parthenopaeus*, produced in 340 BC as part of a set of two tragedies that won first prize,[23] was so successful that the city of Athens bestowed on him the exceptional honour of having his statue set up at the theatre of Dionysus.[24]

---

[21] Cf. Ov. *Met.* 8. 435–6 *ne sit longe tibi captus amore | auctor*, 'lest this captive of love [=Meleager] may turn out to be far from a champion for you [=Atalanta]'.

[22] See further Stephanopoulos 1988b: 4–5 and 2013: 67.

[23] See *IG* ii² 2320, col. ii (20–2) = *TrGF* I, DID A2 (20–2) = Millis and Olson 2012: 65 (22–4) with their commentary on p. 67; Hanink 2014b: 51–2. The star actor Thettalus, who performed in *Parthenopaeus* as protagonist, was victorious at the actors' contest in the same year. Hornblower (2015: on Lyc. *Alex.* 1189–213) observes that there may have been political, as well as artistic, reasons behind the success of *Parthenopaeus*: in 340 BC, an alliance between Athens and Thebes looked imminent, and indeed only two years later the two cities for once in their history fought side by side at the battle of Chaeronea; so, a play on a Theban theme (Parthenopaeus was one of the Seven against Thebes) was likely to garner popular acclaim.

[24] Further on Astydamas' statue, and on the story of the self-congratulatory epigram he supposedly composed for it, see Duncan and Liapis, this volume.

Astydamas came from a line of distinguished dramatists. His family tree comprises several tragic poets going back (indirectly) to Aeschylus himself: his father was the tragic poet Astydamas Senior (*TrGF* I, 59), his grandfather was Morsimus (*TrGF* I, 29) and his great-grandfather was Philocles (*TrGF* I, 24), the son of Aeschylus' sister. What is more, Astydamas' brother, the junior Philocles (*TrGF* I, 61), was also a tragic poet.[25]

If Astydamas did in fact produce 240 plays, as later sources claim, he must have been astonishingly prolific. It has been argued that the uncommonly high number may be no more than a copyist's error, and it is true that it does represent a staggering productivity rate,[26] even though comparably high or even higher numbers are attested for the tragic poet Carcinus (160 plays) and for the comic poets Antiphanes (260, 280 or even 365 plays) and Alexis (245 plays).[27] He reportedly won fifteen victories in dramatic contests, and inscriptions show that five of those victories, in both Dionysian and Lenaean contests, were spread over a period of more than thirty years (372, ca. 370, 347, 341, 340), which suggests unflagging creativity.[28] However, all that has survived of this apparently prodigious output is a total of seventeen titles, together with a handful of fragments. We know very little about the context or plot of the relevant plays, and all we can say is that five of the surviving titles are also attested for Aeschylus,[29] nine for Sophocles,[30] seven for Euripides[31] and three for other fifth-century dramatists;[32] indeed, in at least seven cases

---

[25] For Astydamas' family tree, with references to the ancient evidence, see *TrGF* I, 12 T 3.
[26] If Astydamas' plays were in tetralogies (which they were not always, see n. 23 earlier in this chapter), then 240 would correspond to 60 tetralogies, i.e., 60 entries in dramatic contests at the City Dionysia, or as many years of continuous writing. In fact, we know that the City Dionysia was not the only festival for which Astydamas produced plays (he also wrote for the Lenaea; see later in this chapter in the text). This means that, rather than entering the dramatic contests every year, he must have produced, in some years, different sets of plays for both the Dionysia and the Lenaea festivals. But of course his productivity is no less astounding for that.
[27] Number of Astydamas' plays: *Suda* α 4264; possible copyist's error: Kannicht, Gauly et al. (1991) 287 n. 2. On Carcinus see *Sud.* κ 394 (*TrGF* I, 70 T 1) and cf. later in this chapter, with n. 68. For the number of Antiphanes' and Alexis' plays see *Sud.* α 2735 (test. 1 K.-A.) and α 1138 (test. 1 K.-A.), respectively. On Antiphanes in particular see further Konstantakos (2000: 177), who rightly dismisses 365 as grossly inflated, and argues that 260 rather than 280 may be closer to the truth.
[28] For the epigraphic evidence see *IG* ii² 2325A.44 (372 BC); 2318.1189 (372 BC), 1477 (347 BC), 1549 (341 BC), 1561 (340 BC); cf. Millis and Olson 2012: 145, 148 (on 44), 42, 44, 46.
[29] *Athamas, Mad Ajax* (cf. Aesch. *Thracian Women*), *Epigoni, Lycaon* (cf. Aesch. *Callisto*), *Parthenopaeus* (cf. Aesch. *Atalantē*).
[30] *Athamas, Mad Ajax* (cf. Soph. *Ajax*), *Alcmeon, Antigone, Epigoni, Nauplius, Palamēdēs, Tyro, Phoenix.*
[31] *Athamas* (cf. Eur. *Ino*), *Alcmeon, Alcmene, Antigone, Bellerophontēs, Palamēdēs, Phoenix.*
[32] *Alcmeon* (also a satyr-play by Achaeus and a tragedy by Agathon; see *TrGF* I, 20 F 12–15 and 39 F 2); *Nauplius* (also a tragedy by Philocles, 24 F 1); *Lycaon* (also a tragedy by Xenocles, 33 F 1).

Astydamas dealt with subjects that, to judge by the plays' titles, were treated by more than one fifth-century tragedian.[33] At first sight, this suggests a desire to emulate the fifth-century masters by covering the same ground as they had and, presumably, by striving to outperform them. This is consistent with the general tendency of fourth-century tragedies to set themselves against earlier (esp. fifth-century) tragic treatments of any given myth.

## Achilles

About Astydamas' *Achilles* (60 T 5) we know virtually nothing, except that it was part of a trilogy that won first prize at the Dionysia of 341. The play is one of several testimonies to Achilles' remarkable popularity as a tragic character in the fourth century: as pointed out in the chapter by Duncan and Liapis, he featured in at least six plays produced in that period.

## Hector[34]

To readers of Homer, Achilles is inextricably bound with Hector, and indeed we know of at least three fourth-century tragedies that take Hector as their principal character. Apart from Astydamas' *Hector*, there is also the pseudo-Euripidean *Rhesus*[35] and *Hector Ransomed* ("Ἕκτορος λύτρα) by Dionysius I, the tyrant of Syracuse, which won first prize at the Lenaea of 367 BC.[36]

Astydamas' *Hector* is one of the few tragedies that are known to have drawn inspiration from the *Iliad*, the others being Aeschylus' Achilles trilogy (*Myrmidons, Nereids, Phrygians*) and the fourth-century *Rhesus*.[37]

---

[33] *Athamas* (also by A., S., and E.), *Ajax* (also by S. and A.), *Alcmeon* (also by S., E., Achaeus, Agathon, Timotheus, Astydamas II, Evaretus and Nicomachus), *Antigone* (also by S. and E.), *Epigoni* (also by A. and S.), *Palamēdēs* (also by S. and E.), *Phoenix* (also by S. and E.). There is also a *Phoenix or Caeneus* by Ion (*TrGF* I, 19 F 36–41b), who also produced a second *Phoenix* (19 F 42–43); it is a puzzle how the former play brought together Phoenix and Caeneus, who belong to entirely different mythic cycles (cf. Snell and Kannicht *ad l.*; Kannicht, Gauly et al. 1991: 276–7 n. 23), and it may be that Ion's Phoenix was a different person from Achilles' tutor, who features in Sophocles' and Euripides' plays.

[34] This section summarizes the argument of Liapis 2016.

[35] For *Rhesus* as a fourth-century play see now Liapis 2012; Fries 2014; also Fries, this volume.

[36] See *TrGF* I, 76 T1, 5 and 3, 4; cf. 76 F 2a. On Dionysius' *Hector* see later in this chapter.

[37] On Hector's *Astydamas* see (apart from Liapis 2016 mentioned in n. 34) Webster 1954: 305–6; Snell 1937: 84–9 and esp. 1971: 138–53; Xanthakis-Karamanos 1980: 162–8. On Aeschylus' Achilles trilogy and its similarities to and divergences from the *Iliad* see further Taplin 2009: 253; cf. Duncan and Liapis, this volume; on *Rhesus* and its models (principally but not exclusively *Iliad* 10) see Liapis 2009a: 273–86 and 2012: xvii–xxvii; Fries 2014: 8–14.

It may be that parts of this play are preserved in the papyrus fragments *TrGF* I, 60 F \*\*1h?, \*\*1i?, and \*\*2a?; their attribution, however, is uncertain. The play must have been famous throughout antiquity, to judge by the fact that Plutarch, writing in first/second century AD, mentions it (as well as Carcinus' *Aëropē*) in the same breath with tragedies by Aeschylus and Sophocles.[38] As far as it can be ascertained, *Hector*'s plot seems to have focused on the build-up to the climactic duel between Hector and Achilles. If fragments 1h and 1i do indeed come from *Hector*, the play must have shown the eponymous character after he had slain Patroclus and stripped him of the shield of Achilles: the former fragment (lines 19–21) mentions Thetis asking Hephaestus to forge a new and more splendid armour for her son, who has been deprived of his weapons; and in the latter (line 6), Hector asks for 'Achilles' shield won in battle' to be brought to him.

The same fragment contains the remains of a seemingly heated altercation between Hector and a messenger, in which the former berates the latter for his alarmist attitude. The messenger has brought news of (evidently) an imminent attack by Achilles himself, who is now about to rejoin the war, and urges Hector to 'take thought for the garrison over there' so that Troy may be prepared 'in well-timed fashion' against the assault. This is reminiscent of Hector castigating the Chorus of Trojan guards for their fearfulness in *Rhesus* 80; indeed, Astydamas' Hector, like his counterpart in *Rhesus*, is also concerned about the effect the messenger's unnerving news may have on the army: 'you are apt to reduce even the bravest man to a hare's mentality', he protests (line 10) – cf. Hector's reproaching the chorus for their panicked apprehension in *Rhesus* 19–22, 34–40, 80 ('if you are afraid of this, then know that you would fear anything'). Significantly, however, this Hector also owes to being shaken by the messenger's news. In what remains of lines 11–13, the hero admits that he feels 'somewhat broken down' (καί πως τ[έθ]ραυσμαι), although he resolutely decides not to appear 'inferior to himself' (ἐμαυτοῦ χείρον[). After all, a few lines before he had asked for his weapons to be brought to him, and in particular for the shield of Achilles, which he has taken as booty from the dead Patroclus. This oscillation between conflicting emotional states may well have been a focal point in this scene.[39] Moreover, the

---

[38] Plut. *Mor.* 349e: 'this is the kind of thing that the city celebrates and performs sacrifices to the gods for, rather than for Aeschylus' or Sophocles' victories, or for the occasion when Carcinus conversed(?) with Aerope or Astydamas with Hector'.

[39] Cf. Snell 1971: 148; Xanthakis-Karamanos 1980: 168; Thum 2005: 217–18.

fact that the scene must have taken place within the walls of Troy, probably before the palace – note the messenger's 'out there', which seems to refer to the battlefield, and Hector's injunction, presumably to a mute attendant, to go 'to the house' to fetch his armour[40] – suggests that Astydamas' play allowed for an intimate farewell scene between Hector and his wife and son – a scene for which we have firm evidence in fr. 2.

In fr. 2, the only fragment whose attribution to Astydamas' *Hector* is assured, and which probably comes from a later point in the play,[41] an armed Hector bids his wife and son farewell, and hands his helmet to an attendant so as to avoid frightening the baby Astyanax.[42] This is an obvious nod to *Iliad* 6.466–75, where Hector removes his helmet to assuage his baby son's fearful agitation at the sight of 'the crest of horsehair [...] waving terribly from the top of the helmet'.[43] Astydamas departs from the epic precedent in having his Hector hand his helmet to an attendant rather than placing it on the ground.[44] This small divergence from the familiar Iliadic scene would no doubt have been perceived by a significant portion of the audience, although it would hardly constitute 'a conspicuous change', as Taplin (2009: 253) argues; if it was meant as such, it is hard to see its dramatic point.[45] One might speculate that the change was due to theatrical practicalities: it would be natural for the actor to hand the helmet over to one of the attendants who would form (as is usual in tragedy) his entourage rather than to have to pick it up again from the ground at the end of the scene. Further, as pointed out by Snell (1971: 142), Astydamas' rearrangement of the chronological order of events by comparison to the *Iliad* means that the helmet that frightens the baby

---

[40] Cf. Xanthakis-Karamanos 1980: 166.
[41] In *Il.* 6.390–496, Hector is armed when bidding his family farewell but his capture of Achilles' armour comes much later (17.85–6, 125); in Astydamas, however, Hector must first put on Achilles' armour (F **1i?), and then bid farewell to his family (F 2), by which time he has his (i.e., presumably Achilles') helmet on. The different sequence of events is, of course, no argument against the attribution of **1i? to Astydamas (*contra* Page 1942: 161): see Taplin 2009: 257–8.
[42] The transmitted text of the fragment is heavily corrupt, though emendations by Porson and Cobet seem to go some way towards restoring it: δέξαι κυνῆν μοι πρόσπολ' †ἐμονδε | <μὴ> καὶ φοβηθῇ παῖς, 'servant, take my helmet ... lest my son is frightened' (the MSS offer a meaningless δέξαι κοινήν μοι πρὸς πόλεμον δέ).
[43] Transl. A.T. Murray and Wyatt 1999a: 309.
[44] The difference (for which see further Taplin 2009: 253) was considered important enough for some ancient critics, reported in the A scholia to *Il.* 6.472, to mark out the Homeric passage for special commentary and comparison with the Astydamas version (II.211.85–7 Erbse).
[45] Taplin (2009: 256) attempts to associate the helmet's presumed conspicuousness in the Astydamas fragment with its undisputed iconographic conspicuousness on a fourth-century Apulian volute-crater, which he argues may echo Astydamas' play. However, the relationship between vase and play is rather unlikely: see Liapis 2016: 84–5; cf. n. 49 later in this chapter.

Astyanax in fr. 2 is not his father's, as in *Iliad* 6, but Achilles' – yet another small change, which however makes for much greater poignancy.

There can be little doubt that fr. 2 would have been part of an extensive and pathetic farewell scene, in which Hector's emotional turmoil would have figured prominently. The play will no doubt have featured a messenger speech describing Hector's fatal duel with Achilles. A part of this narrative may be preserved in fr. **2a?, in which Hector is the first to throw his spear against Achilles (10) but the Greek ducks and dodges the shot (12), so that the spear passes just over his shield's rim (13). Achilles retaliates, and his own spear hits Hector's shield – Achilles' erstwhile possession – but fails to pierce it (18: 'the shield did not let (the spear) through but kept it there').[46] The shield, the messenger continues, 'did not forsake its new owner' (19–20) – though surely his narrative will have ended with Hector's eventual defeat and death. Remarkably, Astydamas reverses the roles, as well as the sequence of events, of *Iliad* 22.273–93, where Achilles throws his spear first, and Hector crouches (275), thereby avoiding the shot; when Hector shoots, his spear strikes 'square on the shield of the son of Peleus'[47] but then glances off it. Astydamas' rearrangement of the Iliadic narrative may have been meant to give Hector an edge over Achilles: in his version, it is Achilles, not Hector, who crouches, thus being cast as perhaps more apprehensive than his opponent.[48] The play may also have included, as Taplin (2009: 254) suggests, 'the return and lamentation of Hector's body immediately after his death', so that its time span would have telescoped 'within a single day events that in the *Iliad* are set several days apart'.[49]

### *Alcmeon; Antigone; Nauplius;* Unidentified Plays

Of Astydamas' *Alcmeon* – a favourite subject in classical tragedy, to judge by the fact that it was treated also by Sophocles, Euripides and Agathon (39 F 2), and in a satyr-drama by Achaeus of Eretria (20 F 12–15) – we

---

[46] Page's supplement for l. 18 ἀσπὶς δ' οὐ διῆκ' εἴσ[ω ξίφος has been accepted by Kannicht, Gauly et al. 1991: 143. Surely, however, εἴσ[ω δόρυ is more appropriate: see Liapis 2016: 71 n. 38.
[47] Transl. A.T. Murray and Wyatt (1999b) 473.
[48] On Astydamas' departure from the *Iliad* see Snell 1937: 86; cf. Xanthakis-Karamanos 1980: 167; 1981: 219. Taplin (2009: 259), who disregards Astydamas' upending of the Iliadic narrative, calls fr. **2a? 'conventional'; on the contrary, it is bold and enterprising.
[49] Further on Astydamas' *Hector* see Liapis 2016, which discusses, *inter alia*, the possibility that Helenus' mantic trance was reported in the lacunose fr. 1h, and argues that neither *TrGF* II, F 649 (adesp.) nor the Apulian volute-crater Berlin Inv. 1984.45 are likely to be connected to Astydamas' play, *pace* Taplin 2009.

know virtually nothing, except that Alcmeon killed his mother Eriphylē without being aware of her true identity: Aristotle (*Poetics* 1453b29–33) classifies *Alcmeon* under those tragedies in which a person does 'a terrible thing' in ignorance, i.e., without realizing, at the time of the deed, that they were slaying a member of their own family.[50]

Astydamas' *Antigone* was part of the trilogy that won him the victory at the Dionysia of 341 BC, the other two plays being *Achilles* and *Athamas*.[51] It was argued by Webster (1954: 304–5) that Hyginus' *Fabula* 72 preserves traces of the Astydamas version of the story, in which Creon had Antigone arrested for burying Polynices against his edict and ordered his son Haemon to kill Antigone himself; disobeying his father, Haemon secretly entrusted Antigone, who was pregnant by him, to shepherds. The play may have opened with the couple's son, now an adult, coming to Thebes, where he was recognized by Creon by the birthmark borne by all descendants of the Sown Men who sprang from the dragon's teeth.[52] Hercules intervened, begging Creon to spare Haemon, whom presumably he had condemned to death for his disobedience; according to Hyginus, Heracles' pleas were unsuccessful, and Haemon went on to kill both himself and Antigone. But as Webster remarks 'unsuccessful intervention by Herakles seems unlikely',[53] and one imagines that the wedding of Hercules and Creon's daughter Megara mentioned by Hyginus would have been combined with official pardon for Haemon and Antigone and recognition of their offspring. If the reconstruction offered here has any validity, Astydamas' *Antigone* must have taken place entirely in Thebes; it then follows that the mention of 'the bronze threshold' at Colonus in Athens in fr. 9 (if indeed this fragment comes from *Antigone*),[54] would be part of a reference to the prehistory of the drama (Oedipus' supernatural end at Colonus, cf. Soph. *Oed. Col.* 57, 1590–1).

The only surviving fragment of *Nauplius* (fr. 5) – a play whose possible relation to Sophocles' own *Nauplius* (fr. 425–438) cannot be established on the evidence currently available – seems to belong to Nauplius' farewell speech to his dead son Palamēdēs. In what was probably meant as self-

---

[50] Cf. Kannicht, Gauly et al. 1991: 287 n. 7; cf. Stephanopoulos 1984: 181–2.
[51] *IG* ii² 2320, col. ii = *TrGF* I, DID A2 (4–6) = Millis and Olson 2012: 65 (ll. 5–8).
[52] In his discussion of 'recognition by signs', Aristotle (*Poet.* 1454b 20–2) mentions 'the spear [i.e., a birthmark in the shape of a spear] which the Earthborn wear' (×—∪ λόγχην ἣν φοροῦσι Γηγενεῖς). One might be tempted to attribute the iambic fragment to Astydamas' play (cf. Webster 1954: 305, 307), although of course this is unprovable.
[53] Webster 1954: 305.
[54] See Snell/Kannicht in app. crit. *ad* F 9, who attribute the suggestion to P. Nikitin.

## Greek Tragedy in the Fourth Century: The Fragments 37

consolation, the speaker argues that the dead must be happy insofar as they can no longer feel the pain they experienced while alive. The idea that death is a deliverer from the sorrows of life first appears in archaic Greek lyric (Mimnermus, Sappho, Theognis), and becomes a standard part of the consolatory discourse only in fourth-century funerary epigrams.[55] The theme is, however, particularly common in fifth-century tragedy: Astydamas' *Nauplius* is performing a tragic *topos*.[56]

One may detect Euripidean influence in F 8 (from an unidentified play), in which the point is made that true nobility is a matter not of bloodline but of character: an entire clan can be exalted through the merits of a single virtuous individual rather than the other way around.[57] 'The surest praise of a family', lines 1–3 claim, 'is to praise a single individual, whoever is just and has the best character; it is he that should be called noble'. Such implicit attacks against old aristocratic ethics are typically Euripidean. In *Electra* 383–4, Orestes states that nobility in people is to be determined on the basis of their 'dealings' (ὁμιλίᾳ) and of their 'disposition' or 'character' (ἤθεσιν). In *Dictys* (fr. 336 Kannicht), an unidentified character, perhaps Dictys, claims that only the morally superior can be truly noble; base characters, even if they are of the noblest ancestry, will in essence be ignoble. Similar sentiments are also put forth in *Captive Melanippē* (fr. 495.40–3) and *Phrixus* (fr. 831).[58]

A glimpse into Astydamas' poetics is afforded by a fragment (F 4) from his satyr-play *Herakles*.[59] 'An accomplished poet', the speaker claims, 'should offer his spectators something resembling the variegated dishes of a refined dinner'; the poet's art (*mousikē*) should not have 'only one kind of dressing'; on the contrary, it should allow everyone to 'eat and drink whatever they prefer'. A similar point is made in a fragment from Metagenes' (fifth-/fourth-century BC) comedy *Philothytēs* (*The Lover of Sacrifices* or *The Festival-Lover*): 'I change my discourse episode by episode so that

---

[55] Sourvinou-Inwood 1995: 393–4.
[56] See esp. Friis Johansen and Whittle 1980: iii.*ad* A. *Su*. 802–3; Sourvinou-Inwood 1995: 394–8; cf. A. fr. 353 and 255.3 Radt; S. *Tr*. 1173; *El*. 1170; *OC* 955; fr. 698 Radt; E. *Alc*. 937–8; *Hipp*. 1047; *Su*. 1004–5; *Tro*. 271, 641–2; *Heracl*. 595–6 (with Wilkins 1993 *ad loc*.); *Ba*. 1360–2; fr. 833.3–4 Kannicht; *TrGF* II, fr. 371 (adesp.).
[57] On the textual corruption in l. 4 see West 1983: 80; Stephanopoulos 1988b: 5–6.
[58] Cf. also fr. 232.3–4 Kannicht: 'an impoverished person does not lose his ancestral nobility'; see Denniston 1939: 81–2 (*ad* E. *El*. 253).
[59] The fragment is in 'choriambic dimetres' or *wilamowitziani*, a metre particularly favoured by Euripides; see further Itsumi 1982.

I can feast the theatre with many new side-dishes'.[60] What is prioritized here is not merely novelty or variety, but a subtle and adroit coordination of different artistic ingredients, so that the resulting work may appeal to as many sections of the audience as possible and (one may infer) increase the poet's chances of achieving victory. The *Herakles* fragment, with its metapoetic statement, seems to be surprisingly close to the parabasis of Old Comedy, which 'was in essence an occasion for comic poets to carry out exchanges with one another, styling themselves in competition for the prize' and asserting their own talent, inventiveness and overall literary significance.[61] As we know nothing either of the speaker or of the context of the *Herakles* lines, we cannot press the point any further, but it would be tempting to see here the traces of cross-genre play and a blurring of boundaries between kindred but distinct dramatic forms.

## Carcinus Junior

Like Astydamas, Carcinus Junior (or 'Carcinus II', *TrGF* I, 70) was born into a family of tragic poets, of which he was the most eminent member.[62] His grandfather, Carcinus I (*TrGF* I, 21), was a choral dancer and a tragic dramatist (21 T 3a), who won first prize at the Dionysia of 446 BC (T 1);[63] he was also a prominent citizen, since he served as a trierarch, or commander of a trireme, around 450 BC (T 7) and as one of the generals of an Athenian naval expedition against the Peloponnese in 431 BC (T 5, 6). Carcinus Senior's three sons were also tragic choreuts (21 T 2a–f, cf. Aristophanes' *Wasps* 1498–1532), and one of them, Xenocles I (*TrGF* I, 33), was the father of Carcinus Junior. This Xenocles was also a tragic poet (33 T 1), one recognizable enough to have one of his plays (*Likymnios*, F 2) parodied in Aristophanes' *Clouds* 1265[64] and to be otherwise satirized by comic poets (T 2, 4a–b, 5). Remarkably, Xenocles came in first at the

---

[60] *PCG* fr. 15; transl. Wilkins 2000: 100; cf. Olson 2007: 109–10. An 'episode' (ἐπεισόδιον) here is an extraneous addition made for the sake of eliciting laughter, without any special connection to the main argument of the play; see Olson 2007: 84.

[61] See Biles 2011: 37, whence the quotation. On the *Herakles* fragment as evidence for the poetics of ποικιλία, or diversity/variety (including 'the structural diversity that comes through the use of digression and contrasting material'), as opposed to integration and uniformity see M. Heath 1987: 105–6.

[62] On Carcinus Junior and his family see J. K. Davies 1971: 283–5 (no. 8254); cf. MacDowell 1971: 326–7 *ad* Ar. *Vesp.* 1501.

[63] It has been argued by Rothwell 1994 that Carcinus Senior was a comic rather than a tragic poet; see, however, Olson 1997 and 2000.

[64] See discussion in Dover 1968a: *ad* Ar. *Nub.* 1264.

Dionysia of 415 BC (T3, F1), leaving Euripides with his Trojan trilogy at second place.

Carcinus Junior (henceforth: Carcinus) must have been born in the last years of the fifth century: the *Suda* places his *floruit* (i.e., possibly, his first victory)[65] at around 380/79–377/6 (70 T 1). This is consistent both with the (lacunose) inscriptional record, which indicates that Carcinus' first victory is to be placed sometime before 372 BC,[66] and with the fact that one of his fragments (fr. 6) is preserved in Lysias (fr. 235 Carey), whose last speech dates from around 380 BC.[67] That a well-established orator such as Lysias should cite lines by Carcinus suggests that the latter had not only begun his career before 380 but also that he must have become well known relatively early. On the other hand, it is remarkable that the otherwise prolific Carcinus did not participate in the Great Dionysia either in 341 or in 340, when two of his fellow-tragedians, the celebrated Astydamas (roughly, Carcinus' contemporary) and the obscure Evaretus, took part in the contests for two years in a row. This may mean either that Carcinus was no longer alive (the more probable explanation) or that he was away from Athens, perhaps in Syracuse, where he paid repeated visits (see later in this chapter).

Carcinus is credited with 160 plays,[68] and the inscriptional record attests that he won eleven victories for plays produced at the Great Dionysia.[69] The later reception of his work is not easy to ascertain, and may not have been unanimously positive. Interestingly, the few available testimonia come from a variety of sources (rather than, as, e.g., in the case of Moschion, from the anthologist Stobaeus) and concern various aspects of his work, such as dramaturgy, performance and song. Already in the

---

[65] See Kannicht, Gauly et al. 1991: 288 n. 4.
[66] On the assumption that the relics ]ΝΟΣ on *IG* ii² 2325A, 43 are to be supplemented as ΚΑΡΚΙ]ΝΟΣ: see further Millis and Olson 2012: 148. On the basis of a didascalic fragment first published in 1971 (Camp 1971: 302–5), Snell conjectured that Carcinus may have won a victory at the Lenaea contest in 376 BC (see *TrGF* I, p. 342, Addenda to p. 27, DID A2b, app. crit. to col. 1, 11).
[67] See Dover 1968b: 44–6; Todd 2007: 1.
[68] The number has been considered too high by some. If 160 is correct, Carcinus must have produced more plays (some three or four?) per year on average than any of the three great fifth-century tragic poets (two at most); he may have written also for performances outside Athens. His prolific output may have something to do with the development of the chorus in post-classical drama: if expected to produce only brief stasima and/or to include pre-fabricated *embolima* (see Duncan and Liapis, this volume) into his plays, a dramatist would surely need to invest less time and effort than his fifth-century predecessors in producing new work.
[69] See *IG* ii² 2325A, 43 in Millis and Olson 2012: 145.

fourth century, five of his works are mentioned by Aristotle in several treatises,[70] while in Menander's *Shield* (407–28), the slave Daos intersperses his affected lament with tragic quotations from Carcinus, as well as from Aeschylus, Euripides and Chaeremon, all of whom are mentioned by name.[71] Carcinus' *Medea* was evidently still performed in the second century AD (though possibly in the form of condensed excerpts, see later in this chapter), while his *Aëropē* could still be mentioned as an example of a first-rate tragedy by Plutarch, who implies that the play's first performance was a triumph (see earlier in this chapter, including n. 38). Indeed, according to Aelian (*Varia Historia* 14.40), *Aëropē* was performed by the great tragic actor Theodorus[72] in so riveting and poignant a fashion that it moved to tears even the bloodthirsty tyrant Alexander of Pherae (*regn.* 369–358) – although the historicity of this anecdote is highly debatable, since the same story is also found elsewhere, with Euripides' *Hecuba* or *Trojan Women* as the cause of Alexander's tears.[73] On a more negative note, in the first century BC, Philodemus of Gadara in his treatise *On Poems*[74] groups Carcinus together with Cleaenetus (*TrGF* I, 84 T 3) as an example of 'low-quality' (πονηρούς) poets who can only be unfavourably compared to the 'outstanding' Euripides. Finally, according to an anecdote related by Athenaeus (351f), the witty fourth-century citharist Stratonicus, when informed that a song he had heard was by Carcinus (which is Greek for 'crab'), quipped: 'that's more like it – this doesn't look like it's by a human being' (πολύ γε μᾶλλον ἢ ἀνθρώπου).[75] Even if the anecdote is true, it is possible that Stratonicus was more interested in cracking a joke than in making a serious statement about the quality of Carcinus' songs.

## *Aëropē; Ajax*

Of Carcinus' most famous drama, *Aëropē*, nothing survives. On the assumption that the adulterous relationship between Aëropē and Thyestes may have featured prominently in it, it has been suggested that *Aëropē* may have been the same play as *Thyestes*. In such a case, Aristotle's mention of 'stars' as a recognition-token in Carcinus' '*Thyestes*' could refer to a scene in *Aëropē* in which Thyestes recognized the butchered body of his son by a

---

[70] *Alopē* (*EN* 1150b10); ?*Amphiaraus* (*Po.* 1455a26–9); *Medea* (*Rh.* 1400b9–15); *Oedipus* (*Rh.* 1417b18–20); *Thyestes* (*Po.* 1454b23). See Hanink 2014b: 200–1.
[71] See further Wright 2016: 124–5.   [72] On Theodorus see Stephanis 1988: no. 1157.
[73] See Plut. *Pel.* 29.5; *Mor.* 334a.   [74] *PHerc.* 994, col. xxv (Sbordone 1976: 87).
[75] Cf. Bélis 2004: 1327–8; West 2013: 347.

star-shaped birthmark on his shoulder.[76] However, the identification of *Aëropē* with *Thyestes* is far from certain, and may be unnecessary or even unlikely for a poet credited with 160 plays.[77]

With regard to Carcinus' *Ajax* we have not much to go on. We hear of a proverb 'Ajax's laughter' (Αἰάντειος γέλως), which supposedly originated in the sarcastic laughter with which Pleisthenes (Stephanis 1988: no. 2069), the tragic actor playing Ajax, reacted to Odysseus' hypocritically moralistic 'one must do what is right' (fr. 1a). Although it is possible that Ajax's laughter was prompted by a stage direction (*parepigraphē*) in the play script, it is likelier that it was the actor Pleisthenes himself who hit upon the idea, hence his mention by name in the sources.

## *Alopē; Amphiaraus*(?)

Our knowledge of *Alopē* relies entirely on Aristotle's *Nicomachean Ethics* (1150b10) and on its ancient commentators. Aristotle mentions Carcinus' Cercyon, together with Theodectas' Philoctetes, as an example of a tragic character succumbing, in spite of initial resistance, to 'extreme grief'. According to later Aristotelian commentaries,[78] Cercyon, upon confirming that his daughter Alopē was raped by Poseidon, became so devastated that he found it impossible to go on living, and so apparently committed suicide.[79] Such a version of the myth would represent a substantial deviation from its treatment in Euripides (where Alopē was put to death), as well as shifting rather drastically the dramatic focus to Cercyon's inner struggle.[80]

According to Aristotle (*Poetics* 1455a 26–9), a play by Carcinus including the seer Amphiaraus – perhaps the play itself was entitled *Amphiaraus* – was 'hissed off the stage' by a disgruntled audience, who perceived an error of stagecraft that Carcinus had evidently missed when composing his play

---

[76] See Arist. *Po.* 1454b19–23 with Lucas (1968) 167 (*ad* 54b22 and 54b23).
[77] See Kannicht, Gauly et al. 1991: 288 n. 1, where it is pointed out that Agathon too is credited with both an *Aëropē* and a *Thyestes* (*TrGF* I, 39 F 1 and 3), and that both a *Cretan Women* (an Aëropē drama) and a *Thyestes* are attested for Euripides.
[78] See esp. *Comm. in Aristot. Graeca* XX, p. 437.2–6.
[79] According to Dirlmeier (1969: 490), the Greek (ἀλλὰ καὶ τὸ ζῆν ἀπελέγετο) may mean either that Cercyon committed suicide or that he killed his daughter (as was apparently the case in Euripides). However, the Greek idiom seems to be used only of suicide, never of murder; and in the partly parallel story of Nycteus (Apollod. 3.5.5), the hero committed suicide on realizing that his daughter Antiopē was pregnant by Zeus. Admittedly, if the play culminated (presumably) in Cercyon's suicide, one would expect it to be named after him rather than after Alopē.
[80] Schmid 1940: 593; Webster 1954: 300–1. Against Xanthakis–Karamanos' (1980: 36–8) unwarranted generalizations (to the effect that Carcinus' Cercyon is an instance of a supposed tendency in fourth-century tragedy to avoid wilful murder of kin) see the criticisms offered by Belfiore 2000: 218. On Carcinus' *Alopē* see also Karamanou 2003.

because he had allowed himself to lose sight of its visual and performative aspects. Carcinus had Amphiaraus come up out of a shrine in a manner that was probably perceived as contradictory or otherwise inappropriate[81] – perhaps because Amphiaraus had already exited the shrine and was not subsequently seen re-entering it.[82] As for the plot, one may surmise that it revolved around the well-known myth of Eriphylē receiving a necklace in return for persuading Amphiaraus to join the doomed expedition of the Seven against Thebes.[83]

## Medea

Even though the relevant evidence is fragmentary and inconclusive, we would not be wide of the mark in assuming that Carcinus' *Medea* put forth a revisionist version of the myth as we know it from earlier tragedians (possibly Neophron, and especially Euripides). One of our sources for the play is Aristotle (*Rhetoric* 1400b9–15), who cites the confrontation between Medea and her accusers in Carcinus' tragedy as an example of both plaintiff and defendant arguing on the basis of 'errors committed' (ἐκ τῶν ἁμαρτηθέντων). According to a probable reconstruction of the play's events, Medea, having sent her children away from Corinth (for their protection?), was accused of having killed them; in her defence, she denied the accusation and resorted to an obvious argument from probability: namely that, had she harboured murderous designs, these ought to have been directed against the unfaithful Jason, who is nonetheless alive, rather than against her children.[84]

Recently, a Louvre musical papyrus of the second century AD[85] has added to the textual evidence by furnishing us with a fragment, or more

---

[81] Arist. *Po.* 1455a 26–9 ὁ γὰρ Ἀμφιάραος ἐξ ἱεροῦ ἀνῄει, ὃ μὴ ὁρῶντα {τὸν θεατὴν del. Butcher} ἐλάνθανεν, ἐπὶ δὲ τῆς σκηνῆς ἐξέπεσεν δυσχερανάντων τοῦτο τῶν θεατῶν. As Lucas (1968: 174) remarks, μὴ ὁρῶντα 'must refer [...] "to anyone who did not see it", i.e., to those who read [the play]. But in the theatre (δέ is now adversative) the result was calamitous'; cf. Bremer 1993: 203; see further Tarán–Goutas 2012: 273.

[82] Thus Webster (1954: 300) and others; for doxography see Lapini 1995/8, Dettori 1997, and Davidson 2003, all of whom offer different interpretations of the *Poetics* passage.

[83] Of the three great tragedians, only Sophocles is credited with both an *Amphiaraus* and an *Eriphylē*. In fact, there may have been two Sophoclean plays entitled *Amphiaraus*, one a tragedy and the other a satyr-drama; see S. Radt in *TrGF* IV, 151–2.

[84] Some scholars have seen Medea's argument as an implicit criticism of the Euripidean version: e.g., Schmid 1940: 359 n. 5, 370; Webster 1954: 301; Xanthakis-Karamanos 1980: 35–6. But the criticism, if such it is, may as well have been directed against Neophron, especially if the latter's *Medea* was earlier than Euripides' (see Stephanopoulos 1984: 181; *contra*, though not with absolute certainty, Mastronarde 2002: 57–64). Against Xanthakis-Karamanos' (*l.c.*) assumption that Carcinus put forth an innovatively humane representation of Medea as one incapable of harming her children see Belfiore 2000: 217–18.

[85] Antiquités égyptiennes inv. E. 10534; *ed. pr.* Bélis 2004; discussion and improvements in West 2007 (rev. in West 2013: 334–50, whence the citations later in this chapter); Martinelli 2010. Cf. also Pöhlmann 2009: 296–9; Burkert 2009: 162–6.

probably a compressed excerpt, from Carcinus' *Medea*. The papyrus contains the remains of some fifteen iambic lines (compatible with Aristotle's passing reference to the play), in which Jason, Medea and evidently a third speaker[86] debate what must have been the play's central question: if Medea has not killed her children, as she keeps asserting, then where are they? Jason asks Medea to prove her innocence by producing the children; Medea swears that, far from killing them, she has entrusted them to a nurse and sent them away; and a third character insists that Medea, who is by her own confession the murderer of Glaukē, has obviously killed her own children too, and deserves to be put to death. In any case, at this point in the play, it would have been unlikely for Medea to claim that she has merely sent her children away, when in reality she has murdered them. Indeed, if the children were still alive at this point, it stands to reason that the truth would have come out later in the play, and even perhaps that the children themselves were produced.[87]

Lately, Taplin (2014: 149–53) suggested that an Apulian volute-krater of ca. 340–330 BC reflects Carcinus' *Medea* (Figure 1). On it, Medea stands inside the shrine of Demeter and Korē in Eleusis conversing with an aged tutor-figure, while her two children (in all likelihood), very much alive, are shown as suppliants at a nearby altar.[88] However, Taplin's assumption that the vase is inspired from Carcinus is problematic in two respects. Firstly, it is hard to accept, without further evidence, that *Medea* took place partly in Corinth (where the Louvre papyrus scene is evidently set) and partly in Eleusis: this would require not only the characters but also the chorus to move from one place to the other, which would have been hard to account for (contrast the mobile chorus of Aeschylus' *Eumenides*, which suits their character of pursuing deities). Secondly, it is even harder to accept that Medea, who has already murdered Glaukē (Louvre papyrus) and is now accused of murdering her children too (Aristotle), should have been allowed to repair, or escape, to Eleusis, while facing extremely serious charges.

*Oedipus*

From an elliptic reference in Aristotle's *Rhetoric* (1417b18–20), one may gather that Carcinus' *Oedipus* contained a scene in which someone, probably Oedipus himself, pressingly asked Jocasta what became of the

---
[86] West (2013: 345) is inclined to identify the third speaker as Creon, the king of Corinth. However, it seems odd that Creon should refer to his dead daughter, somewhat aloofly, as 'Glaukē' (line 8) rather than, more paternally, as 'my daughter'.
[87] Cf. Revermann 2010: 83; see also McHardy 2005: 137. For a conjectural reconstruction of the plot of this play see West 2013: 341–5; for a response see Martinelli 2010: 72–3.
[88] See further the discussion in Giuliani and Most 2007.

Figure 1  Red-figure volute-krater attributed to the Darius Painter, ca. 340–330 BC. Princeton University Art Museum, Carl Otto von Kienbusch Jr., Memorial Collection Fund, y1983-13. Photo: Trustees of Princeton University.

infant she once gave birth to.[89] If this is so, then Carcinus will have in all likelihood constructed a scene along the lines of Sophocles' *Oedipus Tyrannus*, in which Oedipus may have urged Jocasta to provide information on the fate of her child, and the queen in response tried to allay his concerns, perhaps by pointing out, as she does in Sophocles, that since Laius' son died in infancy and cannot have killed his father, the credibility of oracles, about which Oedipus is so concerned, is seriously undermined;

---

[89] For the argument that Oedipus himself, rather than Laius (as Webster 1954: 301 thought), is meant by Aristotle's πυνθανομένου τοῦ ζητοῦντος τὸν υἱόν see Cooper 1929: 176–80; cf. Stephanopoulos 1984: 180. If Laius were the enquirer, the play's action would probably have had to cover, implausibly, the whole range of events from Oedipus' exposure to the revelation of his crimes.

she may also have advised Oedipus to desist from the search.[90] Moreover, as Cooper (1929) 179 speculates, Carcinus may have gone Sophocles one better by providing Jocasta with a long speech of advice to Oedipus, which is why Aristotle used the Carcinus play to illustrate his argument that an orator making a point his hearer may find incredible should profess to tell the truth and at once corroborate that statement with an explanation.[91]

### The 'Sicilian Fragment'

The most extensive of Carcinus' surviving fragments is fr. 5 (from an unknown play), which relates the foundation myth of the Sicilian cult of Demeter and Korē. The ten-line fragment, which is introduced by a formula reserved for stories, folktales, anecdotes and suchlike (λέγουσι, 'they say'), relates how Demeter roamed the earth in search of her daughter, who had been carried off by Pluto into Hades. Demeter's wanderings were accompanied by an eruption of Aetna: 'the earth around Aetna's Sicilian crags, which was filled with streams of fire hard to approach, groaned all over' (lines 6–8). The goddess' sorrow caused the crops to fail, as a result of which the inhabitants started to perish; in response, the Sicilians instituted a cult in honour of the two goddesses. The fragment's aetiological function is made explicit in its last line: ὅθεν θεὰς τιμῶσιν ἐς τὰ νῦν ἔτι, 'on account of this, they honour the two goddesses down to this day'. It is impossible, however, to determine whether the fragment comes from a tragedy dramatizing the myth of Demeter and Korē, or (the likeliest possibility) whether it is an *en passant* reference to their Sicilian cult. We are equally uncertain about the play's setting: Wilamowitz's change of the fragment's last word into ἐκεῖ ('there, in that place') would mean that the play was *not* set in Sicily, although the fragment's narrative is obviously associated with it. However, Wilamowitz's conjecture is unwarranted: ἐς τὰ νῦν ἔτι is a formulaic expression, which (like similar expressions such as ἔτι καὶ νῦν, εἰσέτι καὶ νῦν, etc.) is often used in aetiological narratives.[92]

It has been argued that the fragment in question comes from the play's narrative prologue, which supposedly replicated a Euripidean mannerism (cf. esp. *Or.* 4–9, where ὡς λέγουσι is repeated twice), and even that these were the play's opening lines.[93] The argument, however, is specious. Carcinus' seemingly self-contained narrative differs unmistakably from the style of Euripidean prologues: it is largely in indirect speech (the initial λέγουσι governs five infinitives in the space of only eight lines); it is

---

[90] See Cooper 1929: 179.   [91] On the Aristotelian passage see Cooper 1929: 170–3.
[92] See Stephanopoulos 1988b: 7 for full documentation.
[93] Thus Xanthakis-Karamanos 1980: 89.

strikingly free of the specific details (such as the speaker's identity, the setting, the account of recent events, etc.) regularly found in Euripidean prologues; and its extensive aetiological narrative is quite unlike anything we find in the opening of Euripidean plays.[94] Similar narratives (minus the aetiological conclusion) are by no means restricted to tragic prologues; for instance, in Sophocles' *Electra* (566–72) an account of Agamemnon's transgression forms part of a debate; and in the pseudo-Euripidean *Rhesus* (919ff.), a comparable narrative (with aetiological elements) is found near the end of the play (see Fries, this volume); cf. also Aeschylus' *Agamemnon* 1583–1611.

Carcinus' account of Demeter's search for her daughter is evidently indebted to Euripides' lyric version of the myth in *Helen* 1301–52, as a number of verbal similarities suggest.[95] However, Carcinus' retelling is significantly different in that it shifts the spatial focus of the mythic incident from Mt. Ida in the Troad (E. *Hel.* 1323–4, with a nod to Demeter's syncretistic fusion with Cybele, the 'Idean Mother')[96] to Mt. Aetna in Sicily. One is tempted to speculate, though this must remain a mere hypothesis for the time being, that the fragment is informed by Carcinus' personal experience of the Sicilian cult of Demeter and Korē, or at least that 'he had an eye to a local audience'.[97] We know, on the authority of the historian Timaeus (*FGrHist* 566 F 164 = Diod. Sic. 5.5.1), that Carcinus sojourned repeatedly in Syracuse, where the cult of the grain-goddesses had been promoted already in the fifth century by the Deinomenid rulers of south-eastern Sicily (especially Gelon, Theron and Hieron), often in the form of festivals commemorating important episodes of the Korē myth, including her rape by Pluto.[98]

As is to be expected from a fourth-century tragic author, the remains of Carcinus' tragic production, meagre as they are, suggest an engagement with myths already dealt with by the three great tragedians.[99] In a few cases, his fragments even contain identifiable verbal reminiscences of specific Aeschylean or Euripidean passages. Thus, the only surviving fragment of Carcinus' *Achilles* (1d) includes a usage (αὐλῶνα = 'ditch') that is otherwise found only in Aeschylus (*TrGF* III, F 419)[100] and also in the fourth-century *Rhesus* (112), in the latter case presumably as an

---

[94] See further Stephanopoulos 1988b: 6–7.
[95] For instance, Carcinus' ἄρρητον κόρην (l. 1) evokes Euripides' ἀρρήτου κούρας (*Hel.* 1307); his μαστῆρ' (l. 5) harks back to μαστεύουσα in *Hel.* 1321; etc. Cf. Kannicht 1969: 2. 327–59; Xanthakis-Karamanos 1980: 87–8.
[96] See further W. Allan 2008: 294–5 (on E. *Hel.* 1301–68) and 302 (on 1323–4).
[97] Quotation from Dearden 1990: 239.
[98] See further Polacco and Anti 1981: 26–7 (on such Syracusan festivals as the Thesmophoria, the Koreia, etc.); Kowalzig 2008: 132–45.
[99] Aeschylus: Oedipus, Semelē. Sophocles: Ajax, Oedipus, Thyestes, Tyro. Euripides: Alopē, Medea, Oedipus, Orestes, Thyestes.
[100] See Radt's commentary *ad loc.* and on Aesch. fr. dub. 465.

imitation of Aeschylean style.[101] The influence of Euripides appears to be (unsurprisingly) more extensive. As we saw earlier in this chapter (cf. n. 95), fr. 5 is a reworking, with noteworthy deviations, of a lyric passage from *Helen*. Moreover, the violently misogynistic fr. 3 from Carcinus' *Semelē* – to the effect that calling a woman simply 'woman' is the vilest insult imaginable – rephrases a sentiment found already in Euripides (fr. 666 Kn.). Finally, fr. 9 (– ⏑ δειλόν ἐσθ' ὁ πλοῦτος καὶ φιλόψυχον κακόν) appears to be an almost verbatim repetition of Euripides, *Phoenissae* 597.[102] On the other hand, as far as we are able to ascertain, Carcinus did not hesitate to diverge from Euripides in interesting ways. As we saw, in his *Alopē* the focus of dramatic interest may have been Cercyon's inner struggle and climactic suicide (as opposed to Alopē's death in Euripides); his *Medea* certainly featured a 'courtroom' scene in which rhetoric played a prominent part; and his *Orestes* also must have included a similar scene, in which Orestes, who no doubt found it hard to confess his matricidal act, responded 'by riddles' to accusations of matricide (fr. 1g), perhaps using the same evasive and ambiguous language his Euripidean predecessor resorts to in *Iphigenia in Tauris* 495–512.[103]

## Chaeremon

Of Chaeremon's life almost nothing is known (*TrGF* I, 71 T 1–5) – neither where he came from, nor the number of his plays, nor the number of dramatic contests he took part in, nor the number of his victories.[104] We do, however, know the titles of nine of his plays, and possess some 40 fragments (or approximately 85 lines), more than half of which are gnomic, mostly one-liners, some of them peculiar (F 32) and some extremely popular (F 2 and 3). Our admittedly fuzzy image of this idiosyncratic playwright comes principally from these fragments, as well as from references in Aristotle and in the comic poets, from a second-century inscription, and from a vase-painting arguably inspired from his work.[105] That he was active around or even before 370 BC is indicated by a quotation in the comic poet Eubulus (*PCG* fr. 128 K.-A. = Chaerem. F 17), who won his first victory in 370 BC, and by a mention in the comic

---

[101] See Liapis 2012: *ad* [E.] *Rh.* 112–15; Fries 2014: *ad* 112.
[102] In *TrGF* I, the fr. is printed as part of a trochee, to reflect the trochaic character of its Euripidean model; but Carcinus may well have chosen to recast the Euripidean line as an iamb, namely δειλόν δ' ὁ πλοῦτος, etc. The feeble ἐσθ', which slackens the line's punchy succinctness, is probably an anthologist's addition.
[103] For a comprehensive appreciation of Carcinus see Seeck 1979: 187–8.
[104] Essential bibliography on Chaeremon: Collard 1970 (the article will be cited in the revised form in which it appeared in Collard 2007: 31–55); Snell 1971: 154–69.
[105] See Seeck 1979: 188; Müller-Goldingen 2005: 88–96. On the inscription and on the vase-painting see later in this chapter.

poet Ephippus (*PCG* fr. 9 K.-A.), who won his first victory in 368 (assuming of course that the Chaeremon mentioned there is the tragic poet).[106] In Menander's *Shield* (407–28, cf. earlier in this chapter), the slave Daos quotes from, among others, Euripides and Chaeremon, specifying that they are 'not just any old poets' (428 οὐ τῶν τυχόντων).[107] Chaeremon shares with other early fourth-century tragic poets both 'the strong influence of Euripidean theatre' and 'the contemporary attempt to outdo Euripides' colours and effects'.[108] Aristotle (*Rhetoric* 1413b12) classifies Chaeremon as an *anagnōstikos*, explaining that he is 'accurate like a prose-writer' (ἀκριβὴς ὥσπερ λογογράφος).[109] Aristotle's *anagnōstikos* was once interpreted as meaning that Chaeremon was one of those tragedians who wrote dramas intended for reading (*anagnōsis*) rather than for performance. However, the modern consensus is that Aristotle's reference to *anagnōstikoi* is simply a stylistic judgment: its point is that certain authors' stylistic accuracy makes them especially suitable for reading, though not necessarily to the exclusion of stage representation (see further later in this chapter, on *The Centaur*).[110] After all, some time in the second century BC,[111] an unknown touring actor-cum-boxer won the first prize at the Naïa festival of Dodona with a performance of Chaeremon's *Achilles*, probably the same play as *Achilles Slaying Thersites*.[112] And a line from that play – 'human affairs are a matter of luck, not of sagacity' (F 2) – became a familiar catchphrase, quoted by subsequent playwrights,[113] who must have counted on its being recognizable by large audiences rather than only by the literati.

One of Chaeremon's most salient traits, it seems, was a bold attention to sensuous detail, which is quite unparalleled in fifth-century tragedy. A case

---

[106] See Snell and Kannicht in *TrGF* I, 71 T 2; cf. Hanink 2014a: 193 with n. 30. Eubulus seems to have been active between 380–335 (Hunter 1983: 7–10) or 375–340 BC (Nesselrath 1990: 196–7). In the fragment mentioned in the text, Eubulus quotes Chaeremon verbatim, and must have mentioned him by name (see Kassel and Austin *ad loc.*), possibly by way of parodying his 'dithyrambic' style; see Nesselrath 1990: 247–8.

[107] See Wright 2016: 125.   [108] Quotations from Collard 2007: 38.

[109] Aristotle associates 'accuracy' with prose style (γραφικὴ λέξις) as opposed to the 'debating' style of oral delivery (ἀγωνιστικὴ δὲ (sc. λέξις) ἡ ὑποκριτικωτάτη): see Zwierlein 1966: 131–4.

[110] The interpretation of *anagnōstikos* as 'particularly suitable for reading' goes back to Otto Crusius in the early twentieth century: see Pfeiffer 1968: 28–9; Collard 2007: 35–6; Snell 1971: 158–9; Jacobson 1981: 167–9, with earlier bibliography and discussion. Cf. Lanfranchi 2006: 35–6; Hunter 2003: 219. For a partly different view see D. J. Allan 1980: 246.

[111] Between 190 and 170: see Le Guen 2007: 98–104.

[112] See also Duncan and Liapis, this volume. Cf. Snell 1971: 159. For a comprehensive attempt to reconstruct Chaeremon's *Achilles*, esp. on the basis of an Apulian red-figure krater in Boston, see Morelli 2001. The play must have included Thersites taunting Achilles with his love for the dead Penthesilea and Achilles killing Thersites as a punishment (cf. Collard 2007: 37). However, the connection with the Boston vase remains uncertain; cf. Taplin 2014: 154–5.

[113] Men. *Asp.* 411 τύχη τὰ θνητῶν πράγματ', οὐκ εὐβουλία (cited together with lines from Aeschylus, Euripides and Carcinus); Nicostratus, *PCG* fr. 19.4 K.-A. Cf. also Pl. *Leg.* 709b; Dem. 2.22. On the afterlife of Chaeremon's line see further White 2007: 227–8.

in point is his apparent predilection for descriptions of flowers (pointed out by Athenaeus, 13. 608d), sometimes in erotic or sensual contexts. Flowers are 'children of blossoming spring' (F 9, from *Io*);[114] or they are 'children of the meadows' (cf. A. *Pers.* 618 'flowers ... children of all-bearing earth') forming 'a boundless army without spears' (F 10, from *The Centaur*). Roses are 'bright-beaming' (ὀξυφεγγῆ, a unique formation, F 8 from *Thyestes*), 'the bodies of the seasons' and 'resplendent nurslings of spring' (F 13 from *Odysseus*).[115] And some young persons, perhaps women, at the height of sexual attractiveness, are said to have 'Cypris' bounteous late-summer ripening in (their) tender grape-vines' (F 12 from *Minyae*) – probably a veiled reference to pubic rather than facial hair.[116] The passages cited also exemplify Chaeremon's bold use of metaphor, further evidenced in F 17, in which the water flowing in a stream is termed 'a river's body' (ὕδωρ ... ποταμοῦ σῶμα, quoted in Eubulus, *PCG* fr. 128 K.-A.).[117]

Chaeremon's characteristic attention to flowers, combined with a somewhat contrived boldness of language, is also evident in his *Dionysus*. That tragedy may have revolved around the same myth as Euripides' *Bacchae*, to judge by F *4: 'Pentheus, whose name presaged his future catastrophe'; cf. E. *Ba.* 508 'your name (i.e., Pentheus) makes you suitable for misfortune' (*penthos*). It is presumably in the context of Bacchic celebrations that the ivy is called 'lover of the dance' and 'son of the year' (F 5), and together with the narcissus is 'twisted three times around garlands' (F 7) – garlands being 'harbingers' or 'heralds of ritual silence' (F 6, cf. F 11 from *The Centaur*).

## The Centaur

This appears to have been an unusual play, both in having probably the Centaur Chiron as its main character (see later in this section) and in being 'a mixed rhapsody combining all sorts of metres' (μικτὴν ῥαψωδίαν ἐξ ἁπάντων τῶν μέτρων), as Aristotle puts it, while Athenaeus, who cites two

---

[114] The metaphor resurfaces as a Shakespearean cliché; cf. *Hamlet* 1.3.38 'the infants of the spring'; *Love's Labour's Lost* 1.1.101 'the first-born infants of the spring'; *The Two Noble Kinsmen* 1.1.7–8 'Primrose, first-born child of Ver'. The similarity is, of course, coincidental.

[115] On these colourful metaphors, and the recherché language in which they are often couched (including new coinages), see Collard 2007: 38–40.

[116] 'Tender' renders Meineke's emendation ἁβραῖσι for MS ἄκραισι; see *TrGF* I, p. 354 (Addenda to p. 220, 71 F 12 2). Pubic hair: West 1983: 80; cf. Stephanopoulos 1988b: 11. Chaeremon's language appears to echo Pindar, *Nem.* 5.6 (with reference to a beardless youth): οὔπω γένυσι φαίνων τερείνας ματέρ' οἰνάνθας ὀπώραν, 'not yet showing on his cheeks late summer, the mother of the grape's soft bloom' (transl. Race 1997: 47).

[117] Cf. Collard 2007: 39.

fragments from this play, calls it a δρᾶμα πολύμετρον, or 'polymetric drama'. This combination of various metres, which Aristotle finds ἀτοπώτερον ('extraordinary', or even 'absurd'), consisted principally of dactylic hexametres, iambic trimetres and trochaic tetrametres, but also perhaps anapaests.[118] The two fragments cited by Athenaeus (F 10, 11) display Chaeremon's unmistakable predilection for flowers. As we saw earlier in this chapter, F 11 refers to garlands in the context of ritual. And in F 10, a group of females take pleasure in gathering flowers, an activity that is paradoxically – and with an almost Hellenistic verbal playfulness[119] – described in the language of typically male activities, such as warfare and hunting (cf. Günther 1999: 587):

> Some of them advanced against the countless,
> spear-less army of flowers, pleasurably
> hunting after the <blossoming?> children of meadows.[120]

Scraps of *The Centaur* are, probably, to be found in a papyrus fragment of 280–250 BC (*PHib* 2, 224 = F 14b), which preserves the beginnings of six gnomic hexametre lines. They would have been eminently suitable to the Polonius-like Chiron, the teacher of Achilles and many other Greek heroes, who even became a fixture in the Greek sapiential tradition through *Chiron's Counsels*, a poem attributed to Hesiod.[121] A remarkable novelty of this fragment, first noticed by Kannicht, is that it forms an acrostic spelling out the beginning of Chaeremon's name (probably ΧΑΙΡΗΜ[ΟΝΟΣ).[122] Given that acrostics 'are a verbal effect most readily available to readers' than to listeners,[123] it is possible that *The Centaur* was addressed to a reading public at least as much as to theatre audiences; or it may have been composed for performance, with additional layers of meaning reserved only to readers.[124]

It is uncertain whether *The Centaur* (F 9a–11) was a tragedy or a satyr-play. That its principal character was a Centaur (probably Chiron) is often

---

[118] See Arist. *Po.* 1447b20–3, 1459b34–60a2 (with Lucas *ad locc.*); Ath. 13, 608e. Cf. Else 1957: 54–61; Collard 2007: 36; Hanink 2014b: 202 (with further doxography in her n. 40).
[119] Cf. Kannicht, Gauly et al. (1991: 154) for Chaeremon providing a link between fourth-century tragedy and the *Buchpoesie* of the third century.
[120] For an extensive commentary on this fr. see Lorenzoni 1995: 45–56; cf. also Cipolla 2003: 307–11.
[121] See Snell 1971: 166–8; cf. Kannicht, Gauly et al. 1991: 290 n. 14.
[122] The fragment is largely mutilated; for tentative supplements see West 1977: 37.
[123] Quotation from Ford 2003: 18. On the acrostic see further Stephanopoulos 1984: 184–5; Collard 2009 (with earlier bibliography on 11 n. 7); Luz 2010: 7–15.
[124] More radically, Snell (1971: 159–60) considers this acrostic as evidence that 'Chaeremon in composing his tragedies had already readers, not listeners, in mind' (my translation).

put forward as evidence for the play's satyric character: we know of no other tragedy entitled *Centaur* or *Chiron*, though there are several comedies so entitled.[125] Still, if *The Centaur* were merely a metrically aberrant satyr-play, it is hard to see how Aristotle could apply to it so specific a term as 'mixed rhapsody': that it consisted partly of hexametres is not, in and of itself, an adequate explanation. It is even harder to see how a satyr-play could be compatible with the gnomic lines of fr. 14b, which were possibly addressed by Chiron to Achilles (cf. the second person singular in 4, 6? and 7) and express fundamental moral principles.[126] Possibly, *The Centaur* was a highly idiosyncratic experiment, impossible to straightjacket into one of the traditional dramatic genres. The piece's idiosyncratic character would explain the difference in the terminology used by Aristotle ('mixed rhapsody') and by Athenaeus ('polymetric drama').

## Alphesiboea

The play's title suggests that it must have dramatized the story of Alcmeon, on which see later in this chapter. Its only surviving fragment (F 1) is transmitted by Athenaeus (13, 608d), who prefaces it with the following remark: 'this poet, who is also prone to (describing) flowers, says in his *Alphesiboea* the following'. He then goes on to cite the text of the fragment:

And the appearance of the body was accomplished(?)
by < ... > that gleamed prominently with their white skin(?).[127]
But modesty altered this, adding a most
mild blush to that radiant hue.
And the hair, like that of a wax-coloured statue[128]         5
moulded together with its curly locks,
revelled in the rustling wind that blew it around.

However, F 1 contains no reference to flowers; moreover, the mention of 'modesty' (αἰδώς, 3), the comparison to a statue (5–6), and especially the imagery in the last line (hair being 'blown around' by the wind) are hardly compatible with a description of flowers. By contrast, flower-related

---

[125] See Snell 1971: 168 and esp. Günther 1999: 580–90 (with speculation on the play's content, on the basis of comparisons to Philostratus and Dio Chrysostom). Cf. Collard 2007: 36; Shaw 2014: 130–3; *contra* Sutton 1980: 75, 85.
[126] Snell (1971: 168) argued unhesitatingly that these gnomic lines were ironical, but there is no indication of this in the text.
[127] Lines 1–2 as transmitted are heavily corrupt: καὶ σώματος μὲν †ὄψεις κατειργάζετο | στίλβοντα λευκῷ †χρώματι διαπρεπῆ.
[128] Reading κηροχρῶτος (Wilamowitz) for the MS κηροχρῶτες; *contra* Primavesi 2004: 226.

references are to be found in abundance in the passages Athenaeus cites immediately afterwards to document Chaeremon's predilection for descriptions of flowers.[129] It is therefore likely that, as Collard (2007: 41–2) has suggested, F 1 originally belonged, together with F 14 from *Oeneus* cited immediately before (Ath. 13, 608d), to the preceding section on the topic of female beauty, and that consequently F 1 offers a description of a woman, not of a flower. After Athenaeus' rather solemn preface about Chaeremon's 'proclivity' (cf. ἐπικατάφορος) for descriptions of flowers, one should probably have expected him to prove his point by quoting not the brief passages now extant (cited in n. 126 earlier in this chapter) but a more extensive passage on flowers, one subsequently ousted by F1.[130] All in all, it seems likelier that F 1, like F 14, offers a description of outstanding female beauty (with reference, perhaps, to Alphesiboea?), which is quite unlike anything found in fifth-century tragedy. Particularly notable is the comparison of the woman's streaming hair to that of a statue, the orderly enumeration of her features with a regular sequence of μέν ... δέ ... δέ, as well as the abundance of compound words (mainly verbs).

## *Oeneus*

The single surviving fragment of this play (F 14) offers a narrative by Oeneus, which contains an unusually explicit description of exhausted young girls slumbering on a meadow in the moonlight.[131] Some are half-naked, exposing their breasts, flanks or thighs; the bare thighs are memorably said to have 'the hopeless desire for the smiling bloom of youth stamped deeply on them';[132] two more girls are lying in each other's arms. The play of shadow and moonlight on the girls' bodies is rendered in amazing detail.[133]

---

[129] F 9, 10, 5, 13, 8 and 12, all of which are appreciably shorter than F 1 (two one-liners, three two-liners, one three-liner).

[130] For a history of the debate and for attempts at emendation see Primavesi 2004; Russo 2008. Snell (1971: 165 n. 18) rightly observes that Chaeremon's affected and precious style makes it impossible to divine what may have once lain underneath the now-corrupt lines.

[131] For a commentary on the fragment, including speculation on the play's subject, see Collard 2007: 43–8.

[132] As Snell (1971: 163) pointed out, Chaeremon's description must inform the story of Apollo and Daphne in Ovid, *Met.* 1.497–592: the god's gaze rests on the Nymph's fingers, hands, and arms 'laid bare more than halfway up'; and his 'fruitless love' for her is 'fed by hope' (*sterilem sperando nutrit amorem*).

[133] Collard (2007: 39, 45, 46, 55) suggests that these chiaroscuro contrasts were prompted by contemporary developments in painting; cf. also Snell 1971: 161–2; Kannicht, Gauly et al. 1991: 290 n. 12; Wright 2016: 129.

It is generally accepted that Chaeremon here echoes the impressively unornamented description of maenads slumbering in Mt. Cithaeron from the first messenger speech in Euripides' *Bacchae* (683–8). It is apparently those Euripidean echoes that have led a number of scholars to assume that Chaeremon's fragment too comes from a messenger speech and contains a description of maenads.[134] However, there is no good reason for such an assumption: Athenaeus expressly states that these lines contain an eyewitness report by Oeneus himself;[135] moreover, their leisurely and relaxed narrative pace is very different from the familiar briskness of messenger speeches, especially Euripidean ones.[136] Moreover, nothing in this fragment points unambiguously to maenads: despite numerous references to dress (2 ἐπωμίδος, 9 χλανιδίων, 13–14 ὑφάσματα | πέπλων), there is no mention of the thyrsus or the fawnskin – or, for that matter, of drums, pipes, ivy or snakes.[137] Finally, of decisive importance are elements that seem incompatible with Dionysiac religion, and suggest that Chaeremon is distancing himself from Euripides. In *Bacchae*, in accordance with Dionysus' demand for universal participation in his rites (207–9), maenads include women of all ages (694 'young women, old women, and girls still unmarried'), whereas Chaeremon's females are designated as 'unmarried girls' (παρθένων) by Athenaeus (13.608b). What is more, the obvious eroticism of Chaeremon's description, focusing as it does on the girls' partly naked bodies, is incompatible with Euripides' maenads, who are emphatically chaste (cf. esp. 685–8). All in all, then, despite appearances to the contrary, this fragment shows in the starkest light the great distance separating Chaeremon from Euripides.

We do not know if *Oeneus* was a tragedy or a satyr-drama; there is nothing, however, in the one surviving fragment that points to satyr-play. The diminutive χλανιδίων (9) has been recently put forward as evidence of satyric style,[138] since avoidance of diminutives is characteristic of tragedy as opposed to comedy and satyr-drama; however, the same diminutive is also attested three times in tragedy (E. *Su.* 110, *Or.* 42; *Trag. Adesp.* 7), probably because χλανίδιον 'may have ceased to be felt as a diminutive'.[139]

---

[134] See Barlow 1971: 69; Snell 1971: 161; Seeck 1979: 189; Xanthakis-Karamanos 1980: 73; Collard 2007: 44–5 (but a change of mind is noted on p. 55).
[135] See Stephanopoulos 1984: 182.
[136] See esp. Barlow 1971: 68–70, although she does not reject the view that the Chaeremon fr. may come from a messenger speech.
[137] Stephanopoulos (2001: 405) remarks that nothing in the fr. points unambiguously to maenads, and that its similarities to the *Bacchae* passage are less important than its differences. See further the detailed and well-argued discussion of Dolfi 2006; cf. Collard 2007: 55.
[138] By Lämmle 2013: 27–8, 66. [139] Quotation from Stevens 1976: 5 n. 12.

A fragment from a tragedy on Oeneus (or on Meleager) is preserved as an *adespoton* (*TrGF* II, F 625). Its style suggests that it might be by Euripides or by a close imitator: there is nothing in it that might evoke Chaeremon's highly individual style.[140]

## Theodectas

We are comparatively well informed about the life and career of Theodectas (the epigraphically attested form of the name, which appears as Theodektēs in the literary sources). A native of Phasēlis in Lycia, Theodectas (*TrGF* I, 72) was active in Athens, where he was taught by Plato, Isocrates and Aristotle, and went on to become an accomplished orator and teacher of rhetoric as well as a tragic poet.[141] He is said to have produced fifty plays overall; he won his first tragic victory some time after 372 BC and he took part in a contest of funerary speeches at the funeral of Mausolus, satrap of Caria, around 353 BC – though it is perhaps unlikely that he also presented a tragedy entitled *Mausolus* on the same occasion.[142]

Of Theodectas' output, only nine titles and some twenty fragments survive, most of them from unidentified dramas. Unsurprisingly for a fourth-century tragic poet, he seems to have vied with the canonical fifth-century tragedians, especially Sophocles and Euripides: his plays include an *Ajax*, an *Alcmeon*, a *Helen*, an *Oedipus*, an *Orestes*, and a *Philoctetes*. He is said to have excelled in riddle-solving (T 10), although this may be an extrapolation from the apparent frequency of riddles in his work: two of the extant fragments contain riddles (F 4, 18), while a third (F 6) contains a riddle-like description, by an illiterate rustic, of the letters making up Theseus' name. This is modelled, down to the level of verbal imitation, on similar passages from Euripides' *Theseus* (F 382 Kannicht) and from Agathon's *Telephus* (*TrGF* I, 39 F 4).[143]

---

[140] See Collard 2007: 33–4; Stephanopoulos 1988a: 238–40.
[141] For the ancient sources see *TrGF* I, 72 T 1, 2, 4, 7, 10, 11, 12, 13; discussion in Müller-Goldingen 2005: 69–70. On Theodectas as an orator see Matelli 2007. On Theodectas and Aristotle see Hanink 2014b: 199–200, esp. n. 31.
[142] For the ancient sources see *TrGF* I, 72 T 1, 2, 3, 5, 6; cf. Kannicht, Gauly et al. 1991: 291 n. 2. Webster 1954: 303 suggests 368 BC as the year of Theodectas' first victory.
[143] See N.W. Slater 2002, esp. 124; Martano 2007: 187–94; Torrance 2010: 246–50.

## Ajax

From what may be gathered from brief mentions in Aristotle and his ancient commentators,[144] Theodectas' *Ajax* (F 1) must have included a version of the 'Judgment of Arms' story, in which Odysseus argued that he was more valiant than Ajax despite appearances to the contrary, while Diomedes undermined Odysseus' claims by disclosing that if he chose Odysseus as his companion in their joint operations,[145] it was not because of his bravery but so that his own excellence might be all the more apparent. One may reasonably speculate that the play will have included Ajax's suicide after his defeat.

## Alcmeon

The story of Alcmeon was treated in Sophocles' *Alcmeon* and in the two Euripidean plays of that title, namely *Alcmeon in Psophis* (438 BC) and *Alcmeon in Corinth* (produced after the poet's death in 406 BC). It was an extremely popular subject, which also spawned tragedies by at least six more playwrights (nn. 30–33 earlier in this chapter). Of Theodectas' play we have only two fragments, one of which (F 2) is a dialogue between Alcmeon and his wife Alphesiboea, daughter of Phēgeus, king of Psophis, who had purified Alcmeon after the latter's murder of his mother Eriphylē. In the fragment, Alcmeon explains that people, albeit convinced that Eriphylē deserved to die, took issue with his murder of her – a nice legal distinction that seems compatible with Theodectas' parallel rhetorical career,[146] although it may just as plausibly derive from Tyndareus' argument in Euripides' *Orestes* (496–525), to the effect that Clytemnestra's murder of Agamemnon deserved to be punished, but not with murder. In the myth,[147] Alcmeon was forced to seek further purification from the river Acheloos, whose daughter Callirrhoē he subsequently married. His bigamy was discovered when he returned to Arcadia to retrieve, at Callirrhoē's insistence, a necklace that had belonged once to his mother, now to Alphesiboea. It may be that the second surviving fragment from Theodectas' play (F 1a) was spoken by Alphesiboea when she realized her husband's

---

[144] See *TrGF* I, app. font. to 72 F 1.
[145] On which see Liapis 2012: *ad* [E.] *Rh.* 565 ff. Further on Theodectas' *Ajax* see Wright 2016: 166–8.
[146] Cf. Webster (1956: 64): 'a point of nice discrimination which perhaps belongs rather to the law court than to the tragic stage'.
[147] For the details of the Alcmeon story see Gantz 1993: 526–7.

treachery: 'there is a simple and clear saying among mortals: there is no creature more wretched than a woman'.[148] The line is unmistakably an allusion to Euripides' *Medea* 230–1 – further evidence, if any were needed, of Euripides' prestige and influence in the fourth century.[149]

## *Helen*

If spoken by Helen, as seems likely, the only extant fragment of this play (F 3) suggests the heroine's proud frustration at being held captive, perhaps in Egypt, or otherwise at her state of enforced submission: 'I have sprung from divine stems on both my father's and my mother's side: who would presume, then, to address me as a slave?' The reference to two divine parents implies that Theodectas cast Helen as the daughter of Zeus and (not Leda but) Nemesis.[150]

## *Lynceus*

All we know about this play (F 3a) consists of a few elliptic and lacunose references by Aristotle (*Poetics* 1452a27–9, 1455b29–32), who was, we recall, one of Theodectas' teachers. The title shows that the plot revolved around Lynceus, the only one of Aegyptus' fifty sons to be spared by his Danaid wife, Hypermestra. A central part of the plot will have been the mortal enmity between Lynceus and his father-in-law Danaus: as Aristotle intimates, the latter led the former to be killed, but Lynceus turned the tables on his seemingly superior enemy and killed him instead. This version of the myth may go back to the Hesiodic *Ehoiai* (fr. 129.2 MW = 77 Most), but it is unclear if it was part of tragic treatments of the myth before Theodectas, notably in Aeschylus' *Danaids*.[151] Aristotle also refers to the 'catching' (λῆψις) of a child, who must be Abas, the son of Lynceus and Hypermestra. The boy's being held captive or hostage must have been significant for the plot, but we do not know how: perhaps Danaus used the boy to blackmail Lynceus into surrendering himself.[152]

It has been argued by C. Del Grande (1933/35: 198) that a fragment from an unknown play by Theodectas (F 8) may belong to *Lynceus*. The fragment addresses the age-old problem of the belated punishment of

---

[148] For the putative attribution of this fr. to Alphesiboea see Welcker 1841: 1075.
[149] For shifts of emphasis in the Theodectas fr. see, however, Stephanopoulos 2013: 67–8.
[150] See Kannicht, Gauly et al. 1991: 292 n. 10; for the mythic details see Gantz 1993: 319–21.
[151] See further Garvie 2006: 165, 179, 206–7, 210 with n. 3; Gantz 1991: 206.
[152] On *Lynceus* cf. Webster 1954: 304; 1956: 64; Karamanou 2007.

sinners: if a transgression, the speaker argues, were followed immediately by its punishment, then most people would be law-abiding out of fear rather than out of true virtue; as it is, people 'follow their nature' since they do not feel that punishment is imminent. The argument might have suited, perhaps, a gloating Danaus, who has captured at long last his enemy Lynceus; but its generality makes it appropriate for any number of different dramatic situations.[153]

### Oedipus; Philoctetes

All that survives from Theodectas' *Oedipus* is a two-line fragment, in hexametres, from a riddle about day and night (F 4): 'there are two sisters, one of whom gives birth to the other, and having given birth is herself born by the other'. It is hard to see how this particular riddle could have fitted the Oedipus plot,[154] although it is of course anything but extraordinary for a play about Oedipus to include references to riddles or even to quote riddles verbatim – as indeed Euripides did in his own *Oedipus* with the Sphinx's hexametre riddle (fr. 540a.5–11 Kannicht). Another riddle, whose phrasing partly resembles that of the Sphinx's riddle as quoted in later sources,[155] is found in F 18: 'what is largest at its youth and at its old age, while being smallest in its prime?' (the answer is 'one's shadow'). From the phrasing of that fragment's source (Athenaeus 10. 451e), it seems unlikely that it comes from *Oedipus*.

*Philoctetes* (F 5b) featured a scene between Philoctetes and Neoptolemus, in which the wounded hero tried (but eventually failed) to hide the painful symptoms of his condition from the young man, presumably in the hope to persuade Neoptolemus to take him on board, as in Sophocles' play (*Philoctetes* 468–503). A novelty of Theodectas' play is that Philoctetes had been wounded by the snake in his hand rather than in his foot. This would have aggravated Philoctetes' misery, since he would have been unable to use his bow, which in Sophocles is his sole means of sustenance and defence. If so, we must probably assume that Philoctetes' abode was not an uninhabited island, or he would have starved to death.[156] Moreover, Philoctetes' inability to use his bow may have encouraged some of his fellow-Greeks to envisage the possibility of absconding with the weapon

---

[153] On this fr. see further Müller-Goldingen 2005: 71–2, esp. with regard to the problem of theodicy.
[154] Cf. C. Robert 1915: 493.
[155] See Kannicht, *app. font.* to E. *Oed.* fr. 540a.4 (*TrGF* V(1), p. 573).
[156] See further Stephanopoulos 1984: 187.

and leaving the hero himself behind (a possibility raised in Sophocles' *Philoctetes*).[157]

### *Unidentified Plays:* Bellerophon *or* Hippolytus(?); Thyestes(?)

In the puzzling F 10, which may or may not preserve the first lines of a tragedy,[158] an unidentified speaker complains of the unjust accusations levelled against him: a woman has accused him to her husband, and both of them are in a superior position (κρατοῦσι) to that of the speaker. As has been remarked,[159] this looks like an instance of the 'Potiphar's Wife' motif: a married woman takes a fancy in a younger man; her advances turned down by him, she accuses him to her husband of rape, attempted or accomplished. The motif is present in many a Greek myth, most notably those of Hippolytus and Phaedra, and of Bellerophon and Stheneboea.[160] Both myths were dramatized by fifth-century tragedians: Sophocles wrote both a *Phaedra* and an *Iobates* (a character in the Bellerophon myth), and Euripides produced two *Hippolytus* plays, a *Bellerophontēs*, and a *Stheneboea*. But it may be that Theodectas' play treated a less well-known myth, such as that of Phoenix (subject of a tragedy by Euripides), or Phineus (also a tragedy by Aeschylus, although its plot is unknown).

Thyestes is mentioned by name in F 9, which may come from a play of the same title (as we have seen, Thyestes-plays are also attested for Sophocles, Euripides, Carcinus and Chaeremon). Here, Thyestes is urged by an unidentified speaker to restrain his anger, presumably after discovering the enormity of the crime he has unwittingly committed (the eating of his own children).

Finally, F 17 offers an explanation of the Aethiopians' black skin and curly hair. These features, we are told, are the result of the sun's heat, as Ethiopia is extremely close (ἀγχιτέρμων) to the point where the sun rises (as in *Od.* 1.23–4). We know nothing of this fragment's context (perhaps a *Phaethon* tragedy?), although it is possible that it comes from a messenger speech.

---

[157] Cf. Wright 2016: 174.
[158] The address to the Sun (ὦ καλλιφεγγῆ λαμπάδ᾽ εἱλίσσων φλογός | Ἥλιε) recalls E. *Ph.* 3 Ἥλιε, θοαῖς ἵπποισιν εἱλίσσων φλόγα and the paratragic Ar. *Eccl.* 1 ὦ λαμπρὸν ὄμμα τοῦ τροχηλάτου λύχνου – both at the beginning of the respective plays; cf. Liapis 2012: *ad* [E.] *Rh.* 59–62; on E. *Ph.* 1–2 as spurious see Haslam 1975: 157; cf. Müller-Goldingen 2005: 73–4. See, however, Stephanopoulos 1988b: 15–16 for arguments against identifying F 10 with the play's beginning.
[159] Cf. Stephanopoulos 1988b: 17; Kannicht, Gauly et al. 1991: 292 n. 13.
[160] See Hansen 2002: 332–52.

## Dionysius of Syracuse

The image that ancient sources present of the dramatic writings of Dionysius I, the tyrant of Syracuse (*TrGF* I, 76), is a predominantly negative, even derisory one.[161] We are repeatedly told, for instance, that the dithyrambic poet Philoxenus took an openly dismissive view of Dionysius' literary skills, at the cost of being condemned by the tyrant to forced labour at the Syracusan stone quarries.[162] Dionysius participated in the Athenian dramatic contests at least once, namely at the Lenaea of 367 BC, where he won the first prize with his play *Hector Ransomed* (*TrGF* I, 76 F 2a), of which we know nothing except that Dionysius diverged from the Homeric account in having Priam approach Achilles' tent on foot (rather than on a chariot) and in the company of Polyxena, Andromache and the latter's children.[163] Dionysius' *Hector* may have been influenced by Aeschylus' *Phrygians or Hector Ransomed* (Φρύγες ἢ Ἕκτορος λύτρα, see *TrGF* III, F 263–272), and/or by Sophocles, if that poet's *Phrygians* (*TrGF* IV, F 724–725) did indeed treat of the ransoming of Hector.[164] It is conceivable that the Athenian judges' verdict was politically motivated, as a means of ingratiating Athens with the lord of Syracuse. At any rate, the victory of a foreign potentate in an Athenian dramatic festival seems to have attracted the lampooning attentions of comic poets, who may have thus initiated, at least in part, the tradition of dismissive references to Dionysius' literary skills that we find in later sources.[165] The comic poet Ephippus (*PCG* fr. 16 K.-A.) lists 'learning Dionysius' plays by heart' as one of several unimaginably harsh punishments,[166] and Eubulus in his

---

[161] For a thorough survey of the (hostile) ancient tradition on Dionysius see Duncan 2012: 138–41, 144–5; cf. Dearden 1990: 234–5. Wright 2016: 130–43 deconstructs the tradition, arguing that 'it is possible to see Dionysius as a versatile and successful writer, not a trivial dilettante or an embarrasing failure' (quotation from p. 138).

[162] See *TrGF* I, 76 T 11, 13, 14; cf. Duncan 2012: 138–9.

[163] *TrGF* I, 76 F 2b (in 'Addenda et corrigenda', p. 354–5). See further Bühler 1973; Papathomopoulos 1981; Grossardt 2005.

[164] For the theme in fourth-century vase-paintings see Dearden 1990: 235 with nn. 23–4 (although theatrical influence is impossible to ascertain). A first-/second-century BC papyrus (*P.Oxy.* 5203; cf. TrGF V/2 p. 1103, DID B 15a) mentions 'songs' (ᾠδαί) composed by a certain Epagathos (Stephanis 1988: no. 846) for, *inter alia*, a play entitled Λύτρα Ἕκτορος.

[165] See Hunter 1983: 116, who also reminds us that Athens had granted citizenship to Dionysius and his sons in 368, one year before Dionysius' Lenaean victory, no doubt as part of their effort to improve relations with Syracuse after the Battle of Leuctra (371 BC), which gave neighbouring Thebes a menacing (if eventually short-lived) ascendancy.

[166] *Contra* Csapo (2010: 171–2), who argues that the speaker in the Ephippus fragment comically condemns himself 'to high-class sympotic bliss', and that 'learning Dionysius' plays by heart' is accordingly envisaged as a pleasurable 'punishment'. But the (mock-)curses the speaker heaps upon

comedy *Dionysius* has the tyrant complain about his critics' mockery of the stylistic defects of his poetry (*PCG* fr. 25 K.-A.).

Among Dionysius' surviving fragments, F 1 from *Adonis*, an extremely rare tragic subject,[167] stands out for its seemingly recherché language (although the transmitted text is corrupt): ἐκβόλειον occurs nowhere else in Greek literature, σπήλυγγα nowhere else in Greek tragedy, and ἀκροθινιάζομαι only in Euripides' *Heracles* 476. The precious style seems, at first sight, compatible with the outrageous coinages Dionysius is elsewhere credited with – for instance, βαλάντιον (properly, 'purse') in the sense 'spear' (from βάλλειν ἀντίον, 'to throw against'), or σκέπαρνον (properly, 'adze') in the sense 'sheep's wool' (from σκέπειν τοὺς ἄρνας, 'covering the sheep').[168]

Otherwise, the scanty remains of Dionysius' tragedies are flat and commonplace: 'if you think you can be free of pain, your life is that of a god' (F 2, from *Alcmene*); 'never call someone happy until after he is dead' (F 3, from *Leda*, another unique tragic title). As already Plutarch saw (*Mor.* 338B), it is stupendously self-contradictory for an authoritarian tyrant to compose lines castigating despotic rule (*tyrannis*) as being 'the mother of injustice' (F 4) or even reproducing the platitude about 'the eye of Retribution (*Dikē*) looking upon all things, albeit with a calm countenance' (F 5).[169] Alternatively, as Duncan has recently argued, Dionysius may have thereby attempted to cast himself, through the medium of drama, as an ideal ruler comparable to, e.g., Theseus or Pelasgus in Greek tragedy.[170]

## Diogenes of Sinopē

A pre-eminent Cynic philosopher, though much maligned in the ancient tradition, Diogenes of Sinopē (*TrGF* I, 88) is credited with a number of plays with run-of-the-mill titles such as *Atreus*, *Helen*, *Medea*, *Oedipus*, etc. However, the seemingly innocuous titles concealed, or so we are told, highly provocative and even outrageous dramas, which seem to have

---

himself also include 'whatever Demophon wrote about Cotys', presumably the king of Thrace, to which an admiring reference seems unlikely. Cf. also Duncan 2012: 140 n. 9.

[167] We know only of one *Adonis* tragedy by Ptolemy IV Philopator (221–205 BC): see *TrGF* I, 119. On Dionysius' *Adonis* see further Olivieri 1950: 91–2; Suess 1966: 313–16; Roux 1967: 260–2; Kannicht, Gauly et al. 1991: 292–3 n. 7.

[168] See *TrGF* I, 76 F 12; Kannicht, Gauly et al. 1991: 293 n. 12. For the argument that these coinages are comic parodies of Dionysius' style rather than quotations from his work see Webster 1954: 298. Further discussion in Suess 1966: 310–13.

[169] Cf. Olivieri 1950: 99–100.  [170] See Duncan 2012: 148–54; cf. Wright 2016: 140–1.

offended conventional sensibilities. This is in line with Diogenes' image as a 'cynic' or 'dog-like' (i.e., shameless) individual, who promoted a way of life according to nature, in which humans could be free from the constraints of civilized conventions, including social values and accepted morality. Such arguments could easily be (mis)represented as a call for depravity, for the debasement of human nature, and for a return to a primitive or animal-like existence.

Thus, for instance, we hear that in Diogenes' *Thyestes* (which may have been the same play as his *Atreus*) someone argued that there is nothing reprehensible about anthropophagy, and thus with Thyestes' devouring of his own children. For one thing, the argument went, elements from the flesh of living bodies insinuate themselves, 'through some invisible pores', into plants, bread and other edibles; for another, anthropophagy is practiced by foreign peoples.[171] Likewise, we are told that Diogenes' *Oedipus* contained an approval of patricide and incest;[172] and that his *Medea* exonerated the heroine from the charge of witchcraft, casting her rather in the role of a 'skilled' or 'expert' (σοφή) practitioner who could restore people to their former strength.[173] On the other hand, it is hard to see how the free-for-all morality supposedly advocated by Diogenes can be made to square with the violently moralizing tone of his F 1h (from an unidentified tragedy), which appears to castigate a perceived vice (either gluttony or male homosexuality) in surprisingly vulgar terminology: 'those weighed down by the pleasures of the unmanly and shit-besmeared wantonness, those completely averse to toil...'

As we saw earlier in this chapter, Diogenes' authorship of the tragedies attributed to him was in doubt, and some attributed them instead to his pupil Philiscus of Aegina. There is also a number of unattributed tragic fragments that seem to convey Cynic ideas and may reasonably be associated with Diogenes or with Philiscus (*TrGF* I, 89), or with the Cynic philosopher Crates (*TrGF* I, 90), also a follower of Diogenes. Thus, we hear, Diogenes saw his own life as a fulfilment of the curses usually found in tragedy, since he roamed about 'deprived of city, home, fatherland, a beggar, a wanderer, eking out a day-by-day living'.[174] He would also half-mockingly hold the philosopher Antisthenes responsible for the uncouth

---

[171] See Diog. Laert. 6.73 and cf. further Snell and Kannicht's *app. font.* to *TrGF* I, 88 F 1d; also Kannicht, Gauly et al. 1991: 294 n. 2.
[172] See *TrGF* I, 88 F 1f with Snell's and Kannicht's *app. font.*
[173] *TrGF* I, 88 F 1e with Snell's and Kannicht's *app. font.*
[174] Diogenes (?), F 4. Noussia (2006: 235–6) points out that here Diogenes seems to present himself (or a character cast as a Cynic philosopher) as a tragic hero.

state he himself was in: 'it was he who dressed me in rags and forced me to become a beggar and drove me from house and home'.[175] A Socratic disciple, Antisthenes preached a lifestyle of ascetic austerity, which was subsequently taken up by Cynic philosophy; and it is precisely the avoidance of gluttony and extravagance, combined with a tough physical regimen, that is put forward as conducive to true wisdom in a couple of tragic fragments that appear to reflect Cynic philosophy and *may* be the work of Diogenes.[176] The importance of hard work in the pursuit of happiness is also stressed in the one fragment that can be securely attributed to Philiscus (89 F 1).

As we saw in the previous paragraph, some of the purportedly tragic lines attributed to Diogenes may have been (impromptu?) summaries of basic tenets of Cynic philosophy, without necessarily being part of full-fledged tragedies.[177] This, incidentally, seems the likeliest interpretation of the one fragment attributed to Crates (90 F 1), in which it is tempting to see an adaptation of, e.g., the tragic *adespoton* 392 K.-S. into a characteristically Cynic advocacy of cosmopolitanism.[178] Even so, it is indicative of the range and flexibility of the tragic genre in the fourth century (and later) that it could be made into a vehicle of philosophic ideas, even in the form of snippets redolent of the tragic style, if not in the form of full-scale tragedies (which is what, e.g., Diogenes' F 1h and F 2 seem to come from).[179]

## Sosiphanes of Syracuse

Often confused with, apparently, a younger namesake, Sosiphanes (*TrGF* I, 92) appears to have been active during the second half of the fourth century, and is said to have composed 73 plays and to have won seven victories.[180] His *Meleager* (like Euripides' and Antiphon's) will have treated the well-known myth of the Calydonian boar hunt and its aftermath.[181] Its

---

[175] Diogenes (?), F 5.   [176] See Diogenes (?), F 6 and F 7.
[177] Noussia (2006: 231) argues that Cynic tragedies were monologue recitations (monodramas), 'a series of talking points, argumentation provided to convince an audience, resulting in brief self-contained dramas composed as fragments'.
[178] The speaker of the *adespoton* is Heracles, and Noussia (2006: 237–42) argues that the Crates fragment presents Heracles as a proto-Cynic wanderer.
[179] Further on Cynic tragedy (and its unconventionality in terms of fifth-century drama) see Noussia 2006, with full bibliography and extended discussion.
[180] On the vexed problem of Sosiphanes' chronology and on the younger Sosiphanes (*TrGF* I, 103), who seems to have been a member of the Hellenistic Pleiad, see further Schramm 1929: 8–10; Kannicht, Gauly et al. 1991: 295 nn. 2, 3; Hornblower, this volume.
[181] Cf. n. 19 earlier in this chapter; Schramm 1929: 10–11.

Greek Tragedy in the Fourth Century: The Fragments 63

only surviving fragment (F 1) refers to the false claim by 'all Thessalian girls' that they can use magical incantations to bring down the moon from the heavens. That Thessalian witches had such powers was a widespread belief as early as the fifth century;[182] but Sosiphanes is our earliest source to dismiss this as a mere trick.[183] It is a matter of conjecture which part of the play's action this fragment may come from.

The rest of Sosiphanes' surviving fragments come from unidentified plays. In F 2 an old man is urged to 'make his spirit young again' and show his anger for an injustice he had suffered in the past.[184] The perennial theme of the mutability of fortune reappears in F 3, albeit admittedly in a more stylish and elegant fashion than is commonly the case. Finally, Sosiphanes may have put forth an innovative version of the Labdacid myth, in which (F 4) Laius seems to have been guilty of the murder of Menoeceus – either Creon's son (who in other versions commits suicide or is devoured by the Sphinx) or Creon's and Jocasta's father. The latter possibility may have provided an 'original sin' that would have explained the evils of the Labdacids.[185]

## Epilogue

To return to our initial question: is there such a thing as fourth-century tragedy? More precisely, can the term be meaningfully used to denote a distinct period of recognizably homogeneous dramatic production? The question does not admit of a simple yes or no answer. On the one hand, 'fourth-century tragedy' is a useful concept insofar as tragedians in that period were conscious of being heirs to the glorious and perhaps unsurpassable legacy of their fifth-century predecessors, and had to deal with the formidable task of proving themselves their worthy successors. On the other hand, 'fourth-century tragedy' may be misleading in that it may seem to lump together a seemingly kaleidoscopic variety of authorial styles and versions of, or attitudes to, traditional mythic or poetic material. To be

---

[182] Ar. *Nub.* 749–52; Pl. *Grg.* 513a (with Dodds 1959: *ad l.*); Hor. *Epod.* 5.45–6 (with Watson 2003: *ad l.*); Sen. *Phaed.* 420–1; Luc. 6. 499–502; Plin. *Nat.* 30.7; Apul. *Met.* 1.8.4 (cf. 1.3.1). See further Schramm 1929: 12. The superstition survived in Thessaly itself until well into the twentieth century.

[183] Cf. also Prop. 1.1.19–20 *at uos, deductae quibus est fallacia lunae | et labor in magicis sacra piare focis*, 'but you, who practice the trick of bringing down the moon and deal in expiatory rites over magic fires' (with Cairns 1974: 100–1); Plut. *Mor.* 145c-d; Hippol. *Haer.* 4.37 (p. 124–5 Marcovich). See Kannicht, Gauly et al. (1991: 295 n. 4), and esp. Hill 1973 with further sources and discussion.

[184] For discussion see Schramm 1929: 14–15.   [185] See Robert 1915: 493–4; Schramm 1929: 11.

sure, a few trends are detectable: e.g., the pervasive influence of Euripides (most notably perhaps in Carcinus [see earlier in this chapter], although such influence may prove illusory, as in the case of Chaeremon's *Oeneus*), or the growing popularity of Achilles, perhaps as a corollary of the tragedians' ambitious engagement with Homer as opposed to the epic cycle.[186] However, the overall picture that emerges is, at once, both too complex and too fragmentary to allow us to identify general developments in fourth-century tragedy. The picture is further complicated by outliers like Diogenes of Sinope, whose Cynic tragedies appear to stretch the tragic genre to unprecedented extremes.

Some of the dramatists examined in this chapter – e.g., Antiphon, Carcinus, and especially Theodectas, who was also a career orator – may appear particularly fond of rhetorical tropes and legalistic niceties (see esp. on Theodectas' *Alcmeon*, earlier in this chapter), which may seem to bear out the oft-expressed view that tragedy became more conspicuously 'rhetorical' in the fourth century. But it would be ill-advised to deduce a trend out of a handful of fragmentary examples, which may or may not have been typical of the era. As Carter argues in this volume, we have no reason to treat fourth-century tragedy as more 'rhetorical' than its fifth-century predecessors, since employment of persuasive speech, as far as we can see, had been a standard feature of tragic discourse since at least the time of Sophocles. The same goes for the perceived predilection of some fourth-century dramatists (e.g., Diogenes of Athens, Dionysius I) for choice words and unusual meanings: it would be methodologically unsound to put forth these scant examples of recherché language (which, in the case of Dionysius, may have been blown out of proportion by hostile authors) as evidence of widespread developments, perhaps prefiguring the forbiddingly dense style of *Alexandra* (on which see Hornblower, this volume).

On the other hand, it would be equally unwise to preclude the possibility that some fourth-century tragedians do display seminal features that would later evolve into full-fledged characteristics of later poetry. The obvious example here is Chaeremon: as we have seen, he offers evidence of idiosyncrasies in language and form (unusual attention to sensuous detail, exotic style and verbal playfulness, the unprecedentedly polymetric *Centaur* and its equally unprecedented acrostic), which have been legitimately seen as a bridge to the more widespread and sustained linguistic and formal experimentations of Hellenistic poetry. And as pointed out at the beginning of this chapter, fourth-century tragedians were no strangers to

---

[186] See further Duncan and Liapis, this volume.

innovation in general: suffice it to mention the startlingly novel plots of Astydamas' *Antigone* and Carcinus' *Medea*.

One way of making sense of this bewildering variety is to assume that the contradictory symbiosis of centripetal and centrifugal forces – with authors now gravitating towards the fifth-century exempla, now pulling away from them – may well have been a defining characteristic of fourth-century tragedy. This of course can only be a tentative and provisional approach, so long as the lack of adequate evidence is not mitigated by new finds. But it may be advisable to see the fourth century as a transitional period in which the invigorating influence of canonical fifth-century drama coexists, in a state of temporarily unresolved tension, with fresh tendencies that would eventually debouch into the neoteric aesthetics of Hellenistic poetry.

CHAPTER 2

# *The* Rhesus
*Almut Fries**

The pseudo-Euripidean *Rhesus* is doubly unique. It is the only extant Greek tragedy whose plot is based on an episode from Homer's *Iliad* (the equally spurious Book 10, also known as *Doloneia*) and in all probability the only one surviving complete from the fourth century BC. Internal criteria tell against Euripidean authorship, whereas our external evidence favours a date between ca. 390 and 370 BC.[1] Going under Euripides' name at least since Alexandrian times, *Rhesus* developed a substantial history of reception and by the second or third century AD had become one of the poet's ten most popular plays. Inclusion in this canon ensured its transmission through the Middle Ages down to us.

This chapter will address the most important questions connected with the play and will try to locate it more firmly within the history of the genre by regular comparison with the practices of fifth- and, as far as it is possible, fourth-century tragedy.

## Scene and Setting; Cast of Characters; Distribution of Roles

*Rhesus* is set in the bivouac which the Trojans put up at the end of the second Iliadic day of battle (*Il*. 8.489–565). The stage represents Hector's sleeping-place, while the stage-building (*skēnē*) is ignored, except when (in accordance with a common practice) its roof is used for the two divine epiphanies in the play. One side-entrance (*eisodos*) leads to the main body of Trojans and further to the Greek naval camp, the other one to the separate Thracian bivouac, Troy and Mt. Ida.

---

* This chapter is a modified and abridged version of the introduction to, and parts of my commentary on, *Rhesus* (Fries 2014), to which I refer for more extensive discussion. I am grateful to the editors of this volume, Vayos Liapis and Antonis Petrides, for incisive comments on the first draft, and to Christopher Collard for reading the final version with characteristic acumen.
[1] See 'Authenticity and Date' later in this chapter.

The time-scale is indicated at once by a reference to the fourth watch of the night (*Rh*. 5–6); it corresponds to *Iliad* 10, where Odysseus and Diomedes set out to spy on the Trojans when 'dawn is near, the stars have moved forward, the night has passed by more than two thirds, and (only) one third still remains' (*Il*. 10.251–3). In a similar way, dawn is announced by the chorus in *Rh*. 527–64, and at 985 the first sunrays herald the new day and the end of the play (cf. *Il*. 11.1–2).

Eleven speaking characters, excluding the chorus, make up the unusually large cast. They are (in the order of appearance) Hector, Aeneas, Dolon, a Shepherd from Mt. Ida, Rhesus, Odysseus, Diomedes, Athena, Paris-Alexandros, Rhesus' Charioteer and Rhesus' mother, a Muse. The Protagonist would have played Hector (1–526, 806–992) and Odysseus (565–637, 675–91); for the other parts different distributions are possible, for example: Deuteragonist: Aeneas (85–148), Shepherd (264–341), Rhesus (380–526), Athena (595–674), Charioteer (728–881); Tritagonist: Dolon (154–223), Diomedes (565–637), Muse (885–982).[2] A fourth actor is required for Alexandros (642–67).[3]

## The Plot

*Rhesus* has no conventional prologue; it begins with the choral entrance-song or *parodos* (1–51).[4] The chorus of Trojan sentries bursts in to wake up Hector and tell him of watchfires and unusual activities in the Greek camp. Hector suspects a stratagem to mask an escape by night, and only the combined efforts of the chorus and Aeneas can persuade him to dispatch a scout instead of attacking immediately (52–148). Dolon volunteers and, after eliciting from Hector the promise of Achilles' horses as a reward and telling the sentries how he plans to approach the enemy in a wolf's disguise, he departs (149–223). No sooner has the chorus finished a hymn to Apollo (224–63) than a Shepherd arrives from Mt. Ida, announcing the approach of Rhesus, whom Hector, prompted by the messenger and the chorus-leader, reluctantly accepts as a belated ally (264–341). An ode, which greets Rhesus in the style of a cletic hymn (a hymn calling upon a god to appear, 342–79), is followed by the entry of the Thracian prince (380–7). Hector reproaches Rhesus for failing to respond to earlier

---

[2] Alternative assignments for the second and third actor are proposed by Liapis 2012: xlv.
[3] See 'Dramaturgy and Stagecraft', later in this chapter.
[4] On the fragments of two spurious iambic prologues transmitted in one of the ancient *hypotheses* to the play see 'Authenticity and Date', later in this chapter.

calls for assistance, while Rhesus explains that he was delayed by a war against the Scythians and, in recompense, promises to defeat the Greeks in one day (388–453). After further choral praise (single-strophe, 454–66), he even proposes to invade Greece, but Hector rejects the offer. They discuss battle dispositions and the most formidable opponents, including Odysseus, before Hector leads Rhesus to the intended resting-place for the Thracians (467–526).

Instead of returning to their posts, as Hector had ordered, the sentries sing a song mixed with chanted or spoken passages ('epirrhematic'), in which they greet the coming of dawn, ask for the relief watch and express their fear for Dolon (527–64). Once they have left to wake up the next shift, Odysseus and Diomedes enter, carrying Dolon's spoils and intent on killing Hector. Unable to find him, they prepare to leave, but are held back by Athena, who redirects them towards Rhesus, noting that no one will be able to check him if he survives the night (565–94 + 595–641). While the Greeks follow her orders, Athena, in the guise of Aphrodite, distracts Paris, who has come to find out the cause of the commotion in the Trojan army (642–67). On their way back from the Thracian bivouac the Greeks are intercepted by the Trojan chorus, but Odysseus cunningly effects their escape (675–91). In their second entrance-song (*epiparodos*, 692–727), the sentries tentatively identify him as the infiltrator; yet further deliberations are prevented by the arrival of Rhesus' badly injured Charioteer, who after lamenting his master's death (728–55) gives a highly subjective account of the assault (756–803). A new conflict arises when Hector returns. He chides the chorus for having let the enemy slip by (808–19) – they defend themselves in a brief song (820–32), which technically is the antistrophe to the chorus' praise of Rhesus in 454–66 – but then he is himself accused by the Charioteer of having killed Rhesus out of desire for his horses (833–81). Resolution for the Trojans comes from Rhesus' mother, the Muse. Carrying her son's body, she appears *ex machina* (885–94), sings a dirge from the *skēnē*-roof (895–914) and reveals Athena as the true force behind Rhesus' death (915–49). She declines Hector's offer of burial for him (959–61), on the grounds that he is destined to become a semi-divine prophet of Bacchus in Thrace (962–73). The play ends with the Trojans preparing for battle at the break of the new day (983–96).

## Sources

Apart from two satyr-plays, Euripides' *Cyclops* (based on *Odyssey* 9) and Sophocles' partly preserved *Trackers* (after the *Homeric Hymn to Hermes*),

*Rhesus* is the only Greek drama where we can study in detail the adaptation of an epic precedent, including what possibilities and constraints the conversion from one genre into the other entailed. In addition to *Iliad* 10, the poet drew on several other sources, both from the Greek tradition and Thracian lore.

A comprehensive analysis of *Rhesus* in relation to its models would be beyond the scope of this chapter. For the Homeric material especially, a few general remarks and salient examples must suffice.[5]

## Iliad 10 and Homer

The most fundamental debt to *Iliad* 10 is apparent from the beginning. Unusually for a Greek tragedy, *Rhesus* takes place entirely at night – a convenient cover for secret actions and, in contrast to the epic, a major source and symbol of human ignorance.[6] In terms of plot structure, the playwright essentially follows *Iliad* 10. His poetic techniques range from the dramatization of an entire episode to the creation of a scene out of a single sentence, and he does not refrain from wholesale invention.

The best examples of continuous borrowing are the *parodos* (1–51) and part of the first 'act' or *epeisodion* (52–148), where the poet, finding no substantial description of the situation among the Trojans in his epic model (the account of Hector's call to assembly occupies only four lines in *Il.* 10.299–302), has created a mirror image of the Homeric introductory episode in the Greek camp (*Il.* 10.1–179). The watchfires that worry Agamemnon in *Il.* 10.11–13 now lie on the Greek side (*Rh.* 41–8), the anxious commotion on that of the Trojans. Only with Dolon (149–94 + 201–23) does the plot turn to the Trojan narrative in *Il.* 10.299–337.

Conversely, the agitated encounter of Odysseus and Diomedes with the chorus (*Rh.* 674–91) is entirely based on *Il.* 10.523–4: 'And a clamour arose from the Trojans and an enormous turmoil as they rushed along in

---

[5] The best account is still Ritchie 1964: 62–81. On Rhesus and the Epic Cycle see also Fenik 1964, although his reconstruction of a full pre-Homeric version of the myth is controversial. The few remains of Astydamas' *Hector* show similar deviations from their sources, *Iliad* 6 and 22 (see Liapis and Stephanopoulos, this volume), as does Ezekiel's *Exagōgē* in relation to the Old Testament episode on which it is based (Lanfranchi, this volume).

[6] Cf. 'Structure and Meaning', later in this chapter. Other nocturnal tragedies may have been Sophocles' *Laconian Women* and Ion's *Guards* (Ritchie 1964: 136–7); likewise, perhaps Aeschylus' *Phrygians*, also known as *Hector Ransomed* (Ἕκτορος Λύτρα), and the homonymous play by Dionysius of Syracuse (*TrGF* 76 F 2a), if the poet(s) followed *Iliad* 24 strictly. Sophocles' *Men Dining Together* (Σύνδειπνοι), apparently the same drama as *The Achaeans in Assembly* (Ἀχαιῶν Σύλλογος), perhaps began in the evening (fr. 143 *TrGF*); cf. Sommerstein 2003: 359–60 and Sommerstein 2006: 89, 92.

confusion', except that in *Rhesus* the Trojans have not yet discovered the Thracian massacre.

Between these extremes, Dolon's description of 'god-like' Rhesus in *Il.* 10.435–41 has been incorporated into the Shepherd's report of his approach in *Rh.* 301–8; it is further elaborated in the chorus' 'cletic hymn' to Rhesus and their subsequent announcement of his arrival (342–79 + 380–7) and confirmed by his appearance at 388. In other words, the poet converted a single Homeric passage into a climactic series of aural and visual impressions.

The first *epeisodion* also illustrates the author's use of other books of the *Iliad*. Hector's speech in which he proposes a nocturnal attack on the allegedly fleeing Greeks (52–75) owes much to that of his epic counterpart in *Il.* 8.497–541, while the prudent advisor Aeneas (87–148) is modelled on Polydamas in *Iliad* 12, 13 and 18. The elaborate guessing-game Dolon plays with Hector about the reward he desires for his expedition (154–94) is informed by the far more consequential proxy negotiations between Agamemnon and Achilles in *Iliad* 9.[7]

Straightforward adaptation of *Iliad* 10 is interrupted by the short Paris scene, invented to cover the time of Rhesus' killing and for the spectacle of Athena's 'transformation' into Aphrodite,[8] and it ends with the Charioteer's accusation of Hector and the epiphany of the Muse. The concluding lines of *Rhesus* (983–96) roughly correspond to the Trojan arming in *Il.* 11.56–66 and so foreshadow the long third Iliadic day of battle.

### Other Greek Sources

The most important non-Homeric sources are two alternative stories about the titular hero, transmitted in the scholia to *Il.* 10.435.

According to the first version, which is ascribed to Pindar, but may well be older, Rhesus enjoyed one day of triumph against the Greeks, whereupon Athena, prompted by Hera, sent Odysseus and Diomedes to kill him.[9] In the second one, Rhesus had to be eliminated because an oracle had predicted that he would be invincible if he and his horses drank from the river Scamander and the animals grazed on the local pastures.[10]

---

[7] Bond 1996: 257–9, Fantuzzi 2006: 259–61.
[8] This would have been achieved by a modulation of voice and maybe a few suggestive gestures.
[9] Pi. fr. 262 Sn.-M. = schol. (bT) *Il.* 10.435 ~ schol. (AD) *Il.* 10.435. Cf. Eust. *Comm. Il.* 817.29.
[10] Schol. (AD) *Il.* 10.435. Cf. Eust. *Comm. Il.* 817.27–8.

## The Rhesus

From the 'Pindar version', it seems, stem Rhesus' boast that he will end the Trojan War in a single day (447–53) and especially the expansion of Athena's role compared to her benevolent presence behind the scene in *Iliad* 10. A trace of the 'oracle version', on the other hand, may be seen when Athena confirms Rhesus' claims by declaring that, for the final success of the Greeks, he must not survive the night (600–4).

Definite borrowings from the Epic Cycle are Odysseus' treacherous exploits referred to by Hector (498–509) and partly again by the chorus (705, 709, 710–19). They are (1) the theft of the Palladion, a protective statuette of Pallas Athena, from the goddess' temple on the Trojan acropolis (501–2; cf. 709), (2) Odysseus' spying expedition to Troy in a beggar's costume ('Ptōcheia'), during which he met Helen (this part of the story is suppressed in *Rhesus*) and killed several Trojan guards (502–7a, 710–19), and perhaps (3) the capture of the seer Helenus at the altar of Thymbraean Apollo on the Trojan plain (507b–9).[11] All three episodes belong to the *Little Iliad* (although the 'Ptōcheia' is first attested in *Od.* 4.242–64) and have been moved in mythical chronology to highlight the Trojans' contempt for Odysseus and provide a foil for his nocturnal attack on Rhesus.[12]

No written source exists for Dolon's wolf-disguise (208–15) as opposed to his donning of a wolf-skin and marten's cap in *Il.* 10.333–5. But three Attic vase-paintings of the early fifth century already show the spy in full camouflage, and one even crawling on all fours.[13]

### Rhesus of Thrace

Rhesus is a native of Thrace (his name very probably means 'king' in Thracian) and of the lower Strymon valley in particular, as his genealogy suggests: he is the son of the river god Strymon or (in *Il.* 10.435) of Eioneus, the eponymous hero of the seaport Eion at the mouth of the

---

[11] For this interpretation of the *Rhesus* passage and the location of the ambush see West 2013c: 180 with nn. 17 and 18.
[12] Accordingly, Diomedes is not mentioned as Odysseus' usual partner in the Palladion theft. He does, however, appear immediately before Odysseus in Hector's list of dangerous Greeks (*Rh.* 498).
[13] Paris, Louvre CA 1802 (ca. 480–460 BC) = *LIMC* III.1/2 s.v. Dolon B 2. The other two vessels are Paris, Cab. Méd. 526 (part), 743, 553, L. 41 (ca. 500–490 BC) = *LIMC* III.1/2 s.v. Dolon E 11 and St. Petersburg, Ermitage Б 1452 (ca. 490–480 BC) = *LIMC* III.1/2 s.v. Dolon E 13, which illustrate Dolon's encounter with Odysseus and Diomedes. On the Paris cup, Athena stands by the Achaeans, while Hermes is abandoning Dolon (cf. *Rh.* 216–17). See further Liapis 2012: xxx–xxxi and Fries 2014 on *Rh.* 201–23, both with earlier literature.

Strymon. This geographical association matches most of the other information we have about him.[14]

The Muse's prediction about her son's future as a cave-dwelling prophet of Bacchus on Mt. Pangaeum (*Rh.* 970–3) is our only evidence for a possible association of Rhesus with the local oracle of Dionysus, which was administered by priests from the Thracian tribe of the Bessi.[15] Yet the temporary existence of a Greek-style hero cult is attested for the nearby Athenian colony of Amphipolis. It was instituted by the city's founder Hagnon in 437/6 BC after an oracle had declared that he would succeed only if Rhesus' bones were returned from Troy (Polyaen. 6.53). The cult probably ceased when Athens lost its hold on Amphipolis during the First Peloponnesian War,[16] and no trace of the monument in honour of Rhesus (*hērōon*) seems to survive. However, the Macedonian historiographer Marsyas of Philippi mentions a shrine of Clio in Amphipolis facing a 'memorial' for Rhesus;[17] this shrine has been excavated and dated to the fourth century BC.

Until 357 BC, Amphipolis remained a focus of Athenian strategic and economic interests, and it is possible that *Rhesus* reflects something of this, although we must beware of seeking any direct connections with historical personages or events.[18] Yet it is likely that part of the audience was familiar not only with the famously rich gold mines and silver mines on Mt. Pangaeum (cf. *Rh.* 921–2, 970), but also with some local lore. In that case, the aetiology of Rhesus' Thracian cult (*Rh.* 962–73), even if not immediately relevant to Athens or Attica, was an excellent way to invest the unpromising 'Homeric' hero with lasting prestige.

## Structure and Meaning

While *Rhesus* is certainly not a 'great' Greek tragedy in the conventional sense, the play by no means lacks any deeper meaning, as many critics have

---

[14] Outside *Rhesus* cf. especially Hippon. fr. 72.7 West: 'lord of Aenia' (Αἰνειῶν πάλμυς) at the mouth of the Hebrus; Strabo 7 fr. 16a (II 366.5–7 Radt): ruler of the Odomantes, Edoni and Bisaltae (all from around the Strymon); *Suda* ρ 146 Adler: 'a general of Byzantium' (στρατηγὸς τῶν Βυζαντίων).

[15] Hdt. 7.111–12. Cf. E. *Hec.* 1267 (with schol. MAB), *Ba.* 298.

[16] Amphipolis fell to Sparta in 424/3 BC and, following the Peace of Nicias, maintained *de facto* independence until Philip II conquered it in 357 BC.

[17] *FGrHist* 136 F 7 = schol. (V) *Rh.* 346.

[18] As was done by Iliescu 1976. Greek tragedies set in the mythical past do not usually allude to specific events (Aeschylus' *Persians* and *Eumenides* being the notable exceptions), although they often reflect the political situation and/or social developments of their time. There is no reason to assume that this changed in the fourth century (see Carter, this volume).

maintained. A carefully constructed network of leitmotifs and structural responsions holds together the seemingly disparate scenes and creates a consistent picture of human weakness and the calamity of war.

By setting his drama in the Trojan camp, the poet has chosen the perspective of the doomed party (as, for example, Euripides did in *Hecuba*, *Trojan Women* and the lost *Alexandros*, and Astydamas in *Hector*), although for the moment Hector is in high confidence and convinced that Zeus or Fate will grant him victory on the following day (e.g., 56–64, 319–20, 331). This trust in his good fortune is maintained to the very end (989–91), despite intermittent challenges by the more sceptical chorus (330–2, 882–4; cf. 995–6) and the Muse's revelation that Rhesus' death was divinely ordained (938–49).

Rhesus is presented as Troy's greatest hope, a sort of anti-Achilles, who is not only capable of vanquishing the 'best of the Achaeans' (315–16, 370–4, 460–2), but also resembles him in many ways.[19] Yet neither Hector nor the chorus ever learn that, far from simply boasting about his martial prowess, he could indeed have altered the course of the war. This crucial piece of information Athena reserves for Odysseus and Diomedes (600–4) – and implicitly for the audience, who thus alone can judge what the Trojans have lost.

The epiphanies of Athena and the Muse, respectively modelled on the prologue of Sophocles' *Ajax*[20] and perhaps the appearance of Eos, mother of Memnon, in Aeschylus' lost *The Weighing of Souls* (*Psychostasia*), are visible signs of the degree to which both Greeks and Trojans in *Rhesus* depend on the gods. Just as Odysseus and Diomedes would never have achieved their goal without Athena, the Trojans need divine assistance to find out how Rhesus died. It is a fine touch, therefore, that in the play Dolon departs before the Thracians arrive and so cannot betray them to the Greeks. Pindar's version, which must have provided the inspiration for Athena's intervention, is more telling than *Iliad* 10 here.[21]

More often than the Greek spies, however, who escape on their own in 675–91, the Trojans and their confederates are seen making false decisions or groping in the dark – literally as well as metaphorically. The night,

---

[19] Like Achilles (according to Pi. *Nem.* 3.43 and Ap. Rhod. 4.812–13), Rhesus was brought up by nymphs (*Rh.* 928–30). His parents opposed his desire to go to Troy, knowing that he was destined to die there (*Rh.* 900–1, 934–5), just as Peleus tried to conceal Achilles on Lemnos (cf. schol. (D) *Il.* 19.326) and Thetis laments his fate in *Il.* 18.54–64. After their death both Rhesus and Achilles (in the *Aethiopis*) are carried away by their mothers to lead a supernatural afterlife.
[20] See 'Language and Style', later in this chapter.  [21] Cf. Strohm 1959: 260–1.

frequently mentioned for the sake of keeping the theatrical illusion,[22] thus becomes a dramatic force in itself, which prevents men from seeing the truth without supernatural assistance. The chorus-leader's words to the approaching Charioteer are significant in this respect (736–7): 'My vision is dim in the darkness, and I cannot see you clearly'.[23]

Structurally, *Rhesus* falls into two halves. The first part (1–564) shows a gradual build-up of Trojan confidence in the characters of Hector, Dolon and Rhesus, while the second (565–996) deals with the destruction of the hopes represented by the last two. The agents of their death, Odysseus and Diomedes, enter suddenly onto an empty stage, engaged in a conversation that resembles a second prologue (565–94).

Scenic doubling underlines the tragic antithesis. Each half of the play contains a messenger speech and a formal debate (*agōn logōn*): from the Shepherd Messenger we learn of Rhesus' glorious arrival (284–316), from the Charioteer of his inglorious death (756–803). Likewise, Hector's reproach of Rhesus for being late in joining the war (388–454) is mirrored by the Charioteer's accusation that Hector himself engineered the death of the Thracian leader (833–81). The reversal is further highlighted by the distantly responding lyric stanzas 454–66 ~ 820–32: in the strophe the chorus enthusiastically greet Rhesus as the saviour of Troy, while in the antistrophe they must face his death and Hector's charge that they let the Greek spies enter the Trojan camp.[24]

Leitmotifs also function as a structural device. Hector's persistent belief in the favour of the gods and the regular juxtaposition of Rhesus with Achilles (and Ajax) have already been mentioned; in addition, Dolon is characterized by wolf-imagery, which produces an ironic contrast when he is killed and robbed of his wolf-disguise (208–11) by Odysseus and Diomedes, who appear in the Charioteer's dream as wolves mounting Rhesus' horses (780–8). By the same token, the watchword 'Phoebus' (521), which Dolon betrays to his captors (573), not only fails to protect the Trojan camp (although Apollo favours their side), but actually helps the Greeks to escape (588). 'Lycian' Apollo, invoked for Dolon's safety and success in 224–63, has become Apollo '*lykoktonos*' ('wolf-slaying'; cf. S. *El.* 6–7).

---

[22] See Ritchie 1964: 137 with n. 2 (where add *Rh*. 45, 765, 774, 788, 824 and 852) and Liapis 2012: xxxiv–xxxv.
[23] Cf. Strohm 1959: 257–66, 274 and, on the ironic interplay of light and darkness in *Rhesus*, Parry 1964.
[24] See in detail Fenik 1960: 84–93, especially 91–3.

The unity of *Rhesus* does not lie in the Aristotelian principle of having one episode follow upon another with probability or necessity (cf. *Poet.* 1450b 22–34, 1451b 32–5), but in the idea of human fallibility and dependence on the gods. This also constitutes the 'tragedy' of the play, as do the prospect of Hector's death and the fall of Troy. In contrast to what we know of fifth-century drama, the characters on stage remain for the most part unaware of their fate, which also perhaps accounts for the absence of a true 'tragic hero' and the fact that none of the Trojans seems genuinely moved by Rhesus' death. He is but an incident in the much larger calamity of their war.[25]

## Dramaturgy and Stagecraft

*Rhesus* is full of rapid action and theatrical excitement. Despite being the shortest extant Greek tragedy, it boasts not only two messenger-scenes (264–341, 728–803), two formal debates (388–526, 804–81) and two divine epiphanies (595–674, 882–982), but also a possible chariot entry (380–7) and an unusually mobile chorus. In all of this, archaizing features mix with elements that have little or no precedent in fifth-century drama.

The chorus of sentries has been created against *Il.* 10.416–20, where Dolon informs Odysseus and Diomedes about the absence of Trojan night-watches. Their role and volatile character easily motivate their movements within the play, especially the *parodos* (1–51) and the first part of the *epiparodos* (675–91).[26]

Both these scenes recall early tragedy. An anapaestic-lyric *parodos* takes the place of the prologue in Aeschylus' *Persians, Suppliants, Myrmidons, Nereids, Niobe* (cf. Ar. *Ran.* 911–15) and the spurious *Prometheus Unbound*. The best tragic parallels for the searching-scene are Aeschylus' *Eumenides* 254–75 (the Erinyes on the hunt) and Sophocles' *Ajax* 866–78, both of which follow a choral exit in mid-play.[27] Even closer overlaps, however, exist with searching scenes in comedy and satyr-play, especially

---

[25] On the general danger of measuring Greek tragedy (classical and post-classical) by modern concepts of 'the tragic' see Lanfranchi, this volume.

[26] The much-criticized lack of military common sense in that all the sentries leave their posts would either have passed unnoticed in the commotion or been accepted as a piece of dramatic necessity. Hector's accusation of the chorus, combined with a threat of capital punishment, that they let the Greek spies slip by (808–19) and their eagerness to defend themselves (820–32) acknowledges the problem.

[27] Otherwise paralleled only in E. *Alc.* 747–860 and *Hel.* 386–514.

Aristophanes' *Acharnians* 204–40 and 280–327 and Sophocles' *Trackers* frr. 314.64–78, 100–23, 176–202 *TrGF*.

This treatment of the chorus seems to run counter to the alleged loss of significance that choral song underwent in fourth-century drama. However, Aristotle's characteristically linear account of this development (*Poet.* 1456a 25–30) needs to be taken with a pinch of salt. Agathon, said to have been the inventor of choral 'interludes' (*embolima*) unrelated to the plot, is presented as composing a lyric chorus-actor dialogue in Aristophanes' *Women at the Thesmophoria* of 411; and several post-classical tragedies bear titles in the plural, which suggests that the chorus was still of some importance in them.[28]

Likewise, the neglect of the stage-building, as part of a realistic setting on the Trojan plain, harks back to the early days of tragedy – before the invention of the *skēnē*.[29] Hector's resting-place is consistently referred to as 'couch' or 'bivouac', not 'hut' or 'tent' as in other military plays (cf. S. *Ai.* 3–4, E. *Hec.* 53, *Tro.* 32–3, *IA* 1, 12, 189–90), and the same applies to the remaining Trojans and their allies.[30] Both Athena and the Muse, however, probably appear on top of the *skēnē*. The surprise effect of Athena's intervention would be much diminished if she simply entered by one of the side-entrances, to be seen by at least part of the audience long before she speaks at 595,[31] and a raised position (more obviously outside the characters' field of vision) would also give physical expression to her divine invisibility (cf. 608–10).[32] The Muse, by contrast, arrives by means of the crane (*mēkhanē*). Beyond her entry 'above the heads' of the chorus (886–8), no stage directions can be deduced from the text, but to have her alight on the *skēnē*-roof rather than on the ground visually stresses her superiority over the Trojans and avoids the bathetic image of her departing

---

[28] On the development of the tragic chorus in the late fifth and the fourth centuries see, with different emphases, the chapters by Dunn, Duncan and Liapis, Griffith, and Liapis and Stephanopoulos in this volume.

[29] See most recently Perris 2012. The stage-building first explicitly appears in the *Oresteia* (458 BC) and was probably introduced shortly before (Taplin 1977a: 452–9). I am not persuaded by Seaford's arguments (2012: 337–9) for the presence of the *skēnē* already in *Persians* and *Seven against Thebes* (both times representing the royal palace), nor by Bakola's (2014) revival of the idea that in *Persians* the *skēnē* was used for Darius' tomb, with the king's ghost appearing from the door. (Would the Elders in *Pers.* 140–1 claim to hold council sitting inside the mausoleum – τόδ' ἐνεζόμενοι / στέγος ἀρχαῖον? Bakola omits the participle in her discussion of the passage.)

[30] Morstadt 1827: 6 n. 1. See also Liapis 2012 on *Rh.* 1–51 and Perris 2012: 152–7.

[31] Mastronarde 1990: 275; cf. Perris 2012: 155 n. 23, 160–1.

[32] This is a desirable side effect, rather than a necessary condition for placing Athena 'on high', since deities in drama can be invisible by convention (cf. Liapis 2012 on *Rh.* 595–674).

on foot, carrying her son (in the form of a dummy corpse) to his posthumous existence as a prophetic hero.

In this archaizing context it would have been fitting for Rhesus to enter on a horse-drawn chariot.[33] Aeschylus was famous for this device (cf. Ar. *Ran.* 962–3), which among his extant dramas occurs in *Persians* and *Agamemnon* and, perhaps inspired by reperformances, saw a renaissance in the later fifth century BC.[34] Yet verbal reference to a chariot in *Rhesus* is limited to the Shepherd's description (301–8), and it may be significant that in 383–4 the bells on the horses' headgear are transferred to Rhesus' shield. Perhaps the exotically attired hero alone was considered impressive enough.

By contrast, one finds innovative traits in the presentation of Athena, the Charioteer and the Muse. While Athena's mid-play epiphany has a definite precedent in E. *Her.* 815–73 (Iris and Lyssa), her masquerade as another goddess, Aphrodite, is unparalleled in both epic and, as far as we can tell, tragedy. A single equivalent exists in the mythical parody of Middle Comedy: Amphis (fr. 46 *PCG*) had Zeus transform himself into Artemis in order to seduce Callisto.

The highly subjective narrative of the Charioteer (756–803), who is himself a victim of the events he reports, goes far beyond the classical messenger speech.[35] Similarly, the Muse is the only known *deus ex machina* who sings from 'on high', although the author of *Prometheus Bound* (perhaps Euphorion, son of Aeschylus)[36] may already have attempted a bolder move in bringing on his chorus of Oceanids via the *skēnē*-roof or indeed the crane.[37]

The number of speaking roles is matched only in the late-Euripidean and much longer *Phoenician Women* (eleven) and, nearly so, *Orestes* (ten). Unlike these, however, *Rhesus* requires a fourth actor to play Paris-Alexandros in 642–67, for even if Odysseus left at 626, his actor (the only one available) would have to change costume and walk to the opposite *eisodos* within fifteen or, between 668 and 675 (681), even fewer iambic trimetres. Other possible four-actor tragedies are Aeschylus' *Libation*

---

[33] For example, Taplin 1977a: 43, 74–8, 287–8, Liapis 2012 on *Rh.* 380–7.
[34] Cf. E. *El.* 988–97, *Tro.* 568–76 and *IA* [590–7] and [598–606]. A. *Eum.* [405] was interpolated so that Athena could arrive on a chariot, and according to schol. (MTAB) E. *Or.* 57, 'some actors' corrupted *Orestes* by giving Helen a procession from Nauplia.
[35] See Strohm 1959: 266–73.
[36] So plausibly West 1990: 67–72 and 2000: 339 = 2013a: 229–30.
[37] For useful reviews of how [A.] *PV* 128–92 and 193–283 could have been staged see Taplin 1977a: 252–60, West 1979: 136–9 ~ 2013a: 262–7 and Griffith 1983 on [A.] *PV* 128–92.

*Bearers* (*Choephori*), where Pylades' crucial lines (900–2) would be infinitely more effective if they came suddenly from Orestes' ever-silent companion,[38] and Sophocles' *Oedipus Coloneus*, although in this case role-splitting cannot be ruled out.[39]

Two entries in *Rhesus* are problematic. Scholars have long debated whether Dolon at 154 arrives by an *eisodos* or simply emerges from among Hector's retinue. Liapis (2012 on *Rh.* 154 ff.) and Perris (2012: 157–8) recently argued for the latter, but Liapis' parallels for a minor character being silently and anonymously on stage for some time are inaccurate,[40] and it seems likelier that Dolon entered in the normal way. Hector's call for a volunteer scout (149–53) could be imagined to have reached the offstage space.[41]

Secondly, it is unclear from which direction Hector arrives at 808 and how he learnt of the Thracian massacre (806–7). He was last seen leading Rhesus to his resting-place (526) and by convention should return via the same *eisodos*. But this would suggest that he was present during the killing, which makes it preferable to think that the poet exploited his open topography and had him come from the other side. The question is unresolvable.

For lack of evidence, we cannot tell how far the eclectic dramaturgy of *Rhesus* was typical of post-classical tragedy. But several sources attest to an increase in spectacle, both in new productions and revivals of old plays (especially, it seems, Aeschylus).[42] *Rhesus* sits well in this development.

## Language and Style

Of all internal criteria, it is the language and style of *Rhesus* that have been examined most closely in the attempt to prove or disprove authenticity. Phenomena are therefore very well documented, and it remains to refine

---

[38] Cf. Taplin 1977a: 353–4.
[39] See in detail Battezzato 2000. Cf. Liapis 2012: xliii–xlv and Fries 2014 on *Rh.* 595–641.
[40] Danaus in A. *Suppl.* 1–176, Cassandra in A. *Ag.* 810–1072 and Alcestis' son in E. *Alc.* 233–393 could all have been identified in principle before they are named or speak: Danaus as the father of the young women forming the chorus (he is mentioned in A. *Suppl.* 11), Cassandra as a noble captive, and the little boy as one of Alcestis' children (entering with her and Admetus at E. *Alc.* 232). Dolon, by contrast, would have been one of a group of silent attendants, indistinguishable from them in costume and behaviour for more than 150 lines. Cf. Fries 2013: 819.
[41] Ritchie 1964: 114–15.
[42] Taplin 1977a: 39–49, 477–9. See also Duncan and Liapis in this volume, including their remarks on stage machinery.

and draw an overall picture. Again, the topic cannot be exhaustively treated here; illustrative examples especially must be highly selective.[43]

The poet's compositional technique is as eclectic as his stagecraft and far more obviously derivative – although less so in the lyrics, where the irregular metres would have inhibited linguistic reproduction. Perhaps the most noticeable feature of especially the iambic trimetres is the large number of verbal repetitions, which only rarely are unavoidable or fulfil a purpose.[44] The poet also shares with Euripides many words and expressions, including set phrases that occupy a specific position in the iambic lines. Often, however, it is impossible to tell whether any given case represents a true borrowing or the common use of what belonged to a developed tragic *koinē*.[45] So the Euripidean traits which scholars have detected in the style of *Rhesus* may be a red herring and, in any event, are overshadowed by the poet's taste for the high-flown, which he shared with some other fourth-century tragedians,[46] and by the extraordinary way in which he exploited his literary predecessors for linguistic material.

Throughout *Rhesus*, poetic archaisms and otherwise remarkable words mix with technical terms and the occasional colloquialism. In addition to the usual sprinkling of epic or epic-style expressions in Greek poetry of the serious kind, the playwright produced many close echoes of his Homeric models[47] and periodically, it seems, attempted to 'epicize' his diction further by the introduction of appropriate verb forms.[48]

From tragedy, we find words and phrases (especially compound adjectives and adverbs) that were favourites of, or probably coined by, Aeschylus,[49] while other singular formulations may at least in part have had

---

[43] See especially Ritchie 1964: 141–258; Fraenkel 1965; Liapis 2012: liii–lxiv; and Fries 2014: 28–39.
[44] Ritchie 1964: 218–25. For an entirely mechanical study of verbal repetition in tragedy, disregarding phrases and poetic necessity, see Pickering 2000. For the Greek attitude towards the 'careless' iteration of words, see Pickering 2003.
[45] A useful term introduced by Stevens 1965: 270; cf. Liapis 2012: lviii–lix. One way to distinguish genuine 'Euripidea' is by comic parody, especially in Aristophanes. Sansone 2013 lists several cases from *Rhesus*.
[46] To judge by our meagre fragments, Diogenes of Athens and the tyrant Dionysius of Syracuse are good parallels (see Liapis and Stephanopoulos in this volume).
[47] For example, *Rh.* 72 καὶ νεὼς θρῴσκων ἔπι (~ *Il.* 8.515), 233–4 στρατιᾶς / Ἑλλάδος διόπτας (~ *Il.* 10.562), 908–9 γέννας ... ἀριστοτόκοιο (~ *Il.* 18.54).
[48] *Rh.* 514 ἀμπείρας, 525 δέχθαι, 629 μεμβλωκότων, 811 ἐξαπώσατε. None is paralleled in tragedy, and the last one, an unaugmented aorist, is unique.
[49] For example, *Rh.* 77, 656, 737 τορῶς, 79, 158, 476 κάρτα, 646 πρευμενής, 724, 805 δυσοίζων, δυσοίζου (~ A. *Ag.* 1316).

Aeschylean precedents.⁵⁰ An important clue for the dating of *Rhesus* was Fraenkel's discovery that numerous tragic rarities have pre-fourth-century parallels only in Euripides' latest plays.⁵¹ The argument is cumulative; we should not forget how much of the evidence has been lost.

At the other end of the linguistic register, *Rhesus* features several military terms, paralleled in the historians, but seldom or never found in tragedy.⁵² They agree with the colloquialisms that cluster mainly in the 'comic-satyric' searching scene (675–91) and the speech of the humble Charioteer (756–803).⁵³ A few more 'everyday' expressions employed by the poet had entered tragic diction with Euripides or other late-fifth-century playwrights.⁵⁴

What really distinguishes *Rhesus* from other surviving tragedies is the manner and extent to which it relies on specific passages from earlier drama and sometimes epic and lyric poetry. We find 1) entire scenes adapted, 2) scattered reminiscences of continuous sections, 3) the 'mosaic-like combination of borrowed expressions'⁵⁵ and 4) peculiarities of usage which seem to stem from purely mechanical reception. Unsurprisingly, war-plays and 'slices from the great Homeric banquets'⁵⁶ prevail among the poet's models. Identifiable overlaps with fragmentary plays, especially Aeschylus' *Myrmidons* (also based on the *Iliad*), show that we might easily be able to expand the selection, if more Greek tragedies were preserved.

1) It has long been recognized that in both structure and wording Athena's epiphany (595–674) is heavily indebted to the prologue of Sophocles' *Ajax* (1–133).⁵⁷ Likewise, the chorus' 'dawn-song' (527–64) follows the first three stanzas of the *parodos* of Euripides' *Phaethon* (63–86 Diggle = E. fr. 773.19–42 *TrGF*),⁵⁸ and the sentries' reverie of peace at *Rh.*

---

⁵⁰ *Rh.* 260 κακόγαμβρον ... γόον ('a lament for her evil brother-in-law') is a strong candidate, and the almost untranslatable αὐτόρριζον ἑστίαν χθονός (288) reflects Aeschylus' fondness for αὐτο-compounds.
⁵¹ Fraenkel 1965: 234, who adduces, e.g., *Rh.* 48 ναυσιπόρος ('seafaring') ~ E. *IA* 172 ναυσιπόρους and *Rh.* 296 προυξερευνητάς ('advance explorers') ~ E. *Phoen.* 92 προύξερευνήσω. On *Rhesus* and *Iphigenia in Aulis* see further later in this chapter.
⁵² For example, *Rh.* 125 (etc.) κατάσκοπος ('scout'), 136 (etc.) ναύσταθμα ('naval camp'), 521 ξύνθημα ('watchword'), 768 ἐφεδρεύω ('besiege').
⁵³ *Rh.* 680 δεῦρο δεῦρο πᾶς, 685 †πέλας ἴθι παῖε πᾶς† (cf. 687, 688, 730), 686 <μὴ> ἀλλά ('No, but ...'), 759 οἶμαι (in parentheses), πῶς γὰρ οὔ; ('of course'), 785 ἔρρεγκον (the horses 'snorted').
⁵⁴ Most clearly *Rh.* 87–9 τί χρῆμα ...; ('Why ...?'), 195 μέγας ἀγών ('a big thing'), 285 φαῦλος and 625 τρίβων ('cunning').
⁵⁵ Fraenkel 1965: 233.
⁵⁶ Ath. 8.347e ~ Eust. *Comm. Il.* 1298.56–8 = A. testt. 112a, b *TrGF* (of Aeschylus' plays).
⁵⁷ See in detail Fries 2014 on *Rh.* 595–674.
⁵⁸ See Macurdy 1943, Ritchie 1964: 255–6, Diggle 1970 on E. *Phaeth.* 63–101 (pp. 95–6), Liapis 2012 on *Rh.* 527–64 and Fries 2014 on *Rh.* 527–64.

360–7 owes something to S. *Ai.* 1185–222 (the third stasimon). How far *Rhesus* depends on Sophocles' *Shepherds* (*Poimenes*), which dealt with the arrival and death of Cycnus at Troy, is impossible to tell from the latter's few remains, but the presence there of a Goatherd-Messenger (S. frr. 502–4 *TrGF*) and an over-confident, and doomed, foreign warrior prince is suggestive.[59]

2) A particular form of borrowing concerns the openings of four tragedies that resemble *Rhesus* in subject matter and/or the general situation. Among the many echoes of Aeschylus' *Seven against Thebes* there is a series which comes only from its prologue (A. *Sept.* 1–77), and almost in the original order of appearance.[60] We also find striking similarities with the entrance-songs of Aeschylus' *Persians* (1–154)[61] and *Myrmidons* (a famous passage; cf. Ar. *Ran.* 1264–77 ~ A. fr. 132 *TrGF*),[62] and with the anapaestic part of the prologue of Euripides' *Iphigeneia in Aulis* (1–48, 115–62).[63] Whether this portion of the play is actually by Euripides or not, the fact that it can be quoted here supports a fourth-century date for *Rhesus* because it is far more probable that the author of the latter exploited a continuous passage than that the revisor of *Iphigeneia in Aulis* gleaned words and phrases from all over *Rhesus*.[64] The large number generally in *Rhesus* of reminiscences from the early parts of fifth-century tragedies (prologues, entrance-songs) is not surprising: the beginnings of texts tend to be much better remembered than the rest.

3) The strongest linguistic argument against the authenticity of *Rhesus* is the poet's habit of combining notable expressions of different origin. Often a contextual relationship to at least one of the assumed models can be found; elsewhere, apparently, a flourish simply stuck in his mind.

One example must suffice. The Charioteer's description of Rhesus' death at 790–1 θερμὸς δὲ κρουνὸς δεσπότου παρὰ σφαγῆς/βάλλει με δυσθνῄσκοντος αἵματος νέου ('And a warm jet of fresh blood hit me from the slaughter of my master, who was dying in agony') may in essence go back to *Il.* 10.484 ... ἐρυθαίνετο δ' αἵματι γαῖα ('... and the earth was dyed red with blood').[65] But its language was inspired by two famous

---

[59] See Fries 2014: 33, with references to earlier literature.
[60] *Rh.* 19 νυκτηγορίαν ('debate by night'), 89 νυκτηγοροῦσι ~ A. *Sept.* 29 νυκτηγορεῖσθαι; *Rh.* 20–2 ~ A. *Sept.* 59–60; *Rh.* 514 ~ A. *Sept.* 33, 58; *Rh.* 632 ~ A. *Sept.* 36, 41 (+ 369); *Rh.* 932 ~ A. *Sept.* 45.
[61] For example, *Rh.* 30 σφαγίων ἔφοροι ~ A. *Pers.* 25 στρατιᾶς πολλῆς ἔφοροι; *Rh.* 58 = A. *Pers.* 54 σύρδην; *Rh.* 375 ~ A. *Pers.* 87; *Rh.* 741 ~ A. *Pers.* 44.
[62] *Rh.* 405 ~ A. fr. 131.3 *TrGF*; *Rh.* 557 ~ A. fr. 132 *TrGF* (= Ar. *Ran.* 1264–5).
[63] *Rh.* 12 = *IA* 143 θρόει; *Rh.* 16 ~ *IA* 2–3; *Rh.* 274 ~ *IA* 36; *Rh.* 529–30 ~ *IA* 7–8.
[64] Cf. Fries 2010: 348 with n. 16 (listing further parallels between *Rhesus* and *IA*).
[65] Ritchie 1964: 77.

tragic murders, namely Agamemnon's in A. *Ag.* 1389–90 κἀκφυσιῶν ὀξεῖαν αἵματος σφαγήν/βάλλει μ' ἐρεμνῇ ψακάδι φοινίας δρόσου ('And gasping out a sharp jet of blood, he hits me with a dark shower of gory dew') and – for the irregular compound participle δυσθνῄσκοντος – that of Aegisthus in E. *El.* 842–3 πᾶν δὲ σῶμ' ἄνω κάτω/ἤσπαιρεν ἠλέλιζε δυσθνῄσκων φόνῳ ('And in his whole body from head to toe he shook with gasps in a bloody death agony').[66] Yet nothing deeply 'intertextual' is made of the juxtaposition; a comparison with the sinister adaptation of A. *Ag.* 1389–90 in S. *Ant.* 1238–9 is instructive in this respect.[67]

4) Certain phrases, verses or even couplets seem to have been adapted without proper regard for the context. A particularly striking case in point is the choral entry announcement for Aeneas in *Rh.* 85–6 καὶ μὴν ὅδ' Αἰνέας καὶ μάλα σπουδῇ ποδός/στείχει, νέον τι πρᾶγμ' ἔχων φίλοις φράσαι ('Look, here comes Aeneas with great haste in his step; he has news to tell his friends'). This remains so close to E. *Hec.* 216–17 καὶ μὴν Ὀδυσσεὺς ἔρχεται σπουδῇ ποδός,/Ἑκάβη, νέον τι πρὸς σὲ σημανῶν ἔπος ('Look, here comes Odysseus with haste in his step, Hecuba, to tell you news') that Aeneas is said to bring fresh information, although in fact he intends to make inquiries himself.[68]

The *Rhesus* poet, it turns out, was familiar with a large portion of classical drama (as well as epic and lyric poetry)[69] and embellished the contemporary tragic vernacular with literary purple patches and bold creations of his own. Sometimes one gets the impression that he went too far or that a phrase imposed itself ready-made on the syntax of his verse.

It is difficult to find parallels for this manner of composition among the scanty remains of fourth-century tragedy. One example of both extended adaptation and individual borrowing is Carcinus the Younger's account of Demeter's search for Kore in Sicily (Carc. II *TrGF* 70 F 5), which largely follows the third stasimon of Euripides' *Helen* (1301–68, especially

---

[66] If Enger's δυσθνῄσκουσα (for συν-) is correct at A. *Ag.* 819, Euripides may have taken over the word from Aeschylus.
[67] Other passages in this category are *Rh.* 430–1 ~ A. *Pers.* 816–17 and E. *Alc.* 851; *Rh.* 440–2 ~ A. *Pers.* 500–1 and E. *Phoen.* 45; *Rh.* 498–9 ~ S. *Ai.* 388–9 and S. fr. 913 *TrGF*; *Rh.* 817 ~ A. *Cho.* 375 and A. *Eum.* 186–7. With non-tragic sources note *Rh.* 72–3 ~ *Il.* 8.512–15, Pi. *Pyth.* 1.28 and Pi. *Isthm.* 8.49–50.
[68] Taplin 1977a: 147 n. 3. See further Fries 2010: 350–1 and Fries 2014: 37.
[69] For choral-lyric reminiscences see especially *Rh.* 72–3 (quoted in n. 67) and *Rh.* 554–6 ~ Pi. *Pyth.* 9.23–5, Bacch. *Pae.* 4.76–8 and probably Alcm. 3 fr. 1.7 *PMGF*.

1301–37) and on one occasion seems to have taken over a unique adjective from elsewhere (Carc. II *TrGF* 70 F 5.3 μελαμφαεῖς ~ E. *Hel.* 518).⁷⁰

For the playwright's 'mosaic technique' Fraenkel (1965: 233) had already compared interpolations like the end of Aeschylus' *Seven against Thebes* (1005–78). 'Composite' lines indeed exist there, but they come mainly from the interpolator's principal models, Sophocles' *Antigone* and Euripides' *Phoenissae* (1625–82).⁷¹ The ancient piece of verse composition that was meant to be an iambic prologue to *Rhesus* (Hyp. (b) *Rh.* 431.34–44 Diggle)⁷² should not be adduced as a parallel either. Our poet was better than that and at present remains a solitary figure in literary history.

## Authenticity and Date

In modern times *Rhesus* was first explicitly declared spurious by J. J. Scaliger,⁷³ who was able to support his claim with one ancient piece of evidence. The learned note that is transmitted as one of the *hypotheses* to *Rhesus* (Hyp. (b) *Rh.* 430.23–431.44 Diggle) begins by telling us that 'some' suspected the play was not by Euripides because it showed rather 'the stamp of Sophocles' (τὸν ... Σοφόκλειον ... χαρακτῆρα). Unfortunately, nothing else is known about these doubters, and while we can discover several echoes of Sophoclean plays in *Rhesus*,⁷⁴ it remains unclear what their statement actually meant.

Otherwise *Rhesus* went unchallenged throughout antiquity and the Middle Ages. In the *hypothesis* to the play, mentioned earlier in this chapter, it is identified as an authentic tragedy of that name recorded in the Athenian state archives of theatre performances (*Didascaliae*). This drama was very probably produced early in Euripides' career (that is, between 455 and 438 BC), since the Pergamene scholar Crates of Mallus of the second century BC is likely to have drawn on the (now lost) chronological data associated with this entry when he excused an alleged astronomical error in *Rhesus* with the poet's youthful ignorance.⁷⁵ At about the same time the Alexandrians Parmeniscus and Dionysodorus seem to

---

⁷⁰ On this fragment see also Liapis and Stephanopoulos in this volume.
⁷¹ For example, *Sept.* [1007–8] and [1037–8] ~ *Ant.* 920 and 891–2; *Sept.* [1013–14] ~ *Phoen.* 1628–30 and E. *El.* 896.
⁷² See 'Authenticity and Date', later in this chapter.
⁷³ Scaliger 1600: 6–7, 8. For a concise review of the debate since then see Jouan 2004: x–xv.
⁷⁴ Cf. 'Language and Style', earlier in this chapter.   ⁷⁵ Schol. (V) *Rh.* 528.

have referred to the play as Euripidean,[76] and one may assume that Aristarchus, the teacher of at least the latter, supported the ascription.[77]

If we grant that neither Euripides nor a namesake wrote the extant *Rhesus*, then there must have been two homonymous plays, one of which disappeared early on and was replaced in the tradition by the other one. This presumably happened in Alexandria, where despite all efforts and the relatively ample documentation for Attic drama, the librarians did not always achieve satisfactory results. We hear of several plays that did not survive; conversely, the Medicean catalogue of Aeschylus' plays lists a 'genuine' and a 'spurious' *Women of Aetna* (Αἰτναῖαι γνήσιοι, Αἰτναῖαι νόθοι), which means that the Alexandrians had copies of both tragedies and felt able to distinguish between them.[78] If, on the other hand, only one anonymous or wrongly inscribed *Rhesus* was at their disposal, it would have been natural to identify this with the play recorded in the *Didascaliae*. The scholars may have been particularly eager to fill a gap among Euripides' early plays, which by their very antiquity were more likely to have perished than later ones.[79]

Conclusions about the date of *Rhesus* can be drawn from the fact that fragments of two iambic prologues are preserved in Hyp. (b) *Rh*. The first consists of the single opening line νῦν εὐσέληνον φέγγος ἡ διφρήλατος ('Now the chariot-borne [*noun and verb missing*] the bright light of the moon'), which the compiler of the note (or his source) gleaned from a *hypothesis* ascribed to Aristotle's pupil Dicaearchus of Messene (Hyp. (b) *Rh*. 430.26–431.29 Diggle).[80] The second fragment, which runs to eleven lines, he was able to judge from autopsy as an actor's interpolation 'unworthy of Euripides' (Hyp. (b) *Rh*. 431.30–44 Diggle).[81] Given the history of their transmission, it is overwhelmingly likely that these extracts come from prologues written for the surviving *Rhesus* and so testify to

---

[76] Parmeniscus: schol. (V) *Rh*. 528; Dionysodorus: schol. (V) *Rh*. 508.
[77] Ritchie 1964: 54. Among the 'anonymous' scholia, Euripides is mentioned in schol. (V) *Rh*. 251, and schol. (V) *Rh*. 430 cites E. *Or*. 220 as if by the same poet.
[78] See Fraenkel 1965: 229–30 and Fries 2014: 23–4, also for other problems the scholars at the Museum could not solve.
[79] Cf. Scullion 2006: 188. According to the calculations of Kannicht 1996 and Scullion (2006: 197–8 n. 7), only two (or three) of the fifteen (or sixteen) dramas by Euripides that did not reach Alexandria were tragedies, the others being satyr-plays.
[80] Δικαίαρχος is Nauck's certain correction of the transmitted δικαίαν. The question whether Dicaearchus wrote any kind of tragic *hypotheses* is highly contentious. It is answered positively in Liapis 2001, negatively in Fries 2014: 25–6, 27–8, Meccariello 2014: 67–82 and Verhasselt 2015 (all with many references to earlier literature).
[81] His view was confirmed by Stephanopoulos 1988a: 208, who exposed the piece as a pastiche of tragic lines and half-lines.

multiple reperformances of the play (for audiences used to the clear iambic expositions of Euripides).[82] This suggests a date relatively early in the fourth century to account for both the initial dissemination of *Rhesus* and later that of texts equipped with either of the two spurious prologues.[83] That Aristophanes of Byzantium, the Alexandrian editor of Aeschylus, Sophocles and Euripides, did not know them can be inferred not only from our standard text, but also from the statement in his *hypothesis* that the chorus of Trojan sentries 'delivered the prologue' (Hyp. (c) *Rh.* 432.52–3 Diggle). The Alexandrians did not normally omit passages they considered inauthentic.

The dating of *Rhesus* to between ca. 390 and 370 BC can perhaps be corroborated by two further sets of witnesses. From the middle of the fourth century (ca. 360–340 BC) we possess three magnificent Apulian vessels with illustrations of Rhesus' death, and at least one of these vase-paintings (Berlin, Antikensammlung, Inv. 1984.39) appears to have been influenced by our play. To the 'Homeric' scene in the Thracian camp it adds in the right margin a male and female figure, who by their iconography are most easily interpreted as Rhesus' divine parents, Strymon and the Muse.[84]

More tenuous is a reference to *Rhesus* in Asclepiades of Tragilus, the author of six books *On Tragedy* (*Tragōdoumena*) and perhaps the same as the tragic victor at the Lenaea of 352 BC. It relies on three almost identical entries in the late-antique and Byzantine lexica of Hesychius, Photius and the *Suda*,[85] where Asclepiades is quoted regarding a garbled Epicharmus verse which mentions a 'lord Rhesus, who †proclaims† divine decrees' (Epich. fr. 206 *PCG* Ῥῆσος ἀρχός, ὃς †τρέει† τὰ θέσφατα). Since it is unlikely that Asclepiades discussed an obscure gloss in Sicilian comedy, the

---

[82] This is the *communis opinio*. Liapis (2001: 328; 2009b: 85–6; 2012: 59–60, 62–5) follows a few earlier scholars in believing that both prologues belong to the genuine *Rhesus* of Euripides (the first presumably the original, the second a spurious alternative), which also helps his idea that the surviving play was first performed in Macedon around 330 BC in that he does not have to account for revivals. Yet it is most improbable that Euripides' *Rhesus* still existed in two versions at the end of the fourth century, but failed to reach Alexandria only a few decades later, and if the 'Dicaearchean' *hypotheses* are in fact a case of later mythography falsely attributed to a famous scholar, the theory becomes entirely untenable. To Liapis' objection that the apparent announcement of dawn in the first prologue does not fit the extant *Rhesus* one might reply that Νύξ (Rusten 1982: 360 n. 17) is as plausible a supplement to the line as Ἕως (Snell, Diggle). Cf. Fries 2013: 815–16 and Fries 2014: 25 n. 17.
[83] Cf. Ritchie 1964: 21, 22–3, 39–40, 57, 58 (although he thinks that the fragment quoted from 'Dicaearchus' is the beginning of a genuine iambic prologue which the extant *Rhesus* has lost).
[84] *LIMC* VIII.1/2 s.v. Rhesos 3, 4, 6. Cf. Giuliani 1995: 31–3, 94–102, Giuliani 1996: 71–86 (with plates 16–20), Jouan 2004: lxi–lxiii and Taplin 2007: 160–5, 283 (notes).
[85] Hsch. ρ 272 Hansen ~ Phot. ρ 103 Theodoridis ~ *Suda* ρ 143 Adler.

note has plausibly been referred to *Rh.* 970–3, where the Muse predicts Rhesus' future as a heroic prophet of Bacchus in Thrace.[86]

To sum up: *Rhesus* was very probably produced in Athens in the first quarter or third of the fourth century BC. Its tragic outlook on the Trojan War and human existence in general may have suited a period of restoration after the Peloponnesian War, but it also afforded dazzling spectacle and seems to have been successful enough to be reperformed at least twice. This popularity will have been instrumental in securing its initial preservation.

## Literary Reception in Antiquity

Several Greek and Latin authors, both poets and prose writers, show the influence of *Rhesus*, suggesting that the play was well known and appreciated in literary circles. In some cases the allusions must also have been intended to be recognized by the audience or readers.

A possible pre-Alexandrian adaptation was recently discovered by Fantuzzi and Konstan,[87] who detect reminiscences of the 'guessing game' between Dolon and Hector (*Rh.* 161–83) in Menander's *The Shorn Girl* (*Perikeiromenē*), 271–91. There Moschion's slave Daos requests a reward from his master for allegedly having moved Glycera, Moschion's beloved, into the house of his foster mother. After going through several options for a 'good life' (including military command) they settle on a cheese stall, and Moschion asks Daos to investigate the situation in the house (295–6 κατάσκοπος ... γενοῦ). The connection with a 'scouting mission' – κατάσκοπος occurs nine times in *Rhesus* – makes it particularly likely that the Menandrean passage is a comic distortion of the Dolon scene in *Rhesus*.

In the first century BC, Parthenius of Nicaea, the author of thirty-six mythological vignettes entitled *Erotika Pathēmata* (*Sufferings of Love*), incorporated the figure of Rhesus into the legend of Arganthone (*Erot. Path.* 36), and numerous parallels suggest that he had the play in mind.[88] Rhesus' earlier campaigns around the Propontis (*Erot. Path.* 36.1 ~ *Rh.* 426–42)[89] brought him to Mt. Arganthon, in the hope of

---

[86] Cf. 'Sources (Rhesus of Thrace)' earlier in this chapter. For a thorough, if sceptical, analysis of the lexicon entry see Liapis 2003.
[87] Fantuzzi and Konstan 2013: 256–74, especially 265–73.
[88] See Lightfoot 1999: 554–8 and already Valckenaer 1767: 104–5 n. 6; also Borgeaud 1991.
[89] Note particularly the use of δασμός for the tribute the hero imposed on the peoples he conquered (*Erot. Path.* 36.1 ~ *Rh.* 435). The word is rare in prose, except Xenophon.

winning the hand of the eponymous heroine Arganthone, a beautiful, but reclusive, hunting maiden. He succeeds by stealth, and later follows a noble embassy to Troy (*Erot. Path.* 36.4 ~ *Rh.* 399–403, 839–40, 935–7, 954–7), against the will of Arganthone, who like the Muse in *Rhesus* (900–1, 934–5) had dire premonitions and desperately tried to hold him back (*Erot. Path.* 36.4). After his death (uniquely in battle with Diomedes on the banks of the Trojan river that would be called Rhesus after him), she is consumed by grief and, in contrast to the immortal Muse, eventually dies from self-starvation (*Erot. Path.* 36.5).

Virgil used *Rhesus*, alongside *Iliad* 10, for the Nisus and Euryalus episode in *Aen.* 9.176–458.[90] Several details of the nocturnal adventure, during which Nisus and Euryalus, on their way through enemy territory, devastate the Rutulian camp, but then succumb to rashness and are killed by an arriving cavalry unit, resemble the play rather than *Iliad* 10. The Charioteer's speech especially seems to have provided Virgil with inspiration. The careless disorder among the Rutulians has a precedent in the way the Thracians sleep without basic camp security (*Rh.* 762–9 ~ Verg. *Aen.* 9.316–19), the deaths of Remus and Rhoetus recall the gruesome end of Rhesus' companions and the wounding of the Charioteer (*Rh.* 789 ~ Verg. *Aen.* 9.332–3, *Rh.* 794–5 ~ Verg. *Aen.* 9.347–8), and Nisus' and Euryalus' reaction to the challenge of Volcens resembles the Charioteer's initial attempt to confront the Greek marauders (*Rh.* 774–5 and 778 ~ Verg. *Aen.* 9.377–8).[91] Before their capture, Nisus had restrained his younger comrade from further killing (Verg. *Aen.* 9.353–6), as Athena restrains the Greeks in *Rh.* 668–74.

The latest author to make conscious reference to *Rhesus* is Longus in the second to third century AD. When the devious cowherd Dorcon in *Daphnis and Chloe* intends to sneak up on Chloe disguised as a wolf, the description of his dressing up (1.20.2) follows Dolon in *Rh.* 208–11 so closely that even the military origin of the scheme is recalled in the comparison of the animal's 'gaping jaws' (χάσμα) with a hoplite's helmet.

---

[90] Cf. Fenik 1960: 54–96 and Pavlock 1985: 207–24.
[91] Volcens' actual words in Verg. *Aen.* 9.376–7 state *viri. quae causa viae? quive estis in armis?/quove tenetis iter?* ('Stop, men! What are you doing here? Why are you armed? Where are you going?') echo those of the sentries to Odysseus (and Diomedes) in *Rh.* 682 τίς ὁ λόχος; πόθεν ἔβας; ποδαπὸς εἶ; ('Which is your company? Where have you come from? Where are you from?'). But military language is universal in this respect.

The phonetic similarity between 'Dolon' and 'Dorcon' will also have played a part.[92]

The illustrious list of ancient authors who have employed *Rhesus* as their model goes some way towards explaining how the play entered the 'Euripidean Selection'. All except Longus (presumably) antedate the firm establishment of this canon in the ancient school curriculum, although preference for the ten plays in question must go much further back. *Rhesus* was certainly not despised.

## Conclusion

It is difficult to draw conclusions about fourth-century tragedy from *Rhesus* without becoming circular. A few characteristics, however, which the play appears to have shared with others of its time, could be identified in the course of this chapter: *Rhesus* delights in spectacle in the way Aristotle (*Poet.* 1453b 7–11) might have disapproved of, its derivative language and manner of composition have at least some parallels in post-classical drama, and its very plot, taken essentially from *Iliad* 10, aligns it with fourth-century productions like Astydamas' *Hector* (after *Iliad* 6 and 22) and Dionysius of Syracuse's *Hector Ransomed* (after *Iliad* 24). Generally, the mythological subjects that had already been treated by playwrights of the fifth century remained in fashion.[93]

The modern criticism of *Rhesus* as in many ways inferior to classical tragedy was evidently not shared in antiquity. The play was successful on stage, appreciated by several later authors, who found in it material worth adapting, and the only doubts regarding its authenticity arose on account of some differences from the style of Euripides. In late antiquity and Byzantine times, *Rhesus* was part of the tragic school curriculum, and one can easily see how the same features that would have appealed to fourth-century theatre-goers (a varied plot based on a well-known episode from Homer, relatively simple language and its brevity compared to other tragedies) made it popular with schoolmasters and independent readers. Perhaps the best way to describe the intention of the *Rhesus* poet (and presumably other fourth-century playwrights) is through the four lines

---

[92] For the relationship of Longus to *Rhesus* (and *Iliad* 10) see Pattoni 2005: 100–5, Liapis 2012 on *Rh.* 208–15 and Liapis, forthcoming.
[93] Xanthakis-Karamanos 1980: 15–18. On the fourth-century preference for 'Homeric' plots see also Duncan and Liapis in this volume.

which Athenaeus (10.411b) quotes from Astydamas' satyr-play *Heracles* (*TrGF* 60 F 4): 'A clever poet should offer his audience, as it were, the rich entertainment of a sumptuous dinner so that everybody eats and drinks whatever he likes before leaving, and his art does not consist of a single course.'[94]

---

[94] Cf. Lesky 1972: 529, Thum 2005: 228 and Liapis and Stephanopoulos in this volume.

CHAPTER 3

# Hellenistic Tragedy and Satyr-Drama; Lycophron's Alexandra

Simon Hornblower*

## Introduction: Hellenistic Tragedy and Society; the General Character of Hellenistic Tragedy

In the Hellenistic period, the writing and performance of Greek tragedy flourished as never before, and on a massive scale.[1] This assertion may seem surprising to anyone who associates tragedy above all with the three great Attic poets of the fifth century BC, and with the choregically financed productions at the classical Athenian festivals. But it is true, if tragedy is considered as a social phenomenon. Nor should we assume that literary quality was necessarily low: we simply lack the evidence to say this, and it is facile to assume that non-surviving automatically means bad. The evidence for the popularity and social importance of tragedy after

---

* This chapter has been read and improved by Christopher Pelling, to whom warm thanks are given, but he is not responsible for any remaining defects. I also thank the editors of this volume for their valuable suggestions.
[1] For the line taken in this first paragraph, see Ziegler 1937: cols. 1967–77, esp. 1967. Habicht 1998: 104 and n. 14 endorses Ziegler generally, and observes that Hellenistic tragedies may have lost popularity merely because later taste preferred Attic Greek. Sifakis 1967 concentrates on epigraphic evidence from Delos and Delphi. For brief accounts, see Fantuzzi and Hunter 2003: 432–7 and (even briefer) Sens 2010: 297–9. Susemihl 1892–3: 1. 269–83 is still useful for the detailed facts; note his opening remark 'there is no poetic genre of this [the Hellenistic] period about which we are so incompletely informed as about tragedy'; cf. Page 1951: 37. Papyrus finds have improved the situation somewhat, as has epigraphically based work by modern Hellenistic historians on the social and cultural importance of tragedy. Lycophron's *Alexandra* is a special case, as we shall see; and for the *Exagōgē* of Ezekiel see Lanfranchi, this volume. But these were generic oddities or crossovers, and it is as true now as it was in 1892 that there is no surviving tragedy of normal type from the Hellenistic period. For performance, see below, on satyr drama. The remains of the Hellenistic tragedians are collected in *TrGF* 1 and 2. Kannicht, Gauly et al. 1991 adopt the numbering of *TrGF* and provide texts and German translations of, and brief introductions to, the main authors whose names are known. Kotlińska-Toma 2015 (a useful work which appeared after the present chapter was submitted) now provides texts of, commentaries on, and thematic discussion of all the Hellenistic tragedians, including the author of the *Alexandra*. (And see now her 'Hellenistic Tragedy' in Oxford Bibliographies Online.) For editions of satyr-plays see later in this chapter.

90

## Hellenistic Tragedy and Satyr-Drama; Lycophron's Alexandra 91

Alexander is primarily epigraphic,[2] and its volume is impressive, even allowing for the greater abundance in the Hellenistic period of all types of inscription. Let us begin with an example. It is richly illustrative, but not untypical.

In the early second century BC, the North Aegean island of Samothrace honoured a tragic poet called Dymas, from Iasus in Caria, praising him in the following terms:[3]

> Because Dymas the poet of tragedies has shown himself piously disposed towards the gods [the locally worshipped but famous Cabiroi[4] are meant] and friendly and kindly disposed towards the city, and is always speaking and writing and doing what is good for the island, and has made a prompt display of his [good] nature, and has composed an account[5] in dramatic form in which he has recorded the greatest deeds of Dardanus...

The decree is one of a pair, and we know from other evidence (also epigraphic) that this same poet was wealthy enough – presumably from his professional activities – to endow his home city of Iasus on a lavish scale.[6] It is likely that his play on the Dardanus theme was performed at one of the dramatic festivals held in the magnificent theatre at Samothrace;[7] such performances at international sanctuaries were not quite always agonistic in the classical manner,[8] but they brought their own rewards, in the shape of recognition, civic honours and sometimes hard cash.[9]

---

[2] It was thoroughly collected by Ziegler 1937: cols. 1970–1. He missed the Zotion inscription, discussed below. Naturally, more have turned up since he wrote, e.g., *SEG* 12. 466, Polyxenus son of Philagrus, twice victor in a contest of 'poets of tragedy', attested at Carian Caunus, second century BC (not in *TrGF* 1). Note the plural: when counting tragic poets, we should factor in Polyxenus' unnamed defeated rivals.

[3] Chaniotis 1988: no. E68, with good commentary (see also *TrGF* 1, no. 130: fuller Greek text of the two inscriptions, but virtually no commentary). See now *I. Iasos* no. 153.

[4] See *OCD*⁴ 'Cabiroi' (A. Sch[achter]).

[5] The Greek is not easy: πραγματείαν σ[υνέ]ταξεν ἐν δράματι τῶν Δαρδάνου πράξεων τὰς μεγίστας μνημο[νεύων]. For the meaning of πραγματεία here, see LSJ πραγματεία III. 3 (a general heading 'systematic or scientific historical treatise'. The roundabout expression (not simply 'drama' or 'tragedy') is interesting: it may be further evidence of an overlap between tragedy and history, of a kind discussed further below.

[6] *I. Iasos* no. 160 lines 5–6.

[7] See Chapoutier, Salac and Salviat 1956: 142 (with discussion of the poems by Dymas and Herodes; on the latter see below).

[8] See Sifakis 1967: 19 (citing L. Robert 1936: 244) for Delos and Delphi, at which the artists offered free performances, ἐπιδείξεις, in honour of the god. But usually (see L. Robert 1936) such performances were by exponents of less prestigious forms of entertainment than tragedy, e.g., conjurors and mime-artists.

[9] L. Robert 1936.

The subject of Dymas' play is of great interest at this moment in history.[10] Dardanus, son of Zeus, counted as one of the founders of Troy, itself the mother-city of Rome. In myth, Dardanus left Samothrace for one reason or another and crossed over to Troy. The topic seems to have been especially attractive to poets of Dymas' generation: it was also dealt with in a surviving tragedy of a most unusual sort, the *Alexandra* of Lycophron (see p. 118 of this chapter), at 72–85. In Lycophron, the reason for Dardanus' departure was a cataclysmic flood, a minority explanation, which made possible an account of marvellous land-sea reversals. The Dardanus theme certainly and naturally appealed to the Samothracians themselves: another epigraphically attested Hellenistic poet called Herodes of Ionian Priene (not necessarily a tragedian) was honoured by the Prieneans' kinsmen the Samothracians for writing about the deeds of Dardanus and his brother.[11] In the years following the Roman defeat of Philip V of Macedon at Cynoscephalae (197 BC), it made good sense for the Samothracians to emphasize their ancient connection with Troy, and thus with the new and victorious Troy, Rome. After all, Aeneas was supposed to have brought the Penates with him from Samothrace to Rome.[12] The precise date of Herodes of Priene is uncertain, and that of Lycophron is not agreed, although the view taken in this chapter will be that the *Alexandra* belongs, precisely like Dymas' tragedy about the deeds of Dardanus, to the early years of the second century BC. If so, the convergence is striking: we shall see that the *Alexandra* is a very political poem, and that the Roman conquest of Greece is its culminating theme.

Dymas belongs to a category of 'wandering poets',[13] attested from earliest times, but particularly a feature of the Hellenistic world. With great virtuosity, such poets made themselves experts in the mythology of cities other than their own. An example is Zotion, son of Zotion of Ephesus, tragedian and author of satyr-plays (see the end of this chapter), rewarded with seventy drachmas at Coronea in Boeotia in the heart of the Greek mainland.[14] The relevant decree, which dates from the mid–second century BC, tells us that he visited the place more than once, and produced his own plays at the festival of Athena Itonia; these 'celebrated in a worthy

---

[10] I. Rutherford 2009: 245–6 argues convincingly for the 'political agenda' of Dymas' tragedy, but treats it in poetic isolation.
[11] *I. Priene* no. 69; Chaniotis 1988: no. E60. See S. Hornblower 2015: *ad* Lyc. *Alex*. 72–3, where the kinship allusion is explained (Cadmus is the key).
[12] *FRHist* 6 Cassius Hemina frr. 6 and 7 with *I. Samothrace*. 16–17 and nn. 66–71.
[13] Hunter and Rutherford 2009. [14] Chaniotis 1988: E69 (bare mention at *TrGF* 1 no. 133).

manner' Athena and the city, i.e., its myths. Boeotia generally, and its main city Thebes in particular, were famously rich in mythology, but the new cities (*poleis*) of the Successor kingdoms were no less fond of dramatic performances. Theocritus praised Ptolemy Philadelphus for his lavish patronage of 'Dionysus' sacred contest' and said that the house of Atreus – which is here a signifier for the entire content of tragedy – might have lost its Trojan treasure, but its fame was secure (*Idyll* 17.112–21).[15] From Ptolemais Hermiou in Egypt, one of the very few Ptolemaic city foundations in Egypt itself, we possess an exceptionally interesting decree on stone dating from the year 246 BC, and passed by the Artists of Dionysus.[16] The artists themselves are all named, and their specialities listed, below the decree, just like so many signatures. They include two tragic poets, Phaenippus and Diognetus.[17] In all, well over sixty Hellenistic tragic poets are known by name, most of them from inscriptions; and from literary sources we know that many of them were as prolific as their classical predecessors. Thus, Homerus of Byzantium alone is credited with forty-five titles (*TrGF* 1, 98 T1), and Ezekiel (*TrGF* 1, no. 128) was 'the poet of tragedies' in the plural,[18] although we have the remains of only one by him (see Lanfranchi, this volume). It has been estimated[19] that several thousand tragedies must have been written in the three centuries from the death of Alexander the Great to the battle of Actium (323–331 BC).

The trouble, for the literary historian, is that so little survives of all this prodigious output.[20] Honorary decrees for tragic poets naturally do not quote extracts from their works; the most we can hope for from this source is summary information about title(s) and contents. Before we turn to what survives – either in fragmentary short quotations, or in longer extracts (plays partially preserved on papyrus or by later authors)[21] or in full (Lycophron's *Alexandra*) – we must ask what can be learnt about Hellenistic tragedy from ancient critics. The sections on tragedy in Horace's *Art of Poetry* (*Ars Poetica*), whatever their Greek or Latin sources (Neoptolemus of Parium or even Cicero?), presuppose Hellenistic theory and practice, and may indicate a greater proneness to melodrama in that period. Horace warns against depicting horrors and bizarre metamorphoses

---

[15] See Fantuzzi and Hunter 2003: 434 and Acosta-Hughes 2012: 397–400.
[16] On the Artists of Dionysus see Le Guen, this volume; further detail in Le Guen 2001; Aneziri 2003 and 2009.
[17] *OGIS* 51 lines 31–3; *DFA*² : 310–11 no. 5b, and discussion at 287.
[18] Eus. *PE* 9.28; Clem. Al. *Strom.* 1.23.155.2–7.    [19] Ziegler 1937: 1971.
[20] See Susemihl 1891–2 (above, n. 1).
[21] In this category is the *Exagōgē* of Ezekiel, for which see Lanfranchi, this volume.

on stage, and recommends greater attention to characterization than was usual in classical drama: Medea must be fierce and undefeated, but she must not kill her children in view of the audience (*Ars P.* 123 and 185).[22] This surely tells us something about Hellenistic dramatic taste: he is presumably warning against excesses which were familiar from Hellenistic tragedy. The latter thought (it is inartistic to seek to generate fear and pity by overt spectacle) is already there in Aristotle (*Poetics* 1453b 1–6), but Horace has sharpened it, and rendered it more dogmatic, and this is thought to indicate a post-Aristotelian source.[23]

History-writing can also be invoked. When in the mid–second century BC the historian Polybius denounced his third-century predecessor Phylarchus for producing emotional effects 'like the writers of tragedy' (2.56.10),[24] he may have had contemporary tragedians in mind; but 'tragic history' was not a monopoly of the post-classical period. (There is no more powerful assault on the emotions than Thucydides' chapter [7.75.4] about the state of morale in the defeated Athenian army as Syracuse, a passage which contains the only two mentions of tears in his whole work. And it says something about Herodotus that, when the — probably Hellenistic – Gyges fragment was published,[25] the distinguished but mistaken advocates of a date in the early fifth century found no difficulty in believing that Herodotus' treatment imitated that of the unknown tragedian, in structure and detailed handling.) In any case, one of Polybius' chief objections to such historiography was that it did not make clear the causes which gave rise to the heart-wrenching effects described (2.56.13). This left room for the sort of writing which generated pity, provided there was good reason for it. Polybius himself offers a sensational picture of Philip V pursued by the Furies (23.10.2; cf. also para. 12, 'Fate, *Tyche*, had a third act of the drama in store...'). As with Herodotus and Gyges, it is unlikely that Polybius' narrative was actually indebted to a recent tragedy, though even this has been suggested. The better view is that 'Philip made tragic', Φίλιππος τραγῳδούμενος, was Polybius' own creation.[26] More broadly, it has been well and wittily said that in this period 'the "tragic" ceased to be

---

[22] Ziegler 1937: 1972–5 is the essential discussion; see also, briefly, Fantuzzi and Hunter 2003: 435. For the *Ars P.*, Brink 1963 and 1971; more manageably, Rudd 1989.
[23] Rudd 1989: 179–80, on *Ars P.* lines 182–8.
[24] 'Tragic history' has been much discussed (was there such a thing, and if so was it specifically Hellenistic?): see esp. Walbank 1955 and 1960; but on Peripatetic, i.e., Aristotelian influence, denied by Walbank, see Fraser 1972: 2. 786 n. 217, part of a discussion of Agatharchides. See also S. Hornblower 1994: 44–5; R. Rutherford 2007.
[25] See below, 'plays on papyrus'. On the implications for Herodotus, Griffin 2006: 50 and 58 n. 38.
[26] Walbank 1958, against Benecke 1930: 254.

the preserve of tragedy', because oratory,[27] historiography and other forms of prose literature also became ever more tragic, in the sense of aiming at pathos.[28]

In recent years, the notion of pervasive social and political 'theatricality', defined as deceitful image-making and manipulation of the emotions, and self-advertising exploitation of actual theatrical space and the borrowing of theatrical and especially tragic techniques, has been fruitfully examined, and claimed as specifically Hellenistic.[29] Certainly, Hellenistic historians were very fond of theatrical metaphors.[30]

## The 'Pleiad'; Moschion

Study of Hellenistic tragedy, as a literary phenomenon, conventionally begins with the so-called 'Pleiad' of tragic poets, who are supposed to have worked at the court of Ptolemy II Philadelphus in early third-century BC Alexandria.[31] Their collective name is first attested in the time of Augustus (Strabo 14.5.15, about Dionysiades of Tarsus), and although Strabo was no doubt drawing on an older source, the notion can hardly be pushed back to the time of Philadelphus. But the identity of these seven is not constant, any more than is that of the Seven Wonders, or of other 'hebdomadal' groupings so loved by Hellenistic compilers of lists ('pinacographers').

As with the Seven Wonders, a few well-known poets make it into all lists.[32] Those mentioned as Pleiad members are the following nine: Homerus of Byzantium; Sositheus of Alexandria in the Troad; Lycophron of Chalcis on Euboea (he is not, on the view taken here, the author of the *Alexandra*); Alexander of Pleuron in Aetolia, a notably versatile figure and the best known of the list;[33] Aeantides; perhaps the younger Sosiphanes of

---

[27] See Chaniotis 2013a, ingeniously arguing from the tone of certain inscribed decrees which are assumed to be based on real speeches.
[28] Ziegler 1937: 1976. It is remarkable (as Pelling points out to me, citing Most 2000: 20–21) that the word 'tragic' came to be a signifier for a certain type of sensationalism and grandiosity – almost as if tragedy's exploration of the human condition was forgotten or considered unimportant.
[29] Chaniotis 1997 and 2009; also, Pelling 2002: 197–206 (esp. on the early Hellenistic king Demetrius the Besieger, as presented by Plutarch). See *OCD*[4] 'theatricality' for a short treatment of the topic.
[30] Chaniotis 2005: 212–13 and 2013b.
[31] See *OCD*[4] 'Pleiad' for a brief account. See further Fraser 1972: 1. 619; Fantuzzi and Hunter 2003: 434–5.
[32] Ziegler 1937: 1970.
[33] For the non-dramatic fragments, see now Lightfoot 2009. For a good short sketch of his literary activity see *OCD*[4] 'Alexander (8) of Pleuron' (K. D[owden]).

?Syracuse (see later in this chapter for his older homonym); Philicus of Corcyra; Dionysiades of Tarsus in Cilicia (*TrGF* 1 no. 105); Euphronius. Civic pride is often at work at the bottom end of such lists, so it would be futile to try to knock any of these definitively off the perch, although Aeantides and Euphronius are the worst attested (*TrGF* 1 nos. 102 and 106), and Homerus, Lycophron and Philicus are the best; it will be seen later that there are problems about Sosiphanes. One big and probably Hellenistic name, Moschion, is absent, but he was an Athenian with no connection to Alexandria that we know of (see later in this chapter, pp. 102–3). If the compatriots of Aeantides and Euphronius hoped to gain fame for their *poleis*, they failed sadly, because their ethnics (indicators of their civic origin) are not preserved. Their names are fairly common everywhere (see *LGPN*), and so we are deprived of one possible clue to their backgrounds.

The idea that some, let alone all, of these poets operated as some kind of organized and self-electing elite literary syndicate is implausible (indeed Sositheus is said, for what it is worth, to have been an opponent or rival, ἀνταγωνιστής, of Homerus: *TrGF* 1 no. 99 T 1). The most that can be conjectured[34] is that some of the Alexandrian tragedians were also scholars (notably Alexander the Aetolian and Lycophron) who might have collaborated at an academic level – not that academics are always friendly and cooperative people. But more probably the Pleiad lists are useful to us merely as an indicator of fame and excellence, as viewed in some later but still Hellenistic generation. The compilation of such a 'canon' of the best writers in any genre (such as the Nine Lyric Poets) is thought to be an Alexandrian pastime.[35] The Pleiad is therefore a special and secondary sort of canon, because its members were themselves products of golden-age Ptolemaic Alexandria, rather than models of earlier excellence. The Pleiad nevertheless provides a convenient point of entry for modern discussion of known individuals. Apart from the Pleiad members, many of the Hellenistic tragic authors are known to us only as names. Only Moschion (*TrGF* 1 no. 97, twelve fragments) is more than that. One non-Pleiad author[36] is famous for other reasons, no less a figure than Ptolemy IV Philopator, king of Egypt from 224–205 BC (*TrGF* 1 no. 119). That 'roi des dilettantes'[37]

---

[34] Fantuzzi and Hunter 2003: 434.
[35] See *OCD*⁴ 'canon' (P. E. E[asterling]). She shows that membership of such canons was not always fixed.
[36] That the philosopher Crates of Boeotian Thebes (*TrGF* 1 no. 90) wrote genuine tragedies is very doubtful; see Liapis and Stephanopoulos, this volume.
[37] Bouché-Leclercq 1903–7: 1. 326.

wrote an *Adonis*. It is startling to be told that his minister and lover Agathocles of Samos, a decidedly sinister figure in Ptolemaic history, wrote some sort of commentary on it. The title is intriguing[38] when we recall that a festival for Adonis featured in one of the most famous poems set in Ptolemaic *Alexandria*, Theocritus' *Idyll* 15, the Συρακόσιαι or Ἀδωνιάζουσαι (*Women of Syracuse* or *Women Celebrating the Adonis Festival*).

If we leave aside the elder Sosiphanes (for reasons given later in this chapter), we are left with very few fragments of Hellenistic tragedy, as opposed to satyr-plays. Pleiad members tend to score better than the rest of the tragic pack in terms of testimonia, but not of actual fragments. Generalization across the whole meagre range of relevant fragments of Hellenistic tragedy is hazardous, but there is general avoidance of metrical resolution, as also in Lycophron's *Alexandra*.[39] (Ezekiel is an exception.)[40] As for titles and topics, traditional mythology continued – as in the classical period – to be milked for subject-matter, although we know of several dramas on historical or contemporary subjects (see later in this chapter on Lycophron's *Cassandrians* and on the *Themistocles* and *Men of Pherae* of Moschion). And the *Alexandra* is an intensely and progressively political poem, with palpable if veiled allusions to real events. But then, Aeschylus and Phrynichus in fifth-century Athens had also taken contemporary successes and disasters for their themes. Finally, it is likely that some, at least, of the known tragedies had choruses.[41]

Let us turn to those individual Pleiadists about whom something can be said. Sosiphanes of Syracuse (*TrGF* 1, no. 92) is alleged to have written seventy-three tragedies, including a fascinating-looking *Meleager*, which talked about Thessalian witches who call down the moon (F 1). But he died in either 336–333 or 324–321 BC, (according to the Suda, which dates by Olympiads), in which case he is in effect pre-Hellenistic; or else 312 (*FGrHist* 239 B 15, the Parian Marble, an inscribed list of dates), in which case he lived well into the early Hellenistic and Ptolemaic period – but not

---

[38] Fraser 1972: 1. 198 draws the connexion between these and other manifestations of enthusiasm for Adonis at Alexandria.
[39] An exception is Moschion, *TrGF* 1, 97 F 10, but this two-line snippet is usually denied authenticity on the grounds that it contains resolution.
[40] Jacobson 1983: 167–9; also, Lanfranchi, this volume.
[41] Sifakis 1967: 123–4. One main reason is provided by plural titles such as *Men of Pherae* (Moschion), *Astragalists* (Alexander of Aetolia) and *Cassandrians* (Lycophron). Sifakis suggested that Ezekiel's *Exagōgē* featured a chorus consisting of Sepphora's six sisters; Jacobson 1983: 31–3 wobbled. See Lanfranchi, this volume. The queen in the Gyges fragment addresses a chorus, according to Page 1951: 30–1, and there is certainly one in the Cassandra tragedy, *TrGF* 2. no. 649; for both these, see 'Plays on Papyrus' later in this chapter.

into the reign of Philadelphus. The ancient biographical evidence appears to be confused as between him and a younger Sosiphanes, possibly his grandson, who was supposedly a member of the Pleiad (*TrGF* 1, no. 103). The younger Sosiphanes was born in 306 BC, again according to the Parian Marble (*FGrHist* 239 B 22). To have featured in that list proves him not only to have existed, but also to have been, like his grandfather (if that is what he was), a literary figure of some fame and importance. Unfortunately, we have not one single fragment of his works. This contradictory state of affairs sums up one main problem about Hellenistic tragedy.

In a way, the most interesting and insistently attested fact about Homerus of Byzantium (*TrGF* 1, no. 98, cf. 109) is his mother Moiro or Myro, herself an epic and elegiac poet.[42] She is not the only female epic poet we know of (Aristodama of Smyrna is epigraphically attested at Delphi from the late third century),[43] and Nossis of Italian Locri wrote epigrams. But we cannot point for certain to a single woman tragic or other dramatic poet (it will be seen that even the pseudonymous *Alexandra*, nearly all of which is convincingly female-focalized, is probably the work of a man). The very public civic role of a writer and producer of plays effectively closed this career path to women.[44] Homerus' father Andromachus was a scholar (φιλόλογος), so it is not surprising that two such literary parents should have called their son after the greatest of all poets, unless that was some kind of professional nickname. Not only do we have no fragments of Homerus; we do not even know the title of any of his many tragedies.

Most of what is preserved of the dramatic output of Sositheus (*TrGF* 1, no. 99) seems to be from satyr-plays (the status of the *Daphnis* or *Lityerses* is disputed), and will be dealt with at the end of this chapter. We have two lines of his *Aëthlius*, a play whose subject was the father of Endymion, beloved by Selene, the moon-goddess in mythology. (For another and very puzzling Hellenistic Endymion poem, preserved only on a stone inscription, see *PMG* 1037.) The sentiments expressed in the *Aëthlius* lines are of a moral, generalizing sort, but that is to be expected, given that the lines owe their survival to the late writer Stobaeus, who collected such maxims. The thought – an eagle scatters a thousand birds, and a noble man does the

---

[42] The Suda identifies him irrelevantly as 'son of Myro' even in its entry for Sositheus (*TrGF* 1, no. 99 T1). For Moiro/Myro see M. L. West 2013d: 329. *LGPN* IV spells her Moiro.
[43] Chaniotis 1988: E56; I. Rutherford 2009. For ancient Greek women poets, see M. L. West 2013d.
[44] For this point see M. L. West 2013d: 316 and (for the Hellenistic period) 329. At *SEG* 54. 787 (first cent. AD) lines 3–4 there is an alleged female writer of 'old comedy' (i.e., adaptations of it?), but supplementation and interpretation are uncertain.

## Hellenistic Tragedy and Satyr-Drama; Lycophron's Alexandra    99

same to a mass of cowards – may echo Sophocles (*Ajax* 167–171);[45] it is also curiously reminiscent of the boast attributed to the aged Antigonus the One-Eyed, who said, just before the battle of Ipsus at which he met his end (301 BC), that he would scatter his enemies with a single stone and a single shout, as if they were a flock of birds.[46]

To the next poet, Lycophron of Chalcis (*TrGF* 1, no. 100),[47] is attributed one of the finest of all surviving Hellenistic tragic poems, the *Alexandra*: wrongly, on the view here taken. The Pleiadist Lycophron was supposed to have 'emended' (i.e., edited?) comedies on the orders of Philadelphus.[48]

Of this, the 'real' Lycophron, we have many tragic titles, but only one tragic fragment, four lines of the *Pelopids* (i.e., the house of Atreus), again preserved by Stobaeus: F5. The sentiment – miserable mortals long for death when it is far off, but when the last wave of our existence laps close to us, we long for life, and cannot have enough of it – is effectively expressed. Up to a point, it evokes Cassandra's poignant cry in Aeschylus' *Agamemnon* (1300), 'the final part of one's time is valued the most'. But a closer parallel is to be found in the *Alcestis* of Euripides (669–72).[49]

Of Lycophron's other tragedies, we have only one-word titles. Speculation about their contents is therefore worth very little. But since we know so many of the titles, compared to the output of any other Hellenistic tragedian, they are worth pausing over, as is the general question of play-titles. Many Hellenistic tragedies presumably revisited or creatively reworked themes familiar from earlier tragedy or the Epic Cycle: Moschion's *Telephus* (F2), Lycophron's *Hippolytus* (1g) or his two *Oedipus* plays and his *Laius* and *Chrysippus* (F 4b, 1i and 9). But historical tragedies continued to be written occasionally, as in the fourth century.[50] Lycophron's *Cassandrians* (1h) was presumably set in near-contemporary Greece. The word Κασσανδρεῖς can only be the plural ethnic of the new north Greek city of Cassandria, founded by Cassander (son of Antipater,

---

[45] On which see Finglass 2011: 188, who gives some earlier poetic parallels.
[46] Plut. *Demetr.* 28. 5 with J. Hornblower 1981: 214.
[47] His father the historian Lycus was from Rhegium in South Italy (*FGrHist* 570 T 1). This is not a problem; Rhegium was founded from Chalcis (see *IACP*: no. 68), and two-way traffic between metropolis and daughter-city was common at all periods.
[48] T 6. On Lycophron's scholarship on comedy, see Lowe 2013.
[49] As Vayos Liapis points out to me.
[50] But against the usual view that Theodectes' *Mausolus* was directly about the fourth-century Hecatomnid Persian satrap, see S. Hornblower 1982: 335–6, suggesting that it resembled Euripides' *Archelaus* in that it may have treated an attested mythical ancestor of the ruler, Mausolus son of the sun-god.

one of the greatest of Alexander's marshals) in about 316 BC, and designed to replace Olynthus, shockingly destroyed and its inhabitants enslaved by Philip II thirty years earlier.[51] A theme has been sought in the terrifying and sadistic behaviour of a tyrant of the city in the 270s BC called Apollodorus; he was eventually suppressed by the Macedonian Antigonus Gonatas.[52] Or was this some equally Hellenistic story of collective displacement, wandering and eventual return, *nostos*? Such *nostoi* were a main theme of the *Alexandra*, written by what I take to be another, probably pseudonymous, Lycophron. But with no evidence whatever for the content of the play, this is mere speculation. A solider link with the *Alexandra* has been sought[53] in the title of another of Lycophron's tragedies, the *Elephenor* (F 1d); this rather obscure mythical king of Euboea features in the *Alexandra* (1034–46) as founder of cities in Illyria, driven out of his home island after killing his grandfather.[54] This coincidence might be evidence for the two Lycophrons being identical; but equally, the author of the *Alexandra* might have taken inspiration and some details from the earlier tragedy. That Andromeda gave her name to a Lycophronic tragedy (F1c), and also appeared in the *Alexandra* (836–41), is less remarkable: she was very popular in poetry and art throughout antiquity.[55] The same is true[56] of Nauplius, father of crafty Odysseus' even craftier enemy Palamedes (Lycophron F 4a): he was prominent in the *Alexandra* (384–6 and 1093–8: after the fall of Troy he lured home-sailing Greeks to their deaths), but was also written about by Sophocles, Euripides, Timotheus of Miletus and – as an Argonaut – by Apollonius of Rhodes.[57] Generally, that *Alexandra* is so full of myths that overlap with known Hellenistic tragic titles proves nothing; one might as well argue that, because Moschion wrote a *Telephus* (F2), he was author of the *Alexandra*, in which

---

[51] Fraser 2009: 354–5.
[52] Ribbeck 1875: 159–60, citing Diod. 22.5 and Ael. *VH* 14.41; see also Tarn 1913: 171–2 and n. 7.
[53] Geffcken 1887: 33–7.
[54] The *Alētēs* ('Wanderer') of Lycophron of Chalcis (F1b) is more likely to be about the son of Clytemnestra's lover Aegisthus than about the mythical founder of Corinth. Again, the *Telegonus* (F 8) might have been about Odysseus' son (see *Alex.* 795–7), subject of the *Telegoneia*, a poem in the Epic Cycle; but even in the *Alexandra*, there is allusion to another Telegonus (line 124, son of Proteus). Neither is named, but that is normal in this poem, as we shall see.
[55] Sophocles and Euripides both wrote *Andromedas* (*TrGF* 4 F 126–36 and *TrGF* 5 F 114–56). Later poetic treatments: Powell 1925: 85; Ovid *Met.* 4.662–738; Manil. 5.558–64. Art: *LIMC* 1.1: 774–90; 6.1: 6–10 and 7.2: 272–309.
[56] Despite Geffcken 1887: 37–42.
[57] Sophocles wrote two plays with Nauplius in the title, and Euripides wrote a lost *Palamedes*. Timotheus: *PMG* 785. Argonaut: Ap. Rh. 1.134. There was in any case another Nauplius, son of Poseidon and Amymone. The two were often confused.

the Mysian king Telephus occurs twice at significant moments (206–15 and again 1245–7, with verbal repetition). Finally, if Lycophron's *Marathonians* (F 1k) was about the Greek victory at Marathon in 490 BC, it will have catered to fourth-century and Hellenistic nostalgia for the Persian Wars; for this phenomenon see later in this chapter on Moschion's *Themistocles*. But was it about the battle? The title is not *Marathon-fighters*, Μαραθωνομάχαι or –μάχοι, but merely *Marathonians*. Callimachus' mini-epic about Theseus, the *Hecale*, also took as its starting-point the Attic deme (village) of Marathon, and that poem had no connection with history. Or we might[58] rather think of the myth of the eponymous hero Marathus (Plut. *Thes.* 32.5).

We have already seen that Alexander of Aetolia (*TrGF* 1, no. 101) was a famous author, prolific in many genres. He is said (T 7) to have 'emended' the text of tragedies and satyr-plays on the orders of Ptolemy Philadelphus (cf. earlier in this chapter for Lycophron's parallel role). It is a great pity that no verbatim quotation survives of Alexander's own tragedy the *Astragalists* (F 1). But for once we do know its subject for sure (from a scholiast on *Iliad* 23.86): it dealt with the accidental killing by Patroclus of a playmate while playing dice, *astragaloi*, lit. 'knuckle-bones'. This developed a passing allusion in Homer (*Iliad* 23.83–90), who had made Patroclus' ghost explain his original presence in the household of Achilles' father Peleus by reference to this youthful act of homicide. Peleus had taken the boy in, much as Croesus in Herodotus took in and purified the ill-fated Adrastus (1.35.1). We should not suppose that this kind of occurrence belonged only in the mists of ancient epic and quasi-mythical early Greek history. Xenophon, matter-of-factly narrating events at the start of the fourth century BC, introduced a minor character, Dracontius of Sparta, who had gone into exile after accidentally killing another boy with a dagger (*Anab.* 4.8.25). The Hellenistic world, perhaps even more than the classical, was full of exiles and other wanderers,[59] who would have made a sympathetic section of an audience for the *Astragalists* (cf. the speculation earlier in this chapter on Lycophron and civic displacement).

Philicus of Corcyra (*TrGF* 1, no. 104) resembles Alexander the Aetolian in that he is better known for non-tragic literary output; some of a hymn survives,[60] but of his tragedies, not a line or even a title. Other names,

---

[58] With Ribbeck 1875: 160. He was in any case right to resist the obvious temptation to associate the play with the battle.
[59] Garland 2014 for the archaic and classical periods; Gray 2015 for the Hellenistic.
[60] *Suppl. Hell.* 676–80, probably a hymn to Demeter.

whether of Pleiadists or others, are so poorly attested on present evidence that even guesses are futile.

We may end this section with the Athenian Moschion (*TrGF* 1, no. 97),[61] about whom biographical evidence is sparse, so that he cannot be confidently placed in the fourth or third century BC; or he may, of course, have straddled the two. We do not know his father's name; his own name is very common and therefore no help: at Athens alone, there are 91 Moschions, most of them Hellenistic (see *LGPN* II; the dramatist is no. 11). On the other hand, we do have twelve fragments of decent length, mostly thanks to Stobaeus. The most substantial, at thirty-three lines (F 6), is an account of the origins of human civilization; it is interestingly reminiscent of Ps.-Aesch. *Prom.* 436–71,[62] mentions primeval cannibalism (lines 14–15)[63] and culminates in the development of funerary ritual. The latter topic recurs among the fragments. The *Men of Pherae* is conjectured[64] to be a historical tragedy based on the life and violent death in 357 BC of the tyrant Alexander of Thessalian Pherae (for this city see *IACP*: no. 414). But this is not a play whose theme is certain from ancient evidence; and – always assuming a historical subject, and even this is far from certain – one could also make an argument for Alexander's more famous predecessor Jason, who in 370 BC was also assassinated, either by his soldiers or perhaps by a brother.[65] F 3 is certainly from the *Men of Pherae*, and says that the living should be punished, not the dead. F 7 seems to be in the same vein: it takes a rationalizing, Epicurean attitude to the folly of dishonouring corpses (note[66] the clear echo at line 2 of *Iliad* 24.54 'dishonouring the dumb earth'). These two fragments have been seen as part of an argument about the propriety of burying a transgressor, on the lines of Sophocles' *Antigone* or *Ajax*.

That Moschion's *Themistocles* was a historical drama is virtually certain; the only certain fragment (F 1) is not informative, but it has been suggested that F 4 might come from the opening lines of an oration by the hero praising Athenian freedom of speech, *parrhēsia* (4.4).

---

[61] For Moschion, see Stephanopoulos 1995/6 and 1997; also Mueller-Goldingen 2005: 75–88, discussing each fr. in detail.
[62] Prometheus is actually named at line 20; Mueller-Goldingen 2005: 83 is not necessarily right to dismiss this ref. as 'marginal'. Kern 1922: no. 292 thought the fragment Orphic. Cf. also Critias (*TrGF* 1, no. 43 F 19).
[63] On this, see the interesting remarks of R. Harder 1944: 29 and 30 n. 1.
[64] Ribbeck 1875: 155–9.
[65] Diod. 15. 60. 5; cf. Xen. *Hell.* 6. 4. 29–32; Xenophon continues the lurid family drama at 35–7, where Alexander's own assassination is narrated.
[66] With Nauck 1926: 815.

It would be good to know the year of this play's production, because early Hellenistic Athens suffered from episodes of tyranny and repression, and this might have been brave and coded encouragement to freedom-loving democrats.[67] In the fourth century, Philiscus of Aegina had written a *Themistocles* (*TrGF* 1, no. 89 T 5), and both then and in the Hellenistic period the Persian wars were constantly being replayed in Greek art and literature, as new enemies were identified with the old barbarian invaders of Greece.[68] There is evidence for continuing Hellenistic attention to Themistocles in particular; an inscription of about 200 BC from Lampsacus attests a festival in his honour, and Plutarch says that he continued to receive honours at Magnesia on the Maeander in his own day, about 100 AD (*Them*. 32.6); for Themistocles' connexion with these two Asia Minor cities see Thuc. 1.138.5. The play did not necessarily deal directly or exclusively with the Persian Wars: Themistocles' later career and his end were dramatic enough.[69] If we are looking for thematic continuity between Moschion's fragmentary plays, we might recall the burial motif in *Men of Pherae*, and note that Themistocles' burial in Attica was controversial because he had been judged a traitor (Thuc. 1.138.6). See earlier in this chapter for this theme.

Moschion's language is sometimes daring and innovative; the compound coinage σαρκοβρώς ('flesh-eating', F 6.14) is of a type favoured in the *Alexandra* (cf. 347, παιδοβρώς and 1066 κρατοβρώς); and with ὄμπνιος ('rich', of corn, F 6.10) cf. *Alex*. 621.[70]

## Plays on Papyrus

The two main tragic fragments about to be examined have more in common with each other than their mode of transmission or their anonymity (there are anyway many *adespota*, i.e., unassignable and often undatable fragments, handed down in the manuscript tradition).[71] They are both fairly recent discoveries, and both are still controversial, although (as often with new literary discoveries) there was in each case an initial flurry of learned interest and publications, soon tailing off.

The first is the iambic 'Gyges fragment' (P. Oxy. 2382; *TrGF* 2, no. 664). It was published in 1949, and its first two commentators, Edgar

---

[67] See *TrGF*n. Mueller-Goldingen 2005: 80 sees in a general way that F4 has political implications.
[68] *OCD*⁴ 'Persian-Wars tradition' (A. J. S. S[pawforth]); S. Hornblower 2010: 317.
[69] So rightly Ribbeck 1875: 147.
[70] See S. Hornblower 2015: *ad l*.: the word had a vogue among Hellenistic poets.
[71] Both types, those known from manuscripts and from papyri, are gathered in *TrGF* 2.

Lobel and then Denys Page, assigned it to the period just before Aeschylus.[72] Almost immediately, Albin Lesky re-dated it to the Hellenistic period. His view has generally prevailed, and will be followed here.[73]

The longest part (column II) is sixteen fairly well-preserved lines of a speech. It opens by naming Gyges, the historical seventh-century BC king of Lydia, and is evidently delivered by the queen of Candaules, from whom Gyges reluctantly seized both throne and wife; he too is named (line 21). The subject-matter corresponds to a remarkable degree with the very first story narrated in Herodotus' *Histories*, after the mythical series of female abductions with which the work actually opens (1.8–12). Herodotus explains that King Candaules was in love with his wife (who is never named) and wanted to convince his favourite bodyguard, Gyges, that she was the most beautiful woman in the world; so he arranged for the protesting Gyges to hide so as to see her naked rear view as she undressed for bed. The queen, who realized what was happening, kept quiet at the time, but in the morning offered Gyges the choice of death, or the kingdom and herself in marriage – after he had killed Candaules. Gyges, again under protest, chose the second way, and that is how his dynasty came to power. In the tragic fragment, the queen describes (to a chorus?) how she saw Gyges and grasped what had happened, because she also perceived that Candaules was still awake; in other words, he had connived at her shame. She 'bridled in silence ... her dishonour's cry' (line 24); compare Herodotus (1.10.2), 'she did not cry out, despite her dishonour'. The root words for dishonour and cry are αἰσχύνη and βοή in both authors. The next day, she sent Candaules about his royal business, and summoned Gyges.

It may seem surprising that famous professors of Greek were and still are unable to tell us for sure whether the Greek of the tragic lines is earlier than Aeschylus or, on the other hand, Hellenistic (the editors of *TrGF* 2 equivocate).[74] There is, however, a simple explanation for this three-century margin of disagreement: the main technical consideration is the presence of a metrical feature[75] found in non-dramatic poetry before the

---

[72] Lobel 1949 and Page 1951.
[73] Lesky 1954. See further Griffith 2008: 69–70, also Lanfranchi, this volume. On the relation to Herodotus, see Travis 2000 (agnostic on the date).
[74] Cf. Griffin 2006: 58 n. 38 (gently chiding them for the guardedness of their conclusion).
[75] The lengthening of a naturally short syllable before a mute with liquid or nasal. The examples in the Gyges fragment are: lines 15, προέδραμεν, 21 ἐγρήσσοντα, 22 ὁ δράσας, 26 ἀυπνίας (but some of these examples of lengthening are more common in fifth-century tragedy than others).

time of Aeschylus and again in Hellenistic tragedy,[76] but hardly at all in the plays of the three great Attic dramatists of the fifth century. Broader considerations can be adduced: if the play followed Herodotus, as it appears to do, then it must have violated the classical unities of time and place: the queen insists that the assassination of Candaules should be carried out on the following night, at the same place as the original visual offence against her honour (Hdt. 1.11.5). There is a good Hellenistic tragic parallel for such a violation: Ezekiel's *Exagōgē*.[77] But this point is hardly decisive.[78]

Since the technical arguments from metre are inconclusive, but the Herodotean parallels are not in dispute, one must simply decide which is likelier: either (a) Herodotus opened his main narrative derivatively, with a mere précis of someone else's work; or (b) a Hellenistic tragic poet followed and adapted Herodotus closely. In view of the general popularity of Herodotus in Hellenistic times,[79] and because of the unacceptable implications for Herodotus' lack of originality, we must surely prefer (b). That conclusion is strengthened by reflection on one Hellenistic poet in particular, the author of the *Alexandra*. It is a commonplace that this poet took Herodotus as one of his main models, especially but not only in the account of the Europe-Asia conflicts which begins at 1283, and which closely tracks the first chapters of Herodotus. We may close this discussion with a detail which links the Gyges tragedy directly with the *Alexandra*. The latter begins λέξω τὰ πάντα, 'I shall tell you everything' (1); there are classical tragic parallels for this, to be sure (see esp. Ps.-Aesch. *Prom.* 609), but note 'Gyges' col. I, at line 13: λέξω τὸ πᾶν. Did the author of the *Alexandra* pay this small tribute to a fellow Herodotean poet of his own time?[80]

The other important papyrus fragment of a tragedy[81] is also in iambics. It was found at Oxyrhynchus in Egypt as long ago as 1903, but not

---

[76] See Page's own concession (1951: 23) that this feature would be consistent with a 'very much *later* date — the age of Tragedy's decadence in the fourth century BC' (*sic*: he cites Moschion in the attached n. 21). To Page's examples add now *TrGF* 2, no. 649 (see below), lines 11 ἀνέκλαγε and 17 παρεπλάγχθης (but not lines 10 and 29). See also Lanfranchi, this volume, for Ezekiel.
[77] Lesky 1953: 6–7; Lanfranchi, this volume. Generally, Page ignored Ezekiel.
[78] Christopher Pelling points out to me that classical tragedies do not always keep the unities of time and place: the *Eumenides* of Aeschylus breaks both.
[79] O. Murray 1972.
[80] Herodotus as model: note that Jacobson 1983: 26, 96–7 and 138–40 argues that Ezekiel, too, was familiar with Herodotus, esp. the Xerxes narrative. On the parallel between the opening of the *Alexandra* and λέξω τὸ πᾶν in the Gyges papyrus, see Gigante 1952: 14.
[81] But Fantuzzi and Hunter 2003: 433 doubt whether it was part of a tragedy in the normal sense; this is part of their general thesis about what they call the 'bookishness' of Hellenistic drama. They

published until 1968.[82] More obviously than the Gyges fragment, it provides a bridge to the *Alexandra*,[83] because – like that poem – it includes a prophecy by Priam's daughter Cassandra of her brother Hector's death at the hands of Achilles (cf. *Alex.* 258–85); or perhaps the papyrus purports to offer a genuine eyewitness account. The ultimate inspiration for both is, naturally, Homer, *Iliad* 22. The papyrus is, however, very different in tone and presentation from Cassandra's uninterrupted monologue in the *Alexandra*, because it consists of rapid, often half-line, exchanges between Cassandra, Priam, Deiphobus and a chorus; the model here may be the Cassandra scene in Aeschylus' *Agamemnon*.[84] The first editor toyed with the idea that this might be part of the *Hector* of Astydamas (fourth century); but there are other short post-classical papyrus fragments on the popular Hector theme, and there is no special reason to pin them all on Astydamas.[85]

Finally, mention should be made of an extraordinary, and very difficult, post-classical poem on a Berlin papyrus published in 1907. It is in anapaests, an excited dramatic metre.[86] The first part is a eulogy of Homer. The second seems to be a tragic lament by Cassandra, addressed to her father Priam. This feature recalls the *Alexandra*, as do certain unusual details of language.[87] In his edition of the fragment, Denys Page asked why Trojan tragic themes inspired imitation after other themes had gone out of fashion. The evidence for this taste goes wider than tragic fragments: two Greek epigrams, the first Hellenistic, the second from the time of the emperor Tiberius and in transparent imitation of the first, allude to female reciters of Trojan War themes;[88] and persistent preoccupation with Troy is

---

cannot mean that literary allusions preclude performance, whether at a symposium or a more public festival context, like that described at Theoc. *Idyll* 15. 96–7 (Syracuse; Hector makes an appearance here too: line 139). Taplin 1977: 127 wonders whether the play was merely a 'curiosity of amateur dramatics', but does not explain this startling idea. See also Gentili 1977; Taplin 2009; Ferrari 2009.

[82] Coles 1968; *P. Oxy.* 2746; *TrGF* 2, no. 649.

[83] But the detailed similarities to the *Alexandra* alleged by Fernández-Galiano 1978 are not compelling. On the other hand, the opening words of the papyrus fragment, Priam's θάρσησον, ὦ παῖ, find an exact parallel in another Hellenistic tragedy, Ezekiel, *Exagōgē* 100; the form of the verb is unusual (Coles 1968: 115; Jacobson 1983: 30 and n. 18 seems to rest on a misunderstanding). If either poet is the debtor, it is more likely to be Ezekiel.

[84] Taplin 1977: 127.     [85] Page 1941: no. 29.

[86] Powell 1925: Lyrica adespota no. 11; Page 1941: no. 93b.

[87] See S. Hornblower 2015: 503–9 (Appendix) for a Greek text, apparatus, translation, and discussion of this strange and interesting poem. It does not rate a mention anywhere in Fantuzzi and Hunter 2003.

[88] Gow and Page 1965: 1471–4 = *AP* 5.138 (Dioscorides) and Gow and Page 1968: 1777–80 = *AP* 9.429 (Crinagoras no. II), both with Fraser 1972: 1. 621 and n. 23.

attested by a remarkable inscribed dedication from Hellenistic Dodona in which a man called Agathon claimed actual kinship with Cassandra herself.[89] An obvious answer to Page's question is in terms of the Trojan origin of the new Roman masters of the Greek world. That is conspicuously true of the next poem we shall consider, which is by far the greatest work of literature treated in the whole of the present volume, not overlooking the Ezekiel fragment.

## The *Alexandra* of Lycophron

The *Alexandra* is a fully preserved iambic poem of 1,474 lines.[90] It takes its title from the Spartan cultic name for Cassandra, who is named just once (ἦρχ' Ἀλεξάνδρα λέγων, 31).[91] Nearly all the poem (31–1460) is a prophecy in direct speech by Cassandra, but this is book-ended by short speeches delivered by a guard, who has been instructed to tell Priam everything she says. The poem can therefore be regarded as one long tragic messenger speech; as a whole, however, it is an odd sort of tragedy; only two characters, no chorus, and the 'action' consists merely of Cassandra rushing in and out of her stone cell before and after delivering her prophetic speech. The whole poem has been called a 'monodrama', not that that solves anything. We will return to the question of generic categorization.

The poem narrates the fall of Troy and the rape or attempted rape[92] of Cassandra herself by Locrian Ajax (348–72, a pivotal passage); she foretells

---

[89] See Fraser 2003, brilliantly connecting this with Agathon son of Priam at *Il.* 24.249.
[90] Greek texts with full apparatus: Kinkel 1880; E. Scheer 1881; Mascialino 1964; Hurst and Kolde 2009. Greek texts with facing English translations and brief apparatus: Mair 1921; Mooney 1922; S. Hornblower 2015. Full-length commentaries on the whole poem: Holzinger 1895; Ciaceri 1901; S. Hornblower 2015; on 648–819 only ('Lycophron's *Odyssey*'), Schade 1999; on 1141–73 (the 'Lokrian maidens' episode), Mari 2000; on 1281–361, Wilamowitz 1924: 2. 154–64. For other recent brief commentaries in French and Italian, all with Greek texts and facing translations, see Fraser in *OCD*[4] (later in this chapter). Ciani 1975 (lexicon) is an essential tool. The outstanding modern study is Ziegler 1927. Good brief account, with long bibliography updated to 2011 by myself: P. M. F[raser], 'Lycophron (2)(b)' in *OCD*[4]. Collections of essays: Cusset and Kolde 2009; Durbec 2011; Hurst 2012. Notable monographs dealing in part or whole with the *Alexandra*: Wilamowitz 1883 (inaugural lecture) and 1924: 2. 143–64; Sistakou 2008 and 2013; Biffis 2012, 2014 and 2015. For the *Alexandra* in the context of Hellenistic tragedy, Fantuzzi and Hunter 2003: 437–43; Sens 2010: 299–313. For an excellent full-length literary monograph on the poem, see McNelis and Sens 2016; on the *Alexandra* and the historical Roman and Hellenistic worlds see S. Hornblower, 2018.
[91] Detailed documentation and justification for assertions in this section can be found in S. Hornblower 2015 (thematic introduction and lemmatic commentary).
[92] The matter is unclear. Iconographic depiction of Cassandra as naked has been taken to indicate actual intercourse, but this nakedness is not invariable. Contrast the two vase-paintings, both from

that for this 'one man's crime' all Greece will suffer (365–6, cf. 1281–2). This is the organizing principle which generates the long series of *nostoi* narratives which follows (417–1282). But Troy will not after all perish in obscurity because Cassandra's kinsman Aeneas will leave behind him a 'race of outstanding strength', ἔξοχον ῥώμῃ γένος (1233, with a play on the Greek name of Rome, Ῥώμη). The Romans will have 'sceptre and kingship of land and sea', 1229, the most famous line in *Alexandra*. The Trojan War is revisited (1362–8), as one of the hostile encounters between Asia and Europe enumerated in the last great section, 1283–1450. A later Roman kinsman of Cassandra, typically unnamed but called a 'unique wrestler', will impose reconciliation by force of arms, and take the 'first choice of the spear-won spoils' (1446–50).

The *Alexandra* is of a famous obscurity; it was called the 'dark poem', σκοτεινὸν ποίημα, by the *Suda* (λ 821 Adler =*TrGF* 1, 100 T 3). The poem's difficulty must be kept in proportion. It is not difficult in the dense and abstract manner of Thucydidean speeches, or in the vertiginous manner of Pindar.[93] The text is not often seriously in doubt[94] (contrast a play like the *Libation-bearers* of Aeschylus); the poem's sentence-construction is simple; the metre consists almost entirely of 'unresolved' iambics;[95] and the absence of thematically discursive choral lyric makes the thought and the content – a kind of sequential narrative of events which are represented as taking place in the future – easy enough to follow. Cassandra leads us from the first Trojan War to the Roman conquest of Greece, with a long middle section 'predicting' the unhappy homecomings (*nostoi*) of Greek heroes after the Trojan War, and the wanderings of Trojan refugees, conspicuously Aeneas the founder of Rome. Of the Greeks, she gives special attention to Diomedes (592–632 and again 1047–153), Odysseus (648–819, Lycophron's '*Odyssey*') and Menelaus (820–76, a passage almost exactly one-third of the length of the '*Odyssey*'). She passes from one hero or group of heroes with plain and predictable formulae of transition like 'and another...', 'and others...'; this is

---

the Naples museum, reproduced as figure 1 of S. Hornblower 2015. Connelly 1993: 103–4 (cf. 88) leaves the question open. See S. Hornblower 2015: on *Alex.* 365.

[93] But note one stylistic feature in common between all three authors, namely *variatio* or ποικιλία. An early example is at 8, θυμῷ καὶ διὰ μνήμης, a dative and a propositional expression used to describe two mental processes; also 59–60. Cf. Pi. *O.* 6.17 and Thuc. 7.59.2.

[94] This would not be true if we were to accept the extensive interpolation theories of S. West 1983 and 1984, but these are not here followed.

[95] That is, metrically 'long' syllables are only rarely replaced by 'double shorts'.

## Hellenistic Tragedy and Satyr-Drama; Lycophron's Alexandra 109

reminiscent of the Epic Cycle,[96] or of Catalogue poetry, on which see later in this chapter. The last main section of the poem reprises Herodotus, as we have seen, and the organization here is for the most part lucid and logical, from Io, Medea and the Amazons, down to the Persian wars and beyond. But the vocabulary is punishingly recondite throughout[97] (hundreds of words used here only, in Greek of any period), and the many individual places, gods, heroes and heroines are almost always referred to by riddling periphrasis; gods, male and female, are often given only their divine epithets (*epiklēseis*). Only very minor mythical figures are named straightforwardly. Even this sort of puzzling allusiveness is not wholly new or peculiar to the *Alexandra* (Clytemnestra's 'beacon-speech' in Aeschylus' *Agamemnon* lines 281–316 contains some challenges to geographical understanding towards its end, and Hellenistic poets like Euphorion enjoyed teasing their readers). But the *Alexandra* takes it to extremes.

An advantage of this obscurity is that it generated an exceptionally rich commentary tradition in ancient and Byzantine times (Tzetzes alone wrote a very full and valuable commentary);[98] this is of great assistance to us in translating all those rare words. As for the roundabout allusions to gods and mythical figures, their elucidation by the scholia and Tzetzes is not only helpful in the same way as the purely grammatical and lexical notes; the explanatory material also constitutes a prime source of knowledge about Greek mythology, and it can be shown from epigraphy that the ancient explanations of the poem's many divine epithets reflect historically authentic local cults.[99] This has implications for the nature of the poem as well as for the reliability of its commentators: the *Alexandra* is no mere puzzle poem but is rooted in cultic reality. Aetiology was a feature of classical tragedy (see, e.g., Eur. *Hipp.* 1423–7 for the premarital cult of Hippolytus at Troezen). The *Alexandra* similarly predicts cults of Diomedes in Daunia (mod. Northern Puglia in South Italy), the siren Parthenope in Italian Campania, Odysseus in Aetolia, Philoctetes in South Italy,

---

[96] Pelling directs me to *AP* 11.130 for cyclic poetry as characterised by formulaic repetitions of 'and then...and then', αὐτὰρ ἔπειτα.

[97] Curiously enough, this applies to the guard (whom we would expect to be an ordinary sort of chap) as well to Cassandra; see Wilamowitz 1924: 2. 147 n. 2.

[98] For the main ancient scholia see Kinkel 1880 (at the back) and E. Scheer 1908 (his vol. 2), and now Leone 2002. For Tzetzes see Müller 1811 and again E. Scheer 1908. E. Scheer vol. 1 (1882) provides (as well as the text of the poem itself) the texts of two ancient paraphrases of the poem.

[99] S. Hornblower 2014. But see McNelis and Sens 2016 ch. 2 for a well-documented argument that the multiple cult titles in the poem are often presented in alphabetical order, and that this may indicate that the poet used a preexisting collection of such titles. But the authors also demonstrate convincingly that the cult titles are frequently chosen with deliberate and appropriate care.

Podalirius (an incubatory healing cult, perfect for a son of Asclepius) also in South Italy, Hecuba in Sicily, and Hector at Boeotian Thebes (630, 720, 799, 927–9, 1051–2, 1181–4, 1212–13). Pride of place must go to the premarital cult of Cassandra herself in Daunia, and that of her 'spouse' Agamemnon at Sparta (1126–30 and 1123–4). Many of these cults are independently attested, either by inscriptions[100] or by other literary sources.[101] Excavation at Amyclae near Sparta has proven that there was indeed a joint cult of Agamemnon and Alexandra/Cassandra there[102] (for a temple at Amyclae to Alexandra see *SIG*³ 932.14–15, second or first century BC). There is a noticeable concentration of these cults in the West (South Italy and Sicily), and this corresponds to the generally western slant of the poem as a whole, beginning with the reference to the 'Ausonian [i.e., Italian] sea' at 44.

One striking feature of the *Alexandra* is its fondness for metamorphoses; there are no fewer than twenty-eight in the poem.[103] Even here we can detect awareness of real-life categories of ritual. Sometimes the poem's metamorphoses merely satisfy a Hellenistic taste for the outré and shocking; see the Introduction to this chapter. But sometimes – like the Aeginetan ants at 176 or the Cypriot wasps of 447 – they conform interestingly to a category of foundation myth. Sometimes – like Io the 'bull-maiden' at 1292 – they may belong to a recognized type of pre-marital ritual; compare the little female 'bears' at Brauron in Attica.

It will have been seen by now that this is a poem spectacularly rich in mythological material – indeed, that is one reason for its survival in the manuscript tradition (but as handbooks go, it is a rather wilful example of the type: often minority or more outré versions of myths are preferred to standard ones). It is also prime evidence for the student of Mediterranean settlement and myths of identity or charter myths;[104] and it is a poem with a political thesis, the apparently welcoming acknowledgment of Rome as a pan-Mediterranean power 'by land and sea' 1229. See further later in this chapter, on Naples).

All this makes it, in a real sense, a work of history on a broad definition, which includes the study of ancient perceptions by communities of their

---

[100] See, e.g., *SEG* 48.692bis-694 for pottery graffiti attesting fifth-century BC cult of Diomedes in the central Adriatic.
[101] See, e.g., Paus. 9.18.5 for Hector at Thebes, and *FGrHist* 269 Staphylos F 8 for Agamemnon at Sparta).
[102] See S. Hornblower 2015: on *Alex.* 30, with figure 2(unpublished sherds from Amyclae).
[103] See S. Hornblower 2015: on *Alex.* 176 for the full list.
[104] And therefore duly exploited by T. Scheer 1993, Malkin 1998 and Lane Fox 2008.

own ethnic origins. After all, the *Alexandra* is the earliest evidence for several features of early Roman tradition[105] which are otherwise first met in prose writers such as Dionysius of Halicarnassus, who in turn drew on the prose historian and mythographer Hellanicus of Lesbos (ca. 400 BC) and the great Greek prose historian of the west, Timaeus of Tauromenium (ca. 300 BC); indeed, Lycophron's *Alexandra* itself is thought to have drawn directly on Timaeus at a number of points.[106]

The *Alexandra* is thus a historical document, if not the work of a historian, unless of a very special sort. So, what – apart from iambic metre, the name of the author,[107] and the poem's suitably tragic length[108] – is the justification for including the *Alexandra* in a book about tragedy at all? One answer is to point to the ways in which the poem conforms to formal, classical models (on this topic see later in this chapter, and Lanfranchi, this volume), such as the adoption of the old device of the messenger-speech; a narrow definition of tragedy as a genre tied to fifth-century Athenian institutions would exclude not only the *Alexandra*, but all the plays discussed in the first part of this chapter. Another answer is to point to actual tragedies on historical episodes, as written by Phrynichus, Aeschylus and perhaps Moschion; see further later in this chapter for direct history in the *Alexandra*. Yet another answer is that Greek tragedy had always used myth to explore the present: the *Oresteia* of Aeschylus had closed with what was in effect a eulogy of imperial Athens, and 'social contextualization' theories of classical tragedy detect contemporary democratic Athenian preoccupations at every turn. A different sort of answer is that insistence on strict single-option generic categorization is modern, for all that the historian Thucydides could refer slightingly to poetic licence to exaggerate (1.21.1), and that Aristotle sought, not very satisfactorily, to demarcate history from poetry. Was Herodotus a historian or an ethnographer? The question is unreal. If the Lycophron of the *Alexandra* made his mantic Cassandra draw on the historian Timaeus, Timaeus may in turn have drawn on the archaic Sicilian poet Stesichorus. It might be objected that the performance context provides a clear criterion for distinguishing

---

[105] See *Alex.* 1250–2 for the 'eating of the tables' by Aeneas' companions (a Greek type of foundation myth, made famous by Virgil but also mentioned by his contemporary Dion. Hal. (*AR* 1.55), and 1259 for Aeneas' foundation of Lavinium.

[106] Geffcken 1892 remains the essential treatment.

[107] If the poem is pseudonymous (see following), the choice of the name of a known tragic poet is informative about the author's view of his own work. Conversely, if it was a genuine production of Lycophron the Pleiadist tragedian, it was yet another of his tragedies, albeit a highly experimental specimen.

[108] With its 1,474 lines, compare, e.g., the 1,471 of Sophocles' *Philoctetes*.

history (i.e., prose) and poetry. But we can only guess at what sort of audience was envisaged for the *Alexandra* (see later in this chapter); and recitation of histories remained common throughout antiquity.[109] As a final answer, we should recall that classical tragedy was itself hospitable to other genres.[110] To that extent the *Alexandra* was not eccentric.

It is therefore worth asking what other genres are co-present with tragedy in the *Alexandra*.[111] Epic is one inspiration, not only Homer but also the Epic Cycle. The Homeric *Odyssey* lies behind the *nostoi* of Odysseus and Menelaus as a matter of course, but the *Iliad* is there too; see esp. *Alex.* 258–97.

We have seen that there is history in abundance. Actual references to clearly identifiable historical events are rare: the 'unique wrestler' of 1447 is cryptically described, and his identity has been endlessly disputed (Titus Quinctius Flamininus or another?). But the striding 'giant' of 1414 is patently Xerxes (cf. Hdt. 7.187.2 for the king's height and beauty); and the murder of Hercules, son of Alexander the Great by Barsine, by Polyperchon, one of Alexander's Successors, in 309 BC, is plainly alluded to at 801–2 (cf. Diod. 20.20 and 28). This is the poem's only mention by name of a historical character; the mythical Heracles is always referred to indirectly.

But to search for such specific events may be the wrong approach. On the date here accepted (the early second century BC, see later in this chapter), it is reasonable to press the poem to yield evidence for the then very recent conflict by which Rome prevailed over Hannibal, and so came much closer to the Mediterranean dominion 'prophesied' by Cassandra; that is, evidence for the Second Punic War of 218–201 BC. And arguably there is such evidence. (See S. Hornblower 2018). One example is the emphatic positioning of the section about Naples and the eponymous Siren Parthenopē, in the run-up to the dead centre of the poem at 737 (Parthenopē was another name for the city). In the long struggle with Hannibal, Carthaginian failure to establish supremacy by sea, and thus the means to reinforce Hannibal, was a crucial factor in the eventual Roman victory. For this reason, Hannibal was desperate to acquire a first-rate port, but failed to do so. In particular, the longstanding loyalty of Naples to Rome since the original alliance of 326 BC – very favourable to Naples – was crucial. After defeating the Roman armies at Cannae, Hannibal tried to take Naples 'so that he would have a maritime city' (Livy 23. 1. 5), but had to abandon the attempt and fix his Campanian base at inland Capua

[109] Momigliano 1980.   [110] Swift 2010.   [111] S. West 2000.

instead. In his own way, Lycophron registers the importance of Naples to Roman sceptre and kingship by land *and sea*. This is history, heavily coded and in iambic trimetres, but nonetheless history.

Another literary genre to be reckoned with is laments for the fall of cities. The best evidence for this is provided by epigrams. A fine surviving example is that composed by Antipater of Sidon on the Roman destruction of Corinth in 146 BC (Gow and Page 1965: 569 = epig. 59). In similar vein, Cassandra utters laments for Troy (31, 52, 69–71, and cf. 1230); and for the 'apostrophe' (direct address in the vocative) to cities, see 968 ('unhappy Segesta!') or the invocation of a long list of Locrian places which will grieve for their daughters (1146–50).

The female element in the poem – especially the emphasis on women as victims of male sexual violence, like Cassandra herself – is ubiquitous and important, beginning with the myth of Hesionē (34). There is surely some indebtedness here (as well as in the poem's repetitive transition-formulae) to the traditional catalogue genre, and in particular to the Hesiodic *Catalogue of Women*. The most obvious specific intertext is the story of Erisychthon's daughter Mestra (1391–6). Only with the publication in 1960 of the Cairo fragment of the *Catalogue* (Hes. fr. 43a Merkelbach-West) was the extent of the relationship revealed.

Cassandra is compared to a Sibyl by the guard near the end of the poem (1464–5), and the Cumaean, i.e., Italian Sibyl herself, immured in her gloomy cavern like Cassandra in her cell, makes a memorable appearance in the course of the prophecy (1279–80). This has prompted generic comparisons.[112] The surviving Greek-Jewish hexametre Sibylline oracles[113] have, as politically motivated prophetic literature, some features in common with the *Alexandra*, so that the poem has even been claimed as an example of the Sibylline genre[114] (this goes much too far, as we shall see). The most important Sibylline oracle for our purposes is the third, the earliest and most historically specific of the set of fourteen: it contains material almost certainly dating from the second century BC. Like the *Alexandra*, which in traditional oracular mode regularly describes mythical characters as birds or animals (wolves, lions, doves, eagles), the Third Oracle refers to a ruler as a 'fiery eagle' (line 611). Like the Oracle (and like the apocalyptic biblical book of Daniel), the *Alexandra* uses cryptic

---

[112] Ziegler 1927: 2379–81; Amiotti 2001; Biffis 2012.
[113] Geffcken 1902 remains the best edition. The secondary literature is vast. The following may be singled out: Rzach 1923; Goodman 1986: 632–41; Momigliano 1987; Collins 1997: 181–97.
[114] Nilsson 1961: 109, followed by Hengel 1974: 2. 125 n. 523.

dynastic enumeration (1446, the unique wrestler will appear 'after six generations'; compare the 'seventh ruler of Egypt' whose coming is more than once foretold in the Oracle). And both Cassandra (*Alex.* 1454–60) and the mouthpiece of the Oracle (lines 815–6) complain that they will be regarded as liars, despite speaking the truth. But these similarities are presentational and superficial. The metre is different, because Cassandra speaks in tragic iambics, whereas the oracle is in hexametres, the usual though not invariable Greek oracular metre;[115] the Oracle is messianic whereas the *Alexandra* shows not the slightest awareness of Judaism; and above all, the attitude to Rome of the Oracle is hostile (see, e.g., lines 356–64), whereas Cassandra looks forward exultantly to the triumph of her Roman kinsmen. More recently, the *Alexandra* has been compared to the so-called 'Oracle of the Potter', perhaps a prose Greek translation of a demotic Egyptian original.[116] It is true that this strange fragment shares some of Cassandra's allusiveness, and is book-ended by short, narrative sections. The closural lines ('having spoken up to this point he [the potter] fell silent'), recall Cassandra's guard at 1461–2, 'this is what she said; then off she went on foot/back into her prison'. But the Potter's targets are, like those of the Third Sibylline Oracle, very different from Cassandra's, and the Oracle of the Potter is a raw vernacular production, whereas the *Alexandra* is a sophisticated work, which never forgets its links to high literature. The guard's final prayer to the god to 'keep safe this Bebrycian [Trojan] heritage' (1474) borrows a device from yet another genre, the hymn: similar prayers form the closures of Callimachus' Fifth and Sixth Hymns, which owe a debt in their turn to one of the Homeric Hymns (no. 13 *to Demeter*, line 3).

It is, however, tragedy which is the dominantly influential genre in the *Alexandra*, despite a forthright and surprising denial by Wilamowitz.[117] The poem's closure may recall hymnal discourse, but we have seen already that the opening words λέξω τὸ πᾶν have a parallel and perhaps a precedent in the Gyges fragment, as they certainly do in Ps.-Aeschylus; this small tragic locution can be seen as a kind of manifesto for the poem as a whole. The *Alexandra*'s repertoire of poetic allusions is formidably wide,

---

[115] For iambic oracles (very rare) see Hdt. 1.174.5; also, Sayer 1998: no. 57, a curious inscribed oracle from Perinthus (? first century BC).

[116] For the Greek text see Koenen 1968; Eng. tr. in Austin 2006: no. 326. For the comparison see S. West 2000: 160–3, cited with approval by Fantuzzi and Hunter 2003: 440. Sens 2010: 300 is slightly more cautious. On the language of the original, see now Ladynin 2016: 172–3 n. 35.

[117] Wilamowitz 1924: 2. 148–9; he meant that there was no plot or action ('Handlung') to speak of. At the other extreme, Durbec 2011: 55–61 sees the *Alexandra* as a drama in five acts.

as we shall see; and we have already noted that the prose writer Herodotus is a constant presence, and that Timaeus was a probable source of foundation myths about the west. But tragedy is never far away.[118] One stylistic habit is conspicuously Aeschylean, the frequency of 'majestic three-word trimeters'. Again, the *Alexandra* takes this to an extreme: there are no fewer than 54 in the poem (= one in 27.3 lines), compared to 54 in the surviving plays of Aeschylus (= one in 81 lines), 23 in Sophocles and 61 in all of the genuine plays of Euripides.[119]

The earlier tragedies which resonate most insistently in the *Alexandra* are those in which Cassandra herself had made unforgettable appearances. Those are the *Oresteia* trilogy of Aeschylus (see esp. the unmistakably Aeschylean lines 1099–1122 of *Alexandra*, foretelling the murder of Agamemnon and Cassandra herself) and the *Trojan Women* of Euripides (this too belonged to a trilogy, and if we had more than a few lines of the lost *Alexandros* we could no doubt add that as an influence as well). In particular, the *Trojan Women* propounds (at lines 427–44) a moral thesis which is crucial to the *Alexandra*, the idea that Odysseus' sufferings are causally linked to those of the violated Cassandra. It was a short but inspired step to extend that notion so as to cover *all* the Greeks who sacked Troy (see above, pp. 107–8). But other classical plays are cleverly played with as appropriate. Telamonian Ajax is the subject of an extended passage of the *Alexandra* (450–68), and the intertextual relationship with Sophocles' *Ajax* is naturally very dense throughout that section. Similarly, Euripides' *Hecuba* must lie behind the metamorphosis of Cassandra's mother Hecuba into a bitch (334, 1176; on metamorphosis as a leading theme in the poem, see earlier in this chapter).

One probably non-classical feature of the *Alexandra* must be noted; it sets it apart from all earlier tragedies (though see later in this chapter), but not from some other Hellenistic poems. The poem has what we may call a detectable internal geometry. We have seen that the narrative of Odysseus' *nostos* takes up almost exactly three times as many lines as Menelaus' (172: 57; an exact 3:1 ratio would be 171:57); as in their model, the Homeric *Odyssey*, the two *nostoi* are thematically linked. Again, the exact half-way point of the poem is reached at 737, the endpoint of the long section about Naples and the Sirens (see earlier in this chapter for the importance of this); and the prophecy about Roman sceptre and kinship (1229) is

---

[118] See Gigante Lanzara 2009 for a very full catalogue of parallels.
[119] R. Rutherford 2012: 403 (whence the quotation in my text) and n. 13. For the statistics about the *Alexandra*, and a complete list of the occurrences, see S. Hornblower 2015: on *Alex.* 63.

positioned five-sixths of the way through. Compare the symmetry of Callimachus' Sixth Hymn: 23 lines for the ritual, 92 (= 23 × 4) for the myth, then 23 for more ritual. If these features are not mere coincidence, then they show that our poet took meticulous care about structure; they also tell against interpolation theories. The *Alexandra* is, in this respect, the heir to the great age of Hellenistic poetry rather than to the old tragedians.[120]

But we have here made large assumptions about the poem's date and authorship. Was the author of the *Alexandra* really later than and aware of Callimachus and the other great names of early Ptolemaic Alexandria? Or was he really Lycophron of Chalcis the Pleiadist? Did he write in the time of Ptolemy Philadelphus (early third century BC) or in that of Flamininus, a whole eventful century later? These questions have been left to the end. In some ways, they are unimportant. The poem's value for the religious historian, and for the student of myths of identity, is hardly affected; all that matters is that it should be Hellenistic, as it certainly is. Nor are its undoubted tragic power and fascination lessened or increased on the one dating rather than the other. But if we are to treat the *Alexandra* as a document of Greek reaction to Roman military and political ascendancy, its date matters a great deal. If, in the aftermath of Cynoscephalae, a second-century Greek poet celebrated Rome and its founder Aeneas so positively, he ran counter to much Greek and other foreign feeling. Anti-Roman writings and prophecies are much more usual in this period:[121] apart from the Sibylline material, there are the stories collected by Phlegon of Tralles (*FGrHist* 257: the author is Hadrianic, but the subject-matter relates to the early second century BC), and hostility to Rome and eager anticipation of its downfall has even been detected, with some exaggeration, in Polybius.[122] The best poetic parallel to the *Alexandra* was long thought to be Melinno's hymn to Rhome/Rome (compare earlier in this chapter for the *Alexandra's* similar play on the name): 'Rome holds with its

---

[120] Note, however, that Irigoin 1983 argued that Sophocles had already played with numbers of lines in the way here discussed. On poetic numerology, see (with modern refs.) Lyc. 737n.

[121] Fuchs 1938 remains the classic treatment. See also Gruen 1984: 323–8. A hexameter Sibylline oracle about Macedon's downfall at Cynoscephalae was in circulation: see Paus. 7.8.9 for the text. This is, in a way, comparable to the line taken in the *Alexandra*.

[122] See Champion 2004: 97–8, relying chiefly on Pol. 6.9.13 (Rome's rise will be followed by a return to the opposite state). It is not in dispute that certain Polybian speakers express anti-Roman sentiments, but note the admiring and authorial 1.3.9: he himself wished nobody to be in any doubt 'by what power and resources the Romans embarked on that enterprise which made them lords *over land and sea*'. The italicised words are, in prose, the language of the *Alexandra*. (See earlier in this chapter on *Alex*. 1229, 'sceptre and kingship of land and sea'.)

## Hellenistic Tragedy and Satyr-Drama; Lycophron's Alexandra 117

strong straps the breasts of the earth and of the grey sea'. But this poet, formerly assigned to the second century BC, is now thought to have been Hadrianic, i.e., second century AD[123]

The attribution of the *Alexandra* to the Pleiadist Lycophron is ancient; but equally, there is ancient authority for doubting it (a scholiast on 1226; see later in this section). We have seen already that the tragic play-titles of the Pleiadist cannot be forced to strengthen the attribution, and the fragments of his satyr-plays are wildly different from anything in the *Alexandra*. The two main reasons for holding the *Alexandra* to be an early second-, not an early third-century BC poem are that (a) the prophecy of Roman 'sceptre and kingship of land and sea' is impossible before the First Punic War (262-240 BC), which gave the Romans their first overseas provinces, Sicily and Sardinia; (b) the *Alexandra* shows detailed awareness of literary works securely datable to the later third century; see later in this chapter. The matter is complex and controversial, and only an outline and a dogmatic conclusion can be given here, with minimal citation of modern work.

There are three approaches to the problem. The first accepts the attribution to the Pleiadist, and argues that 'land and sea' is a merely conventional formula.[124] As to literary echoes (b), they must either be denied altogether, or else the – surely counter-intuitive – reverse relationship must be assumed: the elusive, cryptic author of the *Alexandra*, a work scarcely mentioned by literary critics[125] in succeeding centuries, was imitated by a whole throng of mainstream third-century authors (but not the Pleiadists), or at any rate was one of a group of like-minded spirits.

The second approach takes its start from the scholiast: 'from here on he speaks about the Romans, and the poem must be reckoned to be by another Lycophron, not the tragedian. For he was acquainted with [Ptolemy] Philadelphus, and would not have discussed the Romans'. This most probably means that the whole poem was by an author who lived much later than the attested Lycophron. If so (but see later in this chapter) the second modern view[126] agrees: it holds that the Roman material is

---

[123] *Suppl. Hell.* no. 541; quotation is from line 10.
[124] Momigliano 1945 (and 1942). His arguments from the Locrian Maidens episode are weak. Against Momigliano see now Jones 2014.
[125] As opposed to grammarians. An interesting exception is the allusion in the second century AD dream-interpreter Artemidorus of Daldis (*Onirocr.* 4.63) to Lycophron as a source for out-of-the way myths. Evidently the *Alexandra* is meant.
[126] This view has often been held. I give only two exceptionally clear and authoritative statements of it: Beloch 1927: 566–74 (but essentially unchanged from ed. 1 of 1904); Ziegler 1927: 2359. A more recent statement in English: Gruen 1984: 326–7.

politically unthinkable in the age of the Pleiadist Lycophron of Chalcis, and that no suitable candidate for the Roman 'unique wrestler' can be identified at the supposed Philadelphan date. This dating is reinforced by literary considerations, to be specified later.

A third and intermediate view reckons that the main part of the poem is third century, but that there are later and perhaps very much later interpolations relating to Rome and Italy.[127] The Italian preoccupations begin very early indeed (see earlier in this chapter on 'Ausonian' at line 44), so the surgeon's knife needs to be wielded with restraint. Ancient support could be found for this, if the scholiast were to be interpreted as meaning 'the [rest of the] poem' is by another hand, but this is an unnatural way of taking the Greek, and in any case the 'Roman' passages have already been subtly prepared for; cf. earlier in this chapter for the two Telephus allusions, one early on, the other (a verbally similar one) in the 'Roman' section. More generally, Trojan mythical woes are needed for Troy's historical Roman resurgence to have its full impact.

Some Hellenistic poems were written for patrons, and if this were ascertainably true of the *Alexandra* also, then we might have a good chronological clue. But there is no authorial prooemium, and, in so indirect and mythologically saturated a poem, attempts to press this or that mythological allusion are ingenious but not compelling. Thus, Telephus of Mysia was exploited by the Attalids of Pergamum, to be sure, and features in the *Alexandra*, but also in a tragedy of Moschion, as we have seen. The name of the mythical Laodicē (*Alex.* 314, 496) was shared by the wife of Perseus the Antigonid king of Macedon, but that is far from proving an Antigonid context, and nor does the early and programmatic presence in the poem of Samothrace, an island in which the Ptolemies no less than the Antigonids were interested.[128] As for the Ptolemies, the young Wilamowitz claimed sweepingly that Egypt was virtually absent from the poem, even in the Proteus section (*Alex.* 110–31), which is admittedly more concerned about Thrace. It is true that the name Egypt occurs only once anywhere in the poem, as an ethnic (576, part of the story of Anios king of Delos; and note the mention of Memphis at 1294, from the Io story, the only passage which reveals real Egyptological knowledge). But Wilamowitz went too far: Hellenistic Egypt was an empire as well as the country of the Nile, and there is a certain amount about Ptolemaic overseas possessions and Cyrenaica, though nothing

---

[127] See esp. S. West 1983 and 1984.
[128] For the Attalids see Kosmetatou 2000; for the Antigonids, Musti 2001.

datable. Most recently, it has been suggested that there is an important Seleucid dimension, and that the poem was prompted by Roman military successes against Antiochus III.[129] If, as the present author suspects, the poem originated in the West (perhaps South Italian Locri, a city with a good literary tradition), then there is no hint of autocratic or other patronage.

Literary affiliations offer a more promising approach. The *Alexandra* draws on older writers extensively: Homer, the epic cycle, Hesiod and the Hesiodic *Catalogue*, lyric poetry (in particular, Stesichorus rewards investigation as a predecessor poet of the West), epinician, tragedy, Timotheus, Antimachus, the classical mythographers and historians (above all but not only Herodotus), Timaeus, Hieronymus of Cardia. But that tells us nothing about the poem's date. It is more significant that the author shows detailed knowledge of the prose writings of Eratosthenes and Philostephanus, authors of the second half of the third century BC; it was this consideration which converted P. M. Fraser to a belief in an early second-century date for the whole *Alexandra*.[130] The poem's connections with other Hellenistic poems have been well examined in recent years:[131] there are parallels, some of them striking, with Callimachus, Apollonius of Rhodes, Theocritus, Euphorion, Nicander, Dosiades. We may confine ourselves to a single example, the neat description of Epeius, maker of the Wooden Horse, as ἱπποτέκτων (*Alex.* 930). The word is extremely rare, though not an actual *hapax legomenon* (unique occurrence):[132] it was used by Callimachus, fr. 197 Pf., from *Iambus* 7.[133] The entire *Alexandra* passage about Epeius, and the entire Callimachean *Iambus*, are marked by striking intertextual closeness. Absolute proof can never be had in such matters, but to the present writer the overwhelming probability is that the *Alexandra* was dependent on and later than Callimachus, rather than vice versa, and the same goes for the other third-century Hellenistic poets listed earlier in this section.

The view here taken, then, is that the poem is a product of the early second century BC, that 'sceptre of land and sea' should be given its full

---

[129] On Egypt see Wilamowitz 1883: 4. The 'Antiochus III' thesis: Jones 2014. I have replied to this at Hornblower 2015: 114, 'Annex' (I agree with and welcome Jones' early second-century dating, but continue to believe that Scipio Africanus is a far less attractive candidate for the victorious Roman 'wrestler' than is Flamininus).
[130] Fraser 1979.    [131] Hollis 2009; Durbec 2014.
[132] It is so described by Ciani 1975: 131, in an uncharacteristic error, perhaps misled by LSJ (the Call. fr. does get into the LSJ 1996 Supplement).
[133] Missed by Hollis 2009, which is a valuable study, but his treatment of Callimachus is incomplete, being largely confined to the *Hecale* and the *Aetia*.

and natural weight, and that the mighty Roman kinsman-wrestler is Flamininus, the victor of Cynoscephalae. That is, the second of the three views listed earlier in this chapter is preferable. Political considerations of a general sort would appear to impose that solution; and there is a particular minor argument from the prominence of a local elite Apulian (Daunian) family, the Dasii, who claimed descent from the Homeric hero Diomedes at a precise moment in history, the early years of the Hannibalic War (220s BC), and whose claim is undoubtedly alluded to in the poem (they are the 'Aetolians' of 623–4).

An objection to this conclusion lies in the need to assume pseudonymity. Most pseudonymous poems in antiquity took the name of a great name such as Homer, Aeschylus, Virgil.[134] Why should the *Alexandra* have been passed off under the name of Lycophron of Chalcis, a much smaller figure than any of those giants? Pseudo-Oppian (the early third-century AD author of a *Cynegetica*, a hexameter poem on hunting and the animals hunted), is perhaps the best parallel case; the real Oppian wrote the *Halieutica* (on sea-creatures and fishing) a few decades earlier. Another way out is to suppose[135] that the author of the *Alexandra* really was called Lycophron (the name is a common one), and was a relation, perhaps grandson, of the Pleiadist; that might do away altogether with the need to explain the pseudonym. We may note here that the otherwise appealing idea of a female author of the *Alexandra* stumbles against the particular difficulty of explaining why an ancient Greek woman writer should have posed as a man (rather than the other way round; there are probable examples of that, such as 'Kleoboulina', parts of 'Theognis', and perhaps Erinna).[136] But if the poem was indeed pseudonymous, then the third-century Lycophron was well enough known as a prolific tragedian for the theft of his literary identity to seem attractive to our nameless but learned and versatile genius of a poet.

## Hellenistic Satyr-Drama

Satyr-drama, like tragedy, flourished in the Hellenistic period, if not to the same society-defining extent. An inscription from Tanagra in Boeotia

---

[134] See *OCD*[4] 'pseudepigraphic literature' (P. J. P[arsons]).   [135] With Ziegler 1927: 2381.
[136] 'Kleoboulina': Sider 1999: 26 n.6, M. L. West 2013d: 317. Parts of 'Theognis': Bowie 1986: 16. Erinna: M. L. West 2013b: 445. The Alexander-historian Nikoboule (*FGrHist* no. 127) was suspected by Jacoby of being the pseudonym of a male writer, but this is not accepted by B. Sheridan in *BNJ*, where s/he is also no. 127.

## Hellenistic Tragedy and Satyr-Drama; Lycophron's Alexandra 121

stipulates that money is to be paid to artists of both tragedy and satyr-drama, τ]οῖς τραγικοῖς καὶ σατύροις (*SEG* 19.335.44, first cent. BC). And Horace's *Art of Poetry* implies, by the length and detail of its comments and recommendations, that the genre was still vigorous in the time of Augustus.[137] Several of the authors reviewed earlier in this chapter, including and especially Lycophron of Chalcis, wrote satyr-plays.[138] Satyric drama enjoyed a special revival in the early Hellenistic period; insofar as well-known people came in for ridicule (Alexander's defaulting treasurer Harpalus in Python's *Agēn* (later in this chapter); the philosopher Menedemus of Eretria in Lycophron's *Menedemus*; see later in this chapter) the satyr-play can be seen[139] as taking over some of the social functions of Athenian Old Comedy, though without the obscenity. An epigram of Dioscorides (T2 = Gow and Page 1965: 1607–16 = *AP* 7.707) praised Sositheus for restoring satyr-drama to its original form, and saving it from recent innovations. We do not really know what these might have been, although it has been suggested that the dropping in 341 BC of satyric plays from the tragic competition at the Dionysiac festival at Athens might have hastened the development towards more openly comic features; Horace's strictures (satyr-drama should avoid shameless and undignified language and jokes) may support this idea of a move towards comedy.[140] The longest surviving fragment of Sositheus' *Daphnis or Lityerses* (F 2, twenty-one lines) may help to illustrate what Dioscorides meant: it blended the usually unrelated mythical stories of Midas and Daphnis, and seems generally to resemble the bucolic satyr-drama of the fifth century more than it does the productions of Lycophron or Python, with their contemporary targets.[141]

---

[137] *Ars P.* 220–39 with Ziegler 1937: 1978 and Shaw 2014: 150–3. Wiseman 1988: 13 argues that Horace's advice implies real performance of satyr-plays at Rome.
[138] The satyric fragments are included in the individual *TrGF* 1 entries. For fuller explanatory material see also Krumeich et al. 1999. See also van Rooy 1965: 124–43; Sifakis 1967: 124–6 (on satyric choruses); Xanthakis-Karamanos 1996 and 1997a; Sutton 1980; Cipolla 2003; Griffith 2008: 75–6, and now Shaw 2014, a monograph treatment of the entire history of the genre, with special attention to its relation to comedy; see esp. his 123–53 for the post-classical satyr-play.
[139] See Shaw 2014: 141 n. 57, cf. 126.     [140] Shaw 2014: 141–2.
[141] Shaw 2014: 140. On the other hand, Sositheos F 4 mocks the philosopher Cleanthes for a fool, so we must be careful not to over-interpret the epigram or the Daphnis fragment as indicators of a reversion to earlier models.

Python's *Agēn*[142] took as its subject a prominent Macedonian called Harpalus, who was Alexander the Great's treasurer after 331 BC, based at Babylon.[143] His extravagant lifestyle and sexual excesses were legendary (see esp. Diod. 17.108, describing his relationships with two Athenian courtesans in turn, Pythionicē and Glykera). When Alexander returned from India, Harpalus decamped to Greece, taking with him large sums of money. He found refuge at Athens in spring 324, where much of the money disappeared into the pockets of leading Athenian politicians, generating a political scandal of the first magnitude (the 'Harpalus affair').[144] This was a wonderful subject for a topical drama, and Python obviously made the most of it. The fragments of the *Agēn* are quoted in the course of an entertaining section of Athenaeus' *Learned banqueters* (ca. 200 AD) about Greek courtesans through the ages, so it is not surprising that this was the main aspect of the play which we hear about; it evidently drew on the same source-tradition as Diodorus. Python described a temple which Harpalus built for Pythionicē when she died (this detail is also in Diodorus, who however speaks less outrageously of a mere tomb).[145] But the reference to Harpalus' gift of wheat to underfed Athenians seems to hint at the contemporary political situation.[146]

Lycophron's *Menedemos* (*TrGF* 1, 100 F 2–4) was also topical. Its subject was a celebrity Eretrian philosopher, known to us from an unusually rich biographical tradition.[147] There are clear sympotic allusions, leading Tarn to remark that 'it it perhaps at his famous suppers that we see him [Menedemos] most clearly';[148] and when Lycophron says (F 4)

---

[142] *TrGF* 1, no. 91 F1; Shaw 2014: 123–9 for very full discussion. On the date and historical context (324 BC, near the end of Alexander's life, not 326), see Beloch 1927: 434–6; Lloyd-Jones 1966a: 16–7, part of a bad-tempered review of Snell 1964.
[143] Athenaeus' statement (595e) that Alexander himself was somehow responsible for the play is surprising; at most, ἐδίδαξε might mean he produced it (rather than wrote it). The relevant sentence may be corrupt.
[144] See Habicht 1998: 30–5; Heckel 2006: 129–31; A. B. B[osworth], *OCD*[4] 'Harpalus' and in *CAH* 6[2] 838 with n. 83 and 856–8.
[145] It is possible (Lloyd-Jones 1966a: 17; Shaw 2014: 125) that the satyrs played the part of the magi who called up the spirit of the dead Pythionicē; see F1 line 6. Python's lines (2–3) about the temple may echo Soph. *El.* 7–8; cf. Shaw 2014: 128.
[146] So rightly Lloyd-Jones 1966a: 16.
[147] Diog. Laert. 2. 125–44 with the excellent commentary by Knoepfler 1991; see also the brilliant portrait at Tarn 1913: 21–6. One main source of our knowledge is the Hellenistic biographer Antigonus of Carystus on the island of Euboea: he was the source of both Diog. Laert. and Ath., who between them supply all the relevant fragments.
[148] Tarn 1913: 24.

that the bird which announced the dawn would still find them talking, the allusion to the 'more famous banquet'[149] in Plato's *Symposium* is transparent. The word συμπότης actually occurs in F 2 line 10. We are a world away from the *Alexandra*, where the only feasts (the usual noun is θοίνη) are of a nightmarish quality.

Perhaps it is right that Menedemos really gave banquets, of the parsimonious sort for which he is teased in the fragments. But perhaps the playwright here makes a simultaneous gesture towards the mode of performance. We have seen that actual and very public performance of tragedies was a pronounced feature of Hellenistic culture. There is no good reason to deny that the tragic fragments which we possess could come from plays which were performed in the usual way; erudition is no bar (see earlier in this chapter n. 81 on 'bookishness'). Even the *Alexandra* could have been designed for recitation; it would take about two hours. But it is not so clear what sort of performance should be imagined for satyr-plays. The *Agēn*, to be sure, was produced for a Dionysiac festival (Ath. 595e), but the event must have been of a strange sort, if the location was the Median river Hydaspes. Alan Cameron has suggested that at Menedemus' symposia, the poets present (and Lycophron was one of these) were expected to contribute their own poems.[150] It is a small step from this to imagining that a short satyr-plays could have been performed sympotically – as a mime? Is this incompatible with the public performance which satyr-drama is usually thought to presuppose? Here we may invoke a recent challenge to sharp distinctions between public and private or elite performance, using an old weapon of eristic logic to do so: how many people, it is asked rhetorically, have to be at a performance before it ceases to be private?[151] Much about satyr-drama is obscure, and it is best to end with questions rather than with assertions.

## Conclusion

It would be tempting to continue the story by discussing Hellenistic writers such as the 'Roman' poet Livius Andronicus. Why not? Andronicus, whose name could not be more Greek, was a half-Greek who came

---

[149] Tarn 1913: 24.    [150] Cameron 1995: 97.    [151] Morrison 2007: 108.

from the ancient Spartan colony of Tarentum, and he produced a drama, perhaps a tragedy, at the Roman Games in 240 BC. This was in Latin, but it must have been an adaptation of Greek material. Ziegler, with whom we began this survey, was right to insist that Roman tragedy is the best proof of the vitality of Hellenistic Greek tragedy.[152]

[152] Ziegler 1937: 1968. On Livius Andronicus and the *ludi Romani*, see now Feeney 2016: 129–31 and, for Livius' 'translation project', *passim*.

CHAPTER 4

# The Exagōgē *of Ezekiel the Tragedian*

Pierluigi Lanfranchi

Arnold Schönberg's unfinished opera *Moses und Aron* opens with an invocation addressed to God by Moses:

> *Einziger, ewiger, allgegenwärtiger,*
> *unsichtbarer und unvorstellbarer Gott...!*
> (One and only God, eternal, omnipresent,
> invisible and inconceivable)

In accordance with the text of *Exodus* 3, God then speaks to Moses from a burning bush. In composing this scene, Schönberg was faced with a major problem: how to represent a God who was invisible and un-imaginable to the Israelites? When putting into Moses' mouth the words that affirm God's unity and singularity, Schönberg chose to represent the divinity musically by using a choir of six male, female and children's voices in an alternation of song and *Sprechstimme*, a cross between speaking and singing. The effect of this mix of voices, of timbres and of vocal techniques is one of extraordinary power, at once musical, dramatic and speculative. In setting the voice of God in music, the composer actually raises the question of divine nature and the ability of man to represent it at all.

Schönberg was not the first to have dramatized episodes from the book of *Exodus*, or to have broached the question of whether the biblical God could ever be represented. Two thousand years earlier, a poet called Ezekiel composed a tragedy on the Exodus of the Israelites out of Egypt, in which God – or at least his voice – features among the protagonists. Seventeen fragments of the *Exagōgē* have come down to us, in all a total of 269 iambic trimetres, the longest specimen of a tragedy that we have from the Hellenistic era.[1]

---

[1] The fragments are to be found in Snell 1971: 288–301. Commentaries: Jacobson 1983; Holladay 1989: 301–529 and Lanfranchi 2006, to which I refer the reader for a detailed discussion of all the

## Ezekiel and His World

Apart from his name, we know nothing about the author of the *Exagōgē*, neither his date nor his geographical origin.[2] It was formerly thought that Ezekiel was identical to the Ezekiel who figures among the seventy-two translators of the Pentateuch in Greek, mentioned in the *Letter of Aristeas* (50), but the most recent studies have not maintained this identification.[3] If one is to believe Clement of Alexandria, who refers to Ezekiel as 'the author of Jewish tragedies' (*Strom.* 1.23.155), the *Exagōgē* was not the only piece that he wrote on biblical subjects. In the Latin translation of the *Praeparatio Evangelica*, George of Trebizond (1395–1472) adds a detail that is highly suspect, namely that Ezekiel is supposed to have written tragedies on the entire Jewish history (*Ezechielus etiam poeta universam Iudaeorum historiam carmine moreque tragico scripsit*).[4] However, no other title has been preserved. And as for Ezekiel's origins, although several hypotheses have been advanced, it has not been possible to settle with any certainty on a specific location. Scholars in the nineteenth century tended to assume that all literary production by Greek-speaking Jews in the Hellenistic era emanated from the Jewish community of Alexandria, who would have been imbued with Hellenistic culture – unlike the Palestinian Jews, who were impermeable to the cultural seductions of their Greek rulers. Historians in the twentieth century, however, have shown that the phenomenon of Hellenization was not restricted to Alexandrian Jews, and that Jewish-Hellenistic literature could have been produced elsewhere – in Asia Minor, for example, or even in Palestine.[5] But even if that is the case, it is nonetheless probable that the *Exagōgē* originated in the Jewish-Hellenistic world of Alexandria or Egypt, where the acculturation of the Jewish population was particularly profound.[6] Besides,

---

questions broached in this chapter as well as for the bibliography. In the following pages I shall refer mainly to works on the *Exagōgē* that have appeared since 2006.

[2] In 2010, Dirk Obbink announced the discovery of an Oxyrhynchus papyrus containing verses from the *Exagōgē*. At the time of this chapter going to press this papyrus has not yet been published, and despite my efforts I have not been able to obtain further information on it. It would seem, however, that it contains no new material. Cf. Whitmarsh 2013: 216, no. 11.

[3] Denis 2000: 1214.

[4] George's translation is more a summary of Eusebius' *Praeparatio evangelica* than a literal translation. He does not translate the verses of Ezekiel quoted by Eusebius. On George's translation technique of Patristic texts, see Monfasani 1976: 78.

[5] The classic study on this subject is Hengel 1974.

[6] For a fuller discussion of the date and place of origin of the author, cf. Jacobson 1983: 5–17 and Lanfranchi 2006: 7–13. In a highly original and stimulating study, Tim Whitmarsh assumes an

Alexandria, as the theatre capital of the Hellenistic era,[7] is the obvious place to situate the encounter between Jewish culture and the Greek theatrical tradition which the *Exagōgē* exemplifies.

In such an environment, as in the rest of the Mediterranean diaspora, Jews spoke Greek, which necessitated the translation of the Torah from the third century BC onwards. The Septuagint is the great monument of Hellenistic Judaism, but by no means its only literary product. There was an extensive Jewish literature which, while taking its inspiration from the Septuagint, adopted the Greek conventions and literary genres: epic poetry, gnomic poetry, tragedy, historiography, philosophical dialogue, prose narrative, etc.[8] These Jewish authors were influenced by the intellectual activity developed in the large Hellenistic *metropoleis* around prestigious institutions such as the Mouseion of Alexandria. Jewish exegetes were thoroughly familiar with the methods that Alexandrian philologists had developed in the study and editing of classical Greek texts. While certain Jewish authors (e.g., Demetrius, Aristobulus) employed the methods of Alexandrian philology for biblical interpretation, others (e.g., the author of the *Letter of Aristeas*) opposed the application of these hermeneutic procedures to the Scriptures.[9]

Poetic production was another means by which these Jewish authors expressed in a creative manner their identity, their cultural specificity and also their resistance to the dominant Hellenistic culture. Besides Ezekiel, there were other poets, whose names are sometimes all that has survived. Sosates is one of them, whose name is cited in the Latin translation of a Greek chronicle composed in the fifth century AD, where he is referred to as the *ebraicus Omirus*, 'Hebrew Homer'.[10] We do have hexametres of a distinctly Homeric character from the poem *On the Jews* by a poet named Theodotus. The verses on Abraham, Joseph and Jerusalem from the poem *On Jerusalem* by a certain Philo (not to be confused with the philosopher Philo of Alexandria) are also in hexametres. His style is obscure and *recherché*, his verses replete with unusual words – precisely, that is, the characteristics of Hellenistic poetry that one finds, for example, in Lycophron's *Alexandra* (see Hornblower, this volume). The poems of Theodotus and of Philo can be compared with the genre of geographical and

---

Alexandrian context for the *Exagōgē*: for Ezekiel, Pharaonic Egypt at the time of the Exodus would be an allegory of the contemporary power of the Ptolemaic dynasty. See Whitmarsh 2013: 211–27.

[7] See Vinegre 2001: 81–95.
[8] Texts by Jewish-Hellenistic authors are assembled in Holladay 1983 and 1989.
[9] See Honigman 2003; Niehoff 2011.
[10] *Excerpta Latina Barbari* in Frick 1892: 278.24–9. Cf. S. J. D. Cohen 1981: 391–6.

ethnographical epic associated with Rhianus, the *Ktiseis* of Apollonius of Rhodes and the poem *Megara* of Pseudo-Moschus. Moreover, Jewish authors modified or straightforwardly invented gnomic verses that they attributed to Greek poets of the past, such as Homer, Phocylides, Aeschylus, etc., in order to express religious ideas that belonged to Judaism. This was, in fact, not an uncommon practice during the Hellenistic and later eras: the *Greek Anthology* preserves epigrams falsely attributed to the great figures of Greek poetry.[11]

One could get the impression that this sort of Jewish poetry in Greek concerned a strictly limited, erudite public. But epigraphic sources suggest that it was remarkably widespread amongst Egyptian Jews. Metrical inscriptions for deceased Jews found at Leontopolis and at Schedia, near Alexandria, contain abundant Homeric formulae and parallels with the funerary epigrams of the *Greek Anthology*.[12] Moreover, the study of poetry was an integral part of the curriculum that the children of the Jewish elite followed at school. Indeed, it was important for the Roman curriculum too: Philo of Alexandria mentions, as part of his 'school curriculum', the 'knowledge of what one finds in the poets' (*De congressu eruditionis gratia* 74).[13]

Philo's knowledge of poetry – and the same holds apparently for other Jews of his class – was not only scholarly and bookish: the Alexandrian philosopher recalls often going to the theatre (*De ebrietate* 177; *Quod omnis probus* 141).[14] During the Hellenistic and Roman era, it was by no means unusual for a diaspora Jew to frequent the theatre. True, the practice is firmly condemned in the rabbinical sources,[15] but attempts to demonstrate that Jews in the Hellenistic and Roman eras never dared to disobey rabbinical laws by frequenting the theatre fail to take into account the fact that rabbinical Judaism only took over at a very late stage. Such attempts also tend to ignore the reality of the Hellenistic diaspora: the study of the

[11] On these and other *pseudepigrapha* cf. Wilson 2005.
[12] For the metrical inscriptions from Schedia and Leontopolis see Horbury and Noy 1992: nos. 23 and 29–40, respectively. Cf. Ameling 2008: 117–33.
[13] In the *Exagōgē*, Ezekiel appears to present Moses as the paradigm of the cultural convergence between Gentile education and Judaism: as Moses says in the prologue (32–8), he was educated in both traditions.
[14] The Alexandrian philosopher's familiarity with drama is also suggested by the numerous quotations from the tragedians and by the images from the world of the theatre that are to be found in his treatises. See, for example, *De opificio mundi* 78; *De posteritate Caini* 104; *De Gigantibus* 31; *De Abramo* 103; *De specialibus legibus* 4.185. On theatrical language in *In Flaccum* see especially Calabi 2003: 91–116. On Philo's knowledge of the *Exagōgē* see Lanfranchi 2007c.
[15] See, e.g., Jerusalem Talmud, *Avodah Zarah* 1.7; Babylonian Talmud, *Avodah Zarah* 18b; Tosefta, *Avodah Zarah* 2.5 and 7.

epigraphic, papyrological, archaeological and literary sources relating to the Jewish communities of the Greco-Roman world has shown that they were profoundly and actively implicated in the political, social and cultural life of the cities in which they lived. In this context, frequenting the theatre was no aberrant phenomenon, but one of the manifestations of active participation of Jews in the collective life of their cities. As a matter of fact, diaspora Jews were not a monolithic entity, and attitudes could differ. For example, in an anecdote concerning the fourth-century BC tragic poet Theodectas (on whom see Liapis and Stephanopoulos, this volume), the author of the *Letter of Aristeas* would seem to condemn the theatrical representation of biblical stories: 'At the very moment he was at the point of introducing a passage taken from the Bible in a play, his eyes developed cataracts. Suspecting the cause of his affliction, he prayed to God, and after a few days he found that he was cured' (316). This passage is not a condemnation of the theatre in itself, but rather of the imprudent use, by a pagan author, of the sacred history of the Jews. It would even appear that Pseudo-Aristeas actually approved of the theatre, since he recommends watching plays at times of relaxation and leisure (*Letter of Aristeas* 284).

The image that emerges from Jewish-Hellenistic literature in general is that of a culture which, far from merely allowing itself to be absorbed into the surrounding cultural environment, is actively engaged in the intellectual life of the polis and seeks to reformulate its own traditions in the Greek language and conceptual framework. It is in this context of profound and creative Hellenization of the diaspora Jewish communities that one has to situate the composition of Ezekiel's *Exagōgē*.

## Transmission of the Text

In Late Antiquity, the Jewish literature composed in Greek during the Hellenistic and Roman eras had been forgotten by Jews, as rabbinical Judaism – with its emphasis on Hebrew and Aramaic language and culture – imposed its religious and cultural hegemony within the diaspora.[16] However, parts of the Jewish literature written in Greek continued to be transmitted by Christians, who exploited it for their own apologetic

---

[16] That does not mean that Greek disappeared entirely. Greek remained the language spoken by Jews in the Byzantine Empire, although they wrote mainly in Hebrew. But the fragments in Greek of the Book of Kings and the Psalms discovered in the Cairo Geniza, which date from the fifth or sixth century AD, show that during that period the Egyptian Jews were still reading the Bible in Greek. Cf. de Lange 1996.

purposes and for their own doctrinal constructions. Ignored by Jewish tradition, the *Exagōgē*, too, is transmitted, in part, by Christian authors, notably by Clement of Alexandria (ca. 150–ca. 215) and Eusebius of Caesarea (ca. 260–ca. 340), both of whom quote extracts from it.[17] Clement of Alexandria, in the section devoted to Moses at the end of the first book of his *Stromateis*, which deals with the correspondences between Greek philosophy and the religious world of the Bible, quotes two passages from the *Exagōgē*. Clement's aim is apologetic: he wishes to show that Greek philosophy is derived from earlier wisdom, notably from Hebraic wisdom, of which Moses is the most important representative. The *Praeparatio Evangelica* by Eusebius of Caesarea also belongs to the genre of apologetics: his aim is to refute paganism and to demonstrate the superiority of Judaism as a preparation for the Gospels. Seventeen passages of the *Exagōgē* are quoted in Eusebius' Book 9 along with other Greek witnesses on the Jews and Israelites, whom Eusebius considered to be the originators of true philosophy. The passage from the *Exagōgē* relating to the mysterious bird (256–69) is also to be found in the *Commentarius in Hexaemeron* by Pseudo-Eustathius of Antioch.

Neither Clement nor Eusebius had direct knowledge of Ezekiel or other Jewish-Hellenistic authors: they knew of them only indirectly, through quotations from their work by the Greek grammarian Alexander Polyhistor (ca. 80–35 BC).[18] Polyhistor's *On the Jews* was an ethnographic compilation for the use of the Roman ruling class. It included information on the geography, history and customs of those regions that the Romans had recently conquered during Pompey's campaigns in the East. Polyhistor's method consisted of assembling excerpts in both prose and verse on a particular subject, introduced by the name of their author. In general, *On the Jews*, like the rest of Polyhistor's ethnographic work, belong to the genre of paradoxography, which was much in vogue during the Hellenistic era. This taste for the wondrous and the exotic would have influenced his choice of passages from the *Exagōgē*: for instance, Moses' dream, the miracle of the burning bush, the description of the oasis of Elim, and the apparition of the marvellous bird (the last two items have close parallels in other paradoxographical works). The verses relating to Libya also seem to correspond to Polyhistor's ethnographical and geographical interests.

---

[17] Cf. Inowlocki 2006; Lanfranchi 2006: 73–99; Frulla 2009: 131–46.

[18] Van de Water's (2000) hypothesis that Eusebius quotes directly from the *Exagōgē* has been refuted by Jacobson 2005.

Thus, Polyhistor's ethnographic and paradoxographical interests determined the choice of passages from the *Exagōgē* that he quoted in his work – just as Clement's and Eusebius' respective choices from Polyhistor's selection were determined by their apologetic programme. In other words, the extant fragments of the *Exagōgē* have reached us through the double filter of a two-layered selection process. Any attempt to interpret the fragments of the *Exagōgē* must take into account this essential fact.

## The Subject of the *Exagōgē*

The subject of the play is derived from the events described in the first fifteen chapters of *Exodus*, which Ezekiel read in the Greek translation of the Pentateuch.[19] But Ezekiel does not slavishly follow the Septuagint: he selects from the biblical material, omitting certain passages and amplifying others. On several occasions, he distances himself from the Greek Bible as well as from the Masoretic Text and follows other exegetical traditions that we find also in other Jewish-Hellenistic authors, in the Targums and in the later Midrashim. Fragments 1 to 3 belong to the prologue, in which Moses explains the background to the story, from the arrival of Jacob in Egypt until his current condition as a refugee in a foreign land. At the end of the prologue he sees Jethro's seven daughters approach, among whom is his future wife, Sephora, who explains to him that the region in which he finds himself is called Libya, populated by the Ethiopians and ruled by her father Raguel (fr. 4). The brief dialogue (fr. 5)[20] between Sephora and a certain Chum, probably her brother, has no parallel in *Exodus*, as is also the case with Moses' prophetic dream and its interpretation by his father-in-law (fr. 6 and 7).[21] In the following fragments a change of scene must be assumed. They present a dialogue between Moses and God, which includes the encounter with the burning bush (fr. 8),[22] God's instructions on how Moses has to persuade Pharaoh to set the people free (fr. 9),

---

[19] On the subject of the *Exagōgē* as 'Jewish myth' cf. Bloch 2011: 141–7.
[20] Cf. Lanfranchi 2007a.
[21] The passage on Moses' dream has caused much ink to be spilled by historians of Judaism seeking in the *Exagōgē* evidence of mystic speculations on the divine chariot (*merkavah*), often isolating this fragment from its context. See, for example, Ruffatto 2006 and 2008; Orlov 2007 and 2008; Bunta 2007. These three authors appear to ignore entirely the context in which the *Exagōgē* was produced and performed as well as the characteristics of its literary genre. More profitably, Heath 2007 tried to interpret the scene of Moses' dream in the cultural context of Hellenism in which Ezekiel wrote the *Exagōgē*. For a discussion of this passage and a critique of traditional interpretations cf. Lanfranchi 2007b.
[22] Van Ruiten 2006.

Moses' hesitation in accepting the mission to Pharaoh (fr. 10), the promise of Aaron's help (fr. 11), the signs of the staff turned into a snake and the equally miraculous cure of the leprous hand (fr. 12) and, finally, God's instructions concerning the plagues of Egypt, the institution of the Passover (fr. 13), the Feast of Unleavened Bread and the Exodus (fr. 14). In a messenger narrative (fr. 15), which is the most successful bit of the play as we have it, a soldier of Pharaoh's army who has survived the catastrophe recounts the miraculous crossing of the Red Sea.[23] In the last two fragments (fr. 16–17), a scout announces the discovery of the oasis of Elim and the appearance of the mysterious bird, of which there is absolutely no mention in the Bible.[24]

## Is the *Exagōgē* Tragedy?

The *Exagōgē* is not simply a paraphrase of the first fifteen chapters of *Exodus* in iambic trimetres. It is rather an original attempt to recast the content of the biblical text into the metrical forms and dramatic structure of Greek tragedy. Although ancient sources characterize the *Exagōgē* as 'tragedy' (τραγῳδία)[25] and as 'drama' (δρᾶμα),[26] scholars have raised doubts as to the 'tragic' nature of this singular work and have asked the question of what literary genre it actually belongs to, arguing that it presents an unusual subject, it violates dramatic conventions[27] and it does not contain the constitutive elements of classical tragedy according to Aristotle's *Poetics* – such as *hamartia* and *peripeteia*. For want of any traditional literary category that could accommodate this work, the category of 'Midrashic drama'[28] has been created, emphasizing the fact that the *Exagōgē* is a totally new kind of dramatic poetry, very different

---

[23] Allen 2007.     [24] Heath 2006.     [25] Clem. Al. *Strom.* 1.23.155.1.
[26] Eus. *PE* 9.29.14; 9.28.3.
[27] It is true that what survives of the *Exagōgē* does not respect the unities of place and time, but these principles were unknown to ancient theories of tragedy, and do not apply to extant Greek plays. The unity of time was mentioned for the first time by Giovan Battista Giraldi Cinzio in his *Lettera intorno al comporre delle comedie e delle tragedie* (1543). Some years later, Ludovico Castelvetro introduced the unities of time and space in his commentary on Aristotle's *Poetics* (Vienna 1570). Given the fragmentary state of the text, it is difficult to evaluate whether Ezekiel respected the unity of action prescribed by Aristotle (*Poet.* 50a 16–19). Robertson 1985 suggests that the figure of Moses, the protagonist and hero of the drama, is the unifying element of the *Exagōgē*. This is far from certain, however, especially if one considers that the title of the drama makes no reference to the protagonist but rather to the collective Exodus of the Israelites from Egypt. See also Hornblower, this volume.
[28] Jacobson 1983: 26; Bryant Davies 2008.

# The Exagōgē of Ezekiel the Tragedian

from Greek tragedy. As has been pointed out, it is in fact a very early anticipation of medieval religious drama, both Christian and Jewish.[29]

Traditional judgements of the literary qualities of Ezekiel's work have tended to be negative:[30] in adapting the *Exodus* story for the purposes of drama, Ezekiel, we are told, was unable to exploit the 'tragic' potential inherent in the biblical events, dissipating this potential in a plot that is more epic than dramatic. However, opinions differ on the tragic or non-tragic nature of the *Exodus* story. Some scholars do not consider the story of *Exodus* to be even remotely 'tragic' and find it fundamentally resistant to any tragic treatment. For Rachel Bryant Davies, for instance, the total absence of tragic elements in the *Exagōgē* should not be interpreted as a failure on Ezekiel's part to cast his material successfully into dramatic form. On the contrary, Ezekiel's intention was not to write a Greek tragedy, for he was well aware, long before Wittgenstein or Steiner, that God's presence in the biblical story neutralizes all tragic potential: the *Exagōgē* 'actively resists its tragic potential, precluding that interpretation through its fidelity to Scripture even as the possibility of divergence is explored'.[31] While some biblical scholars have stressed the analogies, even at the structural level, between *Exodus* and Greek tragedy,[32] others have tried to find a universal definition of the tragic genre, one that would apply both to fifth-century Greek tragedy and to certain books or episodes from the Bible.[33] But all these definitions, which lead to conflicting conclusions, are based on a conception of tragedy that was unknown to the ancient world and is tied rather to a modern idea of the 'tragic' developed primarily in nineteenth-century German philosophy.

Whether or not modern scholars problematize the classification of the *Exagōgē* as part of the tragic genre, for Ezekiel's contemporaries as well as later readers it certainly was a tragedy. One therefore needs to understand why it should be presented as tragedy before asking oneself why it should not. In the classic Athenian period of their history, tragedy and other dramatic forms were essentially defined by the institutional and festive context in which they were performed, whereas in the Hellenistic era other criteria come into play (cf. Le Guen, this volume). On the one hand, the fact that tragedy was no longer bound to the institutional context of Athenian festivals opened up new possibilities for its development and performance;[34] on the other hand, the crystallization of a tragic canon compelled authors to refer constantly to the great models of the past. For

---

[29] Free 1999.   [30] Zwierlein 1966: 141.   [31] Bryant Davies 2008: 402.
[32] Cf. Kellenberger 2006: 139–44; Dafni 2008.   [33] Utzschneider 2010.   [34] Cf. Kuch 1993.

Ezekiel's contemporaries, therefore, tragedy was not only defined by the context in which it was performed, but also as a codified literary genre with its own history, themes and conventions, which were distinct from other forms of poetry and drama.[35] Seen in this perspective, i.e., from the point of view of the spectators and readers of antiquity, the *Exagōgē* could legitimately be called a tragedy, for it is consistent with classical models and conforms to the conventions of the genre in its literary as well as its dramatic characteristics. The influence on Ezekiel of fifth-century Athenian tragedy – particularly Euripides, the author most read and imitated during the Hellenistic era – has been widely documented.[36] The analysis of the messenger speech will help us understand the relation between Ezekiel and his models as well as the procedures he used to dramatize the text of *Exodus*.

## The Dramatization of the Biblical Text[37]

As we have seen, what Ezekiel attempted to do was to recast the biblical text into a literary form that was part of the Greek tradition. This endeavour involved a whole series of more or less substantial transformations of the source text, with which the *Exagōgē* maintains a dialectical relationship that is simultaneously one of fidelity and innovation.[38] This procedure has a dual aspect: on the one hand there is the theatralization of the text, i.e., an interpretation staged by means of scenery and actors; on the other hand, there is the dramatization which, by contrast, is effected entirely through dialogue, which must create dramatic tension and conflict between protagonists.[39]

One could try to analyse the techniques by which Ezekiel dramatizes the *Exodus* text: the addition or suppression of *dramatis personae*, the treatment of character, changes of place, the compression of time, the omission or addition of scenes, the connections with the original language, the relations between dialogue and narrative, etc. One of the more significant changes was that of the point of view: what the Bible relates through the voice of an external and omniscient narrator is necessarily communicated in the *Exagōgē* by the voice of one of the characters. Undoubtedly influenced by Aeschylus' *Persae*,[40] in which the Queen is informed of Xerxes'

---

[35] Fantuzzi and Hunter 2003: 433.  [36] Already by Wieneke 1931.
[37] The following section draws on Lanfranchi 2003.  [38] Cf. Frulla 2007.
[39] Pavis 1998: s.vv. 'dramatization' and 'theatralization'.
[40] The sole survivor who lives to tell the tale is a motif found also in Sophocles' *Oedipus Tyrannus* and (in the fourth century BC) in *Rhesus*.

The *Exagōgē* of Ezekiel the Tragedian 135

defeat at Salamis through a messenger speech, Ezekiel opted to have the debacle of Pharaoh's army related by an Egyptian soldier,[41] even though this solution to a certain extent betrays the biblical text, for in fact, according to *Exodus*, not a single Egyptian survived (*Ex* 14:28). Philo of Alexandria writes more precisely that there remained 'not a single torch-bearer to carry back to the people of Egypt the news of this sudden catastrophe' (*Mos.* 1.179). This information is similarly found in Josephus (*AJ* 2.344). It is worth quoting the *Exagōgē* passage (193–242) in its entirety.[42]

> When King Pharaoh rushed from his palace
> with his host of countless armed men,
> with all the cavalry and four-horsed chariots                                195
> and with soldiers both in the front ranks and on the flank,
> there was an awesome host of men arrayed in battle order:
> footmen and phalanxes in the middle,
> leaving passages for the chariots to pass through.
> He stationed a part of the cavalry on the left,                              200
> on the right all the rest of the cavalry of the Egyptian army.
> I inquired about the total number of the army.
> There were a million valiant men altogether.
> When our army encountered the Hebrews,
> they were lying gathered in groups                                           205
> near the edge of the Red Sea.
> The men, exhausted from exertion, were giving food
> to their children as well as to their wives.
> There were countless flocks and household goods.
> But they were all unarmed for fighting,                                      210
> and on seeing us, they cried out
> tearfully in unison toward the heavens,
> their ancestral deity. The turmoil among the people was enormous.
> We by contrast were jubilant.
> Then, we pitched camp behind them                                            215
> (people call that city Baal-Zephon).
> Since Titan Helios was setting,
> we waited, since we wanted a morning battle,
> fully confident of our numbers and dreadful weapons.
> But then, wonders of divine portents                                         220
> began to occur! Suddenly, a large
> pillar of cloud rose to the West

---

[41] The narrator refers to Pharaoh's army as 'my' army (204) and uses the first person plural with reference to the Egyptians (211, 214, 218, 230, 231, 235, 238, 240).
[42] The translation is mine, but it is based on the translation by Jacobson 1983 and Holladay 1983.

> midway between our camp and that of the Hebrews.
> Then, their leader Moses, took
> the rod of God with which he had previously 225
> wrought signs and awful wonders against Egypt,
> struck the surface of the Red Sea and split it deep
> in the middle; and all of them in full force
> rushed forward quickly through the path of the sea.
> And we immediately entered upon the same path, 230
> on their tracks. We entered at night
> shouting and running. Suddenly, the wheels of our chariots
> refused to turn, as if bound by chains.
> And from heaven a great flame, like fire,
> appeared to us. As far as we could guess, there came 235
> to them the God who helps them. And just as they were already
> well beyond the sea, a great wave rushed in,
> closing around us. And someone, seeing this, shouted:
> 'Let us run back home before the hand of the Most High!
> For He is helping them, but on us 240
> he has wrought destruction. The path of the Red Sea
> closed over us and completely destroyed our army.'

Ancient commentators (cf. the scholium on Aeschylus' *Eumenides* 1) already recognized that Euripides was the first truly to give shape to the messenger's speech, which in his plays has a fixed structure organized according to very precise rules.[43] If Ezekiel owes his inspiration to Aeschylus' *Persae*, his debt to Euripides is evident in the technique of the messenger speech. First of all, the form of the long, continuous narration is typical of Euripidean narratives, while the news of the Persian army's defeat in Aeschylus' *Persae* is in the form of a dialogue consisting of short passages by the messenger, the chorus and the Queen. The messenger in the *Exagōgē* begins his speech rather abruptly: he is evidently responding to questions put by an interlocutor whose identity is difficult to ascertain.[44] Even if line 193 ('When King Pharaoh rushed from his palace...') is not the very beginning of the speech, the fact that the messenger begins with a temporal phrase introduced by ὡς indicates that he has just begun to speak. In fact, Ezekiel seems here to be following the way in which Euripides also often introduces messenger speeches: out of a total of twenty-four such speeches, fifteen open with a subordinate temporal clause

---

[43] Cf. Di Gregorio 1967: 86–97; Rutherford 2012: 200–16.
[44] In Greek tragedy 'messengers typically respond to a request to tell how the events occurred' (J. Barrett 2002: 184); cf. also De Jong 1991: 33 with n. 81.

introduced by ἐπεί.[45] Another Euripidean characteristic shared by the *Exagōgē* is the messenger's insistence on having personally witnessed the events he reports. This is not simply a stylistic effect. The movement from an omniscient narrator (inherent in biblical narrative) to a *dramatis persona* as the focalizing voice makes it necessary for the playwright to explain how the messenger came by the information he is relating.[46] To achieve this end, Ezekiel employs different verbal means: as well as using first person pronouns, he uses verbs of vision to emphasize the narrator's actual witnessing of the events as they develop (221: ἰδέσθαι; 235: ὤφθη). The position of the Egyptian camp behind that of the Israelites (ὑπ' αὐτούς, 'below their camp', at line 215 corresponds to ὀπίσω αὐτῶν, 'behind them', in *Exodus* 14:10) provides a vantage point from which the messenger was able to observe the events that he is relating.[47] The use of the present tense at significant moments in the narrative – the pillar of fire, and the splitting of the Red Sea – also helps to enhance the impression of an eyewitness report.[48] However, making the messenger an eyewitness of the events he reports creates a problem: how to account plausibly for the fact that, as an involved participant, this messenger possesses information that one would not normally expect him to be privy to? Hence the need to explain his prior knowledge of the number of soldiers (223: 'a million valiant men') in the Egyptian army (222: 'I inquired about the total number of the army').

As has already been remarked, the messenger is not an omniscient narrator in the way that the biblical narrator is. As a result, his narrative is subject to the same restrictions as messenger speeches in Euripides.[49] In the first place, there are restrictions related to space: because of his position, the messenger cannot know of certain circumstances, such as the movement of the pillar of fire to the rear of the Israelites (*Ex* 14:19), the protestations of the people against their leader (*Ex* 14:11–14) or the orders given by God to Moses (*Ex* 14:15–18). Nonetheless, in casting the

---

[45] Cf. *Med.* 1136; *Andr.* 1085; *El.* 774; *IT* 260, 940; *Ion* 1122; *Hel.* 1526; *Ph.* 1359. See Rijksbaron 1976: 293–308. Sophocles prefers ὅπως to introduce messenger speeches (cf. *OT* 1241). Cf. also Liapis 2012 on *Rh.* 762–4.

[46] For a definition of 'focalization' cf. Genette 1986: 49: 'by focalisation, I certainly mean a restriction of "field", – actually that is, a selection of the narrative information with respect to what was traditionally called *omniscience* [. . .]. The instrument of this possible selection is a *situated focus*, a sort of information-conveying pipe, that allows passage only of information that is authorized by the situation (Marcel on his steep slope outside the window of Montjouvain).'

[47] Euripides too takes care to signal to the spectator the point of view of a messenger taking part in a battle. Cf., e.g., *Supp.* 651–2, *Ph.* 1139–40, 1164, 1170–1.

[48] Cf. Rijksbaron 1994: 22–4.

[49] For subtle analyses of messenger speeches in Euripides see de Jong 1991 and J. Barrett 2002.

messenger as a pagan who recognizes the power of God, Ezekiel finds an effective means of capturing in a dramatic form the essence of divine speech; cf. *Exodus* 14:18: 'Thus the Egyptians shall know that I am the Lord, when I am glorified at the expense of the Pharaoh, his chariots and his horsemen'. Secondly, the messenger is limited in his ability to understand fully the events he has witnessed, notably the divine signs and manifestations. Even if he senses the divine character of these wonders, the Egyptian is unable to sense behind the pillar of cloud the presence of the Angel of the Lord spoken of in *Ex* 14:19. The pillar itself is described in a rather vague, imprecise manner.[50] And when finally the messenger recognizes that God is on the side of the Israelites, his admission is qualified by a cautious 'it would seem' (235: ὡς μὲν εἰκάζειν). The same parenthetical phrase is found in the messenger's speech in Euripides' *Bacchae* 1078, in relation to Dionysus' voice from the sky. The messenger is excluded from a real understanding of divine manifestations because he is a pagan, as evinced by the fact that he calls the sun 'Titan' (217) and identifies the God of the Israelites with the sky (212–13).

Let us now look at the organization of time in the messenger's speech. The type of narrative that predominates in it is, in modern narratological terms, of the 'actorial narrative type', meaning that the agent serves as the centre of orientation with regard to perception, space and time in the narrative.[51] The chronological ordering of the messenger's narrative is linear and, with minor variations, keeps to the essential chronology of *Exodus* 14. The sequence of events – articulated by temporal conjunctions and other indicators of time – allows us to subdivide the text into the following segments: the Egyptian army leaves in pursuit of the Israelites (193–203 = *Exodus* 14:6–8); they camp by the edge of the sea (204–13 = *Exodus* 14:9–10); at sunset the pillar of smoke settles between the two camps (220–3 = *Exodus* 14:19–20); Moses causes the waters to split (224–8 = *Exodus* 14:21); the Israelites pass through the sea (228–9 = *Exodus* 14:22); the Egyptians follow them during the night (230–2 = *Exodus* 14:23). Ezekiel introduces a slight variation by putting the blockage of the Egyptian chariots before the appearance of the pillar of fire, whereas in the Septuagint the blockage follows the appearance: 'And it happened in the early morning watch that the Lord looked at the camp of the Egyptians

---

[50] Note that Ezekiel employs an indefinite pronoun (221–2: τις ἐξαίφνης μέγας στῦλος νεφώδης) where *Exodus* uses the definite article (ὁ στῦλος τῆς νεφέλης). Cf. also 234–5: ἀπ' οὐρανοῦ δὲ φέγγος ὡς πυρὸς μέγα ὤφθη τι ἡμῖν.

[51] Cf. Lintvelt 1981: 67–99. As an example of the 'actorial type of narrative' in the modern novel one could cite Dr Watson, who relates as a witness the exploits of his friend Sherlock Holmes.

in the pillar of fire and cloud, and he threw the camp of the Egyptians into disarray. And he bound together the axles of their chariots and led them violently' (*Ex* 14:24–5;1 trans. J. Perkins). But the sequence of the respective events in the *Exagōgē* is consistent if considered from the messenger's point of view: only after observing the impossibility of pursuing the Israelites by chariot did the Egyptians realize what the force behind this miracle was. The Israelites then walk out of the Red Sea, and a huge threatening wave gathers above the Egyptians, at which point one of the soldiers urges his comrades to flee before the divine power that evidently protects the Israelites; this represents yet another divergence from the sequence in *Exodus*, in which the Egyptians are urged to flee before the sea begins to return. The sense of anticipation introduced here by Ezekiel helps enhance the pathetic effect.

The analysis of the Egyptian messenger's speech allows us to see how Ezekiel proceeded to dramatize the account of *Exodus*, which tragic models he turned to for inspiration, and which techniques he employed. In translating biblical events into dramatic structures, the poet was particularly concerned with the verisimilitude and the coherence of his work. In doing so, he was evidently following the guidelines formulated by the literary theorists of the Hellenistic era. We know, for instance, that Neoptolemus of Parium (third century BC) wrote a treatise on the art of poetry with a view to systematizing the precepts formulated by Aristotle, in which the preeminent notion was that of ἀκολουθία, coherence (Porphyrio *ad* Hor. *A.P.* 1, p. 162 Holder).

## The *Exagōgē* and the Evolution of Tragedy in the Hellenistic Era

Can one point to other elements in the *Exagōgē* that show its links with post-classical dramatic production? Situating the *Exagōgē* in the development of the tragic genre during the Hellenistic era is not an easy task. The near-complete loss of the dramatic texts produced in that period prevents us from following in any detail the genre's evolution.[52] There remain no more than a few fragments of dramas staged after the fourth century. Unfortunately, papyrological discoveries, which have made decisive contributions in other literary domains, have not led to any radical change in our knowledge of Hellenistic tragedy.[53] Nevertheless, scholars have

---

[52] See Sens 2010: 297–9; also, Hornblower, this volume.
[53] Xanthakis-Karamanos 1997b. The papyrological sources, however meagre, remain fundamental to any reconstruction of the characteristics of post-classical theatre; see Tedeschi 2003.

amassed a considerable collection of indirect testimonies, literary, epigraphic and archaeological, which allow us to follow the evolution of the Hellenistic theatre in broad outline with regard to the composition of dramas, their performance, recitation techniques, the structures of theatrical buildings, etc.

Is the *Exagōgē* part of this evolution of the tragic genre? There are several elements that lead us to think that it is. As we have already seen, Ezekiel shares with other Hellenistic dramatists a predilection for the tragedies of Euripides. For example, the Euripidean-style monologue and metres that Moses utters at the beginning of the play are also found in the *Daphnis* or *Lityerses* by Sositheus (*TrGF* 99 F 2), one of the poets of the Pleiad, who lived in the era of Ptolemy II Philadelphus.[54] The taste for the miraculous and the pathetic found in certain passages of the *Exagōgē* (e.g., the burning bush, Moses' dream, the crossing of the Red Sea, etc.) as well as the interest in the aetiology of religious traditions (e.g., the passage on the Passover) are tendencies shared by other Alexandrian literature too.[55] Jane Heath has convincingly brought out the affinities between Ezekiel and the Hellenistic genre of *ekphrasis* and has demonstrated that 'Ezekiel had a distinctively contemporary and Hellenistic visual imagination'.[56]

Besides, the contamination of literary genres and the combination of different elements in a new literary type, as seen in Ezekiel's 'translation' of an essentially epic narrative (*Exodus*) into the tragic form, are characteristic of Hellenistic aesthetics.[57] The author of the so-called 'Gyges tragedy' (*P.Oxy.* 2382 = *TrGF* adesp. 664) seems to have achieved a fusion of literary genres very similar to that of Ezekiel's. Just as the *Exagōgē* closely follows the text of *Exodus*, the fragments of the 'Gyges tragedy' are closely connected with the Gyges tale in Herodotus (1.8–12).[58] Similarly, a fragment from a Hellenistic tragedy preserving a piece of dialogue between Priam, Cassandra and the chorus (*P.Oxy.* 2746 = *TrGF* adesp. 649) is clearly modelled on a passage from the *Iliad* (*Il.* 22.226 ff.).[59]

[54] Cf. Hornblower, this volume.
[55] An interest in the origin of rituals is also evident in *fabulae praetextae*, Latin tragedies with Roman subjects. According to a passage in Varro (*De lingua latina* 6, 18), a *praetexta* explained to the people (*docuit populum*) why women during the Nonae Caprotinae carry out a sacrifice under a male fig tree (*sub caprifico*) and use a branch taken from this tree. Cf. Wiseman 1998: 8–11.
[56] Heath 2006: 26.
[57] See, however, Hornblower, this volume, for the argument that classical tragedy itself was hospitable to other genres, and that *Alexandra* (and by implication the *Exagōgē*) is not eccentric in this respect.
[58] On the Gyges fragment, see Lesky 1953; Garzya 1993; Travis 2000 ; Hornblower, this volume.
[59] See Catenacci 2002; Liapis and Stephanopoulos, this volume. It should be remarked that the expression θάρσησον, ὦ παῖ found in v. 100 of the *Exagōgē* similarly features in the first verse of *P.Oxy.* 2746.

No choral song has been preserved among the surviving fragments of the *Exagōgē*. Thus, we do not know whether Ezekiel had envisaged the presence of a chorus.[60] The absence of choral parts further prevents us from establishing whether the *Exagōgē* was organized in five acts, as was common practice at least since New Comedy. Nevertheless, taking account of the changes of location and of the number of characters present on stage at any given time, one may organize the fragments of the *Exagōgē* into seven or eight scenes.[61] I have already pointed out that these scenes unfold in places that are sometimes very far apart and over a long period of time. This violation of the unities of time and place has to be seen in relation to the evolution of dramatic conventions and of tragic structure in general. Indeed, the events of the *Exagōgē* extend over several years (from Moses' arrival in Madian to the Exodus from Egypt) and include at least three changes of location (Madian, the burning bush, a place not far from Elim). As an explanation for this broad temporal and spatial span, it has been suggested that the fragments transmitted by Eusebius belong not to a single tragedy but to a tetralogy.[62]

As Bruno Gentili has argued, the Hellenistic practice of staging selected episodes from Athenian dramas rather than complete tragedies could plausibly have obviated the need for 'regular' tragedies to be composed and may have favoured the development of new dramatic forms.[63] On this assumption, one can imagine that the *Exagōgē* could have been organized in relatively autonomous sections, in 'tableaux' separated by the temporal intervals dictated by the story of *Exodus*. One can detect this tendency already in certain tragedies of Euripides, e.g., the *Trojan Women*. But the phenomenon has primarily been observed in the archaic Latin tragedies, which are more or less contemporary with the *Exagōgē*. Examples here include Ennius' *Medea exul*, a fragment of which has the heroine in Athens, while the others take place at Corinth,[64] and the same author's *Hectoris lytra*, for which it has been suggested that it had a triptych structure, with three separate, autonomous parts. This structure would be analogous to that of Plautus' comedies, which are also organized in relatively autonomous scenes. There is a strong temptation to see the

---

[60] Some scholars believe that line 59 (ὁρῶ δὲ ταύτας ἑπτὰ παρθένους τινάς) is an internal stage direction to introduce the *parodos* (entrance-song) of the chorus, which would have consisted of the six daughters of Raguel. On the question of the chorus cf. Lanfranchi 2006: 28–9. On the chorus in post-classical tragedy, cf. Griffith, this volume.
[61] Cf. Lanfranchi 2006: 31–2. [62] Kohn 2002–3. *Contra* Jacobson 2002–3.
[63] Gentili 1979a and 1979b. *Contra* Nervegna 2007 and Nervegna 2013: 78–88.
[64] Cf. Rosato 2005: 140–4.

*Exagōgē* as part of this evolution of drama, but prudence is called for: the impression of segmentation suggested by the *Exagōgē* and by the tragedies of Ennius could well be the result of the fragmentary state in which they have come down to us.

Even in terms of prosody and metre, the *Exagōgē* shares the trends of post-classical tragedy, even if it is more conservative in this respect, contrary to the poets of the Pleiad.[65] According to K. Mras, *Exagōgē*'s iambic trimetres are closer to that of Attic comedy, whose rules are freer,[66] but B. Snell has shown that Ezekiel fundamentally follows the metrical rules of classical tragedy, in particular of Euripides.[67] Porson's law is violated in only four instances (62, 163, 174, 233), one of which is mitigated by elision (62) and one by a monosyllable (233).[68] Concerning resolutions, anapaests are more frequent in the first foot and dactyls in the third foot. We find also tribrachs in the second foot. All these resolutions are common in fifth- and fourth-century tragedy.[69] Still, we find in the *Exagōgē* some metrical features unusual in classical tragedy, for instance the absence of 'Attic correption' (the lengthening of a short vowel before a combination of mute and liquid consonants), which is typical of Hellenistic tragedy, and occurs again in the 'Gyges tragedy'.[70]

### The *Exagōgē*: Possible Performance Contexts

It is a hotly debated question whether the *Exagōgē* was originally conceived to be read or to be staged. Those who consider it a *Buchdrama* (a drama meant for reading) do so on the strength of various arguments – ideological (e.g., the presence of God on stage would have been unacceptable for a Jewish public), dramaturgic (the violation of the unities of time, place and action) and technical (the difficulty of staging the miracles of the burning bush, or the rod transformed into a snake, etc.). These arguments are not decisive, however, and one has to consider the possibility that the *Exagōgē* was indeed written for the theatre. The analysis of the messenger scene

---

[65] On Ezekiel's metre cf. Snell 1966 and Jacobson 1983: 167–73; Strugnell 1967.
[66] Mras 1954: 525 (in the critical apparatus).   [67] Snell 1966.   [68] Snell 1966: 29–30.
[69] D'Angelo 1983: 82–4.
[70] Among the examples of unusual lengthening given by Xanthakis-Karamanos 1997b, only Ἑβραίοις in 110 and 152 (lengthening before voiced plosive and liquid) is relevant because it would normally demand *correptio Attica* in classical tragedy. By contrast, ἐκλάμπει (99), τέφραν (136), ὄχλῳ (193), and ἄνοπλοι (210) are less relevant because lengthening before voiceless plosive or fricative and liquid is normal in fifth-century tragic authors. See West 1982: 16–17. Lengthening before voiced plosive and nasal, as in λελεγμένα, 117, is common in Sophocles and Euripides (cf. λελεγμένα in the final position of the iambic trimetre in S. *El.* 1011, E. *Med.* 453, *IA* 1425).

The Exagōgē of Ezekiel the Tragedian 143

earlier in this chapter shows that the trouble taken by Ezekiel to ensure coherence in the organization of his material, as well as in his dramaturgic solutions, appears to have been dictated by the exigencies of adapting the biblical text for the stage. The presence of internal 'stage directions' (implicit instructions incorporated within speech), locative adverbs or deictic pronouns also suggests the possibility of staging.

But what kind of public did Ezekiel intend the *Exagōgē* for? It is unlikely that the play was performed in a public theatre before pagan spectators, as Jacobson suggests.[71] In the first place, the *Exagōgē* assumes a thorough knowledge of *Exodus* on the part of its audience. Apart from its general content, the play's constant references to the text of the Septuagint and the long section on the institution of the Passover lead one to think that the spectators must have been familiar with the Bible and with Jewish traditions. Moreover, Moses' use of the first person plural pronoun to refer to the Jewish people ('Having seen that *our* people had greatly increased, the king Pharaoh devised against *us* a great stratagem', 7–9) was probably meant to encourage, from the outset, the identification of the spectators with Jewish characters on stage.[72] In other words, the play assumes the viewpoint of a Jewish spectator, for whom it would indeed have been 'his' people who had been oppressed in Egypt: the formulation would hardly have made sense if Moses was addressing a pagan audience. In addition, one knows of no other example of a Hellenistic tragedy whose subject was not drawn from Greek mythology or history.[73] Moreover, performances in the Hellenistic era still took place during religious festivals, and it is difficult to imagine that a tragedy based on a biblical subject would have been admitted in such a dramatic competition.

---

[71] For evidence against a Greek pagan audience see Brant 2005: 132–3.

[72] That the first person plural is not a case of 'royal plural' is confirmed by the fact that in what follows Moses consistently uses the singular (14, 16, 18, 27, 32, 34, 45, 53, 56, 57), the sole exception being εἴχομεν in line 36.

[73] Admittedly, Jacobson 1983: 4 cites two Hellenistic tragedies on non-Greek subjects, namely Dymas' *Dardanos* (*TrGF* 130 T 1,19) and the anonymous 'Gyges tragedy' (*Trag. Adesp.* fr. 664 Sn.). But neither play is comparable to the story of Moses, as they are both linked to Greek mythology or history. Dardanos, as ancestor of the Trojan kings, was linked to Greek mythology: he figures in the *Iliad* (20.304–5), and also in Hellenistic literature (Lycoph. 72–3). As for Gyges, his story must have been well known to the Greek public, as it had been related by Herodotus (1.8–12). Eustathius of Thessalonica attributes a play entitled *Susanna* (Σωσάννα) to a certain Damascene (*Commentarium in Dionysii periegetae orbis descriptionem*, 976 Müller). This Damascene may or may not be Nicolaos Damaskenos, the Greek historian who was a friend of King Herod, to whom Suda attributes the composition of 'celebrated tragedies and comedies' (αὐτός τε τραγῳδίας ἐποίει καὶ κωμῳδίας εὐδοκίμους).

What, then, could have been a suitable performance context for the *Exagōgē*? Can one imagine a festive occasion in which Jews would have been able to attend a performance of *Exodus*? Unfortunately, we have no idea whether performances were organized by diaspora Jews in public places during the Hellenistic era. For the pagan world, we know not only that Hellenistic theatres were used for a variety of cultic activities,[74] but also that in cultic contexts, particularly in sanctuaries for Eastern divinities, there were small *theatra* capable of accommodating spectators who came to attend performances of sacred stories or religious plays.[75] Could the Jews have exploited the cultic potential of the theatre to enact their religious history on the occasion of a Jewish celebration? The content of the *Exagōgē* would seem to support this idea.

We have already pointed out that the subject of the *Exagōgē* made the play eminently suitable for a Jewish public. This is particularly true for the section that Ezekiel devotes to the institution of the Passover. In lines 152–74, God dictates to Moses the rites that the Israelites are to carry out during the night of the Passover, and gives instructions for the Feast of Unleavened Bread and the redemption of the firstborn. These same prescriptions are repeated with variations and the addition of certain details in the ensuing lines (175–92). The reference to the Passover rite is not there simply out of fidelity to the biblical story, which Ezekiel generally follows. In fact, *Exodus* 12 is not the only source for this section: Ezekiel not only introduces a detail (162–6) drawn from a different part of *Exodus* (3:21–2), but also combines elements from *Exodus* with material from *Deuteronomy*, and even offers explanations of rites that are not to be found in the Bible (e.g., the association of the seven-day duration of the Feast of Unleavened Bread with the seven-day journey after the Exodus). By means of these variants, Ezekiel obviously intends to present his public with an aetiological explanation of certain aspects of the Feast of the Passover, although in doing so he runs the risk of introducing a dramatic anticlimax. In fact, the long ritual section placed just after the account of the plagues that will fall on Egypt neutralizes the dramatic tension of the list of plagues, and at the same time expands the time frame of the drama to include future generations, when the events of *Exodus* will have become merely ritual observances. In other words, the prescriptions for an annually repeated rite (170–1) disrupt the dramatic fiction, as they look outwards to the spectators themselves. The division between the time of the dramatic

---

[74] Chaniotis 2007: 48–66.   [75] Nielsen 2000; Izenous 1992.

events, the time of the performance and real time will thus remain in suspension.

But the part on the Passover is not simply a digression or a poorly conceived passage disrupting the economy of the tragedy. On the contrary, this passage may provide the key to understanding the nature of the *Exagōgē* and the occasion of its performance; indeed, it is of pivotal importance, both ideologically and structurally. In my opinion, it was the very nature of the Exodus story and its annual evocation during the Feast of the Passover that may have suggested to Ezekiel the idea of casting the biblical events in dramatic form.[76] In fact, the celebration of the Passover, as instituted in the book of *Exodus*, comprises mimetic actions through which the events of the original Passover are commemorated and re-enacted.[77] Even if this remains in the realm of hypothesis, we can imagine that the *Exagōgē* could have been performed as a peripheral event (not necessarily as institutionalized rite) on the occasion of the celebration of the Passover, whose mimetic elements Ezekiel could have exploited in addition to its commemorative value.

Once again, one may detect here parallels with the theatrical production of Rome in the Republican era. Archaic Latin theatre is a product of the encounter between the national rites of Rome (*ludi*) and the kind of literary drama that was introduced from Greece.[78] In particular, there is good reason to compare the *Exagōgē* and the *fabulae praetextae*, which represent the most advanced stage of 'Romanization' of the archaic Latin theatre. The authors of the *praetexta* freed themselves from the Greek themes and took as their subject what Horace calls *domestica facta* (*Ars poet.* 287), i.e., Roman legends of origin or recent events from Roman history.[79] The surviving fragments suggest that the *fabulae praetextae* largely derive from Greek tragedy, whose structure, dramaturgical conventions and stylistic features they adopt.[80] The performance context of the

---

[76] According to Bryant Davies 2008, Ezekiel's decision to dramatize episodes from *Exodus* is part of his project to resolve 'the question of liturgical/dramatic replacement of sacrificial rite', which biblical law forbade outside of the Temple of Jerusalem. Ezekiel's work would thus be a 'verbal sacrifice', which in a liturgical context could replace the 'sacrifice of blood'.

[77] In his *De vita contemplativa* 85–9, Philo of Alexandria describes the mimetic dance, accompanied by choral chants, performed by the Therapeuts at the dawn of their Feast of Weeks – a dance that was directly inspired by the dance of the Israelites after the crossing of the Red Sea. Egyptian Judaism thus practised 'ritual dramatizations' on the occasion of religious festivals.

[78] On the Latin theatre of the Republican era cf. Manuwald 2011.

[79] On the *fabulae praetextae* cf. Manuwald 2001.

[80] In that part of *Brutus* which recounts Tarquin's dream and its interpretation by his advisers, Accius took as his model the celebrated scene of the Queen's dream in Aeschylus' *Persae*, which is also the intertext of Moses' dream in the *Exagōgē*.

*fabulae praetextae* was the religious festivals of Rome – a connection that is also evident in the choice of subjects, which was sometimes related to the festival during which the plays were staged.[81]

The content, form and performance contexts of the *praetextae* are in every way comparable to those of the *Exagōgē*. In staging the story of the *Exodus*, Ezekiel employed the language, rhetorical devices, images and structural elements of classical Greek tragedy, just as the authors of the *praetextae* did. Moreover, by situating itself at the intersection between religious mimetic performances and literary spectacle, the *Exagōgē* helped shape the national and religious identity of its audience, just as the *praetextae* did – although in very different political, social and cultural contexts.

[81] As we have seen, the *praetextae* could have an aetiological function in explaining the origin of customs and rites on the occasion of festivals that were often connected to a certain temple or cult. Two anonymous pieces belong to this category, one concerning the arrival of the Magna Mater and the other the origins of the *Nonae Caprotinae*; they were performed at the *Ludi Megalenses* and the *Ludi Apollinares*, respectively. See Flower 1995: 170–90.

PART II

*Contexts and Developments*

CHAPTER 5

# Beyond Athens
## The Expansion of Greek Tragedy from the Fourth Century Onwards

*Brigitte Le Guen**

The time is no more when we thought that Greek theatre, having reached its glorious peak in fifth-century Athens, entered subsequently a period of slow decadence. In fact, over the last fifteen years or so, several scholars have shown that, after the end of the fifth century, theatrical activity, far from losing its vigour, was spread far and wide beyond the city of Athens.[1] But what about tragedy, more specifically?

This chapter will deal with the expansion of tragedy from the fourth century onwards, starting with the regions for which tragic performances are attested for that period, and exploring the contexts in which such performances took place. Next, we shall discuss the even broader diffusion of tragedy in the Hellenistic era and the reasons behind this phenomenon. Finally, we shall look at what the term 'tragedy' signifies during this entire period, and at the evidence for or against the use (and the make-up) of choruses in tragic performances.[2] This will allow us to reflect on the meanings and functions of tragedy after the fifth century in the Greek and the Hellenized worlds alike. The following discussion will entail fully laying out the documentary evidence on which my analysis relies, its nature and its problems.

### The Expansion of Tragedy in the Fourth Century

#### Sicily and South Italy

First of all, we must emphasize the paucity of precise and incontestable evidence on the performance of tragedy in the Western Mediterranean

---

* The author wishes to extend her warm thanks to Vayos Liapis for the English translation of this chapter and to Mark Griffith for corrections on points of style.
[1] Easterling 1993; Green 1994: 49–88; Le Guen 1995; Dearden 1999; Taplin 1993: 12–20 and 1999; Revermann 1999–2000; W. Allan 2001; Csapo 2010; Petrides in the Introduction to this volume.
[2] On the issue, see also Griffith, this volume.

during the fourth century BC.[3] Still, there was original and advanced theatre activity in that area already in the fifth century. Indeed, the influence of Athenian drama in Sicily merely superimposed itself as an additional layer on earlier local traditions,[4] mainly as a result of Aeschylus' extended visits to the island.[5] We know that the great Athenian tragic poet died in Gela after 458,[6] but he had also paid an earlier visit to Hieron's court at Syracuse, where he produced his tragedy *Aetnean Women* in 475/4[7]. On the same occasion he may even have put on a performance of his *Persians*, according to an old (1852) hypothesis by E. J. Kiehl, recently revived with new and solid argumentation by Kathryn Bosher (2012b: 103–8), since that play does not seem to have been originally conceived for performance in Athens.[8] Moreover, Dearden (2012: 275) wonders if Hieron had turned to the Athenian dramatist in order to rouse Sicilian interest in tragedy, since comedy was already popular there, or because Aeschylus' plays were, in the tyrant's eyes, more sophisticated and innovative than local dramas.

For the fourth century, the inscriptional record is dismally deficient, and the archaeological evidence presents us with undeniable limitations. The remains of theatrical buildings, however numerous before the end of that period both in Sicily and in South Italy,[9] do not, in and of themselves, constitute evidence for theatre performances, or for tragic performances at that. Nor do they allow us to conclude, if need be, that the events hosted in those venues were exclusively or for the most part Athenian plays, or rather plays composed and produced, entirely or in part, along Athenian lines.

The little archaeological evidence we possess – terracotta figurines representing actors, masks, theatre-related reliefs and mosaics[10] – does of

---

[3] See now on this point Csapo and Wilson 2015: 328–44. Their comprehensive study had not been published when I finished writing the present chapter, two years ago.
[4] Kowalzig 2008; Bosher 2012a; Dearden 1990.
[5] Further evidence for intense artistic activity in Sicily prior to that era, and for the Syracusans' passion for Athenian tragedy even before the late fifth century, may be found in Jordan 2007: 335–50; Wilson 2007b: 351–77; Dearden 2012: 280.
[6] Another Athenian tragic poet, Phrynichus, was also perhaps invited to the Deinomenid court (Bosher 2012b: 102).
[7] Vahtikari 2014: 79–82. In his recently published doctoral dissertation, Vesa Vahtikari evokes also the case of the *Prometheus Bound*, whose performance in Sicily is possible but not very probable (pp. 84–6).
[8] On the Athenian production, see Vahtikari 2014: 82–4.
[9] Todisco 2002: 139–92; Marconi 2012, with earlier bibliography.    [10] Todisco 2002: 101–4.

course attest to a public with a taste for such objects and decorations, but can by no means be used as indisputable evidence for actual theatre performances either at the sites where such findings have turned up or in their immediate vicinity. This holds good also for the numerous vases unearthed in those areas and depicting scenes from the theatre, whether they were imports or imitations produced by local craftsmen. After all, such vase-paintings have given rise to entirely different interpretations by specialists.[11] For example, whereas Oliver Taplin (2012: 229–36) is convinced that they reflect Athenian tragedies performed by troupes of touring actors upon invitation,[12] Luigi Todisco (2012: 251–71) dwells on the fact that a great number of vases found in South Italy are of non-Greek provenance and that, far from preserving reminiscences of known dramatic performances, they served above all to make the Greek myths known to populations unfamiliar with them.

All the same, the fact that in the fourth century there were actors and tragic poets who could come from cities as different as Thurii, Metapontium, Acragas, Syracuse and Catana,[13] and who could nonetheless try their hand in Athenian dramatic contests and win prizes there indicates that those areas, in which local forms of theatre had left their mark from a very early stage, had undoubtedly known the expansion of Athenian tragedy, either directly (through performances by acting troupes upon invitation) or indirectly (through the circulation of dramatic texts). There is no doubt that one man played a decisive role here – namely, Dionysius I, the tyrant of Sicily, who won first prize at the Lenaea contest in Athens in 367 and was apparently an innovative tragic poet.[14] He seems to have been the first poet to grasp the potential of this dramatic genre and to utilize in his own

---

[11] For further details, see Duncan and Liapis, this volume. Here, I simply want to underline the different nature of pre-Hellenistic and Hellenistic sources.
[12] See also Vahtikari 2014: 20–48 (evidence from vases).
[13] See Todisco 2002: 65–6. Mamercus, the tyrant of Catana, 'bragged about his writing skills as a poet and an author of tragedies', according to Plut. *Tim.* 31 (cf. *TrGF* 87). Achaeus II of Syracuse, author of ten tragedies according to the *Suda* (α 4682), won first prize at the Lenaea contest in 330 (*IG* ii² 2325.242; *TrGF* 79). His contemporary Sosiphanes, also of Syracuse, produced 73 dramas and won seven victories (*TrGF* 92). The tragic poets of Sicily and South Italy also include Patrocles of Thurii (*TrGF* 58) and Carcinus II of Acragas (*TrGF* 70), the latter having won eleven victories at the Great Dionysia. Noteworthy among tragic actors are Aristodemus of Metapontium (Stephanis 1988: no 332) and Archias of Thurii (Stephanis 1988: no 439).
[14] *TrGF* 76 T 1.5, 3.3–4; Duncan 2012: 143.

plays the figure of the monarch idealized in Athenian tragic theatre as part of his programme to cast himself as the embodiment of the righteous sovereign.

According to Plato's *Laws* 659b, a work dated in the mid–fourth century, theatre performances in Sicily and South Italy at that time were competitive events, just as they were in Athens, although victors in those regions were proclaimed in a different manner, namely by a show of hands by the spectators.[15]

In view of the dearth of direct (and thus incontestable) evidence, we must rely on a nexus of indirect but solid and consistent indications for an account of the expansion and performance of tragedy in the Western Mediterranean.

## From Macedon to the Kingdom of Alexander

Let us now turn towards Macedonia, where Athenian tragedy was introduced at the end of the fifth century at latest, on the initiative of King Archelaus (413–399 BC). It is actually Archelaus who founded the festival of Olympia at Dion, in which dramatic contests took place (Diod. Sic. 17.16.3; Dio Chrys. 2.2), and invited to his court the tragic poets Agathon and Euripides. To honour his host, the latter produced a tragedy named after Archelaus' ancestor.

Archelaus' successors, following in his footsteps, contributed, for their part, to the promotion of the theatre in the Macedonian kingdom.[16] This tendency is evidenced by the theatrical buildings and the archaeological findings from the fourth century (with the reservations expressed earlier in this chapter),[17] but also by a number of literary sources. For instance, Diodorus of Sicily says that Neoptolemus, the famous Athenian tragic actor, was among the invitees at the royal dinner party thrown by Philip II at Aegae on the occasion of his daughter Cleopatra's wedding to Alexander of Epirus. Neoptolemus would have no doubt participated, on the following day, in the 'musical contests' (ἀγῶνες μουσικοί) that Philip had proclaimed, if the king had not been assassinated as he entered the theatre (Diod. Sic. 16.91).[18] In 335, before his expedition to Anatolia and

---

[15] Todisco 2002: 17; Wilson 2007b: 335; Dearden 2012: 279.   [16] See Moloney 2014: 231–48.
[17] See Adam-Veleni 2010.
[18] I make no mention of the festival of Olympia organized by Philip after the fall of Olynthus at 348, although Diodorus 16.55 (and cf. schol. on Dem. *On the False Embassy* 192) says that they included 'contests': the programme of that festival is not known. However, if it was modelled on the Olympia at Dion, it will have included tragic contests too.

in the context of the Olympia at Dion, Philip's son Alexander organized scenic contests, including tragic competitions in honour of Zeus and the Muses.[19] During his expedition, Alexander also organized some twenty more contests, some of which are termed 'musical' (μουσικοί) in our sources and may thus have included dramatic competitions, while others are certain to have done so.[20] In March/April 331, on his return journey from Egypt, Alexander actually organized a contest (ἀγών) of dithyramb and tragedy, which was by and large an imitation of the famous Great Dionysia of Athens.[21] It was surely no accident that two star actors of the Athenian theatre, namely Athenodorus and Thessalus,[22] were invited and distinguished themselves in that event. In late December 325, having crossed the harrowing Gedrosia desert, Alexander organized again, according to Diodorus, athletic and musical (in the narrow sense) but also dramatic contests (σκηνικοί ἀγῶνες) in the Salmous area.[23] Apparently, there were also dramatic contests at Memphis, Ecbatana and Babylon, although we know nothing of their programme of events.[24] In April 324, during the famous mass weddings at Susa, although there were no real contests, there were certainly performances by comic and tragic troupes,[25] the tragic protagonists being Athenodorus, Thessalus and Aristocritus.[26] Finally, according to Athenaeus (13, 586d and 595e), Alexander himself was believed by some to be the real author of the satyr-drama *Agēn*, which was also attributed to Python of Catana or of Byzantium.

What is important for our purposes is to emphasize what a powerful magnet Alexander's itinerant court was for athletes and artists alike. The king is said to have invited three thousand expert performers to Ecbatana (October 342), according to Plutarch (*Alex.* 72.1), and just as many to Babylon (early 323), according to Arrian (*Anab.* 7.14.10), although it is possible that only one of these places saw the confluence of so many skilled performers. On the other hand, Arrian states (*Anab.* 3.1.4, 3.5.2) that only

---

[19] Diod. Sic. 17.16.3–4. However, Arrian (1.11.1) situates the festival at Aegae. See further Mari 1998.
[20] See Le Guen 2014: 257–63, and independently Vahtikari 2014: 99–115.
[21] Plut. *Alex.* 29.5; *De Alex. fort.* 2.334e).
[22] See Stephanis 1988: no 75 and no 1200, respectively.
[23] Arr. *Anab.* 6.28.1–3; *Ind.* 8.36.3; Diod. Sic. 17.106.4.
[24] Memphis: Arr. *Anab.* 3.1.4 and 3.5.2. Ecbatana: Arr. *Anab.* 7.14.1; Diod. 17.110.4; Plut. *Alex.* 72.1. Babylon: Arr. *Anab.* 7.14.10; Diod. 17.115.6.
[25] Ath. 12.4.538b–539a; cf. Le Guen 2014: 256, 264–6.
[26] On Aristocritus see Stephanis 1988: no 352.

the most famous artists were summoned to join Alexander at Memphis in late 332/early 331, and then in the spring of 331. We know, moreover, that the actor Athenodorus was present at Tyre and at Susa but returned to Athens in the intervening period in order to participate in the Great Dionysia of 329.[27] By contrast, the tragic poet Neophron of Sicyon, whom *Suda* (v 218) credits with the composition of 120 dramas, accompanied Alexander in his campaigns, as did, probably, the tragic actors Thessalus and Aristocritus, both of whom served as ambassadors as well as actors according to their sovereign's whims.

Thus, theatrical activity was of cardinal importance in Alexander the Great's campaign. It is to him rather than to his Ptolemaic successors that we should attribute the genesis of 'monarchic Dionysism', which assimilated the monarch to the god of theatre, itself a venue for contests intended to proclaim winners, and thereby lent ideological legitimacy and authority to the link between theatre, victory and monarchic power.[28] As well as being an essential link in the chain of the development of Hellenistic dramatic contests, both tragic and comic (see later in this chapter), Alexander the Great also bears the principal responsibility for propagating Athenian drama from the Balkans to the Indus River.

### *Other Locales*

Only a handful of ancient documents attest, more or less clearly, to the dissemination of tragedy outside of the areas we described earlier in this chapter.[29] As in the previous cases, its geographic range may be deduced from the ethnic designations attaching to the names of tragic poets and actors that have reached us. The dramatists we hear of include Apollodorus of Tarsus (*TrGF* 64), author of six tragedies mentioned by title in *Suda* (α 3406), who won five victories at the Lenaea and six victories perhaps at the Great Dionysia from the 380s onwards; also, Theodectas of Phaselis, who won first prize at the rhetorical contest organized by Artemisia to honour the memory of her dead husband, although his tragedy *Mausolus* was held in higher esteem, according to Hyginus,[30] than his laudatory prose

---

[27] *IG* ii² 2318.360. See Tritle 2009: 122–9.
[28] See, e.g., Dunand 1986: 85–103; Musti 1986: 111–28.
[29] See, independently, Vahtikari 2014:116–20.   [30] Fr. 12 Funaioli, as cited by Gellius 10.18.5.

(*TrGF* 72 T6); and finally, Diogenes of Sinope (*TrGF* 88), Philiscus of Aegina (*TrGF* 89) and perhaps Heraclides of Pontus (*TrGF* 94). As for the actors, pride of place must be given to the star performers Neoptolemus of Scyrus and Polus of Aegina, to whom we might have added Hippasus of Ambracia, if he were not a figment of Alciphron's imagination, and Timotheus of Zacynthus, if he really was active between the end of the fifth and the beginning of the fourth century (Stephanis 1988: no 2416).[31]

The inscriptional record suggests, however, that tragedy was even more widespread. For instance, a decree from Samos (ca. 350 BC) stipulates that the honours conferred by the Athenian cleruchs of the island on their compatriot Diotimus be publicly proclaimed during the tragic contests at the Dionysia festival (Διονυ[σίων τ]οῖς τραγωιδοῖς).[32] One sees here a characteristically Athenian practice (proclamation of public honours in the theatre) being translocated outside of the city, though still in a strictly Athenian context, since cleruchs were landowners living outside Athens but without loss of Athenian citizenship. And we may reasonably suppose that other cleruchs too would have desired likewise to reproduce, at their new place of residence, customs familiar to them.

If we are to credit a passage from a puzzling and lacunose agonistic list found in Rome,[33] which makes reference to theatre performances at the beginning of the fourth century BC, a tragic actor by the name of Aristomedes, of whom we know nothing else, competed at the Lenaea festival in Athens, but also in the city of Rhodes, against a certain Kleandros.[34] However, we know nothing of the context in which the Rhodian performance took place. Thanks to Diodorus (20.84), we are only informed that Dionysia existed in the city before the end of the fourth century.

Finally, at Cyrene, tragic choruses are mentioned twice in inscriptions containing financial reports by the *dāmiergoi* (civic officers responsible for managing sacred property) dating from 335 BC.[35] In their analysis of these documents, Paola Ceccarelli and Silvia Milanezi (2007: 196) stress

---

[31] For Neoptolemus, Polus, Hippasus and Timotheus see Stephanis 1988: nos 1797, 2187, 1280 and 2416, respectively.
[32] *IG* xii 6.253.11.  [33] *IGUR* 223 + 229 = Mette 1977: 194.
[34] Aristomedes: Stephanis 1988: no. 363. Kleandros: Stephanis 1988: no. 1413.
[35] *SEG* 9, 13.13–14 and *SEG* 48, 2052.9–10. Cf. *SEG* 43, 1186; 38, 1875; Dobias-Lalou 1993: 30; Wilson 2000: 290 and n. 120.

that it is hard to know which god was honoured by these choral performances and in which context exactly. Cautioning against the temptation to associate these performances, systematically but rashly, with Dionysus, Ceccarelli and Milanezi argue (p. 197) that '*even before Hellenistic times*, dramatic performances were associated *in various cities* with divinities *other than Dionysos*' (my emphasis), citing as proof the contests established at Dion by the Macedonian king at the end of the fifth century. However, this is a special case: it is a decision by a monarch with a view to promoting the Macedonian kingdom in the context of a broader rivalry with Athens. This last point has been very well brought out by Manuela Mari (1998). Thus, we cannot use the Macedonian example as evidence for non-Dionysiac dramatic performances 'in various cities'. Ceccarelli and Milanezi go on to cite a second example, affirming that 'There were tragic performances for Athena at Coronea.' In fact, however, the honorific decree they cite (*TrGF*, DID B 12) seems to date from the mid–second century BC, and it is worth re-examining. The document in question mentions Zotion, son of Zotion, an Ephesian poet of tragedy and satyr-drama, who (following a practice that is abundantly attested from the third century BC onwards) demonstrated his talent, not in a competitive context, at Coronea, where he was a visitor, and was deemed worthy both of the city and of Athena Itonia, the patron goddess of the Boeotian *koinon*. This text, then, is not earlier than the Hellenistic period and, what is more, it is not concerned, strictly speaking, with 'tragic performances for Athena'. The rest of the evidence cited by Ceccarelli and Milanezi comes, again, from the Hellenistic era.[36] Thus, on the strength of the available evidence, one can maintain only that from that period onwards Greek cities begin to introduce dramatic contests into all sorts of festivals. There is no unambiguous evidence for dramatic contests in honour of gods other than Dionysus before the mid–third century BC, and that according to a chronology that I tried to establish in Le Guen 2010a.

This is why – without discarding the possibility that Cyrene followed different practices from the rest of the Greek world, and despite the fact that the two extant lists from the second half of the fourth century do not mention the god being honoured – I believe that the three tragic choruses and the one dithyrambic chorus mentioned in these sources are to be

---

[36] *SIG*³ 1080 must now be dated to 190–170; see Le Guen 2007c.

associated with Dionysus, patron god of the theatre but also of the dithyramb.

As for the make-up of these tragic choruses, I concur with Peter Wilson (2000: 290) in seeing them as local outfits, each one recruited from one of the three Cyrenian tribes, along the lines of the tribal make-up of Athenian dithyrambic choruses. They must have been an integral part of plays performed by specially hired actors, who would have been remunerated in some specific fashion, although the inscriptions say nothing about this.

All in all, there can hardly be any doubt that already in the fourth century, Greek tragedy had spread well beyond Attica, especially thanks to powerful rulers (tyrants or monarchs), who were dramatists themselves (real or imagined) and could muster sufficient funds to sponsor poets and actors, in the deeply held belief that theatre could be a means of promoting their respective ideologies. Unsurprisingly, tragedy in the fourth century has an equally strong presence in wealthy cities, such as Gela and Cyrene, or in areas associated with Athens and its practices. In any case, we should never lose sight of the fact that the expansion of the theatre is a question of power and money.

## The Dissemination of Tragedy in the Hellenistic Era

In the Hellenistic era, we have evidence for numerous theatrical buildings in most Mediterranean cities, whether ancient or more recent: Babylon, Aï-Khanoum in Afghanistan, but also Seleucia on the Tigris and Tigranocerta in Armenia,[37] where the sparse archaeological findings attest to an extraordinary enthusiasm for theatrical spectacle,[38] and where the ethnic names of actors and tragic dramatists provide information on new cities into which tragedy had made its way.[39] Here, there are three important factors that contributed to the proliferation and further expansion of theatrical activity in general and of tragedy in particular. First and foremost, there is the large number of festivals in honour of Dionysus (Dionysia) throughout the Greek world, which included contests for actors and/or tragic poets. Second, there is also the introduction of theatrical contests, including tragic competitions, into festivals in honour of gods other than Dionysus, either on their own or in conjunction with him in a sort of twin festival.[40] Third, there is the establishment of a new kind of guild, both professional and religious in character, as a response to the

[37] Le Guen 2003: 331–41.   [38] Green 1994: 105–41.
[39] Stephanis 1988: nos 556–61; Snell 1986: 263–312; Le Guen 2007b.   [40] Cf. Le Guen 2010a.

exponential demand for scenic artists caused by the proliferation of dramatic contests. At the same time, these guilds were absolutely instrumental in the dissemination of the theatrical tradition and equally indispensable in supporting artistic creation.[41] In what follows, we shall examine each of these three factors separately.

*Proliferation of Festivals with Theatrical Components and Tragic Contests*

It would appear that after the death of Alexander the Great, the Dionysia came to be celebrated throughout the Greek world. But this may be merely a false impression created by what sources we possess, since the majority of the Greek cities of the classical period had not adopted yet the Athenian habit of transferring onto stone parts of the documents they kept in their archives. As a result, it often happens that we are ignorant of the exact number and the precise content of the festivals held in those cities before the Hellenistic period.

However this may be, from the third century BC onwards, a number of inscriptions mention the Dionysia, including the performance of tragic contests. These inscriptions are mainly cities' decrees stipulating that honours bestowed on a fellow citizen or a stranger be proclaimed in public during the tragic contests of the (following) Dionysia festival. In the case of decrees granting various privileges to strangers, it happens sometimes that the promulgating authorities ask the respective cities of origin of the persons honoured to make public announcements, too, on the same occasion. The epigraphic record also includes catalogues and lists of victors mentioning the contestants or the winners of tragic contests, laws or testamentary regulations regarding the recruitment of various artists, or even accounts established by magistrates to record expenses incurred during the festival.

Without claiming to be exhaustive, here (see Tables 1 and 2) are lists of cities, geographically and alphabetically arranged, for which we know for certain that they held Dionysia festivals featuring tragic contests.[42]

---

[41] Le Guen 2001, 2004a, 2004b; Aneziri 2003.
[42] See also the honorific decree from an unknown city in honour of foreign judges from Iasos, which stipulates that they be crowned on the first day of the contest of tragedy during the Dionysia and that the relevant announcement be made by the organizer (*agōnothetēs*) of the contest of *mousikē* (*IK* 28.1-Iasos, 83.18–22; cf. *IK* 28.1-Iasos, 72). There was perhaps also a contest of tragedy at the Dionysia held at Epidaurus, described as *theōrikois* on a first-century BC inscription (*IG* iv² 1, 67.14).

Beyond Athens: The Expansion of Greek Tragedy 159

Table 1 *Aegean and Ionian cities with Dionysia festivals featuring tragic contests*

| Place | Nature and date of the document[a] | References[b] |
|---|---|---|
| **Aigyalē** (Amorgos) | Honorific decree, end of third century BC. | *IG* xii 7, 386.34–6. |
| **Andros** | Honorific decree, 275–225 BC? | *SEG* 44, 699.10–1 (*IG* xii 5, 714 and *IG* xii *Suppl.*, 119). |
| **Cos** | Lists of victors, end of third–beginning of second century. | *IG* xii 4, 2, 452A.22–4; 452B.82–5. |
| **Delos** | Archons' list mentioning *chorēgoi* for tragedy and comedy from 284 to 169. | *IG* xi 2, 105–33 (minus the inscriptions 117, 119, 121, 125, 127, 131, which are unrelated to the Dionysia). |
| **Eresos** (Lesbos) | Decree from Paros, third–second century? | *IG* xii *Suppl.*, 121.30–5. See further, among honorific decrees: *IG* xii *Suppl.*, 125.21–3 (second century BC). |
| **Euboea** (Oreos, Chalcis, Eretria, Karystos) | Law on the recruitment of artists, between 297 and 288 BC. | *IG* xii 9, 207 + *ad*. p. 176 et 178 (Le Guen 2001: i, TE 1). |
| **Ios** | Honorific decree, third century BC. | *IG* xii 5, 1010.2–3. See further, among honorific decrees: *IG* xii 5, 1011.7 (restored in its entirety, third century BC). |
| **Ioulis** (Keos) | Honorific decree, second century BC. | *IG* xii 5, 599.7–10. See further, among honorific decrees: *BÉ* 1999: 659, no 422 (ca. 200); *IG* xii 5, 604.4, where *Dionysiois* is all that is legible. |
| **Karthaia** (Keos) | Honorific decree, third century BC. | *IG* xii 5, 531/1063.9–10 (restored almost in its entirety). See further, among honorific decrees: *IG* xii 5, 529/1064.6–7 (restored almost in its entirety; third century BC); *SEG* 48, 1130.10–13 and 28–9 (ca. 194–192?). |
| **Lepsia** | Honorific decree by the Milesian *dēmos* living at Lepsia, ca. 169 BC. | *IIsolMil* 18.24–5. See also the decree *IG* xii 5, 653.47–50, first century BC. |
| **Naxos** | Honorific decree, ca. 280 BC. | *SEG* 49, 1106B.15–17. |

## Table 1 (cont.)

| Place | Nature and date of the document[a] | References[b] |
|---|---|---|
| Paros | Decree recognizing the *Leukophryēna* of Magnesia on the Maeander, end of third century BC. | Rigsby 1996: no100.39–42. See further, among honorific decrees: *IG* xii 5, 129.33–4 (second century BC). |
| Rhodes | Undated honorific inscription, mentioning a victorious tragic *chorēgos* at the *Alexandreia kai Dionysia*. | *IG* xi 1, 71.2–4. See also the undated honorific inscription: *Tit. Cam.* 63.24–7. |
| Salamis | Honorific decree, 131/0 BC. | *IG* ii²1227.30–2. See also *IG* ii²1008.82. |
| Samos | Honorific decree, 306/5 BC? | *IG* xii 6, 1, 56.28–9 (*SEG* 1, 362). See further, among honorific decrees, *IG* xii 6, 1, 150.3 (end of fourth century); *IG* xii 6, 1, 141.32–4? (extremely mutilated; early third century); *IG* xii 6, 1, 95.25 (ca. 280); *IG* xii 6, 1, 156. 15–16 (ca. 245/4); *IG* xii 6, 1, 11.55–6 (after 243/2); *IG* xii 6, 1, 151.29 (after 241); *IG* xii 6, 1, 152.9 et 21 (ca. 200–150); *IG* xii 6, 1, 153.8 and 12–14 (ca. 200–150); *IG* xii 6, 1, 6.34? (restitution of *Dionysiois*; after 167); *IG* xii 6, 1, 154.27 et 31 (ca. 150–100). For victors' lists see *IG* xii 6, 1, 176.1–5 (shortly after the middle of the third century); *IG* xii 6, 1, 178.9–11 (second century BC); *IG* xii 6, 1, 177.6–8 and 15–17 (second half of second century BC). |
| Siphnos | Honorific decree, ca. 274/3–270. | *IG* xii 5, 481.19–20. See further, among honorific decrees: *IG* xii 5, 482.3–4 (restored almost in their entirety; second/third century); *IG* xii 5, 471.11–12 and 26–7 (second century BC). |
| Syros | Honorific decree, first century BC. | *IG* xii 5, 653.47–50. |
| Tenos | Decree in honour of Melesias, son of Melesias, of Mytilene, third century BC. | *IG* xii 5, 798.12–14. See further, among honorific decrees: *IG* xii 5, 800.8–10 (third century BC). |

Table 1 (*cont.*)

| Place | Nature and date of the document[a] | References[b] |
|---|---|---|
| **Corcyra** | Foundation[c] of Aristomenes and Psylla, end of third/beginning of second century BC. | *IG* ix 1, 694 (*IJG* ii, 25B); new edn. *IG* ix 1², fasc. 4, 798. |

*Note*: In the Aegean and Ionian Seas
[a] This column mentions the date of the earliest Hellenistic document to attest to the existence of tragic contests.
[b] In what follows, 'TE' followed by an Arabic numeral refers to the classification of epigraphic testimonies in Le Guen 2001.
[c] That is, a private endowment managed by a city or sanctuary. In this case, interests accruing from the capital donated helped defray the costs of hiring artists for the biannual Dionysia.

Table 2 *Cities in continental Greece and Asia Minor with Dionysia festivals featuring tragic contests*

| Place | Nature and date of the document | References |
|---|---|---|
| **Didymes** | Honorific decree, very lacunose, end of Hellenistic period. | *I.Didyma*, 234AI.2–3. |
| **Iasos** | Decree of the Artists of Dionysus, second or third quarter of the second century BC. | *IK* 28.1-Iasos, 152.11–16. |
| **Smyrne** | Honorific decree, second century BC. | *IK* 24.1-Smyrna, 579.22–3. |
| **Priene** | Honorific decree, 328–ca. 200 BC. | *IPriene* 8.30-2, 51–3 et p. 308. See further, *IPriene* 18.8–9 (ca. 285–280); *IPriene* 17.41-3 (278–ca. 260); *IPriene* 22.15–17 (ca. 262); *IPriene* 23.14-5 (third century); *IPriene* 75.8–10, if correctly restored (second century BC). |
| **Miletus?** | Honorific decree mentioning an *agōn skānikos*, but we know nothing of the contests it involved (first half of the second century BC). | *Milet* I 3, 152 A-B.53–4. |
| **Teos?** | If Brixhe's restoration is correct (probably second half of third century BC). | *BÉ* 1996: 621, no 351. |

*Note*: In continental Greece and Asia Minor

Still, as we saw earlier in this chapter, in the Hellenistic period the Dionysia are no longer the only festivals to include tragic contests. There are also the following festivals (see Table 3), in chronological order.

Table 3 *Cities with festivals (other than the Dionysia) featuring tragic contests*

| Place | Festival | Dates and references[a] |
|---|---|---|
| Athens | Dionysia–Demetrieia in honour of Dionysus and of Demetrius Poliorcetes. Musical contest (*agōn mousikos*) instituted by the Technitai of Athens for Ariarathes V of Cappadocia. | 295 BC. Plut. *Dem.* 12, 1–2; *IG* ii², 649 + *Dinsmoor* 1931: 7–8, l. 42. Shortly before 130 BC. Le Guen 2001: i., TE 5.43–6. |
| Samos | Antigoneia and Demetrieia Heraia. | Decree, probably 306/5 BC. *IG* xii 6, 1, 56.28–9; cf. *SEG* 1, 362. List of victors, shortly before the first half of the second century BC. *IG* xii 6, 1, 173.3 and 9 (Mette 1977: 49–50). |
| Delos | Ptolemaia of the Island League (Koinon of the Nesiotes). | 291–287 BC. *IG* xi 4, 1043.14–16. |
| Euboea: Oreos, Chalcis, Eretria, Karystos | Demetrieia (together with Aristonikeia, only at Karystos). | Between 297 and 288 BC. *IG* xii 9, 207 + *ad.* p. 176 and 178 (Le Guen 2001: i, TE 1). |
| Delphi | Amphictionic Soteria in honour of Zeus the Saviour (*Sōtēr*) and Pythian Apollo. | ca. 265 BC. *Nachtergael* 1977: *Actes* 2, 3 and 5; also, *Actes* 7 to 10 (Mette 1977: 67– 71). Cf. Le Guen 2001: ii, 181, s.v. *Sôteria de Delphes*. |
| Thespiae | Mouseia. | Before 230–225 or mid–third century BC. *Schachter* 1986: ii, 163; Mette 1977: 58–61. Cf. Le Guen 2001: ii, TE 22 and 23; ii, 177, s.v. *Mouseia*. |
| Epidaurus | Asklepieia–Apollonia. | End of third or beginning of second century BC. *IG* iv² 1, 99 iii and 100. |
| Ilium | Panathenaia organized by the League of Trojan cities. | Decree of ca. 202 BC. *IK* 3-Ilion, 2.40–1. Cf. L. Robert 1966: 26–30. |
| Dodona | Naia, in honour of Zeus Naios and Dione. | List of victors, ca. 190–170. *SIG*³ 1080. |
| Argos | Heraia. | Ditto. |
| Caunus (Caria) | Letoa-Rhomaia in honour of the goddesses Lētō and Rhōmē. | Agonistic inscription (base of a statue of Polyxenus commemorating his victory at a contest of tragic poets); after 167 BC. |

Table 3 (cont.)

| Place | Festival | Dates and references[a] |
|---|---|---|
| | | SEG 12, 466.1–6 (=I.Kaunos 62). |
| **Magnesia on the Maeander** | Rhomaia. | Lists of victors from ca. 150–100 BC. Mette 1977: 46–48. |
| **Tanagra** (Boeotia) | Sarapieia. | List of victors, 100/90–85 BC. Mette 1977: 53–4. |
| **Orchomenos** (Boeotia) | Charitesia. Homoloia. | First century BC. IG vii, 3195–7. IG vii, 3196, 3197 (Mette 1977: 54–5). |
| **Akraiphia** (Boeotia) | Soteria in honour of Zeus the Saviour (*Sōtēr*). | List of victors 'at the first trieteric contests after the war' (probably Sulla's victorious campaign in Greece against the followers of Mithradates VI). IG vii, 2727 (Mette 1977: 62). |
| **Oropos** | Amphiaraia–Rhomaia. | Lists of victors for the years 85–84 or after 73 BC. I. Oropos, no 523, 524, 525, 526, 528, 531. |

[a] In what follows, '*Nachtergael 1977*' followed by '*Actes*' signifies the epigraphic evidence cited under 'Corpus des actes relatifs aux Sôtêria de Delphes' at the end of that book.

We may possibly need to add to the list earlier in this chapter the Rhomaia of Thebes, of which we know only that they included, between ca. 146 and ca. 87/86, a contest of satyr-drama;[43] also, the Panathenaia, which, according to a list of victors from 162 BC, included 'scenic contests' (*skēnikoi agōnes*), though we do not know what they consisted of (*Hesperia* 60, 1991: 188–9, col. iii, l. 39 and commentary on pages 203–4).

## The Guilds of the Artists of Dionysus

All these festivals could not have been held without the existence of authorities capable of regulating supply and demand, and of furnishing

---

[43] BÉ 2006: 659–60, no. 204. At the time, satyr-drama was performed independently of tragedy, and so we cannot establish whether there were also contests of tragedy or not.

the artists required by the communities organizing dramatic contests – in other words, without the existence of the Artists of Dionysus. These guilds were constituted like miniature cities, established inside states, and regulated by authorities of an essentially religious, financial and administrative character. They issued decrees, negotiated contracts for their members,[44] dispatched embassies and received, in their turn, missions sent by the various political authorities of the time. By virtue of their elaborate structure and the diverse skills of their members, these guilds were privileged interlocutors for the various contest organizers, whose tasks were complicated by overlaps between different event calendars and by the ever-increasing distances that entrants in two different contests were sometimes obliged to cross.

These guilds first appeared around the beginning of the third century BC, according to our sources. They went by the name of Artists (*Technitai*) of Dionysus,[45] were under the protection of Dionysus and, in the case of Egypt, of a Hellenistic monarch,[46] and comprised solely performance specialists possessed of expert skills (*technē*).

Four of those guilds were operative in the Eastern Mediterranean. These were:

1) The *Technitai* based in Athens – perhaps the oldest of these associations and in any case the earliest attested in the sources.[47]

2) The *Technitai* of Egypt, under the tutelage of Dionysus and of the Ptolemaic rulers in their capacity as 'Sibling Gods' (*Theoi Adelphoi*), then as 'Prominent Gods' (*Theoi Epiphaneis*). This association perhaps preceded the one in Athens and was based in Ptolemais and most certainly Alexandria, with a branch in Cyprus between the middle of the second and the beginning of the first century BC.[48]

3) The *Technitai* active at (or travelling to) Isthmus and Nemea, with branches subsequently in Argos, Thebes, Thespiae, Opous, Chalcis and probably also in Sicyon and at Dion in Macedonia.[49]

---

[44] See Le Guen 2004b: 91–4.
[45] In Greek, σύνοδοι or κοινὰ τῶν περὶ τὸν Διόνυσον τεχνιτῶν. See Sifakis 1967: 136–46; Pickard-Cambridge 1988: 279–321; Le Guen 2001; Lightfoot 2002; Aneziri 2003 with Le Guen 2004a.
[46] Aneziri 1994; Le Guen 2003: 353–5 and 2007a: 275–8. See also Le Guen 2016.
[47] Le Guen 2001: ii, General Index, s.v.; Aneziri 2003: 25–51; Le Guen 2007d.
[48] Aneziri 1994; Le Guen 2001: ii. 5–9 and her General Index, s.v.
[49] Le Guen 2001: ii, General Index, s.v.; Aneziri 2003: 51–70.

4) Finally, the *Technitai* active at (or travelling to) Ionia and the Hellespontine region and 'those devoted to Dionysus *Kathēgemōn*', with one branch on Teos and the other in Pergamum.[50]

The titulature used by this last guild is particularly interesting, as it makes evident the artists' privileged area of activity rather than the pool from which they were recruited, since all these associations admitted members from all over the Greek world. Nonetheless, the Artists of Dionysus based in Teos and Pergamum were by no means limited to that geographic area, large as it may have been. A decree issued around 171 BC states in general terms that the *Technitai* took part 'in the contests in honour of Pythian Apollo, the Heliconian Muses and Dionysus, at Delphi during the Pythia and the Soteria, at Thespiae during the Mouseia, and at Thebes during the Agrionia'[51] – that is, in contests held in mainland Greece.

At the end of the second or the beginning of the first century, the Artists of Dionysus appear also in Magna Graecia, namely Rhegion,[52] and in Sicily, namely Syracuse,[53] where there is also evidence for an Artists' guild under the tutelage of Aphrodite *Hilara*, 'the Mirthful'[54] – hardly a banal epithet. Although at about this time our evidence on the older guilds becomes rarer, probably as a result of economic and financial difficulties experienced by numerous Greek cities, the *Technitai* of the Western Greek world seem to thrive: as a result of the conclusion of the Carthaginian Wars, the multiple repercussions of the Roman conquests, and the policies of Roman generals who favoured the 'Dionysiac' triumph, theatrical performances are all of a sudden multiplied, and the demand for scenic artists increases accordingly.

For our purpose, it is important first of all to enumerate the specializations of the members of the Dionysiac guilds that could have had an import on the performance and dissemination of tragedy. All in all, we possess only a single catalogue (lacunose in its lower portion) of artists with a corporate affiliation,[55] one drawn up by the Dionysiac artists of Ptolemais in Egypt towards the end of the reign of Ptolemy II. Among the artists related to the performance of tragedy we find two poets (col. i, 31–3), one actor or protagonist (col. ii, 29–30), four *synagonistai* (actors

---

[50] Le Guen 2001: ii, General Index, s.v.; Aneziri 2003: 71–109; Le Guen 2007d: 260–8.
[51] See *IG* xi(4), 1061.14–16.   [52] *IG* xiv, 615.6–7; cf. Le Guen 2001: i. 317–19, TE 72.
[53] *IG* xiv, 12.1–2; *IG* xiv, 13.4–5; *SEG* 34, 974; cf. Le Guen 2001: i. 319–23, TE 73, 74, 75.
[54] Cf. Le Guen 2001: i. 323–26, TE 76 et 77. A different, but convincing, interpretation of this particular association is to be found in Dimartino 2010 (with previous bibliography).
[55] *OGIS* 51; cf. Le Guen 2001: i. 296–300, TE 61.

other than the protagonist who could not claim the victor's prize),[56] an aulos-player (col. iii, 30–1), one or more chorus trainers (*chorodidaskaloi*) without further specification. Our documentary evidence on the other guilds of the Eastern Mediterranean[57] confirms that these comprised the same kind of artists, including *chorodidaskaloi* specifically designated as tragic chorus trainers,[58] but mentions further the *hypodidaskaloi* of tragedy,[59] whom Photius describes as chorus trainers that appeared in the fourth century BC, when the poets no longer trained the chorus themselves. Still, as noted by Sifakis (1967: 119–20), nearly contemporary inscriptions, dating from the late second and early first centuries BC, mention the same type of artists, who are termed now tragic *chorodidaskaloi*, now tragic *hypodidaskaloi*, but are also associated with non-dramatic choruses. This leads to a twofold conclusion. On the one hand, from the end of the second century onwards, the term *chorodidaskalos*, which originally would have designated, according to Sifakis, the leader of the dithyrambic chorus, becomes interchangeable with the term *hypodidaskalos* – a development that became possible and was even encouraged, in my view, by the fact that the members of the Dionysiac guilds were professionals whose expertise extended to more than one artistic domain, and so were often interchangeable.[60] On the other hand, what characterizes the *chorodidaskaloi/hypodidaskaloi* is their ability to train choruses.

These observations are particularly interesting since they imply that tragic performances in the Hellenistic era could still include choruses and that the guilds of Dionysiac artists were capable of providing the specialists necessary for such performances – with one exception: the sources at our disposal make no mention of tragic chorus-members. How are we to explain this? And what type of tragic performance are we talking about anyway? Before attempting to answer these questions, I would like to add one last point.

If the guilds of Dionysiac artists could contribute, as they did, to the theatre life of the Hellenistic era, it is because they offered their members numerous privileges that were often vital for the exercise of their art. For all of their members as a whole, they requested the respective competent authorities (the Amphictionic council managing the Delphic sanctuary, the sovereign of Cappadocia, the Roman generals such as L. Mummius and Sulla) to confer, to confirm or to prorogue some of those privileges,

---

[56] Cf. Aneziri 1997: 59–60.  [57] Cf. Le Guen 2001: ii. 104–8.
[58] Cf. Le Guen 2001: ii. 125, 128.  [59] Cf. Le Guen 2001: ii. 107.
[60] Le Guen 2001: ii. 105–30.

which had previously been awarded individually and sparingly. Some of the most important privileges were the *asphaleia*, a security pledge prohibiting the arrest of *Technitai* in times of war, and the *asylia* (inviolability), which protected them from uncontrolled acts of seizure (of persons or goods) or reprisal in times of peace, except in the case of debts privately incurred. Thanks to these privileges, the Artists of Dionysus could move about in safety in a world continuously torn by conflict, and exercise their *métier* to the best of their abilities.[61] There were also other advantages, just as valuable and related to the itinerant nature of the Artists' profession, such as the exemption from military service and from the obligation to provide shelter to soldiery (both requirements were regarded as especially onerous by those who had to shoulder them).

## New and Old Tragedies

Thanks principally to the evidence for Athens, we know that the programme of the Great Dionysia and the Lenaea was modified over time, as indeed was the case with a number of other festivals too.[62] With regard to our subject, tragedy, a contest for tragic actors, with a prize for the victor, was instituted alongside the contest of tragic poets around 449 in the Great Dionysia and around 432 in the Lenaea. Further, the *Fasti* for 387/6 attest to a novelty of capital importance for the history of Greek theatre: namely, the performance, before the dramatic contests and *hors concours*, of an 'old tragedy' staged by actors.[63] This is a crucial innovation, since it is the point of origin of the dramatic repertoire of ancient Greece and also of the literary patrimony to which we are heirs.[64] According to our sources, these revivals of 'old tragedy' became a regular feature of the festival ca. 341/0. They were subsequently incorporated into the competitive part of the festival, in the course of the third century BC (see later in this chapter). In any case, the fact is that the distinction between 'old' and 'new' tragedy introduced at that time in Athens is found again in victors' lists from other cities in the Hellenistic period, and not only with regard to Dionysiac festivals (see further later in this chapter).

In view of the sources available, what can we claim to know of the place these two types of performance occupied in the festivals and also of the way in which the plays, both old and new, were performed? Was the chorus always an inalienable feature of tragedy, and if yes, were its members

---

[61] Le Guen 2001: ii. 69–71.   [62] W. J. Slater 2007.   [63] See Duncan and Liapis, this volume.
[64] Cf. Easterling 1997.

selected from the organizing community or were they professional choreuts recruited for the occasion, as actors were? After attempting to answer such questions, we shall reflect, finally, on the meanings that tragic performances could still carry several centuries after the birth of tragedy.

### Known Contests for New and/or Old Tragedy

I begin with some methodological points. In the absence of formal indicators, it is impossible to deduce from the simple epigraphic attestation of the word 'Dionysia' that the festival thus designated was modelled on the Athenian Dionysia and that it included similar contests, that is, a contest of 'old' tragedy, where only the actor was entitled to a prize, and a contest of new tragedy, where both poets and actors were competing for prizes.

Thanks to the Archons' lists from Delos' second period of independence (314–167 BC) we know, for instance, that the programme of the Delian Dionysia, apart from a dithyrambic contest for boys (παῖδες) only, included also contests for tragedy and comedy, with two troupes competing in each category. Our sources mention repeatedly *chorēgoi* for performances in both genres, which means that the plays performed included choruses; however, the evidence does not allow us to determine whether they were choruses of old or of new tragedy. All the same, there is at least one inscription (*IG* xi 2, 120.50, 236 BC) attesting, for this period, a performance by one tragic poet *hors concours*, alongside comic and dithyrambic poets, and so we can suppose that, among these artists, there were more than one who had previously taken part in real contests.[65] The Dionysia on Delos could thus have included a contest of new tragedy, securely attested for a different period (the year 111/10, that is, during the second period of Athenian dominance) on the basis of a dedicatory inscription by the Athenian tragic poet Dionysius, son of Demetrius, after his victory 'over the poets of tragedy and satyr drama'.[66] However, according to Sifakis, the vast majority of actors mentioned in the Archons' lists, compared to the number of poets, seems to suggest that poets' competitions (and so new plays) were not a regular feature at the Dionysia on Delos.[67]

The island of Cos has also yielded an interesting piece of evidence in this respect.[68] The extant choregic inscriptions from the late third and early

---

[65] Cf. Sifakis 1967: 24.   [66] See *ID* 1959.   [67] Cf. Sifakis, n. 65 earlier in this chapter.
[68] *IG* xii 4, 2, 452A–B. Cf. Ceccarelli 1995: 287–305 and 1998: 121–5.

second centuries allow us to conclude that the Dionysia of Cos required three *chorēgoi* for tragedy (one from each tribe, as the dithyrambic and dramatic contests were organized according to tribal standards). Comedy, by contrast, was the responsibility of an *epimelētēs*, which seems to support the assumption that comedies at Cos, unlike tragedies, were performed without a chorus.[69] And from the fact that we know the names of some comic and tragic actors, but never those of playwrights, I would be willing to deduce that only repertoire pieces were performed on the island, complete with choruses (in the case of tragedy).

Moreover, whereas contests could differ from one year to the next in one and the same city for various political and/or financial reasons,[70] festivals in which tragedies were performed did not necessarily include a real agonistic component. The best illustration of this point comes from the Carian city of Iasos, which has yielded an exceptional corpus allowing us to gauge the cultural and theatrical activity of a Hellenistic polis. The corpus, which has been made the object of numerous studies,[71] comprises today fifty-six lists of voluntary financial contributions tendered by magistrates and/or *chorēgoi* (both citizens but also metics in the case of dramatic (as opposed to dithyrambic) *chorēgiai*), while they were in office or after they had retired, by way of sharing in the financing of theatrical activities during a large part of the second century.[72] These texts throw light not only on the programme of events organized by the city of Iasos but also on the ways in which it managed first to adapt its choregic system, in a period of great financial stress, and then to rationalize it. During a first period, which extends, according to Léopold Migeotte (1993: 268–78), from 199 to 185 BC, the generous donors mentioned in the lists were apparently willing to finance only *hors concours* performances, as suggested by the term θέα, 'spectacle' (as opposed to ἀγών, 'contest'), found repeatedly on the inscriptions, as well as by the fact that the city recruited, for engagements of one or more days, performers of both sexes, some of whom could never have been allowed to perform at the dramatic contests of the Dionysia. Such is the case of the *choropsaltria*, or harpist accompanied by a chorus, who was recruited in the same way as comic actors, cithara and aulos-players, and a tragic actor. As this was a troubled period – an earthquake in

---

[69] Cf. Wilson 2000: 290.   [70] Cf. W.J. Slater 2010: 276.
[71] Crowther 1990: 143–51; 1995: 225–34; 2007: 294–334; Migeotte 1993: 267–94; Delrieux 1996: 371–88; Maddoli 2000: 15–32; 2007: 353–61; Maurizi 2000: 42–68.
[72] The corpus includes also a decree by the Dionysiac *Technitai* of Anatolia (*IK* 28.1-Iasos, 152), found *in situ* by Le Bas 'sur la base du mur du théâtre', as well as four lists mentioning donations for reconstruction works in the theatre (*IK* 28.1-Iasos, 179, 180, 182, 183).

199/8, armed conflict marking the wresting of the city from Philip V by Antiochus III in 197, lack of 'concord' among citizens[73] – this must have affected public finances, and so it seems to me highly unlikely that the authorities of Iasos would have sought to lend, by means of subscriptions, even more splendour to the city's festivals, i.e., to add a further set of performances to the contests that traditionally formed part of their programme (of which, however, we know next to nothing).[74] I would rather tend to believe that their repeated appeals to the generosity of *agōnothetai* and *chorēgoi*, whether still in office or retired, were intended, for lack of a better alternative, to furnish the city's Dionysia with musical and/or dramatic performances at a time when it would have been absolutely impossible to finance real dramatic contests. As for the donors' pledges, they were, in those uncertain times, a formal guarantee that the Dionysia of the following year would feature stage performances by musicians and/or actors. Little did it matter that this was not a contest in the full sense of the term.[75] Although not under entirely comparable circumstances, we know that on different occasions artists (including tragic actors) could showcase (*epideixeis*) their talent in performances on the fringe of the main event.[76] And we know also that during the winter festival of Soteria at Delphi, there were no contests, properly speaking.

To return to Iasos, after a second period of adjustment during 185–180 BC (which should be inserted between the two periods already identified by Léopold Migeotte, i.e., from 199 to 185 and from ca. 185/80 to 120/115 BC), the system was finally rationalized: indeed, a set of inscriptions dating from 125–120 no longer mention the names of artists involved or of their specialities, and the word θέα disappears. Mention is now made only of the amounts (strictly identical from one year to the next) paid by the *agonothetēs* in office and by the former *chorēgoi*. These amounts were to be expended according to the needs and wishes of the Iasians, and so they must have served, in my opinion, either to supplement public funds towards the celebration of Dionysia complete with lyric

---

[73] Cf. Migeotte 1993: 276.
[74] We do know, however, that around 270–260 BC, the programme comprised a contest of choral song (*IK* 28.1-Iasos, 82.20).
[75] It is symptomatic that the term θέα, 'spectacle', is used in lieu of ἀγών, 'contest', in the corpus of documents dating from ca. 190–180 – for instance, in a decree from Skepsis in the Troad reporting a decision by the community to organize, during the Dionysia, choral performances in honour of the god, without however including an *agōn* properly speaking; for supplements in lines 26–8 see Wilhelm 1900: 54–7 and 1940: 61.
[76] Cf. (*inter alia*) for Delos, *IG* xi, 105.16–18 (284 BC); *IG* xi, 108.17–19 (279 BC); for Perinthos or Herakleia see *Perinthos-Herakleia*, 2 (third/second century).

and/or dramatic contests, or to make up for the lack of public funds towards non-competitive displays, or to finance partly or entirely *hors concours* performances intended to lend splendour to the contests.

At any rate, it is certain that during the 150s or in the second or third quarter of the second century, the Iasians were faced once more with a tricky situation (an inscription makes reference to ἀναγκαιοτάτοις καιροῖς, 'most urgent circumstances').[77] Unable to organize their own 'contests in honour of Dionysus',[78] they asked the Guild of *Technitai* of Ionia and the Hellespont for help. They responded by offering – without financial compensation and in the name of their long-standing friendship – two tragic protagonists, two comic protagonists, a cithara player, a citharode, as well as assistants to all of those. The participation of two troupes, one for each dramatic genre, made sure that dramatic contests would be held, while that of the cithara player and the citharode suggests performances by at least two choruses (the word is in the plural in l. 16), the latter apparently supplied by the city and performing to accompaniment by the two aforementioned professionals.

In light of the previous specifications, the victory lists, the contestants' lists and the dedication that have survived, to which we should add a decree by the Dionysiac *Technitai* of Athens, allow us to affirm with absolute certainty the existence of the following contests, at least for the periods to which our sources correspond:

- **Old and new tragedies**: At the Heraia of Samos, at the Mouseia of Thespiae, at the Soteria of Akraiphia, at the Sarapieia of Tanagra, at the Charitesia of Orchomenos, at the Amphiaraia–Rhomaia of Oropos and at the musical contest established by the *Technitai* of Athens in honour of Ariarathes V of Cappadocia.
- **Old tragedies**: At the Amphictionic Soteria of Delphi, at the Naia of Dodona, at the Heraia of Argos and at the Homoloia of Orchomenos.
- **New tragedies**: At the Rhomaia of Magnesia on the Maeander and at the Letoa–Rhomaia of Caunus.

It is possible that the Naia of Dodona and the Heraia of Argos also included contests of new tragedy, and that the Rhomaia of Magnesia on the Maeander and the Letoa–Rhomaia of Caunus included, inversely, contests of old tragedy; however, there is no such documentary evidence to date. We may add that the Mouseia of Thespiae and the Amphictionic Soteria of Delphi, just like the Agrionia of Thebes (see later in this

---

[77] *IK* 28.1-Iasos, 152.27–8.   [78] *l.c.* (n. 77), ll. 12–13.

chapter), were co-organized, respectively, by the cities of Thespiae, Delphi and Thebes in collaboration with the *Technitai* of Isthmus and Nemea, a guild whose members also took part in the contests – as indeed did the members of other guilds.[79]

In the case of decrees stipulating that there be a public proclamation of privileges accorded by a city just before the contest of tragedy at the Dionysia, I am convinced that the relevant events were contests of new rather than old tragedy, as was the case in Athens since the fourth century (or the late fifth, according to Wilson and Hartwig 2009: 17–27),[80] and as evidenced also by an honorific decree of the Milesians living at Lepsia dated to ca. 169 BC (*IIsolMil* 18.25).[81] The occasion chosen for the proclamation of public honours (just before the performance of the contest of new tragedy) was surely significant, and it revealed the deep links between tragedy, politics and civic community, since the tragic choruses were composed of members from the entire citizen body (Ceccarelli 2010 also stresses this point).

As the large majority of Hellenistic cities took Athenian usage as their model both for their theatrical practices and for the proclamation of honours conferred, I seriously doubt that they could have found a moment

[79] See Le Guen 2001: i. 173; Aneziri 2007: 77.
[80] From the beginning of the fifth century to the first decade of the fourth, the City Dionysia included only contests of new plays, be they tragedies, satyr-dramas or comedies. However, in 387/6 an important change occured, a '*palaion drama*' (i.e., a previously performed tragedy) was staged again, this time by tragic actors, as the first item of the festival and *hors concours*. This is the reason why, in 330 BC, (*Against Ctesiphon* 34) specifies the contest of new tragedies as the event chosen for the announcement of public honours (τραγωιδιῶν γιγνομένων καινῶν), distinguishing the non-competitive performance of 'old tragedy' from the contest of new tragedy. A second major change occurred between 283/2 and 270/69, as shown by two epigraphic sources. The crowns awarded by the Athenian People to the poet Philippides of Kephale in 283/2 (*IG* ii³ 1, 877.62–3) and to Kallias of Sphettos in 270/69 (*IG* ii³ 1, 911.93–4) were to be announced, respectively, 'at the tragedy competition of the Great Dionysia (Διονυσίων τῶν μεγάλων τραγῳδῶν τῷ ἀγῶνι)' and 'at the new tragedy competition of the Great Dionysia (Διονυσίων τῶν μεγάλων τραγῳδῶν τῷ ἀγῶνι τῷ καινῷ)'. The latter expression, which is also attested in another honorific decree dated to 259/8 (*IG* ii³ 1, 985.76–7), underlines the specific nature of the contest in question and clearly indicates that the programme of the City Dionysia had been expanded to include old tragedies. Afterwards two formulas of the same meaning alternate in the honorific decrees (and sometimes even in the same inscription, cf. *IG* ii³ 1, 1256.31 et 59) referring to the new tragedy competition as the appropriate time for proclaiming honours and crowns: ἀνειπεῖν τὸν στέφανον (*vel sim.*) Διονυσίων τῶν ἐν ἄστει καινοῖς τραγωιδοῖς (cf. *IG* ii³ 1, 1150.10, *IG* ii³ 1, 1178.16–17, *IG* ii³ 1, 1185.21, *IG* ii³ 1, 1218.12–13, *IG* ii³ 1, 1290.93–4, *IG* ii³ 1, 1292.48–9, *IG* ii³ 1, 1313.39–40, *IG* ii³ 1, 1362.8–9, *IG* ii³ 1, 1392.14–15, etc.); and ἀνειπεῖν τὸν στέφανον (*vel sim.*) Διονυσίων τῶν ἐν ἄστει τραγῳδιῶν τῶι καινῶι ἀγῶνι (cf. *IG* ii³ 1, 1147.37–8, *IG* ii³ 1, 1215.8–9, *IG* ii³ 1, 1256.31, *IG* ii³ 1, 1281.5–6, *IG* ii³ 1, 1348.2–3, *IG* ii³ 1, 1390.9, *IG* ii² 1039.62, *IG* ii² 1040.37, *IG* ii² 1041.29, *IG* ii² 1042.frg d.8, *IG* ii² 1043.53–4, etc.
[81] The adjective καινοῖς implies a distinction between new plays and revivals of old plays similar to that obtaining in Athens at the beginning of the third century BC.

less symbolically laden to grant awards. Thus, I conclude that in the case of Aigyalē on Amorgos, Andros, Eresos, Ios, Ioulis, Karthaia, Lepsia, Naxos, Paros, Salamis, Samos, Siphnos, Syros, Tenos, and also of Didyma, Smyrna, Priene and perhaps Miletus and Teos, the tragic contests attested in the sources mentioned earlier comprised – at least in the periods to which those sources correspond – only new pieces composed specifically for those occasions. I shall go even further.

## Old and New Tragedies, Choruses and Dionysiac Artists

When a city chose the contest of new tragedy as the occasion on which to announce the names of those to whom honours were awarded, the new tragedies in question were always performed, in my opinion, with choruses consisting of citizens, as in Athens. My hypothesis relies on the prominence of civic choruses in Hellenistic sources. On Samos, for instance, an honorific decree for Telestratos, son of Diogenes from Magnesia (second half of the second century BC), specifies that he be crowned 'on the occasion of the tragic contests at the Dionysia, when the city will assemble its next choruses in honour of the god' (ὅταν τοὺς πρώτους χοροὺς ἡ πόλις τῷ θεῷ συντελῇ, l. 31–2).[82] The importance of the chorus may also be deduced from an inscription of Eresos (*Milet* I 3, 152C.88), which specifies that a *khorostatas*[83] shall be responsible for the public proclamation of honours (crowns) during the Dionysia and in particular, as another passage in the same text indicates (l. 75 ff.), on the occasion of the contest of tragedy.

By contrast, when the proclamation of honours is held before the dithyrambic contest in cities known to celebrate the Dionysia, I consider this as evidence for the (temporary or longer-lasting) absence of contests of new tragedy in which citizen choruses would have participated. Such absence may be the result of the high cost (too high sometimes) involved in holding a Dionysia festival complete with theatrical performances;[84] indeed, lack of sufficient funds would have made it especially difficult to

---

[82] *IG* xii 6, 1, 154. The text of the inscription is partly restored on the basis of the previous lines and of parallel texts (cf. *IPriene* 75.8–10); further sources demonstrate that a choregic system was in place on the island of Samos.

[83] The same official appears again, in a similar context, in *IG* xii Suppl 34, 121 and in *IK* 25-Parion, 2.

[84] Already in the classical era, some demes were unable to produce, at the Rural Dionysia, contests comprising both dithyrambic and dramatic performances (the latter including both tragedy and comedy). For example, there is no evidence for dithyramb in Thorikos. In Aixone, there appear to have been comedies only in either 339 or 312 BC (*IG* ii² 1202), again with no evidence for dithyrambs at those dates.

hire professional actors and chorus trainers.[85] One may reasonably imagine that chorus rehearsals, under the baton of a specially hired *chorodidaskalos* or a *hypodidaskalos* (for the terms see earlier in this chapter), involved high expenses, especially when added to those already incurred towards actors' salaries, no matter in which direction the tragic chorus may have evolved in the meantime.

This, at any rate, is how I understand the set of inscriptions from Priene, which give an account of the Dionysia and the rewards announced on that occasion. Whereas in the third century the *agonothetēs* announced the honours bestowed either before the beginning of the tragic contests (e.g., *IPriene* 23.14) or before the beginning of the dithyrambic contest (*IPriene* 21.19), in the second century, those inscriptions that contain a time reference mention only the dithyrambic contest, even with specific reference to the category of 'boys' choruses' (*IPriene* 53 II.70).

If Greek cities continued, during the Hellenistic period, to emphasize more particularly that choral performances were held in honour of Dionysus, I do not think we ought to be surprised (*pace* Ceccarelli 2010) if it is to the contest of dithyramb (or of any other choral song for that matter) that the proclamation of honours should have been transferred whenever it proved impossible to organize a contest of (new) tragedy. We find such transferals in, for instance, Iasos during the 270s–260s, on Kyme after 130 BC, and even at Delphi.[86] And I would be prepared to believe that the unspecific phrasing used in certain decrees, to the effect that the proclamation of honours will take place (in the theatre)[87] during the (following) Dionysia festival,[88] or during the following Dionysiac contests,[89] with no further details provided, allowed the organizers some necessary leeway, since they had no way of knowing which contests they would actually be able to hold in the end.

What is true of the Dionysia must also be true, it seems to me, for those dramatic festivals that were held in honour of other gods too. The proclamation of the honours bestowed on Thrasycles by the Island League between 291 and 287 during the tragic contests of the Ptolemaia[90] makes

---

[85] As W. J. Slater (2010: 249, 251) puts it, 'drama is more expensive than most other entertainment, and particularly when it is connected with choral singing and dancing'; 'it is immediately obvious that a Dionysia-type festival with its separate dramatic troupes and choruses was a far more difficult and expensive project than a thymelic or even gymnastic festival'.
[86] Iasos: *IK* 28.1-Iasos, 82.20–1. Kyme: *IK* 5-Kyme, 13.7. Delphi: *CID* 4, 87.32–3 and 88.6–7.
[87] Cf. (*inter alia*) the Dionysia of Olbia in Pontos, *SEG* 34, 758. 49–50; the Dionysia of Kalchedon, *IK* 20- Kalchedon, 1.70–1 and 2.11; the Dionysia of Cyzicus, *IMT* 1437.11–12, etc.
[88] For example, *Milet* I 3, 153.24–5; *IPriene* 61.17.   [89] For example, *IK* 30-Keramos, 9.10–11.
[90] *IG* xi 4, 1043.14–16.

me think that that was a contest of new tragedy. And the same conclusion must hold also for the Panathenaia of Ilion in the last third of the third century.[91]

Let us now move to the Demetrieia, established, in addition to the Dionysia, by the Euboean cities of Chalcis, Eretria, Oreos and Carystus. For their individual celebrations of this festival, the cities hired choruses of boys and men, aulos-players, tragic and comic actors, *chorodidaskaloi* and *didaskaloi* for comedy and tragedy[92] – but no playwrights. This leads me to conclude that on those occasions there was no contest of new plays, either tragedies or comedies. This conclusion is corroborated by the fact that, on the island, the tragic contests of the Dionysia, at least on the evidence of post-fourth-century sources, are no longer dedicated to the proclamation of honours. However, the Euboean inscription documenting the contests contains a curious reference to 'choruses of male tragedians' (χοροὶ τῶν ἀνδρῶν τραγῳδῶν, l. 31), for which Sifakis (1967: 116, and 2007: 211) has provided what I think is the only plausible explanation: namely, that these were hired professionals who took part in the contest for cyclic choruses of men but also doubled as members of the tragic choruses. This, then, would be proof that the dramatic festivals held in the four principal cities of Euboea comprised performances of old tragedy complete with professional choruses – provided perhaps, as the actors were, by a guild of Dionysiac artists, which counted among their number dithyrambic choreuts, if not tragic ones.[93] And we can better see the point of the high salaries paid to each of the three aulos-players who performed at the Euboean festivals: they were hired in order to accompany not only choruses of boys and men, but also the arias of tragic actors and the songs of tragic choruses.

At Delphi, during the Amphictionic Soteria established to commemorate the Greek victory over the Galatians, the occasion chosen for the

[91] *IK* 3-Ilion, 2.41.
[92] The *didaskaloi* were probably trainers of actors, as a parallel for the Delphic Soteria suggests (*SIG*³ 424 = Nachtergael, *Actes*, 7; ca. 260–256 BC). Sometimes, *didaskaloi* (instead of the usual *protagonistai*) directed revivals of 'old' tragedies.
[93] In any case, there is no evidence against the existence of a guild of *Technitai* on Euboea at the time of the inscription discussed earlier in this chapter. Indeed, we only have a *terminus ante quem* for the date in which these guilds were introduced (279/8 or 278/7). By contrast, we know that the *Technitai* of Isthmus and Nemea provided for the Dionysia of Thebes (renamed Agrionia when they were promoted to an *agōn stephanitēs*: see Le Guen 2001: i. 139) aulos-players and choreuts for the dithyrambic contest as well as tragic and comic actors – whose mention, in and of itself, does not allow us to determine the nature of the scenic pieces performed. There is no mention, in contemporary sources, of a proclamation of honours during the festival, which may suggest that no new tragedies were performed.

proclamation of honours was not the tragic contest but either the dithyrambic or the gymnic contest. This is to be explained, as in the case of Euboea, by the nature of the plays performed, which were repertoire pieces rather than new creations.[94] Indeed, on those festival lists that include the names not only of victors but also of all other participants, we notice that (leaving comedy out of the discussion) two or three troupes of tragic actors, depending on the vagaries of the hiring process, annually competed against each other. We may ignore the precise status of each of the artists listed under 'Tragic Actors' on those lists, but we do know that each troupe of tragic actors always included a principal actor (protagonist) flanked by a second and a third actor (the deuteragonist and the tritagonist, respectively), an aulos-player and a *didaskalos*. The presence of the *didaskalos* corresponds to the absence of a poet-director and suggests on the one hand that at the Amphictionic Soteria the actors performed only repertoire pieces, not new plays, and on the other hand that the staging of those pieces was not the responsibility of actors, as was the case in Athens and elsewhere, but of a person charged with that specific task, namely the *didaskalos*.[95] There is nothing in these lists, however, to suggest either that those old tragedies were performed with a chorus or that they were not. One could subscribe to K. von Jan's proposal, cited with approval by Sifakis,[96] that, as was the case on Euboea, the members of the adult male dithyrambic chorus doubled as tragic choreuts too; alternatively, one could adopt Peter Wilson's thesis,[97] to the effect that choruses on certain occasions consisted not of hired professionals but of citizens belonging to the organizing communities. Still, there is a third alternative, namely that proposed by William Slater, who argues that old tragedies were performed without choruses.[98] For my part, I shall refrain from associating myself with one or the other position, since the one thing I am certain of is that in this matter there was no general rule that could be held valid regardless of time and place. In the current state of our evidence, it would be, I think, extremely risky to attempt a distinction between, on the one hand, contests modelled on the Dionysia (regardless of their actual appellation) and featuring dithyrambic and dramatic contests, albeit the latter's tragic component may have been reduced to the production of old tragedies

---

[94] This important point is disregarded by Ceccarelli 2010: 122.
[95] The list of victories, found at Tegea, by an anonymous tragic actor also testifies to the existence of a contest of old tragedy at the Soteria, albeit at the time of the festival's reorganization by the Etolians (*SIG*³ 1080, dated to 190–170).
[96] Sifakis 1967: 116 n. 3; 2007: 212, n. 10.    [97] Wilson 2000: 289.
[98] W.J. Slater 2010: 254 with n. 18.

without choruses,[99] and on the other hand contests, for instance those called *stephanitai* or *hieroi* ('crown-games' and 'sacred games', respectively), which were open to participants from all over the Greek or Hellenized world and included contests both of old and of new tragedy. The reason for this is a simple one: as I have shown, there was no strictly defined programme typical of all Dionysia festivals in the Hellenistic period, even if we limit our account only to the dramatic component of the festivals: in some cases, the Dionysia included only 'old' tragedies, while in others only new ones. As for the sacred contests, it is impossible to prove that they all included contests both of 'old' and of new tragedy, performed in all cases in the same manner.

As for the Antigoneia and the Demetrieia of Samos – in which as famous an actor as Polos of Aegina agreed to take part, on the request of special envoys and for a lower fee than his usual rate – there is nothing to suggest that real contests were part of their programme. We may nonetheless suppose that, if the Antigonids wished to give maximum splendour to the festivities they had established to celebrate their victory over the Lagids at Salamis in Cyprus, then they would have surely organized proper dramatic contests, as Alexander had done before them after his military victories. The inscription documenting the event (*IG* xii, 6,1, 56, ?306/5 BC) is crowned by a relief depicting a man with a club, and so one reasonably speculates that the actor may have played the role of Heracles. It is, however, impossible to determine whether the play in question was Sophocles' or Euripides' *Heracles* (and so an 'old' tragedy) or a play composed by a fourth-century author, which could have been classified either as an 'old' or as a new tragedy. Indeed, a number of later tragedians are credited with tragedies entitled *Heracles*: Demetrius, Astydamas II, Diogenes of Sinope and Lycophron.[100] We can go no further than that, however, especially since we are not even certain that the role Polos of Aegina performed was actually the title-role.

Finally, in the case of the Asklepieia-Apollonia of Epidaurus, which we associate with tragic contests only because two tragic actors appear in the epigraphic lists of artists fined for violating the terms of their contracts during the festival,[101] there is no way for us to determine the type of tragedy or tragedies performed.

---

[99] For these contests, W.J. Slater (2010: 264) uses the term *nemētoi agōnes*, as the artists were contracted well in advance of the relevant events.
[100] See Le Guen 2007b: 93.   [101] See Le Guen 2004b: 99–101.

## Conclusion

What are we to conclude from the preceding analysis? First of all, obviously, that tragedy became a considerably widespread phenomenon from the fourth century onwards: at the end of the Hellenistic period, we find its traces throughout the eastern and the western Mediterranean. Further evidence, if any was needed, is provided by the famous episode reported by Plutarch in his *Life of Crassus* (33. 1–7). In the year 53 BC, after the battle of Carrhae, a banquet was held at the court of the Armenian ruler Artawazd II (no doubt at the capital Artaxata) to celebrate the wedding of the king's sister with the son of the Parthian king Arsacides, sealing the alliance between the two kingdoms. On that occasion, while the tragic actor Jason of Tralles sang the role of Agave from Euripides' *Bacchae*, the satrap of Mesopotamia entered the hall with the head of Crassus, the defeated Roman general, in his hands. The actor, we are told, took hold of the head and incorporated it into the action, as if it were the head of Pentheus. Regardless of the truthfulness of this report, or of the specific reasons for which the Armenian king, himself a tragic poet, wished to have Greek artists at that event, or of the exact way in which *Bacchae* was performed, the event is evidence for the widespread dissemination of the art of drama and for the far-reaching activities of artists, promoted by the establishment of the guilds of Dionysiac artists.[102]

As we have seen, both old and new tragedies were performed in various cities and at various times, in numerous festivals, in honour both of Dionysus and (now) of other gods, although the link with the theatre god *par excellence* was never broken, since tragedies were most often produced with the aid of Dionysiac artists, who were expressly under the god's tutelage.[103] All the same, we cannot reduce those 'old' tragedies to the works produced by the three great fifth-century Athenian poets, Aeschylus, Sophocles and Euripides. True, an anonymous tragic actor had it inscribed on his list of victories that, between the second half of the third century and the years 190–170, he won the day with his performances in Euripidean dramas at Athens, Delphi, Argos and Dodona; still, he also mentions an occasion in which he performed, equally triumphantly, Chaeremon's *Achilles* and Archestratus' *Antaeus*, the latter being virtually impossible to date, as we have no secure information about him. In any case, the evidence suggests that the 'old' tragedies performed by later actors, who included them in their repertoire as old favourites,

---

[102] Cf. Easterling 1997: 221–2.   [103] See Le Guen 2003: 353.

were by no means limited to those pieces that have come down to us after a process of selection made by philologists and grammarians according to very different criteria.

With regard to the evidence discussed earlier in this chapter, we shall need to remember two more things. First, that during the last three centuries BC, one could still produce performances of both old and new tragedies complete with choruses, the choreuts being often ordinary citizens rather than professionals – although I must stress again that members of dithyrambic choruses, hired from the guilds of Dionysiac artists, could also double, at least in part, as members of tragic choruses too. Second, that the Hellenistic period is not, in my view, the end of the symbiosis between city and tragedy.[104] As long as the cities possessed the financial means to organize Dionysia festivals featuring theatrical events that included new tragedies, they continued to use those events as the occasion on which to proclaim honours and awards bestowed. Having said that, I do not mean to suggest that Hellenistic tragedy underwent no formal developments. On the contrary, the importance of song increased considerably, as suggested indirectly by the fact that a number of Dionysiac artists had the double specialization of singer and of tragic actor.[105] The predominance of song, in its turn, explains the success of choral performances in a very large number of cities.

Finally, I wish to emphasize that the expansion of tragedy, both old and new, led to the dissemination of various plays, which had won first prize in the past, as well as to the continuation of a long creative tradition, throughout the Greek and the Hellenized world. This phenomenon continued under the Roman Empire too. Among the victors at the Mouseia festival of Thespiae, ca. 160–9 AD, we find both an actor of ancient tragedy and a poet and an actor of new tragedy.[106]

---

[104] The opposite conclusion is reached by Ceccarelli (2010: 143–6), who fails, however, to take into account the previous considerations on the nature of the tragedies performed.
[105] Le Guen 2001: ii. 126–9 and 2007b: 115–19.   [106] *IG* vii, 1773.21–2, 24–7.

CHAPTER 6

# Theatre Performance After the Fifth Century

## Anne Duncan and Vayos Liapis*

### The Formation of a Canon and the Emergence of a Repertory Tradition

In 340 BC, the tragic playwright Astydamas the Younger won first prize in the tragedy competition at the Great Dionysia with *Lycaon* and *Parthenopaeus*, the latter a play about the son of Atalanta who was one of the Seven against Thebes. This was Astydamas' second victory in a row at the Dionysia; in 341, he had won with his *Achilles*, *Athamas* and *Antigone*.[1] It is a mark of Astydamas' popularity that the people of Athens voted to set up his portrait statue in the Theatre of Dionysus. (All that remains of the statue is the base, with only the first four letters of Astydamas' name legible.[2]) Reportedly, Astydamas composed an inscription for his own statue, but it was so self-congratulatory that the Athenians refused to have it inscribed on the statue.[3] In the inscription, Astydamas complained that the only reason he is not considered the equal – or superior – of Aeschylus, Sophocles and Euripides is that they all lived before his time, and are thus immune to the 'envy' of Astydamas' contemporaries. Astydamas' epigram seems to have become a byword for extravagant self-praise, as suggested in a fragment by the fourth-century comedian Philemon: "You're praising

---

* The sections on 'The formation of a canon and the emergence of a repertory tradition', 'Innovation in later tragedy', 'Canonization and Lycurgus', 'Architecture of the theatres', 'Theatrical machinery', 'The rise of the actor', 'Acting style', 'Standardization of masks' and 'Conclusion' are by Duncan. The rest of the chapter is the work of Liapis. Both authors have read and commented on each other's sections but remain responsible only for their respective contributions.
[1] *IG* ii² 2320 = Millis and Olson 2012: 65; see Pickard-Cambridge 1988: 107–9.
[2] See *TrGF* I, 60 T 2a; Papastamati-von Moock 2014: 23–34; Scodel 2007: 148; Pickard-Cambridge 1946: 135–6. Astydamas' statue must have been erected shortly after his victory in 340 BC; Papastamati-von Moock (*l.c.*); Hanink 2014b: 51–2, 183–8, 198.
[3] For sources and discussion see Snell 1971: 152; Page 1981: 33; Papastamati-von Moock 2014: 28–31; Scodel 2007: 148; most recently, Hanink 2014b: 183–8.

yourself like Astydamas, woman!"[4] Whether exaggerated by comic poets or not, Astydamas' conceitedness does not diminish the significance of his back-to-back victories in the tragic competition, nor, indeed, the boldness of his self-promotion. One prominent scholar of the Greek theatre, T. B. L. Webster, has called Astydamas' inscription 'a manifesto' for fourth-century tragedy.[5] To understand why, it is helpful to note that in the years 341, 340 and 339, i.e., at the time of Astydamas' victories, three 'old tragedies' by Euripides were also revived at the Great Dionysia: *Iphigenia*, *Orestes* and a third play whose title has not been preserved.[6] By this time, the works of Euripides had become canonical, along with those of Aeschylus and Sophocles. By praising himself as the equal (at least) of the 'Big Three,' Astydamas was challenging the canon, and implicitly questioning the valuation of fifth-century tragedy over contemporary, fourth-century tragedy.

## Fourth-Century Tragedy and the Tragic Canon

It is during the fourth century that we see the crystallization of a tragic canon, in which the three great tragedians of the fifth century have pride of place. Their dramatic output becomes part of a body of texts considered authoritative and magisterial: they are generally acknowledged as paragons of literary creativity for subsequent generations to aspire to and to draw inspiration from. This is a development that seems to begin already in the late fifth century. The three contestants seriously considered in Aristophanes' *Frogs* for the distinction of being brought back to the upper world are Aeschylus, Euripides and Sophocles.[7] And a few decades later, in the mid-to-late fourth century, Heraclides of Pontus, a pupil of Aristotle's, could write a treatise entitled simply *On the Three Tragic Poets* (Περὶ τῶν τριῶν τραγῳδοποιῶν), evidently on the assumption that the identity of the 'Big Three' needed no further specification.[8] More important, as early as 386 BC, performances of 'old tragedy' – i.e., a tragedy by one of the canonical

---

[4] fr. 169 KA. See Hanink 2014a: 205–6; 2014b: 183–8; Scodel 2007: 148; Capps 1900: 41–2.
[5] Webster 1954: 306.
[6] See *IG* ii² 2320, col. ii (= *TrGF* I, DID A 2), 2–3, 18–19, 32–3 = Millis and Olson 2012: 65 (ll. 3–4, 20–1, 34–5). Cf. Pickard-Cambridge 1988: 99–100. See Duncan 2015; Nervegna 2007: 15; Xanthakis-Karamanos 1980: 21. Vahtikari 2014: 172 and Taplin 2007a: 149 argue that the Iphigenia play was more likely *Iphigenia in Tauris* than *Iphigenia in Aulis*.
[7] See Pfeiffer 1968: 204. Further on Aristophanes as both reflecting and fostering the canonization of certain tragic poets see Rosen 2006.
[8] Heraclid. Pont. no. 17 (36) in Schütrumpf 2008: 66–7.

fifth-century tragic dramatists – were introduced into the Great Dionysia, though as an *hors concours* event rather than as part of the regular contest.[9] This explains the aforementioned performances of Euripides' plays in the Dionysia of 341–339 BC (see n. 6 earlier in this chapter), with contemporary actors, one of whom was the famous Neoptolemus of Scyros,[10] being responsible not only for starring in but also apparently for organizing and producing the revivals.[11] This is presumably the general context in which the Athenian orator Aeschines (ridiculed as a third-rate actor by his political rival Demosthenes) performed in revivals of Euripides' *Cresphontes*, *Oenomaus* and *Hecuba*, as well as of Sophocles' *Antigone*, no doubt in the third quarter of the fourth century.[12] In about the same time, between 336 and 324 BC, the statesman Lycurgus passed a decree whereby the Athenian state was to set up bronze statues of the three great tragic poets in the Theatre of Dionysus and to have official copies of their tragedies deposited in the state archive and read out to actors by a state official.[13] This measure was reportedly intended to prevent actors from inserting interpolations into the authoritative texts of the canonical tragedies; however, it was also as an act of cultural appropriation asserting a vision of the recent Athenian past as an era of memorable greatness.[14] The Athenian city thus granted official recognition to the canonical status of Aeschylus, Sophocles and Euripides, and also took it upon itself to

---

[9] See *IG* ii² 2318, col. 8 (= *TrGF* i, DID A 1), 201–3 = Millis and Olson (2012) 40 (l. 1009–11) with 56, n. on 1010–11. Recently, Hanink (2015) argued that the introduction of reperformances of fifth-century tragedies in 386, with its manifest evocation of Athens' golden era, was part of a broader state-sponsored effort to revive notions of Athenian cultural supremacy as a means of bolstering anew (unsuccessfully, as it turned out) Athenian imperial claims in the context of the opportunities offered by the Peace of Antalcidas (spring of 386 BC). The ancient tradition according to which the Athenians, as an exceptional token of respect for Aeschylus' memory, decreed that anyone wishing to produce plays by Aeschylus should be granted a chorus automatically (presumably already in the fifth century) has been forcefully questioned by Biles 2006/2007.

[10] On Neoptolemus see, e.g., the second Hypothesis to Dem. 29; Dem. 5.6 with schol. *ad loc.*; D.S. 16.92; Ghiron-Bistagne 1976: 156–7, 345; Stephanis 1988: no. 1797; Easterling 1997: 218.

[11] In the inscription cited in n. 9 earlier in this chapter, the phraseology (παλαιὸν δρᾶμα πρῶτο[ν] παρεδίδαξαν οἱ τραγ[ῳδοί]) suggests that the tragic actors themselves were responsible for 'producing' (παραδιδάσκειν) the old plays; cf. Millis and Olson 2012: 56, n. on 1010–11. According to Pickard–Cambridge 1988: 124, 'παρεδίδαξαν must imply that [the 'old tragedy'] was an "extra"'; cf. Nervegna 2007: 15 with n. 7 (with further bibliography).

[12] Dem. 18.180, 267 (*On the Crown*, 330 BC) with Wankel 1976: ii.891–2; Dem. 19.246–7 (*On the False Embassy*, 343 BC).

[13] On the monument of the Three Tragedians (cf. *TrGF* I, 60 T 8a) see further Papastamati-von Moock 2007: 312–24 (with Figs. 7 and 8 on pp. 308–9) and 2014: 35–60; Hanink 2014b: 74–83.

[14] [Plut.], *Vit. Dec. Orat.* (=*Mor.* 841F); see further Scodel 2007: 130, 149–52.

guarantee the authenticity of their texts.[15] On this topic see further 'Canonization and Lycurgus', later in this chapter.

## The Influence of Euripides and Aeschylus on New Tragedy

If the three great tragedians of the fifth century become undisputable paragons of tragic dramaturgy in the fourth century, it is Euripides who (at least on the strength of the evidence available) stands out as a particular favorite with audiences in that era and later. We saw earlier that, between 341 and 339, the 'old tragedy' performed at the Great Dionysia was consistently a play by Euripides; what is more, as has been recently pointed out, Aphareus, one of the contestants in 341, entered the contest with three tragedies whose titles (*Peliades, Orestes, Augē*) are also attested as titles of Euripidean plays.[16] And in the second century BC (some time between 190 and 170),[17] a dedicatory inscription from Tegea in Arcadia by an unknown actor commemorating his victories in various dramatic contests mentions performances of three Euripidean plays (*Orestes, Heracles, Archelaus*), the last two repeated twice in different venues.[18] Literary sources also provide evidence for repeats of Euripidean plays in the fourth century (or somewhat later).[19] It is therefore unsurprising that echoes from Euripides should appear in the sparse remains of fourth-century tragedy (see further Liapis and Stephanopoulos, this volume).

More generally, on the basis of the little that remains from their considerable output, it would appear that fourth-century tragic authors staked their own claim on excellence by vying with the canonical playwrights of the previous century (as we saw earlier in this chapter in the case of Astydamas), but also with the canonical author *par excellence*: Homer. This tendency may perhaps be exemplified in the comparatively large number of fourth-century tragedies that draw their plot from Homer

---

[15] See further Hanink 2014b: 192, 230, 245 and in this volume. For a detailed account of revivals of fifth- (and fourth-) century drama in later times see Nervegna 2007. The canonical status of fifth-century tragedy is also implicitly highlighted by its being treated as paradigmatic of the tragic genre in fourth-century comedy: see Hanink 2014a: 191–200.

[16] See Stephanopoulos 2014: 200.

[17] For the date see Le Guen 2007e: 98–104 with earlier bibliography.

[18] *IG* V(2), 118 = *TrGF* i, DID B 11. See Ghiron-Bistagne 1976: 102; Revermann 1999/2000: 462–5; Le Guen 2007e; Nervegna 2007: 19.

[19] For example, Euripides' *Trojan Women* after 367 BC (Plu. *Pel.* 29.9); his *Andromeda*, after 306 BC (Luc. *Hist. Conscr.* 1); and unspecified Euripidean tragedies 'sung' in Asia after 330 BC (Plu. *De gen. Alex.* 5 = *Mor.* 328D). For accounts of the reception of Euripides in antiquity see now Lauriola and Demetriou 2015. See also: Schmid 1940: 823–32; Easterling 1994; Revermann 1999/2000; Mastronarde 2010: 1–9; Nervegna 2014: 162–3, 165–6.

rather than from the epic cycle, as was commonly the case in the fifth century. Characteristically, at least five plays of that period (including tragedies by such major authors as Astydamas and Carcinus) took Achilles as their principal character,[20] and at least some of them must have done so in a bid to outperform each other in recasting Homer into tragic molds. By contrast, we know of only three fifth-century tragic works with Achilles as their subject, most notably Aeschylus' Achilles trilogy (*Myrmidons*, *Nereids*, *Phrygians*).[21] As Taplin (2007: 254) remarks, it was evidently important for a new fourth-century tragedy 'to set itself against earlier versions of the story, both reflecting and rejecting them' – although, remarkably, Aeschylus' undisputable primacy in the fifth century seems not to have led to a corresponding number of revivals of his plays, at least in mainland Greece.[22]

Much as fourth-century tragedy seems to have evolved under the sign of the canonical authors of an earlier era (Homer and the three great tragedians, particularly Euripides), it would be rash to dismiss it as merely derivative. As Taplin (2014: 141–2) has recently reminded us, there is unmistakable, if rather sparse, evidence suggesting that such fourth-century tragedians as Chaeremon, Theodectas and Astydamas were highly esteemed; indeed, they were popular on the stage, they were as memorable and quotable as, say, Euripides, and they could be evoked in serious critical

---

[20] We know of Achilles tragedies by: Astydamas (*TrGF* I, 60 T 5); Carcinus Junior (70 F 1d); Cleophon (77 F (3), unless it is a mistake for Iophon, 22 F 1a); Evaretus (85 T 1); and Diogenes of Sinope (88 F 1a). Cf. Michelakis (2002) 13–16. Chaeremon's *Achilles Slaying Thersites* (71 F 1a–3) will probably have relied on non-Iliadic (cyclic) material; Sophocles' *Lovers of Achilles* is thought to have been a satyr-drama. A recently published musical papyrus from the third/second century BC (Pöhlmann and West 2001: 22–5, no. 5) bears the subscription '*Achilles* by Sophocl[es]'; but this must be the younger Sophocles (*TrGF* I, 62): see West 1999: 43–4. Of unknown date and authorship (but possibly postclassical) is an Achilles tragedy published in 1987 from a 150–100 BC Köln papyrus (*P. Köln* 6.241 = 1711.01 Mertens-Pack³ = *Trag. adesp.* fr. 640b, published in *TrGF* v/2, p. 1131–4). Its scant fragments contain a dialogue commenting on Achilles' intransigence and on efforts by his circle to persuade him to rejoin the battle (cf. *Iliad* 9); they also preserve a report of a Trojan attack which forces the Greeks to start hauling their ships to the sea to prevent the enemy from setting them on fire (clearly, a reworking of *Il.* 15.300–746).

[21] Fifth-century dramatic production also includes an Achilles-tragedy by Aristarchus of Tegea (14 F 1a), now known only through the fragments of Ennius' *Achilles* (cf. Nervegna 2014: 185, with earlier bibliography).

[22] For the scanty evidence on Aeschylus' performance reception in fourth-century theatre see Scodel 2007: 130–3 and now Nervegna 2014: 166–76 and Vahtikari 2014: 153–63, 175–81, Appendix III. Scodel has pointed out that the rarity of Aeschylean reperformances seems predominantly a phenomenon of mainland Greece; West Greece presents a different picture, and South Italian vases suggest that Aeschylus was considerably more popular on South Italian stages (Nervegna 2014: 172–6).

discussion as masters of the tragic art.²³ The canonization of fifth-century tragedy by no means implies that fourth-century tragic production was somehow of lesser quality or vitality.²⁴ As we saw earlier, Astydamas enjoyed incomparable success in his time, and had public honors lavished on him. Chaeremon was, alongside Euripides, among the authors whose plays secured victorious performances for the anonymous actor of the Tegea inscription mentioned earlier in this chapter, including n. 18); he is also quoted, together with Aeschylus, Euripides and the fourth-century Carcinus Junior, in Menander's *Shield* and also in other authors; and he is mentioned or parodied (a sign of general recognizability) by Eubulus and Ephippus. Carcinus produced, among other things, a startlingly innovative version of the Medea myth, in which the heroine did *not* kill her children; and his *Aëropē* was apparently a classic in its own right. Finally, passages from plays by fourth-century tragic authors – including not only those mentioned earlier in this chapter but also, e.g., Dicaeogenes and Antiphon – are brought to bear on topics discussed by Aristotle in his *Poetics* and in his *Rhetoric*, and not only in disparaging ways at that (though see the next section on 'Innovation in later tragedy').²⁵

## Innovation in Later Tragedy

As we saw earlier, the development of the repertory tradition of fifth-century 'old tragedies' during the fourth century by no means suggests that 'new tragedy' was in the shadow of 'classic,' canonical tragedy: the momentum, during the time of Astydamas' back-to-back victories, seems to have been on the side of 'new tragedy.' It can be difficult to appreciate this state of affairs, between the almost complete absence of any preserved fourth-century tragedies and the tremendous influence of Aristotle's *Poetics*, which sometimes may seem to value 'old tragedy' over the tragedy of Aristotle's

---

²³ As observed by Ceccarelli (2010: 118–19) and Hanink (2014a: 204–5), Aeschines' *Against Ctesiphon* 34 (330 BC) suggests that, on at least one occasion, the proclamation of public honors at the City Dionysia was reserved for the time-slot before the contest of 'new' tragedies (τραγῳδῶν γιγνομένων καινῶν) rather than before the revival of the 'old' tragedy, which suggests that the former were thought to be more prestigious or popular than the latter.
²⁴ See further Easterling 1993: 562–9.
²⁵ For references and further discussion see Liapis and Stephanopoulos, this volume; cf. Hanink 2014a: 201–2.

own time.[26] In the *Poetics*, Aristotle compares modern tragedy, sometimes unfavorably, with what he sees as the best of fifth-century tragedy, plays like Sophocles' *Oedipus the King* and Euripides' *Iphigenia among the Taurians*. He says that modern tragedy often lacks ἦθος (1450a15),[27] that modern tragic characters speak more like rhetoricians than like statesmen (1450b23),[28] and that modern tragedies do not treat the chorus like a full character (1456a19–20). He implies that many modern tragic playwrights rely too much on spectacle (1450b28),[29] that their plots are often episodic rather than organically connected, partly due to pressure from actors (1451b11), and that they occasionally cave in to the sentimentality of the audience by rewarding the 'good' characters while punishing the 'wicked' ones (1453a4). To be fair, Aristotle, who has very precise ideas about what the perfect tragedy should look like, applies these criticisms to some fifth-century playwrights and plays as well; and his reservations do not, in any case, amount to a wholesale dismissal of the tragedy of his time, nor are they necessarily representative of audience opinion, which surely will have varied. Furthermore, some of the attributes he seems to associate principally with fourth-century tragedy can actually be detected already in the fifth century (see Carter, this volume).

It may be helpful for our purposes to read the *Poetics* not as the prescriptive text it often is (i.e., a set of guidelines for producing the best kind of, mainly, tragedy), but rather, descriptively, as evidence for the ongoing changes and developments in fourth-century tragedy. We do not have to subscribe to Aristotle's judgments about 'the best kind' of tragic plot, or his teleological view of tragedy's development, to discern a vibrant, active theatrical culture during the period when he was writing. Reading between the lines of the *Poetics*, it seems that playwrights were experimenting with different sorts of diction, plot, character, and structure from what was common in fifth-century tragedy, and that they may have catered to popular tastes by ceding to actors' demands.[30] The competitive festival context in which plays were performed in Athens made it highly likely that playwrights would respond to audience

---

[26] See Webster 1954: 307. See, however, Carter, this volume, for the view that, for Aristotle, the fourth century represents no meaningful landmark since he considered tragedy to have remained essentially unchanged since the early career of Sophocles.
[27] See Schütrumpf 1970 and 1987; Held 1985.   [28] On this issue see further Carter, this volume.
[29] See Petrides 2014: 102–7.
[30] Cf. Aristotle's famous remark (*Rh.* 1403b33) that 'actors nowadays have greater power than playwrights', and his reference to a famous actor's trick for capturing audience attention (*Pol.* 1336b27–31); cf. Hanink 2014b: 214.

pressures. At the same time, and in the same festivals, audiences enjoyed non-competitive performances of 'old tragedies,' which continued to influence new tragedy. Presumably the performances of 'old tragedies' were also due to popular interest, which suggests a sort of push-and-pull: pressure on contemporary tragedians to differentiate themselves from 'classic' tragedy, and, at the same time, an interest in keeping 'the classics' alive in a repertory tradition. This push-and-pull may explain Aristotle's observation that most tragedies in his day concerned the same few mythological cycles of stories (1453a17–22); tragedians might try to differentiate themselves, but within a narrower range of material, as Carcinus did with his *Medea* (on which see Liapis and Stephanopoulos, this volume).

The only extant fourth-century tragedy is the *Rhesus*, formerly attributed to Euripides (see Fries, this volume). From the point of view of performance history and staging, it is a fascinating play. Set entirely during nighttime, with possibly four speaking actors, it includes one goddess impersonating another and a Muse singing a dirge over her son Rhesus' corpse while on the *mēkhanē*.[31] The play's plot, lyrics and unusual staging features provide a glimpse into the state of fourth-century tragedy: an interest in finding new aspects of familiar material, an emphasis on spectacle and the heavy influence of the 'classic' canon, especially Euripides.

The *Rhesus* may have been written in fourth-century Macedon, possibly at the royal court, for a Macedonian audience.[32] We might consider other experimental tragedies from the fifth century onwards as evidence of the genre's flourishing and adaptability to different venues and markets. Although tragedies on non-mythical subjects were not unknown in the fifth century (cf. Phrynichus' *Sack of Miletus*, Aeschylus' *Persae*), it is in the fourth century that this subgenre seems to acquire new vitality. We know of several historical tragedies written during the fourth century, including Theodectes' *Mausolus* and Moschion's *Themistocles*.[33] In the *Poetics*, Aristotle notes in passing that 'the poet should lay out the whole story for both

---

[31] See Parry 1964; Wiles 1997: 156; Battezzato 2000; Walton 2000; Liapis 2012.
[32] Liapis 2009b; *contra* Fries 2014: 18–21.
[33] On *Mausolus* see Gel. 10.18.5; cf. Xanthakis-Karamanos 1980: 17. On *Themistocles* see Hornblower, this volume, who also discusses historical tragedies by Philiscus (*Themistocles*) and Lycophron of Chalcis (*Cassandrians*).

traditional tales *and made-up ones*, and then expand the episodes,' which suggests that he took it for granted that playwrights of his time might invent their plots;[34] indeed, elsewhere (*Po*. 1451b19–23) he refers to Agathon's *Antheus* or *Anthos*, a tragedy in which both plot and characters were entirely made up, and Aristotle's language here suggests that he knew of other similarly made-up tragedies. He does not mention in which circumstances playwrights might work with invented plots, but creating works on commission for powerful patrons is one plausible reason. Moving past the fourth century, we see further evidence of the ever-expanding market for tragedy in Ezekiel's *Exagōgē*, a Hellenistic Greek tragedy about the Exodus of Moses and his followers which was most probably composed in Alexandria, Egypt,[35] and a tragedy by an unknown author about Gyges, the sixth-century BC ruler of Lydia, whose story was most famously recounted by Herodotus in his *Histories*.[36] All of these historical tragedies can be thought of as evidence for the flexibility and variety of postclassical tragedy. They can also be thought of as the forerunners of Roman historical tragedy, *fabula praetexta*, which dramatized significant events and 'great men' from Rome's legendary early days and its more recent history.

## Canonization and Lycurgus: Why 338 BC?

Given this picture of fourth-century tragedy's flourishing, it might seem surprising that just a few years after Astydamas' portrait statue was erected in the Theatre of Dionysus alongside statues of the fifth-century war heroes Miltiades and Themistocles, the politician (and, for lack of a better term, 'financial overlord'[37]) Lycurgus set about fixing the canon of 'old tragedy', which apparently had already been crystallizing since 386 BC (see the section on 'Fourth-century tragedy and the tragic canon' and n. 9). As discussed earlier in this chapter, he had bronze statues of Aeschylus, Sophocles and Euripides made and placed in the Theatre of Dionysus,

---

[34] τούς τε λόγους καὶ τοὺς πεποιημένους δεῖ καὶ αὐτὸν ποιοῦντα ἐκτίθεσθαι καθόλου, εἶθ' οὕτως ἐπεισοδιοῦν καὶ παρατείνειν: Arist. *Poet*. 1455a34–b1 (emphasis added).
[35] See Lanfranchi 2006, and in this volume.
[36] Hdt. 1.8–12. Some scholars, such as Lloyd-Jones 1966: 24–31, have argued for an early fifth-century date for the Gyges tragedy, others for a post-fifth-century date; see Travis 2000: 330–1 and n. 2. On the Gyges tragedy see also Kotlińska-Toma 2015: 178–85; Hornblower, this volume.
[37] Bosworth 1994: 850.

ordered that the texts of their tragedies be deposited in the state treasury for safekeeping and mandated that actors not deviate from the official text in public performances. This canonization process was not simply a matter of enshrining the theatre-going public's current tastes in bronze; it was more a matter of fixing the list of Great Playwrights, those whose work *ought* to be remembered and respected. The canonization process is also evident in the visual record; Csapo has calculated that 'Aeschylean, Sophoclean, and Euripidean plays account for close to 75 percent of all tragedy-related vase-paintings.'[38] The move to canonize the 'Big Three' suggests that the culture's heritage is envisioned as having already peaked, despite the constant production of new plays. It is a nostalgic move, at some level. Along with fixing the tragic canon and the canonical texts, Lycurgus also undertook the work of replacing the wooden walls, seats and buildings in the Theatre of Dionysus with stone ones – another move toward prestige, permanence and fixity.[39]

What prompted this impulse to canon-formation, celebration of the 'classics' of fifth-century tragedy, and textual (and theatrical) fixity at this moment in Athenian history, just a few years after Astydamas' statue was erected as a celebration of 'new tragedy'? Why did the Athenians, under the direction of Lycurgus, look back to their past at this moment? In 338 BC, Athens, together with several other Greek city-states, rose up against the control of Philip II of Macedon, who was expanding his rule outside of his home territory. The Athenians and their allies fought Philip's army at the Battle of Chaeronea, and were crushed. Philip treated Athens more mildly than he did the other city-states that had defied his control, because of Athens' political and cultural importance, but he did set up Lycurgus, an Athenian politician, as financial administrator of Athens. The year 338 marked a turning-point for Athens: the city already had been stripped of its empire at the conclusion of the Peloponnesian War in 404, but it had continued as an autonomous, sovereign city-state after its loss to Sparta.

---

[38] Csapo 2010: 39.
[39] On the Lycurgan Theatre of Dionysus, see Hanink 2014b: 92–125; Papastamati-von Moock 2014; Pickard-Cambridge 1946: 134–74. Papastamati-von Moock demonstrates that Pericles seems to have begun the rebuilding of the seats in the Theatre of Dionysus in stone, but was interrupted rather quickly by wartime exigencies, and that work on the western section of the parodos retaining wall and *theatron* must have begun under Lycurgus' predecessor Eubulus and then finished during Lycurgus' tenure. Hanink (2014b: 99) notes that the restructuring did not simply replace wooden seats with stone ones, but significantly expanded the theatre's seating capacity, which must have been desirable for accommodating more foreign spectators. Lycurgus embarked on a building program to improve and monumentalize many of Athens' most important public spaces; see O'Sullivan 2009: 14–15; Bosworth 1994: 851.

Now, the political autonomy of Athens was gone, and all that was left of its former greatness was its cultural legacy, in which tragedy had pride of place. New Greek tragedies continued to be written and performed for centuries after the 330s BC, but once the impulse to canonize the 'Big Three' of the fifth century was institutionalized, there were two sets of tragic texts: the 'classics,' and everything else. Despite the painstaking work of generations of ancient scholars and editors, most of the latter set of texts has not survived.

## The Theatrical Environment and Equipment

### Drama as an International Art Form

Another major development in fourth-century tragedy was the spread of drama beyond the confines of Attica to other Greek (and later even non-Greek) cities, as a result of which tragedy became a Panhellenic and later an international medium of high prestige and recognizability. True, already in the fifth century major Athenian tragic playwrights were invited to produce their plays outside Athens – for instance, Aeschylus at Syracuse, or Euripides at the court of the Macedonian king.[40] At that era, however, Athenian drama, for all its Panhellenic appeal and prestige, is predominantly an Athenian cultural product, even when produced outside Athens: it is composed to a very large extent by Athenian playwrights, even when performed before non-Athenian audiences, and carries with it the allure of its perceived birthplace, the sophisticated cultural metropolis that was Athens. By contrast, from the fourth century onwards, drama, and especially tragedy, gradually sheds its associations with its Athenian origins to become a truly international medium, spreading not only throughout the Greek peninsula but also as far as South Italy and Sicily, the Black Sea or the Middle East.[41] The recent survey of 116 sites outside Athens in Csapo

---

[40] On the spread of Athenian tragedy outside Athens already in the time of Aeschylus, and on a fairly significant scale from the last half of the fifth century onwards, see Easterling 1994: 73–80; Taplin 1999; Dearden 1990 and 1999; Allan 2000: 149–60 and, with the *Heraclidae* as a case-study, 2001. Especially on Aeschylus at Syracuse see Bosher 2012b and Smith 2012: 129–33; on Euripides at the court of King Archelaus (and on his homonymous play) see Harder 1985: 129–31; Duncan 2011; Moloney 2014: 236–40.

[41] The spread of theatre around the Greek (and non-Greek) world, on which see further Le Guen in this volume, is a vast topic, whose history remains to be written; a major undertaking in this direction is the University of Sydney project 'The Theatrical Revolution: The Expansion of Theatre Outside Athens', implemented by E. Csapo, J. R. Green, S. Nervegna, E. G. D. Robinson, and P. Wilson. See now Csapo and Wilson 2015, which is by far the fullest survey so far of the diffusion of theatre in Attica and beyond (116 sites in South Italy and Sicily, Isthmus and Peloponnese,

and Wilson 2015 (see n. 41) demonstrates both that Athens had no clear or longstanding monopoly on drama and that performance of drama continued to grow, exponentially, in the Greek world and beyond even before the spread of Greek culture through Alexander's successors bolstered the dissemination of dramatic performances even further.

This is evidenced first of all by the international spread of the professional associations known as 'the Artists (*Tekhnitai*) of Dionysus' – a network of guilds comprising actors, directors/producers, musicians, dancers and other related experts, and intended to protect the safety, considerable privileges and prestige of theatre professionals internationally.[42] Such experts now come not only from Athens but also from Boeotia, Thebes, Thespiae, Sicyon, Argos and other parts of the Greek world, including Asia Minor, and the cities of South Italy and Sicily.[43] Fourth-century developments in the acting profession in particular are especially instructive. As Taplin points out, whereas in the fifth century Athens seems to have had an almost total monopoly in outstanding actors (the only noteworthy exception being, apparently, Mynniskos of Chalcis in Euboea), in the fourth century there is a more sizeable specimen of actors of non-Athenian origin who rise to superstardom, amass great wealth and enjoy international fame and the patronage of powerful figures; these include Aristodemus of Metapontum, Neoptolemus of Skyros, and Polus of Aegina.[44] There seems to be a comparable (though perhaps less sharp) disparity among tragic authors too: we know of at least ten

---

Aegean Islands, mainland Greece, Asia Minor, Hellespont, Propontis, Black Sea, and Africa) down to ca. 300 BC, the more so as it takes an inclusive view of the evidence (inscriptions, historical and literary texts, theatre architecture and art). There is also a considerable body of work on specific aspects, such as, e.g., Greek theatre in Macedonia (Revermann 1999/2000; Moloney 2014; cf. Liapis 2009b and 2014: 290–4); the crucial role of Alexander the Great in spreading theatre in the Middle East, West Asia and Egypt (Le Guen 2014); Greek theatre in the Black Sea region (Braund and Hall 2014); Greek theatre in South Italy and Sicily (Bosher 2012a) and its reception by native (non-Greek) populations (Robinson 2014), etc. See also the recent survey of scholarship in Csapo et al. 2014: 1–10.

[42] On the *Tekhnitai* see now principally Le Guen 2001 and Aneziri 2003; cf. Nervegna 2007: 18–21; full annotated catalogue in Stephanis 1988. Cf. also Le Guen, this volume. See also Lightfoot 2002 on the different local union branches as evidence of the continued spread of performance culture in the Hellenistic period, on pay scales for comic vs. tragic actors and for protagonists vs. other actors, and on the higher prestige of tragedy vs. comedy.

[43] See Taplin 1999: 35 n. 6, on the basis of the ethnic designations of 'Artists of Dionysus' catalogued in Stephanis 1988: 530–56.

[44] For the ancient sources and some modern literature on Mynniskos, Aristodemus, Neoptelmus and Polus see Stephanis 1988: nos. 1757, 332, 1797, and 2187, respectively.

playwrights from the fourth century who certainly originated in regions outside Athens (including, again, Asia Minor and Magna Graecia)[45] as opposed to some four from the fifth century.[46]

The significance of vase paintings (and other artifacts) from South Italy and Sicily as evidence for the spread of theatre in those areas has been a hotly debated topic during the last decades. For a considerable number of scholars, such artifacts are potentially a treasure trove of information on the ways in which theatre was disseminated beyond Athens, and a crucial tool for contextualizing Greek drama within a performance-oriented frame of reference. This approach – pioneered by Webster and given a new impetus thanks to the studies of Taplin, Green, Csapo, Revermann and others – has led to all-important discussions and analyses of a wide range of vase-paintings, sculptures, terracottas and mosaics as tools with which to explore the reception of drama in Magna Graecia and its place in and interactions with local populations.[47] The degree to which such artifacts reflect a viewer's experience of actual theatre performances will be open to debate, but at least in some cases it is practically certain that the depictions reflect or are inspired by actual stage productions of tragedies or comedies. A case in point is the famous 'Würzburg Telephus' vase, which undoubtedly testifies to a performance or performances of Aristophanes' *Thesmophoriazusae* in South Italy in the early fourth century.[48] More germane to this volume's concerns is the 'Cleveland Medea' calyx crater, a Lucanian

---

[45] Spintharus of Heraclea in Pontus (*TrGF* I, 40); Apollodorus of Tarsus (64); Theodectas of Phaselis in Lycia (72); Dionysius I the tyrant of Syracuse (76); Achaeus II of Syracuse (79); Mamercus the tyrant of Catane (87); Diogenes of Sinope (88); Philiscus of Aegina (89); Sosiphanes of Syracuse (92); and Phanostratus of Halicarnassus (94). To these may be added, perhaps, Patrocles of Thurii (58), unless he is the same person as Patrocles of Athens (57); Carcinus of Acragas (235; cf. Suda κ 394), unless he is to be identified with Carcinus the Athenian (70); Heraclides of Pontus (93), who is said to have passed off his own tragedies as Thespis'; Python of Byzantium (or Catane), who is credited only with the satyr-play *Agen* (see Hornblower, this volume); and Polyidus of Selymbria (78), who may not, however, have produced tragedies. Non-Athenian tragedians from the early third century include Homerus of Byzantium (98) and Sositheus of Alexandria in the Troad (99). See also Le Guen, this volume.

[46] Aristarchus of Tegea (*TrGF* I, 14); Neophron of Sicyon (15); Ion of Chios (19); and Achaeus I of Eretria (20). Cf. Taplin 1999: 35.

[47] See Webster 1960, 1961 and 1962, followed by second and, in some cases, third editions (see bibliography); also, Trendall and Webster 1971; cf. Trendall (1959). See further the studies of Taplin 1987, 1993 and 1997; Green 1991 and 1994. For a book-length study of theatre-inspired vases, and of the (not always straightforward) interplay between theatre and the visual arts see Taplin 2007; important insights in Csapo 2010: 1–82. For recent contributions on the subject see Taplin 2012 and 2014; Dearden 2012; Green 2012. On comic figurines from Boeotia, Corinth and Cyprus as evidence for regional theatrical activity in the fourth century (a topic which is only now beginning to receive the attention it deserves) see Green 2014.

[48] See Csapo 1986; Taplin 1987; further bibliography in Nervegna 2007: 16–17 nn. 19–20.

vase dated to ca. 400 BC and depicting scenes from Euripides' *Telephus* on one side and from the same author's *Medea* on the other.[49] Nonetheless, this category of evidence is problematized by the possibility (however remote) that theatre-inspired images may not reflect directly the experience of performance but may be mediated by various renderings of myth, ranging from written dramatic texts or funerary declamations to mythic oral traditions.[50]

## Expansion of Theatres Across the Greek-Speaking World

The spread of the theatre in the fourth century is further exemplified by the proliferation of stone theatre buildings both in continental Greece beyond Athens and in non-mainland Greek cities. Indeed, it is only from the second half of the fourth century that Greek cities invest in the construction of theatre buildings from durable materials, as opposed to the predominantly wooden structures found in the fifth century. And by contrast to their rarity in fifth-century non-Attic theatres (e.g., Argos, Metapontum), stone buildings mushroom all over the Greek world during the fourth century: almost throughout the Peloponnese, at Thebes, in Acarnania, in Thessaly, on Euboea, in Asia Minor (Ephesus, Priene), in Pontus (Olbia, Heraclea), on Cyprus (Paphos), and of course in South Italy (Locri, Metapontum, etc.) and Sicily (Catana, Morgantina, etc.).[51] Indeed, it is in the second half of the fourth century that two important innovations in the architecture of theatre auditoria are introduced: namely, the construction of horizontal passageways dividing the auditorium into

---

[49] See Revermann 2005 and 2010.
[50] See Small 2003 (arguing for a variety of sources, including oral narratives, that merely happen to coincide with myths dramatized in tragedy); Giuliani 1996 (arguing for mythic matrices influenced, inter alia, by drama, and even embedded into funerary declamations); 2001: 33–4; 2013: 243–5 (on tragic myth as conveyed by written texts rather than by performances of tragedy). The latest contribution to the 'anti-theatrical' interpretation of such vases is by Todisco 2012, who argues, improbably, that the meaning of drama-related vases was explained by the ceramic artists themselves to native South-Italian populations, who could not follow the Greek of the dramatic performances. For a survey of the debate see Liapis, Panayotakis and Harrison 2013: 11–13. Add now Carpenter 2014, who argues for 'some sort of performance of tragedies at Ruvo di Puglia' (quotation from p. 266).
[51] The bibliography on Greek theatre buildings is vast. An excellent starting point is Moretti 2014, who offers a thoroughly documented survey of Greek theatre architecture in the fourth century. Especially on the stone theatres of Sicily, whose remains date from the mid–fourth century, see Marconi 2012 with an exhaustive catalogue of ancient sources and modern literature; on the newly excavated theatre at Montagna dei Cavalli (ancient Hippana) in West Sicily see Vassalo 2012.

several sections, and (in conjunction to this) the provision of outside access to these passageways and to the upper part of the auditorium. These innovations must have arisen from the need to accommodate large audiences, and thus attest to the growing popularity of the theatre outside Athens in that era.[52]

### Architecture of the Theatres: The Innovation of the Raised Stage in Hellenistic Times

In the fourth century, the Theatre of Dionysus in Athens was renovated and expanded, its front rows of seats constructed of marble.[53] The stage building (*skēnē*), which was a temporary structure made of wood during the fifth century, was converted to a permanent stone structure, with one central door and perhaps two other doors flanking it on either side. Some scholars believe that the stage itself was raised a bit higher during the fourth century than it had been during the fifth century, which suggests that the actors needed to be more visible to larger audiences,[54] and may provide indirect evidence for the 'rise of the actor' in this time period. Hellenistic and Roman-era theatre buildings came to have multiple stories, multiple doors and windows, architectural details such as columns, alcoves, and niches, and an even higher stage.[55]

### Theatrical Machinery

There is some evidence for changes in other physical properties of dramatic performance after the fifth century. An interest in special effects, such as the thunder-machine (*bronteion*), appears in the evidence for this period.[56] Aristotle, Demosthenes, Plato and other fourth-century sources suggest that the crane was a popular theatrical device during their lifetimes;[57] in

---

[52] See Moretti 2014: 117–22 (esp. 120), citing Papathanasopoulos 1986.
[53] Csapo and Slater 1995: 80; Pickard-Cambridge 1946: 134–74.
[54] Csapo and Slater 1995: 258 estimate the fifth-century stage at the Theatre of Dionysus as approximately one metre off the ground. Most scholars believe that the archaeological evidence points to the Theatre of Dionysus in Athens being one of the last stages to be raised considerably higher: see Petrides 2010: 96 and n. 72.
[55] Csapo and Slater 1995: 81–8; Bieber 1961: 54–73; Pickard-Cambridge 1946: 175–264; see also Mastronarde 1990: 254.
[56] See Vahtikari 2014: 212–14; Scott Smith and Trzaskoma 2005 and the reply of Griffith 2008. See also Csapo and Slater 1995: 261 (translating Cramer, *Anecdota Parisiensia* 1.19).
[57] See Mastronarde 1990 and the *testimonia* in his Appendix 1 VII.

fact, the phrase 'the god from the machine,' which has come to us through its Latin translation *deus ex machina*, seems to have hardened into a cliché during the fourth century due to its use (Aristotle would say over-use)[58] in Athenian tragedy and its parody in comedy beginning in the fifth century.[59] Vahtikari estimates that more than half of the fifth-century tragedies performed outside Athens in the late fifth and fourth centuries used the crane.[60]

## Performance

### The Rise of the Actor

The fourth century is often referred to by theatre historians as 'the rise of the actor.' The art of acting acquired, in essence, official approval in 449 BC, when a separate prize at the Great Dionysia was instituted for the best actor, as distinct from the best play.[61] The fourth century saw the emergence of superstar actors like Theodorus, Neoptolemus and Polus, who commanded hefty fees for their performances and donated equally hefty amounts to public works, and who were sometimes entrusted with diplomatic missions because of their speaking ability, stage presence and fame.[62] By 275 BC at the latest, actors and dramatic musicians had formed a union, the Artists of Dionysus (see earlier in this chapter).[63] As actors began to attract attention for their skills, tragedy began to change to showcase those skills. Aristotle notes this ruefully in the *Poetics*, when he laments the contemporary (i.e., fourth-century) trend of 'vulgar

---

[58] Arist. *Po.* 1454a37–b6.
[59] See Ley 2007: 273–4. For examples of the use of the crane in fifth-century tragedy and (parodically) in comedy see Mastronarde 1990: 40–2. For the cliché 'god from the machine' in the fourth century cf. Alexis fr. 131.9 K.-A; Men. *Theophor.* fr. 5 Sandbach; fr. 213 K.-A; Com. Adesp. fr. 1089.12 K.-A; [Dem.] 40.59.
[60] Vahtikari 2014: 213.   [61] Slater 1990; Dearden 1999: 225; Easterling 2002; Csapo 2004.
[62] In 363 BC Theodorus donated 70 drachmas toward the rebuilding of the temple of Apollo at Delphi, far more than any other individual donor and more than some city-states; see Csapo and Slater (1995: 231–8) for further ancient evidence of payouts to actors. On actors (Aristodemus, Ctesiphon, Neoptolemus) serving as ambassadors in inter-state relations in the era of Philip II and Alexander the Great see the second Hypothesis to Dem. 19 (I.3, p.397–8 Fuhr); Dem. 19.315 (with MacDowell 2000: on §12); ancient Hypothesis to Aeschines' *On the False Embassy* (2 Arg. §1, p.8 Dilts); Aeschin. 2.15–19; Dem. 18.21 (with Yunis 2001 *ad l.*); Dem. 5.6–7.
[63] Some scholars are willing to date the beginning of the Artists of Dionysus to the fourth century rather than the early third century: see Webster 1954: 294 and n. 3.

overacting', although he does indicate that overacting began in the last decades of the fifth century with Kallippides.[64] We have already discussed Aristotle's comment that actors sometimes pressured contemporary playwrights to change the plots of their plays. Presumably, actors wanted playwrights to give them scenes that would garner them positive attention: big entrances, challenging songs, highly emotional speeches or intense arguments.

Another sort of evidence for the rise of the actor is the evidence for private performances. There are many accounts of actors being employed outside of the theatre in small-scale performances, usually at drinking-parties (*symposia*) hosted by members of the elite. In these performances, we most often hear about actors performing famous songs from tragedy: for example, Philip II had Neoptolemus perform some of his most famous lines and sing a tragic ode at the symposium Philip hosted the night before his assassination in 336 BC.[65] Philip's son Alexander the Great performed a portion of Euripides' *Andromeda* from memory at a symposium he hosted the night before he slipped into a coma in 323 BC.[66] Climactic scenes were another favorite excerpt from tragedy; there is a famous story in Plutarch's *Life of Crassus* that the Parthian king responsible for Marcus Licinius Crassus' military defeat and death had an actor perform the recognition scene from Euripides' *Bacchae*, in which Pentheus' mother Agave realizes that the 'lion's head' she is displaying proudly is actually the head of her own son whom she killed in a Bacchic frenzy. In the Parthian performance, according to Plutarch, the actor actually held Crassus' severed head instead of a prop (or mask) of Pentheus' head. The story may or may not be true; what is significant for tragedy's enormous spread and prestige at that era is Plutarch's assumption that a foreign king would want a tragic scene performed at an important banquet in the first century BC.[67]

Some scholars have concluded that dramatic performance eventually came to include these private performances of 'highlights' as much as, or

---

[64] Arist. *Po.* 1461b26–62a1. On elite prejudice against performance see Csapo 2002; Hunter 2002; Green 2002. On Aristotle's vexed efforts to defend theatre against Plato's attacks by arguing that there was a 'right way' to do acting and spectacle see Petrides 2010: 89–91.
[65] Diod. Sic. 16.92; see Easterling 1997: 217–20; Moloney 2014: 243–4. [66] Ath. 12.537d–e.
[67] Plut. *Crass.* 33.2–4. The actor was Jason of Tralles. For the appeal of Greek drama for autocrats (in Sicily, Macedon, Black Sea and elsewhere) see now Csapo and Wilson 2015. On private performances of tragedy see also Easterling 1997: 217–24. It is, of course, a favorite trope of Plutarch's *Lives* to present historical narrative as real-life drama, or as the real-life equivalent of a tragedy performance. See de Lacy 1952: 159–71; Mossmann 1988: 83–93. Specifically on the *Life of Crassus* see Braund 1994: 468–74; Zadorojniy 1997: 169–82.

more than, large-scale public performance in theatres – although exactly when this shift occurred is a matter of debate. Other scholars have argued that the fashion for a single actor performing 'highlights' at private functions had existed alongside traditional, large-scale dramatic performance for hundreds of years.[68] Whether it was prevalent or not, this sort of performance suggests that wealthy individuals sought the services of famous actors to impress their friends (or their courtiers, in the case of kings); the prestige of tragedy, combined with the exclusivity of a small audience, meant that an actor's private performance became a status symbol.

## Acting Style

Fourth-century tragedy saw a continuing interest in 'realism,' which began in the late fifth century with the later works of Euripides and Aristophanes (see also Dunn, this volume). 'Realism' in this case means a wide range of acting styles (including gesture and delivery) and of vocabulary, as well as an interest in vocal mimicry, all of which combined to give the effect that there were many different kinds of 'people' (that is, characters) on stage.[69] Aristotle notes that the late-fifth-century tragic actor Kallippides was nicknamed 'The Ape', and Csapo argues this was not for his over-acting but for his amazing range of mimicry, including mimicry of 'low' people, such as poor women.[70] Anecdotes about fourth-century actors suggest that there was a great deal of audience interest in virtuosic vocal mimicry: Plutarch notes that the tragic actor Theodorus and the comic actor Parmenon were both renowned for their ability to imitate the sounds inanimate objects made;[71] and Aristotle mentions a fourth-century tragedian named Cleophon whose tragedies used a 'low' diction with 'common' words.[72]

The ancient scholia (comments by scholars) on tragic texts provide further evidence for the development of acting trends in fourth-century

---

[68] Csapo 2010: 168–204 discusses the history of 'private' theatrical performance in the ancient world, beginning with complicating the distinction between 'private' and 'public.' Nervegna 2007 argues against the 'highlights' theory, claiming that it was only schoolteachers, students, and musicians who engaged in this practice, while actors still performed entire plays in theatres for public performances.
[69] See Csapo 2002, who mostly discusses the late fifth century; Green 2002; Csapo and Slater 1995: 262–4.
[70] Arist. Po. 1461b34–5; Csapo 2002: 127–30.    [71] Plut. Mor. 18c.    [72] Arist. Po. 1458a18.

tragedy, as do actors' interpolations (lines usually made up and inserted by actors).[73] Some scholia on tragic texts can be dated with reasonable confidence to the Hellenistic period, and they are valuable for the light they throw on Hellenistic performances of 'classic' tragedy. Some scholia condemn contemporary (i.e., Hellenistic) performance culture for its emphasis on spectacle and emotion, while others claim that lead actors reassigned lines to themselves that were originally supposed to be spoken by other actors or by the chorus.[74] Interpolations also may shed light on tastes and trends in fourth-century and later acting, insofar as they are *ipso facto* evidence for a play's popularity in later times, and may even allow a glimpse into actors' efforts to increase the appeal of a play to audiences. The text of Euripides' *Orestes*, for example, has a relatively large number of suspected actors' interpolations, at least some of which have been attributed to the actor Neoptolemus, who is known to have performed in the play in Athens in 340.[75] Regardless of who authored them, it seems reasonable to take the interpolations in *Orestes* as evidence of the play's ongoing popularity after the fifth century.[76] Indeed, *Orestes* combined many elements that fourth-century audiences must have enjoyed: a novel treatment of a familiar myth; use of stage space such as the roof of the stage building; and characters ranging from highborn Greek princes to singing Phrygian eunuchs.

The taste for 'realism' in acting, the scholia and actors' interpolations provide evidence that supports Aristotle's general picture of fourth-century tragic performance in the *Poetics*. Playwrights experimented with different sorts of diction for their characters, even as they stuck to a few famous stories for their plots. Professional actors sought to give virtuosic displays of their speaking and singing abilities, sometimes by rearranging or rewriting the play text. Audiences were interested in displays of intense emotion and exciting ways of staging scenes. None of this is, properly speaking, a break with fifth-century tragedy; rather, it is a heightening of tendencies that were already present at the end of the fifth century (see also Dunn, this volume).

## *Standardization of Masks*

Theatrical masks changed over the course of the fourth century, gradually developing into standard 'types.' The tragic mask developed the *onkos*

---

[73] On the scholia see Hanink, this volume.    [74] See Falkner 2002.    [75] See Kovacs 2007.
[76] See Vahtikari 2014: 56, 190–1.

(ὄγκος), an elongated tower of hair on the top, for all of the important characters.[77]

One reason for the standardization of masks may have been philosophical. Aristotle's *Poetics* describes the tragic hero as someone better than the average person, but not morally perfect. This heightened moral stature ensures that the audience cares about what happens to the hero, while the hero's imperfection explains his reversal of fortune.[78] Aristotle's *Nicomachean Ethics* provides a typology of character in its discussion of 'the great-souled man', where Aristotle lays out not only the moral qualities but also the actual behaviors of his type: the great-souled man engages in few but significant endeavors, would prefer to render a favor than to benefit from one, and conducts himself with honor as his only point of reference. He walks slowly, with dignity, and speaks in a deep voice, whereas the 'vulgar man,' his opposite type, trots hurriedly and speaks shrilly.[79] We might be tempted to consider Aristotle's rather generic 'great-souled man,' who has all the behaviors and tastes of the elite ('He likes to own things that are beautiful and useless') without any individuality, to be consistent with the stock tragic hero. The 'great-souled man's' generic traits (high social position, concern for his honor) make him easily represented by the mask of the young tragic hero, visually marked as youthful, aristocratic, and male, but devoid of any individuality.

Contemporary art may also have influenced the standardization of masks. Conventionally, fifth-century sculpture and vase-painting depicted human and divine faces as perfectly symmetrical, beautiful, and virtually expressionless, even in the midst of violent action. Fifth-century tragic masks seem to have been similarly beautiful and bland. In the fourth century, however, artistic ideals and theories began to change. In Hellenistic sculpture, with its statues of drunk old women, satyrs, and children, we see an interest in representing emotions and bodies that do not meet the classical ideal.[80] Mask-makers began to make tragic masks with emotional states represented, like anxiety or suffering, and the comic masks of

---

[77] See Pickard-Cambridge 1988: 193–6. According to Pickard-Cambridge (1988: 179), a statue from Mantua dating around 400 BC provides evidence for the development of *onkos* as early as the end of the fifth century. On the *onkos* of the postclassical tragic mask see Petrides 2014: 138–41.
[78] Arist. *Po.* 1452b34–53a12.    [79] Arist. *EN* 1124b6–25a16.
[80] See Wiles 2007: 65; Fowler 1989; see also McNiven 2000; Cohen 2000b.

low-status characters (slaves, pimps, cooks, parasites) were distinctly grotesque.[81] The second-century AD Greek rhetorician Julius Pollux made a list of the types of theatrical masks known to him, which has survived and is based on Hellenistic sources, but scholars dispute Pollux's accuracy as well as his list's applicability to earlier time periods.[82] The material evidence is also tricky to interpret in terms of pinpointing the emergence of stock character masks. Some scholars have argued that a set of terracotta theatrical masks excavated in Lipari and dated to about 350 BC represent the characters from a particular fourth-century play, or many of the mask types from Pollux's catalogue, while others have cautioned against attempting these sorts of identifications.[83]

Another possible reason for the standardization of masks after the fifth century was a practical one. In an era of travelling theatrical troupes and multiple venues for performances, having a standard set of masks that would fulfil most or all of a company's needs would have been a more attractive and economical option than having to create masks anew for each new play.

## The Chorus in Fourth-Century Tragedy

It is often claimed that the fourth century saw the decline of the dramatic chorus, and that this erstwhile essential component of drama now became peripheral to the plays' action and themes. This claim is based mainly on Aristotle's strictures on his contemporary tragedians' use of stock 'interludes', or *embolima*, which according to Aristotle had originated with Agathon, the late-fifth-century dramatist (*Po.* 1456a27–30). The evidence of Menandrean papyri (but also, e.g., of the manuscripts of Aristophanes' *Assemblywomen* 729, 876 and *Wealth* 322, 626, 770, 801, 1096) would seem consistent with Aristotle's complaints: where we should have

---

[81] Neiiendam 1992: 63–93 analyzes some of the surviving visual evidence for Hellenistic theatrical performance, such as mosaics, wall-paintings and vase-paintings, with particular attention to the ways in which the masks depicted fit Pollux's typology of theatrical masks. See also Foley 2000.

[82] See Appendix A in Csapo and Slater 1995: 393–402 with translation and discussion of Pollux's text. On the reliability of Pollux see mainly Green and Seeberg's introduction in Webster 1995: 1. 8–51. See also Bernabò Brea (1981, 2000) and, for a skeptical approach, Poe 1996 (with the response by Petrides 2014: 157–63).

[83] Xanthakis-Karamanos (1980: 169) argues that the Lipari masks include many of the characters from Astydamas' *Hector* and 'may be related' to that play. Webster (1970: 45–96) attempts to match archaeological and artistic evidence of masks to Pollux's catalogue. Wiles (2007: 52–5) discusses the Lipari masks at length, noting that they lack the *onkos* and cautioning against trying to identify them with particular characters from particular plays; Vahtikari 2014: 166, 183 and Pickard-Cambridge 1988: 193 also urge caution.

expected a choral song, we find no more than the indication '(song) of the chorus' (ΧΟΡΟΥ or ΧΟΡΟΥ ΜΕΛΟΣ). This is usually taken to suggest that Menander (or Aristophanes in his late plays) did not compose original choral songs for his comedies, and that the chorus performed some sort of song-and-dance routine, perhaps as part of a standard repertoire (see also the chapters by Dunn and Griffith, this volume).

Whether Menander's perceived practice was also followed by other comic playwrights or not (and the latter possibility must seriously be taken into account),[84] there is no reason to assume that the *tragic* chorus underwent a process of general marginalization, as Aristotle seems to imply, or even that the development of the tragic chorus in the fourth century (and later) was a uniform one. There are a number of post-fifth-century tragedies named after what may well have been their chorus: for instance, Cleophon's *Bacchae*, Dicaeogenes' *Cyprians*, or Moschion's *Men of Pherae*. If this surmise is accurate, then it suggests that the chorus here must have been thematically important and, presumably, integrated[85] – as indeed it is in *Rhesus*, the only fourth-century tragedy to have been preserved intact.[86] Further, in a tragic *adespoton* (*TrGF* II, F 649), which surely comes from a postclassical, perhaps Hellenistic piece,[87] we find a terse three-way dialogue between Priam, Cassandra and a chorus, no doubt represented here by its coryphaeus, who speaks in what appear to be snippets of iambic trimetres.[88] It is, of course, impossible to ascertain whether in this anonymous drama the coryphaeus, let alone the chorus, functioned as 'one of the actors', as Aristotle's famous injunction has it (*Po.* 1456a25–7). And it is *a fortiori* impossible, on the basis of the meager remains of post-fifth-century tragedy, to extrapolate any kind of general trends with regard to the development of the chorus in that period.

---

[84] For cautious approaches see, e.g., Hunter 1979; Rothwell 1992.
[85] See Sifakis 1967: 113–14. However, caution is advisable here, since some of these titles may have referred to collective entities other than the chorus; in Menander's *Sicyonians* (admittedly a comedy), the title's plural obviously cannot refer to the identity of the play's chorus.
[86] On *Rhesus* see further Fries, this volume. On the chorus in fourth-century and later tragedy see Griffith, this volume.
[87] That F 649 may be a Hellenistic reworking of an earlier tragic excerpt in iambic trimetres originally meant to be recited rather than sung is argued by Ferrari 2009: 24–6. For further possibilities cf. Fantuzzi and Hunter (2004: 433): 'we may have to do rather with a brief "Singspiel", or even a bookish reconstruction of the tragic manner.'
[88] See now Kotlińska-Tomà 2015: 195–8; Liapis 2016: 77–84.

True, there are a small number of papyrus fragments in which choral songs of tragedy have been replaced, as in Menandrean papyri, by the indication 'song of the chorus'. A case in point is a second-century BC Hibeh papyrus, thought to transmit portions of *Hector* by Astydamas,[89] for which it is often presumed that Astydamas composed no choral song (hence the mere note ΧΟΡΟΥ ΜΕΛΟΣ), leaving the gap to be filled by a set piece from the chorus' repertory – no doubt the kind of stock *'entr'acte'* that Aristotle, as we saw, calls *embolimon*. This may well be right, but there are other possibilities. For instance, 'song of the chorus' may suggest that, whether Astydamas did or did not compose original lyric songs for this tragedy, the papyrus in question was meant to be used as a 'promptbook' for a later performance, in which it was thought preferable for the chorus to perform a set piece rather than the original choral songs, perhaps because the latter would have no doubt required special training and/or virtuosity.[90] Evidence for such 'promptbooks' is admittedly sparse, but a third-century AD papyrus of Euripides' *Cresphontes* is likely to preserve the remains of precisely such a text;[91] and a ca. 250 BC papyrus of Euripides' *Hippolytus* (*P. Sorb.* 2252 = no. 393 Mertens-Pack³), which transmits lines 1–106 but omits the lyric portion 58–72, may also have been used as a 'promptbook' to aid rehearsals only of the spoken, iambic passages of the play.[92] Alternatively, it may be that the poets themselves 'simply inserted χοροῦ in the circulated texts, perhaps to ensure common adaptability on stages throughout the Greek world with their varying theatrical resources, as Attic drama was spreading significantly in the fourth century.'[93]

---

[89] *P. Hib.* ii 174 = no. 171 Mertens-Pack³. For the Astydamas fragment see *TrGF* 60 F **1h?, esp. 9–11; cf. Liapis 2016 and Liapis and Stephanopoulos, this volume.

[90] Cf. Taplin 1999: 38.

[91] *P.Oxy.* 2458 (= *TrGF* V/1, E. fr. 448a), identified as an acting copy by its first editor (Turner 1962: 75–6). See further Marshall 2004: 34–5, who also discusses extensively *P.Oxy.* 4546, of which he argues that, as it preserves (with omissions) only lines spoken by Admetus in E. *Alc.* 344–82, it must have been an actor's copy used in rehearsal.

[92] See Marshall 2004: 30, 33, who also raises the alternative possibility of 'a pared-down, non-musical version of *Hippolytus* – a "touring version", for example, when the chorus is not available' (quotation from p. 30). It is immaterial for the purposes of this discussion whether the omission in the *Hippolytus* papyrus was signalled by ΧΟΡΟΥ / ΧΟΡΟΥ ΜΕΛΟΣ (the crucial portion of the papyrus is missing; see further Barrett (1964) 438 with n. 2; Taplin 1976: 49. For tragic papyri containing the indication ΧΟΡΟΥ (ΜΕΛΟΣ) see again Taplin 1976; also, Kannicht and Snell on *TrGF* II, adesp. fr. 625.9 (from Euripides' *Oeneus* or *Meleager*?); adesp. fr. 640b.28 (published in *TrGF* V/2, p. 1132).

[93] Quotation from Revermann 2006a: 281; cf. Marshall (n. 91).

## Conclusion

To return to Astydamas' 'manifesto': the vitality of fourth-century (and later) tragedy can be hard to discern in the extremely fragmentary remains of the texts and the heavy influence of Euripides. Indeed, it was hard even in the fourth century for some to appreciate their contemporary tragedy without seeing it as arrogantly comparing itself to 'classic' fifth-century tragedy. It is no wonder Astydamas sounds like he had a bit of a chip on his shoulder. 'If only he had lived' in the fifth century, as he says in his poem, we might have his tragedies to read and watch today.

CHAPTER 7

# Music and Dance in Tragedy After the Fifth Century

### Mark Griffith*

Greek tragedy first came into existence in the sixth century BC out of choral song and dance. The plays of Aeschylus, Sophocles, Euripides and their contemporaries were highly musical: usually between half and one-third of the lines in every play of theirs were sung or half-sung rather than spoken in normal tones. The singers, whether chorus or solo actors, usually also moved their bodies expressively – i.e., danced – while they sang. This is what the celebration of Dionysus required and what audiences expected.[1]

It is often stated – wrongly – that Greek tragedy steadily evolved throughout its history, to become less musical and more purely rhetorical and speech-focused. But in fact, to judge from what the limited evidence tells us, tragedy appears to have maintained its musical focus even during the course of manifold changes and innovations, right up until Late Antiquity. That is to say, for anyone going to see a Greek tragedy performed, it would usually have been taken for granted that there would be singing, pipe-playing and dancing. This was musical theatre. But musical styles, then as now, kept on changing, and the theatre was always one of the most innovative areas of experimentation; so the music of postclassical tragedy sounded very different, and was employed in different ways, from that of Aeschylus in the early fifth century, and probably was different too even from the music of Euripides, Sophocles and Agathon in the later fifth century.

The play-texts that survived from antiquity into the Middle Ages and were recopied during the Byzantine and Renaissance eras, thus evolving into the manuscripts on which modern editions of the three great

---

* I am very grateful to Donald Mastronarde, Sarah Olsen, Nikolaos Papazarkadas, Naomi Weiss two anonymous referees and especially the editors of this volume, for corrections and valuable suggestions.
[1] The standard Greek words for 'dance/dancing' were *choros*, *choreuō* (whence *choros* = 'dance-group') and *orchēsis*, *orcheomai* (whence *orchēstra* = 'dancing-area', the term used also for the central performance space in a Greek theatre).

tragedians are based, contained no stage directions from the original authors and no musical or choreographic notations. But we can usually tell from the metres used and from slight variations in dialect forms of speech exactly which portions of the plays were originally composed to be sung (lyrics), and which were spoken without melody or instrumental accompaniment (iambic trimeters) or were delivered in a kind of recitative chant (anapaests; perhaps trochaic tetrameters too).[2]

The sung portions of the tragedies were accompanied by an *aulētēs* (player on the *auloi* = double-pipes). Occasionally other instruments may have been used as well, if the play-action demanded it;[3] but the *auloi*, with their 'hot', breathy sound, were always regarded as the standard instrument for theatrical performances.[4]

The chorus members for tragic performances at the City Dionysia during the fifth and fourth centuries BC were always Athenian citizens, whereas the actors and *aulētēs* could be, and often were, from elsewhere.[5] There were hundreds of relatively skilled and experienced Athenian singer-dancers available in the 'talent pool' for the playwrights and *chorēgoi* (producers) to choose from;[6] but we are also informed that the best dancers and singers in a chorus might be strategically arranged to be most prominently in the audience's view, and that some of the less talented singers might only pretend to sing at times so that the best voices could dominate.[7]

Unfortunately, we know very little about the specific melodies composed for fifth-century tragedy, and even less about the dance steps and bodily movements.[8] Occasionally, the words of the text indicate particular

---

[2] For discussion of tragic actors' delivery of anapaests and trochaic tetrameters see Dale 1968: 47–52, 69–72, 87–93; also Michelini 1982; T. Moore 2012.
[3] For example, percussion in Aesch. *Edonians*, Eur. *Bacchae*; a syrinx in [Aesch.] *Prom.* (Io's monody 566–88), Soph. *Inachus*; kithara or lyre in Aesch. *Bassarids* (Orpheus), Eur. *Antiope* (Amphion), Soph. *Thamyris, Ichneutai*; cf. too Aristoph. *Frogs* 1284–95, 1304–28.
[4] The *auloi* also accompanied dithyrambic choruses that performed at the same festivals at Athens and elsewhere. The melodies and rhythms of dithyramb and tragedy often had much in common.
[5] Many of the best *aulētai* came from Thebes: see West 1992: 366–8; Wilson 2007a; and later in this chapter.
[6] Wilson 2000; Revermann 2006b: 107–12.
[7] Menander *Epikleros* fr. 130 K.-A., Aelius Aristides *On Behalf of the Four* 154 (with schol.); cf. Hesychius s.v. ψιλεῖς, Photius *Lex.* s.vv. τρίτος ἀριστεροῦ, ἀριστεροστάτης; Pickard-Cambridge 1988: 241–2, Csapo and Slater 1995: 353–4, 361–4.
[8] The terms *strophe* and *antistrophe* that are regularly applied to metrically equivalent pairs of lyric stanzas were explained by some ancient commentators as referring to a chorus' alternate clockwise 'turning movement' (*strophe*) and 'counter-turning' (*antistrophe*) within the orchestra (e.g., schol. Eur. *Hec.* 647, Atilius Fortunatianus *Grammatici Latini* 6.294); but modern scholars are generally skeptical about this as reliable evidence for Athenian theatre choreography.

movements – e.g., beating the breast and tearing the hair in grief; leaping and prancing in excitement, etc., or even lying on the ground – and sometimes the words may also give some clue as to the flavor and idiom of the melody (e.g., Eur. *Or.* 1395–99, 1425–30 'in Asian style ... like a Phrygian', cf. *Tro.* 511–67; Aesch. *Cho.* 423–28 'like an Aryan or Cissian mourner'). These textual indications will of course have prompted the audience to imagine the 'real-life' equivalents of such behavior, whether or not the actors and chorus-members will always actually have replicated these sounds and movements in an 'authentic' manner.[9] But we have virtually no information about the choreography that was employed at any period of Greek tragic or dithyrambic performance. One type of rather stately step or sequence of steps, the *emmeleia*, was said by later sources to have been basic to tragic choreography throughout the centuries, as distinct from the more exuberant *sikinnis* that was widely used in satyr-drama and the raunchy *kordax*, common in comedy.[10] But only in the case of the *sikinnis* do we have even the roughest idea of what the actual steps may have looked like (thanks mainly to red-figure vase-paintings of satyr-choruses in action).[11]

Up until the late fifth century, it appears that each tragic playwright composed his own music and choreography[12] (and may have designed the masks and costumes too, as far as we know), and he was also the stage director of the performance, working with a 'producer' (*chorēgos*) who financed the whole production (four plays in all during the fifth century –

---

[9] Weiss 2018: *passim*, esp. 10–11.
[10] Names and brief – often vague – descriptions of several dances allegedly employed in drama are attested in late authors (see Lawler 1964, Csapo and Slater 1995: 364–8): on the tragic *emmeleia*, e.g., Bekker *Anecd. Graeca* 1.101.17 (= Aristoxenus fr. 104), Athenaeus 630c–e. See further Fitton 1973; Lawler 1964; Pickard-Cambridge 1988: 239–57; Naerebout 1997: 174–253, 269–89.
[11] Festa 1918; Krumeich, Pechstein and Seidensticker 1999: 21–3, with Figs; Seidensticker 2010. The dancing chorus member on the Pronomos Vase (*ARV*² 1336,1) is likely to be performing the *sikinnis*. In the case of tragedy, in contrast to satyr-play, only two or three scenes of dancing choreuts at most survive from Athenian fifth-century vase painters: (i) the rows of paired dancers on a Basel column-krater (Basel BS 415 = Csapo and Slater 1995, Fig. 1A) – not necessarily a tragic chorus at all; (ii) two young men rehearsing in female costume and masks on a pelike found at Cervetri (Boston, MFA 98.883 = Pickard-Cambridge 1988, Fig. 34 = Csapo and Slater 1995, Fig. 7B); (iii) another scene of two young choreuts on a bell-krater from Valle Pega (Ferrara T. 173C = Pickard-Cambridge 1988, Fig. 33): but the postures of these latter two may not represent actual dance movements. See too Taplin 2007: 29–30; and in general Green 1991; Naerebout 1997: 209–53.
[12] During the later part of his career, Euripides is said to have worked with a musical collaborator, Cephisophon; see Kovacs 1994, Sommerstein 1996: 239–40. We do not know whether other playwrights did the same. For Aeschylus as choreographer, Athenaeus 21e2–22a4 is of ambiguous value.

things changed in later eras) and in some cases a chorus-trainer, too (*chorodidaskalos*).[13] In the early fifth century, tragic poets also acted in their own plays (Ar. *Rhet.* 3.1.1403b23); but Sophocles is said to have abandoned this quite early in his career because of his weak voice (*Life of Soph.* [*TrGF* T1] 21–2), and Euripides never seems to have been an actor at all. Agathon, on the other hand, is presented by Aristophanes (*Thesm.* 39–268) as possessing a lovely, versatile singing voice. In later periods, tragic poets do not seem to have acted in their own plays – though, as we shall see, actors did themselves quite often engage in rewriting the plays they performed, sometimes adding or subtracting musical and choreographic elements. The word for a 'tragic playwright' in the fifth century was *tragōidopoios* ('tragedy-maker'), or simply *tragōidos* (lit. 'goat-singer', i.e., performer of tragedies);[14] the idea that a tragedian was a 'writer' was not emphasized. To complicate the questions of composition, authorship and casting still further, play-making tended to run in families, which doubtless involved extensive collaboration; but as in most other areas of the history of the Greek theatre, we know all too little about the process.[15]

This chapter will address three main issues that are somewhat separate but closely interrelated:

1) How much music and dance was there in later tragedy? Did the amount, or the structure and general character, of the sung and danced scenes in relation to the spoken dialogue change significantly after the fifth century?

2) What in general were the main harmonic and melodic (and choreographic) developments in Greek music between the fifth century BC and later periods?

3) What do we know about the use of music and dance in reperformance of classical (fifth-century BC) plays in later periods? What kinds of changes did actors, directors, singers and reciters of 'old tragedy' make in their performances?

---

[13] Wilson 2000; Marshall 2012; see too Pickard-Cambridge 1988: Index s.v. *chorēgos*; Csapo and Slater 1995: 352–3.

[14] The term 'goat-singer' probably referred originally to the prize awarded to the victorious poet and chorus, which included a goat (*tragos*), to be sacrificed and barbecued at the celebratory feast afterwards; Burkert 1966.

[15] Sutton 1987a; Griffith 2013: 28–31.

## How Much Music and Dance Was There in Post-Fifth-Century Tragedy?

The dialogue and long speeches of Greek tragedy throughout the centuries were all composed in the same basic metre, the iambic trimeter or occasionally in the closely related trochaic tetrameter.[16] These regular 'stichic' metres[17] were regarded as coming closest to the rhythm of everyday speech, and in the fifth century were delivered accordingly, i.e., without musical enhancement. By contrast, the rhythms of ancient Greek songs in general, and the lyrics of tragedy in particular, whether sung by the chorus or by individual character-actors, employ a wide variety of cola of different metrical types, sometimes in regular stanzas (alternating in strophic responsion)[18] or at other times in freer-flowing nonstrophic forms. Lyric passages may combine multiple metres in unique patterns and sometimes switch quite radically from one rhythm to another within the same ode, or even stanza. In addition, chanted passages in the 'recitative' anapaestic metre (a regular, 4/4 rhythm that often accompanies entrances or exits of characters – hence sometimes described as 'marching' anapaests) seem to have occupied an intermediate position on the musical spectrum between spoken and sung.

The metrical patterns not only inform us which passages were musically enhanced, but also give us clues as to the rhythms of that music. Unfortunately, however, we do not know how exact the timing of long vs. short quantities was in actual performance, nor how pauses between phrases may have been managed. This, together with our uncertainty about the ways in which the pitch accent may have affected oral delivery – a factor that almost certainly changed over time (especially between ca. 300 BC and 100 AD), as pitch-variation gave way to simple stress within the spoken

---

[16] These two metres were adopted also by Roman playwrights both for tragedy and comedy, though in the Latin context they are usually termed *iambic senarius* and *trochaic septenarius*. See further later in this chapter.

[17] That is, regular 'one-line' metrical structures that were repeated over sustained passages of spoken dialogue or longer speeches, unlike the varied cola of lyric or the continuous flow of recitative anapaests. (The dactylic hexameter is another example of a 'stichic' metre, but is not employed in tragic dialogue.)

[18] This standard pattern of strophic responsion of stanzas in tragedy (AA BB CC, etc.) is explained in more detail later in this chapter. By contrast, the 'triadic' structure (repeated sets of two metrically equivalent stanzas followed by a metrically dissimilar 'refrain,' in the pattern AAB AAB ... etc.) that was most commonly used for choral lyric performance in the sixth and fifth centuries BC (e.g., Stesichorus' narrative lyrics, and Pindar's Epinician Odes) is relatively rare in tragedy; and it seems to have died out from all forms of Greek musical performance after the fifth century, for unknown reasons.

Greek language – means that we can only very approximately recreate or imagine the actual rhythms of the 'lyrics' written in our surviving Greek texts.[19] Nonetheless, the rhythmical character of any particular lyric sequence can be recognized, and we can track changes from one stanza to another or even from one metrical period to another, sometimes quite clearly linked to particular shifts in mood or pacing within the play.[20]

In addition to the metres themselves, another important structural feature that helps a reader grasp some of the musical character of tragic songs is the presence or absence of strophic responsion, i.e., the arrangement of choral or actors' songs into matching pairs of stanzas, with changing metrical patterns for each successive pair. Although strophic pairs in responsion originally comprised the standard structure of most of the musical passages in tragedy, it became increasingly common in the later fifth century for this structure to be modified or abandoned, with non-strophic, 'free-flowing' lyrics (*apolelumena*) taking their place. This development was closely associated with innovations in dithyrambic and citharodic performance of the later fifth century,[21] and among the tragedians, Euripides and Agathon were the most conspicuous proponents of this musical style, especially for the arias of their solo actors. Further freedoms were adopted also in the use of vocal melismas (two or three different notes assigned to a single metrical syllable), which we also find parodied by Aristophanes' 'Aeschylus' in *Frogs* (1309–63). Thus, by the late fifth century, actors' songs had become more rhythmically variable, extensive and unpredictable, while the regular structure of the chorus' songs tended to be more strictly maintained. Overall, too, the number and length of the choral passages in later-fifth-century tragedy tend to be considerably smaller than what we find in Aeschylus and early Sophocles, whereas the amount of actors' lyrics is much greater.[22]

So, against the background of this general picture of the late-fifth-century context, how do the remains of post-fifth-century tragedy look?

---

[19] In general, we know enough to tell that most modern attempts at reconstructing and performing ancient Greek music (including the bits of musically annotated papyri that survive), usually in simple 3/4 or 4/4 rhythm, are quite inaccurate.

[20] The best guide to the lyric metres of Greek tragedy remains Dale 1968.

[21] West 1992: 359–72; Csapo 2004a, 2004b; Power 2010: 500–16; LeVen 2014 *passim*. These musical innovations are often referred to by modern scholars as the 'New Music', though that term is not found among the ancient critics, for whom 'theatre music' was often employed as a term to designate innovative and/or vulgar musical idioms.

[22] Rode 1971: 85–115; Barner 1971; Csapo 2004a. These are tendencies, not invariable rules: thus, e.g., in *The Bacchae* we find Euripides maintaining quite an 'old-fashioned' manner in his lyrics: relatively little actors' song (only Agave, near the end), but rather extensive strophic singing from the chorus.

What proportion of the lines of poetry that survive in quotations or on papyrus are in lyric metres, and what can we tell about the relative frequency of strophic responsion vs. 'free' lyrics, or of choral vs. actors' songs? What can we learn from *Rhesus*, from Lycophron's *Alexandra* and from Ezekiel's *Exagōgē*? What does the comparative evidence of New Comedy tell us? And how does all of this direct textual evidence stack up against the indirect testimony of inscriptions and of later authors who happen to have reason to write about performances of tragedy in their respective eras?

In general, the direct textual evidence is very mixed.[23] At one end of the spectrum, we find two very unconventional dramas, *Alexandra* and *Exagōgē (Exodus)*. Lycophron's *Alexandra*, composed supposedly in third-century BC Alexandria, was obviously an anomaly in many respects (see Hornblower in this volume), and its complete lack of music is only one of many indications that it was not designed for performance in a theatre. In the case of Ezekiel's *Exagōgē* (also probably from the third century BC, or possibly the second; see Lanfranchi, this volume), the substantial fragments that survive are likewise all in iambic trimeters, and we have no evidence that a chorus or any lyric metres were employed at all. This may be simply an accident of preservation; but in any case we can make no definite pronouncement about the music of this play.

At the other end of the spectrum, *Rhesus* looks very much like a conventional fifth-century tragedy, in terms of the quantity and nature of its lyrics. This play presents its own particular problems and questions, of course: but whatever its date and authorship – and current scholarly opinion seems to be leaning strongly towards a fourth century date – its metrical-musical structure and character appear fairly straightforward, unadventurous and conservative (or imitative of older fashions).[24] The choral odes and 'interludes' are mainly arranged in strophic responsion, employing standard lyric metres without radical shifts of rhythm or other evidence of the mannerisms associated with late Euripides and the 'New Music'.[25] Only at 675–703 do we find a brief section of nonstrophic lyrics; and this is nothing unusual by fifth century standards for such moments of high-energy lyric exchange between two or more characters engaged in vigorous stage action – in this case, one of the characters being the Chorus

---

[23] The texts are collected in Snell *TrGF* I (Minor Tragedians), Snell-Kannicht *TrGF* II (*Adespota* = Unattributed Fragments). For general discussion, see Sifakis 1967; also Xanthakis-Karamanos 1980 – though with little attention to lyrics or music.
[24] Ritchie 1964: 319–27; Liapis 2012: lxiv–lxv; Willink 2002/3.
[25] For fuller metrical analysis and comparison to the lyrics of Euripides, see esp. Liapis 2012 *ad locc*.

in frenzied pursuit, capture, confused discussion and then release of Diomedes and Odysseus.[26] The choreography must have involved rapid running movements, as the chorus, re-entering in full 'seek and destroy' mode, engages in quick back-and-forth interaction with the disguised Greek pair. More unusual, however, is the use of anapaestic metre, intermingled with exclamations and occasional trochaic elements, for the wounded Charioteer's entry at 728–53, as he groans aloud, presumably with some musical enhancement, before going on to deliver his vivid 'messenger speech' in the standard iambic trimeters.

Among the other – much shorter and more disjointed – remains of post-fifth-century tragedy, we find approximately thirty fragments out of the thousand or so contained in Snell-Kannicht's two volumes that appear to be in lyric metres rather than iambic trimeters.[27] This seems quite a small number, which might suggest that relatively little music was contained in these plays overall. But we should recall that a high proportion of these tragic fragments are cited in later authors for their ethical/gnomic neatness and quotability, and that iambic trimeters were always the most suitable medium for such quotation – as is demonstrated by the quoted fragments from Euripides' and Sophocles' lost plays as well.

Papyrological finds actually tell a rather different story from these quotations: more than a dozen papyri of tragedy by unknown authors of different dates contain lyric passages, and several of them actually have some musical notation. A fair number of satyr-play fragments also exist on papyri; several of these contain lyric passages and at least a couple have musical notation. Satyr-drama may be a separate issue from tragedy (especially after the fifth century BC): but the two genres were closely related, and this evidence does seem to indicate that musical – and in this case, specifically choral – components (since the satyr chorus seem always to be the prime musical-choreographic element in satyr-drama) were

---

[26] Liapis 2012 *ad loc.* compares Aesch. *Eum.* 254ff, Soph. *Ajax* 866ff for this excited reentry into the orchestra of the Chorus, and remarks on the 'agitated mood' and 'bustle' of 'this supremely agitated scene'.

[27] In *TrGF* I (Minor Tragedians), I count the following post-fifth-century tragic fragments, of varying lengths and characters, that appear to be in lyric metre and hence presumably to have been accompanied by music: 60 F1h (Astydamas' *Hector*); 72 F4 (Theodectas' *Oedipus*), F18; 101 F2 (Alexander Aetolus); in *TrGF* II (*Adespota* = Unattributed Fragments) F126, 127, 129, 130, 136 (= *PMG* 1027a), 137, 167a, 167b, 167c.3–5, 185a, 243 (= *PMG* 1028), 279f–g?, 279h, 373? (= *PMG* 994), 377 (= *PMG* 999), 415a, 482, 499, 500, 509, 644.21–49 (anapaests), 649, 678, 679, 680, 681?, 682, 684, 691, 692. In addition, several musically annotated papyri of tragic fragments have appeared since the publication of Snell-Kannicht (1971, 1981): see later in this chapter.

commonly included in post-fifth-century Greek drama.[28] Altogether, of the sixty-one items contained in Pöhlmann and West's collection of *Documents of Ancient Greek Music*, at least fifteen (i.e., 25 percent or more) are definitely or probably from tragedies, although as we shall see, their nature and contexts vary considerably, and some may constitute recital repertoires for 'tragedy-singers' *(tragōidoi)* rather than continuous playscripts.[29]

Aristotle's testimony in the *Poetics* can help us here, in two different ways. Writing in the mid–fourth century (perhaps in the 340s), Aristotle acknowledges that for many theatre-goers, the visual and musical dimensions of a theatre performance (*opsis* and *melos* are the shorthand terms that he employs) are the most exciting and attractive (*Poet.* 6.1449b21–29, 1450b16–20; 26.1461b26–62a17), even while he sees his own main original contribution to the appreciation of *tragōidia* as being his focus on plot-construction (*muthos*), which he regards as the subtlest and most sophisticated mechanism for achieving the key 'pleasures' of pity, fear and 'affect' in general (*pathos*). He also acknowledges that the more sophisticated critics of tragedy before him have tended to emphasize 'character portrayal' (*ēthos*) and 'ideas' (*dianoia*), even while he himself seems to share wholeheartedly the elite disdain for spectacle and musical variety that his teacher Plato had previously expounded in several contexts (*Republic*, *Laws*, etc.). Modern critics of tragedy have often interpreted Aristotle's remarks as constituting an active antipathy, or even obliviousness, to the multidimensional appeal of live, musical theatre. As Book 8 of the *Politics* makes clear, however, this is a misunderstanding of Aristotle's appreciation for the emotional power and cultural value of music in general. For our purposes here, all that matters is that Aristotle does in fact recognize that music and visual spectacle are two important extra ingredients that epic poetry lacks, and that therefore render tragedy more complete and satisfying as an art form.[30]

The tragedians whom Aristotle discusses the most (in both the *Poetics* and the *Rhetoric*) and whom he regards as having attained the pinnacle of

---

[28] For the musical dimensions of satyr-drama, see Krumeich, Pechstein, Seidensticker 1999, esp. 16–17; Völke 2001; Lämmle 2013: 313–26; Griffith 2015: 12, 32, 38–9, 42–3, 135–8, 140–1, 144, 152, 154, 157, 159, with further references.

[29] Pöhlmann and West 2001: nos 2, 3, 4, 5, 6, 8, 9, 17–18, 39, 40, 41(?), 42–3, 53, 54. For solo actors' singing, see esp. Hall 2002; also further later in this chapter.

[30] Sifakis 2001: 54–71 argues convincingly (with reference both to the *Poetics* and the *Politics*) for Aristotle's consistently high regard for music as a vital component of the fullest tragic effect. See too Petrides 2014: 102–7, on the importance of *opsis* in Aristotle's views on drama.

Music and Dance in Tragedy After the Fifth Century 213

the genre are Sophocles and Euripides; but he does also admire several playwrights of the fourth century, esp. Theodectas, Carcinus, Chaeremon and Astydamas.[31] And it appears overall that in his prescriptions in the *Poetics* for the best kind of tragedy he does not see a radical disjunction between its fifth-century and fourth-century proponents. But Aristotle does mention one particular phenomenon in relation to the choral songs of tragedy that is quite intriguing: at *Poetics* 18. 1456a25–32, he refers to tragedians composing choral songs that are mere 'inserts' (*embolima*), i.e., self-standing lyrics that have no particular connection to the plot of the play in question – a tendency for which he blames Agathon as the originator. Aristotle gives the impression that this tendency has become common in his own era, though he does not go into any detail.[32]

Further material for comparison is available to us from developments in the separate but related genre of fourth-century Attic comedy, about which we are rather better informed than we are about the tragedy of that period.[33] The two latest plays of Aristophanes that are preserved (his career began in the 420s and ended in the 380s) show radical changes in his use of the chorus. In his *Assemblywomen* (ca. 390 BC), the chorus has only a small role, singing just three very short songs plus another for which only the bare entry '[Song] of the Chorus' (ΧΟΡΟΥ) exists in our medieval manuscripts. In *Wealth* (385 BC), that bare statement 'of the Chorus' is all that is found by way of a choral presence in our manuscripts. Apparently, then, Aristophanes did not compose any script/libretto for these interludes, and consequently to later generations of scholars and copyists, the choral interludes did not count as integral components of the play-text. All of this is in sharp contrast to the prominence and extravagant brilliance of the lyrics that Aristophanes had composed for his choruses in such earlier plays as *Birds*, *Clouds* and *Frogs*. It may well be that this indicator (ΧΟΡΟΥ) would also have been employed for transmitting play-texts of fourth-century tragedies containing 'inserts' (*embolima*) as their choral component; and indeed a similar notation (ΧΟΡΟΥ ΜΕΛΟΣ = "song of the chorus") is found in a second-century BC papyrus containing fragments

---

[31] Xanthakis-Karamanos 1980: 38–41; Hanink 2011, 2014b: 191–220.
[32] See further Liapis and Stephanopoulos, this volume, with particular reference to Astydamas' *Hector* (*TrGF* 60 1h).
[33] On the fourth-century comic chorus, see in general Hunter 1979: 23–38, Rothwell 1992: 209–25; and on Menander in particular, Lape 2006: 89–109.

that seem to belong to Astydamas' *Hector* (*TrGF* 1 60 \*\*1h? = *P. Hib.* ii 174 = no. 171 Mertens-Pack³).³⁴

In the decades that followed, it looks as if choral songs continued to be of relatively small importance in so-called 'Middle' and 'New' Attic Comedy, though we cannot assess what kinds or scale of musical 'interludes' may have sometimes been included between the by now standard five acts.³⁵ Our papyrus texts of Menander's plays (which were composed between ca. 320 and 300 BC) contain no written-out choral songs, only the indications of XOPOY; and only very occasionally do we seem to encounter actors' lyrics. We note, too, that almost none of the fairly numerous, though generally quite short, fragments of Menander's plays that are quoted from other sources appear to be written in lyric metres, i.e., designed to be sung.³⁶ Wall-paintings and mosaics from the Hellenistic and Roman periods that present scenes from Menander's plays do sometimes depict an *aulētēs* with characters (or a chorus) dancing.³⁷ So music and dance certainly continued to be an important part of the productions, even while these components seem often by now to have been largely someone else's business, not the playwright's. On the other hand, it appears that the scenes in Menander's plays that we find written in trochaic tetrameters or iambic tetrameters were actually semi-sung with *aulos* accompaniment.³⁸ This was later to be the case also for trochaic *septenarii* in the plays of Plautus and Terence in third/second century BC Rome, where the accompanying double-pipe instrument was called a *tibia*. Roman comedy in general, like Attic New Comedy, seems to have

---

[34] In another papyrus, from a Hellenistic tragedy of unknown authorship (*TrGF* II adesp. F 649 = P. Oxy 2746), we find ᾠδή ('song') written repeatedly in the margin: but these entries appear to indicate only that the words (of Cassandra) in the text are to be sung; they are not a substitute for the words themselves; see further Kotlińska-Toma 2015: 195–8.

[35] Nervegna 2013: 63–99.

[36] At Men. *Theophoroumene* 36–41, 50–7 Austin we find dactylic hexameters apparently lyrics, probably sung by the 'possessed' girl; and Σ Eur. *Andr.* 103 mentions τὰ ἐν Θεοφορουμένῃ ᾀδόμενα. At Men. *Leukadia*, fr. 1.10–16 Austin (recovered from Strabo and Hesychius) we find anapaests, possibly of the 'melic' kind (i.e., sung). Of a different character is P. Oxy LIII 3075, which preserves part of a line from Menander's *Perikeiromene* with musical notation (see Huys 1993); this is presumably a later actor's or musician's arrangement, and probably does not reflect Menander's original design for these lines.

[37] Nervegna 2013: 136–58, 264–7.

[38] So, for example, the final scene of *Dyskolos* is introduced by the notation in the papyrus AYΛEI (i.e., 'the piper starts playing'), and the aulete is actually addressed later in the scene by the characters in the play; see further Handley 1965 *ad loc.* It is not known whether or not the trochaic tetrameter scenes in fifth-century tragedy, which are found occasionally in Aeschylus and then fairly frequently in Euripides' later plays, were likewise sung/chanted and accompanied by the *auloi*. Such scenes do tend to be more lively and full of movement than iambic trimeter scenes: Drew-Bear 1968; Michelini 1982; Wilson 2002: 61–2.

involved no regular chorus; but the actors' *cantica* ('sung scenes'), especially in Plautus' plays, are often very extensive and elaborate.[39]

The case of Greek drama in Sicily is particularly tantalizing and baffling. The comedies composed in Doric dialect by Epicharmus of Syracuse in the early fifth century came to be widely known all over Greece. Quite extensive fragments of his plays survive from ancient quotation. Yet it has not been possible to determine whether or not his plays included a chorus or any sung portions. The existence of huge Sicilian theatres (Syracuse, Acragas, Segesta, etc.) with large orchestra-spaces, together with accounts of invitations by Sicilian tyrants to famous Athenian playwrights to present their plays there, all suggest that the theatre scene was vibrant throughout the fifth century and included substantial musical/choreographic components. This was certainly true of later centuries.[40] Polyxenus' *Cyclops* was one famous and unusual case of a theatrical work (either a satyr-play or a dithyramb) composed and presented in Sicily during the fourth century that apparently involved two singing actors in alternation, plus an *aulētēs*.[41] Presumably there were many other (less controversial) dramas, performed there too, including both new tragedies and reperformances/revivals of older plays.

As for tragedy at Rome during the Republican era, which presumably reflected to some considerable degree post-fifth-century trends in Greek tragic performance as well as indigenous Italian traditions, the evidence for music and dance is spotty, but there can be no doubt that they were both strongly present from the beginning.[42] The earliest tragedies in the Latin language (those of Livius Andronicus and Naevius in the later third century BC) were composed by bi- or multilingual authors in environments that were heavily Hellenized, and they probably also drew from Etruscan forms of performance, many of which employed the *tibia*. It appears from the surviving fragments that their plays in fact resembled Plautus' subsequent comic practice of including extensive *cantica* (sung or semi-sung scenes for actors) rather than choral odes – though of course we cannot tell whether they may have included also some choral 'interludes' of the Menandrian type.[43] Some of Ennius' tragedies seem to have included a

---

[39] Wilson 2002: 64–7; Moore 2012, who also helpfully discusses Greek practice(s).
[40] W. Allan 2001; Taplin 2012; see in general the papers in Bosher 2012; also Le Guen, this volume.
[41] *PMG* 815–24; Hall 2002: 8; LeVen 2014: 233–42.   [42] Wilson 2002: 64–7.
[43] For the texts and testimonia, see now Schauer 2012; for general discussion, Beare 1968; Beacham 1991; Erasmo 2004; Boyle 2006; and, for the later period, Kelly 1979. On Roman music in general, Wille 1967; see also Hall 2002: 24–7. The architectural elements of Roman theatres generally presented much smaller spaces for dancing than Greek theatres did.

more old-style 'chorus' of the Euripidean kind (e.g., his *Medea*, with a chorus of Corinthian women).[44] The fragments of Accius and Pacuvius, a few generations later, appear to contain little or nothing by way of separate songs composed in lyric metres, but include extensive *cantica* for the actors.[45] Later (mid–first century AD) Seneca returned to a model closer to that of Sophocles and Euripides, with formal strophic songs from his chorus, either in anapaests or in conventional lyric metres, as well as occasional arias for actors (Cassandra in *Agamemnon*; Andromache in *Trojan Women*). It is not known, and is continually debated, whether Seneca's plays were performed in a theatre by actors, or recited by a single person, or perhaps presented in some kind of mixed, quasi-performed mode; and likewise, we can only speculate as to whether or not any instrumental accompaniment or dance steps were employed.[46]

What exactly did the (ultra-Hellenizing) Roman Emperor Nero's notorious stage performances consist of? The question is intriguing and hard to answer, given the multiplicity, vagueness and confusion of our sources; but this confusion highlights the range of options available to musical stage performers in that period (first century AD). Some of Nero's performances were certainly citharodic (i.e., concert pieces sung to cithara accompaniment), and thus not at all similar to tragedy. But he is also credited with composing an *Oresteia* and an *Antigone*, and with acting such roles as *Orestes the Matricide*, *Oedipus Blinded* and others from the tragic repertoire.[47] As we shall see, such a range of talents and contexts seems to have been somewhat typical of a *tragōidos* (however we choose to translate this term) – and presumably Nero could and did perform some of his pieces in Greek.

Overall, then, the musical picture that emerges from the surviving texts themselves is extremely varied. From *Rhesus* – a tragedy with a chorus singing mid-fifth-century-style choral odes of rather conservative metrical form – to the extended actors' *cantica* of Roman tragedy and the *aulos*-accompanied tetrameters of Greek comedy, along with the lively musical tradition of Greek satyr-plays (visible to us only from papyri) and the

---

[44] Jocelyn 1967, Beacham 1991: 119–20.
[45] Sung material from Pacuvius' and Atilius' tragedies is said to have been performed at Julius Caesar's funeral (Suetonius *Iul.* 84.2): Nervegna 2013: 87. See too Beecham 1991: 125 (including discussion of Horace's recommendations for the tragic chorus in *AP* 180–2, 193–5, 338–9).
[46] See, e.g., Zimmermann 2008: 218–26, with further references.
[47] Suetonius *Nero* 21; 10.2; Tacitus *Annals* 16. 65; Philostratus *Life of Apollonius* 4.39, 5.7; Dio Cassius 62.29.1–2, 62.18.1; etc. See further Kelly 1979; Hall 2002: 25–7; Power 2010: 90–103, 163–81; Nervegna 2007.

various roles and concert opportunities of a famous 'tragedy-singer', the options for playwrights and performers seem to have been wide open. Yet we find also a musicless *Exodus* play that borrowed extensively from Aeschylus and Euripides but seems to have eschewed completely all their musical elements. 'Tragedy' had certainly become a capacious category, with very variable musical potential.

*Documentary Evidence for Post-Fifth-Century Music and Dance in the Theatre*

So far I have discussed mainly the internal evidence of the surviving dramatic texts, fragmentary or entire, exploring to see where we find or do not find lyric metres being employed, or other clear indicators of sung and danced passages. But at this point we need to consider also another body of evidence: the monuments, inscriptions and other documentary and literary testimonials concerning dramatic festivals, musical competitions and the guilds of performers who presented plays, segments of plays or musical recitals of dramatic texts, to audiences large or small in the multiple available venues all over the Greek world.

Revivals of 'old tragedy' (*palaia tragōidia*) – most frequently of Euripides' plays – were common in the fourth century and later, in many different contexts. Inscriptions record some of those that were successfully staged in the annual City Dionysia at Athens between the 380s and 330s BC,[48] while prizes for performers in 'old tragedy' are also recorded at various other festivals as well around the Greek world.[49] The question, to what extent the musical elements of the original productions were preserved or whether later producers revised and 'updated' them so as to introduce newly composed music instead, will be discussed later in this chapter.

Celebratory inscriptions dedicated by victorious *chorēgoi* (lit. 'chorus-masters', i.e., 'play-producers') as well as contracts recorded between local *agōnothetai* (lit. 'competition-organizers', i.e., festival officials) and the Artists of Dionysus (*Dionusou Technitai*), provide us with spotty but valuable information about the conditions of performance for the new dramas that were presented in specific contexts during the Hellenistic and Roman periods, including in some cases their musical dimensions.[50] For

---

[48] Pickard-Cambridge 1988: 105–6, Csapo and Slater 1995: 228–9, Millis and Olson 2013.
[49] See Le Guen, this volume.
[50] Stefanis 1988; Kotsidou 1991; Wilson 2000; Le Guen 2001 (and this volume); Manieri 2009; also Csapo and Slater 1995: 121–206; Aneziri 2007; Ma 2007: 220–45; Rutherford 2007; Crowther 2007; Rotstein 2012; Bosher 2012 *passim*.

Athens and the annual competitions at the City Dionysia and Lenaea, the fragmentary remains of the epigraphic compilations known nowadays as the 'Fasti', 'Didaskaliai' and 'Victors List' between them confirm that dithyrambs, tragedies (along with satyr-dramas) and comedies continued to be performed, right through into the Roman period.[51] These inscriptional records provide no direct information about the specifically musical features; but the fact that a *chorēgos* was still involved as the official 'leader' for the whole production, and that dithyrambs were still being performed as well as tragedies and comedies (and satyr-plays), leaves little room for doubt that the tragic performances likewise involved an *aulētēs* as well as singing actors and chorus.[52]

Outside the main Theatre of Dionysus, additional contests (*kat' agrous Dionysia* = 'Rural Dionysia') also were held at the smaller deme theatres of Attica throughout the fourth and third centuries BC, as a number of choregic victory dedications show, some of them specifically including mention of a 'chorus'.[53] Similar conventions seem to have obtained at other venues outside Attica.[54] Whether or not non-Attic forms of drama were already being performed earlier in the fifth century (as seems likely) at sites such as Syracuse, Argos, Sicyon, Cyrene, etc., by the later fifth century Athenian-style tragedy was certainly being exported quite widely to other regions of Greece, and before long theatres large and small came to be standard features of any Greek polis of note.[55] Ever since the archaic period, too, 'musical competitions' (*mousikoi agōnes*) of various kinds had been a vital part of Greek performance culture, from the huge Panhellenic Games at Delphi (and later at Nemea and the Isthmus of Corinth as well, though not at Olympia) to other large-scale regional events such as the Panathenaia at Athens and the festival of the Heliconian Muses near Thespiae, down to many other smaller-scale venues.[56] Several of these

---

[51] 'Fasti'-inscription = *IG* II² 2318; 'Didaskaliai'-inscription(s) = *IG* II 2319–23a + *SEG* XXVI 203; 'Victors List'-inscription = *IG* II 2325 + *SEG* XLVIII 183 (see further Hanink, this volume). See Pickard-Cambridge 1988: 101–25; Csapo and Slater 1995: 133–7, 226–9; Wilson 2000; Millis and Olson 2013, with reviews by S. D. Lambert *BMCR* 2013.06.10 and D. Summa *CR* 64 (2014) 67–9.
[52] Wilson 2000: 68–70, 85–93, 130–1, 214–15.
[53] Csapo and Slater 1995: 121–56; Wilson 2000 *passim*; and Goette 2014 (including full discussion of the archaeological evidence for the various deme theatres), esp. Fig. 2.10 and Plate 2.2, with *SEG* 36, 187 (Sphettos); also Fig. 2.11 and *IG* I 969.
[54] Wilson 2000: 265–302; Le Guen 2010a.
[55] Easterling 1997; W. Allan 2001; Dearden 1990, 1999; Duncan 2011; papers in Bosher 2012 (esp. Marconi 175–207; Vassallo 208–25).
[56] The full inscriptional evidence is collected in Kotsidou 1991 for the Panathenaic festival, and in Schachter 1987 and Manieri 2009 for the multiple musical festivals in Boeotia. In general, see

included contests in tragic performance – whatever that might have entailed.

The surviving victory records often mention contests among *tragōidoi* – a term which, in some cases, seems to refer to tragic playwrights, while in others to performers, who might be troupes of actors or individual 'singers' performing selections of dramatic texts set to music[57] – as well as *aulētai* (pipe-players) and sometimes *choreutai* (choral singer-dancers).[58] These features are confirmed also by some of the contracts recorded between local festival-organizers and the guild of Artists of Dionysus, specifying that a certain number of performers of particular kinds (often including *tragōidoi* and/or *aulētai*) will be provided for a particular occasion.[59]

So, for example, even as late as the Roman period, in a catalogue of the victors at the Festival of the Muses at Thespiae (Boeotia) ca. 160 AD,[60] after mention of a victorious trumpeter, herald, various poets, rhapsode and cithara-player (*kitharistēs*), we find:

> ... Comedian of old comedy: Cl. Apollonius of Miletus; Tragedian of old tragedy: Metrobius ... of Athens; Poet of new comedy: L. Marius Antiochus of Corinth; Actor of new comedy: Fl. Ennychus of Thespiae; Poet (*poiêtês*) of new tragedy: Apollonius ... of Aspendus; Actor of new tragedy: L. Marius Antiochus of Corinth; Singer-to-the-cithara (*kitharōidos*): Memmius Leon of Larissa; Choric piper (*choraulēs*): M. Antius Artemidorus of Alexandria; Writer of satyr-play (*saturographos*): L. Marius Antiochus of Corinth.

At this festival, clearly, there were separate competitions in old and new tragedy, prizes for actors and a prize for the best *aulētēs* for chorus, who perhaps was involved in accompanying old and/or new tragedies and/or comedies.

At a festival for the Egyptian god Sarapis held in Tanagra (likewise in Boeotia) ca. 85 BC,[61] there were contests for trumpeters, heralds, rhapsodes, poets, pipe-players (*aulētai*), lyre-players, as well as for 'poet of

---

further Le Guen 2001, Aneziri 2003, 2007, 2010, Rotstein 2012; Power 2012: 31–3. A useful English translation and discussion of much of the material most relevant for our purposes is provided by Csapo and Slater 1995: 186–220.
[57] Gentili 1979; Hall 2002; Prauscello 2006; Taplin 2012; Nervegna 2007, 2013.
[58] Plutarch (*Mor*. 63a) mentions *tragōidoi* performing with a chorus; see also Lucillius *Anth. Pal.* 11.11.1–3; Wilson 2002; Nervegna 2013: 85.
[59] Le Guen 2001; Aneziri 2007; see also Csapo and Slater 1995: 186–220 and Le Guen, this volume.
[60] *SEG* III. 334; Csapo and Slater 1995 no.160, p. 192; Manieri 2009: 414–16 (*Thesp*. 43).
[61] *IG* VII. 540 = *SEG* XIX. 335: new edition by Calvet and Roesch 1966 (*SEG* XXV. 501); Csapo and Slater 1995: no. 161, pp. 193–6; Manieri 2009: 268–77 (*Tan*. 2).

satyrs', 'poet of tragedies', 'actor', 'poet of comedies', etc.; and later in the same inscription it is stated:

> For the tragic [chorusmen?] and satyrs 100 Attic [sc. silver drachmas were awarded]. For the chorus directors (*chorodidaskaloi*) who produced the new tragedies and satyrs 50 [drachmas]; for the pipers (*aulētai*) who [played for] the tragedy 28 [drachmas]; and for the comic [pipers] 12 Attic [silver drachmas] . . . [Also other expenses] for the daily oaths and the feasting of the daily participants, judges and . . . choruses and victors . . . .

Here again we find confirmation that choral and instrumental music were important components of the tragedy competitions.

At Delphi in the mid-third-century BC biennial performances of a competitive nature were apparently held,[62] including choral contests, pipers, *chorēgoi*, tragedians (each one with *aulētēs*, actors and *chorēgos*), comedians (etc.) and 'comic choreuts'. We do not know whether tragic choreuts were involved as well. It has been argued that this mention of seven specifically named 'comic choreuts' might refer to a song-and-dance troupe who performed the 'entr'acte' segments such as we find marked XOPOY in our manuscripts of Menander (discussed earlier in this chapter). This would leave open the question of who composed their music and choreography, and whether or not the poet and *chorēgos* had anything to do with the musical selection; also, whether or not a similar arrangement was in place for the performance of tragedies.

Competitions in tragedy were thus held in many venues all over the Greek world, and at least in some cases the festival organizers (*agōnothetai*) paid a certain number of professional performers to participate and/or offered prizes for the victors, probably leaving it up to the performers themselves (poet, *aulētēs*, *chorēgos*, etc.) to incorporate additional resources if they so wished. So presumably a playwright or play-adapter or lead-actor (a *tragōidos* could be any or all of these at once), along with his team of fellow actors (usually, it seems, amounting to three in all),[63] plus an *aulētēs*, would all travel to the festival, whether with a new play or with the script of an 'old tragedy' – most often one by Euripides – and they would perhaps select and rehearse from among the local population a chorus of

---

[62] *SIG* 424A and 690; Csapo and Slater 1995 nos 165A and B, pp. 200–2.
[63] That is, the *tragōidos* himself who signed the contract, plus two *synagōnistai* (e.g., *SIG*³ 659.10, *SIG*³ 585.128–30, from Delphi), who might sometimes be described as *deuteragonistēs* and *tritagonistēs*; cf. Aneziri 1997. In Roman contexts, similar arrangements for acting troupes seem to have obtained; e.g., in the case of the Emperor Nero's theatrical endeavours (Suet. *Nero* 24.1; ps.Lucian *Nero* 9); see Nervegna 2013: 81–2.

appropriate size and talent.⁶⁴ (We will consider later in this chapter what the consequences might have been for the degree of adaptation of the original script, music and choreography of 'old tragedy'.) It may be noted that the victorious playwright, *aulētēs* and actor in these records do not usually come from the same city; so perhaps they did not regularly work together as a team, unless the Artists of Dionysus comprised a sufficiently tight-knit network to make this possible. Alternatively, the prizes may have been divided between different productions (as are, e.g., the Oscars nowadays), so that a victorious actor might have performed in a tragedy that did not itself receive a first prize. From the end of the third century BC at least, and perhaps earlier, the Artists of Dionysus were organized regionally (Athens, Nemea, Teos, Rhodes, etc.), so that it must have been possible for most Greeks who lived somewhere near an urban site to see and hear tragedies being performed at least a couple times a year; and these performances would usually have involved plenty of music.

Overall, then, it looks as if the range of musical possibilities in performances of post-fifth-century drama was large and quite open-ended. The general expectation would be that a festival performance of tragedy should include song and dance, whether from actors or chorus or both. Professional actors devoted many hours to the training of their voices and bodies,⁶⁵ and they relished the opportunity to sing, as well as to employ a full range of gesture, bodily movements and dance steps, not simply in order to demonstrate their own technical prowess (a sneer that many ancient and modern critics have expressed) but as effective and appropriate ways of conveying emotional excitement or distress, as well as differences of gender, age, character-type (*ēthos*) and social class. A nonsinging, unmusical actor in the ancient Greek world had small or no chance of success. Indeed, the modern Western style of 'naturalist/realistic' acting associated with Stanislavski and his followers, and with, e.g., contemporary TV and Hollywood movies, or even standard Shakespearean performance conventions, is more the exception than the rule in the history of theatre: in the performance traditions of, e.g., India, Indonesia, China or Japan, as well as those of Commedia dell'Arte or vaudeville, 'acting', 'dance' and 'singing' have not usually been divided among three different groups of practitioners: the practices are more often than not combined into a single

---

⁶⁴ Wilson 2000: 289–90 (citing Plato *Laws* 7. 817a–d and also third-century BC inscriptions regulating performances at the Dionysia in Kos = Segre 1993: ED 52, ED 234); Taplin 2012: 240–2; Nervegna 2007, 2013: 81–3.
⁶⁵ Hall 2002.

performance mode. It appears to have been so for the most part in Greece throughout antiquity.

## Changing Melodies, Tunings, Musical Styles

What about the actual music, especially the melodies, of all those choral and actors' songs? What kinds of changes did Greek vocal and instrumental music undergo after the fifth century BC, and how might these changes have been reflected in the performances of tragedy, new and old? Of course, we have much less by way of direct evidence about the melodies from the surviving texts of the fifth-century plays themselves than we do about the rhythms and metres, since our medieval manuscripts do not contain any musical notation at all. (The same is true of the choreography.) But a certain amount can be said on the basis of our general knowledge of ancient Greek music theory and practice; and for the Hellenistic and later periods we do have a handful of papyri that contain musical notation for bits of tragedy – including some short passages from Euripides' lyrics, though we cannot be certain whether these are Euripides' own original melodies or those of later adapters.

Most Greek music involved voices and instruments performing melodies in unison – or at intervals of an octave, if male and female, or men's and children's, voices were combined. The accompanying instruments might sometimes play 'fills' between sung phrases, or might add occasional harmonies (often at the interval of a fifth) or counterpoint; but for the most part Greek music, like the music of the rest of the Middle East until fairly recently, remained basically monophonic.[66]

Music for the theatre in general, and for Athenian tragedy in particular, involved only male singer-dancers and a male piper (*aulētēs*) as accompanist. The *auloi* were ubiquitous in Greek society for performance both in private and in public contexts, and there were many different types, some simple and inexpensive, others more complicated and made of more precious materials. The *auloi* played in the Theatre of Dionysus were obviously 'state of the art' (see further later in this chapter).[67] Several ancient educationalists and philosophers (especially those based in Athens,

---

[66] For good general accounts of the basics of ancient Greek music, see esp. Barker 2012; West 1992; more detailed and technical are Matheson 1999; Hagel 2010. The ancient musicological sources are collected (in English translations) and well discussed in Barker 1984, 1989; all the musically notated Greek texts are assembled and discussed in detail in Pöhlmann and West 2001.

[67] Modern relatives of the ancient *auloi* are the Sardinian *launeddas* (which have three pipes) and the Armenian *duduk* (single pipe), as well as the medieval *shawm* (single pipe); see further Moore 2012.

including Plato and Aristotle) stated preference for the crisper, dryer, exactly regulated and less affective sounds of strings, as against the hot, breathy and more emotionally versatile pipes, for the education and entertainment of the young men of the polis; so the *auloi* were sometimes demonized as being overly 'expressive/imitative' of vulgar sounds, moods and behaviors.[68] But for the vast majority of Greek audiences, such complaints made no impression. Theatre performances – or any Dionysian celebrations – without the enhancement of *aulos*-music would be almost inconceivable.

Did 'theatre music' have a distinctive character, different from other kinds of Greek musical performance? Athens/Attica itself seems not to have possessed much of a distinctive musical tradition of its own, as compared, e.g., with Lesbos, Miletus, Thebes, or the northeastern Peloponnese; but the fifth-century Athenian tragedians clearly drew on the widest possible range of musical styles from all over the Mediterranean world to replicate within their plays – though how closely and authentically, we cannot tell. Thus, we find in extant fifth-century tragedy choruses of Persian elders (Aesch. *Pers.*), female Phrygian/Trojan captives (Eur. *Hec., Tro.*), Asian domestic slave-women (Aesch. *Cho.*), Egyptian refugees (Aesch. *Supp.*), Bacchantes from Anatolia (Eur. *Ba.*), even the Furies (Aesch. *Eum.*), as well as imaginary Greeks from many different cities, all singing hymns, prayers, laments, invocations to the dead, magical spells, condolences, victory songs – almost the entire range of song-types that the traditional repertoire possessed. Presumably, this eclecticism and relish for variety persisted into later centuries and other venues throughout the Greek world.[69]

Greek music went through continual processes of innovation and experimentation, starting at least as early as the seventh century BC.[70] Both because of the far-flung geographical extent of Greek culture – i.e.,

---

Among more familiar modern Western instruments, the general character of the *auloi*'s sound may best be compared with that of the bagpipes or the alto saxophone.

[68] The term *mimēsis* (or the verb *mimeisthai*) was often employed with reference to the capacity of the *auloi* to 'convey, represent, express' strong emotions, and 'imitate' different kinds of 'voices'. For Plato's (and to a lesser degree, Aristotle's) disapproving remarks about the *auloi*, see Plato *Rep.* 3. 398c–9e; Ar. *Pol.* 8.1341a10–1342a15, with further discussion at, e.g., Barker 1984: 128–35, 177–9; Wilson 1999; Martin 2003; see too Pelosi 2010: 16, 45–6. For discussion of the different valences of *mimēsis*, *mimeisthai* in ancient Greek aesthetic theory see Halliwell 2002.

[69] Timotheus' exoticizing *Persians* (*PMG* 788, composed ca. 400 BC) was probably a citharodic nome, not a tragedy; but it appears to have been widely admired and trend-setting for its musical character: see Hordern 2002; Power 2010: 516–54; LeVen 2014: 87–101.

[70] See esp. Barker 1984: 93–8; West 1992: 327–85; Franklin 2002; Martin 2003; Csapo 2004a; Hagel 2010: 80–98, 442–50.

different regions' music coming into contact with one another, and with the music of non-Greeks as well, and merging/adapting accordingly – and also because of the competitive environment in which music was often performed, including the theatre, there seems to have been considerable variety and innovation even within the well-established harmonic and melodic conventions that all Near Eastern societies, including mainland Greece itself, shared at that period. Unfortunately, most of our information about ancient Greek instruments, tunings, scales and modes (*genē, tonoi, harmoniai*) comes from authors of the fourth century BC or later, whose reports may not always be accurate. But some broad outlines of the major changes can be traced.[71]

In general, the melodies of ancient Greek music, like those of most societies in the world, were structured around the three basic intervals that are universally recognized as being 'concordant' with one another: the fourth (as, e.g., on a modern piano keyboard, the interval from C up to F), the fifth (as in C up to G) and the octave (as in middle C up to the next, higher C'). Within those larger intervals (i.e., the fourth and fifth), however, the smaller intervals that were used in Greek scales and melodies were much more variable than we are generally accustomed to in conventional/mainstream Western music. That is to say, in addition to the 'whole-step' or whole-tone (i.e., an interval such as that between the notes C and D, or D and E, etc., on a conventional Western keyboard) and the 'half-step' or semi-tone (i.e., an interval such as C to C#, C# to D, etc., which are the smallest intervals playable on a piano, e.g., the interval between any black key and a white key adjacent to it), Greek scales and melodies also employed smaller intervals (microtones, or 'in-between' notes, such as quarter-steps, one-third steps, etc.) that do not generally occur in the classical or popular scales and harmonic systems familiar to most Westerners nowadays and therefore tend to sound 'out of tune' to them.[72]

---

[71] See Barker 1984, 1989; West 1992. The most influential, and perhaps the most authoritative, expert on Greek musical history and theory was Aristoxenus of Tarentum, a student of Aristotle who in the late fourth century wrote several books on various aspects of musicology, including a full-scale *Harmonics*, of which substantial fragments survive from quotations by others.

[72] See in general (for the Greek tunings) Barker 1989 and 2012, West 1992: 160–89; Hagel 2010 *passim*; and for discussion (and audio specimens) of different ancient Greek microtonic tunings, Franklin 2005. For other comparable world music/tuning systems, see, e.g., Wade 1999 on Indian ragas; Shiloah 1995: 110–20 on various Persian and other Middle Eastern tunings. In the West, African American–based Blues and jazz do in fact constantly employ microtones, esp. in the so-called 'blue' notes of the flattened third and fifth.

The Greek system of scales and tunings was based on the tetrachord: four notes tuned/pitched so as to span a fourth. Apart from the top and bottom notes of any given tetrachord, the other two notes could notionally be set at any interval that the performer or composer wished – whole-steps, half-steps, a double-step, or various combinations of smaller intervals (microtones). The overall span of the fourth must always amount to the equivalent of two-and-a-half steps, i.e., five semi-tones (as in, e.g., C C# D D# E F, on a modern keyboard), even while the exact intervals of any particular tuning within the tetrachord could (unlike on a modern keyboard) be altered almost infinitely. An octave scale was made by combining two tetrachords, usually with one whole-step in between ('disjunct', as in C-F, G-C', with F-G as the linking whole-step), or, less often, by having the top note of one tetrachord serve as the bottom note of the other ('conjunct'), and then adding one whole-step at the top (as in C-F, F-Bb + one whole-step = C'). All these tunings and ratios were relative to an arbitrarily chosen 'root' note, which might vary from one instrument or singer to another: there were no fixed pitches equivalent to our 'middle C' or 'concert A'.[73]

According to ancient authorities (most of them probably based on Aristoxenus, on whom see n. 71 earlier in this chapter), three basic 'types' (*genos*, plural *genē*; or in Latin, *genus*, pl. *genera*) of scales/tunings of the tetrachord were all in common use during the archaic and classical periods. These were named diatonic, chromatic and enharmonic. In the diatonic, the intervals were relatively evenly spaced; in the chromatic, the 'coloring' (*chrōma*) of the lower intervals was more finely shaded, i.e., using closer-spaced microtones; and in enharmonic this feature was even more pronounced, as the microtones of the 'densely packed' (*puknon*) intervals for the lowest three notes, plus large interval (two whole-tones) up to the top note, were quite distinctive.

Variations also existed within diatonic between the 'tighter, tense' and the 'soft' versions, and within chromatic likewise between three slightly different versions, the 'tonic', the 'hemiolic' and the 'soft'. We can sketch the main alternatives available in the fifth century as follows, with the different intervals within the tetrachord indicated (half-step, whole-step, or other microtonal fractions), proceeding upwards from the root-note:

---

[73] Thus, even when we possess written annotation for an ancient Greek melody, we can only guess approximately the particular pitch of the setting on the basis of the normal range of a man's or woman's singing voice. See further West 1992: 273–6; Hagel 2010: 68–96.

| | | | |
|---|---|---|---|
| 'Tense' diatonic | ½ | 1 | 1 |
| 'Soft' diatonic | ½ | ¾ | 1¼ |
| 'Tonic' chromatic | ½ | ½ | 1½ |
| 'Hemiolic' chromatic | ⅜ | ⅜ | 1¾ |
| 'Soft' chromatic | ⅓ | ⅓ | 1⅚ |
| Enharmonic | ¼ | ¼ | 2 |

(Barker 2012: 980)

Aristoxenus and other ancient historians of Greek music inform us that the enharmonic was extensively used in archaic and classical times (i.e., previous to the fourth century), especially for theatre music, but then largely gave way to the diatonic, which was apparently the dominant 'kind' (*genos*) of tuning employed throughout the Hellenistic and Roman eras; and this is confirmed by the surviving texts (papyri, inscriptions and the medieval manuscripts of the songs of Mesomedes) that contain musical annotation.[74]

But even while this narrowing-down of the types of tuning might seem to imply that Greek music-making became simpler and more limited in its range after the fifth century, there were other developments that moved in the opposite direction, towards greater complexity and fluidity. For, in addition to the three different 'kinds' of tunings, Greek music also employed a number of different modes (sometimes labeled *harmoniai*), depending on where within the octave, or more often, two-octave range, the root-note of a scale or melody was to be set. These ancient Greek modes were conventionally given regional/ethnic names, though these seem to have had little or no historical basis: thus 'Lydian', 'Dorian', 'Phrygian', 'Ionian' and various subdivisions and modifications thereof ('Hypo-Dorian', 'Hyper-Phrygian', 'Mixo-Lydian', etc.).[75] Some of these modes were regarded as possessing particular ethical and affective characteristics: thus, the Dorian was supposed to be dignified, courageous and manly; the Ionian relaxed, luxurious, more feminine; etc. But as with

---

[74] The documents are collected and fully discussed in Pöhlmann and West 2001; a good summary of most of them can be found in West 1992, though several new papyrus fragments were discovered between the times of these two publications. See too Hagel 2010: 256–326 for more detailed and technical discussion.

[75] These ancient labels have nothing to do with the modern usage of such terms for different 'modes' within the standard Western musical system.

many modern assumptions about major and minor modes ('happy' vs. 'sad') or particular keys (F major = bold and cheerful; C# minor = somber, even agonized... etc.), there was considerable variation within these stereotypes. Theatre music was supposed to feature the Mixolydian and Phrygian modes above all;[76] but we do not know if this was in fact always the case. In their discussions of musical tunings and practices, the ancient theoreticians of Greek music took many decades, even centuries, before they worked out a single comprehensive and agreed-upon 'Greater Perfect System', in which all the possible tunings and modes were coordinated and labeled.[77] Previous to that, musical practices and theories appear to have been very variable, and we can be sure that the theatre was one of the places where experimentation was most extensive.

The melodic instruments chiefly used for public performances during the archaic and early classical period, the seven-string cithara and the double-pipes (*auloi*), were quite limited in their capacity to play in more than one *genos* and *harmonia* without retuning or replacement. In the case of the double-pipes (*auloi*), which were used for all theatrical performances, the early instruments had only four or five finger-holes for each pipe, whose placement determined the possible scales and melodies that could be played,[78] and an *aulētēs* might therefore require a different instrument to accompany two separate songs if they were set in different tunings and modes, though, unlike a kithara- or lyre-player, whose strings were exactly fixed and could not be 'bent', an *aulētēs* could vary the pitch of a note slightly by means of his or her fingering or embouchure (positioning of lips and mouth, and blowing technique) – just as a modern saxophonist or clarinetist can 'bend' notes, play 'blue' notes, etc., in ways that a pianist cannot.[79] Thus the *auloi*, in addition to being highly

---

[76] [Plut.] *On Music* 16.1136c–d; Aristotle *Pol.* 8.1340b, 1341a–42b; [Aristotle] *Probl.* 19.48; cf. Barker 1984: 221–2.

[77] Barker 1989; Mathieson 1999: 429–95; Hagel 2010: 134–216.

[78] We might compare the modern penny-whistle or recorder, with their six or seven finger-holes requiring the performer to play, e.g., in the key of C major or A minor, while another instrument with slightly shorter cylinder but the same spacing of finger-holes can be played only in D major or B minor, etc. Similar restrictions attend the (nonchromatic) harmonica, as employed in folk or blues contexts, so that performers usually possess half a dozen or more separate instruments for playing in different keys.

[79] This was apparently one significant reason why Plato and others preferred the stringed instruments: a teacher or legislator or chorus-master could regulate exactly the modes and scales that could be played on them, whereas the *auloi* were more flexible and versatile (*polychordos*, i.e., 'multitoned', and *panharmonios*, 'involving all of the modes'): Plato *Rep.* 3. 399d–e, cf. Barker 1984: 132) – i.e., uncontrollable. Stringed instruments with necks, such as lutes, ouds, guitars, etc., can allow a performer to bend or play 'in-between' notes, and thereby play microtones; but the Greeks seem

expressive in their breathy and affective timbre, were always more versatile in their tonal range and capacity to modulate than were the stringed instruments.

During the later fifth century BC, developments in instrument design and manufacture, along with increasing virtuosity among the performers, increased still further the range and flexibility of what could be played on one pair of *auloi*.[80] Many of the most distinguished *aulos*-players came from Thebes (and Boeotia was also the chief center of reed-production for this instrument).[81] The Theban virtuoso Pronomos was credited with having designed extra keys and sliding sleeves, so that a greater number of holes could be employed, and modulation from one scale or mode to another could thus be achieved in mid-performance; and other Theban *aulos*-players also achieved great acclaim at Athens and elsewhere for their performances, many of them theatrical.[82]

Meanwhile, vocal technique for actors had likewise been developing during this same period,[83] and here, too, non-Athenian professionals were increasingly attracting audiences' attention, so as even to rival the prestige of the playwrights themselves. A prize for the best actor (possibly meaning, the best team of three actors)[84] was instituted at the City Dionysia in 449 BC, and from that point on audiences came to the theatre as much to see and hear the star actors as to see and think about the plays (much as is often the case nowadays with movies and even plays). And these star actors in the Greek context were of course expected to sing and to move expressively.[85]

All these technical developments in the musical capabilities of the performers and their instruments meant that by the late fifth century a

generally to have eschewed such instruments (e.g., the *pandoura*) for public performance, at least before the Hellenistic period.
[80] Extra strings were also added during this period to the concert cithara, from seven up to as many as eleven or even more: West 1992: 62–4, 356–72, Power 2010: 331–50, etc.
[81] Theophrastus *Hist. Plant.* 4.11.1–7; Pausanias 9.27.5; 29.1–30.3; 31.3–5; Dio Chrys. *Or.* 7 (*Euboikos*) 119–22; further Mathiesen 1999: 198–203; West 1992: 85–9, 366–7; Wilson 2007c.
[82] On Pronomos, Potamon, and their achievements, see West 1992: 366 and n. 39; Wilson 2007c; also, Taplin and Wyles 2010 *passim*. Athenian authors of the fifth and fourth centuries, in response to such Theban preeminence, tended to downplay the value of the *auloi* in favor of cithara and lyre: hence, e.g., the popularity in Athens of the stories of the contest between Apollo (playing cithara/lyre) and Marsyas (playing *auloi*) and of Athena's rejection of the *auloi*; see, e.g., *LIMC* 6 s.v. 'Marsyas' (A. Weis), Arist. *Pol.* 8. 1341b; Plut. *Alcib.* 2.4; Hyginus *Fables* 165.
[83] For a good account of voice-training techniques for ancient Greek actors, see Hall (2002) 22–4, with further references.
[84] Sifakis 1995; see earlier in this chapter, n. 63.
[85] It is likely too that, as the actual theatre structures and performance spaces grew bigger, the sheer decibel-production required of pipe-players and singing actors needed to be greater.

tragedian could compose melodies that shifted moods and modes much more rapidly and radically than had been possible during the earlier careers of Aeschylus and Sophocles, and that made greater demands on the skills of the soloists and accompanist. This was clearly a key factor that contributed to the tendency we noted earlier, whereby Euripides and other late-fifth-century innovators (practitioners of what modern scholars have dubbed the 'New Music') reduced the amount of strophically responding choral lyric in favor of more 'free-flowing' solo songs for actors.[86] This was probably true of other theatre contexts as well.

So the most ambitious musical moments of a tragic performance increasingly tended to be arias sung by individual actors. An extraordinarily elaborate example of this is the Phrygian's 'messenger-song' in Euripides' *Orestes* (1358–1602), with its extravagant variety of different metres; more typical are Electra's lyric laments in both Sophocles' and Euripides' *Electra* and Antigone's sung passages in Eur. *Phoenissae* (103–92; 301–54; 1485–581). All of these are plays dating to the last two decades of the fifth century. The mannerisms of this style were extensively parodied by Aristophanes and other comic poets; and 'Aeschylus' in *Frogs* (405 BC) complains that Euripides has 'prostituted' the musical art and utterly debased the dignity of tragedy (*Frogs* 1044–364). But quite soon – probably by the early fourth century – these mannerisms had become accepted as mainstream theatre practice, just as the constantly modulating late-fifth-century citharodic and dithyrambic music of Philoxenus and Timotheus – previously much maligned by Athenian conservatives – had by now become accepted by all as 'classic'.[87] Whether equivalent innovations of virtuoso dance technique were also developed during this period we cannot tell; but it seems likely (as, e.g., Ar. *Frogs* 1298–328 might suggest).

## Musical Notation and the Evidence from Papyri

The ancient Greek system of musical notation, which was presumably first introduced during the later–fifth and early–fourth century BC, fortunately for us was described in detail, with a key, by Late Antique authors such as Alypius, Gaudentius, Bacchius, 'Bellermann's Anonymi' and Boethius.

---

[86] A late source (Aristides Quintilianus 30.2, 23.3) states that melodies composed for tragedy were generally pitched lower than citharodic songs; Sifakis (1967: 77) has suggested that this refers to choral passages of tragedy, rather than actors' arias. There were some tragic actors who commanded an unusually high register and large vocal range in general; cf. Hall 2002: 23–4; also West 1992: 42–6, Hagel 2010: 68–75.

[87] West 1992: 356–72, esp. 371–2; Csapo 2004a; LeVen 2014 *passim*.

This notation system uses symbols (many of them letters of the Greek alphabet), written above the individual syllables of the words in the text, to specify the exact pitch and (to some limited degree) the duration of individual notes. Even though this notation tells us nothing about the style of vocalizing and phrasing, and little about the rhythmic pulse, it does make it possible for modern scholars to establish fairly exactly the melody (i.e., sequence of pitches) for the text in question, including what tuning-*genos* and mode it was set in.[88]

Of the surviving pieces of notated ancient Greek music, which range from the Hellenistic to the late Roman periods, more than a dozen come from tragedy – all of these in a very fragmentary state.[89] One contains a choral passage in the dochmiac metre from Euripides' *Orestes* (lines 338–44) and is apparently set in the enharmonic (or possibly chromatic) *genos*, with frequent use of microtones within the *puknon*.[90] Also in enharmonic are the small and badly damaged fragments from Euripides' *Iphigenia at Aulis* (containing bits of lines 784–92 and 1499–509).[91] Another Hellenistic papyrus (*Pap. Ashm.* inv. 89B/31, 33) contains tiny bits of lyric passages that may come from a tragedy about Achilles, with notation that seems to be in chromatic or enharmonic.[92] Probably set in chromatic *genos* too is a very fragmentary Hellenistic papyrus, with a text in dochmiacs that appears to be from a tragedy (*P. Zenon* 59533),[93] while another third-century BC papyrus – from the same provenance as the *Orestes* fragment and containing a female Trojan character's (Andromache's?) complaints about an Achaean man (Neoptolemus?) – seems again to be composed in chromatic.[94] Some or all of the melodies notated in these papyri might well be the ones actually composed for the original production of those plays.

---

[88] All the surviving musically notated texts from Greek antiquity (about sixty in all) are collected and discussed in Pöhlmann and West 2001. The two main notation systems (one for voices, the other for instruments) are well described in West 1992: 254–76, Hagel 2010: 1–102.
[89] In some cases, the text is too short and/or fragmentary for us to determine whether a passage is specifically tragic or just more generically 'lyric'.
[90] *P. Vindob.* G 2315, written in the third century BC; see West 1992: 284–5 no. 3 for a clear description and transcription into modern notation.
[91] *P. Lugd.* inv. 510, also probably written in the third century BC.; West 1992: nos. 4 and 5; Pöhlmann and West 2001: no. 4; discussed further later in this chapter.
[92] Pöhlmann and West 2001: no. 5; the papyrus scraps are very lacunose, but the title '*Achilleus* of Sophocles' is written on the back of one piece. Since the fifth-century Sophocles did not write any play of that title, M. L. West has suggested that these fragments may come from a fourth-century tragedy about Achilles written by Sophocles' grandson, who was also named Sophocles; see further West 1999.
[93] Pöhlmann and West 2001: no. 8; cf. West 1992: no. 7.
[94] Pöhlmann and West 2001: no. 10; West 1992: no. 8(a–f), p. 279.

Of the musical tragic papyri from later periods, almost all appear to be composed in the diatonic *genos*. We often cannot tell whether these are the original settings for these songs, or whether the words from an older play have been set to newer music at a later period. Nor can we tell in most cases whether the texts we have were actually the lyric parts of whole dramas that were copied in their entirety, or were short excerpts arranged for recital by a solo singer (as seems definitely to be the case for the *Iphigenia at Aulis* excerpts). So, for example, an Oslo papyrus from the first or second century AD contains one passage in anapaests, in which the ghost of Achilles is described rising from his tomb and terrifying some Trojan women, and another in iambic trimeters apparently set on Lemnos and involving Neoptolemus (and Philoctetes?), all set to music (diatonic) in arrangements which would be unimaginable in the fifth or fourth centuries BC (since the iambic trimeters of dialogue at that period were never sung). Whether they both come from the same play is unclear.[95] A Berlin papyrus of the second century AD contains bits of a play about Ajax and Tecmessa, whose verbal text seems to date back to the fourth or third century BC (including lyrics apparently in strophic response), while the music (in diatonic *genos*) seems to be set for a female vocalist to deliver, presumably a much more recent composition.[96] A Yale papyrus from the second century AD, again set in diatonic *genos*, is written in extremely 'florid' musical style, with melismas that extend over as many as six syllables and some unusually large plunges of the melodic line from high to low pitches – all characteristic of 'late' musical tendencies, though the language itself (composed in dactyloepitrite metre) is not obviously post-Hellenistic and might even date to the fourth century BC.[97] Another example of tragic iambic trimeters (probably written originally to be spoken) that have been adapted so as to be sung (again, in diatonic *genos*), is a second-century AD Michigan papyrus involving Orestes and a servant (tutor?) in dialogue, in this case including several instrumental interludes between some of the passages.[98]

---

[95] *P. Oslo.* 1413 = Pöhlmann and West 2001: nos. 39 and 40 (West 1992: 311–14, nos. 30 and 31). A similar musical setting of iambic trimeters is found in a papyrus (*P. Louvre* inv. E 10534), which appears to contain a partly notated fragment from Carcinus Junior's *Medea* (a tragedian of the fourth century BC); see Bélis 2004; West 2007; Martinelli 2010. My thanks to Vayos Liapis for drawing this to my attention.

[96] *P.Berol.* 6870 = Pöhlmann and West 2001: nos. 17 and 18 (cf. West 1992: no. 42; Snell-Kannicht *TrGF* II, F 683a).

[97] *P. Yale* inv. 4510 = Pöhlmann and West 2001: no. 41, who emphasize the 'extraordinary rhythmic distortions' of the musical setting in relation to the Greek text; cf. too Johnson 2000 (with audio rendering of the vocal melody at http://classics.uc.edu/music/yale/index.html).

[98] *P. Mich.* 2958 lines 1–18 = Pöhlmann and West 2001: no. 42 = West 1992: no. 32, pp. 314–15.

Overall then, the assertion of Aristoxenus and others that classical theatre music (i.e., the tragedies of the fifth or early fourth centuries) favoured enharmonic over diatonic, whereas later composers (including tragedians) opted increasingly for diatonic, seems to be confirmed by the extant examples on papyri.[99] And other tendencies too, towards melismas (i.e., greater freedom to embellish the written text with extra melodic ornamentation, much as J. S. Bach and Mozart and Puccini do in their cantatas and arias), greater fluidity and range of vocal pitches, and reduced use of strophic responsion – tendencies that are all already noticeable in later Euripides – are amply confirmed even by these small remains of Hellenistic and (especially) Roman-period musical papyri.

## Developments in Dance

Whether analogous developments also took place within the dance repertoire – i.e., increasing virtuosity on the part of actors, and a greater degree of versatility and fluidity in the types of steps and choreography, corresponding to the shifts in metre and harmonic modes – is impossible to assess. We have much less evidence to work with, as we possess no educational handbooks or technical discussions comparable to the harmonic studies of the Pythagoreans, Aristoxenus and the other musicologists; and no actual notation for choreography existed. Aristoxenus did compose one work *On Tragic Dance* (Περὶ τραγικῆς ὀρχήσεως) and another on *Comparisons (of Dances)*; but almost nothing survives from these.[100] A large number of different names for particular dances existed, and also an extensive terminology for different types of bodily 'movements' or 'patterns' (*schēmata*).[101] We may assume that from the beginning, Greek tragedy had employed a wide variety of dances, adapted from choral performances of different parts of the Mediterranean world, according to the dramatic requirements of each play; and doubtless this practice continued throughout antiquity. But we have no hope of reconstructing any of them.[102]

The distinction between gesture and dance is not always a sharp one, and actors certainly did develop a more extensive repertoire of movements

---

[99] For further discussion of the two Euripides musical papyri, and what they can tell us about the performance of his plays in later centuries, see later in this chapter.
[100] Wehrli 1967: frs 104–6; fr. 109.
[101] For example, Plutarch *Mor. (Table Talk)* 747b–8d; Pollux *Onom.* 4.95–110. See further Lawler 1964; Fitton 1973; Naerebout 1997: 274–89; Zarifi 2007.
[102] Naerebout 1997: 64–145.

in the postclassical age. (This expansion of expressive movement had already begun during Euripides' career, and was frowned upon by conservative critics.)[103] The training of a professional actor (*hupokritēs*) certainly included rigorous training for the whole body, not just the voice;[104] but we do not know much about the actual dance technique. With the development of the pantomime, solo dance certainly became an enormously popular and competitive genre, and presumably there was some overlap between this and the performance of tragedy.[105] In general, we may observe that similar elite prejudices to those we find being expressed in disapproval of the new harmonic and metrical innovations (discussed earlier in this chapter) are apparent in remarks by Plato, Plutarch and others about the excessively 'mimetic' and/or morally reprehensible aspects of certain kinds of dancing that appealed to mass audiences.[106] These complaints were also directed against *aulētai* who moved their whole bodies to enhance the emotionality and excitement of their playing – in itself a kind of choreography.[107] All of this evidence confirms that skilled solo dance was both multifaceted and enormously popular, though we may assume that a *pantomimos* and a *tragōidos* maintained significant differences between their respective physical performances – not least because a *tragōidos* had to sing as well as move, while the words for a pantomime performance were not sung by the dancer himself.

## Reperformance of 'Old' Tragedies

As mentioned earlier, revivals of 'old tragedy' (*palaia tragōidia*) – most frequently of Euripides' plays – were common in the fourth century and later, in many different contexts. This raises the interesting question: how scrupulously did the performers of 'old tragedies' attempt to preserve the text, music and dance of the original fifth-century versions?[108]

---

[103] For example, Arist. *Poet.* 26.1461b32–62a4; cf. Csapo 2002.
[104] This was especially true for comic actors, whereas in tragedy, vocal power and stamina were perhaps more important than physical agility: Fantham 2002: 364–7. But for the varied physical as well as vocal demands that actors (like orators) needed to be able to meet, see Pickard-Cambridge 1988: 171–6, Csapo 2002, and Fantham 2002 *passim*; also, earlier in this chapter.
[105] Webb 1997; Garelli-François 1995, 2001; Zanobi 2008; Lada-Richards 2007; Petrides 2013.
[106] For example, Lucian *On the Dance*; Ath. 628c; see further Zarifi 2007.
[107] Arist. *Pol.* 26.1461b30–1; Thphr. fr. 92; Dio Chrys. *Or.* 78.
[108] As remarked in n. 9 earlier in this chapter, the text itself in some cases prompts an audience to expect particular kinds of sounds or movements, even while there may often have been much left to the imagination in actual performance.

The most likely answer seems to be: not at all scrupulously. Given the conventions of theatrical and musical performance in the ancient Greek contexts, we would expect adaptation and updating to be the norm, rather than antiquarian or purist conservatism. Even while admiration of the classics of the past was widespread, the idea of maintaining an 'authentic' and 'original' style of performance was rarely articulated as an artistic goal in antiquity; rather, an actor or *chorēgos* would generally seek, quite properly, to entertain the audience and show off the artistic talents at his disposal as fully as possible.[109] And in any case, even while the verbal text (script) might be maintained in a somewhat accurately authentic state, it would generally have been impossible, in practical terms, to replicate most of the musical, visual and choreographic elements of a production first staged hundreds of years earlier, even had this been felt to be desirable.[110]

Scholarly opinion is divided as to whether or not the original colometry of fifth-century plays (i.e., the division and arrangement of lyric 'cola', or metrical units, in choral and actors' songs) was maintained when the plays were copied in columns onto a papyrus roll (or later a parchment codex) by the author or any other interested parties: i.e., was the tragedian's own colometry preserved into the Hellenistic period? The majority opinion is negative; instead, the colometry found in our medieval manuscripts was produced by editor-scholars working several decades or even centuries later than the playwrights themselves (Aristophanes of Byzantium was apparently one of these scholars, in the late third century BC), and previously these lyric passages were written out continuously as if they were prose, i.e., indicating nothing to the reader about their rhythms, let alone the melodies or choreography, of the songs.[111] And as for musical notation, very few scholars believe that this would have been included as part of the textual transmission even of late-fifth-century tragedies. Musically annotated texts would generally have circulated only among expert musicians,

---

[109] As Antonis Petrides points out to me, this must be true for at least one crucial element of *opsis*: it is very likely that 'old tragedies' were performed using the new, standardized system of masks developed in the course of the fourth century. Furthermore, the fifth-century classics were also performed in quite different theatrical venues, which means adaptation in the construction of stage space as well.

[110] Opinions differ widely among scholars as to how accurately the verbal texts of tragedy have been transmitted to us: this is not the place to enter into detailed discussion of this issue; but see nn. 112, 119.

[111] Fleming and Kopff 1992 and Fleming 1999 have argued that the original authors' colometry of lyric passages was generally preserved; but for convincing counterarguments see esp. Prauscello 2006: 7–83.

Music and Dance in Tragedy After the Fifth Century 235

many of whom had little interest in the dialogue portions of a play and therefore had no need for a complete text.[112]

When Aristophanes presents 'Aeschylus' and 'Euripides' in *Frogs* competing in the Underworld for the chair of tragedy, he includes some bits of Aeschylean choral song in the course of his extravagant parody of both authors' respective styles. It is clear that these song-excerpts were comically performed in a musical manner that the theatre-goers in 405 BC would immediately recognize as quasi-Aeschylean – otherwise the parody would be ineffective. Some modern critics have concluded that this must mean that it was still possible to perform Aeschylus' music just as he composed it (and this would presumably include the choreography, too). If this was indeed the case, then it must have been by direct oral/aural and visual demonstration, decade after decade, from father to son or expert to apprentice (among actors and *aulētai*), that the melodies, phrasings and dance steps were taught to Aristophanes' cast of performers.

A story narrated by Plutarch about Euripides' training of a chorus to perform one of his plays is illuminating (*On the Right Way to Listen to Poets* 46b), for, whether or not it is historically accurate, it provides reliable testimony as to how Plutarch himself (ca. 100 AD) assumed choruses learned their songs:

> 'When Euripides the poet once was suggesting/demonstrating (ὑπολέγοντος) to his chorus-members (χορευταῖς) a song composed in enharmonic [tuning], one of them burst out laughing. Euripides remarked, "If you weren't completely stupid and tasteless/tone-deaf (ἀναίσθητος), you wouldn't be laughing while I sang in mixo-Lydian (ἐμοῦ μιξολυδιστὶ ᾄδοντος)".'

In this scenario, the playwright himself is singing the melody and words to his chorus for them to learn; there is no need for any written text at all, neither words nor musical notation. (We are told nothing about the dance element, unfortunately.)

So, it would not be impossible for such songs to be handed down accurately over the generations, especially since tragedy-writing tended to run in families.[113] And in some theatre traditions in which exact replication of fixed melodies and gestures is obligatory (e.g., Japanese Noh or Chinese Kunqu drama),[114] this is how the art is taught and fostered, and

---

[112] See Prauscello 2006: 83–183, *passim*; Nervegna 2013: 85–8.
[113] For example, in the fifth and fourth centuries BC, Aeschylus' two sons were both distinguished playwrights themselves, as were several of his nephews and grandchildren; and Sophocles, Pratinas, Euripides, Carcinus and Astydamas likewise all had sons and/or other relatives who were successful in tragedy: cf. Sutton 1987a.
[114] See, e.g., Keene 1966; Royall 1993; Li 2005.

the specialized acting schools are famed for maintaining such authenticity. But it does not appear that this was in fact the approach in classical Athens, nor in Greece in general, any more than it was in, e.g., Shakespeare's England or in Weimar and Saxony during the career of J. S. Bach. Instead, adaptation, resetting of old pieces for new contexts, borrowing of predecessors' and rivals' ideas and even complete pieces were common practice, always keeping one eye and ear on the available resources, human, financial and technical, and the other on the expected audience and its tastes. Musical notation of some kind was probably in existence by the end of the fifth century (as we noted earlier in this chapter), but not so in Aeschylus' day; and it has always been next to impossible to denote dance steps through writing (i.e., through symbols or words for others to read and interpret) – in almost all cultures a dance is learned from watching another dancer or from the original choreographer, and this is usually true of musicians as well.[115]

We are told by a not-very-reliable source (pseudo-Plutarch, *On the Ten Ancient Orators* 841f) that new restrictions concerning the reperformance of old tragedies at the City Dionysia were instituted in the 330s BC by the Athenian politician Lycurgus, requiring 'that the tragedies of Aeschylus, Sophocles and Euripides be written out and conserved in a public depository (ἐν κοινῷ), and that the secretary of the city read them out aloud to the actors for comparison (παραγιγνέσκειν τοῖς ὑποκρινομένοις); for it was not allowed to perform the plays contrary to those [authorized texts]'.[116] This account clearly implies that up until then, considerable liberties had sometimes been taken with those old play-texts. As for the official texts that were allegedly deposited for future consultation by actors, as we have seen, modern scholars differ sharply in their understanding of what these may have been like.[117] It is also unclear how effective this authorized text will have been in the long run in controlling the behaviour of performers of 'old tragedy' all over the Greek world.[118]

---

[115] Even the most sophisticated modern Laban notation for dance is of limited precision and effectiveness: nearly all reconstructions of previously staged dance pieces make use either of the memories of those previous performers or of video, or both.

[116] See Prauscello 2006: 68–78, Hanink 2014b: 60–89 for recent, full discussion of this text and its implications.

[117] See earlier in this chapter and specifically nn. 110, 111, 112.

[118] Prauscello 2006: 68–78. It should be noted that the amusing story (oft-repeated in the modern era, but unattested before Galen in the first century AD) that King Ptolemy III enabled the Alexandrian scholars to acquire these original, authorized texts from Athens in the mid-third century BC while they were compiling their (alleged) Great Library, has rightly been called into question by Bagnall 2001; see further Johnstone 2014: 347–52.

Our medieval manuscript texts of Greek tragedies certainly appear to present abundant evidence of extra lines being interpolated and other kinds of rewriting of the original, especially in the case of Euripides' most popular plays; and some of the ancient papyri confirm that such interpolation occurred quite early on.[119] Mostly these modifications occur in scenes of spoken dialogue, not lyrics, though there are a few possible cases of apparent adaptation of lyric passages, even possibly of wholesale addition of one or more stanzas (e.g., Eur. *Ph.* 1581ff, [Aesch.] *Pr.* 425–30, and perhaps some of the lyrics at the end of *IA*). The ending of Aeschylus' *Seven against Thebes* is a remarkable case, where apparently the popularity of Sophocles' *Antigone* impelled a later (fifth- or fourth-century?) playwright or acting troupe to compose a whole new scene for Aeschylus' older play (1005–78, including anapaests at 1054–78), and to adapt some of the singing parts leading up to this scene to be sung by two solo voices (Ismene and Antigone) rather than the Chorus (961–1003).[120]

We have already taken note of Aristotle's remarks about lyric 'inserts' (*embolima*) that some tragedians employed instead of composing definite scripts for a play's choral songs; and we may assume that when these plays were reperformed, such inserts would often be replaced by others, to suit the skills and tastes of the available performers. Such a process would presumably make it all the easier and more natural for actors and *chorēgoi* to 'insert' new songs (or choral interludes of some kind) even for 'old tragedies' which did possess their own author-composed lyrics. For a possible case in point one may turn to a Sorbonne papyrus from ca. 250 BC, which transmits Eur. *Hipp.* 1–106 but omits the lyric portion 58–72; the omission is likely to have been signalled by ΧΟΡΟΥ/ΧΟΡΟΥ ΜΕΛΟΣ, although the crucial portion of the papyrus is missing.[121]

In general, teams of actors must have been fairly free to adapt the plays they undertook to perform at festivals and elsewhere, especially in contexts where they may have had limited choral resources. This was obviously even

---

[119] See, e.g., Page 1934; Reeve 1972–3; for a somewhat more conservative picture, see Mastronarde and Bremer 1982.

[120] See, e.g., Hutchinson 1985: *ad locc.* At Eur. *Or.* 1384 the manuscripts contain the phrase '*harmateion harmateion melos* ', literally 'chariot-, chariot-melody' (or else 'Harmateios', Harmateios' melody', if we believe one ancient tradition that there was a Boeotian piper of that name), apparently referring to a particular type of high-pitched musical phrase played on the *auloi*. Whether this is a self-referential comment from the singing Phrygian slave, or an ancient commentator's remark about the melody that Euripides composed for this passage, has been much discussed. But this is not a large-scale insertion into the text of a different piece of music or new musical arrangement.

[121] *P. Sorb.* 2252 = no. 393 Mertens-Pack³; see W.S. Barrett 1964: 438 with n. 2; *contra* Taplin 1976: 49; see also Duncan and Liapis, this volume. I am grateful to Vayos Liapis for reminding me of this text.

more true of those individual *tragōidoi* who did not perform whole plays but gave recitals of dramatic (and other?) songs, excerpted from their original contexts, whether in public theatres or for private 'dinner-theatre' occasions.[122] In the second century AD, we find the citizens of Miletus honouring Gaius Aelius Themison for being 'the first and only one to have set to music for himself Euripides, Sophocles and Timotheus'; whether this involved performance as a *tragōidos* (i.e., presumably with *aulos* accompaniment), or more radical adaptations of these texts for citharodic performance (as the mention of Timotheus might imply), we do not know.[123]

Such singers continued to be popular throughout Late Antiquity and into the Byzantine era; for example, St. Augustine mentions how alluring their performances could be.[124] We are told by various ancient critics that some of these performers even modified passages written in iambic trimeters or trochaic tetrameters (i.e., passages composed originally to be spoken), by adding melodies and singing them; and as we have seen, some of our extant musical papyri confirm this.[125] In some cases it is impossible to tell who was writing and using these musical texts: were they for actors who actually performed scenes or whole plays in public? Or were they part of a quite separate process of reception and reperformance carried on among musicians (singers and *aulētai*)? The latter seems generally the more likely. In a few cases, they may even be school exercises, never intended for performance at all.

Overall, it is striking and surely significant that of all the hundreds of papyri that have been discovered containing more or less substantial continuous passages from the plays of Aeschylus, Sophocles and Euripides, whether from lost plays or from ones that we happen to possess in their entirety in medieval manuscripts, almost none contain any musical notation at all. That is to say, the standard copies of ancient tragedies were not musically annotated (and as we remarked earlier in this chapter, they do

---

[122] Nervegna 2013: 76–99, 169–77, 183–8; for 'dinner theatre' at Roman *convivia* see also Jones 1991.
[123] *SEG* XI 52c; cf. Hall 2002: 15–16; Prauscello 2006: 111–16; Nervegna 2013: 87. We may compare also Satyrus' performance – with chorus – of a *kitharisma* adapted from Euripides' *Bacchae* (*SIG*³ 648B; cf. Sifakis 1967: 96–7, Prauscello 2006: 104–8).
[124] Augustine *Conf.* 36, 4.2; Puchner 2002; see further Hall 2002: 4–12, who provides a lively account of the widespread popularity of a 'Flying Medea' aria, performed in many different contexts over the centuries.
[125] Dion. Hal. *Comp.* 63–4; Xenophon *Symp.* 6.3 (on Nicostratus' performances in the fourth century BC); Luc. *Hist. Conscr.* 1; etc.; see further Prauscello 2006: 85–116. For examples of tragic iambics or anapaests with musical notation, see my discussion of the Oslo and Michigan papyri earlier in this chapter.

not usually seem to have been presented with much attention to metrical detail in the lyrics, either). By contrast, the 'musical' papyri that have been found containing annotated bits of tragic texts look as if they were prepared by and for specialist singers (and perhaps for *aulētai* as well) and do not contain any of the dialogue passages of the plays in question. When iambic trimetres and anapaests are included, they are often converted into sung passages. Furthermore, in several cases the lyrics apparently were not even intended to be sung in the same order as they occur in the play – they were recital pieces, and no longer being considered as parts of actual dramas.

This is true of the two most famous surviving musical papyri of tragic texts, those from Euripides' *Orestes* and *Iphigenia at Aulis*, both of which date from the third century BC and raise intriguing questions of their own. In the *Orestes* papyrus (*P. Vind.* 2315), the order of some of the lines (338–40) has been transposed, and the writing-out in full of the melismas (as in 343 *hō - ōs pontou*, and 344 *e - en kumasin*) is an orthographical procedure never encountered in those other, non-'musical' papyri or in our medieval manuscripts.[126] The fragment also contains in a couple of places what appear to be separate musical indicators for the *auloi* in addition to those for (one or more) singer(s).[127] So we may conclude that this papyrus 'text' was designed specifically for a musical recital, rather than for a dramatic performance of the whole play. (Certainly it is hard to imagine why a chorus-member in an actual theatre production would need the pipe-player's part to be included in his 'script'.)

In the *IA* musical fragment (*P. Lugd.* inv. 510), the recital elements are much more obvious: we find two completely separate, short lyric passages from the play, written one right after the other (i.e., with no indication of the missing passages in between), first lines 1500–9 (which were originally written to be sung by Iphigenia, near the end of the play) and then lines 784–94 (from an ode sung by the chorus). Thus, whereas the displacement of lines in the *Orestes* fragment might be accidental (the sense there is not seriously impaired), in the *IA* papyrus it must be a matter of deliberate choice and must indicate that the sequence was not intended to be part of a performance of the whole play. It is worth noting also that neither this

---

[126] Such melismas are parodied at Ar. *Ra.* 1309–22, 1331–63, where the MSS do write the protracted syllables out in ludicrous exaggeration (1314 *eieieieieilissete*, 1349 *eieieilissousa*...); see nn. 21 and 22 earlier in this chapter.

[127] The pitch notations for the *auloi* involved a different set of symbols from those used for vocal performance: both kinds of notation are found on the *Orestes* papyrus. See further West 1992: 254–76; Pöhlmann and West 2001; Hagel 2010: 1–102.

nor the *Orestes* papyrus presents the words in an arrangement within the papyrus columns that makes any metrical sense: that is to say, the focus is entirely on the melody (pitches, 'notes'), not on the structure of metrical cola and strophe/antistrophe. All of this proves that the notated texts are not intended as part of a complete performance of the play (for which the metrical structures would be highly relevant to the choreography as well as to the overall meaning of the words), but involve 'some sort of concert performance of musical highlights'.[128]

The case of another of our musical papyri (*P. Berol.* 6870, from the second or third century AD) is especially illuminating of the ways in which musicians (singers and/or *aulētai*) might assemble a recital collection that included pieces of tragic song but had nothing to do with an actual performance of any particular play.[129] The surviving pieces of this papyrus include four lines of lyrics sung by the character Tecmessa in a tragedy about Ajax; the style and metre (dactylo-epitrite) seem to place the play in the fifth or fourth century BC, but the melody is pitched so high that it seems to be set for a female voice – in which case obviously it cannot be the original musical score, since only male actors were involved in stage productions.[130] By the Roman period, however, and perhaps earlier, a *tragōidos* might sometimes have a female 'assistant' (*hupotragōidos*);[131] and it is possible that just as female citharodes could perform independently, female tragedy-singers might have done so likewise.[132] In addition to this short passage of tragic song, this same papyrus contains also a paean, two instrumental pieces for *auloi* and another very short piece of tragic lyric. The Ajax-tragedy lines are introduced with a *paragraphos* (paragraph-punctuation mark) and the marginal note ΑΛΛ(Ο) ΧΟΡ(ΟΥ), i.e., 'another [melody] for a Chorus'.

In the second century AD, the Syrian-Greek satirist Lucian, in his essay *How to Write History*, provides us with a remarkable account (exaggerated and ludicrous, but clearly based on a recognizable social phenomenon) of a

---

[128] Pöhlmann and West 2001: 20.
[129] Pöhlmann and West 2001: nos. 17 and 18; cf. *TrGF* II, F 683.
[130] M. L. West and others have suggested that this may be a play originally authored by Sophocles' tragedian son, also named Sophocles; see n. 92 earlier in this chapter.
[131] Lucian *Zeus Tragōidos* 1–2; *A.P.* 5. 138 (anon.); also a third century AD inscription from Dura (*Dura* 940, fr. 5, col. 1.5, 7–9 = Stefanis 1988: no. 448); see further Nervegna 2013: 86; Le Guen, this volume.
[132] For female *kitharōidoi*, see Power 2010: 57–71.

Music and Dance in Tragedy After the Fifth Century    241

kind of 'tragedy-fever' that might infect a whole community. It is worth quoting at length:

> They say ... that in the reign of King Lysimachus, the people of Abdera [NE Greece, bordering on Thrace] were smitten by a kind of epidemic fever ... Around the seventh day ... the fever broke ... but it left them in a severely afflicted mental state. All of them went overboard for tragedy, spouting iambic lines and bellowing mightily. Most of all, they were solo-singing Euripides' *Andromeda* (τὴν Εὐριπίδου Ἀνδρομέδαν ἐμονῴδουν) and going all the way through Perseus' long speech in song,[133] and the whole city was full of all those pale, thin, seventh-day-feverish tragedy-singers (*tragōidōn*), bawling out "You, o tyrant of gods and humans, Eros!" and all that other stuff in a mighty voice, over and over again, until finally winter and the cold weather put a stop to their craziness ... I think it was Archelaus the tragedy-performer (*tragōidos*) who was to blame for all of that; he was very famous at that time, and he had given a tragedy-performance (*tragōidēsas*) for them of Andromeda at mid-summer, in the blazing heat, so that most of them caught fever from the theatre, and then later after they had left and gone home they later relapsed into that state of 'tragedy', with Andromeda still dwelling prominently in their memories and Perseus plus Medusa's head still flying all around each of their minds ... (Lucian, *How to Write History* 1)

It seems from this frivolous (and indignant) account that an individual *tragōidos* (tragedy-performer), such as Archelaus, could present – on his own, or backed by a troupe of fellow-actors, though the former seems most likely – a number of scenes from a famous Euripides play, apparently concentrating especially on the female lead character's sung solo-laments (*monōidia*) but also including some lengthy passages from the male hero's spoken role (*rhēsis*), or possibly even including the whole play, while converting some or all of the spoken parts into song (*en melei*). The audience was enraptured. This is what it means to be a 'tragedian' (*tragōidos*) by this period – just as we find them recorded in the festival records of competitions and prizes.

## Conclusion

Tragedy began in the sixth century BC as (in large part) choral song and dance, and even while the notion of 'tragedy' became by the Hellenistic

[133] The MSS are divided here between *en melei* ('with melody') and *en merei* ('in turn'). See Hall 2002: 36, Prauscello 2006: 94 n. 296; Nervegna 2013: 85. A similar anecdote (likewise involving a solo performance of Eur. *Andromeda* by a *tragōidos* to an impressionable audience) is offered by the fourth-century AD historian of culture Eunapius = *Hist. Graec. Minores* fr. 54.

period (as in our own era) commonplace in everyday Greek usage as referring to any kind of sad and pathetic or sensational catastrophe, public performances by *tragōidoi* never ceased to include musical expectations. (And in Modern Greek, as has often been noted, the standard word for 'song' is *tragoudi*.) Whether we choose nowadays to characterize all these postclassical performances as 'tragedy' is a delicate matter of definition. If we mean by 'tragedy' a fully staged production of a complete play, or even a written play-text carefully read in school or in the privacy of one's home or library, then we obviously should exclude many of the phenomena that I have been discussing in this chapter. But if we expand our horizon to include all kinds of adaptations and musically enhanced dramatic scenes, performed by a skilled singer with or without a chorus, then the picture looks quite different. From that perspective, tragedy without music – and without moving, singing bodies to look at – would be almost unthinkable. The Artists of Dionysus knew what they were doing and what their audiences were hoping for.

CHAPTER 8

*The Fifth Century and After
(Dis)Continuities in Greek Tragedy*

Francis Dunn

Discussing fourth-century tragedy can be a dicey proposition. Lacking as we do complete tragedies – with the likely exception of *Rhesus* (see Fries, this volume) – we must extrapolate from other sources, working out from surviving fragments, back from New Comedy, and forward from the more abundant remains of Sophocles and Euripides. Extrapolation attempts to fill a void by extending observable patterns beyond their known domain, and thus it regularly runs the risk of oversimplifying.

For example, the procedure of working forward from the surviving tragedies of fifth-century poets has long been dominated by a conviction that the genre underwent a rapid decline after the deaths of Sophocles and Euripides.[1] Today that normative approach has largely been abandoned, but we are in danger of replacing it with a reductive notion of continuity. Thus Edith Hall argues that from the fifth to fourth centuries, the technology of dramatic performance changed considerably while its content remained largely the same (Hall 2007).[2] I shall argue, however, that innovations in the late fifth century were both real and varied, and that this variety precludes discerning an overriding trend; in fact, for each development we encounter, we are likely to find another moving in a contrary direction. And although we may assume that fourth-century tragedy was indebted to some of these innovations, there is no reason to think that it was less diverse than tragedy of the preceding era. I shall therefore describe as broadly as possible some developments in the late fifth century and examine whether or not they carried over into drama of the following period. I shall be covering, or revisiting, some familiar ground, but in avoiding normative judgments, I hope to present the innovations in these

---

[1] The conviction arguably goes back to Aristophanes' *Frogs* and was given prominence by Nietzsche's *Birth of Tragedy* (see the Introduction, this volume).
[2] Likewise, Carter in this volume proposes that we view all tragedy after c. 450 synchronically.

plays as important explorations, neither symptoms of decline or decay nor mere ripples in a tide of continuity.

My approach thus differs to some extent from other contributions in this volume. I describe developments in surviving late-fifth-century tragedies and ask to what extent these carry over into the fourth, whereas my colleagues discuss what we know of tragedy from the fourth century and frequently compare instances from the fifth. Starting from two different bodies of material means that, despite some overlap, our approaches usefully complement one another. I begin with two relatively narrow topics, aspects of song and plot in late-fifth-century tragedy, and then consider broader developments in naturalism, self-consciousness, and ethical contingency.

## Song

The later plays of Euripides assign a greater proportion of the lyrics to actors, increasingly in the form of astrophic monody; for example, in *Orestes* the messenger's report of the Argive assembly (866–956) is followed not by a choral *stasimon* but by Electra's lyric lament (960–1012),[3] of which the greater part is astrophic (982–1012). The changing role of the chorus has been the subject of much speculation (for the fourth century see Duncan and Liapis, this volume). The internal evidence of fifth-century tragedy suggests a general increase in actors' song and a corresponding decrease in choral song (see later in this chapter). Speculation enters when we try either to extrapolate from this internal evidence developments in the fourth century, or to connect it with external evidence such as remarks in Aristotle (esp. *Po.* 1456a 25–31, quoted and discussed later in this chapter).[4] In what follows, I point rather to varied experiments than to a single line of evolution.

The internal evidence has been assembled by Eric Csapo in tables showing 1) lines sung as a percentage of total lines in the plays of Euripides and Sophocles, and 2) lines sung by actors as a percentage of all lines sung in the same plays.[5] A first and simplest observation is that, although the amount of song in a play remains largely the same over time, the proportion sung by actors increases considerably in the later years of the fifth century. A second observation is that, although the increase tends to be

---

[3] Diggle 1994: 244–5, following Weil, assigns the strophic section 960–81 to the chorus.
[4] So Lucas 1968: 193–4; Xanthakis-Karamanos 1980: 8–10.
[5] Csapo 1999/2000 with Figures 1a, 1b and 2a, 2b, respectively.

associated with Euripides and his fondness for astrophic monodies, there is an equally steady increase in actors' song in Sophocles. Can we assume that this observable trend continued into the fourth century, and continued to a point where the chorus played a minimal part in the drama? I shall in a moment consider some external evidence which bears on this assumption, but I begin by looking more closely at the internal evidence.

Although the overall trend in Euripides and Sophocles is toward less choral song, there is an opposite tendency in their latest plays. Thus for both dramatists, the greatest use of actors' lyrics does not occur in their latest plays, but rather in Euripides' *Orestes* of 408 BC (68.2 percent of all song) and Sophocles' roughly contemporary *Electra*[6] (49.9 percent). In subsequent plays, we find a steady decline in actors' song (with a corresponding increase in choral lyrics): in Euripides down to 22.7 percent in *Iphigenia at Aulis* and 8.3 percent in *Bacchae*, and in Sophocles down to 34.9 percent in *Philoctetes* and 29.2 percent in *Oedipus at Colonus*. In other words, this pattern of premature maximum followed by downturn is not an anomaly involving one or two plays, but a trend encompassing the last three plays of both tragedians during the same period. It would be just as reasonable to extrapolate from these plays into the fourth century a decline in actor's song and a corresponding increase in choral lyrics, as it would be to extrapolate the reverse from the plays composed earlier in their careers.

Our external and indirect evidence is no more decisive than the direct, internal evidence. Central here is Aristotle's observation:

> The chorus should be treated as one of the actors; it should be a part of the whole and should participate, not as in Euripides but as in Sophocles. With the other poets, the songs are no more integral to the plot than to another tragedy – hence the practice, started by Agathon, of singing interlude odes [*embolima*]. Yet what is the difference between singing interlude odes and transferring a speech or whole episode from one work to another? (Arist. *Po.* 1456a 25–31, tr. Halliwell 1995)

In connection with his general criterion of organic unity, Aristotle is here arguing for the (subjective) relevance of choral odes. First he favours the practice of Sophocles over that of Euripides (thinking, perhaps, of *stasima* such as E. *Hel.* 1301–68, on Demeter and Persephone), and then he brings in the limit-case of Agathon's *embolima*: the less (subjectively) relevant an ode, the closer it approaches the latter's experimental use of apparently

---

[6] Stylistic features of Sophocles' *Electra* align it with those of his latest period, *Philoctetes* (409) and *Oedipus at Colonus* (before Sophocles' death in 406), and most critics thus place it near the end of his career: e.g., Jebb 1924: lvi–lviii; Kamerbeek 1974: 6; March 2001: 21.

inserted songs. We may like to think, with Else (1957: 554–6), of four stages in the decline of the chorus – a high degree of integration with the action in Sophocles, a looser connection in Euripides, a total lack of connection after Euripides and finally the insertion of irrelevant *embolima* – but Aristotle himself presents no such picture. (By the way, it is as wrong to conclude from this passage that Agathon regularly used *embolima* as it is to infer from *Poetics* 1451b 1 that he never used mythological plots; note his *Aëropē TrGF* I, 39 F 1, *Alcmeon* F 2, *Thyestes* F 3 and *Telephus* F4.)

The notion of a progressive decline in the chorus rests in part on a different piece of external evidence, namely the notation in some texts χοροῦ or χοροῦ μέλος, evidently indicating a point at which a choral ode would have been performed. Yet in any given case it may be debated whether this is a later scribe's observation or conjecture that the original ode is missing from the text, or a version of the author's indication where a song should be inserted; in Aristophanes' *Plutus*, given the active role of the chorus and discrepancies among the manuscripts, the former is more likely; in Menander, given the complete absence of the chorus otherwise, the latter.[7] And in any case, this notation is extremely rare in tragedy, occurring once in a papyrus that may contain Astydamas' *Hector* (60 F 1h?, 10 *TrGF*), and twice among the *adespota* (F 625.9, 640b.28).[8] Given the tiny sample of relevant fragments, their uncertain attributions, and their lack of context, we cannot safely conclude that tragic authors in the fourth century wrote nonspecific choral odes; on the contrary, the omission of a choral ode from a papyrus of Euripides' *Hippolytus*[9] suggests that the same may have happened in the papyrus ascribed to Astydamas (cf. in this volume Duncan and Liapis).

It follows that external evidence does not alter the conclusion that use of the chorus may have increased *or* decreased after the end of the fifth century.[10] Furthermore, if the surviving *Rhesus* was a fourth-century composition (so Liapis 2012: lxvii–lxxv; Fries, this volume), then we have direct evidence for the chorus playing an important part in the action and singing odes relevant to it.

---

[7] On the former understanding of XOPOY, see Beare 1954; on the chorus in fourth-century comedy more generally, see Hunter 1971 and Rothwell 1992.

[8] *Trag. Adesp.* 667a Kannicht/Snell, once considered tragic (Hunter 1981), has been shown to be satyric (Sutton 1987b: 9–53, followed by Kannicht in *TrGF* 5.2 pp. 1137–42).

[9] *P. Sorbonne* 2252; cf. W.S. Barrett 1964: 438–9, n. 2.

[10] Additionally, titles such as Dicaeogenes' *Cyprians* (52 F 1 TrGF) and Cleophon's *Bacchae* (77 F 1) may reflect the identity of a chorus in those plays. Cf., in this volume, Duncan and Liapis.

Finally, although a statistical analysis such as Csapo's is not possible for the remains of fourth-century tragedy, it is worth noting that innovative forms of monody continued. The Muse's 'song from the machine' in *Rhesus* may be metrically unadventurous,[11] but it is formally quite unusual, with no transition from or to speech, and lament in the strophe answered by curses in the antistrophe. The fragment attributed to Astydamas' *Hector*, by contrast, marks a choral ode with χοροῦ μέλος but follows this with a monody apparently in the uncommon galliambic metre,[12] thus registering cultic associations of the region around Troy.

## Plot

It is often observed that the melodramatic plots of Euripides' later plays anticipate those of fourth-century tragedy and also of New Comedy. Satyrus in his *Life of Euripides* speaks of the poet's innovations later adopted by comic poets: the domestic relationships of husband 'to wife and father to son and servant to master, or the matter of reversals, rapes of virgins, substitutions of children, recognitions through rings and necklaces, for these are clearly the content of New Comedy, things which Euripides perfected' (*P.Oxy.* 1176, fr. 39.7). Although today we can observe similarities between surviving plays of Euripides and Menander, we cannot do the same with regard to fourth-century tragedy; it is nevertheless tempting to see tragedians such as Astydamas and Theodectas bridging the gap between Euripides and New Comedy, and exhibiting typically Euripidean 'melodramatic intrigues' and 'coups de théâtre'.[13] I shall argue in what follows that such a picture is misleading, and that there is in fact a closer affiliation between fourth-century tragedy and Sophocles.

Among our surviving plays, the quintessential 'intrigue plays'[14] are those of Euripides, namely *Ion*, *Iphigenia among the Taurians* and *Helen* – at least if we think of the components of Aristotle's complex plots: recognition, reversal and averted disaster (*Poetics* 14 and 16). Yet this general class of plays also includes lost works by Euripides and Sophocles.[15] Sophocles' *Tyro* (F 648–69 *TrGF*) featured a woman, who had been raped and exposed her children, being reunited with them by means of tokens, while the stepmother is killed. In Euripides' *Chresphontes* (39 *TrGF*), a mother is

---

[11] So Liapis 2012: lxiv.    [12] Xanthakis-Karamanos 1980: 162–5.
[13] Xanthakis-Karamanos 1980: 48; on comedy more specifically, see Csapo 2000.
[14] On this category of dramas see Solmsen 1932 and Diller 1962.
[15] For an overview emphasizing these plays' novelistic features see Winkler 1984.

about to kill her child, but the murder is averted at the last minute, leading to their reunion and the murder instead of a usurper; likewise in Sophocles' *Thyestes in Sicyon* (F 247–69 *TrGF*), the murder of a father by son is averted and leads to their reunion and the murder of their opponent. In Sophocles' *Chryses* (F 726–30 *TrGF*) a brother's destruction of his siblings is averted by recognition, reunion and the murder of their opponent; likewise in his *Alētēs* (F 93–103 N²),[16] a woman is about to blind her sister but recognition intervenes and their opponent is killed. In Euripides' *Ino* (32 *TrGF*), by contrast, a woman's attempt to murder her enemies is foiled when she is made to kill her own children, leading to disaster all around.

Several fourth-century plays seem to follow similar patterns.[17] In Astydamas' *Antigone* (*TrGF* I, 60 F 1e), Maeon the son of Antigone and Haemon comes to Thebes for the games but is recognized by Creon, who orders that Haemon and Antigone be killed; Haemon, after pleading in vain that Heracles rescue them, kills Antigone and himself.[18] In the same poet's *Alcmeon* (F 1b–c), the protagonist kills his mother Eriphyle unawares. Presumably an unfamiliar woman is identified to Alcmeon as responsible for his father's death; in a fit of anger he kills the woman, only to learn afterward that she was his mother. In Theodectas' *Lynceus* (72 F 3a *TrGF*), the discovery of Abas, son of Hypermestra and Lynceus, leads to the discovery of his father also; Lynceus is about to be executed but is somehow rescued, and Danaus is killed instead. In the same poet's *Tydeus* (F 5a), a father is about to be killed by his long-lost son when he utters words that lead to a last-minute recognition and reunion. In Carcinus' *Alopē* (*TrGF* I, 70 F 1b), the protagonist had been raped and exposed her child; a quarrel among shepherds inadvertently leads to their reunion, but when Alopē's father learns she has borne an illegitimate child, he kills himself.

In most of these plays (as far as we can tell), the outcome is double insofar as a protagonist is saved or rediscovered and an enemy is killed; only in Euripides' *Ion, Iphigenia among the Taurians* and *Helen* is there a fully happy ending, with the villain or antagonist merely deceived (Xuthus)

---

[16] Snell in *TrGF* rejects Sophoclean authorship (see adesp. F 1b), following Wilamowitz 1962; the latter's only arguments, however, are that ἐχρῆν is poorly attested in Sophocles, that the proper name Ἀλείτης in Stobaeus cannot stand since ἀλείτης in Homer means criminal (1962: 483–4), and that the fragments strike him as trivial (1962: 291 n.1).

[17] Reconstructions in Webster 1954. See further Liapis and Stephanopoulos, this volume.

[18] So Hygin. *fab.* 72; however Webster 1954: 305 proposes that Heracles does indeed rescue Haemon and Antigone, on the ground that it is unlikely that Haemon's plea should fail.

or outwitted (Thoas, Theoclymenus). These three surviving plays are thus anomalous among the larger group of intrigue plays, and unlike them, they prefigure the fully happy endings of New Comedy. Rather than a continuum from Euripidean plays such as *Helen*, to fourth-century tragedies, to New Comedy, we thus find two separate and distinct trajectories: a continuity on the one hand between lost plays of Sophocles and Euripides and tragedies of the following period, and a similarity on the other between three surviving plays of Euripides and the considerably later comedies of Menander.

A related development is peculiar to the very end of the fifth century. Euripides' *Orestes*, *Phoenician Women* and *Iphigenia at Aulis* and Sophocles' *Oedipus at Colonus* are none of them intrigue plays like those we have been considering, yet all exhibit a burst of complexity and a multiplication of incident. In the last of these, for instance, a chorus of elderly citizens first tries to drive Oedipus from the sacred ground where he stands. Then Ismene arrives, bringing news from Thebes that her brothers are preparing to wage war for the throne and that Creon, because of an oracle, is determined to bring Oedipus back to Thebes. Next Theseus enters, accepts the blind man's offer of a powerful grave, and promises to protect him. No sooner does Theseus leave than Creon appears and, failing to persuade Oedipus to return with him, takes Ismene hostage. He then seizes Antigone and is about to carry her off, but the old men of the chorus hamper him long enough for Theseus to return and demand he give back the sisters. Creon departs, hurling threats, and before long Polyneices himself arrives and, after much debate, is allowed to plead his case. Oedipus, in a fiery speech, denounces the treachery and hypocrisy of his sons and repeats his curse that Polyneices and Eteocles will die by one another's hands; soon afterward, Oedipus departs and a messenger reports his mysterious end.

We cannot tell, from our meager remains, if a significant proportion of fourth-century tragedies were equally eventful or 'overstuffed'.[19] Yet *Rhesus*, most likely our only surviving example from the period, is, as Fries notes in this volume, 'full of rapid action and theatrical excitement', with two messenger scenes, two agons and two divine epiphanies, all in under a thousand lines.

At the same time two late plays, Sophocles' *Electra* and Euripides' *Bacchae*, tend in the opposite direction, reducing stage action to a

---

[19] The expression comes from the end of the Hypothesis to E. *Ph*. τὸ δρᾶμά ἐστι μὲν ταῖς σκηνικαῖς ὄψεσι καλόν, ἐπεὶ καὶ παραπληρωματικόν.

minimum. In *Electra*, the plot to avenge the murder of Agamemnon against Clytemnestra and Aegisthus is discussed in the prologue by Orestes and the Tutor, but on hearing Electra's off-stage cry they withdraw, ceding the stage to Electra and her grief. The women of the chorus, Chrysothemis, and Clytemnestra all try in turn to silence Electra, without success. The Tutor finally enters to begin the deceptive scheme at line 660, intensifying Electra's suffering, and she in turn disabuses Chrysothemis who believes Orestes has returned. We are two-thirds of the way through the play before Orestes enters, and he does not enter the house to exact revenge for another 270 lines; the murder of Clytemnestra is thus postponed to the very last minute, and that of Aegisthus has not taken place when the play ends. By contrast with *Oedipus at Colonus*, in *Electra* almost nothing happens (cf. Dunn 2012). Euripides' *Bacchae* is similar. In the prologue Dionysus, in disguise, announces his intent to demonstrate his divinity in Thebes. All the subsequent scenes, from the palace miracle to the messenger speeches, from the temptation of Pentheus to the final *deus ex machina*, do nothing other than reveal, with progressively greater power, the god's divine nature. In different ways and to different effects both late plays strip the drama of incident. The approach to some extent hearkens back to Aeschylus, whose *Persians*, for example, involves a series of crucial entrances but little in the way of action.

Again, we cannot know whether fourth-century tragedies minimized dramatic incident to quite this extent. Perhaps the strongest candidate is Astydamas' *Hector*, which seems to have included news from the battlefield, Hector's arming, his farewell to his family, and a messenger's report of his duel with Achilles, but little demonstrable stage action.[20]

## Naturalism

Euripides' relative naturalism has been noted ever since the remark, attributed to Sophocles, that he creates characters as they ought to be, Euripides as they are (Arist. *Po*. 1460b 33–4).[21] Many aspects of his plays may be considered under this rubric.

---

[20] Reconstructions in Webster 1954: 305–6, Xanthakis-Karamanos 1980: 162–7. See also Liapis and Stephanopoulos, this volume; Liapis 2016.
[21] See Michelini 1987: 181–5 and Goff 1999/2000, with sources they cite.

## Language

In his handling of the iambic trimetre, Euripides is freer than Aeschylus and Sophocles (more often admitting anapaests and resolution, and allowing resolution in more word shapes) and is progressively freer in the course of his career,[22] with the result that a metre which more than any other has the rhythm of speech (μάλιστα γὰρ λεκτικὸν τῶν μέτρων τὸ ἰαμβεῖόν ἐστιν Arist. *Po.* 1449a 4) is all the closer to ordinary conversation in the late plays of Euripides. Similar but less quantifiable is the more frequent use of colloquial diction in Euripides and Sophocles (esp. *Philoctetes*) by contrast with Aeschylus.[23] An interesting passage in Aristotle's *Rhetoric* praises Euripides' natural diction, implies that subsequent playwrights followed him, and associates with this the natural delivery of the fourth-century actor Theodorus:

> As a result, authors should compose without being noticed and should seem to speak not artificially but naturally. (The latter is persuasive, the former the opposite; for [if the artifice is obvious] people become resentful, as at someone plotting against them, just as they are at those adulterating wines.) An example is the success of Theodorus' voice when contrasted with that of other actors; for his seems the voice of the actual character, but the others' those of somebody else. The 'theft'[24] is well done if one composes by choosing words from ordinary language. Euripides does this and first showed the way' (Arist. *Rh.* 3 1404b 18–25, tr. Kennedy 1991).

The implication seems borne out by rates of resolution comparable to those of late Euripides in Chaeremon (35 percent), Theodectas (24 percent)[25] and, so far as we can tell from their smaller samples, in Diogenes and Carcinus as well.[26] Colloquial diction is harder to track in our fragmentary remains; Collard cites one instance each in Chaeremon and Theodectas, five in *Rhesus*, one in Ezekiel and two in Lycophron.[27]

Yet at the same time there is an opposing trend in Euripides and later in Sophocles, where the language of courts and assemblies constitutes a marked and elevated register. This may take the form of familiar

---

[22] West 1982: 82, 85–8.  [23] Stevens 1945 and 1976; Collard 2005.
[24] By 'theft' or 'deception' (κλέπτεται δ' εὖ) Aristotle means unnoticed artifice.
[25] West 1982: 86, counting 25 in 72 lines and 14 in 58, respectively.
[26] I count 4 resolutions in 11 lines in Diogenes and 5 in 25 complete lines in Carcinus.
[27] Chaeremon F 20, Theodectas F 6.2, *Rhesus* 195, 499, 690, 730, 759, Ezekiel *Exagōgē* 128.24, Lycophron 763, 1464 in Collard 2005: 365–80.

rhetorical tropes. Thus Polyneices, rationalizing his expedition in *Phoenician Women*, begins:

> Telling the truth is by nature simple
> and justice needs no fancy explanations;
> it is itself appropriate; but the unjust argument,
> being sick, needs clever medicines.
> (E. *Ph.* 469–72)[28]

The rhetorical disavowal of rhetoric lends weight to his plea. Another device is imitating a particular genre, as when Sophocles' Electra adopts the language of public encomium as she tries to persuade her sister to help kill Aegisthus:

> What citizen or foreigner, after seeing us,
> will not welcome us with praise like this:
> 'Look at these two sisters, friends,
> who saved their father's estate,
> who when their enemies were riding high,
> risked their lives to champion revenge.
> Everyone should love these two and venerate them!'
> (S. *El.* 975–81)

In vainly trying to win over Chrysothemis, Electra dignifies her proposal with elevated language that helps equate the sisters with the famous tyrannicides (cf. Juffras 1991). And a speaker may reinforce an argument by turning to abstract generalizations or *sententiae*, as when Lycus disparages Heracles' bravery:

> ... and [he is] especially cowardly
> because he never wore a shield on his left arm
> or came near a spear, but holding his bow
> (that worthless weapon) stood ready to flee.
> A bow is no test of a man's courage –
> but one who stands and looks unflinching
> at the spear's swift swathe and holds his rank.
> (E. *HF* 158–64)

The general statement about archery gives the tyrant's claim the added force of universal truth as well as the authority of cultural values concerning warfare. Thus even as drama, in general, leaves behind the ponderous language of Aeschylus, it adopts a new kind of elevated speech.

---

[28] Translations from the Greek are my own, except where noted.

Fourth-century tragedy continued to use the elevated register of oratory. In his *Medea*, Carcinus used a variation of the argument from *eikos*, as we learn from Aristotle:

> Another topic is to accuse or defend on the basis of mistakes that have been made. For example, in the *Medea* of Carcinus some accuse her on the ground that she has killed her children. At any rate, they are not to be seen; for Medea made the mistake of sending the children away. But she defends herself on the ground that [it is improbable she has killed them, because] she would have killed Jason [then as well], not [only] the children; for she would have made a mistake in not doing so if she had done the other thing (Arist. *Rh.* 2 1400b 9–15, tr. Kennedy 1991).[29]

Related to Medea's defensive strategy is the trope of turning an opponent's argument against them. Aristotle reports that in Theodectas' *Ajax*, as Ajax and Odysseus debate for the arms of Achilles, Odysseus claims that his own valor is proven by Diomedes' choice of him as a companion in the Night Raid, to which Ajax replies 'that Diomedes chose Odysseus not out of honor to him but in order that his companion might be inferior; for he could have done it for this reason' (Arist. *Rh.* 2 1399b 29–31, cf. 1400a 27–9).

The use of gnomic *sententiae* as in Euripides' *Heracles* clearly continued in the fourth century; a character in one of Astydamas' plays, for example, declares:

> The surest praise of a family
> is praising an individual – whoever is just
> and best in character, calling him noble.
> (fr. 8.1–3)

Yet this fragment comes to us thanks to Stobaeus, and it is therefore prudent to observe that fragments of tragedy from all periods were selected by compilers such as Stobaeus precisely for their gnomic utterances. As for more specifically oratorical *topoi*, Theodectas and Astydamas were both students of Isocrates,[30] and the former was an orator as well as playwright, so it is quite possible (but not demonstrable, given our evidence) that their use of rhetorical language exceeded that of Euripides.[31]

---

[29] On possible reconstructions of the plot, see Liapis and Stephanopoulos, this volume.
[30] 72 *TrGF* T1 and 60 *TrGF* T1.
[31] *Pace* Xanthakis-Karamanos 1980: 59–60, it does not follow from Arist. *Po.* 1450b 7–8 (οἱ μὲν γὰρ ἀρχαῖοι πολιτικῶς ἐποίουν λέγοντας, οἱ δὲ νῦν ῥητορικῶς) that rhetorical tendencies intensified in the fourth century. Carter in this volume proposes a single 'rhetorical turn' around 450, but does so by defining rhetorical tragedy as that 'populated by people who are frequently trying to persuade other people'; this criterion is so broad as to be virtually useless.

## Characters and Situations

In Euripides, events are by and large portrayed with greater naturalism.[32] For example, the prologue of *Heracles* naturalistically depicts the anxious fears of Megara and Amphitryon, the latter hoping against hope that Heracles will return to rescue them from Lycus (Dunn 2007: 98–9 on *HF*; more generally 65–110 on Euripides' realistic portrayal of dramatic action 'in the present'). Agamemnon is credibly uncertain in the prologue of *Iphigenia at Aulis*, finally deciding to countermand his letter asking for his daughter to come to Aulis; and the beginning of Sophocles' *Oedipus at Colonus* effectively conveys the cautious steps of blind man and young girl over unfamiliar terrain (Dunn 1992). More generally, *Orestes* positions itself as a naturalistic alternative to Aeschylus' *Eumenides*, portraying a sequel to *Libation Bearers* populated not with gorgon-like Furies, the queen's ghost, and the gods Apollo and Athena, but with a sick young man, his attentive sister, and his self-centered uncle.

Such naturalism is harder to identify in the fragments and testimonia of lost plays. One reasonably credible example is Carcinus' *Medea*, where the playwright reverts to an older version of the myth in which Medea hides her children to prevent the people of Corinth from killing them; the change from Euripides' version offers a more naturalistic protagonist, a woman ready and able to avenge her husband's infidelity but not prepared to take the more shocking step of killing her own children. Similar is the same author's *Alopē*, where Cercyon, distraught at learning of his daughter's illegitimate child, kills himself; in Euripides, by contrast, he orders that Alopē be killed, an extreme reaction rejected by the fourth-century playwright. In the *Alcmeon* of Astydamas, the protagonist kills his mother unawares in a striking departure from the traditional plot, where he does so in full knowledge and at his father's command, and is consequently pursued by Eriphyle's Furies; the fourth-century version, in which Alcmeon presumably wants to avenge his father's death, but not by committing matricide, is more plausible and naturalistic. Finally it is arguable, at least, that Hector in Astydamas' play of the same name confesses a realistic (and novel) fear as he prepares to fight Achilles, saying καὶ πως τ[έθ]ραυσμαι, 'even though I am rather rattled' (60 F 11.12).[33]

---

[32] The phrase 'by and large' does not seek to deny the complications and contradictions in Euripides' naturalism, which I observe in my discussion here and which are addressed in Goff 1999/2000.

[33] On Hector's emotional conflict in Astydamas see Snell 1971: 148; Liapis and Stephanopoulos, this volume.

Yet the trend toward naturalism is not universal. In the fifth century, two plays move in an opposite direction. *Helen* and *Iphigenia among the Taurians* both rest on unusual premises, Helen in the former being replaced at Troy by a phantom, and Iphigenia in the latter being forced to conduct human sacrifice; the settings of both plays are exotic and remote, namely Egypt and Crimea; and the foreigners Theoclymenus and Thoas are clichéd stereotypes rather than naturalistic individuals – or, rather, doubled stereotypes, being first described as barbaric savages intent on killing all strangers, then appearing onstage as harmless dupes easily outwitted by the female protagonist. There is little sign of a comparable fantastic or anti-naturalistic bent in the fourth century. Perhaps the closest thing is in *Rhesus*, if composed in that period. In this play, Hector enters as a clichéd braggart soldier, and must be dissuaded by the chorus and then Aeneas from leading a charge against the Greeks at night; when Rhesus appears, he outdoes Hector in foolish boldness and must himself be dissuaded by Hector from rushing at once into battle. Rather than a cartoonish antagonist, as in *Helen* and *Iphigenia among the Taurians*, here we have two cartoonish protagonists (cf. Liapis 2012: xlv–ix).

## Secular Content

An important aspect of naturalism is the largely secular plot. Prologues and epilogues aside, divinities play a relatively minor role. Not only do gods seldom appear onstage (by contrast with, e.g., Aeschylus' *Eumenides* or *Prometheus Bound*), their offstage influence is largely absent. For example, whereas Orestes in *Libation Bearers* is motivated in large part by Apollo's threats of dire punishment, his counterparts in Sophocles and Euripides are driven by a personal desire for revenge; and whereas Orestes in *Eumenides* is pursued by a chorus of Furies, in Euripides' *Orestes* he imagines them in a realistic delirium. The exception that proves the rule is *Heracles*, where Iris and Lyssa enter mid-way through the play to impel the hero to kill his own children; their role in this play is analogous to that of a *deus ex machina* since they do not take part in the action and instead personify his abrupt and unexpected fit of madness.

Comments by Aristotle (*Po.* 1454a37–b6) and Antiphanes (fr. 189 *PCG*) suggest that the *deus ex machina* remained in frequent use in the fourth century, and it is possible that such epiphanies likewise stood in contrast with a largely secular plot. This is certainly true in the surviving *Rhesus*, although in this case the playwright experiments with the device twice over. The epilogue featuring Rhesus' mother the Muse combines a narrative explanation of the hero's death with a lyric lament on his behalf; and the entrance of Athena mid-way through the play includes her unparalleled impersonation of Aphrodite.

Moving in the opposite direction from this general tendency, however, is *Bacchae*, where the god Dionysus is onstage throughout, and the plot consists entirely of a divinity revealing his power. More generally, the trend toward naturalism and secularism is opposed by an interest in the transcendent. As I have argued elsewhere, *Bacchae* and Sophocles' *Oedipus at Colonus* allow the audience gradually to perceive the ineffable power of a god in the former, and of a mysterious death in the latter (Dunn 2010). Thus at the end of *Oedipus at Colonus*, the protagonist's death finally gives the stage space its full meaning – even as that meaning explicitly transcends the space. Sophocles does not convey the meaning of a real place, as Aeschylus did in *Eumenides* by capturing the democratic significance of the Athenian law-court; instead, he evokes recognition of a transcendent meaning that cannot be contained by the theatrical space.

There is no reason to assume, by the way, that a tendency which swims against the general tide is for that reason aberrant and inconsequential; interest in the transcendent realm may or may not have played a part in fourth-century tragedy, but it certainly did so in Plato's philosophy and arguably also in religion of the period. And although we are not in a position to judge whether they fully tend to the metaphysical, at least one play addresses ecstatic aspects of religious experience. Diogenes wrote a *Semelē* presumably set in Thebes and describing the exotic worship of Cybele and Artemis in Asia (*TrGF* I 45 F 1). Furthermore, Carcinus wrote a play, title unknown, dealing with the worship of Demeter and Kore in Sicily (70 F 5); our fragment recounts the myth – abduction of the daughter, the mother's grief, and the resulting famine – concluding with a Euripidean-style aetiology, ὅθεν θεὰς τιμῶσιν ἐς τὰ νῦν ἔτι, 'hence they worship the goddesses to this very day', suggesting that mother and daughter somehow played an important part in the play (see further Liapis and Stephanopoulos, this volume).

### Self-Consciousness

A broad development in later tragedy is literary self-consciousness, which can take many forms, and which I discuss here under three headings: choral self-reference, metatheatre, and allusion.

## Choral Self-Reference

Not uncommonly, a tragic chorus alludes to the part it plays singing and dancing in the orchestra (Henrichs 1994/5). Most famously, the chorus in *Oedipus the King* responds to Jocasta's conclusion that the oracle concerning Laius was wrong by saying, in part, εἰ γὰρ αἱ τοιαίδε πράξεις τίμιαι,/τί δεῖ με χορεύειν; 'if actions like these are honored, why should I dance?' (S. *OT* 895–7). Such references are especially common in late Euripides (Csapo 1999/2000). Thus in *Iphigenia at Aulis*, the chorus, recalling the marriage of Peleus and Thetis, sings and dances to the words, 'and along the white sand, whirling in a circle, the fifty daughters of Nereus performed the wedding dance' (E. *IA* 1054–7). Likewise in *Bacchae*, the maenadic chorus, singing (and presumably beating drums) to the music of the *aulos*, proclaims:

> Sing of Dionysus
> to the deep-roaring drums,
> joyfully exalting the god of joy
> with Phrygian cries and calls,
> when the sacred sweet-sounding pipe
> booms its playful, sacred tune.
> (E. *Ba.* 155–62)

Choral self-reference frequently occurs in the context of the 'New Music' pioneered by Phrynis and Timotheus and closely associated with Euripides (West 1992: 356–72, Csapo 2004).[34] Passages like that in *Iphigenia*, which mentions fifty women dancing in a circle (as in dithyramb), and like that in *Bacchae*, which refers to Dionysus and suggests a cultic context, were probably accompanied by music in the new style. Several passages in Sophocles suggest a dithyrambic context but are not generally taken to reflect the New Music; for example, the women of Trachis, on hearing the news of Heracles' safe return, call out to Apollo and Artemis, and then continue:

> I am lifted up and shall not reject
> the pipe, master of my heart.
> See, the ivy arouses me,
> *euoi,*
> whirling me around
> in the Bacchic contest.
> *Io, io, paian.*
> (S. *Tr.* 216–21)

---

[34] Needless to say, I make no claims about developments in music per se; for an overview of this topic, see Griffith in this volume.

We find similar language in *Ajax* (693–705) and *Antigone* (1146–52). And of course self-reference alone (as in *Oedipus the King*) tells us nothing at all about the music which accompanied that passage. Hence although the New Music was canonical by the fourth century (West 1992: 371), it does not follow that the practice of drawing attention to choral performance continued after Sophocles and Euripides.

One of Euripides' late plays does something quite different, using mention of music and dance not to advertise the role of the chorus, but to try to silence it. In *Orestes*, as the women of the chorus enter, Electra says, 'My dear women, walk with quiet feet, don't make a sound, no noise at all.' (E. *Or.* 136–7), thus referring to the noise of fifteen players marching onstage, afraid they might awaken her diseased brother. When they comply, she continues, 'Oh, oh, please, my friend, play the pipe gently like the breath of a reed!'(145–6), speaking now of the *aulos* which accompanies their movements.

*Metatheatre*

Passages may refer not to music and dance in particular but to the play's general status as theatrical performance. Sophocles in several tragedies portrays a plot within the plot, in which two characters discuss the scheme they are inaugurating, and thus play a role like that of dramatist or stage manager. Thus Athena in *Ajax* brings the deluded protagonist onstage for Odysseus to look at, just as the playwright will bring him onstage for the spectators at large. Orestes and the Tutor in the prologue of *Electra* rehearse the scheme for revenge they will belatedly carry out in the course of the drama. And Odysseus in *Philoctetes* coaches Neoptolemus on the part he must play to obtain the precious bow of Heracles; here Odysseus shows great forethought as stage manager, adding to his instructions a promise that, if the scheme takes too long, he will send a proxy with new directions (S. *Ph.* 126–31); he even mentions that he will give him a ship owner's appearance (128–9), thus alluding to a new costume one of the actors must wear.[35] A similar device is not found in Euripides, presumably because its place is taken by the divine prologue which frequently plays a

---

[35] Allusion to costume makes it reasonably certain we are meant to realize that the actor now playing Odysseus will later re-enter (if necessary) as the captain (cf. Pavlovskis 1977/8: 119, Ringer 1998: 112).

similar role, as a god announces to the audience the action he or she is setting in motion (Apollo in *Alcestis*, Aphrodite in *Hippolytus*, Poseidon and Athena in *Trojan Women*, Hermes in *Ion*, Dionysus in *Bacchae*). In all such examples, a god outside the action, or a character within it, suggests the role of the author; similar is the prologue of *Iphigenia at Aulis* where Agamemnon, anxiously writing and rewriting a letter, suggests the author's fraught task in restaging a story so powerfully represented in Aeschylus' *Agamemnon* and elsewhere.[36]

Metatheatre may also exploit specific aspects of performance. For example, the powerful scene in which Sophocles' Electra mourns over her brother's ashes draws attention to the empty urn's status as a stage property, not an actual funeral implement; when Electra says 'I hold you in my arms now that you are nothing' (S. *El.* 1129), and 'so welcome me into this, your house, I nothing into it, nothing'(1165–6), she ironically underscores the gap between stage prop and dramatic meaning (cf. Ringer 1998: 185–98). Two of our latest surviving tragedies, Euripides' *Bacchae* and Sophocles' *Oedipus at Colonus*, push the limits of metatheatre with sustained and searching interest in the semiotics of dramatic costume and theatrical space, respectively. In the prologue of *Bacchae*, an actor in Asiatic costume announces that he is in fact the god Dionysus disguised as a mortal, come to teach the people of Thebes to worship him. The play's opening lines thus foreground the semiotics of performance, drawing attention to the difference between the actor onstage and the dramatic meaning of the role he creates; as the play continues, and as Pentheus fails to recognize the god before him, the stakes grow progressively higher as we come to realize just how vast is the gulf between this mere actor and the transcendent power of Dionysus (cf. Segal 1982: 215–71). *Oedipus at Colonus* is, if anything, more radical. The entrance of a blind old man at an unfamiliar place (one he has never before visited in his life, or in myth) is a theatrical correlative to the spectators' initial ignorance of what the stage space represents, and the long and eventful plot centers on discovering its meaning. Thus we learn, first, that we are near Athens, then that the *skēnē* represents a grove of the Eumenides in Colonus, but only very gradually do we learn the power of this place – that if Oedipus ends his life here, the spot will protect Athens from any threat from Thebes. The mystical ending, in which a messenger reports the old man's

---

[36] The authenticity of the prologue of *IA* continues to be debated; it was well defended by Mellert-Hoffmann 1969: 91–155, and more recently by Pietruczuk 2012; cf. Michelakis 2006: 108–10.

disappearance, finally suggests the full meaning of the place – and the huge gap between stage space and its theatrical meaning (Dunn 2010).

There are no indications of metatheatre among the remains of fourth-century tragedy, but the phenomenon is so complex that we would need much longer fragments to judge the matter one way or the other.

## Allusion

Greek tragedy is pervaded with allusion to epic, lyric and tragic predecessors (Garner 1990); characteristic of Euripides is allusion so overt it is sometimes described as parody. Best known (and sometimes decried) is the recognition scene in *Electra* which debunks the logic of its Aeschylean counterpart.[37] Thus when the Old Man announces signs of Orestes' return, Electra rejects them immediately: how could a man's hair resemble a woman's, she objects, how could his footprint match a woman's, how could he still wear clothing made when he was a child? (E. *El.* 527–44). Exact repetition of the tokens from *Libation Bearers* juxtaposes the symbolic world of the *Oresteia* with the critical slant of Euripidean theatre.[38] Likewise in *Orestes*, the speeches in assembly concerning the matricide challenge the premises of the trial scene in *Eumenides*; rather than Olympian gods and chthonic Furies, the participants are average citizens, and rather than appealing to abstract or divine principles (the rites of Hera and pledges of Zeus, A. *Eu.* 214; the tablet-writing mind of Hades, 275; oaths versus justice, 432), the speakers appeal to the crowd's base interests (fork-tongued Talthybius, E. *Or.* 890; fence-straddling Diomedes, 899; a loud-mouthed demagogue, 903). In *Phoenician Women*, Euripides first offers in the words of Eteocles a brief and self-conscious allusion to the scene (A. *Th.* 375–676) in which, as a messenger names each Argive and describes his shield, Eteocles names the Theban warrior he will place against him:

> Agreed. After going to the seven-gated town
> I shall position the leaders at the gates, as you say,
> matching the same men against their enemies.
> But it takes too long to say each one's name,
> with the enemy camped beneath the very walls.
> (E. *Ph.* 748–52)

---

[37] Some find the allusion offensive and delete the scene; its authenticity is defended by (among others) M. Davies 1998 and Gallagher 2003.
[38] For a very full recent discussion, see Torrance 2013: 14–33.

Yet having distanced himself from Aeschylus, Euripides proceeds to imitate him: when a messenger later arrives to report the battle, he begins by naming each Argive in turn and describing his shield (1104–40), the shield designs correcting and 'capping' those in *Seven*. In Aeschylus, for example, the warrior Parthenopaeus carries a shield showing the Sphinx devouring a Theban, loosely symbolizing the Argive threat to the city; in Euripides, by contrast, the hero's mother Atalanta is shown killing the Calydonian boar, both wishfully anticipating her son's own success and illustrating the derivation of his name (Torrance 2013: 113–29).

Allusion in its various forms pervades all Greek poetry, so we should expect it to occur in fourth-century tragedy; the same is not necessarily true of the self-conscious and pointed form of allusion we find in Euripides.[39] Yet Athenaeus preserves an instance of Theodectas pointedly alluding to and capping two passages at once – a passage in Euripides' *Theseus*, and a self-conscious allusion to that same passage in Agathon's *Telephus*. In Euripides, an illiterate herdsman is able to report the arrival of Theseus in Crete (cf. test. iiia *TrGF*) by describing the letter-forms on his ship:

> I am ignorant of writing,
> but I'll tell you the shapes and give clear signs.
> There's a circle measured out as if on a lathe,
> having a clear mark in the middle.
> As for the second, there are, first, two lines,
> and then, separating them, one more in the middle.
> The third is like a curling lock of hair;
> as for the fourth, one line stands up straight,
> and three slanting ones lean against it.
> The fifth letter is not easy to describe:
> there are two lines standing apart
> but they run together in a single base.
> And the last letter is just like the third.
> (E. fr. 382 Kn.)

The speaker's ignorance of these strange signs is registered in his language ('signs' 2, 'mark' 4), his apologies ('I am ignorant' 1, 'is not easy to describe' 10), his plodding enumeration ('second', 'third', 'fourth', 'fifth') and syntax (δέ in almost every line), and his resort to thinking of them as physical objects ('as if on a lathe' 3, 'separating them' 6, 'slanting . . . lean against' 9, 'standing apart' 11, 'run together' 12). When Agathon copied

---

[39] On allusion of the former kind in fourth-century tragedy (by contrast with self-conscious and pointed allusion), see in this volume Liapis and Stephanopoulos (esp. on Astydamas' *Hector*) and Fries (on *Rhesus*).

this scene, again spelling out Theseus' name, he compressed it to one line per letter:

> The inscription began with a circle with a navel in the middle;
> two upright rulers were yoked together,
> and the third was like a Scythian bow.
> Beside was a trident lying on its side;
> on one ruler were two leaning back,
> and the last was like the third again.
>
> (Agathon, *TrGF* I, 39 F 4)

The bare enumeration (were ... was ... etc.) is enlivened by various metaphors ('with a navel in the middle' 1, 'yoked together' 2, 'like a Scythian bow' 3, 'a trident' 4), giving the compressed report more the tenor of a riddle for the audience than an expression of rustic simplicity.

Theodectas simultaneously echoes and revises both his predecessors, as an 'illiterate rustic' again spells out 'Theseus':

> The inscription began with a circle with an eye inside.
> Then two rulers of quite equal length;
> these a ruler on its side joins in the middle.
> The third like curling lock of hair.
> The next looked like a trident on its side,
> fifth were two wands of equal length above,
> and they lead together to a single base.
> The sixth just like the lock I mentioned before.
>
> (Theodectas, *TrGF* I, 72 F 6)

The first line is almost identical to the first in Agathon, and the penultimate verse is equally close to the same in Euripides, thus making Theodectas' response to the previous poets more explicit and self-conscious than that of Agathon to Euripides. The fourth-century poet's chief revision is to describe the letters as if explaining how to write them: the two uprights of H are 'quite equal in length' with a crossbar in the middle; likewise the arms of Y are of equal length, leading to a single base. Whereas Agathon presents the listener with a series of riddles, Theodectas repeats terminology (ἰσόμετροι 2, 6, κανόνες 2, κανών 3, πλάγιος 3, 5) and phrasing (πρῶτος ... ἔπειτα ... τρίτον ... ἔπειτα ... ) as if patiently schooling a student, and closes with the gentle reminder 'just as I said before'.

I suggest elsewhere (Dunn, 2017: 449–51) that the passage in Euripides' *Theseus* proved so memorable because of the increasingly close association of literacy with Athenian democratic and cultural institutions, an association ironically foregrounded by the herder's inability to recognize the name of

Athens' archetypal hero. Yet whereas Euripides uses the passage to contrast Athenian culture and Cretan ignorance, Theodectas instead draws upon the language and techniques of the familiar institution of γραμματική.[40]

## Ethical Contingency

The last development I consider could fall under the broad rubric of naturalism, but deserves special mention. Elsewhere I discuss a pronounced trend in Euripidean drama toward relatively open or contingent situations, that is, those which enact the uncertainty of living in the present (Dunn 2007: 65–110); by portraying characters who must act without reliance on the past or confidence in the future, Euripidean plots give us a naturalistic version of human experience. Here I further explore the changeable nature of affective relationships.

A few late plays enact a change in the affective bonds between individuals, as man and woman gradually fall in love, or two men slowly become close friends. Whereas an act of supplication may draw upon existing bonds to extract an oath (Medea and Aegeus in *Medea*) or a confession (the Nurse and Phaedra in *Hippolytus*), in tragedy it is very uncommon for a new bond to arise where none existed before – and thus potentially cause an adjustment in other preexisting bonds.

In connection with Euripides' fragmentary *Andromeda*, John Gibert observes in passing that an 'unusual if not unprecedented aspect of the play is that Perseus began to love Andromeda on stage' (Gibert 1999/2000: 76). I would like to elaborate on this. *Andromeda* begins with the protagonist alone on stage, tied to a cliff as prey for a sea monster. After an experimental prologue in which she exchanges laments with Echo, then the entrance of a Chorus of Ethiopian maidens, Perseus eventually enters, flying and carrying in a bag the head of Medusa. When Perseus first catches sight of Andromeda he takes her for a carving, and the drama thus begins with a situation where an affective relationship between man and woman is impossible:

> What? What hill is this I see, with sea foam
> washing round and what likeness of a girl
> chiseled from stone in her very form, splendid
> image by a clever hand?
>                                             (E. fr. 125 Kn.)

---

[40] Compare the dancing letters and choreographed syllables of Callias' *Alphabet Show* (*PCG* T 7), on which see Ruijgh 2001; Gagné 2013; Dunn 2017: 448–9.

The apparently inanimate object causes surprise but does not and cannot engage him emotionally. In his curiosity he then comes closer to inspect, finding she is a woman, while she is properly ashamed to be approached and addressed by a strange man, and therefore remains silent. The initial interaction between man and woman is thus restricted by social norms:

> You are silent? Silence is ineffective at explaining words. (E. fr. 126 Kn.)

Although her modesty is culturally appropriate, Perseus knows that in her predicament, shackled in this remote spot, she will not easily find πόρος, a 'way out', and the tautology that silence cannot communicate expresses his confusion at her reticence. Somehow, Andromeda is induced to reply, and the two now engage in conversation. What is probably our next fragment[41] shows Perseus taking a further step, confessing that the spectacle of her suffering arouses his pity:

> Young woman, I pity you, seeing you hanging there. (E. fr. 127 Kn.)

What will the hero do now? Both the content of the myth and the story-pattern of 'man meets damsel in distress' lead us to expect that he will rescue her from her bonds, slay the monster to which she has been exposed and fly away with her in triumph. Yet our expectations are defeated, not by a novel turn of events, but by attention to how people normally interact. Perseus would like to help the young woman, but so far knows nothing about her — and therefore does not even know if she wants to be rescued, or whether she will be grateful if she is. Hence the following famous exchange:[42]

> — Young woman, if I rescue you, will you be grateful?
> — Take me, stranger, either as servant, wife or slave,
>     as you like ...
>                                                          (E. frr. 129, 129a Kn.)

To Perseus' surprise, the woman welcomes freedom at almost any price, and says so boldly, forgetting all her prior modesty. Rhetorically, Andromeda's request is a global expression, encompassing the various social ties between a woman and man not related by blood, and it thus amounts to

---

[41] The fragment is accepted by Bubel 1991 and Kannicht (the latter thinks 127 and 128 are 'perhaps by Euripides'), rejected by Klimek-Winter 1993.
[42] Fr. 129 is parodied by Eubulus (*PCG* fr. 26), and the exchange was wittily appropriated by Crantor and Arcesilaus (D. L. 4.29).

'Rescue me, as long as you accept a social obligation between us – and the nature of that obligation may be whatever you wish'. Yet by mentioning, among these social ties, that of wife to husband, Andromeda either arouses or encourages a romantic interest on the young man's part.

We cannot know in detail how the relationship developed, given the meager nature of what remains, but it must have required time and patience since we next find Perseus trying to reassure the woman of his good intentions:

> I have never abused the misfortune of those
> in distress, fearing I could suffer the same.
> (E. fr. 130 Kn.)

At some point the conversation turned to embrace not just the present feelings of man and woman for one another, but also the future challenges to which their developing relationship might lead. These would include, of course, the major datum of the myth, the danger posed by the sea monster to which Andromeda has been exposed; Euripides' version adds a lengthy dispute between the young hero and the woman's parents as well.[43] Some such concerns are reflected in lines probably spoken by Andromeda:

> Do not, by holding out hope, call forth my tears;
> many things could happen we do not expect.
> (E. fr. 131 Kn.)

And her sentiment, if not exact words, is addressed in lines about the uncertain future probably spoken by Perseus:

> Day by day, the future surely terrifies you,
> since the approach of evil is greater than the suffering.
> (E. fr. 135 Kn.)

By the time he prepares to fly off and battle the monster, Perseus openly professes his love for Andromeda and reflects on the obligations this gives rise to. He invokes Eros, calling on the god who inspired his quest to help him succeed, yet goes beyond the usual expression of reciprocity in prayers (such as *do ut des*, 'I give so you will give'; see, e.g., Pulleyn 1997: 28). Instead he outlines a complicated relationship between Love and lovers. It is Eros, according to Perseus, who causes beautiful things to seem beautiful, thus arousing desire in lovers and consequently giving rise to their attempt to obtain the object of their desire. Yet since lovers run risks

---

[43] In Ovid (*Met.* 5.1–235), Andromeda's fiancé Phineus with his many followers is another obstacle Perseus must overcome.

impelled by love, Eros has a reciprocal obligation to help them succeed; if he does not, thus failing to follow through on teaching humans to love, lovers will reject him:

> And you, Eros, ruler of gods and humans,
> either do not teach beautiful things to seem beautiful,
> or labor well along with lovers as they struggle
> in those struggles you have crafted.
> If you do, you'll be honored by <mortals>;[44]
> if not, by the very act of teaching them to love,
> you'll lose the gratitude with which they honor you.
> (E. fr. 136 Kn.)

The convoluted syntax conveys the complexity of this relationship, and the role of Eros in instigating the relationship is expressed by two striking phrases: Love causing beautiful things to appear so, τὰ καλὰ φαίνεσθαι καλά (136.2), and Love as a craftsman, δημιουργός (136.3), of lovers' travails.[45]

From here on, the plot is harder to trace except in broad outline. Most likely Perseus, after killing the monster, returns and tries to persuade Andromeda's parents, Cepheus and Cassiopeia, to let her leave with him; Andromeda takes part in the dispute, as do both her parents,[46] and she plays a decisive role ('after being saved by Perseus, she refused to stay with her father or mother, but left with him for Argos by her own choice, showing nobility of mind', Eratosth. *Catast.* 17). The play closes with Athena *ex machina* announcing that all shall become constellations. The dispute over Andromeda, apparently Euripides' contribution to the plot, is a counterpart to the meeting of Perseus and Andromeda insofar as relationships are built up in the earlier scene and loosened in the later one; it also contrasts with Perseus' defeat of the sea monster, one being a heroic exploit requiring strength, assisted by magic (winged sandals and Medusa's head), and narrated by a messenger, the other being a very human disagreement involving competing affections and performed through dialogue. That the human challenge is more important and more difficult is underscored by the fact that, technically, it is unnecessary: Perseus could simply have flown off with Andromeda, ignoring her parents' objections.

---

[44] The context seems to require βροτοῖς or θνητοῖς (Dobree) rather than received θεοῖς.
[45] In both expressions, Euripides gives bold new form to the traditional notion of love as teacher; cf. E. fr. 663 Kn. ποιητὴν δ' ἄρα / Ἔρως διδάσκει, κἂν ἄμουσος ᾖ τὸ πρίν, 'Eros can teach one to be a poet, even if he was previously unskilled in art'; Klimek-Winter 1993: 251–2.
[46] As the dispute thus involves four speaking roles, it must have extended over more than one scene; cf. Bubel 1991: 56.

His decision to remain and argue shows his respect for social obligations. The course of this debate is unknown, but it included issues of wealth versus poverty (frr. 142, 143) and legitimate versus illegitimate children (fr. 141) and presumably Andromeda's wealth and security in Ethiopia versus an uncertain future in Greece. Her parents seem to have shared Perseus' respect for social relations, allowing Andromeda to decide the matter herself since, as noted earlier, she 'left with him for Argos by her own choice'.

Three years later, Sophocles did something very similar in *Philoctetes*. In that play's prologue, Odysseus instructs the young Neoptolemus in the art of deception so he can swindle Philoctetes of Heracles' bow, which is reportedly required if the Greeks are to take Troy. In the course of the play, Neoptolemus comes to sympathize with the suffering Philoctetes, and as their friendship develops he finds that honoring that bond requires him first to return the bow and then to sail back to Greece with the older man. At the same time, respecting this new relationship means no longer obeying Odysseus and the leaders of the Greek expedition; as in *Andromeda*, one evolving bond runs up against another, but in Sophocles' play the growth of friendship and decline of duty are largely simultaneous rather than sequential. One might take Neoptolemus as 'an example of character development and change of mind that is rare in surviving Greek literature' (Schein 2013: 23), but more important, to my mind, is the portrayal of developing and changing affective ties between the young man and those he interacts with.

Initially Neoptolemus intends to treat Philoctetes as Odysseus advises, employing him as an instrument for his own ends. The scheme works almost at once. Neoptolemus tells a false tale suggesting that his own experiences are much like Philoctetes', thus gaining his trust and a promise to lend him the bow. The older man proclaims that Neoptolemus has saved his life, and compares their relationship with his own to Heracles (662–70). What Philoctetes describes is a newly formed bond of friendship, and in what follows the bond is cemented as Philoctetes lends the young man his bow, and Neoptolemus embraces his diseased and raving companion until he comes to his senses (817–18). The tipping point comes when Philoctetes awakes and asks his companion to help him to his feet, thus invoking the physical and affective bond between them. As he helps the cripple to his feet, Neoptolemus begins to regret his initial deception: 'Ah, me! What can I possibly do after this?' (895). This moment of ethical crisis, which will cause Neoptolemus to reveal the truth and consequently break his allegiance to Odysseus and his fellow Greeks, follows from a deepening affective relationship cemented by physical contact (cf. Taplin 1971; Kosak 1999).

The dramatic tension of the following scenes results from the strains placed upon this new relationship. Neoptolemus thinks that the gestures of telling Philoctetes the truth, and of returning the bow in defiance of Odysseus, will earn him enough trust to persuade the older man to come willingly to Troy; Philoctetes, by contrast, views these as attempts by his companion to evade his obligation to sail back to Greece. Thus important obligations grow, develop, and come into conflict – a conflict so deep and irresolvable that it issues in a *deus ex machina*.

As with several developments discussed earlier in this chapter, we are not in a position to judge whether this novel attention to evolving attachments has parallels in the fourth century. But one or two tantalizing hints point in that direction. In Antiphon's *Andromache*, the protagonist gave up her child to be raised by someone else; although the child does not know his mother, and therefore can never requite her love, she continues to observe him and sees him prosper (Arist. *EN* 1159a 27–33, *EE* 1239a 37). A mother's love is portrayed as persisting, still being felt by the woman – and presumably demonstrated in the course of the drama – despite the length of time from infancy to an age at which a child could be said to prosper. The situation seems to be the converse of the latter half of Euripides' *Andromeda*: there the natural affection of a daughter for her parents cannot withstand the development, over time, of her competing love for Perseus, while in Antiphon a mother's natural feelings are able to withstand the separation over time, and the lack of reciprocal conduct, that would normally doom the relationship.

Incremental effects upon human character are perhaps significant in two further plays. Aristotle, in a discussion of responses to pleasure and pain, points out that, although succumbing is usually considered a weakness:

> If someone is overcome by powerful and excessive pleasures or pains, it is not astonishing; on the contrary, one excuses them if they resisted, as did Theodectas' Philoctetes when bitten by a viper, or Cercyon in Carcinus' *Alopē*. (Arist. *EN* 1150b 6–10)

The ancient commentator explains that Philoctetes had been bitten in the hand, and for a long time withstood his pains and sufferings, but was eventually defeated and cried out 'Cut off my hand!' Cercyon's afflictions, by contrast, were emotional: after learning that his daughter Alopē had an adulterous relationship (presumably discovered, as in Euripides' version, when she gave birth to a child), he compelled her to name the man; when she did so (it was Poseidon), Cercyon in his suffering could no longer endure to live and committed suicide (*Comm. in Aristot. Graeca* XX, p. 437.2–6, on Arist. *EN* 1150b.9).[47] In both cases, a particular (and commendable) ethical attitude is altered by the unrelenting force of great physical or emotional distress.

Ethical issues are central to Greek tragedy, and are normally played out through a clash of individuals (Agamemnon versus Clytaemestra) or principles (Antigone's duty to her brother and to the ruler); in Antiphon, Theodectas and Carcinus, however, we find a novel attention to the effect of circumstances, over time, on one person's ethical stance. Yet these developments are not entirely new, as their precursor seems to be the interest in changeable ethical attachments in the latest plays of Sophocles and Euripides.

## Conclusion

The late fifth century was a period of exciting, sometimes radical, innovation in tragedy as in other spheres. In some cases the connection with fourth-century tragedy is self-evident, as in the use of rhetorical language – although I have insisted that this is not a decline, and is in fact part of a paradoxical development in which dramatic language becomes simultaneously more prosaic and more elevated. In some cases, a connection with the following century is virtually impossible to trace, since metatheatre, for example, will not be evident in fragments or testimonia. More generally it is worth noting, on the one hand, that there are numerous intriguing connections between developments in the late fifth century and what we know of fourth-century tragedy, while on the other hand it is also well to remember that the latter was probably as varied and unpredictable as the former.

---

[47] See further Liapis and Stephanopoulos, this volume.

CHAPTER 9

## Society and Politics in Post-Fifth-Century Tragedy

### D. M. Carter

Was Greek tragedy differently conditioned by social and intellectual trends in the fourth century in comparison to the fifth? My argument in this chapter will be that, in the absence of strong evidence to the contrary, we must assume that changing social and political conditions during the hundred years or so after the end of the Peloponnesian War had, for the most part, little effect on ethical or intellectual emphases within the plays. I shall illustrate this point through particular consideration of the politics of post-fifth-century tragedy: although one can take the view that tragedy became a shade more rhetorical in the fourth century, there is really not enough evidence to establish this point without doubt (cf. Dunn, this volume, on rhetorical language as a point of continuity between fifth-century and fourth-century tragedy); and the Athenian self-image, both in tragedy and other literature, appears unchanged by the loss of empire.

Post-fifth-century tragedy, on one reading of Aristotle's *Poetics*, was similar in form and content to the tragedies of Sophocles and Euripides; which is not to say that nothing changed but rather that nothing essentially changed. In the first part of this chapter I take this reading a stage further, arguing that when Aristotle talks of 'poets nowadays' he is referring to a continuum of tragic poetry that stretches all the way from the mid–fifth century to his own time. This is not a point that I can claim to prove with any degree of certainty; rather, my intention is to question the assumption that post-fifth-century tragedy needs to be significantly different. In particular, when Aristotle draws a distinction between old-style 'political' and new-style 'rhetorical' tragedy, it cannot automatically be taken as a distinction between the fifth and fourth centuries; it is equally plausible that the divide came at the start of the career of Sophocles, or even earlier. From around this time tragedy became, in some sense of the word, rhetorical, and the people of tragic drama can, at times, show themselves to be highly conscious of their ability to argue a point of view. This preoccupation with argument and debate helps us to understand tragedy as something characteristically Athenian, for all that Athens and the Athenian democracy appear relatively infrequently in the surviving plays and fragments. That tragedy continued to be a rhetorical art form beyond the fifth century can be illustrated by taking Moschion fr. 6 as a case study. Finally, in the last part of my chapter, I consider the portrayal of Athens as a receiver and defender of foreign suppliants. This is the principal political role that is given to Athens in fifth-century Athens, and it does not appear to have changed in the hundred years or so after that, for all that the foreign policy context shifted with the loss of empire.

Underpinning my argument is a more basic point: it is too easy to assume that the deaths of Sophocles and Euripides in 406 BC mark a turning point in the history of the genre. Doubtless the almost simultaneous passing of two well-established poets could have been seen as the end of an era, but it does not follow that there is a natural generic division between fifth-century and fourth-century tragedy. That the deaths of Sophocles and Euripides more or less coincided with the fall of the Athenian empire and (by our calendar) the turn of the fourth century tempts us to draw such a line. We should resist this temptation.[1]

## Aristotle on 'Poets Nowadays'

By 'the absence of strong evidence' I mean, of course, the fragmentary nature of the surviving tragic texts in the fourth century and beyond. However, next to a lack of direct evidence we do have a wealth of indirect evidence, and especially the earliest dedicated work of literary criticism: Aristotle's *Poetics*.

One obvious objection to my view, that the changing social and intellectual context had little effect on the drama, comes with Aristotle's lack of interest in tragedy's political function. In the view of Hall (1996), Aristotle is *deliberately* silent on questions of tragic politics; in doing so he diminishes the political function of tragedy and anticipates a state of affairs in which it becomes a more universal and self-sufficient art form. There is a fair amount of corroborating evidence for Hall's view: during Aristotle's lifetime, democracy would come to an end at Athens and Greece would be brought together under Macedonian rule; and the principal focus of artistic and intellectual activity in the Greek world was fairly soon to shift from Athens to Alexandria. Throughout the fourth century,

[1] Cf. Easterling 1993.

Athenian drama was being performed more widely around Greece, as evidenced by the building of new theatres such as the famous one at Epidaurus. As the fame and prestige of professional actors grew, they formed themselves into companies that toured widely around the Mediterranean (see Le Guen, this volume). Although Athens remained a hub of dramatic activity, and the City Dionysia the largest dramatic festival, this outward spread of activity was bound to render the drama more universal and less prone to political specificity. This is certainly what happened to Greek comedy, which appears to have lost some of its political edge during the period between the death of Aristophanes and the earliest victory of Menander.

We might be unsurprised to find the same happening to tragedy. But, of course, tragedy was never political in the same way as comedy. I have argued elsewhere that the political interest of tragic drama was not confined to the democratic *polis*, and that this is explained in terms of a genre that already had international – or certainly Panhellenic – appeal by the middle of the fifth century.[2] Foreign visitors came to the Dionysia each year, foreign poets produced work there, and Aeschylus was visiting Sicily to produce drama for a tyrant as early as 470 BC, or thereabouts.[3]

An alternative explanation for Aristotle's relative silence on tragic politics is that it simply reflects his own priorities.[4] Modern critics of Greek tragedy have their own particular interests: it is perfectly possible to focus on, for example, form and character without much reference to the political or religious importance of the festival where the plays were performed. The same can be said of Aristotle, who is more interested in the construction of tragedy (form, subject matter, plot, character) than he is in its performance, and has almost nothing to say about its religious and political significance. It is a tightly focussed piece of criticism.

Aristotle also reveals his priorities in the historic scope of the *Poetics*. It is striking that, within the particular framework of dramatic and ethical concerns that Aristotle prioritizes, he draws no particular distinction between the generation of Sophocles and the generations of poets that followed him. At *Poetics* 1449a7–30, Aristotle considers tragedy to be a fully evolved genre, the most recent changes being the introduction of the

---

[2] Carter 2004a, 2007; cf. Taplin 1999. For a fuller response to Hall, on similar lines to mine here, see Hanink 2011: 321–4, cf. Heath 1999: 472–3.
[3] Foreign poets at Athens: Griffith 1999: 64–5; Kaimio 1999: 54–61. Aeschylus in Sicily: Herington 1967; Poli Palladini 2001; Duncan 2011.
[4] On what these priorities might have been, see Heath 1999.

third actor and of scene painting by Sophocles.[5] Assuming it to be true that the third actor was a Sophoclean innovation, it must have come early enough in his career to influence Aeschylus, who included a third actor in the *Oresteia* in 458. If we further assume the early introduction of scene painting, it looks as if – as far as Aristotle was concerned – tragedy did not change very much between the 450s and the 320s. Now, we know that this is not entirely true because we have the evidence of the plays – especially the later dramas of Euripides – to suggest that all sorts of melodramatic and new musical elements made their way into the genre in ways that would have been unheard of fifty years before. And Aristotle himself attributes the introduction of *embolima* (choral interludes) to Agathon (1456a28–9). Aristotle was not unaware of all these things; but to him, I suspect, they were mere details. Tragedy was complete in all its essentials of form and staging by the death of Aeschylus, and was recognizably the same well over a hundred years later.

In his discussion of tragic plot, Aristotle appears to distinguish between the 'early poets' and other poets and to include Sophocles and Euripides in the latter category (1453b26–31). In his discussion of 'what sorts of incidents strike us as terrible or pitiable' (1453b14) he says that (1453b26–31):

> The action can occur as in the early poets (οἱ παλαιοί), who made the agents act in knowledge and cognisance (as Euripides too made Medea kill her children). Alternatively, the agents can commit the terrible deed, but do so in ignorance, then subsequently recognise the relationship, as with Sophocles' *Oedipus*: here, of course, the deed is outside the play, but cases within the tragedy are, for instance, Alcmeon in Astydamas, or Telegonus in [Sophocles'] *Odysseus Wounded*.[6]

Aristotle seems to have no difficulty here comparing Sophocles with Astydamas, a poet of the fourth century. Further, although he associates Euripides' *Medea*, produced in 431 BC, with the 'early poets', he does so in such a way as to suggest that he takes Euripides as a separate category: 'as

---

[5] Brown 1984 considers the words τρεῖς δὲ καὶ σκηνογραφίαν Σοφοκλῆς ('three and scene painting Sophocles') to be interpolated, arguing that the text makes more sense if we ignore them. If that is the case then it would appear that Aristotle considers tragedy to be fully formed at some time during the career of Aeschylus. This would alter some of the detail of my argument here, although (as I note later in this chapter) the careers of the two poets overlapped.

[6] Tr. Halliwell 1995. Translations of other Greek passages are my own except where indicated.

in the early poets, who made ... as Euripides too made' (καθάπερ καὶ Εὐριπίδης ἐποίησεν).⁷

Something similar appears to be going on in Aristotle's discussion of the ideal tragic plot. 'Poets nowadays' tend to restrict themselves to a smallish number of mythological storylines that lend themselves to complex plots (1453a17):

> Originally (πρῶτον μέν) the poets recounted any and every story, but nowadays (νῦν δὲ) the finest tragedies are composed about only a few families, such as Alcmeon, Oedipus, Orestes, Meleager, Thyestes, Telephus, and as many others as have suffered or perpetrated terrible things.⁸

He makes it clear that this is not meant to be an exhaustive list, merely a list of subjects presented in the 'finest tragedies', but a comparison is made nonetheless. We can observe that many of the mythical figures associated with the finest poets 'nowadays' were favourite tragic subjects in the second half of the fifth century as well as in the fourth century. All of the figures listed here either appear in the surviving plays of Sophocles or are the titles of attested Sophoclean dramas. Exactly the same can be said of Euripides. We know also from the surviving plays that certain tragic subjects were already particular favourites in the second half of the fifth century. Of the twenty-three extant plays of Sophocles and Euripides (excluding the satyric *Cyclops*, pro-satyric *Alcestis* and spurious *Rhesus*), nine of them – roughly two-fifths – directly concern the houses of Laius or Atreus.

Hall observes that none of the characters in Aristotle's list is Athenian, and wonders if this reflects a fourth-century development.⁹ But Athens is not a particularly recurrent city in surviving fifth-century tragedy. Where Athens does appear in extant tragedy, it tends to fill a particular role: to receive and defend suppliants. And, where Athenians appear in tragedy in roles other than as receivers of suppliants, the drama tends to be set away from Athens: Sophocles' *Ajax* and Euripides' *Hippolytus* and *Ion*. Ajax, who comes from the island of Salamis, also appears in fourth-century tragedy.[10]

---

[7] Denniston 1929 argues that views such as this are based on a misreading of the word καί, and that a correct translation should be, not 'Euripides as well as the ancients', but 'Euripides as well as other ancients'. But he makes the assumption that I discuss later: Euripides can only qualify as a modern poet on Aristotle's terms by being 'born out of due time'. Denniston implies that the Greek of this sentence will bear either meaning: context suggests 'as well as the ancients'.

[8] Tr. Halliwell 1995.    [9] Hall 1996: 300.

[10] Xanthakis-Karamanos 1980: 15–16; Hall 1996: 308 n. 24; cf. Liapis and Stephanopoulos, this volume.

So far I have given reasons to believe that Aristotle places the divide between 'the early poets' and 'poets nowadays' roughly at the start of the career of Sophocles. From Aristotle's peculiar perspective – teleological and overwhelmingly concerned with matters of literary form, subject matter, plot and character – there were no significant changes in the genre for over a hundred years. This is a much earlier date for the divide than the one proposed by many commentators on the *Poetics*, for whom the deaths of Sophocles and Euripides in the same year 'would afford a natural dividing line between old and new'.[11] One difficulty faced by those who make this distinction is the apparent modernity of Euripides. The only route out of this difficulty is to say that Euripides was in some way ahead of his time: the rhetorical features of his plays anticipate fourth-century drama; no wonder then that his work increased in popularity after his death.[12] A more likely possibility is that, on Aristotle's terms, *both* Sophocles *and* Euripides were of their time and of the modern period.

The assumption that tragedy changed at the turn of fourth century is, I think, informed by a more basic assumption on a methodological level: that tragedy must be studied diachronically and with precision. We simply do not have the evidence, most of the time, to embark on such an exercise. Occasionally a year-by-year historicism is possible: for example, in the early comedies of Aristophanes where we have one play a year for the years 425 to 421, a plentiful supply of political reference within the plays, and the detailed historical account of Thucydides for comparison. When it comes to tragedy, we have some sense of the changing political and intellectual context but very little ability to say, beyond mere guesswork, how much influence these contexts had at particular times and on individual dramas. The great exceptions to this, the *Persians* and the *Oresteia*, which in different ways can be linked to recent events, are noticeably Aeschylean. From the fifth century we have a handful of dramas from just three poets, and from the fourth even less; for both centuries there is also some evidence from the comedians, prose authors and inscriptions. Given the nature of the evidence, and the perspective of two and half millennia, it is usually more instructive to stand back and appraise the dramas synchronically; or, adopting a modestly diachronic approach, to try to work

---

[11] Lucas 1968: 152–3. He concedes that 'in view of the large number of complex plays which Euripides wrote it would seem inappropriate to consign him to the category of the ancients', but goes on to argue that, if it is acceptable to consider Sophocles (who also wrote complex plots) an ancient poet, so Euripides must be one too. On the contrary, it seems to me that this gives grounds to include both poets among 'poets nowadays'.
[12] Essentially the view of Xanthakis-Karamanos 1980.

out which are the really significant and lasting changes. Our project should be akin to viewing the broad shape of the continents from a satellite's orbit in space. We should not take a small number of isolated geographical features and try to reconstruct the entire map.[13]

Aristotle, who did have enough information to draw a detailed map, similarly prefers to give us broad outlines.[14] For him, as we have seen, tragedy has been the same in all its essentials since the early career of Sophocles. This includes a tendency among the better poets to present complex plots based on mistakes made by heroic individuals, leading to recognition and reversal of fortune; and the tendency of tragic heroes to make mistakes gives cause for disagreement, which is fertile ground for rhetoric. There is, however, one place where Aristotle shows an interest in how tragedy might have changed since the time of Sophocles and Euripides. This is at *Poetics* 1450a25, where 'the works of most of the recent poets (τῶν νέων τῶν πλείστων) are lacking in character'. Here Aristotle appears to extend the rhetorical trajectory on which (as we are about to see) tragedy has been placed: in recent tragedy, speech explains action more than it reveals character.

One fourth-century development that Aristotle does not mention is the introduction from 386 BC of reperformances of tragedy at the City Dionysia.[15] It seems to me that the production of old plays by Sophocles or Euripides alongside new ones by Astydamas or Theodectas is partly what allows Aristotle to consider the previous 130-odd years of tragic drama as recognizably one single thing. In doing so he is not denying that there are short-term trends within the genre. Rather, he is ignoring trends that may not matter so much, precisely because they have only short-term significance.

## Post-Aeschylean Tragedy as a Rhetorical Art Form

We now have some context in which to appraise the only thing, more or less, that Aristotle has to say on tragic politics. Having considered plot and

---

[13] I hope not (in Francis Dunn's words, this volume) therefore to have adopted 'a reductive notion of continuity'. There will of course have been elements of variety, innovation and discontinuity in the fourth century just as much as in the fifth.
[14] Cf. Halliwell 1986: 93: 'If some of the precise historical details get garbled (or lost) in the course of the argument, that is of less importance to Aristotle than the discernment of the larger pattern.'
[15] On this, and other developments behind the reperformance of the canonical tragic poets after the fifth century, see Nervegna 2014.

Society and Politics in Post-Fifth-Century Tragedy 277

character as, respectively, the first and second elements of tragedy, Aristotle moves briefly to consider the third (1450b4–8):

> The third element is thought (διάνοια). This is the ability to say what is relevant and fitting, which in speeches is the work of politics and rhetoric. For the early poets made people speak politically (πολιτικῶς); poets nowadays (οἱ δὲ νῦν) make them speak rhetorically (ῥητορικῶς).

It is hard to know exactly what Aristotle means by this enigmatic statement, although one must assume from the passages already discussed that 'the early poets' (οἱ μὲν ... ἀρχαῖοι) at the very least predate Sophocles.[16] The more difficult question is around 'poets nowadays' (οἱ δὲ νῦν). At face value this would appear to refer to poets active at the time of the *Poetics*. But, in the light of the previous discussion, it is possible that Aristotle means anyone from Sophocles onwards. A third possibility is that Aristotle is generalizing about early tragedy and making a contrast with his own time, while saying nothing at all about tragic drama in the intervening period. Aristotle says that *dianoia* (thought, reasoning) is revealed in both political and rhetorical speeches. Elsewhere, Aristotle defines *dianoia* as whatever needs to be communicated (*sc.* to an audience) through speech: for example, proof or refutation, as well as a range of emotional effects and value judgments (1456a34–b1). Aristotle describes the *ēthos* (character) and *dianoia* of tragic figures as collectively explaining the nature of their actions (1449b38–9).[17]

Whatever Aristotle's precise meaning, it is not hard to see how Aeschylus can be considered a more political (or an even more political) poet than Sophocles and Euripides, taking 'political' to mean 'concerned with the affairs of the *polis*'. Equally, it is possible to consider both Sophocles and Euripides as frequently rhetorical poets. It depends on what is meant by rhetorical, of course. One available definition of rhetoric in tragedy is simply: 'anything that is said with the intent to persuade'.[18] If we want to narrow the definition slightly, then it matters that a great deal of tragic persuasion is not conversational or informal, but is conducted through set speeches in a public or semi-public context.[19] The public context is

---

[16] For a general discussion of the distinction between politics and rhetoric in Aristotle, see Halliwell 1994.
[17] Halliwell 1986: 154–5.
[18] Cf. Bers 1994: 183. Pelling 2005 uses a narrower definition of 'rhetoric that shows signs of contrivance, artificiality, acquired technique' (p. 85), but it is interesting that his examples, in common with mine, are Sophoclean as well as Euripidean and include only the *Oresteia* from the extant dramas of Aeschylus.
[19] Cf. Halliwell 1997: 124–6.

conditioned by the choice of scene (outside a building, not inside it); by the presence of the chorus, most of the time, as partial or impartial observers; and by the need to make the entire action intelligible to a vast theatre audience, for all that these audience members are not acknowledged by the speakers. In the following I shall assume that plays in which much of the action is driven by persuasive speech can be considered on a basic level to be rhetorical, even if the rhetoric is less conspicuous for being embedded in the plot. It seems to me that, if we wanted to follow a trajectory of tragic rhetoric that extends beyond the fifth century, then we would want to identify more conspicuous examples of rhetoric: either where the argument is tendentious or where it is gratuitous or otherwise inessential to the plot. In fact, it is hard to find examples of this kind in post-fifth-century tragedy, suggesting to me that there is no obvious difference over time in the quality of tragic rhetoric.

That tragedy is populated by people who are frequently trying to persuade other people is easily argued, perhaps even self-evident, when it comes to Euripides, but I think it is equally applicable to Sophocles. To take one example, in *Antigone* Sophocles presents first the title character unsuccessfully trying to persuade her sister to help her bury Polyneices (1–99); then Creon's defence of his own political philosophy (162–210), followed soon after by Antigone's critique and further argument (446–525); then Ismene's unsuccessful attempt to claim a share in the deed (531–81); then a blazing row between Creon and Haemon (631–765); and finally, a further debate between Creon and Teiresias (1023–90). All but one of these exchanges take place in public, before a chorus of elders. The exception is the prologue: here Antigone says that she has brought Ismene out of the house so that they cannot be overheard (18–19) but, in doing so, she also demonstrates her own move into public life, necessitated by a rhetorical position of challenge to civic authority. There is certainly more to the drama than a series of debates: the choral odes; descriptions of events offstage by the guard (249–77, 407–40), Teiresias (998–1022) and the messenger (1192–243); and the twin tragedies of Antigone and Creon (*kommoi* at 806–82 and 1260–353). But the plot itself is driven through individual argumentation.[20] The speeches given are never gratuitously rhetorical, contributing nothing to the drama. Rather, persuasive speech in Sophocles is fully situated within the context of character and plot.

[20] Cf. Griffith 1999: 16–17.

Contrast Aeschylus' *Seven against Thebes*.[21] This play, like Sophocles' *Antigone*, begins with a crisis for the city and ends with individual tragedy, but the drama is to a far lesser extent composed of disagreements or misunderstandings between people. More space is given simply to describing the nature of the political threat. This applies especially to the lengthy report of the seven heroes at the gates in lines 369–676, during which Eteocles posts his own heroes one by one, finishing with his own decision to fight Polyneices. The only possibly rhetorical exchanges in the play are between Eteocles and the chorus.[22] At lines 182–202, Eteocles reproaches the chorus for dampening morale in the city. We then have a dialogue on how and why to trust the gods to look to the city's salvation (203–63), a passage of drama that can be described as deliberative rather than persuasive. A more genuine attempt at persuasion comes at 677–719, a brief series of exchanges in which the chorus plays the role (seen far more extensively in Sophoclean tragedy) of the tragic warner, urging Eteocles not to fight.[23]

It should be stressed that these examples are merely illustrative and that any systematic survey of rhetoric in the surviving fifth-century plays is beyond the scope of this chapter. It is not my intention here to try to unravel Aristotle's dichotomy of political/rhetorical in any satisfactory way, nor to map Aeschylus and Sophocles onto these categories with the pretence of exactness. My main argument is that Sophoclean and Euripidean tragedy is frequently rhetorical. It does not follow, and it is not the case, that Aeschylean tragedy is never rhetorical. We should observe, for example, that the plot of the (late-Aeschylean) *Oresteia* is frequently driven by argumentation; indeed, *peithō* is often considered a theme of the trilogy.

The identification of tragedy as a rhetorical art form is a position Aristotle shares with Plato. And Plato does not contradict the view that tragedy had become rhetorical during the fifth century. The *Gorgias*,

---

[21] For Halliwell 1997: 127–9, this play features usefully in a discussion of tragic rhetoric. However, Halliwell's position here does not directly contradict my own. In relation to Arist. *Po.* 1450b4–8, Halliwell (pp. 125–6) says that he will 'interpret "rhetoric" in a sense which embraces the whole domain demarcated by Aristotle's two terms' (*sc. politikē* and *rhetorikē*). And his discussion of the *Seven against Thebes* demonstrates that Eteocles' speech-making drifts from an 'overtly political perspective' (p. 127) to an exercise, towards the end of the drama, in '*self*-persuasion' (p. 128, Halliwell's emphasis).

[22] The arguments for and against the burial of Polyneices that fill the exodos are highly unlikely to be part of the original play. In fact, the scene appears to have been inspired by Sophocles' *Antigone* or Euripides' *Phoenissae*: see, e.g., Dawe 1967; *contra* Lloyd-Jones 1959; also, Taplin 1977a: 169–70, 180–4; Hutchinson 1985: 209–11; Sommerstein 2010: 90–3; Judet de la Combe 2011; Garvie 2014.

[23] On the Sophoclean tragic warner, see Lardinois 2003.

written in the 380s and set vaguely in the late fifth century, includes the following exchange (502c–d):

SOCRATES: Now then, if someone were completely to strip away from the poetry the music and the rhythm and the metre, is there anything left but words?
CALLICLES: That must be right.
SOCRATES: And aren't these words spoken to a great crowd, a *dēmos*?
CALLICLES: I agree.
SOCRATES: Then poetry is a kind of public speaking (δημηγορία)?
CALLICLES: So it seems.
SOCRATES: And wouldn't it be a rhetorical public speaking? Or don't you agree that the poets practice rhetoric in the theatres?
CALLICLES: I do.
SOCRATES: So now we have found a kind of rhetoric (ῥητορικήν τινα) addressed to such a *dēmos* as composed of children together with women and men, both slave and free; one that we do not at all admire. I mean, we did call it pandering.

This is a much less obscure statement than Aristotle's at *Poetics* 1450b4–8. Plato makes it abundantly clear that his objection to tragedy, just like his objection to rhetoric, is that it panders to the audience. Indeed, for Plato the real difference between tragedy and rhetoric – apart from the musical and metrical elements – is the composition of this audience: in the former case broadly conceived, in the latter composed of citizens only. Commentators on this passage tend to assume that Plato is thinking of the dramatic *agōn* (especially in Euripides) when he says: 'don't you agree that the poets practice rhetoric in the theatres?'[24] However, I have shown elsewhere (taking Euripides' *Medea* of 431 BC as a case study) that this description can be applied plausibly to tragic performance more broadly: people are trying to persuade other people of things for much of the time.[25]

Aristotle does not share Plato's distaste either for rhetoric or for tragedy (nor does he necessarily mean the same things all the time by 'rhetoric'). However, they were men of broadly the same place and time, and so some of the assumptions behind their views are likely to be shared. Sophoclean and Euripidean tragedy is certainly rhetorical in that it is full of persuasive speech. Therefore, when Aristotle says that 'the earliest poets made people speak politically, present day poets make them speak rhetorically', he plausibly includes Sophocles and Euripides among present-day poets.

---

[24] See, e.g., commentaries by Dodds 1959, Irwin 1979 or Canto 1987.   [25] Carter 2011a.

Turning now to some examples of apparently rhetorical language in post-fifth-century tragedy, we find that they do not appear very different from what we see in Sophocles and Euripides. Taken in isolation, some of these speeches may appear more rhetorical in the sense that they are gratuitously rhetorical, contributing nothing to the drama. But, of course, we cannot tell because we must take these lines out of context. Perhaps it helps in each case if we can find a Sophoclean or Euripidean *comparandum*, where the need to persuade is plausibly linked to the needs of the drama. I shall discuss three examples.

The first example is Astydamas, *TrGF* I, 60 F 8 (from an unidentified play):

> The surest way to praise a family is
> to praise an individual; to call
> noble whoever is most just and best
> in his habits (τρόπους); to find one person in
> a hundred, although thousands may seek him.

There is something of an echo here of Orestes' remarks on the peasant in Euripides' *Electra*.[26] Orestes begins his speech by saying that wealth is no guide to a man's true worth; good men can be born to bad parents and *vice versa* (E. *El.* 367–72). He continues (380–5):

> For this man, neither great among the Argives,
> nor boosted by his family's name, but one
> of the crowd, was found to be excellent.
> (ἐν τοῖς δὲ πολλοῖς ὢν, ἄριστος ηὑρέθη.)
> Do not be foolish, you who wander full
> of empty views, but judge men noble by
> their habits and the company they keep.
> (τῇ δ' ὁμιλίᾳ βροτοὺς
> κρινεῖτε καὶ τοῖς ἤθεσιν τοὺς εὐγενεῖς.)

Orestes thus plays on a tension between ideas of poverty and nobility, which is felt elsewhere within this drama (37–8, 253, cf. *Andr.* 319–20, fr. 495.40–3 from *Captive Melanippe*). This tension does not seem to be present in Astydamas fr. 8, but there are otherwise clear echoes: the man who stands out from the crowd as best (ἄριστος) and is judged by his manners or way of life (τρόποι, ἤθη); nobility is in the eye of the beholder (cf. E. fr. 336 from *Dictys*).[27] The speech Orestes gives is certainly

---

[26] Cf. Xanthakis-Karamanos 1980: 148–9, with views on whether the divergence from the 'traditional link of high birth and ἀρετή' begins with Euripides.
[27] Cf. Liapis and Stephanopoulos, this volume.

rhetorical, and might be judged to be gratuitously rhetorical in the sense that it does not advance the plot or explain anyone's actions. However, it does pick up earlier themes and helps to characterize the peasant by showing us how others see him (cf. 404–5).

My second example comes from Theodectas, *TrGF* I, 72 F 1a (from *Alcmeon*):

> The point is often made and is well known
> that no living thing is more wretched than
> (ὡς οὐδέν ἐστιν ἀθλιώτατον φυτόν)
> a woman.

The second line alludes to E. *Med.* 231: γυναῖκές ἐσμεν ἀθλιώτατον φυτόν.[28] The famous speech in *Medea* is most certainly rhetorical in that it seeks to persuade. It is also dramatically necessary: Medea persuades the women of the chorus that she is just like them and shares their socially disadvantageous position; in doing so she seeks to win their sympathy, which she will need later so they can be complicit in her plans. The speaker in Theodectas fr. 1a is, if anything, speaking less rhetorically inasmuch as he or she appears to distance himself or herself from the sentiment.

My third example is Moschion, *TrGF* I, 97 F 3 (from *Men of Pherae*):

> There's no point maltreating a dead man's ghost;
> it's right to punish the living, not the dead.

The most obvious echo here is from Sophocles' *Ajax*, although there are doubtless others. In the final scene of that play, Odysseus persuades Agamemnon that Ajax must be buried on the grounds that it is right to treat the dead with respect, even dead enemies (S. *Aj.* 1344–5). It is possible that Moschion's *Men of Pherae* was equally concerned with a burial crisis.[29] However, the point made by the Sophoclean Odysseus is in two ways slightly different from the point made in Moschion fr. 3. First, the topic of conversation in *Ajax* is the avoidance of *humiliation* of an enemy once dead, as opposed to the avoidance of *punishment* of the dead, although the logic is very similar. Second, Odysseus is careful to couch his remarks in terms of Ajax's nobility (ἄνδρα δ' οὐ δίκαιον, εἰ θάνοι,/βλάπτειν τὸν ἐσθλόν),[30] whereas the example from Moschion effectively treats all dead people the same. We cannot recover the context of the Moschion fragment.[31] We can, however, observe that the Sophoclean Odysseus'

---

[28] Cf. Liapis and Stephanopoulos, this volume.
[29] On this possibility, see Stephanopoulos 1995/96: 146–7.   [30] Cf. Finglass 2011: *ad loc.*
[31] On the possibility is that *Men of Pherae* was a historical drama based on the life and death of Alexander, tyrant of Pherae, see Ribbeck 1875: 155–9; also, Hornblower (this volume).

speech is rhetorical in the sense that it is designed to persuade someone, and that this rhetoric is dramatically necessary: the burial of a noble man must take place for his rehabilitation to be complete.[32]

To sum up: on the basis of comparison with similar sentiments in Sophocles and Euripides, all three of these fragmentary texts can be discussed as examples of rhetoric in drama, but we cannot assume that any of them is gratuitously rhetorical. For this reason, I do not think the rhetoric in the context of these dramas would have been any more conspicuous than in Sophocles or Euripides. Therefore, if we assume 'more conspicuously rhetorical' to equal 'more rhetorical', there does not seem to be any detectable increase in the level of tragic rhetoric as we leave the fifth century. These examples also reveal thematic commonalities with Sophoclean or Euripidean drama: that nobility is revealed in how people conduct themselves; that we should respect the dead without prejudice. If these sentiments come across as somewhat bland or platitudinous, then perhaps this is precisely because we do not have them in their true dramatic context. This context would have given the ideas some point and also, perhaps, tested them through dialogue.

### Free Speech and Democratic Discourse

So far, I hope, not perhaps to have proved, but certainly to have established the plausibility of the view that tragedy took a rhetorical turn at some point in the middle of the fifth century, and that this position was maintained throughout the fourth. I have argued elsewhere that this culture of rhetoric and debate was a characteristically Athenian feature of tragedy.[33] Whether or not tragedy can be considered essentially democratic – a position that I think can be overstated – there is certainly something of the culture of the Athenian democracy in the way different positions are argued for and against. This tendency to settle matters through debate was conditional on an Athenian ability to speak freely: the quality of *parrhēsia*. This word, which literally means 'saying everything', has connotations of unrestrained and even unwanted frankness and candour.[34] It is reasonably easy to demonstrate that characters in Greek tragedy speak with *parrhēsia*; it can also be shown that Sophoclean and Euripidean figures show, at times, a certain self-consciousness around their

---

[32] On Ajax's rehabilitation as a theme of the play, see Garvie 1998: 10–11; Finglass 2011: 51–3.
[33] Carter 2011a, and cf. Burian in the same volume.
[34] On *parrhēsia*, see esp. Carter 2004b; Saxonhouse 2006. The following extends my argument in Carter (2018).

ability to say what they want. This occasional tendency is, as far as we can tell, continued into the fourth century.

Athenian *parrhēsia* emerges in tragedy as a quality, inherited from one's parents, that depends on the status and respectability of the individual speaker (E. *Hipp.* 419–25, *Ion* 671–5). In tragedies set away from Athens, by contrast, *parrhēsia* is not automatic. There are times when it has to be negotiated on a case-by-case basis. This is most frequently the case where a speaker of low status is addressing royalty, for example, the messenger in Euripides' *Bacchae*, who is about to bring unwelcome news from Mt Cithaeron (668–71):

> I want to know: may I describe events
> up there frankly, or should I curb my tongue?
> I fear the swiftness of your temper, sir:
> too domineering and too quick to anger.

Something similar occurs where the enslaved Hecuba addresses her Greek captors (E. *Hec.* 234–8, *Tro.* 903–13) or where Electra wishes to argue with her mother, Clytemnestra (S. *El.* 552–7, E. *El.* 1055–9). In each of these cases the speaker wins from a more powerful figure the temporary right to speak on equal terms. Very occasionally, a weaker figure fails to secure this licence to speak, for example, the guard speaking to Creon in *Antigone* (S. *Ant.* 315–16) or Orestes, in Euripides' play of that name, who desperately tries to get Tyndareus' attention (E. *Or.* 544–50). Finally, there are at least two examples where the ability to speak freely is negotiated between social equals: Sophocles' *Ajax* 1328–31, where Odysseus presents the case for burial to Agamemnon; and *Oedipus Tyrannus* 543–4, where an exasperated Creon expects Oedipus to hear his side of the story before leaping to judgment.

This idea of *parrhēsia*, as something not automatic but rather a freedom that has to be negotiated or asserted, continues into the fourth century and beyond. This can be observed in prose literature as well as tragic fragments. On more than one occasion Demosthenes pleads with the Athenian assembly to be allowed to speak openly and frankly about the Macedonian crisis, for example, in the *Third Philippic* (9.3):

> I claim for myself, Athenians, that if I tell you something of the truth with *parrhēsia* you will take no displeasure at me because of this. For look at it this way. In other matters you think it proper that there should be such a general *parrhēsia* for everyone in the city that you even grant it to aliens and slaves, and one can see many household slaves among us saying what they

want with greater licence than citizens in some other cities; but you have banished it completely from your deliberations.

Demosthenes is of course adopting a rhetorical position, that of the respected statesman who is prepared to tell his audience what they need to hear instead of what they want to hear (cf. Dem. 6.31, 9.2, Isoc. 8.14). But this extract is in other respects similar to the fifth-century tragic examples already discussed: before a hostile or sceptical audience, *parrhēsia* is not an automatic right but rather something that needs to be asserted at the outset.

This provides the context in which to consider two fragments of tragedy from after the fifth century. The speaker in Moschion *TrGF* I, 97 F 5 (from an unknown play) is similar to the messenger in Euripides' *Bacchae* in his fear of an angry response. He also shares Demosthenes' wish to get his audience onside:

> Just listen to the words I bring to you
> without anger; a speech (μῦθος) made to a well-
> disposed hearer is not spoken in vain.

We do not know as much as we would like to about these lines. The speaker may, as in several Euripidean examples, be a powerless figure speaking from a position of weakness, or an exasperated social equal such as Creon in the *Oedipus Tyrannus*. We also do not know whether these lines introduce an *agōn* speech, although they evidently introduce a set speech (μῦθος) of some kind. What is reasonably apparent is that the fifth-century tragic self-consciousness around free speech extends at least a little bit into the fourth.

The speaker in Moschion *TrGF* I, 97 F 4 (again from an unidentified play) is even more assertive:

> But never shall I pass in silence over
> what's right and just; for it is fitting to
> protect nobly the free speech (παρρησίαν) nurtured by
> the men of Athens and the town of Theseus.

This speaker, like Demosthenes, appears to be preparing to make a speech that his or her audience does not want to hear. He or she goes further than other characters in asserting the general principle of *parrhēsia* as well as (presumably) the present opportunity to exercise it. It is relevant that the speech is evidently given in Athens, and one wonders whether an assertion of this kind could be made in any other tragic city. We can compare Iolaus in Euripides *Heraclidae*, a foreigner who attempts to assert Athenian values before an Athenian king (181–3):

> In your land, sir, it is the rule that I
> should speak and hear in turn. And nobody
> will drive me out, as is the case elsewhere.

A difference in Moschion fr. 4 is that the speaker presents the protection of *parrhēsia* as a general duty, and a noble one at that (καλὸν φυλάξαι γνησίως παρρησίαν), rather than asserting his own ability to speak freely. It is arguable that a foreign visitor to Athens would not feel this particular sense of duty; we might then conclude that the speaker, unlike Iolaus, is an Athenian.[35]

On admittedly slim evidence I would therefore suggest that a certain self-consciousness around free speech, which is readily apparent in Sophocles and Euripides, survives into fourth-century tragedy and probably beyond. This self-conscious engagement with *parrhēsia* reflects a broader rhetorical tendency in Greek tragedy throughout this period.

**Moschion on Burial**

As a case study on how rhetorical later tragedy can be, and on some thematic continuity from the fifth century, we can now consider Moschion *TrGF* I, 97 F 6 (from an unknown play):

> But first an explanation, looking back,
> of the beginnings and establishment
> of human life. For there was once a time
> when people's lives resembled that of beasts,
> living in caves found in the mountains and       5
> in sunless gullies. There were not as yet
> houses constructed with a roof, nor broad
> cities, buttressed with towers made of stone.
> Nor yet were lumps of black earth, grower of

---

[35] Cf. Stephanopoulos 1995/96: 150–1, who argues that the location of the scene is uncertain but that the speaker is clearly Athenian. It seems to me, taking E. *Hcld.* 181–3 as a comparable speech, that if anything there is greater certainty around the location of the scene. It is hard to think of a secure tragic example of an Athenian making a strenuous argument that Athenian values of free speech can apply outside Athens. We do, however, have two examples (E. *Ion* 671–5 and *Hipp.* 421–4) where the implication is that *parrhēsia* flourishes only in the peculiar political environment of Athens, contingent on one's reputation within that city.

>     nourishing grain, carved with a curvy plough. 10
>     Nor did the iron tool, hard-working, tend
>     the blooming rows of Bacchic vines. Instead
>     the senseless(?) ground was like unrippled water.
>     For food, they killed each other and produced
>     banquets of human flesh. *Nomos* was held 15
>     in low regard: force shared the throne with Zeus.
>     And so the weak were food to stronger men.
>     But when time, mother of all things and nurse,
>     effected complete change in mortal life –
>     whether by embracing Prometheus 20
>     and his concerns, or through necessity,
>     or taking, through length of experience,
>     nature herself as teacher – then was found
>     the fruit of cultivation, holy to
>     Demeter, and the sweet spring of Bacchus. 25
>     The land, until that time unsown, was now
>     ploughed by yoked oxen. Cities were built up,
>     houses constructed, people changed their lives
>     from savagery to cultivated habits.
>     Since then *nomos* determined that we should 30
>     conceal the dead in tombs and give their share
>     of earth to the unburied, leaving no
>     reminder of the old impious feast.

The most obvious continuity with fifth-century tragedy is the subject matter. The speech, which would not look out of context as one-half of a dramatic *agōn*, is evidently presented by a less powerful to a more powerful figure in the hope of securing the burial of a dead person, perhaps a friend or relative of the speaker. The burial crisis is a topic in Greek literature that goes back as far as the *Iliad*, a poem that ends with the resolution of such a crisis. Likewise, in fifth-century tragedy burial crises never go unresolved, no matter what other horrible things may happen in the vicinity: cf. Sophocles' *Antigone* and *Ajax*, and Euripides' *Suppliants*. It would, I suggest, grate even in the context of tragedy to leave bodies unburied. Part of the reason for this, one assumes, is that an unburied body poses problems for society at large, not just for individuals. Tragedy is about not only the suffering of individuals but also (almost always) the continuity of society and social norms; therefore, bodies must be buried.

Hence the burial of the dead, even of bitter enemies, in Greek tragedy is justified in terms of *nomos* – whether this means divine law or simply human law or custom. The Sophoclean Antigone draws attention to Creon's deliberate use of the word *nomos* at the beginning of her 'unwritten laws' speech. This is the only time in the play that she applies the word *nomos* to what is, after all, only a decree (S. *Ant.* 446–55):

CREON: Now you, explain briefly and not at length:
were you aware of the decree against this?
ANTIGONE: How could I not be? It was public knowledge.
CREON: And even so you dared to break these laws?
(καὶ δῆτ' ἐτόλμας τούσδ' ὑπερβαίνειν νόμους;)
ANTIGONE: For Zeus did not decree these things to me,
nor did Justice, living with the gods
below, determine 'laws' like these among
men. Nor did I consider your decrees,
made by a man, enough to overrule
the safe, unwritten statutes of the gods.

Plenty has been written on exactly what is meant here.[36] For the present purpose it is enough to observe the play on several ambiguities in the word *nomos*: divine/human; unwritten/written; law/convention. For Antigone, burial of the dead is not simply a matter of local custom but of absolute necessity. In Euripides' *Suppliants*, by contrast, burial is required both by 'the law of all the Greeks' (526–7, 671–2, cf. 311) and by divine law (561–3, cf. 301–2).

In Moschion fr. 6 there is a similar sense of ambiguity in the use of the word *nomos*. The speaker presents the custom of burying the dead as a necessity, both in terms of human progress and in some sense of divine law. In early human society '*nomos* was held in low regard: force (βία) shared the throne with Zeus' (15–16), which is to draw an implicit dichotomy between the rule of the stronger and some sense of divine justice. The implication is that, when laws were later established to prevent force always getting its way, this had the effect of enhancing the authority of the Olympian gods. This is the case, even though (as Xanthakis-Karamanos points out) the changes described here occur as part of some sort of evolutionary process through time rather than on divine authority.[37]

The other use of the word, towards the very end of the passage, presents *nomos* more purely in terms of human custom (28–31: 'people changed their lives from savagery to cultivated habits. Since then *nomos* determined that we should conceal the dead in tombs ...').[38] The account of human progress that precedes this statement appears to be noncommittal on

---

[36] See, e.g., Tyrrell and Bennett 1998: 69–70; Griffith 1999: 201–2; Harris 2004. On unwritten laws more generally, see Ostwald 1973; Craik 1993.
[37] Xanthakis-Karamanos 1980: 118–19.
[38] On *nomos* as custom in this passage cf. Xanthakis-Karamanos 1980: 115. There is a curious Sophoclean echo here: compare S. *Ant.* 452 (τοιούσδ' ἐν ἀνθρώποισιν ὥρισεν νόμους) with Moschion fr. 6.30 (κἄκ τοῦδε τοὺς θανόντας ὥρισεν νόμοις).

whether civilization came about through accident or design (20ff.). However, the constant assumption in ancient sources is a more or less Aristotelian view that evolution from savagery to agriculture and finally city life is a natural process (cf. Arist. *Pol.* 1252a24–53a7). The underlying argument, therefore, is not just that we *happen* to bury the dead, but that we *ought* to bury the dead. This view of human progress is consonant with some of the key texts of the fifth-century enlightenment, including several tragic texts.[39]

This ought to be enough on its own to win the debate in which Moschion fr. 6 was presumably situated. Overlying the view of human progress, however, is an argument that seems rather more strained. The argument is fairly carefully framed in a loose ring-composition: once upon a time people did not live in buildings, still less cities (3–8), nor farm the land (9–13), but ate each other (14–17); in time things changed (18–22); they farmed the land (23–6) and lived in houses and cities (27–9).[40] The somewhat tenuous conclusion of this argument (30–3) is that we must not leave the dead unburied because it would serve as an uncomfortable reminder of the cannibalistic habits of our distant ancestors.

The assumption that prehistoric man was a cannibal is not in itself an odd one to make. The ancient Greeks, just as we do today, saw cannibalism as something that happened far off or long ago, or perhaps the food of last resort during a famine or a siege.[41] The remoteness of cannibalism, however, is precisely what makes it useful as a debating point in the present example: it allows the speaker to define modern civilized life through opposition.[42] The difficulty with the argument is therefore not in the assumption but in the way it is applied: the speaker argues strenuously enough around the assumption as to suggest that the cannibalism of primitive human society is not already widespread knowledge; this is a problem for the conclusion since, if we did not already know our ancestors to have been cannibals, then we would not automatically consider dead bodies to be a source of shame. Another possibility is that we are dimly aware of a prehistory of cannibalism, and that the presence of unburied dead bodies serves as an unwelcome memory jogger. But it does not seem

---

[39] For example, [A.] *PV* 442–68, 478–506; S. *Ant.* 332–71; E. *Supp.* 201–13; Critias fr. 25.1–8 D–K. These and similar texts are collected at Guthrie 1969: 79–84. On Moschion fr. 6 as a text on human progress, see Xanthakis-Karamanos 1980: 116–19.

[40] Cf. Xanthakis-Karamanos 1980: 107.

[41] Far off: Pl. *Laws* 782c (ἔτι καὶ νῦν ... πολλοῖς). Long ago: *Orph. Frag.* 292 Kern. Food of last resort: Garnsey (1988) 28–9 with further references.

[42] Cf. Parker 1983: 305.

to me that the presence of unburied bodies in itself, unless they appear half-eaten, automatically puts one in mind of killing people for food.

This argument seems to me slightly more of a stretch than what we are used to in Euripides. Can we therefore say that this tragic speech is more rhetorical than it might have been in the fifth century? Certainly we can, if we assume a more rhetorical speech to be one that appears to be more desperate in its assumptions and conclusions: the product of someone arguing for argument's sake rather than to reach a sensible conclusion. This being the case, we might assume this speech to extend a trajectory towards more and more rhetorical speech that began in the fifth century. The trouble with this view, of course, is that it is based on an isolated example. If we had more evidence from the fourth and third centuries, then this speech might sit on or near the line of best fit, or it might be an outlier. The example is also isolated, in the same way as the fragments discussed in the previous section, in that we do not have the proper dramatic context. This context may well have helped us to explain the apparent excesses of rhetoric, which might have been necessitated by the plot or consistent with the character of the speaker. Moschion fr. 6 presents us with insecure evidence of change in post-fifth-century tragedy (a tendency to be more and more rhetorical); but fairly solid evidence of continuity (a burial crisis; some faith in human progress).

## Suppliant Drama and the Imperial Legacy

In the rest of this chapter I want to consider one other political aspect of tragedy. We have seen that tragedy can be considered a characteristically Athenian art form through its culture of argumentation and debate, a position that was enhanced by the rhetorical turn that tragedy appears to have taken in the 450s. As for Athens herself, the city is cast in one particular role throughout Sophoclean and Euripidean tragedy: as a receiver and defender of suppliants. The evidence suggests that this role continued into the fourth century.

In extant fifth-century tragedy we have just four dramas (*Eumenides*, *Heraclidae*, the Euripidean *Suppliants*, and *Oedipus at Colonus*) that are set in or around Athens. All of these demonstrate the role of Athens as a receiver of suppliants. In each of these plays the decision to receive suppliants is made by the city – or on behalf of the city – so that the suppliants are not simply the responsibility of one Athenian.[43] For this

[43] Tzanetou 2012: 9–10.

reason it is the Athenians collectively who may be called to defend this decision on the field of battle. It has been argued plausibly by Angeliki Tzanetou (2012) that this presentation of Athenian benevolence towards needy foreigners should be read against the historical context of Athenian imperialism. The plays were performed at the City Dionysia, which also happened to be the point in the calendar when ambassadors came to Athens with tribute money. On at least one occasion in the fifth century, this tribute money (or the surplus from it) was displayed in the theatre before the performances began.[44] It was an outward-facing festival with a significant foreign component in its audience. Small wonder then that, where Athens features in tragedy, we see an idealized presentation of Athenian foreign policy more often than we see a democracy in action.

In the fourth century, Athens was still a democracy, albeit one recovering from the rule of the Thirty, but it was no longer a significant imperial power. We might therefore expect the portrait of a city that is active in support of foreign suppliants to be diminished, but it is not. The mythical defence of the Children of Heracles by Athens against their father's enemy Eurystheus, dramatized by Euripides in the early 420s, was celebrated in funeral orations and similar prose works of the fourth century (Lys. 2.11–16; Isoc. 4.56–60; Dem. 60.8; Pl. *Mx.* 239b). Another Euripidean burial crisis occurs in the *Suppliants*, where the Athenians assert Argive interests in the face of Theban opposition; this story also is mentioned by fourth-century orators (Lys. 2.7–10; Dem. 60.8; Pl. *Mx.* 239b). The argument made in defence of this action is strikingly similar in both Euripides and Lysias (E. *Supp.* 522–30; Lys. 2.7–9):

> For I did not begin this war, nor come
> upon the land of Cadmus with these men.
> Burying these dead men is right, I say,
> with no harm to your city, bringing no
> deadly battle, but keeping safe the law
> of all the Greeks. What's wrong in that? Although
> you suffered at the hands of Argives, they
> are dead. You rightly kept your enemy
> at bay, and shame on them. Justice is done.

> When Adrastus and Polynices campaigned against Thebes
> and were defeated, the Thebans would not allow the bodies
> to be buried. The Athenians believed that if those men had
> done anything wrong, they had paid the ultimate penalty by

[44] Isoc. 8.82 with Carter 2004a: 6–8.

dying; but that the gods below were not receiving their dues, and the gods above were being treated with impiety because the sacred rites were being polluted. First, they sent heralds and asked to take up the bodies, believing that honourable men should punish their enemies while alive, but that to display courage at the expense of dead bodies was the sign of those who lack self-confidence. They could not get what they requested, so they made war against Thebes, even though no previous quarrel existed between the Thebans and themselves. They did not do this to please the Argives who were still alive, but because they believed that those who died in war deserved to receive the customary rites. So, they risked danger from one side on behalf of both: on behalf of the Thebans, so they should no longer display arrogance towards the gods by wronging the dead; on behalf of the Argives, so that they should not return home prematurely without the honour due to their fathers, without proper Greek rites, and without the common hope of burial.[45]

Theseus, like the speaker in the Lysian funeral oration, is at pains to say that the Argives have been adequately punished and now deserve burial, and that the Athenians have no particular quarrel with the Thebans but feel compelled to go to war in defence of what is right. Both speakers use the language of *nomos*. Theseus considers it just to bury the dead, upholding the law of the Greeks (θάψαι δικαιῶ, τὸν Πανελλήνων νόμον/σᾠζων, 526–7). Likewise, the Athenians in the Lysian funeral oration 'believed that those who died in war deserved to receive the customary rites' (τοὺς τεθνεῶτας ἐν τῷ πολέμῳ ἀξιοῦντες τῶν νομιζομένων τυγχάνειν).[46]

In view of the popularity of the topic in fourth-century prose literature (some of which at least was intended for delivery in public), it is hardly surprising if suppliant dramas were produced, from time to time, in post-fifth-century Athens. The *Suda* records that Apollodorus, who was active in the 380s, produced a *Suppliant Women* (*TrGF* I, 64 T 1); and that Lycophron produced a *Suppliants* in the third century (*TrGF* I, 100 T 3). In view of the commonalities between fifth-century suppliant drama and fourth-century prose treatments of the topic, it is reasonable to assume that each of these dramas likewise presented the Athenians as members of a benevolent city with military resources, which they were prepared to deploy in defence of suppliant foreigners and of what they believed to be right.

[45] Tr. Todd 2000: 28–9.   [46] Cf. Mills 1997: 59.

The presentation of Athens as the friend of suppliants in post-fifth-century texts would appear at first sight to create problems for Tzanetou's thesis that suppliant drama must be read in the context of the Athenian empire. It could be objected that, if the Athenians continued to celebrate themselves in this way, including in the theatre, then we should not assume that the theatrical self-presentation of Athens was conditioned by the city's imperial power and status. However, this objection would be too simplistic. In the modern world the great European powers, Britain and France, have continued to have military and diplomatic pretentions and to present themselves as a force for good in the world, decades after the loss of their empires. Similarly, the Athenian self-image of greatness was relatively untarnished up until the Macedonian conquests and lingered on in art and literature after that (see, e.g., Dem. 2.24).

## Conclusion

The idea of tragedy as a political art form tends to meet with general agreement in scholarship, even if there is widespread disagreement over exactly what counts as political. I have argued elsewhere that tragedy shows itself to be political through its engagement with the concerns of the Greek polis in general, rather than through a narrow interest in the Athenian democracy; where Athens does appear in tragedy it tends to fill a particular role as the defender of suppliants, and is only occasionally represented as any kind of democracy; this tragic focus on the Athenian treatment of foreigners, rather than on internal political mechanisms, is perhaps appropriate given the international nature of the festival where the plays were first performed.[47] However, if the institutions of democracy are not particularly apparent in tragedy, then its defining culture of opposition and debate pervades the dramas.

Aristotle suggests to us that this culture took a rhetorical turn at some point in the middle of the fifth century. On my reading, Aeschylus emerges as a transitional figure; his plays show a healthy concern with the continuity of the polis alongside the suffering of individuals. Sophocles and Euripides, however, present dramas where much of the action is driven through argumentation. Aristotelian *dianoia* – the thought that explains action – is often presented by opposing speeches, both in the formal *agōn* and elsewhere. This tendency seems to have been maintained in the fourth century and beyond.

[47] Carter 2004a.

# PART III
*Reception and Transmission*

CHAPTER 10

# Attitudes Towards Tragedy from the Second Sophistic to Late Antiquity

*Ruth Webb**

### Setting the Stage

Commenting on the grace of the pantomime dancers' gestural performance, Lykinos, the main speaker in Lucian's dialogue *On the Dance* (27), draws a striking and disconcerting portrait of the tragic actors of his day: 'What an odious and terrifying spectacle is a man dressed up to give him a disproportionate height, mounted on high shoes, wearing on his head a tall mask with a gaping mouth so wide that it looks as if he is about to swallow up the spectators.'[1] This sketch of a second-century AD actor certainly gives a glimpse of the costumes current in the period: the characteristic mask with its gaping mouth and high crown above the face (*onkos*), the shoes with their thick soles, and then the padding worn around the body to balance this exaggerated height. Going on to evoke the performance style of the tragic actor, Lykinos draws our attention both to the sound and to the movement: '...then from inside the man himself shouts out, bending forwards and backwards, sometimes even singing his iambics and, what is most shameful, making a melody out of his calamities'. Where the pantomime dancer was silent, portraying the whole range of action and emotion through gesture, movement and rhythm, the actor vocalized, even breaking into song; perched on his high shoes, his torso bound in padding, he could do little more than lean his upper body backwards and forwards, sometimes breaking into sung arias in the characteristic manner of the postclassical *tragōidoi*.[2]

---

* I would like to thank the editors and the referees for their careful reading and many valuable suggestions.
[1] The translation is my own.
[2] On these, see Hall 2002. The sixth/seventh-century *Etymology* of Isidore of Seville 1.18 45 defined *tragoedi* as 'those who sang the ancient deeds and crimes of wicked kings with a mournful song while the people watched'.

Lykinos' words are a powerful reminder that tragedy was still a familiar *performance* art in the second century AD (and it remained so well into the sixth century in the Eastern parts of the Empire), sharing theatre stages with the more popular and more recent forms of pantomime and mime. He evokes vividly the contrast between the aesthetic of tragedy and that of these other forms: the singing of the *tragōidoi* in contrast to the silent dancer, the static posture and stately movements (simultaneously enforced and reinforced by the costume and high shoes) in contrast both to the lithe athleticism of the dancers' leaps, turns and dramatic changes of height and to the frenetic activity of comedy and mime.[3] Most importantly, however, this comparison between the pantomime and the tragic actor relied for its effect on the prestige that tragedy still retained as part of the classical canon studied in schools and as the source of a wealth of stories and linguistic forms for the common culture of the educated elite. At the same time, in criticizing tragedy to the advantage of a new and controversial art like pantomime, Lucian (through his *alter ego* Lykinos) is presenting a highly paradoxical argument in favour of the latter and, incidentally, inviting his own audience to look at tragedy itself from a fresh perspective, reevaluating its stylized features and its appropriateness as an art form.[4]

Two other authors who remind us of the centrality of tragedy to the culture of the High Empire are Tertullian and Tatian, both Christian converts who urge their audiences to reject the traditional culture of the Empire. In his oration *To the Greeks* (24), Tatian lists tragedy alongside comedy (Menander in particular) and athletics as undesirable and, whereas Lucian's speaker criticizes tragedy in order to praise pantomime, Tatian categorically rejects both. Tertullian focuses on the entertainment culture of the Empire, which he links to the persecuting machinery of the Roman state. In the spectacular finale to his treatise *On the Spectacles*, he imagines the whole range of traditional performers roasting on a bonfire of the vanities, among them the *tragoedus*.[5] These two authors, one writing in Greek, the other in Latin, set the stage for the rejection of tragedy and theatre in general by Christians. However, this rejection was neither immediate nor generalized and, in the case of tragedy in particular, the prestige of the written form complicated the picture considerably.

---

[3] See Hunter 2002 on the kinetic aesthetic of comedy.
[4] See Petrides 2013 (esp. 433–9) on Lucian's strategies in this dialogue.
[5] Tertullian, *On the Spectacles* 30. On this text and what it, along with Lucian, tells us about the spectacle culture of the Empire see Goldhill 2001.

Lucian's comparison of the grotesquely bending and wailing tragic actor to the pantomime dancer thus brings together various strands of the reception of tragedy in the Imperial period, up to and including Late Antiquity, that we will see emerging throughout this chapter. On the one hand, tragedy remained a living performance art with its characteristic performance aesthetic, while on the other hand it enjoyed a particular prestige due to its roots in classical Athens and to its status as a canonical genre studied in schools (on the ancient scholarly tradition see further Hanink, this volume). This dual existence, as *performance* on stage and as *text* pored over in schools and by adult members of the elite in private, characterizes tragedy in the Imperial period and emerges in different ways. So I will start by looking briefly at the practical background represented both by the continued performance of tragedy in the Imperial period and by the didactic uses made of it in the schools on the basis that these two sets of practices represent the context against which to evaluate the uses made of tragedy by authors such as Dio Chrysostom, Lucian and the Church Fathers. These practices, moreover, involved a constant dialogue with the past, which took many different forms. It is also clear that tragedy, like pantomime (Lada-Richards 2008), proved good to think with, and the chapter will conclude with some remarks on the idea of tragedy and the tragic actor.

## Tragedy Performed

The type of performance that Lucian evoked for his readers took place at the many festivals that had multiplied in the cities and towns of the Greek-speaking regions of the Empire, and Italy, from the Hellenistic period on (see Le Guen, this volume). *Tragōidoi*, like those caricatured by Lucian in *On the Dance*, competed at regular festivals throughout the Greek world and beyond, as anecdotes and inscriptions show.[6] The inscriptions record the names of victorious *tragōidoi* and list the programmes of particular festivals, setting out the value of the prizes for each discipline. It is noticeable that in two cases in Asia Minor where we have this information, at Oenoanda and at Aphrodisias, a higher amount of prize money is allotted to tragedy than to comedy, while mime and pantomime do not

---

[6] For references in contemporary texts to tragic performances see Artemidorus, *Oneirocritikon*, 4.33 mentioning a performance by Heracleides of Thyateira in Rome; Philostratus, *Life of Apollonios of Tyana*, 5.9 on a tragedian travelling to Spain.

even figure among the contests on offer.[7] As well as giving us an insight into the relative prestige attached to the various art forms (and the rates that the artists' guilds were able to negotiate to ensure the presence of artists at the festivals), these inscriptions show the range of different types of tragedy that were performed. These encompassed both revivals of classical tragedy and the new compositions which continued to be written well into the second century AD, as we see from the inscriptions celebrating victories in *kainē tragōidia* ('new tragedy') at the festival of the Muses (the *Mouseia*) at Thespiai in Boeotia and at Aphrodisias, among other places (see Griffith, this volume).[8] Even the lowest-rewarded artist among those listed could at least console himself that his art was dignified by the status of contest; in contrast to these, the newer form of mime (a comic form in which women appeared alongside men) appeared at Oenoanda among the far less prestigious hired acts whose representatives received payment for their services instead of competing nobly for a prize. Pantomime is not even mentioned in the programme for this festival, although it was beginning to spread from Italy to the Greek East, first as a paid 'fringe' performance and then as a fully fledged competition piece (Slater 2007).

Tertullian and Tatian's rejection of traditional performance culture, including tragedy, did not prove effective. Like other theatrical forms, tragedy survived the spread of Christianity at least into the sixth century in the Greek East, despite both the decline in the number of the local festivals after the third century AD and the opposition of the Church to all forms of theatrical entertainment. John Chrysostom, for example, remarks on the performances of *tragōidoi* at Antioch in the late–fourth/early–fifth century AD, although these shows caused him far less concern than did those of the pantomimes and mimes and consequently feature less

---

[7] For the Greek text of the Oenoanda inscription (second century AD) see Wörrle 1988 with the English translation in Mitchell 1990. For the Aphrodisias inscription see Roueché 1993: 168–73 (no. 52 = *IAph* 11.305).

[8] Two victors at Thespiai were Agathemeros, actor of new tragedy (third quarter of the second century; Stephanis 1988: 16) and Apollonios of Aspendos, *tragōidos* and poet of new tragedy in the same period (Stephanis 1988: 274). The combination of the two roles (poet and *tragōidos*) shows that some performers at least had an education close to that of the educated élites. For Aphrodisias, see *IAph* 11.305 and 11.21.ii and iii both of the second to third centuries (= Roueché 1993 no. 53). In this second example, prizes of 2,500 denarii and 1,500 denarii are stipulated for the best *tragōidos* and the best *kōmōidos*, respectively. Another example from second- or third-century Aphrodisias is particularly interesting as it stipulates prizes for tragic chorus (500 denarii), new comedy (500 denarii), old comedy (350 denarii) and new tragedy (750 denarii), but there is no mention of old tragedy, an absence that does not seem to be due to subsequent loss or damage in the inscription.

frequently in his sermons.[9] Later still, the diptych commemorating the celebration of the New Year festival of the Kalends at Constantinople in 517, now in the Cabinet des Médailles in Paris, shows what appears to be a group of tragic actors, one seated and two standing, distinctive in their tall masks and high shoes, alongside mimes.[10] That both tragedy and comedy featured in the entertainments put on by consuls in Constantinople is shown by Justinian's *Novella* of 536/7.[11] The images on the diptychs are not of course unmediated representations of *realia*, and it may be that the theatrical scenes are chosen to represent the comic and the tragic, that is, as a metonymic representation of 'theatrical shows'; still, it is significant that tragedy, if the figures on the diptych of 517 are indeed to be thought of as tragic actors, and mime should be selected in place of pantomime and traditional comedy. The presence of these performers at the celebrations marking the consul's entry into office and their depiction in proximity to the imposing portrait of that consul and of members of the Imperial family is a sign not only of survival but of their continuing cultural centrality.

If the continued presence of tragedy is clear, it is less clear what form these performances took. When we hear of a *tragōidos* on stage, it is not always easy to know whether he is to be thought of as a soloist performing extracts or as a member of a group presenting an entire play, or whether the play is classical or contemporary with the performer.[12] In his essay *On*

---

[9] See Lugaresi 2008: 70; Pasquato 1976: 161–5; Theocharidis 1940: 49–62. Csapo (2010: 154) argues on the basis of Libanios, *Or.* 64.112 that 'tragedy survived *only* in the classroom' (my italics) by the fourth century, but I am not convinced that the passage provides such categorical evidence. Barnes 1996: 170–2 is justifiably sceptical about passages in Arnobius and Augustine that have often been interpreted as evidence for tragic performance in the fourth century but the evidence of Chrysostom and of Justinian's *Novella* 105 (see later in this chapter) show that it would be rash to assume that tragedy was completely absent from the stage after the third century.

[10] Delbrück 1929: no. 21; Olovsdotter 2005: 48–50. Seeberg (2002–3) identifies these figures as comic actors on the basis of the similarity to the poses in the *Sunaristosai* mosaics, following the reidentification of two figures on another consular diptych of 517, now in St Petersburg, as comic, rather than tragic, actors by Green 1985 (see also Green 1994: 167–8). However, as Dunbabin (2016: 256) points out, the figures on this particular diptych are clearly wearing the thick-soled *kothornoi* characteristic of tragedy. She concludes that 'it seems more likely that the craftsmen who designed these scenes used whatever models for a theatrical scene were available, and dressed them up in what seemed the appropriate costume'.

[11] Justinian, *Novella* 105.1 sets out the programme of entertainment to be put on by the consul at the Kalends and mentions *gelōtopoioi* (actors of mime or, perhaps, comedy) and performers of tragedy (*tragōidoi*) with choruses alongside unspecified theatrical entertainments (*theamata* and *akousmata*).

[12] On the tragic papyri and their relation to performance see Nervegna 2007 and 2013: 80–8. She argues convincingly that the anthologies of tragic passages used as evidence for theatrical practice by Gentili 1979a, among others, are not in themselves evidence for the performance of excerpts in the theatres. She does, however, conclude (2007: 36–9; 2013: 83) that excerpts may have been sung. See Griffith, this volume, for analysis of the musical papyri and for discussion of the evidence of Lucian, *How to Write History*.

*his love of listening*, Dio Chrysostom notes that in tragedy, unlike comedy, only the iambic sections remained in his day (*Or.* 19.5), and he compares the surviving parts of the plays to the bones of a body that are left behind after the softer parts (the lyrics) have rotted away.[13] However, the existence of a prize for a 'tragic chorus' at Aphrodisias (*IAph* 11.21) shows that the chorus was not yet dead and buried. As Christopher Jones has argued, the picture is likely to have been complex: new forms, like pantomime, or new ways of performing tragedy did not necessarily mean that complete plays had ceased to be put on.[14]

## Tragedy and Other Performance Types

If Lucian chose to contrast pantomime with tragedy, then it was because of the fundamental similarities between the two. As Lykinos states a little further on in the dialogue, the two shared a common stock of stories, although the pantomime repertoire was even more varied.[15] Marie-Hélène Garelli (2006) has also drawn attention to the role of pantomime in preserving and disseminating knowledge of the traditional stories at the very beginning of the Imperial period. This claim is borne out by the list of recorded subjects for the pantomime, which include some performances that seem to have been quite close reworkings of known classical tragedies: an epigram describing a pantomimic performance of the *Bacchae* implies an arrangement that kept remarkably close to the order of events in Euripides' play.[16] Elsewhere, we find titles of pantomime dances that are identical to well-known plays by Euripides and Sophocles (*Ion, Trojan Women, The Madness of Heracles, Ajax, Tympanistai* or *Drummers*), but it is impossible to be sure whether there was any intergeneric relationship or whether the pantomime performances were entirely independent.[17] However, the promoters of pantomime and the organizers of pantomime contests in the late second century certainly liked to claim that pantomime was a close relation to tragedy, labelling it 'tragic rhythmic movement'.[18]

---

[13] On this passage see Hunter 2009a: 15–16 and Hanink 2017: 28, as well as my remarks later in this chapter.

[14] Jones 1993; see also Easterling and Miles 1999.

[15] Lucian, *On the Dance*, 37–61 gives a long catalogue of the subjects represented in pantomime. Garelli (2007: 271–80) gives a full list of the known subjects for pantomime. On tragedy and pantomime see Hall 2002: 27–30; Lada-Richards 2007: 32–7; Petrides 2013.

[16] *Planudean Anthology* 289.

[17] *CIL* 5 5889, with Cadario 2009; *CIL* 14 4254, with Garelli 2007: 274.

[18] The elaborate epitaph of an Egyptian pantomime dancer named Krispos (*IK* 47.9; Stephanis 1988: 1504) defines his art as 'rhythmic tragedy' (ἔvρυθμος τραγῳδία). Other inscriptions recording

This title enabled the dance to benefit from some of the prestige of the older form while clearly marking the differences, namely the rhythm and movement, in contrast to tragedy's words.

Mime at first sight seems to be so far removed from tragedy as to share no common ground with it at all. In terms of its visual and kinetic aesthetic, mime performance was the polar opposite to tragedy: the actors were unmasked and wore no shoes, in stark contrast to the exaggerated mask and high shoes of the tragic actors; their movements are generally described as rapid, in contrast to the stately tragedian; and in contrast to both tragedy and comedy, female parts were played by women rather than masked men. Yet some significant similarities exist between tragedy and mime too at various levels. First, at the level of plot, mime, like New Comedy, was a successor to classical tragedy in its focus on family dramas: adultery, actual and desired, and conflict between generations.[19] In its depiction of female desire and destructiveness, mime came far closer to tragedy than did New Comedy or its Roman descendants. The difference lay in the dénouements which in mime, as far as we can tell, led to the reestablishment of the preexisting order (instead of the radical changes depicted in tragedy)[20] and, again as far as we can tell, in the fact that the characters remained miraculously unscathed by their various brushes with violence and murderous intent. Rather than being members of long-distant families from a heroic age, the characters of mime were ordinary people: housewives, tradesmen, craftsmen, professionals. But the two worlds could and did collide: one fragment of a mime preserved on a papyrus from Oxyrhynchus contains a plot line – a Greek girl being rescued from an exotic land by her brother – that has obvious affinities with Euripides' *Iphigeneia in Tauris*.[21]

More important than any formal similarities or differences, however, are the similarities in function. As tragedy had done in classical Athens, mime brought out onto the public stage problems and tensions that were otherwise unsayable and, if anything, the application to contemporary society was more direct in that the settings and characters were close to the audience's experience.[22] The pantomime, for its part, did not just share with tragedy a repertoire of stories from the mythical past, but, like

---

victories in 'tragic rhythmic movement' (τραγικὴ ἔνρυθμος κίνησις) include those of the star dancer Tiberios Ioulios Apolaustos (*IK* 16.6, 2070–1; Stephanis 1988: 236). On this dancer and his victories see Slater 1996 and Strasser 2004.

[19] On the mime see, for example, Wiemken 1972; Webb 2008: 95–138; Andreassi 2013.
[20] See Chorikios, *In Defence of the Mimes* 55.   [21] See Santelia 1991; Hall 2010.
[22] See Webb 2008: 116–38.

tragedy, it used these stories to arouse emotion.[23] It has also been argued by Alessandra Zanobi (2014), in relation to Seneca's plays, that the interaction between pantomime and Imperial tragedy was a two-way process, and that aspects of the aesthetics of pantomime, such as the episodic treatment of plot and the focus on single characters, were absorbed into tragedy.[24] It would not be surprising if this were true also of the Greek tragedies composed for competitions in the second and third centuries AD, when pantomime was becoming more and more widespread in the East; unfortunately, the lack of evidence for the nature of these plays makes it impossible to know with any certainty whether this was the case.

## Tragedy on the Page

The other half of tragedy's double life was, of course, as part of the canon of classical texts. The fact that élite education was oriented primarily towards enabling students to produce their own rhetorical compositions in the classical Attic dialect affected the ways in which tragedy was read. Plays were mined for examples of Attic usage and for the stories of the mythical past, which still had resonance for the Greek cities of the Empire. They were also used as sources of moral exempla and read through a rhetorical lens with an eye for the credibility, or otherwise, of their stories and the persuasive qualities of their speeches. Euripides' plays were evidently the most suited for this type of treatment, but those of Sophocles and, to a lesser extent, Aeschylus were still read.[25] Reading tragedy was by no means confined to schools, and two passages from the writings of Dio Chrysostom are characteristic of different strands of the reception of tragic texts in the Imperial period.

In one treatise, Dio wrote about the different *Philoctetes* plays by the three major tragedians that he was still able to read in their entirety, claiming that he 'enjoyed the spectacle'.[26] A similar understanding that

---

[23] It is important, however, to note that the arousal of emotion was ascribed to various different arts, including rhetoric and the visual arts, and was not necessarily seen as the preserve of tragedy. See, for example, Schlapbach 2008. In particular, Aristotle's *Poetics*, which has made such an important contribution to the modern association of emotion with tragedy, seems to have been much less well known at this period than it is today. See Halliwell 1986: 287–90; Tarán and Gutas 2012: 32–5.

[24] On Seneca's relation to pantomime see also Zimmermann 2008 (originally published in German in 1990).

[25] Cribiore 2001b: 244. On the ancient reception of Sophocles see Mauduit 2001 with Jouanna 2001 on the scholia; on Aeschylus and the *Agamemnon* see Easterling 2005.

[26] Dio Chrysostom, *Or.* 52.3: εὐωχούμην τῆς θέας. On the treatise as a whole see Luzzatto 1983; on this passage and Dio's relation to the classical theatre see Hunter 2009a: 39–48.

the transmitted texts were just one element of what had been a multi-sensory performance art emerges on occasion from the ancient scholia on the plays, as we shall see. Elsewhere, however, it is clear that Dio also saw tragedy as a rich source of useful sayings. In his *Oration* 18, addressed to a man involved in public life who wanted to catch up on the literate education that he missed in his youth, Dio recommended that his addressee confine himself to Menander among the comic playwrights and to Euripides among the tragedians on the grounds that both excelled in the representation of character. Both are characterized as 'useful' (ὠφέλιμος), a term that occurs twice within a few lines, Euripides being singled out as a rich source of useful maxims (*gnōmai*) that reveal his knowledge of philosophy (*Or.* 18.7). It is significant that Dio recommends that his addressee have the plays read to him by people (in the plural) who are skilled in this rather than reading them himself, as he will be able better to focus on the words. He thus reminds us of the existence of an intermediate stage between a staged performance and an entirely private, individual reading, the use of the plural suggesting that this could have taken the form of a dramatized reading.[27]

These two passages reveal rather different stances towards the texts of the tragedians. On the one hand, they are traces of performances that took place in the classical past and that are recoverable, to some extent, through an effort of the imagination; on the other hand, they are a mine of information to be used in the present or to be adapted to suit the needs of readers of the Imperial period in order to become 'useful' (ὠφέλιμοι). Those needs took various forms (notably, linguistic and ethical) and involved reading practices that were far removed from the performance contexts of tragedy.

## Teaching Tragedy: Grammar, Morality and Rhetoric

An educated man had to be able not only to read and understand texts written in classical Attic but also to produce his own compositions, both written and spoken, in that dialect. Attaining this goal, or even a

---

[27] This type of practice might be behind the Menander mosaics in a private house at Mytilene showing scenes from staged productions (deriving from a much older iconographic tradition) of Menander and the characters from Plato's *Phaedo*. See Charitonides, Kahil and Ginouvès 1970 and for analysis of the mosaics within the context of the ancient reception of Menander, Nervegna 2013: 120–200, who concludes that these mosaics served as general representations of Greek culture. On the evidence for the reading and performance of the Platonic dialogues see Charalabopoulos 2012.

semblance of it, meant studying and absorbing models of classical diction from both poets and prose writers: in Lucian's *Lexiphanes* or 'The Flaunter of Words' (22), Lucian's alter ego Lykinos recommends that his pretentious and hyper-Atticizing interlocutor read first of all 'the best poets' with the guidance of teachers, then the orators, before moving on to Plato and Thucydides. The tragedians were certainly included among the 'best poets' and, as this suggests, the accepted norms of Atticizing prose encompassed the use of words found in the Attic tragedians (and comic poets).[28] At the same time, there were limits to the use of poetic vocabulary by authors: when Lucian criticizes the use of 'poetic' words by contemporary writers of history, the terms he singles out are found in epic but also in tragedy, particularly Aeschylus and Sophocles.[29] Lucian goes on to associate this 'poetic language' with tragedy in particular by comparing writers who mix this register of language with the recounting of banal actions to a limping actor wearing only one of the high shoes that serve to signify tragedy. The image is rich in its use of the costume of contemporary tragedy to express a register of language associated with tragedy both as it was written and as it was performed. Most of its effect lies in its evocation of the limping movement that derives its comic force from the disruption and syncopation of the stately progress of the tragic actor.[30] The choice of image here reveals the extent to which contemporary *performance* conditions were bound up with the reception of tragedy at all levels: in order to express a linguistic incongruity, Lucian has recourse to an image that relies on the reader's knowledge of the stylized and physically elevated style of the players. As if to illustrate his own point, Lucian reserves the thorough imitation of tragic diction for his parody of tragedy, *Podagra* (*Gout*), which treats an everyday ailment in mock tragic diction.[31]

## The Utility of Tragedy

As well as being treated as linguistic models, the texts of classical tragedies were used as moral authorities and as a mine of information on the stories

---

[28] On the presence of tragic vocabulary in Lucian's texts see Karavas 2005 esp. 31–131.
[29] Lucian, *On how to write history* 22: the terms ὄτοβος and κόναβος are used by Homer and Hesiod and also by Aeschylus (*Sept.* 151, 160, 204) and Sophocles (*Ajax* 1202, *OC* 1479).
[30] Lucian uses the same image at *Saturnalia* 19 for a different purpose: in order to express the ups and downs of an individual's fortune.
[31] On the *Podagra* see Karavas 2005: 235–327; Tedeschi 1998.

and topography of the past.[32] Some of the best evidence for the ways in which tragedy was approached in schools comes from the ancient commentaries that have been transmitted along with the texts in the medieval manuscripts (see also Hanink, this volume). Dating these commentaries or their component parts is extremely difficult but, whatever their exact date and place of composition, it is reasonable to suppose that they are representative of methods of reading used in and beyond the schools of the Imperial period.[33]

This teaching often focussed on the plot and the mythological background of each play and on details of the language. In both cases, the text provided a starting point for wider discussions of mythology, topography and vocabulary. As Cribiore notes (2001: 250–3), this approach encouraged a fragmentary, centrifugal reading, using particular terms and mythological allusions as starting points for more general discussions that did not necessarily contribute to the appreciation of the work as a whole.

Another, highly tendentious, source of information is the Sceptic philosopher Sextus Empiricus, who contests all the stages of the traditional curriculum from grammar up to music, astrology and various schools of philosophy and, in so doing, tells us a great deal about the approaches commonly used. It is no surprise to find Sextus accusing the grammarians of being unable to fulfil even the basic task of explaining difficult vocabulary.[34] His greatest scorn, however, is reserved for their claims that poetry contained improving moral lessons. Although tragedy is not the only genre discussed by Sextus in this section – the Homeric poems underwent the same treatment – the majority of his examples are drawn from plays by Euripides. Even allowing for a certain amount of exaggeration and bad faith on Sextus' part, it is clear that the grammarians had no hesitation in taking lines out of their dramatic context and presenting them as examples of both good grammar and good conduct.[35] Sextus' specific objections are multiple and frequently technical: on the one hand, these sayings are mere

---

[32] Cribiore (2001: 246–7) notes that lists of places in commentaries of the Hellenistic period reflect Alexander's conquests or planned conquests, while in the later period they reflect the classical and Homeric worlds implying a different vision of the past as inscribed in space.

[33] See Easterling 2015 on the use of the scholia as evidence for modes of reception of the classical texts. In the case of the Homeric scholia, authors of the Imperial period actively engage with the commentary tradition: see, for example, Hunter 2009c.

[34] Sextus Empiricus, *Against the Grammarians*, 308 on Euripides fr. 682 Kannicht and ibid., 313 on Sophocles fr. 515 (Radt).

[35] The concern for moral examples is visible in the treatments of Homer which attempt to explain potentially embarrassing incidents through allegory; see, for example, Heraclitus, *Homeric Problems*. It also underlies Plato's rejection of poetry (first and foremost Homeric epic) in the *Republic*.

assertions and are not backed up by argument – unlike the use of quotations by philosophers as a means of 'sealing' their argument (*Against the Grammarians*, 271). Sextus is also able, very easily, to demolish one of the claims for the utility of tragedy, arguing that, if grammar is said to be useful because poetry contains expressions of morally useful sentiments, then, by the same token, it can be said to be harmful because of other lines that express opposite ideas: if a character in Euripides' *Aeolus* rejects wealth (fr. 20 Kannicht), then other characters in other plays express the opposite opinion, praising wealth and denigrating poverty (*Phoenician Women* 403; *Danae*, fr. 324 Kannicht; *Trag. Adesp.* 464 Kannicht/Snell).[36] Moreover (*ibid.* 280), he argues, when such statements are presented out of context with no accompanying arguments, it is likely that the hearers will choose the morally worse.

This is not the place for an analysis of Sextus' claims; his discussion is interesting for what it reveals about the uses made of tragic texts by his contemporaries. Their antiquity and their status as classics made them authorities not only on linguistic but also on ethical matters, but this status came at the expense of their nature as *dramatic* texts. The extraction of gnomic lines from their larger context was done at the expense of the unity of their source texts and entirely neglected the polyphonic nature of tragedy.[37] From this perspective, Sextus' own argument is interesting in that he attempts to restore the plurality of opposing views that is characteristic of tragedy and thus to argue that any attempt to identify a given statement as an opinion attributable to the poet – and bearing the stamp of his authority – is vain. This view finds an echo in the advice given a century earlier by Plutarch in *On Listening to Poetry*, which was also written against the background of predominantly moralizing readings. Although Plutarch concentrated on Homer, he insisted on the importance of understanding the nature of the speaker and the dramatic situation in each case, explaining that, in their imitation of life, poets necessarily portrayed both positive and negative characters. Rather than excising or allegorizing problematic passages, including expressions of ideas judged as immoral, he recommends explaining them in their contexts.[38] Significantly, the examples that Plutarch draws specifically from tragedy (*Mor.* 27F–28D) are of arguments used by female characters (Phaedra in

---

[36] Sextus Empiricus, *Against the grammarians* 279.
[37] On this extraction of lines from their dramatic contexts and its effects on the process of reading and interpretation see further Liapis 2007 (esp. 272).
[38] Plutarch, *On Listening to Poetry* 7–9 (*Moralia* 25B–28D).

Euripides' first *Hippolytus* and Helen in *Trojan Women*) in order to shift the moral responsibility for their actions onto others.[39] No doubt the speakers' gender made it easier to single out these speeches as negative exempla to be avoided. Plutarch's approach was still that of a moralist moved by the anxiety that young readers would be drawn inexorably to imitate actions and ideas that they read about (28C; cf. 3E–F and Plato, *Republic* 395C–D). His solution, however, was to preserve the integrity of the dramatic text by positing the teacher as a mediator of the poetic text, who was to supply the moral evaluations necessarily omitted by the tragic (and epic) poet.

Outside the realm of education and reflections on education, Dio Chrysostom's writings offer several examples of the use of tragedy as a source of useful quotations that he mentions in his own *Oration* 18 (it is noticeable that he avoids citing lines as if they were reflections of the poets' thought and is generally careful to specify the identity of the speaker in each case).[40] These uses take different forms. In his *Oration* 15 (*On Slavery*), two characters debate the definition of slavery by citing examples drawn from the mythical past: when one character draws attention to the fact that the tragic poets are being appealed to as witnesses, the other replies that this is reasonable because of the esteem with which 'the Greeks' hold them. Here, Dio is not speaking in his own voice, and it is unclear to what period we are supposed to assign this dialogue between two Athenian characters. In *On his exile* (*Oration* 13.20–1), the reflections on the ethical lessons offered by tragedy, whose plots show the sufferings of the rich and powerful, are placed in the mouth of Socrates himself. In the same discourse, Dio cites a brief passage of dialogue from Euripides' *Electra* as an illustration of the commonly held view that exile is a misfortune, only in order to distinguish his own position from this general one. The philosopher thus distances himself from the commonly accepted position as represented by the tragic character. In *Oration* 17 (*Against covetousness*), Dio cites at length Jocasta's warning to her sons from the *Phoenician Women*, one of the most widely read plays in the Imperial period.[41] In the light of Plutarch's discussion, it is interesting to note that Dio is careful to specify the speaker and the situation and to attribute to the poet the role of producer who 'brings on' (εἰσάγει) Jocasta rather than speaking in his

---

[39] As Hunter and Russell note in their edition ad loc. (Hunter and Russell 2011: 157) Plutarch could have quoted the chorus' critical assessment of Helen's speech at *Trojan Women*, 967–8.
[40] See Gotteland 2001.
[41] On the popularity of *Phoenician Women* in antiquity see Cribiore 2001b.

own voice. Euripides' presence is not, however, entirely negated: the description of him as more 'esteemed', or one whose opinions are more respected (ἔνδοξος), than any other poet places emphasis on his authority as well as his fame. The familiarity of the play, and the prestige of its author, did not, however, prevent Dio from adapting the lines in question to his own needs, changing the noun φιλοτιμία ('ambition') in *Phoenician Women* 532 to πλεονεξία ('covetousness'), to suit the subject of his discourse.[42] That this was not simply a result of poor memorization or a variant textual tradition, and that Dio was fully aware of this piece of editing and expected his audience to notice it too, is suggested by the way in which he introduces the quotation with the words 'something like this' (οὕτω πως, 17.8), as if to draw attention to his own unreliability as a source. In his use of this quotation from the play to back up a moral point, Dio was very much in keeping with the common reading practices that began at the first stage of elite education, in the schools of the grammarians, and his treatment of the text shows how the needs of the present could take precedence over the writings of the past. In the bid to lay claim to the authority of the poet in support of his own argument, Dio feels free to adapt the text to fit its new context. Together, Plutarch and Dio illustrate a tension inherent in the transition from the stage (where the enunciative situation of each statement is immediately clear) to the page that is only intensified by the continuing desire to make use of the texts of the past. This tension makes necessary the strict policing of reading and interpretation that we see in Plutarch and that is reflected in Sextus' attack on the grammarians.[43]

A comparable approach to texts reappears in a seminal Christian text, Basil of Caesarea's *Letter to the Young Men on How to Profit from Greek Literature*. The moral lessons to be learned from select passages of different texts, expressed through the image of the bee collecting nectar from various flowers, represent the only justification Basil can offer for reading the Greek texts (4.8). Like Dio before him, he is prepared to adjust these texts to make them more suitable to his purpose, as we see in his use of Homer. Tragedy, however, is striking for its absence among the positive models offered by Basil and, where it is cited, it is as an illustration of attitudes to be avoided. At 6.6, for example, Hippolytus' notorious statement (Euripides, *Hippolytus* 612) that his tongue swore and not his heart is given as a negative example. This difference in treatment is certainly not due to the

[42] See Gotteland 2001: 105 and 109.
[43] See Hunter 2009a: 41 on the need for control of the past inherent to classicism.

higher moral value of Homeric epic (it too was excised from the reading programme offered to Basil's sister, Makrina, by her mother, along with tragedy and comedy, on the grounds of its unsuitable content, particularly with respect to the portrayal of female characters).[44] If Basil is not willing to make the same interpretative efforts to justify the reading of tragedy that he applies to the Homeric epics, it is surely because of its continued associations with the living stage and all that it represented (Webb 2007).

## Tragedy and Rhetoric

One further reason why Dio recommends Euripides as suitable reading for a man active in public life is the plausibility (πιθανότης) of his plays – a concern for the fit between characters, their actions and their words that was typical of a critical approach shaped by rhetoric.[45]

Remarks on the *ēthos* (character) and *pathos* (suffering or emotion) of the characters are also common in the scholia; these phenomena (both treated as essential to argumentation, *pistis*, by Aristotle) were highly relevant to the study of rhetoric. It is not surprising, then, to find that, in the exercise of *ēthopoiia*, students could be called upon to compose the words that a certain character from tragedy might have said in the emotional state brought on by a particular situation. In the extant rhetorical handbooks and collections of model exercises, some situations derived from tragedy are treated: Libanios' model *ēthopoiiai* include two derived from the plot of Sophocles' *Ajax* (the words that Ajax might have said after his madness and just before his suicide) and one from Euripides' *Medea* (the speech of Medea when she is about to kill her children).[46] Such compositions required the students to project themselves into the mythical (or rather, in the eyes of many ancient readers, historical) time and place depicted in the plays in question. Libanios' model *ēthopoiia* of Medea, however, shows the limits of this engagement.[47] The speech avoids its obvious model, taking very little from the famous Euripidean monologue (*Med.* 1019–80) in which Medea wavers between sparing her children and

---

[44] Gregory of Nyssa, *Life of Makrina* 3.
[45] Dio's *Trojan Oration* (*Or.* 11) applies the criterion of plausibility to the Homeric epics and finds them wanting. In other authors of the period, comedy and mime are more usually singled out as models of plausible plots. See, for example, Quintilian, *Institutio Oratoria* 4.2.53 and Asclepiades as quoted by Sextus Empiricus, *Against the Grammarians* 253.
[46] Libanios, *Progymnasmata* 11.5 and 6. On the treatment of situations from the Trojan War see Webb 2010.
[47] The same is true of Libanios' version of Andromache's lament in his *Progymnasmata* 11.2: see Webb 2010: 140–3.

her chilling resolve to slaughter them.[48] Libanios instead makes his Medea into an orator concerned for justice, and as a result echoes arguments that are found elsewhere in the play, namely in her *agōn* (debate) with Jason (465–519): the injustice of the treatment she has suffered at his hands, the catalogue of all that she has done for him and all that she has sacrificed for him.

Tragedy also provided the raw material for exercises in argumentation, as shown in Theon's choice of the plot of Euripides' *Medea* for his demonstration of how to argue that a story is or is not plausible.[49] He breaks the story down into its basic elements (the who, what, when, where and why) and proceeds to show how it is improbable that a mother would kill her children, that she would do it at that particular time and place, and so on. In so doing, he makes use of the bare bones of the plot and ignores the psychological complexity of the character of Medea in his search for the starting points for arguments.

This is all done, of course, for the sake of argument and, like the *ēthopoiiai*, shows how the extreme and singular aspects of tragic character and plot could be negated in order to fulfil readers' needs, while, as we saw earlier in this chapter, some of the key functions of tragedy in the classical world were performed by the newer genres of mime and pantomime and, as we shall see later in this chapter, by the rhetorical art of declamation.

## Tragedy and Imagination

These uses of tragedy as a source of quotations to be plundered and re-used in very different contexts appear anachronistic – perverse even – to the modern reader, but they can be seen as part and parcel of a widespread method of reading classical texts in antiquity by which they were treated as part of a common (to the elite) cultural capital to be adapted and used rather than being preserved in some original state. Possession of this cultural capital allowed members of non-Greek élites to lay claim to a share in Hellenic culture and its prestige.[50] However, such uses of the texts coexisted with other reading practices that did allow for the fact that the texts were originally intended for performance, and this understanding was no doubt aided by the continued presence of tragedy – as well as other

---

[48] This monologue was well known in antiquity as shown, for example, in Callirhoe's speech in Chariton (*Chaereas and Callirhoe*, 2.9), which adapts the situation. Chariton and his readers were not necessarily familiar with the whole play.
[49] Theon, *Progymnasmata*, 94, 7–33.   [50] See Morgan 1998.

*Attitudes Towards Tragedy* 313

performance genres – on stage.⁵¹ It is surely significant that there is some overlap between the plays that were the most often read in schools and those most often performed in the postclassical period: Euripides' *Orestes* and *Medea* fall into both categories.⁵² In these readings, as evidenced in scholia and in other sources, we can see attempts to reconstitute phenomena beyond the words of the text.⁵³ Sometimes these take into account what the scholiast understood to be the original performance conditions, while at other times they add information that would have been visible to an audience in a theatre, or explain what both the reader of the text and a theatre audience needed to imagine in order to follow the play.

Some of these comments show that readers were well aware that the play scripts were part of a multisensory phenomenon that obeyed very particular practical constraints. Scholia comment on the sound of the voice at certain moments,⁵⁴ on gestures,⁵⁵ and on the qualities demanded of the actors of certain roles.⁵⁶ Dio Chrysostom again, in his *Oration* 74, *On Distrust*, appears to imagine a staging of the opening scene of Euripides' *Orestes* (211–59) as he describes how Electra resists the weeping Orestes' attempts to draw her to him because she is still wary of his state of mind. It has been suggested (see discussion in Gotteland 2001: 104) that Dio here was influenced by a production of the play that he had seen for himself; however, it would not be impossible to deduce these details from the surrounding text.

Other comments draw attention to the difference between what was present in the text and what was visible to the audience in the theatre. The opening of Euripides' *Orestes* presented a particular challenge in this respect, as Orestes' intermittent visions of the Furies pursuing him did not correspond to the reality within the fictional world of the play. The scholia to line 257, where Orestes refers to the Furies using the deictic (αὗται γὰρ αὗται, 'these women here'), explain that the poet 'has represented the Erinyes pursuing him unseen in order to present to us the thoughts of the madman', and point out that if the Furies were present on

---

⁵¹ One might also add that Theon's choice of Euripides' *Medea* as an example of confirmation and refutation reflects the contrasting versions of her story current in antiquity as well as the uncertainty that Euripides creates in his play about Medea's intentions and the competing visions of her offered by other characters throughout the play.
⁵² On the performance tradition see Nervegna 2014: 162; also, Duncan and Liapis, this volume.
⁵³ On the tragic scholia see Meijering 1987; Easterling 2015; Falkner 2002; Jouanna 2001.
⁵⁴ Scholia to E. *Or.* 176 (see Falkner 2002: 345–6).
⁵⁵ Scholia to E. *Or.* 643 (see Falkner 2002: 359); scholia to S. *El.* 823 (see Easterling 2015: 3 n. 8).
⁵⁶ Scholia to S. *Aj.* 864a; see Nervegna 2014: 165; Jouanna 2001: 22 n. 42.

stage, Orestes would be sane, as he would merely be able to perceive what was real within that same fictional world.[57]

The previous examples suggest how the texts of tragedies could form a basis for the type of ideal, imaginative reconstruction that Dio alludes to when comparing the three *Philoctetes* plays. The readers clearly understand the plays as theatrical performances, and their understanding of them is informed by their familiarity with the continued performance tradition, but the imagined spectacle is complete in itself and dispenses with the need for performance, just as Aristotle claimed should be the case (*Poetics*, 1450b: 18–19). In fact, both Dio and Aristotle seem to reflect an important characteristic of classical tragedy, which often evoked unseen characters and events through words alone, both in messenger speeches and elsewhere (see Hunter 2008: 663–77). Such readings, or internal performances, thus generalize this characteristic and apply it to the play as a whole. These imagined, internal performances are also, as Porter (2006: 303–4) has noted in the case of Aristophanes' *Frogs*, an example of the 'classical fantasy' of contact with the past. When Dio claims that the spectacle of the three *Philoctetes* plays that he 'enjoyed' was superior to anything that could have been seen in ancient Athens itself, since the plays were never staged simultaneously (*Or.* 52.3), he is placing himself imaginatively on an equal footing with a classical Athenian audience, able to judge between three performances and in possession of the shared expertise necessary for such discrimination. He also simultaneously displays the ability to control the past that his knowledge and his chronological distance from it confer on him.[58]

A slightly different form of imaginative engagement is to be found in the treatise *On the Sublime* attributed to Longinus, an Imperial author whether one dates him to the first century AD or accepts a third-century dating.[59] Longinus discusses tragic examples in his chapter on *phantasia*, which he defines as the capacity to imagine and to transmit the resulting mental image to an audience (*On the Sublime*, 15.1). Longinus is highly appreciative of the tragic text's ability to achieve the sublime by transporting its readers in imagination to the times and places of the mythical past and even to take them beyond the realms of normal human experience. One particularly striking passage is taken from the messenger speech of Euripides' lost play *Phaethon*. In it, a witness to the catastrophe recounts the growing panic of Helios as he saw his son lose control of the chariot in his

---

[57] Scholia to E. *Or.* 257; see Meijering 1987: 129.   [58] See Hunter 2009a: 41.
[59] On the dating see Heath 1999. On Longinus' reading of tragedy see also Hanink, this volume.

fatal flight. As is often the case in ancient criticism, Longinus contents himself with a quotation of the passage and an evocation of his own response to it, but this response is particularly interesting in this case, as he claims that the text gives access to the experience of the poet himself: 'Wouldn't you say', he asks, 'that the soul of the writer has mounted the chariot and, sharing in the horses' danger, has taken flight along with them? For otherwise, if it had not been carried along, running beside such deeds, it would never have imagined such things.'[60]

In a very similar fashion, he claims the cries of the mad Orestes, imagining that he is pursued by the Furies (Euripides, *Orestes*, 255–7), as proof that Euripides had 'seen the Furies himself' (*On the Sublime*, 15.3).[61] Whereas the scholia to the same passage of Euripides' *Orestes* draw attention to the poet's aesthetic choices as composer of the text, Longinus sees Euripides as a conduit allowing access to the events depicted.[62] What is more, he proposes his own reading as a means of sharing the poet's experience at the moment of composition that is thus placed almost on a par with the mythical past. Access to the texts of classical tragedy thus made it possible for the expert reader to bypass the performer entirely and to gain access to two different strata of the past: the mythical past of the events depicted and the classical past of the moment of composition (for Longinus) and/or first performance (for Dio). This does not mean that tragedy was no longer a living performance tradition but instead reflects the desire to do away with the contemporary tragic actor with his bodily presence, in the same way as Dio (*Or.* 19.5) conceived of tragedy as free from the 'soft' flesh represented by the choral odes. Dio is, of course, referring to present-day performances which put onstage the 'hard' remains of the plays, but his choice of image reveals a desire to remove the body – and the sensory impact that must have been particularly intense in the case of choral song and dance – from the communication between poet and reader/spectator.[63]

---

[60] Longinus, *On the Sublime*, 15.4; the translation is my own.
[61] Longinus, *On the Sublime*, 15.5–7 also cites passages from Sophocles and Aeschylus as examples of *phantasia* in poetry.
[62] A comparable strategy can be seen in play in the Elder Philostratus' *Imagines*, where the (fictional) paintings in the gallery are portrayed as giving a similar access to the events related in various tragedies, particularly in messenger speeches. Philostratus' viewers become as it were witnesses not of a performance but of the actions themselves, seeing Hippolytus' fatal chariot ride (2.4) or Phaethon's fall to earth (1.11). See Elsner 2007; Webb 2013.
[63] In Lucian's *Teacher of Rhetoric*, 9–11, the 'hard' body of the traditional teacher who forces his students to read classical texts is contrasted with the body of the contemporary teacher, described in terms that are elsewhere associated with softness and effeminacy. Lucian's treatment, in which both are subject to criticism, reveals the complexity of this binary opposition.

## Tragedy in Rhetorical Practice

Many of the intellectuals of the Imperial period were, of course, themselves performers. The mainstay of Second Sophistic output was represented by the declamations and epideictic speeches that made the reputations of the sophists profiled by Philostratus in his *Lives of the Sophists*. There was a clear link between tragedy and declamation: like actors, the declaimers played the role of a familiar individual from the past, and they did so on stage and as a form of spectacle. There are, moreover, some indications that tragedy may on occasion have provided the raw material for declamations: when Longinus (*On the Sublime*, 15.8) criticizes orators in his day who acted as if they, like Orestes, could see Furies but failed to realize that Orestes did so because he was mad, he may have in mind declamations on the theme of Orestes' trial. Others certainly came close to tragedy in the structure of the stories dealt with as in the often-repeated case of the young man who commits suicide in order to save his country, which recalls the suicide of Menoeceus in Euripides' *Phoenician Women*.[64] The language of later declamation in particular is full of overt allusions to the 'tragic' nature of the situations the characters find themselves in and of exclamations, such as οἴμοι ('woe is me') more often found in classical tragedy than oratory.[65] All of the passages of this type suggest that 'tragic' meant, above all, transgressive events with painful results, very like our colloquial use of the term.

Rhetoric of all types and at all periods demanded skills close to those of actors: it is interesting to note that Philostratus in his *Lives of the Sophists* (607) likens the ability to take on the correct tone and style in the composition of imperial letters to the skills of a tragic actor.[66] Practice in role play in fact started at an earlier stage in education, with the preliminary exercise of reading which, according to Theon, required the student to think himself into the persona and the situation of the orator, just as tragic

---

[64] See Bernstein (2013: 91, 138–9) on the similarity between the types of family dramas found in declamation and tragedy. Cribiore (2001: 247) notes the importance of the theme of dying for the fatherland in the scholia to Euripides' *Phoenician Women*, an interest that is likely to reflect the common declamation theme.

[65] The teacher of rhetoric Sopater Rhetor (fourth century AD) uses the term *tragōidia* several times in his demonstrations of how to treat declamation themes. One example in Walz (1835: 70) is particularly interesting in that the story defined as 'tragic', involving a woman's affair with a slave, is in fact closer to the mime. The speaker of Lucian's *Tyrannicide*, 22, a particularly dramatic declamation, compares the different agents of the tyrant's demise to parts in a play, as noted by Kokolakis 1960: 55. On this declamation see the excellent discussion in Guast 2018.

[66] Kokolakis 1960: 64.

actors do (Theon specifically mentions the actor Polus as an example to be followed).[67] However, as a performance art in which the orator played a role, declamation had deeper affinities with drama in general and tragedy in particular.

The line between acting and oratory was fine and needed to be guarded closely, precisely because of the vigorous continuing tradition of stage performance (Fantham 2002). Tragedy, despite its prestigious origins, was no exception to this rule. There were clear boundaries to the use of vocal and verbal styles associated with tragedy in high-style compositions and performances. We hear complaints about singing sophists (Philostratus, *Lives of the Sophists* 513; Aelius Aristides 34.47); more surprisingly perhaps, no classical tragedian figures among the models of style recommended by Hermogenes in his treatise *On Types of Style*.

## Tragic Actor as Sophist

To return to the boundaries between Imperial sophists and actors, contrasts between the two groups are drawn by Dio Chrysostom, Lucian and Plutarch. For Dio (in the passage in which he discusses the loss of the choral odes in contemporary performances), the words sung by actors (he includes comedy here alongside tragedy) have been composed by wiser men than the men of his own day.[68] Immediately before this (19.4), Dio had praised the enunciation (φωνή) and style (λέξις) of actors in comparison with that of contemporary sophists who improvised their words. On the surface, Dio argues for the superiority of the actor who transmits words written by wiser men from a better era – men who, what is more, had free time (σχολή) to reflect on their compositions and did not have to compose them on the spot as the sophists did. In other contexts, however, the figure of the tragic actor as reciter of the words of others has less positive connotations. In the passage of the dialogue *On the Dance* with which we began, Lucian's speaker goes on to develop the unfavourable comparison between the tragic actor and the pantomime dancer by complaining that the former is 'accountable only for his voice since the rest has been taken care of by poets who lived a long time ago'.[69] A similar point was made slightly earlier by Plutarch in the opening section of the essay on *The*

---

[67] Theon, *Progymnasmata* 13, ed. Patillon and Bolognesi (1997: 103). This part of the treatise only exists in an Armenian translation. Quintilian makes a similar comparison between orators and actors when speaking of emotion at *Institutio Oratoria* 6.2.35.
[68] Dio Chrysostom, *Or.* 19.5.    [69] Lucian, *On the Dance* 27.

*Glory of the Athenians* (345E), in which he discusses the question of whether action itself or the representation of action was more worthwhile. Here, he contrasts historians, like Xenophon who 'became his own history' (αὐτὸς ἑαυτοῦ γέγονεν ἱστορία), with those who merely write and thus 'have been for the actions of others what actors (*hypokritai*) are to plays (*dramata*), representing the deeds of generals and kings and taking on (*hypoduomenoi*) their memory (like masks or costumes)'.[70]

Plutarch's mention of 'the deeds of kings', and the general tone of the comparison between two modes of representation of the past, certainly imply that these ventriloquizing *hypokritai* are to be thought of primarily as tragic actors. As in Lucian's *On the Dance*, these actors are dismissed as mere mouthpieces incapable of creating anything for themselves or of matching their actions to their words. Dio, as we saw, put a positive gloss on the actor's function at the expense of contemporary orators, and it is tempting to see a potential critique of sophists running beneath the figure of the actor elsewhere too. The charge of merely speaking about the deeds of the past and repeating the words of better authors could easily be applied to the sophists themselves who devoted so much time and energy to composing and performing speeches set in the distant past.[71] One of the worst things that could happen to a sophist was to be exposed as a mere repeater of scripts (even of their own works), that is, to be reduced to the level of an actor.[72] To return to the tragic actor for a moment, the gulf between him and the tragic poet – the better man – who had written his words appears nowhere more clearly than in Dio Chrysostom's *Euboicus* (*Or.* 7). The speaker of this oration includes tragic and comic actors along with mimes and dancers among the professions to be excluded from his ideal city (*Or.* 7.119), reflecting not only the Platonic suspicion of theatrical mimesis but also the Roman legal exclusion of performers of all types from full civic rights.[73] It is important to note that in the context of the *Euboicus* a clear distinction is made between the *actors* of tragedy and comedy and the classical *poets*, as the speaker insists that his rejection of the former is not to be taken as a criticism of the latter (*Or.* 7.120).

---

[70] Plutarch, *Moralia*, 345E.
[71] See, for example, the remarks of the first speaker in Lucian's *Teacher of Rhetoric* 10, who dismisses the traditional methods of teaching as the 'imitation (*mimesis*) of the ancients' producing speeches that are distant to contemporary concerns.
[72] See Lucian, *Pseudologistes*, 5–6 and Philostratus, *Lives of the Sophists*, 579 on sophists caught reciting a declamation from a script instead of improvising.
[73] For discussion and further bibliography see Leppin 1992; Webb 2008: 44–57.

Intellectuals could claim to re-enact tragic plots and even classical productions in their minds, bypassing the paraphernalia of the stage. The image of the actor, by contrast, brought with it associations of exaggeration, grotesquery and incongruousness, which consequently attached to the *idea* of tragedy as a whole in certain contexts.

## Tragedy and Alterity

As we have seen, educated readers of the texts of classical tragedy such as Dio and Longinus engaged freely in the fantasy of being brought into the presence of the deeds of the heroes of the mythical past, or of sharing the experience of the audience of the original production in classical Athens. In both cases, the act of reading both abolishes the radical differences in time and place and allows the inconvenient constraints of chronology (in the case of the impossible contest between the three *Philoctetes* plays) and of the material conditions of performance to be bypassed. The figure of the tragic *actor* is excised from this classical fantasy, and when it is evoked it is most often as a jarring symbol of distance and dissonance, in contexts that draw attention to the lack of identity and of the fundamental *disjunctions* between the performer and his text and between the actor and his role. Here, it is interesting to return to the bonfire with which Tertullian's *On the Spectacles* ends and where each performer consigned to the flames is characterized by one aspect of his art: in the case of the *tragoedi*, Tertullian remarks sourly (30) that 'then they will be more worth hearing as they will naturally be more vocal in *their own* sufferings'.

The use of the tragic actor in particular to illustrate the idea of the unbridgeable gap between external appearance (the role played) and the true nature of the player is ubiquitous in Imperial literature, both in Latin and in Greek.[74] Although such comments can be made of most actors (the case of the pantomime raised different problems), the *tragōidoi* are often singled out for the contrast between their social status on the one hand and the grandiose style of costume and acting and the high-ranking characters they played on the other. As Lucian himself says in his *Apologia* (5), actors who, on stage, are Agamemnon, Creon or Herakles become mere 'hired tragic performers' (ὑπόμισθοι τραγῳδοῦντες), subject to public humiliation once they remove their masks. Elsewhere (*Saturnalia* 28), he speaks

---

[74] See, for example, Seneca, *Letter* 80.7 with Edwards 2002: 381–2; Libanios, *Or.* 30.28.

of tragic actors' costumes as 'all gold on the outside but rags on the inside'.[75] The discrepancy between the tragic actor and his role could also, on occasion, be used as a positive example, as when Maximus of Tyre treats the players' versatility as a model throughout his seventh dissertation.

In the passage with which we began (*On the Dance* 27), Lucian notes a further incongruity, this time between the singing of the *tragōidoi* of his age and certain of the characters they played, when he describes as a form of solecism the use of song to depict characters like Heracles. Again, this critique of tragedy has to be read in the light of the praise of pantomime that is Lucian's aim in this work. It is interesting, however, to compare the emphasis on the lack of identity between the tragic actor and his role (whatever the cause) that we see here with the widespread view that the pantomime dancer was merged with his role, *becoming* (or almost becoming) feminine when he took on female roles. Defenders of the dance draw attention to this difference when they point out that tragic actors also play female roles without attracting criticism.[76] The contrast is striking and must be attributable at least in part to the force of the dancer's bodily mimesis, which created the sense that he *was* the character whose actions he not only portrayed but executed through the motions of the dance.

The plays themselves could also attract accusations of incongruity, particularly regarding the disparity between the respect shown to them as works of the classical past and the details of their narrative content. Lucian, again, compares the rich Romans who employ Greek intellectuals to volumes of tragic plays which, under their splendid covers, contain Thyestes feasting on his children or Oedipus marrying his mother (*On Salaried Posts* 41). A recognition that, without their veneer of classical prestige, the tragic plots were immoral and entirely unsuitable for schoolchildren is found in the arguments in defence of the mime put forward by Chorikios of Gaza (*In Defence of the Mimes* 36–41 and 141), where tragic plots are characterized as 'a son killing his mother, a mother raising a sword against her own children out of jealousy in love'. Like Lucian in his critiques of tragedy in *On the Dance*, Chorikios here is resorting to a paradoxical argument, which, however, could carry real weight as we saw in the rejection of tragedy in Gregory of Nyssa's *Life of Makrina* (earlier in this chapter). The scandalous nature of tragic plots, combined with their depictions of vengeful deities and heroes, must also lurk behind Tatian's comments at the end of his tirade against classical culture, when he invites

---

[75] On this topic in Lucian see further Schmitz 2010.
[76] See, for example, Lucian, *On the Dance*, 28.

his pagan readers either to embrace fully the lessons of their plays or to reject them.[77] All of these comments invite a questioning of the classical canon and its place in education and culture, and it is no accident that this questioning appears to be most acute in the case of tragedy, which remained a living art on the stages of the Empire.

## Laughter and Fear

The sense of incongruity attaching to the tragic actor and the enhanced cognitive dissonance that it entailed led to two different types of responses. One is to be seen in the expressions of fear surrounding tragic actors that emerge in the famous anecdote in Philostratus' *Life of Apollonius of Tyana* (5.9) concerning an actor who caused panic among the inhabitants of Hipola (Seville) when he opened his mouth.[78] Although the event itself is distanced from Philostratus' own day in time and is placed at the very edges of the civilized world, the terms in which it is related are not totally removed from those of the passage of Lucian with which we began. Philostratus tells us how, as long as the actor simply strode across the stage with his gaping mouth (i.e., of the mask), his high shoes and his impressive costume, the naïve spectators simply felt afraid, but that once he opened his mouth they fled in terror as if they were being shouted at by a demon (ὥσπερ ὑπὸ δαίμονος ἐμβοηθέντες). The point of the anecdote is, ostensibly, to show how uncultivated these particular barbarians were, but the feeling of terror at the spectacle of a gaping mask is also present in Lucian's image of the mask's open mouth as capable of swallowing up the audience.[79] The juxtaposition of Philostratus' terrifying *tragōidos* with Lucian's ironic portrait of the grotesque foil to the dancer brings out their common traits: a sense of the incongruity that can lead either to anxiety or to laughter.

Lucian's corpus in fact contains one of the compositions that best illustrate the comic potential that lies in the tragedy, specifically, in the mismatch between language and content. The mock tragedy *Podagra*, or *Gout*, which features as its *dramatis personae* the personification of the disease herself, a sufferer, a chorus of gouty men, a pair of Syrian doctors, and Suffering personified: the central conflict is between the doctors and

---

[77] Tatian, *To the Greeks*, 24.
[78] On the fear of the mask and its close relationship to laughter see Wyler 2008.
[79] Epictetus' use (*Discourses*, 2.1.15) of the tragic mask and the fear that it inspires in children as an illustration of the empty fears that stem from ignorance also implies that such reactions could be felt to have a general application.

Gout whom they claim to be able to vanquish. Lucian takes the mimesis of classical texts to its logical conclusion, using the vocabulary and diction inspired by tragedy in iambic verses and in lyric choral passages. The tragic language, however, is mixed with medical vocabulary from the very first lines which place the illness within a Hesiodic genealogy: Ὦ στυγνὸν οὔνομ', ὦ θεοῖς στυγούμενον,/Ποδάγρα, πολυστένακτε, Κωκυτοῦ τέκνον..., 'Oh, hateful name, hated by the gods, Gout, source of many groans, child of Kokytos...'[80] The joke, of course, lies in the transposition of the tragic hero's suffering (one thinks of Oedipus and Philoctetes in particular) onto the level of the everyday malady of the prosperous. As often in Lucian's works, the targets of his wit are potentially multiple: in addition to the doctors with their empty claims and useless remedies, the sufferers are identified as the butt of jokes – and of the *Podagra* itself – at the very end of the piece (ll. 332–5). However, the choice of the paratragic form in itself suggests other targets, such as the traditional tragic language and form (as in the final resigned and banal comments of the chorus which conclude the piece) and their incongruity as a medium for expressing contemporary concerns. If this is, indeed, the case, the traditions under fire from Lucian's wit may well include contemporary performances of tragedy just as much as the classical texts. The similarities between actors and sophists also add another item to the potential list of targets of Lucian's *Podagra*: the educated elites (*pepaideumenoi*) themselves, who could imitate the language and the literary forms of the past but who fell far short as regards the content.[81]

## Conclusion

These final examples show how the values that could attach to theatrical performances of all types often emerged in high relief in the case of tragedy: the gap between reality and fiction was all the more acute when the jobbing actor took on the roles of kings and heroes, and the feeling of unease that can be provoked by any mask was more acute in the case of the tragic mask. As these examples suggest, the particular complexity of the reception of tragedy stemmed from its double life as sketched out at the beginning of this chapter: the coexistence of classic texts with a continuing

---

[80] Other examples of medical vocabulary include ἰχώρ and χυμός (l. 18). For a full analysis of the vocabulary see Tedeschi 1998 and Karavas 2005: 243–99.

[81] See Schmitz 2010, esp. 308 and, for a stimulating discussion of paratragedy in Lucian, Whitmarsh 2013: 176–85.

performance tradition involving both reperformances of old tragedies in new ways (including pantomimic reworkings) and entirely new compositions. The ancient texts, in themselves, set in motion a multileveled interaction between the Imperial present and different moments in the past: the mythical-historical past to which the characters and events belonged, and the classical past – itself partly heroized – during which the plays were originally composed and performed. It was their classical provenance that gave the tragic texts their authority as linguistic and ethical models, but this same provenance gave rise to a gulf between the extreme situations and transgressive acts which formed the centre of tragic plots and the needs of the present. The negotiation of this gulf was fraught with difficulties. The use of classical tragedy as an ethical model involved considerable interpretative effort on the part of the grammarians who needed to stand guard between the young reader and the text. The only safe tragedy in this context was the disembodied fragment, extracted from its dramatic context and safely embedded in a moralizing interpretation. Such a use of tragedy (and other poetic texts), which reached its peak in the fifth-century anthology of John Stobaeus, and the status of these collections of extracts as potentially works of literature in their own right, are confirmed by the weaving of tragic lines into a new narrative in the *Khristos Paskhōn*.

It is striking that, in many of the sources from the second and third centuries AD, the sense of distance and incongruity attaching to tragedy was projected onto the figure of the contemporary *tragōidos*, aided by the effect of estrangement created by the appearance and performance style of these artists. *Readers* of the texts preferred to emphasize the sense of imaginative proximity they achieved both to the narrative content and to the original classical moments of composition and performance once the actor, with his inconvenient wailing and bending body, was removed from the equation and once the bodily senses were replaced by their internal, mental equivalents. In so doing, the educated Greek-speaking 'spectators' like Dio were creating their own imagined community with its own, very particular, rights of access, distinct from the communities brought together in the material theatres of the Empire.

CHAPTER 11

## Scholars and Scholarship on Tragedy

Johanna Hanink

Handbooks of classical scholarship tend to sweep discussions of ancient work on tragedy into accounts of Homeric, or more generally 'Alexandrian', scholarship: the editing of tragic and epic texts took place alongside each other in Alexandria, but the city's great librarians and scholars were always most concerned with textual criticism and exegesis of Homer.[1] On the other hand, much of the important new work on performance in postclassical antiquity makes little use of the evidence for the scholarly tradition, and instead focuses on the material (epigraphic, architectural and visual) records. But the ancient scholars who 'corrected' and commented on the tragic plays laboured while lively dramatic performance traditions, discussed by others in this volume, carried on in the world outside the walls of the Museum: they, too, belong to any picture that we might seek to piece together of tragedy's (re)performance and reception in antiquity.

The present chapter aims to provide an overview of ancient scholarship on tragedy, but also to highlight some of the respects and instances in which it differed from scholarship on other kinds of texts. By its very nature, drama presented scholars with challenges unlike those of the Homeric poems: dramatic texts constituted only the archived remains of performances, which once had real historical contexts and significant aural and visual dimensions.[2] These more evanescent aspects of performance seem to have been the subject of the very earliest writing about the theatre. Vitruvius reports that during Aeschylus' lifetime Agatharchus invented, and wrote a treatise on, scene-painting, and that Anaxagoras and Democritus wrote theoretical treatments of perspective-drawing and its implications for

---

[1] Studies of tragedy dedicated to 'texts and transmission' tend to focus upon the complications of the medieval manuscript traditions. For extended discussions of transmission in antiquity see Wartelle 1971 and Tuilier 1968: 23–127; for broader overviews which highlight ancient scholarship see esp. Kovacs 2005 and Finglass 2012.
[2] I follow Taylor 1993 in distinguishing the dramatic 'archive' (i.e., the range of material traces of performance) from the 'repertoire' (i.e., the store of embodied memory of performance).

set design.³ Classical tragedians were also remembered for having studied and theorized their craft: Sophocles is said to have written a prose treatise *On the Chorus*, 'in competition (ἀγωνιζόμενος) with his colleagues Thespis and Choerilus'.⁴

Other texts from the fifth and early fourth centuries, such as comedies by Aristophanes and the tragedians' own highly allusive plays, indicate that careful *reading* of tragedy was taking place while the classical playwrights still lived. Comedy contains some of our earliest evidence for tragic citation in other genres, as well as for the kinds of 'theatrical' debates (about tragic style, characterization, tragedy's effects on its audiences, the tragedians' use of stage machinery, etc.) that were taking place in fifth-century Athens. Euripides was reputed to have had a large personal library, and his poetry reveals him to have been an exceptionally attentive student of his colleagues' work.⁵ And while plays themselves do not constitute true literary scholarship as Pfeiffer famously defined it, that is, as 'the art of understanding, explaining, and restoring the literary tradition',⁶ they do tell us about how tragedy was informally studied in the decades before the field of scholarship took full shape.

These texts also exerted a traceable influence on later critical thought, and the comic playwright Aristophanes is a particularly important resource for the early evolution of critical and 'scholarly' ideas about tragedy. Hunter has discussed how *Frogs* 'set the parameters of discussion' for many areas of literary criticism in antiquity,⁷ and Wright has detailed 'the surprising amount of common ground' that Old Comedy shares with later critical traditions.⁸ Plato, too, proved influential in this respect: in the *Republic* alone, Socrates provides accounts of mimesis, the negative effects of tragedy on spectators (tragedy provokes excessive and unseemly emotion) and the tragedians' predilection for praising tyrants. Each of Socrates' arguments about tragedy and drama more generally would be taken up and disputed in later, more recognizably 'scholarly' works.⁹

---

³ Vitr. 7.11. On the sources for scene painting (*skēnographia*) in antiquity see Small 2013.
⁴ *Suda* σ 815.
⁵ Athen. 1.3a, cf. Knox 1985: 9; explicit references to Euripides' use of books appear at Ar. *Ran*. 943 and 1409. For recent studies of Euripides' engagement with plays by other tragedians see, e.g., Torrance 2013 and Lamari 2009; for the fifth-century 'comedian as reader' see Wright 2012: 141–71.
⁶ Pfeiffer 1968: 3.   ⁷ Hunter 2009a: 2.   ⁸ Wright 2012: 2.
⁹ For an overview see G. R. F. Ferrari 1989: esp. 103–41.

## Taking Stock: Athenian Archives and Editions

The beginnings of scholarship, and of scholarship as a 'state-sponsored' institution, are often associated with the third-century BC Ptolemaic court in Alexandria. Yet to a certain extent, the early Ptolemies had been able to look back to a model in Athens, where work towards assembling the history of the Athenian theatre began under the city's own aegis. Sometime between 346 and 343 BC, the *dēmos* decided to install on the Acropolis a monumental inscription that listed information about victories at the Great Dionysia. This inscription, *IG* ii$^2$ 2318 or the *Victorum Dionysiorum Fasti* – conventionally referred to as the *Fasti* – survives today in a number of fragments.[10] Originally the monument displayed the following information for each celebration of the Great Dionysia from the festival's beginning (note that the comedy category was not introduced until 486 BC, and that a prize for best tragic actor began to be awarded in the middle of the century):

1  name of the eponymous archon
2  victorious boys' chorus
3  *chorēgos* of the victorious boys' chorus
4  victorious men's chorus
5  *chorēgos* of the victorious men's chorus
6  Comedy (entry heading) (from 486 BC onwards)
7  *chorēgos* for the victorious comic playwright
8  victorious comic *didaskalos* (i.e., playwright)
9  Tragedy (entry heading)
10  *chorēgos* for the victorious tragic playwright
11  victorious tragic *didaskalos* (i.e., playwright)
12  victorious actor (from between 450 and 447 BC onwards)

The monument's prestigious location on the Acropolis indicates the pride that Athens was taking in its own cultural history, but the very existence of the *Fasti* also suggests that the city had long been keeping assiduous records of at least the *victors* at the Great Dionysia.[11] In roughly the same era, Aristotle was also using those records to compile historical results of Athens' dramatic festivals. Diogenes Laertius reports that Aristotle

---

[10] For an edition and commentary see Millis and Olson 2012: 5–58.
[11] On the *Fasti* see most recently Tracy 2015, with p. 559 on the inscription's date and location (Tracy 'down-dates' the inscription to the end of the fourth century BC); for an edition see Millis and Olson 2012.

composed two works on Athenian theatrical history: one book of *Victories at the Dionysia* and another called *Didascaliae*.[12] This latter title, which translates roughly as 'Theatrical Performances', implies a more detailed assemblage of information than was preserved in the *Fasti*, which did not record titles of plays or names of non-victorious poets. Such information could also have been kept by the city, perhaps by the archon responsible for choosing which playwrights would receive choruses for (and thus be allowed to compete at) the festival.[13]

Archival theatre history, as pursued by the state and by private individuals alike, marks an important point of intellectual contact between fourth-century Athens and Hellenistic scholarship. The surviving dramatic *hypotheseis*, or plot summaries often accompanied by information about performance (see later in this chapter), drew their own didascalic information from sources that ultimately derived, however mediated through Aristotle, from the Athenian records.[14] Take, for example, this second sentence of a *hypothesis*, attributed to Aristophanes of Byzantium, to Euripides' *Hippolytus*:

> It was [first] produced (ἐδιδάχθη) during the archonship of Epameinon, in the fourth year of the 87th Olympiad [i.e., 429/8 BC]. Euripides came in first, Iophon second, Ion third. (Eur. *Hipp. hyp.* lines 25–7 Diggle)

Here the name of the archon, the play's premiere-date and the names of Euripides' competitors mark the sort of details that the Athenians' original records presumably noted.

The display of the *Fasti* on the Acropolis should also be contextualized as part of more widespread efforts made in this era to curate the city's theatrical heritage (on those efforts see also Duncan and Liapis in this volume).[15] That decision probably should be viewed in the context of the cultural programme undertaken by the politician Lycurgus in the 330s and 320s. Lycurgus, a contemporary of Aristotle's, steered a number of other initiatives directed at reorganizing the city's festivals and spotlighting its illustrious 'dramatic' history.[16] His most famous legacy is his sponsorship

---

[12] D. L. 5.26. Hesychius of Miletus' alternate title for the *Victories at the Dionysia* is *Victories at the City Dionysia and Lenaea* (Hsch. Mil. *Vita Aristotelis* 147). For Aristotle's work on Athenian theatre history see Blum 1991: 24–42, with 26–7 for Aristotle's reliance upon the Athenian records.
[13] Arist. *Ath. Pol.* 3.56; cf. Sickinger 1999: 43 and Millis and Olson 2012: 1.
[14] Cf. Pfeiffer 1968: 81.   [15] See esp. Hanink 2014b.
[16] For a survey of theatre reforms and management under Eubulus and Lycurgus (i.e., in the third quarter of the fourth century) see Csapo and Wilson 2014.

of a law aimed partially at ensuring the accurate preservation of the fifth-century tragic scripts.[17] According to Pseudo-Plutarch, the law ordered that bronze statues of the poets Aeschylus, Sophocles and Euripides be put up and that their tragedies be written down and kept publicly (ἐν κοινῷ γραψαμένους φυλάττειν), and that the city's secretary check them against (παραναγινώσκειν) the actors for the purpose of comparison.[18] ([Plu.] *Lives of the Ten Orators* 841f)

The bronze statues prescribed by the law were erected at the eastern *parodos* of the Theatre of Dionysus as adornments to the new theatre building.[19] Even in the fifth century many of the playwrights who competed at the city's theatre festivals (such as Pratinas of Phlius, Achaeus of Eretria, Ion of Chios et al.) came from abroad, but the three now chosen to stand for the tragic tradition had all been Athenian citizens. For Lycurgus and his circle, the fifth century's Golden Age of Tragedy was necessarily and entirely an Athenian achievement. This early decision to seize upon Aeschylus, Sophocles and Euripides – a decision foreshadowed and partially determined by Aristophanes' *Frogs* – was largely responsible for the survival of works by those tragedians alone.

The Lycurgan law thus marked a truly watershed moment in the history of the dramatic texts. Not only did it signal the city's imprimatur upon a narrative of tragedy that bound the plays and playwrights to Athenian civic identity, it also called for the establishment of the first official copies of tragedies.[20] Though not fully fledged editions, these texts will have required some degree of editing, for the years since the tragedians' deaths had seen the 'Decree of Archinus' (403/2) institute the use of the Ionian alphabet in Athenian official documents.[21] Lycurgus' legislation also forbade actors from improvising with respect to the state scripts, and the 'Lycurgan recension' is therefore to be viewed as an attempt to prevent the entry of *further* 'histrionic interpolations' into the texts.[22] We can only

---

[17] For general discussions of the law see Scodel 2007 and Hanink 2014b: ch. 2.
[18] Pseudo-Plutarch glosses this last clause: 'for it was not allowed for these plays to be performed out of accordance with the official texts'.
[19] On the statues and their context in the theatre space see Papastamati-von Moock 2014. For an analysis of putative Roman copies of the Lycurgan originals see Zanker 1995: 43–57.
[20] On the law's significance for the tragic texts see esp. Wartelle 1971: 101–15; Battezzato 2003: 9–19; Prauscello 2006: 68–78.
[21] Finglass 2012: 11 underscores that this 'almost certainly did not involve a critical recension of the text'. Wartelle 1971: 110–12 discusses the implications for the texts – including confusion between ε and η, and ο and ω, which the old Attic alphabet did not distinguish. On the reform generally see D'Angour 1998–9.
[22] The authoritative study of such interpolations remains Page 1934; see now also Finglass 2015.

wonder who was called upon to produce the official versions of the scripts, and which credentials recommended them – were they actors, scholars or playwrights? Some tragedians active in this period descended from Aeschylus, Sophocles and Euripides, and may still have had access to family copies of their ancestors' works.[23] In any case, the Lycurgan texts were products of efforts that were highly political and of the *polis*: this early form of scholarship sought to preserve the authentic words of the fifth-century poets, but also to shore up Athens' status as the texts' rightful home and guardian.[24]

## Aristotle and the Scholarly Turn

During the Lycurgan era, Aristotle was also refining his theories of poetry and drama, some of which are preserved in the *Poetics* (on which see also the chapters by Dunn and by Duncan and Liapis in this volume). In its surviving form the *Poetics* is generally thought to date to Aristotle's 'second Athenian period', which began after he returned from Macedon in 335.[25] Despite the efforts underway in Athens to construct Attic tragedy as a phenomenon that belonged wholly to the city, this text famously makes no mention of dramatic festivals, nor does it in any way emphasize Athens' unique relationship with its tragic tradition.[26] Aristotle's aim was instead to construct a 'universal' and abstract account of drama and dramaturgy,[27] as part of a narrative which defined tragedy against other forms (epic, dithyramb, comedy, etc.) and explained the plays in terms of component parts: plot, character, diction, thought/meaning, spectacle and song.[28] The *Poetics* therefore omits detailed discussions of many other aspects – the gods, choral lyric,[29] contexts of theatrical production, etc. – that occupy scholars of tragedy today, and which had also interested earlier 'cultural commentators' such as Aristophanes and Plato. Nevertheless, the *Poetics* has enjoyed incomparable influence as an early work of tragic scholarship: it set literary-critical parameters and agendas for generations of subsequent

---

[23] See Sutton 1987a, with family trees of 'tragic' families.
[24] In the late fourth century, local historians of Attica (Atthidographers) used tragedy as a source for myths and legends; cf. Rusten 1982: 361–2.
[25] On the date of the *Poetics* see esp. Halliwell 1998: 324–30.   [26] Hall 1996.
[27] For Aristotle's 'universalizing' approach to poetry see M. Heath 1991 and 2009; Donini 1997.
[28] Arist. *Po.* 1450a9–10.
[29] The chorus is discussed only briefly at Arist. *Po.* 1456a25–32; cf. Mastronarde 2010a: 146 n. 116 with references.

scholars in antiquity and beyond, and even seems to have had an indirect hand in shaping the selection of Greek tragedies that survive to this day.[30] Despite its focus on tragic drama, the *Poetics* is enormously expansive in the range of material that it covers, from epic composition to figures of speech to grammatical morphology and beyond. From our vantage point it does therefore seem to herald, as Ford has described, 'the full arrival of literary criticism as a systematic map of all forms of literature (mimetic arts in words) and a technical account of how each achieves its particular effects'.[31] In view of the breadth of coverage, we might ask: what in the *Poetics* belongs most properly to the domain of tragic scholarship? Under this rubric we can place, for example, Aristotle's (frustratingly) brief accounts of the history and evolution of tragic drama (ch. 4), his taxonomies of tragic plot and character types (chs. 6–11), his classification of parts of a tragedy (prologue, *parodos*, etc., ch. 12) as well as his observations about the style of tragic poetry, both generally and with reference to individual tragedians (ch. 22).[32]

Aristotle is not the first, even to our knowledge, to comment on any of these areas.[33] Yet he is the first to do so systematically, and the first *not* to embed his observations in a dramatic framework of his own (such as a comedy, dialogue or rhetorical performance). In his era we do still find 'theories' of tragedy alluded to in comedy, fragments of which explicitly reflect upon the nature and purpose of tragic drama. A character in Antiphanes' *Poetry* laments the potted nature of tragic plots: tragic playwrights have it easier than comedians, he complains, because mythology has already written their *mythoi*.[34] On the other hand, the unknown speaker of a fragment of Timocles' *Women at the Dionysia* praises tragic spectatorship as a balm for daily distress: in viewing tragic characters

[30] About half of the tragedies that Aristotle mentions in the *Poetics* have survived. Montanari 2009 emphasizes the persistent influence of Aristotle (and the Peripatos) on ancient Aeschylean scholarship down to Didymus. For an overview of the history of interpretation of the *Poetics* see Halliwell 1992. Later playwrights mined its pages for prescriptive advice on their craft; for evidence that Menander was familiar with Aristotle's ideas see, e.g., Cinaglia 2014, Munteanu 2002 and Webster 1974: 59.

[31] Ford 2002: 251; cf. 20–2; cf. Pfeiffer 1968: 75. See also Depew 2007 on Aristotle's taxonomy of poetic genres and Nünlist 2009: 95–9 for its influences on later ancient scholarship.

[32] See Halliwell 1989: 165–75 for a concise account of Aristotle's treatment of tragedy in the *Poetics*.

[33] Cf. Russell 1981: 31: 'in much [of the *Poetics*] Aristotle is responding to predecessors – on the one hand, sophists and grammarians; on the other, Plato.' Hunter 2009a: 15 also notes that tragedy's development from lyric poetry/dithyramb is also assumed in *Frogs*; cf. Hunter 2009a: 20–2 for other ways in which *Frogs* anticipated Aristotelian ideas about tragedy.

[34] Antiphanes fr. 189 K.-A. See Handley 1985: 412–13 on similarities between Aristotle's ideas and the 'theory' expressed by Antiphanes' character.

## Scholars and Scholarship on Tragedy 331

experience utter ruin and the most extreme of hardships, we see our own sufferings pale in comparison. Tragedy thus affects both education (*paideusis*) and enchantment (*psychagōgia*).[35]

But again, Aristotle's treatise is our earliest text to contain a clear attempt at a definition of tragedy, and the first 'scientific' account of its effects: by arousing pity and fear, tragedy accomplishes the 'purgation' (*katharsis*) of those emotions. Many have seen in these words a response to the arguments made by Plato's Socrates about tragic drama's dangerous effects upon the souls of spectators.[36] Even so, Aristotle's account is not *sui generis*. The fifth-century sophist Gorgias of Sicilian Leontini celebrated the 'deceptive' power of tragic *mimesis*, claiming (according to Plutarch) that 'the deceiver is more correct (δικαιότερος) than the non-deceiver, and the deceived is wiser (σοφώτερος) than the one not deceived'.[37] In his *Encomium of Helen*, Gorgias had also identified the peculiar power of *logos* to inspire 'fearful shuddering, tearful pity and longing for grief' (φρίκη περίφοβος καὶ ἔλεος πολύδακρυς καὶ πόθος φιλοπενθής) whereby the soul experiences 'its own particular emotion' (ἴδιόν τι πάθημα).[38] Aristotle ascribes similar qualities specifically to tragedy,[39] but a real innovation lies in his use of this definition to launch an account and analysis of tragedy's constituent parts.

The *Poetics* thus marks the first surviving document of literary scholarship as we know it, that is, research undertaken for the explicit purpose of advancing and expanding knowledge.[40] In his *Discourse* on Homer, Dio Chrysostom indicates that Aristotle, 'with whom they say *kritikē* and *grammatikē* first began', was regarded in antiquity as the father of literary criticism and scholarship.[41] Aristotle's 'objective' observations in the *Poetics* are typically accompanied by aesthetic judgments: the chorus should act

---

[35] Timocles fr. 6 K.-A.; cf. Gutzwiller 2000: 112–13. Rosen 2012 reads the fragment as a comic parody of dramatic theory.
[36] For an overview see Halliwell (1984), who also discusses some of Plato and Aristotle's common ground.
[37] 82 B. 23 Diels-Kranz, *ap*. Plu. *Mor*. 15d (*De audiendis poetis*)=348c (*De gloria Atheniensium*).
[38] Gorg. *Hel*. 9; for discussion see Russell 1981: 22–4. For bibliography on Gorgias and his formulations of 'the contract between poet and audience, which constitutes dramatic illusion', see Hunter and Russell 2011: 78.
[39] Arist. *Po*. 1449b24–8.
[40] Aristotle probably never produced a critical edition of any classical text, though one source claims that he produced an *ekdosis* of the *Iliad*: see Pfeiffer 1968: 71.
[41] D. Chr. 53.1. Pfeiffer 1968: 67–74 notes the many problems with Dio's claim and discusses the nature of Aristotle's work on Homer, which Dio has in mind. On the term *grammatikē* see esp. Schenkeveld 1993 and later in this chapter; for *kritikē* see later in this chapter.

as a character 'not as in Euripides, but as in Sophocles';[42] Euripides' use of more obscure poetic language is in one instance to be preferred over Aeschylus' poetic straightforwardness (a notable reversal of the 'Aristophanic' view of the two poets' styles);[43] and the best kind of recognition (*anagnōrisis*) is one that brings about reversal (*peripeteia*).[44] At certain points Aristotle even seems to be writing with first-hand knowledge of theatrical spectatorship, which speaks against the common charge that he was bookish and ignorant about the realities of performance.[45] No armchair scholar himself, Aristotle did nevertheless provide a set of methods and frameworks and a lexicon of critical vocabulary that enabled successive generations to begin to pursue their own tragic scholarship in the comfort of schools, studies and libraries.

After the *Poetics*, the *Rhetoric* is our most important surviving source for Aristotle's study of tragedy; it is also the work in which he most often refers to fourth-century tragedians.[46] The *Poetics*, despite its ostensibly universalizing approach to poetry and to the classification of tragic plots, is conspicuously dominated by examples selected from the works of Sophocles, Euripides and (to a lesser extent) Aeschylus – the same three poets whose scripts were kept in the Athenian archive.[47] Four fourth-century tragedians (Astydamas II, Carcinus, Chaeremon and Theodectes) are mentioned, but in nearly every case it is only to reaffirm a point about plot or character that Aristotle has already made by means of a fifth-century example.[48] We do possess a clue as to why the fourth-century tragic playwrights receive more attention in the *Rhetoric*: in *Poetics* ch. 6 Aristotle observes that, whereas the 'old' tragedians (οἱ ἀρχαῖοι) portrayed characters who spoke 'like citizens' or 'in a civically minded way' (πολιτικῶς), contemporary playwrights (οἱ νῦν) produce characters who speak 'rhetorically' (ῥητορικῶς) (though see Carter in this volume on tragedy's 'rhetorical' nature in the fifth century, too).[49] In the portion of *Rhetoric* III dedicated to enthymemes, or schemata of rhetorical persuasion, the later

---

[42] Arist. *Po.* 1456a25–7.   [43] Arist. *Po.* 1458b17–24.
[44] Arist. *Po.* 1452a32–3. For Aristotle's 'favourite tragedies' as judged by his own criteria see White 1992.
[45] Cf., e.g., Baldry 1969; Hanink 2011; Sifakis 2013.
[46] On Aristotle and fourth-century tragedy see esp. Webster 1954; Kitto 1966; Karamanou 2011. The sole monograph on fourth-century tragedy is Xanthakis-Karamanos 1980.
[47] Cf. Green 1994: 50: 'Aristotle refers to five plays of Aeschylus, twelve of Sophocles and twenty of Euripides'.
[48] An exception is Aristotle's remark on Carcinus' poor staging of a play about Amphiaraus (*Po.* 1455a26–9), cf. Green 1990; Liapis and Stephanopoulos, this volume.
[49] Arist. *Po.* 1450b7–8; cf. Hunter 2009a: 43.

tragedians are cited more frequently than their predecessors to illustrate rhetorical principles.[50] Nevertheless, almost no trace of scholarly commentary upon these playwrights, who were enormously prolific and famous in their own time, survives outside of Aristotle. They are very occasionally referred to in Homeric and tragic scholia (on which see later in this chapter),[51] and Plutarch invokes the names of Astydamas and Carcinus, alongside those of Sophocles and Aeschylus, as bywords for Athens' great tragic tradition.[52] Yet fragments of Hellenistic scholarship are all but silent about them, and not until Athenaeus' eclectic third-century AD *Deipnosophists* do their names resurface in force.

## From the Athenian Archive to the Alexandrian Library

Aristotle's *Poetics* stands as the first great testament to the transformation of tragedy into an object of scholarly study. His work was carried on by the next generation of Peripatetics, who also undertook inquiries into tragedy's history, poetics and *mousikē* (an ancient category that included all aspects of song, music and dance).[53] The polymath and prodigious scholar Aristoxenus of Tarentum is said to have written monographs *On Tragic Dance* and *On the Tragic Poets* (on Aristoxenus as theoretician of dramatic music and dance see Griffith in this volume).[54] Heraclides of Pontus wrote a number of works on poets and poetry; these included *On Euripides and Sophocles* (three books) and *On the Three Tragedians* (one book).[55] Works *On Aeschylus* are attributed to Theophrastus, Aristotle's successor as head of the Lyceum in Athens,[56] and to Chamaeleon of Heraclea Pontica, another high-volume literary scholar and former student of Aristotle's.[57] Duris of Samos, a historian and tyrant, wrote further treatises *On Tragedy* and *On Euripides and Sophocles*.[58] Studies named for individual tragedians seem to reflect a general Peripatetic interest in biography, particularly in the kind of literary biography that mined an author's works for evidence of

---

[50] See Hanink 2014b: 204–7.
[51] The b-scholion to H. *Il.* 6.472 preserves a fragment of Astydamas' *Hector* (F 2), on which see Taplin 2009 and Liapis 2016; cf. also the scholion to Soph. *OC* 57.
[52] Plu. *Mor.* 349e (*On the Glory of the Athenians*).
[53] For tragic scholarship associated with the Peripatos esp. Wartelle 1971: 125–34. For an overview of Peripatetic scholarship generally see Pfeiffer 1968: 87–95. References to Peripatetic scholars in this chapter follow Wehrli's edition unless otherwise indicated.
[54] Cf. Aristoxenus fr. 103–12 and fr. 113–16, respectively.
[55] D. L. 5.88.3 = Heraclid. Pont. fr. 22.16 (Περὶ τῶν παρ' Εὐριπίδῃ καὶ Σοφοκλεῖ); D. L. 5.50.2 = Heraclid. Pont. fr. 22.17.
[56] D. L. 5.50.2.   [57] Chamaeleon fr. 39.
[58] *BNJ* 67 fr. 28 and 29; both fragments relate to music.

his personal experiences and qualities (Hunter 2009a: 105 put it well: 'for most of antiquity, "you are what you write" was a self-evident truism').[59] The surviving titles – surely only a small portion of the era's scholarship on tragedy – also imply that from early on the tragic scholarly agenda was centred upon the playwrights of Lycurgus' triad.[60] Nevertheless, more 'general' works (such as Duris' *On Tragedy* and Aristoxenus' *On the Tragic Poets* and *On Tragic Dance*) may well have engaged with contemporary theatrical trends.

Traces of work by late fourth- and early third-century Peripatetic scholars are fossilized in the tragic scholia, which contain occasional references to their opinions. In some instances, those opinions must have resulted from detailed exegetical work: the scholion to line 900 of Sophocles' *Oedipus at Colonus*, for example, deems that Praxiphanes of Mytilene, a pupil of Theophrastus (and an adversary of Callimachus), had proposed the best poetic interpretation of the verse.[61] The name of Dicaearchus of Messene, who in antiquity was credited with a book of Sophoclean and Euripidean *hypotheseis* as well as a work *On the Competitions at the Dionysia*, also appears in the scholia. In the twentieth century, a papyrus containing plot summaries of Euripides' plays (*PSI* 1286, nicknamed 'Tales from Euripides', after Charles and Mary Lamb's 1807 *Tales from Shakespeare*) was pronounced a collection of Dicaearchan *hypotheseis*. The attribution of these summaries remains controversial. Rusten argued that these summaries date to a later period, when the 'Alexandrian edition' (see later in this chapter) of Euripides' plays was in circulation; Liapis has elaborated the possibility that Dicaearchus was their ultimate source, if not the actual author.[62] More recently, Verhasselt (2015) concludes that these *hypotheseis* cannot be ascribed to the fourth century BC (and *a fortiori* not to our Dicaearchus), and revives an old hypothesis that the texts are

---

[59] Leo (1990 [1901]) 104–5 referred to the genre as Περὶ τοῦ δεῖνα; cf. Pfeiffer 1968: 146. The 'method' of inferring biographical information from a writer's output is so associated with Chamaeleon that it has come to be known as the 'Chamaeleontic method': on its origins see Arrighetti 1987: 141–59.

[60] Cf. Pfeiffer 1968: 204. The mid-Hellenistic Peripatetic biographer Satyrus also wrote a *Life of Euripides* in dialogue form; Schorn 2004 contains an edition and commentary. See later in this chapter about the tragedians' later *Vitae*.

[61] Σ *LRM ad* Soph. *OC* 900 = Praxiphanes fr. 23. On Praxiphanes and Callimachus see Pfeiffer 1968: 95.

[62] Rusten 1982, building on Zuntz 1955: 135–6; Liapis 2001: 321–8. For early mythographical scholarship based on plots of tragedies see van Rossum-Steenbeek 1998 (on *hypotheseis* on papyri, such as the 'Tales') and Cameron 2004: 58–9, with references to further ancient works.

owed to a second-century BC grammarian and pupil of Aristarchus – also named Dicaearchus (hence the confusion).[63]

Surer signs of Dicaearchus' own interests and investigations appear elsewhere: he is cited as the source of notices to the effect that Euripides' *Medea* was based on Neophron's;[64] Aristophanes' *Frogs* was reperformed in Athens after its premiere at the Lenaea festival of 405;[65] *Death of Ajax* was an alternate title for Sophocles' *Ajax*;[66] and in the year that *Oedipus Tyrannus* premiered, Sophocles was defeated by Philocles in the tragic competition.[67] Each of these valuable bits of information may well derive from Dicaearchus' own research into theatre history, and the preservation of such material in the scholia testifies to persistent interest – on the part of early scholars and later scholiasts alike – in the plays' original historical and performance contexts.

Scholars such as these also provided a link between the modes and methods of study developed in the ambit of the Athenian Peripatos and the early days of scholarship at the Library in Alexandria.[68] This library, really an entire complex (one thinks of a modern Institute for Advanced Study), aspired to be *the* centre for learning in the Greek world. Under the patronage of the Ptolemies, the scholars of the library undertook to assemble the Greek literary patrimony and to study it systematically and comprehensively. In the early third century Callimachus, a scholar-poet who worked at the library, compiled the *Pinakes*, a bibliographic register of the institution's extensive holdings. The work included brief biographies of authors (precursors to the surviving *Vitae*: see later in this chapter) as well as lists of their works; it filled 120 papyrus rolls – one indicator of the collection's massive and ever-increasing size.[69]

During the same era, in the reign of Ptolemy II Philadelphus (r. 282–246), the scholar-cum-tragic-poet Alexander Aetolus supposedly

---

[63] Verhasselt 2015.
[64] Arg. in Eur. *Med.* line 23–25 = Dicaearchus fr. 63 (62 Mirhady) = Arist. fr. 635 Rose: Aristotle claimed the same in his *Commentaries*. See Mirhady 2001: 134–5 for Dicaearchan testimonia preserved in scholia.
[65] Arg. in Ar. *Ran.* 44 = Dicaearchus fr. 84 (104 Mirhady); cf. Sommerstein 1993.
[66] Arg. in Soph. *Aj.* 12–13 = Dicaearchus fr. 79 (113 Mirhady).
[67] Soph. test. 39 Radt = Dicaearchus fr. 80 (101 Mirhady); cf. Soph. test. 40.Verhasselt 2015: 65 argues that the testimonium most likely derives from Dicaearchus' *On Dionysiac Contests* rather than from a hypothesis.
[68] Cf. Pfeiffer 1968: 95. Pfeiffer's account provoked much debate over the degree of influence and contact between Aristotle's school and Alexandria, see, e.g., Richardson 1993 with valuable material in the 'Discussion.' Demetrius of Phaleron may have embodied a critical bridge between Lycurgan Athens and Ptolemaic Alexandria: see Mossé 2000. For an overview of the library at Alexandria see Fraser 1972: 1.305–35.
[69] See Pfeiffer 1968: 127–34.

'corrected' the tragedies and satyr-plays (Lycophron, also a practicing tragedian, did the same for comedy).[70] A famous anecdote recounted by the physician Galen (second century AD) tells of how in later years the great bibliophile Ptolemy III Euergetes (r. 246–221) deceived the Athenians out of their official texts of the three great tragedians: under the pretence that the texts were merely to be copied he put down an exorbitant deposit – which he then happily forfeited.[71] Though perhaps of dubious truth, Galen's story is illuminating on two counts: first, it allegorizes a transfer of the centre of textual authority for the tragedians' works from Athens to Alexandria; second, it suggests that Athens had been successful in convincing other Greeks that the city's copies of the dramatic scripts were to be prized as the 'authorized' versions.

No document of early Alexandrian scholarship has been fully preserved, and any conclusions about work on tragedy in this period must be inferred from citations in the tragic scholia or by way of parallels with the better-documented case of Homer. We do not know to what extent scholars made editions and wrote commentaries upon tragedians other than the great three,[72] nor whether the surviving *corpora* of those fifth-century three were edited in their entirety. We can, however, surmise that the Alexandrians will have been preoccupied with authenticity, regarding both the ascription of plays to the correct poets as well as the genuineness of individual lines and passages (lines deemed spurious were retained in editions, but marked with critical signs).[73] One word for an 'edition' of a work was *diorthōsis*: this noun comes from the verb διορθόω, which literally means 'to make straight' (Hippocrates uses it of bone-setting) and hence 'to correct' or 'to restore' something to its original state. Tzetzes (n. 70), our source for Alexander Aetolus' and Lycophron's editorial work

---

[70] The source is John Tzetzes, who lived in Constantinople in the twelfth century AD (the text is most easily accessed in Kaibel 1899: *Prolegomenon* Pb I 19).
[71] Gal. *In Hippocratis epidemiarum* iii 17a.607.5–17 Wenkebach.
[72] See, e.g., Griffith 1977: 235 with 351 nn. 83–4 on the (thin) case for Ion and Achaeus' presence in the early canon.
[73] See Kovacs 2005: 386, with examples of imputed plays. The authenticity of the *Rhesus* is questioned in a *hypothesis* (Eur *Rh. hyp.* b Diggle; though the play was one of Euripides' 'select' ten: see later in this chapter); on the issue and for bibliography see Liapis 2012: lxvii–lxxv, who suggests that the play may have been authored by the famous fourth-century actor Neoptolemus. The *Life of Euripides* declares the (now lost) *Tennes, Rhadamanthys* and *Perithous* to be inauthentic (the verb used is νοθεύομαι): Eur. test. A1.IA.9 Kannicht. Aristophanes of Byzantium supposedly deemed 17 of Sophocles' 130 plays spurious: Soph. test. A1.18 Radt = Aristophanes of Byzantium test. 385 Slater.

## Scholars and Scholarship on Tragedy 337

reports that the pair 'corrected' the dramatic texts (τὰς σκηνικὰς διώρθωσαν βίβλους);[74] one wonders whether they would have worked alone or collaboratively, even with help from assistants or pupils. Editors explained their decisions, recorded variant readings, offered explanations of difficult words and passages, and provided supplemental mythological and historical information in commentaries (*hypomnēmata*), which were written on separate scrolls.[75] If Alexander Aetolus himself produced commentaries as a complement to his 'restorative' work on the tragic texts, no remnants of them survive.

Aristophanes of Byzantium, who assumed the post of head librarian early in the second century BC, is the first Alexandrian scholar of tragedy about whose work we can speculate in some detail.[76] He is thought to have created an edition of tragedy, the so-called 'Alexandrian edition', but Finglass rightly cautions that there is no direct evidence for this.[77] We might nevertheless pause to imagine what virtues might have characterized such an edition, which Zuntz called 'the fountainhead of the whole subsequent tradition'.[78] If there is any truth to Galen's story about Ptolemy Euergetes' bibliomania, Aristophanes' work on tragedy will have profited from the addition to the library of Athens' Lycurgan texts. An edition by Aristophanes will also have benefitted from his pioneering use of accentuation and breathing marks, as well as his innovations in (though perhaps not invention of) lyric colometry, i.e., the division of lyric passages into separate lines according to metrical units.[79] A notoriously vexed question, discussed at length in this volume by Griffith, is whether scholars of this era had access to tragedies' original musical scores, or if their analyses were based exclusively on a theoretical understanding of metre.[80] We also do not know to what extent someone such as

---

[74] For the terms used of editions (ἐκδόσεις; διορθώσεις) and 'formally independent commentaries' (ὑπομνήματα) see Fraser 1972: 647–8 n. 3. For insight into the mechanics of Alexandrian edition-making see esp. Montanari 2011.

[75] Perrone 2009: 205–6 and McNamee 2007: 32–6 provide succinct accounts of the characteristics of Alexandrian *hypomnēmata*.

[76] For Aristophanes of Byzantium's work on tragedy see esp. Kovacs 2005: 384–6 and Wartelle 1971: 143–61.

[77] Finglass 2012: 12.

[78] Zuntz 1965: 249; at 249–51 he discusses instructive cases in which pre-Alexandrian papyri reveal a sense of the confusion and errors which the edition corrected.

[79] Lyric passages were once written continuously, but Aristophanes may not have been the first to divide them: cf. Reynolds and Wilson 2013: 15. See also Pfeiffer 1968: 188–9. Battezzato 2008 provides a useful introduction to the subject, with practical examples.

[80] This question is the subject of intense debate; Fleming 1999 provides an overview of previous opinions and argues for optimism about the long survival of notation, but Prauscello 2006 makes a detailed and important case for scepticism.

Aristophanes had first-hand experience of tragic performances, though comments attributed to him do touch upon aspects of staging.[81] For example, the Aristophanic *hypothesis* to Euripides' *Orestes* observes that the play begins with Electra ministering to Orestes and sitting at his feet. It continues: 'One is at a loss as to why she does not sit by his head: surely she would better look after her brother by sitting closer to him. But the poet likely did this to accommodate the chorus'.[82] Athenaeus' *Deipnosophists* also preserves a reference to Aristophanes' treatise *On Theatrical Masks* (Περὶ προσώπων).[83] All of this does suggest that Aristophanes attempted to engage with and to preserve knowledge about aspects of tragic drama which transcended the poetry on the papyrus.

The *hypotheseis* attributed to Aristophanes (such as the one to Euripides' *Hippolytus*, excerpted earlier in this chapter) tend to give information along the following lines:

1) A concise account of what happens in the play
2) Indications of which other playwrights (if any) treated the same material
3) Where the play is set
4) Didascalic information
5) Identifications of the chorus and the character who delivers the Prologue[84]

The *hypotheseis* and scholia also preserve references to opinions of Aristophanes which together allow us some idea of his framework for literary criticism. We find, for example, judgments as to the overall quality of certain plays: Euripides' *Hippolytus* is 'one of the best' (τῶν πρώτων) but his *Andromache* is 'of the second rank' (τῶν δευτέρων, i.e., the next-best

---

[81] Performances of old tragedies continued into this period in Alexandria; Falkner 2002 discusses how the worlds of the scholar and the actor potentially overlapped. Prauscello 2006: 118 rightly cautions that the scenic and Alexandrian scholarly tragic traditions may not have been as distinct as we often presume.
[82] Eur. *Or. hyp.* lines 35–40 Diggle = Arg. 2c Mastronarde 2010b. A scholion to the play (*MTAB ad* 279) also records an amusing anecdote about an acting mishap at the play's premiere.
[83] Mentioned *ap.* Ath. 14.695a = Aristophanes of Byzantium F 373 Slater.
[84] Trendelenburg 1867: 4–5; cf. *EM s.v.* πίναξ. For overviews of the *hypotheseis* and Aristophanes' scholarly work see also Schneidewin 1852; C.H. Moore 1901; the series of studies by Achelis 1913a; 1913b; 1914; Pfeiffer 1968: 192–6; Dickey 2007: 92–4. Kovacs 2005: 385 notes that whether these texts were 'intended to be prefixed to the plays in his edition or to stand alone in the commentary volume is unclear'. See also Bing 2011, who reads the Euripidean *hypotheseis* as signs of the poet's widespread popularity and Mossman 2010, on both the relation of the *hypotheseis* (Aristophanic and otherwise) to Euripidean prologues and their potential use in rhetorical training.

class – i.e., *not* English's more pejorative 'second rate'). In the latter case we receive this justification for the relatively positive judgment:

> The prologue is delivered clearly and eloquently. The elegies in Andromache's lament are also done well (εὖ). In the second part, Hermione's *rhēsis* on royalty and her speech to Andromache are not bad (οὐ κακῶς ἔχων). And Peleus also does well (εὖ) in rescuing Andromache.

Euripides' *Alcestis* and *Orestes* both receive criticism in the Aristophanic *hypotheseis* on account of their endings: that of *Alcestis* is 'more [properly] satyric', while *Orestes* concludes in a 'more [properly] comic' way.[85] The *hypothesis* to *Orestes* further notes that, although the play was popular on stage, it is 'terrible in terms of its characters (χείριστον δὲ τοῖς ἤθεσι): all of them except for Pylades are unsavoury (φαῦλοι)'.[86] Criticism elsewhere in the scholia does show considerable interest in the poets' adherence to the constraints of tragic 'decorum' (τὸ πρέπον), or the appropriateness of lines both to the character who delivers them (i.e., whether the utterance is οἰκεῖον, 'suited to' him or her[87]) and to tragic drama generally.[88] In *Poetics* chapter 2, Aristotle had explained that tragic characters ought to be 'better' than people are in real life, and the scholiasts tended to agree.[89] One was accordingly glad to see the Polyxena of Euripides' *Hecuba* preserve her 'heroic character' (τὸ ἡρωικὸν ἦθος, schol. MA ad 342) when she gives a speech accepting her fate. On the other hand, a comment upon his *Phoenissae* (*MAB ad* 1539) finds fault with the wretched appearance of Oedipus at the end of the play: 'Euripides always makes everyone a beggar, and now Oedipus has no one to guide him, even in his own country!' The adjective used of Euripides, 'beggar-maker' (πτωχοποιός), is an insulting label with which 'Aeschylus' had branded Euripides in Aristophanes' *Frogs*.[90]

---

[85] Eur. *Alc. hyp.* line 24 Diggle; *Or. hyp.* line 2 Diggle = Arg. 2c Mastronarde 2010b. For reactions of ancient commentators against such violations of 'tragic sublimity' see esp. Fantuzzi 2014. Cf. Arist. *Po.* 1453a33–9: the pleasure of plot resolutions that turn out badly for bad characters and well for the good is more 'appropriate to' (οἰκεία) comedy, where even the bitterest of enemies depart as friends (φίλοι).

[86] *Or. hyp.* lines 43–4 Diggle = Arg. 2d Mastronarde 2010b, cf. Arist. *Po.* 1449a32: it is comedy that more properly treats of characters who are base (φαῦλοι).

[87] Cf. Arist. *Po.* 1461a4–9. For the use of τὸ πρέπον and τὸ οἰκεῖον as near-synonyms see Plu. *Mor.* 853d (*Comparison of Aristophanes and Menander*) and Dio 12.52. See too Hunter 2009a: 32–6 for a discussion of Euripides and the *oikeion*, with *oikeion* understood in its other important sense, namely as related to an 'everyday' style that used ordinary words and avoided metaphor and other rhetorical constructions.

[88] For discussion of the term πρέπον and the related term καιρός ('opportuneness') see Ford 2002: 16–21, who observes that terms such as these are slippery: 'The *prepon* or *kairos* names a central but unsystematizable value for which one must have a "nose"' (20).

[89] Arist. *Po.* 1448a17–18; cf. Fantuzzi 2014.   [90] Ar. *Ran.* 842.

His *Acharnians* had even featured an entire scene dedicated to the premise: in need of rags for his own 'tragic' performance, Dicaeopolis turns up at Euripides' house to borrow a beggar's costume from an old production.[91] It is admittedly impossible to know which anonymous opinions in the scholia had their origins in Aristophanes of Byzantium (and to what extent the citations and *hypotheseis* are genuine),[92] and a comprehensive account of his work on tragedy is still to be desired. Nevertheless, the *hypotheseis* and scholia do offer a panorama of varied Alexandrian interests in and research on tragedy, and a glimpse into certain persistent aesthetic and literary-critical orientations.

Legend has it that Aristophanes of Byzantium was thrown into prison as a means of preventing King Eumenes from poaching him for the Attalid library at Pergamum.[93] The king finally managed to fill the post with Crates of Mallus, a contemporary of Aristarchus, Aristophanes' pupil and successor in Alexandria.[94] We know less about the scholarship (and still less about the tragic scholarship) carried out in this rival library, where some of the scholars were dubbed 'critics' (κριτικοί) as opposed to the Alexandrian 'philologists' (φιλόλογοι) and grammarians (γραμματικοί).[95] As scholars working in a Stoic tradition their methods and interests differed somewhat from those at Alexandria: they pursued allegorical interpretations,[96] placed a premium upon poetic euphony (the pleasantness of sounds) and favoured 'anomaly' over analogy (reliance upon parallels) in their correction of texts.[97] Like all great ancient editor-librarians, Crates dedicated himself to the Homeric texts, but tragic scholia also preserve a few of his observations upon plays of Euripides (*Orestes*,

---

[91] Ar. *Ach.* 393–489.
[92] Scholia which explicitly cite Aristophanes of Byzantium are collected as frr. 385–402 in W. J. Slater (1986), who does not include the *hypotheseis* attributed to him.
[93] *Suda* a.3936 (*s.v.* Ἀριστώνυμος, an ancient error).
[94] Aristarchus probably based his own tragic commentaries on his teacher's edition: we have evidence of his work on Aeschylus' *Lycurgus* tetralogy (Σ *ad* Theoc. 10.18e: cf. Wartelle (1971) 164–5) as well as on a few Sophoclean and Euripidean plays; see Finglass (2012) 12 and Tuilier (1968) 62–6, respectively.
[95] Cf. Pfeiffer 1968: 159.
[96] For an example of scholia (not necessarily Pergamene in origin) that preserve allegorical readings of tragic poetry see Hunter 2009b, a discussion of the scholia to Eur. *Hipp.* 73–87.
[97] See esp. Janko 2000: 120–7, Porter 1995 – a full reappraisal of the evidence for the *kritikoi* – and Pfeiffer 1968: 156–9 (Eratosthenes coined the term φιλόλογος in Alexandria). On Pergamene scholarship generally see Nagy (1998) and Sandys (1903) 144–62.

*Phoenissae* and *Rhesus*).[98] It is unsurprising that Crates should have been most interested in Euripides, a perennial favourite among the Stoics.[99]

## Rome and Back Again

Crates was famed in antiquity as the first to introduce the Greek study of grammar to Rome. During an ambassadorial mission there he fell into an open sewer on the Palatine, broke his leg, and kept himself busy while he convalesced by delivering a series of lectures.[100] In the next century, the immensely prolific Alexandrian scholar Didymus served as another potential conduit of Greek learning. In Alexandria he composed works *On Tragic Vocabulary* and *On Comic Vocabulary*; he also must have written a number of commentaries, given the scores of references in the scholia to his opinions[101] – not to mention his own staggering rate of production (he was reputed to have written some 3,500 books).[102] Didymus' great contribution was to compile the results of earlier Alexandrian literary scholarship, which he supplemented with further historical and mythological information, often to discredit Euripidean versions of stories. Of the tragedians he preferred Sophocles,[103] and his negative judgments of Euripides only served to exacerbate the hostile line of criticism that is curiously forceful in the Euripidean scholia (no other poet is so great an object of his own ancient commentators' disdain).[104] Scholia betray Didymus' especial irritation at Euripides' anachronisms,[105] as well as his characters' failure to speak in ways appropriate to their gender and status.[106] He was also attentive to the tragedians' consistency with Homer, and

---

[98] Σ *ad.* Eur. *Or.* 1233; *Ph.* 208; *Rh.* 5 and 528. *Orestes* and *Phoenissae* both belong to Euripides' Byzantine triad (see later in this chapter), but the scholia to the third play in the triad, *Hecuba*, preserve no mention of Crates.

[99] The third-century Stoic philosopher Chrysippus was notorious for citing Euripides excessively: D. L. 7.180.

[100] Suet. *De Gramm.* 2.1.

[101] The *subscriptio* at the end of Euripides' *Medea* in ms. B claims that the scribe was working from 'various copies (ἀντίγραφα) of Dionysius and an entire one [*sc.* commentary] of Didymus'. This Dionysius is a mysterious figure: cf. Kovacs 2005: 386.

[102] Ath. 4.139c, who reports that he was nicknamed 'Book-forgetter' (*Bibliolathas*) because he could not recall all that he had written; cf. *Suda* δ.872. On Didymus' work on tragedy see Wartelle 1971: 185–95 (with a focus on Aeschylus), Zuntz 1965: 253–4. Pfeiffer 1968: 277–8, Trendelenburg 1867: 56–8. Didymus tended to blame suspected interpolations on actors: Zuntz 1965: 254 n.†; cf. Finglass 2015.

[103] Cf. Pfeiffer 1968: 277.

[104] Elsperger 1906: 108–27 collects Didymus' negative criticisms of Euripides. For a brief overview of ancient criticism's hostile stance towards Euripides see Mastronarde 2010a: 3–4; cf. also Fantuzzi 2014.

[105] Trendelenburg 1867: 64–7; Elsperger 1906: 147–52.   [106] Elsperger 1906: 33–54.

points of Homeric cross-reference are often indicated in our tragic manuscripts with the letter χ.[107]

The *Suda* claims that Didymus 'was born in the era of Antony and Cicero, and lived until the time of Augustus'.[108] His lifetime thus ran roughly parallel to that of King Iuba II of Mauretania, who as a child was paraded at Rome in Caesar's 'quadruple triumph' celebrating victory over, among other kings, Iuba's own father. Iuba II went on to become a member of the circle of Augustus and to enjoy a reputation as a most learned king and historian.[109] Among his many works was a treatise on theatre, the *Theatrical History* (Θεατρική ίστορία),[110] and today he is often regarded by theatre historians as one of their discipline's founders.[111] The meagre surviving fragments belong to the work's fourth book, and each has only to do with musical instruments and dance, i.e., with tragic *mousikē*.[112] Julius Pollux, who held the imperial 'Chair in Rhetoric' at the Academy in Athens in the second century AD, drew upon Iuba's *Theatrical History* in his own monument to antiquarianism, the ten-book *Onomasticon*, a thematically arranged lexicon of Attic words and phrases.[113] Its fourth book contains a section on the terminology of the theatre, arranged under headings (e.g., types of dance; actors' costumes, footwear and masks) that indicate a strong interest in performance.[114] Pollux's many sources included, in addition to Iuba, Didymus' lexica of tragic and comic words and Aristophanes of Byzantium's *On Theatrical Masks*.

Authors who lived between the lifetimes of Iuba and Pollux also exhibited an interest in how tragic drama had contributed to what today we would call 'cultural history', as classical tragedy came to be seen as a product and symbol of Athens' great yet faded achievement. Plutarch's *Lives* contain colourful vignettes set at celebrations of the Great Dionysia in the fifth and fourth centuries BC. In the *Life of Cimon* we hear of how Cimon, along with the other elected Athenian generals, once presided as

---

[107] Trendelenburg 1867: 67–9.   [108] *Suda* δ 872.
[109] For example, Plu. *Caes.* 55.3. On Iuba II of Mauretania see *BNJ* 275 and Roller 2006.
[110] Iuba II of Mauretania *BNJ* 275 fr. 15–19 and 80–6; cf. Roller (2006) 174–7. Amarantos of Alexandria's c. 100 AD work *On the Stage* (Περί σκηνής) mentioned Iuba: Ath. 8.343e–f = *BNJ* 275 fr. 104; cf. Roller 2006: 80–1.
[111] Schoch 2012 discusses how Iuba's treatise 'has been used to construct disciplinary myths of origin' in the field of theatre history (5).
[112] *BNJ* 275 fr. 15–17 and possibly 80–6.
[113] Rohde 1870: 33–5 for Iuba as the source behind Poll. 4.78–82, on *auloi* and auletic tunes; cf. *ibid.* 56–63 for Pollux's more general use of Iuba as a source. In the second century AD Palamedes also compiled a lexicon of tragic words, the λέξις τραγική: see Matthaios 2015: 241.
[114] See Csapo and Slater 1995: Appendix A for an introduction and English translation.

judge of the tragic contest: this was the contest at which Aeschylus is said to have grown so upset over losing to Sophocles that he decided to quit Athens for Sicily.[115] And when sycophants of Demetrius 'the Besieger' supposedly renamed the Dionysia the Demetria in the late fourth century BC, Athens suffered an unseasonable cold snap on the day of the festival's procession, and frost destroyed all the crops.[116] Plutarch is one of the first authors since the comic playwright Aristophanes to consider – as Aristotle famously had not – the role that tragedy and theatre festivals had played in the life of Athens.[117] In a comparison of the three great tragedians' *Philoctetes* plays, Plutarch's contemporary Dio Chrysostom delighted in imagining (as many of us still do) what it must have been like to be a spectator at the early Great Dionysia, and to judge for oneself the tragic choruses (on Dio and tragedy see Webb in this volume).[118] Though we tend to class either Plutarch or Dio as a 'scholar' of tragedy, their works open a window into how Athens' tragic heyday was understood and romanticized in the first century AD. For Dio, at least, 'modern' performances of old tragedy were disappointing: theatres still hosted performances of tragic dialogue (τὰ ἰαμβεῖα), but the lyric songs (τὰ μέλη) had fallen away (ἐξερρύηκε).[119]

Some writers thus took pleasure in envisioning what the Great Dionysia must have *looked* like and even what its atmosphere might have *felt* like, and Pollux, though a 'professor of rhetoric', also helps us to imagine the sights and sounds of ancient theatre through his descriptions of costume, scenery and song.[120] But with other authors of the Imperial Era (and even in other texts by Dio and Plutarch), the 'dramatic' element of dramatic poetry becomes largely effaced in the interest of rhetorical analysis.[121] For example, in his discussion of poetic 'imagery' (φαντασία), the author of *On the Sublime* (first century AD?) compares the three tragedians with an eye to how successfully they used poetry to convey the images of their imaginations (such as the furies in Euripides' *Orestes*, or Dionysus'

---

[115] Plu. *Cim.* 8.7–8; the *Vita Aeschyli* also reports the story: test. A.1.8 Radt.    [116] Plu. *Dem.* 12.
[117] In *On the Glory of the Athenians* Plutarch extensively faults the Athenians for having poured more resources into their tragic plays than into the military maintenance of their empire.
[118] Cf. Hunter 2009a: 39–48.    [119] Dio 19.5. See esp. Hunter 2009a: 15–16.
[120] See Porter (2005) on the desires of ancient audiences and critics to feel the presence of the 'classical'.
[121] A notable exception occurs at Demetr. *Eloc.* 195, where Demetrius describes the 'histrionic' possibilities offered by Eur. *Ion.* 160–9, part of a monody that Ion sings as he chases birds away from the Temple of Apollo: Demetrius claims that the 'configuration' (διαμόρφωσις) of the scene is 'made for the actor' (πρὸς τὸν ὑποκριτὴν πεποιημένη).

possession of Lycurgus' palace in Aeschylus' now-lost *Lycurgus* tetralogy).[122] 'Longinus' describes the effectiveness of this poetry in the context of recitation, not dramatic performance: the vividness (ἐνάργεια) of the verses causes 'listeners' (ἀκούουσιν) to 'think that they see' (βλέπειν δοκῇς) the events described. *Opsis* in this passage refers to the spectacle perceived not on the stage (the word's sense in Aristotle's *Poetics*) but rather in the mind's eye. Other teachers of rhetoric, such as Quintilian (first century BC), were most interested in what the aspiring orator might learn from each of the tragedians. Quintilian reserves judgment about the ultimate superiority of Sophocles or Euripides, but admits that 'Euripides will be much more useful for anyone preparing himself to speak in court'.[123] In the second century BC the Alexandrian Dionysius Thrax had defined *grammatikē* as 'familiarity with what is commonly said in the poets and prose writers',[124] and for later literary critics and rhetorical instructors the purpose of studying the ancient poets was to gain insight into rhetoric, 'style' and language. Though still used to illustrate aspects of those subjects, tragedy now no longer constituted a significant research field of its own.[125]

The use of tragedies as educational texts in the early centuries of the Roman era is clearly borne out by the kinds of orations, letters and treatises discussed by Webb in this volume; tragedy's perceived 'instructional' value is also documented by papyrus finds from Egypt.[126] These indicate, as Cribiore has observed, that 'members of the cultivated public were very fond of Euripides; they read Aeschylus rarely, and Sophocles even more infrequently'.[127] Euripides was the most popular author after Homer in schools,[128] and his *Phoenissae* was the most widely read play of all.[129] Additional tragedies that are well represented in the Egyptian papyri (e.g., *Medea, Orestes, Bacchae*[130]) also belong to the 'canon' of ten Euripidean

---

[122] [Longin.] 15.2–3; see Hunter 2009a: 30–1.
[123] Quint. *Inst.* 10.1.67 (the tragedians are discussed at 66–9), cf. D. H. fr. 31.2.11, from *On Imitation*, which bears many similarities to Quint. 10.1.46–84: cf. Bonner 1939: 39. Quintilian's advice represents a practical extension of the old and entrenched view of the 'usefulness' of Euripidean poetry (cf., e.g., Ar. *Ran.* 971–8); on such ideas and their influence upon subsequent literary criticism see Hunter 2009a: 17–25.
[124] D. T. 629b Uhlig.
[125] Cf., e.g., D. H. *Comp.* and Plutarch's triad of educational treatises: *On the Education of Children, How to Listen to Poetry* and *On Listening to Lectures*. Hunter and Russell 2011: 2–17 provide a survey of Plutarch's views on poetry and pedagogy. Morgan 1998: Table 19 quantifies the citations of Greek authors (including Sophocles and Euripides) in rhetorical treatises of the Imperial era.
[126] Authors in annotated papyri are generally the same as those recommended by rhetoricians such as Quintilian: McNamee 2007: 56–8.
[127] Cribiore 2001a: 198. [128] Cf. Morgan 1998: Table 15.
[129] Cribiore 2001a: 198–9 and 2001b with bibliography. [130] Morgan 1998: Table 22.

plays that were singled out for reading and study in later antiquity – perhaps as the medium of textual transmission shifted from papyrus roll to codex, between the second and fourth centuries AD.[131] Some of these papyri preserve marginal scholia and interlinear glosses and notes,[132] the character of which is generally similar to that of the scholia in the manuscripts.[133] Euripides' other surviving plays, whose titles all begin with ε, ι or κ, come down to us by chance in a single early fourteenth-century manuscript (Laurentianus 32.2). These so-called 'alphabetic plays' were copied without scholia from an (alphabetically arranged) exemplar of Euripides' 'complete works'. Despite Euripides' predominance on the ground in this period, the symposiasts of Athenaeus of Naucratis' *Deipnosophists* (second/third century AD) still cite a variety of dramatic fragments, many of which are credited to lost playwrights of both the fifth and later centuries. A range of tragic texts was therefore still in circulation, even if those texts were now largely reduced to excerpts gathered in anthologies and gnomological collections.[134]

## Tragic Scholia and Tragedians' *Lives*

The *corpora* of ancient tragic scholia (*scholia vetera*) that survive in medieval manuscripts constitute, from our perspective, accumulated end-products of centuries of ancient scholarship on the plays of Aeschylus, Sophocles and Euripides. The early compilers of scholia (from Greek σχόλιον: a 'comment' or 'short note') consolidated information from a variety of resources in a process that involved, as Montana describes, 'selective *transfer* of a multifaceted array of ancient erudite materials (*hypomnēmata, syngrammata* [i.e., monographs], *lexeis* and so on) into the margins of the editions of literary texts'.[135] Scholia were copied into

---

[131] See esp. Reynolds and Wilson 2013: 34–7.
[132] These are collected in McNamee 2007: 131–6 (Aeschylus), 253–7 (Euripides) and 362–71 (Sophocles).
[133] Maehler 1993 and McNamee 2007: 127–8. Correspondences are not exact, and notes in papyri tend to be shorter than their respective scholia. Perrone 2009 discusses papyrus scholia and commentaries to *adespota* plays. The ongoing *Commentaria et lexica graeca in papyris reperta* (*CLGPR*) aims to produce a comprehensive *corpus*; Part I Vol. 1 fasc. 1 (Bastianini et al. 2004) includes the Aeschylean *commentaria*; we await Euripides (Vol. 2) and Sophocles (Vol. 4). Athanassiou 1999, an unpublished UCL PhD thesis, does collect marginalia and commentaries in papyri of Sophocles and Euripides (and Aristophanes).
[134] On the development of poetic anthologies – another large source of tragic fragments – see Hunter and Russell 2009: 15–16.
[135] Montana 2011: 110–11, who provides an excellent account of 'the making of Greek scholiastic *corpora*'; see also the brief overview of Mastronarde 2010b: 'Home'.

the marginal space around the ancient texts (again, commentaries had first been written on rolls separate from editions). This new combined and condensed format was a direct result of the hugely significant transition in late antiquity from the roll to the bound codex: *corpora* of scholia were amassed in about the same period (fifth–sixth century AD, the first centuries of the Byzantine Empire) that saw the codex completely replace the roll as the standard book format.[136] The scholia themselves cite scholars from the fourth century BC to the early Common Era.

Because *corpora* of scholia contain so many accreted layers of ancient learning, it is often difficult or impossible to identify the ultimate sources of their judgments and information.[137] Even in cases for which a source is explicitly named we often must doubt how *much* of the material really derives from that particular scholar. The *hypotheseis* ascribed to Aristophanes of Byzantium were altered, augmented and in some cases almost certainly written by others, but still retain their single attribution to him in the manuscripts. Yet studies in recent years have begun to examine collections of scholia holistically with a view to what light they shed upon ancient practices of reading and literary criticism.[138] To give but one example, Papadopoulou has identified tension in tragic scholia between two ideas about the nature of poetic fiction and license (πλάσμα): one line of thought sees fiction as dishonest (Euripides himself is frequently charged with 'lying' in the Euripidean scholia) whereas another regards it as a marker of creativity and 'part of the poet's job'.[139] Scholia have also come to be mined for information about ancient approaches to performance history and practice. Nünlist devotes the last chapter of his pathbreaking *The Ancient Critic at Work* to questions of 'staging, performance and dramaturgy'. He highlights the considerable efforts that scholars made to understand practical issues such as entrances, exits and who delivered which lines, but also to think about the nontextual, 'embodied' aspects of performance (e.g., gesture, posture and acting 'method')[140] and the physical *Realien* of dramatic production (masks, props, the crane and *ekkyklēma*, etc.). Like Pollux's *Onomasticon*, the scholia are not an immensely reliable source for tragic performance in classical Athens, but are more

---

[136] Roberts and Skeat 1983.  [137] This difficulty is outlined by Nünlist 2009: esp. 4 and 18–19.
[138] See esp. Nünlist 2009, with references to earlier work at 1 n. 4, and with specific regard to tragic scholia; Easterling 2006, with a bibliography of previous work in this area at 21–2 nn. 4–5.
[139] Papadopoulou 1998–9: 203. Easterling 2015 is an illuminating exploration of how the scholiasts imagined tragedy's performative space, especially in the case of Sophocles' *Ajax*.
[140] Sifakis 2002 also discusses Aristotle's works as a source for 'the actor's art'; Aristotle's comments on contemporary acting practice (in the fourth century) may also have influenced the scholia.

## Scholars and Scholarship on Tragedy 347

illuminating of later (ideas about) theatrical practice. They also happen to serve as an encouraging reminder that early scholars, too, struggled in their attempts at recovering and visualizing the experience of tragic performance in the fifth-century Theatre of Dionysus.

The collections of tragic scholia are not as rich as the *corpora* for Homer, Pindar and Aristophanes; those other traditions are, however, also valuable for tragic scholarship. They contain many references to, citations of and comparisons with works by the three tragedians (the particular take of the Aristophanic scholia upon the tragedians – especially Euripides – would be one fruitful line of future enquiry). Dickey has now provided an excellent and clear overview of the surviving scholia for the three tragedians, as well as the nature and extent of their usefulness. Only a few of the points which she covers can be rehearsed here.[141] It should be highlighted, for example, that tragic scholia have been particularly helpful to textual critics, as they often preserve readings preferable to those which have come down in the manuscripts.[142] Later Byzantine scholarship and scholia (which lie beyond the scope of this overview) are most copious for plays that belonged to each tragedian's 'Byzantine triad', the three texts most studied and taught in schools.[143] This vast tradition culminates in the work of late medieval (thirteenth–fourteenth century AD) scholars, principally Thomas Magister, Maximus Planudes, Manuel Moschopoulos and Demetrius Triclinius, and offers great insight into the state of the tragic texts and the preoccupations of scholarship in that period;[144] Byzantine metrical work (especially by Triclinius) has proven particularly useful for analyses of tragedy's lyric parts. From the perspective of intellectual history, this scholarship is also of immense interest – and perhaps under-exploited potential – because it dates to an era not long before Greek learning started to make its way once more to an eager public in Italy: at the close of the fourteenth century, in 1397, Manuel Chrysoloras accepted an invitation from the University of Florence to deliver lectures there on Greek literature.[145] Just over a century

---

[141] Dickey 2007: 31–8, arranged by tragedian with extensive (and usefully annotated) bibliography; ch. 6 consists in a useful 'Glossary of Grammatical Terms' that are used in the scholia but which are not always fully explained in modern dictionaries of Ancient Greek.

[142] Tuilier 1972 compares the transmitted texts and the readings preserved in scholia.

[143] Aeschylus: *Persians, Seven Against Thebes, Prometheus*; Sophocles: *Ajax, Electra, Oedipus Tyrannus*; Euripides: *Hecuba, Orestes, Phoenissae*. In some cases, it is difficult to distinguish Byzantine from ancient scholia.

[144] See also Papaioannou 2013: 115–17 on the work of Michael Psellos (eleventh century): 'Among middle Byzantine writers, Psellos is the first to devote considerable critical energy to the discussion of ancient drama.' A work *On Tragedy* has been transmitted under Psellos' name: see Perusino 1993.

[145] For a concise account see Reeve 1996: 32–4.

after that, the first printed editions of the tragic playwrights began to appear with the Aldine Press in Venice.[146]

It is mostly the Byzantine manuscripts that preserve for us short texts on the 'life' (βίος) or 'origins and life' (γένος καὶ βίος) of each of the three tragedians;[147] these biographies are known as *Vitae*. Those of Sophocles and Euripides may be the product of Byzantine scholars, but they also cite earlier and in some cases Alexandrian authorities.[148] The tragedians' *Vitae* evolved in parallel with each other;[149] it seems that they contain little reliable information about the poets' lives.[150] Nevertheless, in some cases they have had a strong hand in shaping the preoccupations of modern scholarship. Their claims that Euripides was forced into a self-imposed 'exile' in Macedon due to his poor treatment in Athens, and that after Aeschylus died a decree was passed granting choruses to anyone who wished to put on his plays, have influenced contemporary accounts of classical tragedy; these stories, however, are more likely products of biographers' imaginations.[151] The picture that Euripides' *Vita* paints of the poet as a reclusive misanthropist also seems to be mostly derived from Aristophanes' comic representations of him, and complements the more antagonistic tone of the Euripidean scholia. The *Vita Aeschyli*, on the other hand, champions its subject: Aeschylus 'adorned' the *opsis* of tragedy, and it was he – not, as Dicaearchus (and perhaps Aristotle) had claimed, Sophocles – who 'discovered' the third actor.[152] Here we find another likely debt to early comic discourse, particularly in the assertion made by the *Vita* that Aeschylus 'first augmented tragedy with most noble sufferings'.[153]

Even the tragedians' *Vitae*, then, attest to the longstanding interest in the performative aspects of drama. These *Vitae* (and those of other ancient poets) are important documents in the history of reception, and are

---

[146] Sophocles (ed. A. Manutius?) in 1502, Euripides (ed. A. Manutius?) in 1503, Aeschylus (ed. F. Asulanus) in 1518. McCall (1985) discusses the sources used to create the Aldine text of Aeschylus' *Supplices*.
[147] Aeschylus test. A1 Radt (βίος), Sophocles test. A1 Radt (γένος καὶ βίος); Euripides test. A1 IA–III Kannicht (γένος καὶ βίος).
[148] Hanink 2008: 121 discusses the Hellenistic sources used by the *Vita Euripidis*.
[149] Hanink 2010: 59–60.
[150] See Lefkowitz 2012: chs. 7–9 and Appendices 3–5 for English translations of the *Vitae*.
[151] Scullion 2003 and Hanink 2008; Biles 2006–7 respectively.
[152] Aesch. test. A1.15 Radt, preserving Dicaearchus fr. 76 (100 Mirhady); cf. Arist. *Po.* 1449a18–19 (though see Brown (1984) for the position that this phrase of the *Poetics* was not written by Aristotle).
[153] Or 'most noble emotions': πάθεσι γεννικωτάτοις, Aesch. test. A1.14 Radt. In *Frogs* 'Aeschylus' harps on his poetry's power to 'ennoble' its audience: cf. esp. 1006–44.

Scholars and Scholarship on Tragedy 349

currently becoming more accessible thanks to the efforts of the *Living Poets* project based at Durham University.[154] New digital formats such as XML are also proving especially useful as platforms for such 'layered' material as *Vitae* and scholia. Mastronarde's on-going *Euripides Scholia* project will eventually also allow open access to comprehensive *corpora* of the Euripidean scholia, different strata of which (e.g., the *scholia vetera* vs. the Byzantine scholia) can be isolated onscreen.[155] The new editions of tragic scholia that have appeared in recent years have also benefitted from the development of imaging techniques that use ultraviolet light ('Wood's lamp'); in some cases this technology has led to new and more accurate readings of the marginalia preserved in the manuscripts.[156] Thus even today we continue to discover ever more ancient material, which happily means that new chapters in the study of classical tragedy – and in the history of ancient tragic scholarship – still remain to be written.

---

[154] Livingpoets.dur.ac.uk, a project headed by Barbara Graziosi.   [155] Mastronarde 2010b.
[156] Merro 2008, on the scholia to Euripides' *Rhesus*, and Xenis 2010a and 2010b, on the scholia to Sophocles' *Electra* and *Trachiniae* respectively. Janz 2005, an unpublished Oxford DPhil thesis, is an edition of scholia to Sophocles' *Philoctetes*.

# Bibliography

Achelis, T. O. H. (1913a) 'De Aristophanis Byzantii argumentis fabularum I', *Philologus* 72: 414–41.
　(1913b) 'De Aristophanis Byzantii argumentis fabularum II', *Philologus* 72: 518–45.
　(1914) 'De Aristophanis Byzantii argumentis fabularum III', *Philologus* 73: 122–53.
Acosta-Hughes, B. (2012) '"Nor when a man goes to Dionysus' holy contests" (Theocritus 17.112): outlines of theatrical performance in Theocritus', in *Theatre Outside Athens: Drama in Greek Sicily and South Italy*, ed. K. Bosher. Cambridge: 391–408.
Adam-Veleni, P. (2010) Θέατρο και θέαμα στην αρχαία Μακεδονία [*Theatre and Spectacle in Ancient Macedon*]. Thessaloniki.
Allan, D. J. (1980) 'ΑΝΑΓΙΓΝΩΣΚΩ and some cognate words', *CQ* 30: 244–51.
Allan, W. (2000) *The Andromache and Euripidean Tragedy*. Oxford.
　(2001) 'Euripides in Megale Hellas: some aspects of the early reception of tragedy', *G&R* 48: 67–86.
　(2004) 'Religious syncretism: the new gods of Greek tragedy', *HSCP* 102: 113–55.
　(2008) *Euripides: Helen*. Cambridge.
Allen, J. (2007) 'Ezekiel the tragedian on the despoliation of Egypt', *Journal for the Study of the Pseudepigrapha* 17.1: 3–19.
Ameling, W. (2008) 'Die jüdische Gemeinde von Leontopolis nach den Inschriften', in *Die Septuaginta: Texte, Kontexte, Lebenswelten*, ed. M. Karrer and W. Kraus. Tübingen: 117–33.
Amiotti, G. (2001) 'Gli oracoli sibillini e l'Alessandra di Licofrone', in *La profezia nel mondo antico*, ed. M. Sordi. Milan: 139–49.
Andreassi, M. (2013) '"Adultery mime": da pratica scenica a modello ermeneutico', *RhM* 156: 293–313.
Aneziri, S. (1994) 'Zwischen Musen und Hof: die dionysischen Techniten auf Zypern', *ZPE* 104: 179–98.
　(1997) 'Les synagonistes du théâtre grec aux époques hellénistique et romaine : une question de terminologie et de fonction', in Le Guen (1997), 51–71.
　(2001–2) 'A different guild of artists: τὸ κοινὸν τῶν περὶ τὴν ἱλαρὰν Ἀφροδίτην τεχνιτῶν', *Ἀρχαιογνωσία* 11: 47–56.

(2003) *Die Vereine der dionysischen Techniten im Kontext der hellenistischen Gesellschaft: Untersuchungen zur Geschichte, Organisation und Wirkung der hellenistischen Gesellschaft*. Stuttgart.

(2007) 'The organisation of music contests in the Hellenistic period and artists' participation: an attempt at classification', in Wilson (2007a), 67–84.

(2009) 'World travel: the associations of Artists of Dionysus', in Hunter and Rutherford (2009), 217–36.

Arnott, W. G. (1996) *Alexis: The Fragments*. Cambridge.

(2000) 'On editing fragments from literary and lexicographic sources', in *The Rivals of Aristophanes: Studies in Athenian Old Comedy*, ed. D. Harvey and J. Wilkins London: 1–13.

Arrighetti, G. (1987) *Poeti, eruditi e biografi: momenti della riflessione dei greci sulla letteratura*. Pisa.

Athanassiou, N. (1999) *Marginalia and Commentaries in the Papyri of Euripides, Sophocles and Aristophanes*. Diss. London.

Austin, M. M. ([2]2006) *The Hellenistic World from Alexander to the Roman Conquest: A Selection of Ancient Sources in Translation*. Cambridge.

Baertschi, A. (2015) 'Epic elements in Senecan tragedy', in *Brill's Companion to Roman Tragedy*, ed. G. W. M. Harrison. Leiden: 171–95.

Bagnall, R. S. (2002) 'Alexandria: library of dreams', *PAPS* 146: 348–62.

Bakola, E. (2008) 'The drunk, the reformer and the teacher: agonistic poetics and the construction of persona in the comic poets of the fifth century', *CCJ* 54: 1–29.

(2014) 'Interiority, the "deep earth" and the spatial symbolism of Darius' apparition in the *Persians* of Aeschylus', *CCJ* 60: 1–36.

Bakola, E., Prauscello, L. and Telò, M. (eds.) (2013) *Greek Comedy and the Discourse of Genres*. Cambridge.

Baldry, H. C. (1969) 'Aristotle and the Greek theatre', *PCA* 66: 34–5.

Barker, A. (1984, 1989) *Greek Musical Writings*. 2 vols. Cambridge.

(2012) 'Music', in *The Oxford Classical Dictionary*, ed. S. Hornblower, A. Spawforth and E. Eidinow, 4th edn. Oxford: 975–83.

Barlow, S. A. (1971) *The Imagery of Euripides*. London.

Barner, W. (1971) 'Die Monodie', in *Die Bauformen der griechischen Tragödie*, ed. W. Jens. Poetica Beiheft 6. Munich: 277–320.

Barnes, T. D. (1996) 'Christians and the theater', in *Roman Theater and Society: E. Togo Salmon Papers 1*, ed. W. Slater. Ann Arbor: 161–80 (reprinted in Gildenhard and Revermann 2010).

Barrett, J. (2002) *Staged Narrative: Poetics and the Messenger in Greek Tragedy*. Berkeley.

Barrett, W. S. (ed.) (1964) *Euripides: Hippolytos*. Oxford.

Bartsch, H. (1843) *De Chaeremone poeta tragico*. Moguntia.

Bastianini, G. et al., eds. (2004) *Commentaria et lexica graeca in papyris reperta (CLGP), Pars I: Commentaria et lexica in auctores; Vol. 1, fasc. 1: Aeschines-Alcaeus*. Munich and Leipzig.

Battezzato, L. (2000) 'The Thracian camp and the fourth actor at *Rhesus* 565–691', *CQ* n.s. 50: 367–73.
  (2003) 'I viaggi dei testi', in *Tradizione testuale e ricezione letteraria antica della tragedia greca. Atti del convegno Scuola Normale Superiore, Pisa, 14–15 giugno 2002*, ed. L. Battezzato. Amsterdam: 7–31.
  (2008) 'Colometria antica e pratica editoriale moderna', *QUCC* 90: 137–58.
Beacham, R. C. (1991) *The Roman Theatre and Its Audience*. Cambridge, Mass.
Beare, W. (1954) 'The meaning of ΧΟΡΟΥ', *Hermathena* 84: 99–103.
  (1968) *The Roman Stage*. 3rd edn. London.
Belfiore, E. S. (2000) *Murder Among Friends: Violation of Philia in Greek Tragedy*. Oxford.
Bélis, A. (2004) 'Un papyrus musical inédit au Louvre', *CRAI* 2004, no. 3: 1305–29.
Beloch, K. J. (1927) *Griechische Geschichte 4² 2*. Berlin.
Benecke, P. (1930) 'The fall of the Macedonian monarchy', in *The Cambridge Ancient History*, vol. 8, *Rome and the Mediterranean 218–133 BC*, ed. S. Cook, F. E. Adcock and M. P. Charlesworth. Cambridge: 241–78.
Bernstein, N. (2013) *Ethics, Identity and Community in Later Roman Declamation*. New York and Oxford.
Bieber, M. (1961) *The History of the Greek and Roman Theater*. Princeton.
Biffis, G. (2012) *Cassandra and the Female Perspective in Lycophron's Alexandra*. Diss. UCL.
  (2014) 'Can iconography help to interpret Lycophron's description of the ritual performed by Daunian Maidens (*Alexandra* 1126–40)'?, *Aition* 4, http://aitia.revues.org/1025, accessed 23.1.15.
  (2015) 'Licofrone: tra parola poetica e realtà storica come memoria di guerra', in *Guerra e memoria nel mondo antico: Collana Quaderni 6*, ed. E. Franchi and G. Proietti. Trento: 211–26.
Biles, Z. P. (2006–7) 'Aeschylus' afterlife: reperformance by decree in 5th C. Athens?', *ICIS* 31–32: 206–42.
  (2011) *Aristophanes and the Poetics of Competition*. Cambridge.
Bing, P. (2011) 'Anecdote, hypothesis, and image in the Hellenistic reception of Euripides', *A&A* 56: 1–17.
Bloch, R. (2011) *Moses und der Mythos: Die Auseinandersetzung mit der griechischen Mythologie bei jüdisch-hellenistischen Autoren*. Leiden.
Blum, R. (1991) *Kallimachos: The Alexandrian Library and the Origins of Bibliography*, trans. H. H. Wellisch. Madison.
Blundell, S. (1986) *The Origins of Civilization in Greek and Roman Thought*. Beckenham.
Bond, R. S. (1996) 'Homeric echoes in *Rhesus*', *AJPh* 117: 255–73.
Bonner, S. F. (1939) *The Literary Critical Treatises of Dionysius of Halicarnassus: A Critical Study in the Development of Critical Method*. Cambridge.
Borgeaud, P. (1991) 'Rhésos et Arganthoné', in *Orphisme et Orphée: en l'honneur de Jean Rudhardt*, ed. P. Borgeaud. Geneva: 51–9.

Bosher, K. (ed.) (2012a) *Theater Outside Athens: Drama in Greek Sicily and South Italy*. Cambridge.
(2012b) 'Hieron's Aeschylus', in Bosher (2012a), 97–111.
Bosworth, A. B. (1994) 'Alexander the Great Part 2: Greece and the conquered territories,' in *The Cambridge Ancient History*, 2nd edn, vol. VI: *The Fourth Century B.C.*, ed. D.M. Lewis, J. Boardman, S. Hornblower and M. Ostwald, Cambridge: 846–75.
Bouché-Leclercq, A. (1903–7) *Histoire des Lagides*. 4 vols. Paris.
Bowie, E. L. (1986) 'Early Greek elegy, symposium and public festival', *JHS* 106: 13–35.
Boyle, A. J. (1997) *Tragic Seneca: An Essay in the Theatrical Tradition*. London.
(2006) *Roman Tragedy*. New York.
Brant, J.-A. A. (2005) 'Mimesis and dramatic art in Ezekiel the Tragedian's *Exagoge*', in *Ancient Fiction: The Matrix of Early Christian and Jewish Narrative*, ed. J.-A. A. Brant, C. W. Hedrick and C. Shea. Atlanta 2005: 129–47.
Braund, D. (1994) 'Dionysiac tragedy in Plutarch, *Crassus*', *CQ* 43: 468–74.
Braund, D. and Hall, E. (2014) 'Theatre in the fourth-century Black Sea region', in Csapo et al. (2014), 371–90.
Bremer, J. M. (1993) Review of R. Janko, *Aristotle: Poetics I* [Indianapolis 1987)], *Gnomon* 65: 201–4.
Brink, C. O. (1963) *Horace on Poetry 1: Prolegomena to the Literary Epistles*. Cambridge.
(1971) *Horace on Poetry 2: The Ars Poetica*. Cambridge.
Brown, A. L. (1984) 'Three and scene-painting Sophocles', *PCPS* 30: 1–17.
Bryant Davies, R. (2008) 'Reading Ezekiel's *Exagoge*: tragedy, sacrificial ritual, and the Midrashic tradition', *GRBS* 48: 393–415.
Bubel, F. (ed.) (1991) *Euripides: Andromeda*. Stuttgart.
Bühler, W. (1973) 'Tzetzes über die Ἕκτορος λύτρα des Dionysios (Mitteilungen aus griechischen Handschriften 5)', *ZPE* 11: 69–79.
Bunta, S. (2007) 'One man in heaven: Adam-Moses polemics in the Romanian versions of the Testament of Abraham and Ezekiel the tragedian's *Exagoge*', *Journal for the Study of the Pseudepigrapha* 16.2: 139–65.
Burian, P. (2011) 'Athenian tragedy as democratic discourse', in Carter (2011), 95–117.
Burkert, W. (1966) 'Greek sacrificial ritual and the origins of tragedy', *GRBS* 7: 87–121.
(2009) 'Medea: Arbeit am Mythos von Eumelos bis Karkinos', in *Mythische Wiederkehr*, ed. B. Zimmermann. Freiburg: 153–66.
Burnett, A. P. (1985) '*Rhesus*: are smiles allowed?' in *Directions in Euripidean Criticism: A Collection of Essays*, ed. P. Burian. Durham, N.C.: 13–51.
Cairns, F. (1974) 'Some observations on Propertius 1. 1', *CQ* n.s. 24: 94–110.
Calabi, F. (2003) 'Theatrical language in Philo's In Flaccum', in *Italian Studies on Philo of Alexandria*, ed. F. Calabi. Leiden: 91–116.
Calvet, M. and Roesch, P. (1966) 'Les Sarapeia de Tanagra', *RA*: 297–332.

Cameron, A. (1995) *Callimachus and his Critics*. Princeton.
  (2004) *Greek Mythography in the Roman World*. Oxford.
Camp, J. McK. (1971) 'Greek inscriptions: tragedies presented at the Lenaia of 364/363', *Hesperia* 40: 302–7.
Canto, M. (ed.) (1987) *Plato: Gorgias*. Paris.
Capps, E. (1900) 'Chronological studies in the Greek tragic and comic poets', *AJP* 21: 38–61.
Carpenter, T. H. (2014) 'A case for Greek tragedy in Italic settlements in fourth-century B.C.E. Apulia', in *The Italic People of Ancient Apulia: New Evidence from Pottery for Workshops, Markets, and Customs*, ed. T. H. Carpenter, K. M. Lynch and E. G. D. Robinson. Cambridge: 265–80.
Carter, D. M. (2004a) 'Was Attic tragedy democratic?', *Polis* 21: 1–25.
  (2004b) 'Citizen attribute, negative right: a conceptual difference between ancient and modern ideas of freedom of speech', in *Free Speech in Classical Antiquity*, ed. I. Sluiter and R. M. Rosen. Leiden: 197–220.
  (2007) *The Politics of Greek Tragedy*. Exeter.
  (2011a) 'Plato, drama and rhetoric', in Carter (2011b), 45–67.
  (ed.) (2011b) *Why Athens? A Reappraisal of Tragic Politics*. Oxford.
  (2018) 'Tragic *parrhesia*', in *A l'Assemblée comme au théâtre. Pratiques délibératives des Anciens, perceptions et résonances modernes*, ed. N. Villaceque. Rennes: 91–109.
Catenacci, C. (2002) 'Un frammento di tragedia ellenistica (*P.Oxy.* 2746 = *TrGF* adesp. 649)', *QUCC* 70.1: 95–104.
Caven, B. (1990) *Dionysius I: War-lord of Sicily*. New Haven and London.
Cawkwell, G. (1978) *Philip of Macedon*. London and Boston.
  (2005) *The Greek Wars: The Failure of Persia*. Oxford.
Ceccarelli, P. (1995) 'Le dithyrambe et la pyrrique: à propos de la nouvelle liste de vainqueurs aux Dionysies de Cos (Segre, *Iscrizioni di Cos*, ED 234)', *ZPE* 108: 287–305.
  (1998) *La pirrica nell'antichità greco romana: studi sulla dansa armata*. Pisa and Rome.
  (2010) 'Changing contexts: tragedy in the civic and cultural life of Hellenistic city-states', in Gildenhard and Revermann (2010), 99–150.
Ceccarelli, P. and Milanezi, S. (2007) 'Dithyramb, tragedy – and Cyrene', in Wilson (2007a), 185–214.
Champion, C. B. (2004) *Cultural Politics in Polybius' Histories*. Berkeley, Los Angeles and London.
Chaniotis, A. (1988) *Historie und Historiker in den griechischen Inschriften*. Munich.
  (1990) 'Zur Frage der Spezialisierung im griechischen Theater des Hellenismus und der Kaiserzeit auf der Grundlage der neuen Prosopographie der dionysischen Techniten', *Ktèma* 15: 89–108.
  (1997) 'Theatricality beyond the theatre: staging public life in the Hellenistic world', in Le Guen (1997), 219–59.
  (2005) *War in the Hellenistic World*. London.
  (2007) 'Theatre rituals', in *The Greek Theatre and Festivals: Documentary Studies*, ed. P. Wilson. Oxford: 48–66.

(2009) Θεατρικότητα και δημόσιος βίος στον ελληνιστικό κόσμο *[Theatricality and Public Life in the Hellenistic World]*. Athens.

(2013a) 'Paradoxon, enargeia, empathy: Hellenistic decrees and Hellenistic oratory', in *Hellenistic Oratory: Continuity and Change*, ed. C. Kremmydas and K. Tempest. Oxford: 201–16.

(2013b) 'Empathy, emotional display, theatricality and illusion in Hellenistic historiography', in *Unveiling Emotions II. Emotions in Greece and Rome: Texts, Images, Material Culture*, ed. A. Chaniotis and P. Ducrey. Stuttgart: 53–84.

Chapoutier, F., Salac, A. and Salviat, F (1956) 'Le théâtre de Samothrace', *BCH* 80: 118–46.

Charalabopoulos, N. G. (2012) *Platonic Drama and Its Ancient Reception*. Cambridge.

Charitonidis, S., Kahil, L. and Ginouvès, R. (1970) *Les Mosaïques de la Maison de Ménandre à Mytilène*. Bern.

Chiasson, C. C. (2003) 'Herodotus' use of Attic tragedy in the Lydian *logos*'. *CA* 22.1: 5–35.

Ciaceri, E. (1901) *La Alessandra di Licofrone*. Catania, Reprinted Naples, 1982.

Ciani, M. G. (1975) *Lexikon zu Lycophron*. Hildesheim and New York.

Cinaglia, V. (2014) *Aristotle and Menander on the Ethics of Understanding*. Leiden and Boston.

Cipolla, P. (2003) *Poeti minori del dramma satiresco: testo critico, traduzione e commento*. Amsterdam.

Cohen, B. (2000a) *Not the Classical Ideal: Athens and the Construction of the Other in Greek Art*. Leiden.

(2000b) 'Man-killers and their victims: inversions of the heroic ideal in classical art', in Cohen 2000a: 98–131.

Cohen, S. J. D. (1981) 'Sosates, the Jewish Homer', *Harvard Theological Review* 74: 391–6.

Coles, R. (1968) 'A new fragment of post-classical tragedy from Oxyrhynchus', *BICS* 15: 110–68.

Collard, C. (1970) 'On the tragedian Chaeremon', *JHS* 90: 22–34.

(2005) 'Colloquial language in tragedy: A supplement to the work of P. T. Stevens', *CQ* 55: 350–86.

(2007) *Tragedy, Euripides and Euripideans: Selected Papers*. Bristol.

(2009) 'P. Köln XI 431 and its "genre": a suggestion', *ZPE* 171: 9–14.

Collins, J. J. (1997) *Sibyls, Seers and Sages in Hellenistic-Roman Judaism*. Leiden.

Connelly, J. B. (1993) 'Narrative and image in Attic vase painting: Ajax and Kassandra at the Trojan Palladion', in *Narrative and Event in Ancient Art*, ed. P. J. Holliday. Cambridge: 88–129.

Cooper, L. 1929. 'Aristotle, *Rhetoric* 3. 16. 1417$^b$ 16–20 (Haemon and Jocasta Advising)', *AJPh* 50: 170–80.

Craik, E. M. (1993) 'Unwritten laws', *LCM* 18: 123–5.

Cribiore, R. (2001a) *Gymnastics of the Mind: Greek Education in Hellenistic and Roman Egypt*. Princeton and Oxford.

(2001b) 'The grammarian's choice: the popularity of Euripides' *Phoenissae* in Hellenistic and Roman education', in *Education in Greek and Roman Antiquity*, ed. Y. L. Too. Leiden: 241–59.
Crowther, Ch. (1990) 'Iasos in the second century, I: the chronology of the theatre lists', *BICS* 37: 143–51.
  (1995) 'The chronology of the Iasian theatre lists: again', *Chiron* 25: 225–34.
  (2007) 'The Dionysia at Iasos: its artists, patrons, and audience', in Wilson (2007a), 294–334.
Csapo, E. (1986) 'A note on the Würzburg bell-crater H5697 ("Telephus travestitus")', *Phoenix* 40: 379–92.
  (1999/2000) 'Later Euripidean music', *ICS* 24/25: 399–426.
  (2000) 'From Aristophanes to Menander? Genre transformation in Greek Comedy', in Depew and Obbink (2000), 115–34.
  (2002) 'Kallippides on the floor-sweepings: the limits of realism in classical acting and performance styles', in Easterling and Hall (2002), 127–47.
  (2004a) 'The politics of the New Music', in *Music and the Muses: the Culture of Mousike in the Classical Athenian City*, ed. P. Murray & P. J. Wilson. Oxford: 207–48.
  (2004b) 'Some social and economic conditions behind the rise of the acting profession in the fifth and fourth centuries BC', in *Le Statut de l'acteur dans l'antiquité grecque et romaine*, ed. C. Hugoniot, F. Hurlet and S. Milanezi. Tours: 53–76.
  (2010) *Actors and Icons of the Ancient Theater*. Chicester, UK and Malden, MA.
Csapo, E. and Slater, W. J. (1995) *The Context of Greek Drama*. Ann Arbor.
Csapo, E. and Wilson, P. (2009) 'Timotheus, the New Musician', in *Cambridge Companion to Greek Lyric*, ed. F. Budelmann. Cambridge: 277–93.
  (2014) 'The finance and organisation of the Athenian theatre in the time of Eubulus and Lycurgus', in Csapo et al. (2014), 393–424.
  (2015) 'Drama outside Athens in the fifth and fourth centuries BC', in Lamari (2015), 316–95.
Csapo, E. et al., (eds.) (2014) *Greek Theatre in the Fourth Century BC*. Berlin.
Cusset, C. and Prioux, E. (eds.) (2009) *Lycophron: éclats d'obscurité*. Saint-Étienne.
Dafni, E. G. (2008) 'Euripides und das Alte Testament: zum überlieferungsgeschichtlichen Horizont der Septuaginta', in *XIII Congress of the International Organization for Septuagint and Cognate Studies, Ljubljana 2007*, ed. M. K. H. Peters. Atlanta: 87–97.
Dale, A. M. (1968) *The Lyric Metres of Greek Drama*. 2nd edn. Cambridge.
D'Angelo, R. M. (1983) *Fra trimetro e senario giambico: ricerche di metrica greca e latina*. Rome.
D'Angour, A. (1998–1999) 'Archinus, Eucleides and the reform of the Athenian alphabet', *BICS* 43: 109–30.
Davidson, J. (2003) 'Carcinus and the temple: a problem in the Athenian theater', *CPh* 98: 109–22.
Davies, J. K. (1971) *Athenian Propertied Families, 600–300 B.C.* Oxford.

Davies, M. (1998) 'Euripides' *Electra*: the recognition scene again', *CQ* 37: 65–75.
Dawe, R. D. (1967) 'The end of *Seven against Thebes*', *CQ* 17: 16–28.
Dearden, C. W. (1990) 'Fourth-century tragedy in Sicily: Athenian or Sicilian?', in *Greek Colonists and Native Populations: Proceedings of the First Australian Congress of Classical Archaeology held in Honour of Emeritus Professor A. D. Trendall, Sydney 9–14 July 1985*, ed. J.-P. Descoeudres. Canberra and Oxford: 231–42.
  (1999) 'Plays for export', *Phoenix* 53: 222–48.
  (2012) 'Whose line is it anyway? West Greek comedy in its context', in Bosher (2012a), 272–88.
De Lacy, P. (1952) 'Biography and tragedy in Plutarch', *AJPh* 73: 159–71.
De Lange, N. (1996) *Greek Jewish Texts from the Cairo Genizah*. Tübingen.
Delbrueck, R. (1929) *Die Consulardiptychen und verwandte Denkmäler*. Berlin.
Del Grande, C. (1933/1935) 'Teodette di Faselide e la tarda tragedia posteuripidea', *Dioniso* 4: 191–200.
Delrieux, F. (1996) 'Remarques sur l'ordre de succession des contributions financières d'Iasos au II$^e$ siècle av. J.-C.', *RÉA* 98: 371–88.
Denis, A.-M. (ed.) (2000) *Introduction à la littérature religieuse judéo-hellénistique*. Turnhout.
Denniston, J. D. (1929) 'καθάπερ καί, ὥσπερ καί, οἷον καί', *CR* 43: 60.
  (1939) *Euripides Electra*. Oxford.
Depew, D. (2007) 'From hymn to tragedy: Aristotle's genealogy of poetic kinds', in *The Origins of Theater in Ancient Greece and Beyond: From Ritual to Drama*, ed. E. Csapo and M. Miller. Cambridge: 126–49.
Depew, M. and Obbink, D. (eds.) (2000) *Matrices of Genre: Authors, Canons and Society*. Cambridge, Mass.
Descroix, J. (1931) *Le Trimètre iambique*. Mâcon.
Dettori, E. (1997) 'Aristotele, *Poetica* 17, 1455a 22–9 (la "caduta" di Carcino)', in *Griechisch-römische Komödie und Tragödie*, vol. 2, ed. B. Zimmermann. Stuttgart: 75–84.
Di Gregorio, L. (1967) *La scena di annuncio nella tragedia greca*. Milan.
Dickey, E. (2007) *Ancient Greek Scholarship*. Oxford.
Diggle, J. (1970) *Euripides: Phaethon*. Cambridge.
  (1994) *Euripides: Fabulae*, vol. 3. Oxford.
Diller, H. (1962) 'Erwartung, Enttäuschung und Erfüllung in der griechischen Tragödie', in *Serta Philologica Aenipontana*, ed. R. Muth. Innsbruck: 93–115.
Dimartino, A. (2010) 'Venus *Felix* a Siracusa? Per una rilettura dei decreti della *synodos* di *technitai* di Afrodite *Hilara*', *Epigraphica* 72: 21–50.
Dinsmoor, W. B. (1931) *The Archons of Athens in the Hellenistic Age*. Cambridge, Mass.
Dirlmeier, F. (1969) *Aristoteles: Nikomachische Ethik* (Aristoteles: Werke vol. 6). Berlin.

Dobias-Lalou, C. (1993) 'Les dépenses engagées par les démiurges de Cyrène pour les cultes', *RÉG* 106: 24–38.
Dodds, E. R. (1951) *The Greeks and the Irrational*. Berkeley.
  (1959) *Plato: Gorgias*. Oxford.
  (1960) *Euripides: Bacchae*. Oxford.
Dolfi, E. (2004) 'Sul fr. 14 di Cheremone', *Prometheus* 32: 43–54.
Donini, P. (1997) 'L'universalità della tragedia in Aristotele (e in Platone)', in *Filosofia, storia, immaginario mitologico*, ed. M. Guglielmo and G. F. Gianotti. Alexandria: 137–47.
Dover, K. J. (1968a) *Aristophanes: Clouds*. Oxford.
  (1968b) *Lysias and the Corpus Lysiacum*. Berkeley and Los Angeles.
  (2000) 'Fragments', *The Rivals of Aristophanes: Studies in Athenian Old Comedy*, ed. D. Harvey and J. Wilkins. London: xvii–xix.
Drew-Bear, T. (1968) 'The trochaic tetrameter in Greek tragedy', *AJP* 89: 385–405.
DuBois, T. A. (2009) *An Introduction to Shamanism*. Cambridge.
Dunand, F. (1986) 'Les associations dionysiaques au service du pouvoir lagide (IIIe s. av. J.-C.)', in *L'Association dionysiaque dans les sociétés anciennes*. École Française de Rome, Rome: 85–104.
Dunbabin, K. M. D. (2016) *Theater and Spectacle in the Art of the Roman Empire*. Ithaca and London.
Duncan, A. (2011) 'Nothing to do with Athens? Tragedians at the courts of tyrants', in Carter (2011b), 69–84.
  (2012) 'A Theseus outside Athens: Dionysius I of Syracuse and tragic self-presentation', in Bosher (2012a), 137–55.
  (2015) 'Political reperformances of tragedies in the fifth and fourth centuries BC', in Lamari (2015), 297–315.
Dunn, F. M. (1992) 'Beginning at Colonus', *YClS* 29: 1–12.
  (2007) *Present Shock in Late Fifth-Century Greece*. Ann Arbor.
  (2010) 'Metatheatre and crisis in Euripides' *Bacchae* and Sophocles' *Oedipus at Colonus*', in *Crisis on Stage: Comedy and Tragedy in Late Fifth-century Athens*, ed. A. Markantonatos and B. Zimmermann. Berlin: 359–76.
  (2012) '*Electra*', in *A Companion to Sophocles*, ed. K. Ormand. Chichester: 98–110.
  (2017) 'Euripides and his intellectual context', in *The Blackwell Companion to Euripides*, ed. L. McClure. Chichester: 447–67.
Durbec, Y. (2011) *Essais sur l'Alexandra de Lycophron*. Amsterdam.
  (2014) *Lycophron et ses contemporains*. Amsterdam.
Easterling, P.E. (1993) 'The end of an era? Tragedy in the early fourth century', in *Tragedy, Comedy and the Polis*, ed. A. H. Sommerstein, S. Halliwell, J. Henderson and B. Zimmermann. Bari: 559–69.
  (1994) 'Euripides outside Athens: a speculative note', *ICIS* 19: 73–80.
  (1997) 'From repertoire to canon', in *The Cambridge Companion to Greek Tragedy*, ed. P. E. Easterling. Cambridge: 211–27.
  (2002) 'Actor as icon', in Easterling and Hall (2002), 327–41.

(2005) 'Agamemnon for the ancients', in *Agamemnon in Performance 458 BC–AD 2004*, ed. F. Mackintosh et al. Oxford: 23–46.
(2006) 'Notes on notes: the ancient scholia on Sophocles', in Συγχάρματα: *Studies in Honour of Jan Fredrik Kindstrand*, ed. S. Eklund. Uppsala: 21–36.
(2015) 'Space in the tragic Scholia', in *Images and Texts: Papers in Honour of Eric Handley*, ed. R. Green and M. Edwards. BICS Supplement 129. London: 1–12.
Easterling, P. E. and Miles, R. (1999) 'Dramatic identities: tragedy in Late Antiquity', in *Constructing Identities in Late Antiquity*, ed. R. Miles. London and New York: 95–111.
Easterling, P. E. and Hall, E. eds. (2002) *Greek and Roman Actors: The Rise of an Ancient Profession*. Cambridge.
Edwards, C. (2002) 'Acting and self-actualisation in imperial Rome', in Easterling and Hall (2002), 377–94.
Else, G. F. (1957) *Aristotle's Poetics: The Argument*. Cambridge, Mass.
Elsner, J. (2007) 'Philostratus visualizes the tragic: some ecphrastic and pictorial receptions of Greek Tragedy in the Roman era', in *Visualizing the Tragic: Drama, Myth, and Ritual in Greek Art and Literature*, ed. C. Kraus et al. Cambridge: 309–37.
Elsperger, W. (1906) *Reste und Spuren antiker Kritik gegen Euripides: gesammelt aus den Euripidesscholien*. Tübingen.
Erasmo, M. (2004) *Roman Tragedy: Theatre to Theatricality*. Austin.
Falkner, T. (2002) 'Scholia versus actors: text and performance in the Greek tragic scholia', in Easterling and Hall (2002), 342–61.
Fantham, E. (2002) 'Orator and/et actor', in Easterling and Hall (2002), 362–76.
Fantuzzi, M. (2006) 'La Dolonia del *Reso* come luogo dell'errore e dell'incertezza', in *I luoghi e la poesia nella Grecia antica: Atti del Convegno Università 'G. d'Annunzio' di Chieti-Pescara 20–22 aprile 2004*, ed. M. Vetta and C. Catenacci. Alexandria: 241–62.
(2014) 'Tragic smiles: when tragedy gets too comic for Aristotle and later Hellenistic readers', in *Hellenistic Studies at a Crossroads: Exploring Texts, Contexts and Metatexts*, ed. R. Hunter, A. Rengakos and E. Sistakou. Berlin: 217–35.
Fantuzzi, M. and Hunter, R. (2003) *Tradition and Innovation in Hellenistic Poetry*. Cambridge.
Fantuzzi, M. and Konstan, D. (2013) 'From Achilles' horses to a cheese-seller's shop: on the history of the guessing game in Greek drama', in Bakola, Prauscello and Telò. (2013), 256–74.
Feeney, D. (2016) *Beyond Greek. The Beginnings of Latin Literature*. Cambridge, Mass., and London.
Feickert, A. (2005) *Euripidis Rhesus: Einleitung, Übersetzung, Kommentar*. Frankfurt a.M.
Fenik, B. (1960) *The Influence of Euripides on Vergil's Aeneid*, Diss. Princeton.
(1964) *Iliad X and the Rhesus: The Myth*. Brussels.

Fernández-Galiano, M. (1978) 'Sobre el fragmento trágico del P. Oxy. 2746', *Mus. Phil. Lond.* 3: 139–41.
Ferrari, F. (2009) 'L'altra Cassandra: *adesp. trag.* fr. 649 *TrGF*', *Seminari Romani* 12: 21–35.
Ferrari, G. R. F. (1989) 'Plato and poetry', in *The Cambridge History of Literary Criticism. Vol. I: Classical Criticism*, ed. G. A. Kennedy. Cambridge: 92–148.
Festa, V. (1918) 'Sikinnis', *Memorie della Reale Accademia di Archeologia* 3: 2–60.
Finglass, P. J. (ed.) (2011) *Sophocles: Ajax.* Cambridge.
  (2012) 'The textual transmission of Sophocles' dramas', in *A Companion to Sophocles*, ed. K. Ormand. Malden, Mass. and Oxford: 9–24.
  (2015) 'Reperformances and the transmission of texts', in Lamari (2015), 259–76.
Fitton, J. W. (1973) 'Greek Dance', *CQ* 23: 254–74.
Fleming, T. J. (1999) 'The survival of Greek dramatic music from the fifth century to the Roman period', in *La colometria greca dei testi poetici greci*, ed. B. Gentili and F. Perusino. Pisa: 17–29.
Fleming, T. J. and Kopff, E. C. (1992) 'Colometry of Greek lyric verses in tragic texts', *SIFC* 10: 758–70.
Flower, H. I. (1995) '*Fabulae praetextae* in context: when were plays on contemporary subjects performed in Republican Rome?', *CQ* 45: 170–90.
Foley, H. P. 2000. 'The comic body in Greek art and drama', in Cohen (2000a), 275–311.
Ford, A. (2002) *The Origins of Criticism: Literary Culture and Poetic Theory in Archaic and Classical Greece.* Princeton.
  (2003) 'From letters to literature: reading the "song culture" of classical Greece', in *Written Texts and the Rise of Literate Culture in Ancient Greece*, ed. H. Yunis. Cambridge: 15–37.
Fountoulakis, A. (2000) 'The artists of Aphrodite', *AC* 67: 133–47.
Fowler, M. H. (1989) *The Hellenistic Aesthetic.* Madison.
Fraenkel, E. (1950) *Aeschylus: Agamemnon*, vols. i–iii. Oxford.
  (1965) Review of Ritchie (1964), *Gnomon* 37: 228–41.
Franklin, J. C. (2002) 'Musical syncretism in the Greek orientalizing period', in *Studien zur Musikarchäologie* 3, ed. E. Hickman, R. Eichmann, and A. Kilmer, 441–51.
  (2005) 'Hearing Greek microtones', in *Ancient Greek Music in Performance*, ed. S. Hagel and C. Harrauer. Vienna: 9–50 (plus CD).
Fraser, P. M. (1972) *Ptolemaic Alexandria.* 3 vols. Oxford.
  (1979) 'Lycophron on Cyprus', *Report of the Department of Antiquities of Cyprus*: 328–43.
  (2003) 'Agathon and Cassandra (*IG* IX.1² 4.1750)', *JHS* 123: 26–40.
  (2009) *Greek Ethnic Terminology.* Oxford.
Free, K. B. (1999) 'Thespis and Moses: The Jews and the ancient Greek theatre', in *Theatre and Holy Script*, ed. S. Levy. Brighton and Portland: 149–58.
Frick, C. (1892) *Chronica Minora.* Leipzig.

Fries, A. (2010) 'The poetic technique of [Euripides]: the case of *Rhesus* 118', *CQ* n.s. 60: 345–51.
  (2013) Review of Liapis (2012), *Mnemosyne* IV 66: 814–21.
  (2014) *Pseudo-Euripides, Rhesus: Edited with Introduction and Commentary*, Berlin and New York.
Friis Johansen, H. and Whittle, E. W. (1980) *Aeschylus: The Suppliants*, vols. i-iii. Copenhagen.
Frulla, G. (2007) 'The language of the *Exagōgē* as an example of cultural exchanges: influences of the Septuagint and of the Masoretic Text', *Henoch* 29: 259–87.
  (2009) 'La "cornice" in cui vengono tramandati i frammenti dell'opera di Ezechiele il Tragico', in *Ricordo di Delfino Ambaglio*, ed. M. T. Zambianchi. Como: 131–46.
Fuchs, H. (1938) *Der geistige Widerstand gegen Rom in der antiken Welt*. Berlin.
Gagarin, M. (2002) *Antiphon the Athenian: Oratory, Law, and Justice in the Age of the Sophists*. Austin.
Gagné, R. (2013) 'Dancing letters: The alphabetic tragedy of Kallias', in *Choral Mediations in Greek Tragedy*, ed. R. Gagné and M. G. Hopman. Cambridge: 299–316.
Gallagher, R. (2003) 'Making the stronger argument the weaker: Euripides, *Electra* 518–44', *CQ* 53: 401–15.
Gantz, T. (1993) *Early Greek Myth: A Guide to Literary and Artistic Sources*. Baltimore and London.
Garelli-François, M. H. (1995) 'Le danseur dans la cité: quelques remarques sur la danse à Rome', *REL* 73: 29–43.
  (2001) 'La pantomime entre danse et drame: la geste et l'écriture', *CGITA* 14: 229–47.
  (2007) *Danser le mythe: la pantomime et sa réception dans la culture antique*. Louvain.
Garland, R. (2004) *Surviving Greek Tragedy*. London.
  (2014) *Wandering Greeks: The Ancient Greek Diaspora from the Age of Homer to the Death of Alexander the Great*. Princeton.
Garner, R. (1990) *From Homer to Tragedy: The Art of Allusion in Greek Poetry*. London.
Garnsey, P. (1988) *Famine and Food Supply in the Graeco-Roman World: Responses to Risk and Crisis*. Cambridge.
Garton, Ch. (1957) 'Characterisation in Greek tragedy', *JHS* 77.2: 247–54.
Garvie, A. F. (1998) *Sophocles: Ajax*. Warminster.
  (2006) *Aeschylus' Supplices: Play and Trilogy*, 2nd edn. Bristol (1st edn. Cambridge, 1969).
  (2014) 'Closure or indeterminacy in *Septem* and other plays?', *JHS* 134: 23–40.
Garzya, A. (1981) 'Sulle interpolazione delle attori', in *Studi Salernitani in memoria di Rafaelle Cataudella*. Salerno: 53–75.
  (1993) 'Dramma di Gige o di Candaule?' in *Tradizione e innovazione nella cultura greca da Omero all'età ellenistica*, 2, ed. R. Pretagostini. Rome: 547–9.

Geffcken, J. (1887) 'Zwei Dramen des Lykophron', *Hermes* 26: 33–42.
  (1892) *Timaios' Geographie des Westens*. Berlin.
  (1902) *Die oracula Sibyllina*. Leipzig.
Genette, G. (1986) *Narrative Discourse Revisited*. Transl. J. E. Lewin. Ithaca.
Gentili, B. (1977) 'Interpretazione di un nuovo testo tragico di età ellenistica (P. Oxy. 2746)', *Mus. Phil. Lond.* 2: 127–46.
  (1979a) *Theatrical Performances in the Ancient World*. Amsterdam.
  (1979b) 'Il teatro ellenistico e il teatro romano arcaico', *Grazer Beiträge* 8: 119–39.
Geuss, R. and Speirs, R. eds. (1999) *Nietzsche's The Birth of Tragedy and Other Writings*. Cambridge.
Ghiron-Bistagne, P. (1974) 'Die Krise des Theaters in der griechischen Welt im 4. Jahrhundert v. u. Z', in *Hellenische Poleis: Krise-Wandlung-Wirkung*, volume 3, ed. E. V. Welskopf. Berlin: 1335–71.
  (1976) *Recherches sur les acteurs dans la Grèce antique*. Paris.
Gibert, J. (1999/2000) 'Falling in love with Euripides (*Andromeda*)', *ICIS* 24/25: 75–91.
Gibson, C. (2008) *Libanius' Progymnasmata: Model Exercises in Greek Prose Composition and Rhetoric*. Atlanta.
Gigante, M. (1952) 'Un nuovo frammento di Licofrone tragico', *PdelP* 7: 5–17.
Gigante Lanzara, V. (2009) 'ἔστι μοι...μυρία παντᾷ κέλευθος', in Cusset and Prioux (2009), 95–115.
Gildenhard, I. and Revermann, M. (eds.) (2010) *Beyond the Fifth Century: Interactions with Greek Tragedy from the Fourth Century BCE to the Middle Ages*. Berlin and New York.
Giuliani, L. (1995) *Tragik, Trauer und Trost: Bildervasen für eine apulische Totenfeier*, Berlin.
  (1996) 'Rhesus between dream and death: on the relation of image to literature in Apulian vase-painting', *BICS* 41: 71–86.
  (2001) 'Sleeping Furies: allegory, narration and the impact of texts in Apulian vase painting', *Scripta Classica Israelica* 20: 17–38.
  (2013) *Image and Myth: A History of Pictorial Narration in Greek Art*, trsl. J. O'Donnell. Chicago.
Giuliani, L. and Most, G. W. (2007) 'Medea in Eleusis, in Princeton', in *Visualizing the Tragic: Drama, Myth, and Ritual in Greek Art and Literature*, ed. C. Kraus, S. Goldhill, H. P. Foley and J. Elsner. Oxford: 197–217.
Goette, H. R. (1999) 'Die Basis des Astydamas im sogenannten lykurgischen Dionysos-Theater zu Athen', *AK* 42: 21–5.
  (2014) 'The archaeology of the "Rural" Dionysia in Attica', in Csapo et al. (2014), 77–105.
Goff, B. (1999/2000) '"Try to make it real compared to what? Euripides' *Electra* and the play of genres", *ICS* 24/25: 93–105.
Gogos, G. (2008) *Das Dionysostheater von Athen: architektonische Gestalt und Funktion*. Wien.

Golden, M. and Toohey, P. (1997) *Inventing Ancient Culture: Historicism, Periodization, and the Ancient World*. London.
Goldhill, S. (2001) 'The erotic eye: visual stimulation and cultural conflict', in *Being Greek under Rome: Cultural identity, the Second Sophistic and the development of Empire*, ed. S. Goldhill. Cambridge: 154–94.
Goodman, M. (1986) 'Jewish writings under gentile pseudonyms', in *The History of the Jewish People in the Age of Jesus Christ*, ed. E. Schürer, revised by G. Vermes, F. Millar and M. Goodman, 3 vols., London, 1973–86: 3. 618–700.
Gotteland, S. (2001) 'Dion de Pruse et la tragédie', in *Lectures antiques de la tragédie grecque*, ed. A. Billault and C. Mauduit. Lyon and Paris: 93–107.
Gray, B. (2015) *Stasis and Stability: Exile and the Idea of the Polis, c. 404–146 BC*. Oxford.
Green, J. R. (1985) 'Drunk again: a study in the iconography of the comic theater', *AJA* 89: 465–72.
  (1990) 'Carcinus and the temple: a lesson in the staging of tragedy', *GRBS* 31: 281–5.
  (1991) 'On seeing and depicting the theatre in Classical Athens', *GRBS* 32: 15–50.
  (1994) *Theatre in Ancient Greek Society*. London.
  (2002) 'Towards a reconstruction of performance style', in Easterling and Hall (2002), 93–126.
  (2012) 'Comic vases in South Italy: continuity and innovation in the development of a figurative language', in Bosher (2012a), 289–342.
  (2014) 'Regional theatre in the fourth century: the evidence of comic figurines of Boeotia, Corinth and Cyprus', in Csapo et al. (2014), 333–69.
Griffin, J. (2006) 'Herodotus and tragedy', in *Cambridge Companion to Herodotus*, ed. C. Dewald and J. Marincola. Cambridge: 46–59.
Griffith, M. (1977) *The Authenticity of Prometheus Bound*. Cambridge.
  (1983) *Aeschylus: Prometheus Bound*. Cambridge.
  (1999) *Sophocles: Antigone*. Cambridge.
  (2008) 'Greek middlebrow drama (something to do with Aphrodite?)', in Revermann and Wilson (2008), 59–87.
  (2013) *Aristophanes' Frogs*. Oxford.
  (2015) *Greek Satyr Play: five studies*. Berkeley.
Griffith, R. Drew (2008) 'Salmoneus' thunder-machine again (Apollod. *Bibl.* 1.9.7).' *Philologus* 152.1: 143–5.
Grossardt, P. (2005) 'Zum Inhalt des *Hektoros Lytra* des Dionysios I (TGrF 1,76 F 2A)', *RhM* 148: 225–41.
Gruen, E. S. (1984) *The Hellenistic World and the Coming of Rome*. Berkeley, Los Angeles and London.
Guast, W. (2018) 'Lucian and declamations', *CPh* 113.2: 189–205.
Günther, T. (1999) 'Chairemon', in *Das griechische Satyrspiel*, ed. R. Krumeich. Darmstadt: 580–90.
Guthrie, W. K. C. (1969) *A History of Greek Philosophy* vol. 3: *The Fifth-Century Enlightenment*. Cambridge.

Gutzwiller, K. (2000) 'The tragic mask of comedy: the metatheatricality of Menander', *CA* 19: 102–37.
Habicht, C. (1998) *Athens from Alexander to Antony*. Princeton.
Hagel, S. (2010) *Ancient Greek Music: A New Technical History*. Cambridge.
Hall, E. (1996) 'Is there a *polis* in Aristotle's *Poetics?*', in *Tragedy and the Tragic: Greek Theatre and Beyond*, ed. M. S. Silk. Oxford: 295–309.
  (1997) 'The sociology of Athenian tragedy,' in *The Cambridge Companion to Greek Tragedy*, ed. P. E. Easterling. Cambridge: 93–126.
  (2002) 'The singing actors of antiquity', in Easterling and Hall (2002), 3–38.
  (2007) 'Greek tragedy 430–380 BC', in *Debating the Athenian Cultural Revolution: Art, Literature, Philosophy, and Politics 430–380 BC*, ed. R. Osborne. Cambridge: 264–87.
  (2010) 'Iphigeneia in Oxyrhynchus and India: Greek tragedy for everyone', in *Parachoregema*, ed. S. Tsitsiridis. Heraklion: 393–417.
Hall, E. and Wyles, R. (2008) *New Directions in Ancient Pantomime*. Oxford.
Halliwell, S. (1984) 'Plato and Aristotle on the denial of tragedy', *PCPS* 30: 49–71.
  (1986) *Aristotle's Poetics*. London.
  (1989) 'Aristotle's *Poetics*', in *The Cambridge History of Literary Criticism. Vol. I: Classical Criticism*, ed. G. A. Kennedy. Cambridge: 149–83.
  (1992) 'The *Poetics* and its interpreters', in *Essays on Aristotle's Poetics*, ed. A. Rorty. Princeton: 409–24.
  (1994) 'Popular morality, philosophical ethics, and the *Rhetoric*', in *Aristotle's Rhetoric: Philosophical Essays*, ed. D. J. Furley and A. Nehamas. Princeton: 211–30.
  (ed. and tr.) (1995) *Aristotle: Poetics* [together with Longinus and Demetrius]. Cambridge, Mass.
  (1997) 'Between public and private: tragedy and the Athenian experience of rhetoric', in *Greek Tragedy and the Historian*, ed. C. B. R. Pelling. Oxford: 121–41.
  (1998) *Aristotle's Poetics*. Chicago.
  (2002) *The Aesthetics of Mimesis: Ancient Texts and Modern Problems*. Princeton.
Hamilton, R. (1974) 'Objective evidence for actors' interpolations in Greek tragedy', *GRBS* 15: 449–77.
Handley, E. W. (1965). *The Dyskolos of Menander*. London.
  (1985) 'Comedy', in *The Cambridge History of Classical Literature. Vol. 1: Greek Literature*, ed. P. E. Easterling and B. M. W. Knox. Cambridge: 355–425.
Hanink, J. (2008) 'Literary politics and the Euripidean *Vita*', *CCJ* 54: 135–55.
  (2010) 'The classical tragedians, from Athenian idols to wandering poets', in Gildenhard and Revermann (2010), 39–67.
  (2011) 'Aristotle and the tragic theater in the fourth century: a response to Jennifer Wise', *Arethusa* 44: 311–28.

(2014a) 'Literary evidence for new tragic production: the view from the fourth century', in Csapo et al. (2014), 189–206.
(2014b) *Lycurgan Athens and the Making of Classical Tragedy*. Cambridge.
(2015) '"Why 386 BC?" Lost empire, old tragedy and reperformance in the era of the Corinthian War', *Trends in Classics* 7: 277–96.
(2017) 'Archives, repertoires, bodies and bones: thoughts on reperformance for classicists', in Hunter and Uhlig (2017), 21–41.
Hansen, W. (2002) *Ariadne's Thread: A Guide to International Tales Found in Classical Literature*. Ithaca and London.
Harder, A. (1985) *Euripides' Kresphontes and Archelaos: Introduction, Text and Commentary*. Leiden.
Harder, R. (1944) 'Karpokrates von Chalkis und die memphitische Isispropaganda', *Abh. Preuss. Akad. ph.-hist. Kl*. no. 14.
Harris, E. (2004) 'Antigone the lawyer or the ambiguities of nomos', in *The Law and the Courts in Ancient Greece*, ed. E. Harris and L. Rubenstein. London: 19–56, reprinted in E. Harris (2006) *Democracy and the Rule of Law in Classical Athens: Essays on Law, Society, and Politics*. Cambridge: 41–80.
Harris, W. V. (1989) *Ancient Literacy*. Cambridge, Mass., and London.
Harrison, G. W. M. and Liapis, V. eds. (2013) *Performance in Greek and Roman Theatre*. Leiden and Boston.
Haslam, M. W. (1975) 'The authenticity of Euripides, *Phoenissae* 1–2 and Sophocles, *Electra* 1', *GRBS* 16: 149–74.
Heath, J. (2006) 'Ezekiel Tragicus and Hellenistic visuality: the Phoenix at Elim', *Journal of Theological Studies* 57.1: 23–41.
(2007) 'Homer or Moses? A Hellenistic perspective on Moses' throne vision in Ezekiel Tragicus', *Journal of Jewish Studies* 58.1: 1–18.
Heath, M. (1987) *The Poetics of Greek Tragedy*. Stanford.
(1991) 'The universality of poetry in Aristotle's *Poetics*', *CQ* 41: 389–402.
(1999) 'Longinus On Sublimity', *PCPS* 45: 43–74.
(2009) 'Should there have been a polis in the *Poetics*?', *CQ* 59: 468–85.
Heckel, W. (2006) *Who's Who in the Age of Alexander the Great*. Oxford.
Held, G.F. (1985) 'The meaning of ἦθος in the *Poetics*', *Hermes* 113: 280–93.
Hengel, M. (1974) *Judaism and Hellenism: Studies in their Encounter in Palestine during the Early Hellenistic Period*, tr. J. Bowden. London.
Henrichs, A. (1994/1995) '"Why Should I Dance?": Choral self-referentiality in Greek tragedy', *Arion* 3: 56–111.
Herington, C. J. (1967) 'Aeschylus in Sicily', *JHS* 87: 74–85.
Hoffmann, H. (1951) *Chronologie der attischen Tragödie*, Diss. Hamburg.
Holladay, C. R. (1983) *Fragments from Hellenistic Jewish Authors, vol. 1: Historians*. Atlanta.
(1989) *Fragments from Hellenistic Jewish Authors, vol. 2: Poets*. Atlanta.
Hollis, A. S. (2007) 'Some poetic connexions of Lycophron's *Alexandra*', in *Hesperos: Studies in Ancient Greek poetry Presented to M. L. West on his*

*Seventieth Birthday*, ed. P. J. Finglass, C. Collard and N. J. Richardson. Oxford: 276–93.

Holzinger, C. von (1895) *Lycophron's* Alexandra. Leipzig.

Honigman, S. (2003) *The Septuagint and Homeric Scholarship in Alexandria: A Study in the Narrative of the Letter of Aristeas*. London.

Horbury, W. and Noy, D. (1992) *Jewish Inscriptions of Graeco-Roman Egypt*. Cambridge.

Hordern, J. H. (2002) *The Fragments of Timotheus of Miletus*. Oxford.

Hornblower, J. (1981) *Hieronymus of Cardia*. Oxford.

Hornblower, S. (1982) *Mausolus*. Oxford.

  (ed.) (1994) *Greek Historiography*. Oxford.

  (2010) *Thucydidean Themes*. Oxford.

  (2014) 'Lykophron and epigraphy. The value and function of cult epithets in the *Alexandra*', *CQ* 64: 91–120.

  (2015) *Lykophron* Alexandra*: Greek Text, Translation and Commentary*. Oxford.

  (2018) *Lykophron's* Alexandra, *Rome, and the Hellenistic World*. Oxford.

Hugoniot, C., Hurlet, F. and Milanezi, S, eds. (2004) *Le statut de l'acteur dans l'antiquité grecque et romaine*. Tours.

Hunter, R. L. (1979) 'The comic chorus in the fourth century', *ZPE* 36: 23–38 (repr. with Addenda in Hunter 2008: 575–92).

  (1981) 'P. Lit. Lond. 77 and tragic burlesque in Attic comedy', *ZPE* 41: 19–24.

  (1983) *Eubulus: The Fragments*. Cambridge.

  (2002) 'Acting down: the ideology of Hellenistic performance', in Easterling and Hall (2002), 189–206.

  (2003) 'Reflecting on writing and culture: Theocritus and the style of cultural exchange', in *Written Texts and the Rise of Literate Culture in Ancient Greece*, ed. H. Yunis. Cambridge: 213–34.

  (2008) *On Coming After: Studies in Post-Classical Greek Literature and Its Reception*. 2 vols. Berlin and New York.

  (2009a) *Critical Moments in Classical Literature: Studies in the Ancient View of Literature and its Uses*. Cambridge.

  (2009b) 'The garland of Hippolytus', *TiC* 1: 18–35.

  (2009c) 'The *Trojan Oration* of Dio Chrysostom and ancient Homeric criticism', in *Narratology and Interpretation: The Content of Narrative Form in Ancient Literature*, ed. J. Grethlein and A. Rengakos. Berlin and New York: 43–61.

Hunter, R. and Russell, D. (2011) *Plutarch: How to Study Poetry*. Cambridge.

Hunter, R. and Rutherford, I. eds. (2009) *Wandering Poets in Ancient Greek Culture: Travel, Locality and Panhellenism*. Cambridge.

Hunter, R. and Uhlig, A., eds. (2017). *Imagining Reperformance in Ancient Culture: Studies in the Traditions of Drama and Lyric*. Cambridge.

Hurst, A. (2012) *Sur Lycophron*. Geneva.

Hurst, A. and Kolde, A. (2009) *Lycophron*, Alexandra. Paris.

Hutchinson, G. O. (ed.) (1985) *Aeschylus: Septem contra Thebas*. Oxford.

Huys, M. (1993) 'P.Oxy. LIII 3705: A line from Menander's 'Periceiromene' with musical notation', *ZPE* 99: 30–2.
Iliescu, V. (1976) 'Zeitgeschichtliche Bezüge im *Rhesos*', *Klio* 58.2: 367–76.
Inowlocki, S. (2006) *Eusebius and the Jewish Authors: His Citation Technique in an Apologetic Context*. Leiden.
Irigoin, J. (1983) 'Structure et composition des tragédies de Sophocle', in *Sophocle: Entretiens Hardt*. Vandoeuvres: 39–76.
Irwin, T. (Tr.) (1979) *Plato: Gorgias*. Oxford.
Itsumi, K. (1982) 'The "choriambic dimeter" of Euripides', *CQ* 32: 59–74.
Izenous, G. C. (1992) *Roofed Theaters in Classical Antiquity*. New Haven.
Jacobson, H. (1981) 'Two studies on Ezekiel the tragedian', *GRBS* 22: 167–78.
  (1983) *The Exagoge of Ezekiel*. Cambridge.
  (2002–3) 'Ezekiel's Exagoge, one play or four?', *GRBS* 43.4: 391–6.
  (2005) 'Eusebius, Polyhistor and Ezekiel', *Journal for the Study of the Pseudepigrapha* 15.1: 75–7.
Janko, R. (2000) *Philodemus On Poems: Book I*. Oxford.
Janz, T. (2005) *The Scholia to Sophocles' Philoctetes*, Diss. Oxford.
Jebb, R. C. (1924) *Sophocles, The Plays and Fragments, VI: Electra*. Cambridge.
Jocelyn, H. D. (1967) *The Tragedies of Ennius*. Cambridge.
Johnson, W. A. (2000) 'Musical evenings in the early Empire: New evidence from a Greek papyrus with musical notation', *JHS* 120: 57–85. (Audio renderings available at: http://classics.uc.edu/music/yale/index.html)
Johnstone, S. (2014) 'A new history of libraries and books in the Hellenistic period', *CA* 33: 347–93.
Jones, C. P. (1991) 'Dinner-theater', in *Dining in a Classical Context*, ed. W. J. Slater. Ann Arbor: 185–98.
  (1993) 'Greek drama in the Roman Empire', in *Theater and Society in the Classical World*, ed. R. Scodel. Ann Arbor: 39–52.
Jones, K. (2014) 'Lycophron's *Alexandra*, the Romans, and Antiochus III', *JHS* 134: 41–55.
Jong, I. J. F. de (1991) *Narrative in Drama: The Art of the Euripidean Messenger-Speech*. Leiden.
Jordan, D. (2007) 'An opisthographic lead tablet from Sicily with a financial document and curse concerning *choregoi*', in Wilson (2007a), 335–50.
Jouan, F. (2004) *Euripide: tragédies* (vol. VII, Pt. 2: *Rhésos*). Paris.
Jouanna, J. (2001) 'La lecture de Sophocle dans les scholies: Remarques sur les scholies anciennes *d'Ajax*', in *Lectures antiques de la tragédie grecque*, ed. A. Billault and C. Mauduit. Lyon and Paris: 9–25.
Judet de la Combe, P. (2011) 'Sur la poétique de la scène finale des *Sept contre Thèbes*', in *Contributi critici sul testo di Eschilo: ecdotica ed esegesi*, ed. M. Taufer. Tübingen: 61–77.
Juffras, D. M. (1991) 'Sophocles' *Electra* 973–985 and tyrannicide', *TAPhA* 121: 99–108.
Kaibel, G. (1899) *Comicorum graecorum fragmenta*. Berlin.

Kaimio, M. (1999) 'The citizenship of the theatre-makers in Athens', *Würzburger Jahrbücher für die Altertumswissenschaft* 23: 43–61.
Kamerbeek, J. C. (1974) *The Plays of Sophocles*, Part V: *Electra*. Leiden.
Kannicht, R. (1969) *Euripides: Helena*, vols. 1–2. Heidelberg.
  (1996) 'Zum Corpus Euripideum', in ΛΗΝΑΙΚΑ: *Festschrift für Carl Werner Müller*, ed. C. Mueller-Goldingen and K. Sier. Stuttgart and Leipzig: 21–31.
Kannicht, R. et al. eds. (1991) *Musa Tragica: Die griechische Tragödie von Thespis bis Ezechiel*. Göttingen.
Karamanou, I. (2003) 'The myth of Alope in Greek tragedy', *AC* 72: 25–40.
  (2007) 'The *lysis* in Theodectes' *Lynceus*: remarks on Arist. *Poet.* 11, 1452a27–29 and 18, 1455b29–32', *QUCC* 87: 119–25.
  (2011) 'Aristotle's *Poetics* as a source for lost tragedies', in *Actas del XII Congreso Español de Estudios Clásicos*. Madrid: 389–97.
Karavas, O. (2005) *Lucien et la tragédie*. Berlin and New York.
Katsouris, A. G. (1974) 'Staging of παλαιαὶ τραγῳδίαι in relation to Menander's audience', *Dodone* 3: 173–204.
Keene, D. (1966) *Nô: The Classical Theatre of Japan*. Tokyo and Palo Alto.
Kellenberger, E. (2006) *Die Verstockung Pharaos: exegetische und auslandsgeschichtliche Untersuchungen zu Exodus 1–15*. Stuttgart.
Kelly, H. A. (1979) 'Tragedy and the performance of tragedy in late Roman antiquity', *Traditio* 35: 21–44.
Kennedy, G. A. (tr.) (1991) *Aristotle: On Rhetoric*. Oxford.
Kenyon, F. G. (1951) *Books and Readers in Ancient Greece and Rome*. Oxford.
Kern, O. (1922) *Orphicorum fragmenta*. Berlin.
Kinkel, G. (1880) *Lycophronis* Alexandra. Leipzig.
Kitto, H. D. F. (1966) 'Aristotle and fourth century tragedy', in *For Service to Classical Studies: Essays in Honour of Francis Letters*, ed. M. Kelly. Melbourne: 113–29.
Klimek-Winter, R. (1993) *Andromedatragödien: Sophokles, Euripides, Livius Andronikos, Ennius, Accius*. Stuttgart.
Knoepfler, D. (1991) *La vie de Ménédème d'Érétrie de Diogène Laerce: contribution à l'histoire et à la critique du texte des* Vies des Philosophes. Neuchâtel.
Knox, B. M. W. (1985) 'Books and readers in the Greek world. I: From the beginnings to Alexandria', in *The Cambridge History of Classical Literature. Vol. I: Greek Literature*, ed. P. E. Easterling and B. M. W. Knox. Cambridge: 1–16.
Koenen, L. (1968) 'Die Prophezeiungen des "Töpfers"', *ZPE* 2: 178–209.
Kohn, T. D. (2002–3) 'The tragedies of Ezekiel', *GRBS* 43.1: 5–12.
Kokolakis, M. (1960) *The Dramatic Simile of Life*. Athens.
Konstantakos, I. M. (2000) 'Notes on the chronology and career of Antiphanes', *Eikasmos* 11: 173–96.
Kosak, J. C. (1999) 'Therapeutic touch and Sophokles' *Philoctetes*', *HSPh* 99: 93–134.
Kosmetatou, E. (2000) 'Lycophron's *Alexandra* reconsidered: the Attalid connection', *Hermes* 128: 32–53.

Kotlińska-Toma, A. (2015) *Hellenistic Tragedy: Texts, Translations and a Critical Survey*, London.
Kotsidou, H. (1991) *Die musische Agone der Panathenäen in archaischer und klassischer Zeit*. Munich.
Kovacs, D. (1994) *Euripidea*. Leiden.
  (2005) 'Text and transmission', in *A Companion to Greek Tragedy*, ed. J. Gregory. Oxford: 379–93.
  (2007) 'Tragic interpolation and Philip II: Pylades' forgotten exile and other problems in Euripides' *Orestes*', in *Hesperos: Studies in Ancient Greek Poetry Presented to M. L. West on his Seventieth Birthday*, ed. P. J. Finglass, C. Collard and N. J. Richardson. Oxford: 258–75.
Kowalzig, B. (2008) 'Nothing to do with Demeter? Something to do with Sicily! Theatre and society in the early fifth-century West', in Revermann and Wilson (2008), 128–57.
Kowalzig, B. and Wilson, P. eds (2013) *Dithyramb in its Contexts*. Oxford.
Krumeich, R., Pechstein, N. and Seidensticker, B. (eds.) (1999) *Das griechische Satyrspiel*. Darmstadt.
Kuch, H. (1993) 'Continuity and change in Greek tragedy under postclassical conditions', in *Tragedy, Comedy and the Polis: Papers from the Greek Drama Conference Nottingham, 18–20 July 1990*, ed. A. H. Sommerstein, S. Halliwell, J. Henderson and B. Zimmermann. Bari: 545–57.
Lada-Richards, I. (2007) *Silent Eloquence: Lucian and Pantomime Dancing*. London.
  (2008) 'Was pantomime good to think with?', in *New Directions in Ancient Pantomime*, ed. E. Hall and R. Wyles. Oxford: 284–313.
  (2009) "By means of performance': Western Greek mythological vase-paintings, tragic 'enrichment', and the early reception of fifth-century Athenian tragedy.' *Arion* 17.2: 99–166.
Ladynin, I. A. (2016) 'Virtual history Egyptian style: the isolationist concept of the Potter's Oracle and its alternative', in *Greco-Egyptian Interactions: Literature, Translation and Culture, 500 BCE-300 CE*, ed. I. Rutherford. Oxford: 163–85.
Lamari, A. (2009) 'Knowing a story's end: Future reflexive in the narrative of the Argive expedition against Thebes', in *Narratology and Interpretation: The Content of the Form in Ancient Texts*, ed. J. Grethlein and A. Rengakos. Berlin and New York: 399–419.
  (ed.) (2015) *Reperformances of Drama in the Fifth and Fourth Centuries BC* (*Trends in Classics* 7, special issue). Berlin.
  (2017) *Reperforming Greek Tragedy: Theater, Politics and Cultural Mobility in the Fifth and Fourth Centuries BC*. Berlin.
Lämmle, R. (2013) *Poetik des Satyrspiels*. Heidelberg.
Lane Fox, R. (2008) *Travelling Heroes: Greeks and their Myths in the Epic Age of Homer*. London.
Lanfranchi, P. (2003) 'L'*Exagōgē* d'Ezéchiel le Tragique: du texte biblique au texte théâtral', *Perspectives* 10: 15–31.

(2006) *L'Exagōgē d'Ezéchiel le Tragique: Introduction, texte, traduction et commentaire*. Leiden.

(2007a) 'Moïse l'étranger: l'image du ξένος dans l'*Exagōgē* d'Ezéchiel', in *L'Étranger dans la Bible et sa culture*, ed. J. Riaud. Paris: 249–60.

(2007b) 'Moses' vision of the divine throne in the *Exagōgē* of Ezekiel the tragedian', in *The Book of Ezekiel and Its Influence*, ed. H. J. de Jonge and J. Tromp. Aldershot: 53–9.

(2007c) 'Reminiscences of Ezekiel's *Exagōgē* in Philo's *Vita Mosis*', in *Moses in Biblical and Extra-Biblical Tradition*, ed. A. Graupner and M. Wolter. Berlin and New York: 144–50.

Lape, S. (2004) *Reproducing Athens: Menander's Comedy, Democratic Culture, and the Hellenistic City*. Princeton.

(2006) 'The poetics of the *kōmos*-chorus in Menander's comedy', *AJPh* 127: 89–109.

(2010) 'Gender in Menander's Comedy', in *New Perspectives on Postclassical Comedy*, ed. A. K. Petrides and S. Papaioannou. Newcastle upon Tyne: 51–78.

Lapini, W. (1995–1998) 'Aristotele e l'*Anfiarao* di Carcino (*Poet.* 17.1455a22–33)', *Helikon* 35–38: 351–62.

Lardinois, A. (2003) 'Broken wisdom: traces of the adviser figure in Sophocles' fragments', in *Shards from Kolonos: Studies in Sophoclean Fragments*, ed. A. H. Sommerstein. Bari: 23–43.

Lauriola, R. and Demetriou, K. N. (2015) *Brill's Companion to the Reception of Euripides*. Leiden and Boston.

Lawler, L. B. (1964) *The Dance of the Ancient Greek Theatre*. Iowa City.

Le Guen, B. (1995) 'Théâtre et cités à l'époque hellénistique: mort de la cité–mort du théâtre?', *RÉG* 108: 59–90.

ed. (1997) *De la scène aux gradins: théâtre et représentations dramatiques après Alexandre le Grand*. Pallas 47. Toulouse.

(2001) *Les Associations de Technites dionysiaques à l'époque hellénistique*. 2 vols. Nancy.

(2003) 'Théâtre, cités et royaumes en Anatolie et au Proche-Orient de la mort d'Alexandre le Grand aux conquêtes de Pompée', in *L'Orient méditerranéen de la mort d'Alexandre aux campagnes de Pompée*, ed. F. Prost. Rennes: 329–55.

(2004a) 'Remarques sur les associations de Technites dionysiaques de l'époque hellénistique (à propos de l'ouvrage de Sophia Aneziri, *Die Vereine der dionysischen Techniten im Kontext der hellenistischen Gesellschaft. Untersuchungen zur Geschichte, Organisation und Wirkung der hellenistischen Gesellschaft*, Stuttgart, 2003)', *Nikēphoros* 17: 279–99.

(2004b) 'Le statut professionnel des acteurs grecs à l'époque hellénistique', in *Le Statut de l'acteur dans l'Antiquité*, ed. Ch. Hugoniot, F. Hurlet and S. Milanezi. Tours: 77–106.

(2007a) *À chacun sa tragédie? Retour sur la tragédie grecque*. Rennes.

(2007b) "Décadence' d'un genre? Les auteurs de tragédie et leurs œuvres à la période hellénistique', in Le Guen (2007a), 85–139.

(2007c) 'Le palmarès de l'acteur-athlète: retour sur *Syll.*³ 1080 (Tégée)', *ZPE* 160: 97–107.

(2007d) 'Kraton, son of Zotichos: artists' associations and monarchic power in the Hellenistic period', in Wilson (2007a), 246–78.

(2010a) 'Les fêtes du théâtre grec à l'époque hellénistique', *RÉG* 123: 495–520.

ed. (2010b) *L'Argent dans les concours du monde grec.* Saint-Denis.

(2014) 'Theatre, religion, and politics at Alexander's travelling royal court', in Csapo et al. (2014), 249–74 and pl. 10.

(2016) 'Associations of artists and Hellenistic rulers: the case of the guild established in Ptolemaic Egypt and its Cypriot subsidiary", *Frühmittelalterliche Studien* 50: 231–54.

Lefkowitz, M. (2012) *Lives of the Greek Poets*, 2nd edn. Baltimore.

Leo, F. (1990 [1901]) *Die griechisch-römisch Biographie nach ihrer litterarischen Form.* Leipzig.

Leone. P. A. M. (2002) *Scholia vetera et paraphrases in Lycophronis Alexandram.* Lecce.

Leppin, H. (1992) *Histrionen: Untersuchungen zur sozialen Stellung von Bühnenkünstlern im Westen des Römischen Reiches zur Zeit der Republik und des Principats.* Bonn.

Lesky, A. (1953) 'Das hellenistische Gyges-Drama', *Hermes* 81: 357–70, reprinted in Lesky (1966), 204–12.

(1966) *Gesammelte Schriften.* Bern.

(1972) *Die tragische Dichtung der Hellenen* (3rd edn.). Göttingen.

Le Ven, P. (2014) *The Many-headed Muse: Tradition and Innovation in late Classical Greek Lyric Poetry.* Cambridge.

Lewis, D. M. (1994) 'Sicily, 413–368 B.C.', in *The Cambridge Ancient History*, 2nd edn., vol. IV: *The Fourth Century B.C.* ed. D. M. Lewis et al. Cambridge: 120–55.

Ley, G. (2008) 'A material world: costumes, properties and scenic effects,' in *The Cambridge Companion to Greek and Roman Theatre*, ed. M. McDonald and M. Walton. Cambridge: 268–85.

Li, X. (2005) *Chinese Kunqu Opera.* San Francisco.

Liapis, V. (2001) 'An ancient hypothesis to *Rhesus*, and Dicaearchus' *Hypotheseis*', *GRBS* 42: 313–28.

(2003) 'Epicharmus, Asclepiades of Tragilus, and the *Rhesus*: lessons from a lexicographical entry', *ZPE* 143: 19–22.

(2007) 'How to make a *monostichos*: strategies of variation in the *Sententiae Menandri*', *HSCPh* 103: 261–98.

(2009a) 'Rhesus: myth and iconography', in *The Play of Texts and Fragments: essays in Honour of Martin Cropp*, ed. J. R. C. Cousland and J. R. Hume. Leiden: 273–91.

(2009b) '*Rhesus* revisited: the case for a fourth-century Macedonian context', *JHS* 129: 71–88.

(2012) *A Commentary on the Rhesus Attributed to Euripides*. Oxford and New York.
  (2014) 'Cooking up *Rhesus*: literary imitation and its consumers', in Csapo et al. (2014), 275–94.
  (2016) 'On the *Hector* of Astydamas', *AJPh* 137: 61–89.
  (forthcoming) 'From Dolon to Dorcon: echoes of *Rhesus* in Longus', in *Literary Memory and New Voices in the Ancient Novel: The Intertextual Approach*, ed. M. Futre Pinheiro and J. Morgan. Groningen.
Liapis, V., Panayotakis, C. and Harrison, G. W. M. (2013) 'Introduction: making sense of ancient performance', in Harrison and Liapis (2013), 1–42.
Lightfoot, J. L. (1999) *Parthenius of Nicaea: The Poetical Fragments and the Ἐρωτικὰ Παθήματα*. Oxford.
  (2002) 'Nothing to do with the *technītai* of Dionysus?', in Easterling and Hall (2002), 209–24.
  (2009) *A Hellenistic Collection: Philitas, Alexander of Aetolia, Hermesianax, Euphorion, Parthenius*. Cambridge, Mass.
Lintvelt, J. (1981) *Essai de typologie narrative: le 'point de vue'*. Paris.
Lloyd-Jones, H. (1959) 'The end of the *Seven against Thebes*', *CQ* 9: 80–115.
  (1966a) 'Problems of early Greek tragedy: Pratinas, Phrynichus, the Gyges fragment', *Cuadernos de la Fundación Pastor*. 11–33.
  (1966b) [Review of Snell 1964], *Gnomon* 38: 12–17, reprinted in *Greek Epic, Tragedy and Comedy*. Oxford (1990), 210–17.
Lobel, E. (1936) 'A tragic fragment', in *Greek Poetry and Life: Essays Presented to Gilbert Murray on his Seventieth Birthday*, ed. C. Bailey. Oxford: 295–8.
  (1949) 'A Greek historical drama', *PBA* 35: 207–16.
Lorenzoni, A. (1995) 'Chaerem. fr. 10 Sn.-K.', *Eikasmos* 6: 45–56.
Lowe, N. (2013) 'Comedy and the Pleiad: Alexandrian tragedians and the birth of comic scholarship', in Bakola, Prauscello and Telò (2013). Cambridge: 343–56.
Lucas, D. W. (1968) *Aristotle: Poetics*. Oxford.
Lugaresi, L. (2008) *Il teatro di Dio: Il problema degli spettacoli nel cristianesimo antico (II-IV secolo)*. Brescia.
Luz, C. (2010) *Technopaignia: Formspiele in der griechischen Dichtung*. Leiden.
Luzzatto, M.T. (1983) *Tragedia greca e cultura ellenistica: L'Or. LII di Dione di Prusa*. Bologna.
Ma, J. (2007) 'A *horse* from Teos: epigraphical notes on the Ionian-Hellespontine Association of Dionysiac Aritsts', in Wilson (2007a), 215–45.
  (2008) 'Paradigms and paradoxes in the Hellenistic world', in *Studi Ellenistici*, XX, ed. B. Virgilio. Pisa and Roma: 371–86.
Macurdy, G. H. (1943) 'The dawn songs in *Rhesus* (527–556) and in the parodos of *Phaethon*', *AJPh* 64: 408–16.
MacDowell, D. M. (1971) *Aristophanes: Wasps*. Oxford.
Maddoli, G. (2000) 'Nuovi testi da Iasos', *PdP* 316–317: 15–32.
  (2007) *Epigrafi di Iasos. Nuovi Supplementi*, I, *PdP* 354–356: 353–61.

Maehler, H. (1993) 'Die Scholien der Papyri in ihrem Verhältnis zu den Scholiencorpora der Handschriften', in Montanari (1993), 95–141.
Mair, A. W. and Mair, G. R. (1921) *Callimachus: Hymns and Epigrams, Lycophron, Aratus*. London.
Malkin, I. (1998) *The Returns of Odysseus: Colonization and Ethnicity*. Berkeley.
Manieri, A. (2004) *Agoni poetico-musicali nella Grecia antica 1: Beozia*. Pisa and Rome.
Manuwald, G. (2001a) *Fabulae praetextae: Spuren einer literarischen Gattung der Römer*. Munich.
  (2001b) 'Römische Tragödien und Praetexten republikanischer Zeit: 1964–2002', *Lustrum* 43: 11–237.
  (2011) *Roman Republican Theatre*. Cambridge.
March, J. (2001) *Sophocles: Electra*. Warminster.
Marconi, C. (2012) 'Between performance and identity: the social context of stone theaters in late Classical and Hellenistic Sicily', in Bosher (2012a), 175–207.
Mari, M. (1998) 'Le Olimpie macedoni di Dion tra Archelao e l'età romana', *RFIC* 126: 137–67.
  (2000) 'Commento storico a Licofrone (*Alex.* 1141–1173)', *Hesperia* 10: 283–96.
Marshall, C. W. (2004) '*Alcestis* and the ancient rehearsal process (P. Oxy. 4546)', *Arion* 11: 27–45.
  (2012) 'Sophocles *didaskalos*', in *Blackwell Companion to Sophocles*, ed. K. Ormand. Oxford: 187–203.
Martano, A. (2007) 'Teodette di Faselide poeta tragico: riflessioni attorno al fr. 6 Snell', in *Influences on Peripatetic Rhetoric: Essays in Honor of William W. Fortenbaugh*, ed. D. C. Mirhady. Leiden: 187–99.
Martin, R. P. (2003) 'The pipes are brawling: conceptualizing musical performance in Classical Athens', in *The Cultures within Ancient Greek Culture*, ed. C. Dougherty and L. V. Kurke. Cambridge: 153–80.
Martina, A. (2003) *Teatro greco postclassico e teatro latino: teorie e prassi drammatica. Atti del convegno internazionale (Roma, 16–18 ottobre 2001)*. Rome.
Martinelli, M. C. (2010) 'Una nuova *Medea* in musica: *PLouvre* inv. E. 10534 e la *Medea* di Carcino', in *Ricerche di metrica e musica greca per Roberto Pretagostini*, ed. M. S. Celentano et al. Alexandria: 61–76.
Mascialino, L. (1964) *Lycophronis Alexandra*. Leipzig.
Mastronarde, D. J. (1990) 'Actors on high: the skene roof, the crane and the gods in Attic drama', *CA* 9: 247–94.
  (1994) *Euripides: Phoenissae*. Cambridge.
  (2010a) *The Art of Euripides: Dramatic Art and Social Context*. Cambridge.
  ed. (2010b) *The Euripides Scholia Project*. Euripidesscholia.org: beta-version released April 2010.
Mastronarde, D. J. and Bremer, J. (1982) *The Textual Tradition of Euripides' Phoenissae*. Berkeley.

Matelli, E. (2007) 'Teodette di Faselide, retore', in *Influences on Peripatetic Rhetoric: Essays in Honor of William W. Fortenbaugh*, ed. D. C. Mirhady. Leiden: 169–85.
Mathieson, T. J. (1999) *Apollo's Lyre*. Lincoln and London.
Matthaios, S. (2015) 'Philology and grammar in the Imperial Era and Late Antiquity: An historical and systematic outline', in *Brill's Companion to Hellenistic Scholarship*. Vol. 1: *History*, ed. F. Montanari, S. Matthaios and A. Rengakos. Leiden: 184–296.
Mauduit, C. (2001) 'Sophocles, l'abeille et le miel', in *Lectures antiques de la tragédie grecque*, ed. A. Billault and C. Mauduit. Lyon and Paris: 27–41.
Maurizi, M. (2000) 'A proposito dei nuovitesti di coregia da Iasos', *PP* 316–7: 42–68.
McCall, M. (1985) 'The sources of the Aldine text of Aeschylus' *Supplices*', *BICS* 32: 12–34.
McHardy, F. (2005) 'From treacherous wives to murderous mothers: filicide in tragic fragments', in McHardy et al. (2005), 129–50.
McHardy, F. et al. eds. (2005) *Lost Dramas of Classical Athens: Greek Tragic Fragments*. Exeter.
McNamee, K. (2007) *Annotations in Greek and Latin Texts from Egypt*. Oakville, Conn.
McNelis, C. and Sens, A. 2016. *The* Alexandra *of Lycophron: A Literary Study*. Oxford.
McNiven, T. J. (2000) 'Behaving like an Other: telltale gestures in Athenian vase painting', in Cohen (2000a) 71–97.
Meccariello, C. (2014) *Le hypotheseis narrative dei drammi euripidei: testo, contesto, fortuna*. Rome.
Meijering, R. (1987) *Literary and Rhetorical Theories in Greek Scholia*. Groningen.
Mellert-Hoffmann, G. (1969) *Untersuchungen zur "Iphigenie in Aulis" des Euripides*. Heidelberg.
Merro, G. (2008) *Gli scoli al Reso euripideo*. Messina.
Mette, H. J. (1977) *Urkunden dramatischer Aufführungen in Griechenland*. Berlin and New York.
Michelakis, P. (2002) *Achilles in Greek Tragedy*. Cambridge.
  (2006) *Euripides: Iphigenia at Aulis*. London.
Michelini, A. N. (1982) *Tradition and Dramatic Form in* The Persians *of Aeschylus*. Leiden.
  (1987) *Euripides and the Tragic Tradition*. Madison.
Migeotte, L. (1993) 'De la liturgie à la contribution obligatoire: le financement des Dionysies et des travaux du théâtre à Iasos au II$^e$ siècle avant J.-C.', *Chiron* 23: 267–94.
Millis, B. W. and Olson, S. D. eds. (2012) *Inscriptional Records for the Dramatic Festivals in Athens: IG II$^2$ 2318–2325 and Related Texts*. Leiden and Boston.
Mills, S. (1997) *Theseus, Tragedy and the Athenian Empire*. Oxford.
Mirhady, D. C. (2001) 'Dicaearchus of Messana: the sources, text and translation', in *Dicaearchus of Messana: Text, Translation, and Discussion*, ed. W. W. Fortenbaugh and E. Schütrumpf. New Brunswick, NJ: 1–142.

Mitchell, S. (1990) 'Festivals, games and civic life in Roman Asia Minor', *JRS* 80: 183–93.
Moloney, E. (2014) '*Philippus in acie tutior quam in theatre fuit*... (Curtius 9, 6, 25): the Macedonian kings and Greek theatre', in Csapo et al. (2014), 231–48.
Momigliano, A. (1942) 'Terra marique', *JRS* 32: 53–64, reprinted in *Secondo contributo alla storia degli studi classici e del mondo antico*. Rome, 1960: 431–46.
  (1945) 'The Locrian Maidens and the date of Lycophron's *Alexandra*', *CQ* 39: 49–53, reprinted in *Secondo contributo alla storia degli studi classici e del mondo antico*. Rome, 1960: 446–53.
  (1980) 'The historians of the classical world and their audiences', in *Sesto contributo alla storia degli studi classici e del mondo antico*. Rome: 361–76.
  (1987) 'Sibylline oracles', *Ottavo contributo alla storia degli studi classici e del mondo antico*. Rome: 349–54.
Monfasani, J. (1976) *George of Trebizond: A Biography and a Study of His Rhetoric and Logic*. Leiden.
Montana, F. (2011) 'The making of Greek scholiastic corpora', in *From Scholars to Scholia: Chapters in the History of Ancient Greek Scholarship*, ed. F. Montanari and L. Pagani. Berlin: 105–61.
Montanari, F. ed. (1993) *La Philologie grecque à l'époque hellénistique et romaine*. Vandoeuvres-Geneva.
  (2009) 'L'esegesi antica di Eschilo da Aristotele a Didimo', in *Eschyle à l'aube du théâtre occidental*, ed. A.-C. Hernández. Vandoeuvres-Geneva: 379–433.
  (2011) 'Correcting a copy, editing a text. Alexandrian *ekdoseis* and papyri', in *From Scholars to Scholia: Chapters in the History of Greek Scholarship*, ed. F. Montanari and L. Pagani. Berlin: 3–15.
Mooney, G. W. (1922) *The Alexandra of Lycophron*. London.
Moore, C. H. (1901) 'Notes on the tragic hypotheses', *HSCPh* 12: 287–98.
Moore, T. (2012) *Music in Roman Comedy*. Cambridge.
Morel, W. (1937) 'Andromacha Aechmalotis', *Philologische Wochenschrift* 19/20: 558–60.
Morelli, G. (2001) *Teatro attico e pittura vascolare: una tragedia di Cheremone nella ceramica italiota*. Hildesheim.
Moretti, J.-C. (2014) 'The evolution of theatre architecture outside Athens in the fourth century', in Csapo et al. (2014), 107–37.
Morgan, T. (1998) *Literate Education in the Hellenistic and Roman World*. Cambridge.
Morrison, A. (2007) *The Narrator in Archaic and Hellenistic Poetry*. Cambridge.
Morstadt, R. (1827) *Beitrag zur Kritik der dem Euripides zugeschriebenen Tragödie Rhesos*. Heidelberg.
Mossé, C. (2000) 'Demetrius of Phaleron: a philosopher in power?', in *Alexandria, Third Century B.C.: The Knowledge of a Single World in a City*, ed. C. Jacob and F. de Polignac. Paris: 74–82.
Mossman, J. (1998) 'Tragedy and epic in Plutarch's *Alexander*', *JHS* 108: 83–93.
  (2010) 'Reading the Euripidean *hypothesis*', in *Condensing Texts, Condensed Texts*, ed. M. Horster and C. Reitz. Stuttgart: 247–67.

Most, G. W. ed. (1997) *Collecting Fragments – Fragmente sammeln*. Göttingen.
  (2000) 'Generating genres: the idea of the tragic', in Depew and Obbink (2000), 1–35.
Mras, K. (1954), *Eusebius Werke, VIII: Die Praeparatio evangelica*. Berlin.
Muecke, F. (1982) "I know you – by your rags': costume and disguise in fifth-century drama'. *Antichthon* 16: 17–34.
Müller, (M.) C. G. (1811) Ἰσαακίου καὶ Ἰωάννου Τζέτζου σχόλια εἰς Λυκόφρονα. 3 vols. Leipzig.
Mueller-Goldingen, C. (2005) *Studien zum antiken Drama*. Zurich and New York.
Munn, M. (2006) *The Mother of the Gods, Athens, and the Tyranny of Asia: A Study of Sovereignty in Ancient Religion*. Berkeley, Los Angeles and London.
Munteanu, D. (2002) 'Types of *anagnorisis*: Aristotle and Menander. A self-defining comedy', *Wiener Studien* 115: 111–26.
Murray, A. T. and Wyatt, W. F. (ed., trsl.) (1999a) *Homer: Iliad Books 1–12 (Loeb Classical Library 170)*. Cambridge, Mass.
  (1999b) *Homer: Iliad Books 13–24* (Loeb Classical Library 171). Cambridge, Mass.
Murray, O. (1972) 'Herodotus and Hellenistic culture', *CQ* 22: 200–13.
Murray, P. and Wilson, P. eds. (2004) *Music and the Muses*. Oxford.
Musti, D. (1986) 'Il dionisismo degli Attalidi: antecedenti, modelli, sviluppi', in *L'Association dionysiaque dans les sociétés anciennes*. Rome: 105–28.
  (2001) 'Punti fermi e prospettive di ricerca sulla cronologia della *Alessandra* di Licofrone', *Hesperia* 14: 201–26.
Nachtergael, G. (1977) *Les Galates en Grèce et les Sôtéria de Delphes*. Brussels.
Naerebout, F. (1997) *Attractive Performances. Ancient Greek Dance: Three Preliminary Studies*. Amsterdam.
Nagy, G. (1998) 'The library of Pergamon as a classical model', in *Pergamon: Citadel of the Gods*, ed. H. Koester. Harrisburg, Penn: 185–232.
Nauck, A. (²1926) *Tragicorum graecorum fragmenta*. Leipzig.
Neiiendam, K. (1992) *The Art of Acting in Antiquity: Iconographical Studies in Classical, Hellenistic and Byzantine Theatre*. Copenhagen.
Nervegna, S. (2007) 'Staging scenes or plays? Theatrical revivals of "old" Greek drama in antiquity', *ZPE* 162: 14–42.
  (2013) *Menander in Antiquity*. Cambridge.
  (2014) 'Performing classics: the tragic canon in the fourth century and beyond', in Csapo *et al* (2014), 157–87.
Nesselrath, H.-G. (1990) *Die attische mittlere Komödie*. Berlin and New York.
Niehoff, M. (2011) *Jewish Exegesis and Homeric Scholarship in Alexandria*. Cambridge.
Nielsen, I. (2000) 'Cultic theatres and ritual drama in ancient Greece', *Proceedings of the Danish Institute at Athens* 3: 107–27.
Nilsson, M. P. (1961) *Geschichte der griechischen Religion. II: Die hellenistische und römische Zeit²*. Munich.

Noussia, M. 2006. 'Fragments of Cynic "tragedy"', in *Beyond the Canon*, ed. M. A. Harder, R. F. Regtuit and G. C. Wakker. Leuven, Paris and Dudley: 229–47.
Nünlist, R. (2009) *The Ancient Critic at Work: Terms and Concepts of Literary Criticism in Greek Scholia*. Cambridge.
Olivieri, A. (1950) 'Dionisio I° tiranno di Siracusa e Patrocle di Turi, poeti drammatici', *Dioniso* n.s. 13: 91–102.
Olovsdotter, C. (2005) *The Consular Image: An Iconological Study of the Consular Diptychs*. Oxford.
Olson, S. D. (1997) 'Was Carcinus I a tragic playwright? A response', *CPh* 92: 258–60.
  (2000) 'We didn't know whether to laugh or cry: the case of Karkinos', in *The Rivals of Aristophanes: Studies in Athenian Old Comedy*, ed. D. Harvey and J. Wilkins. London: 65–74.
  (2007) *Broken Laughter: Select Fragments of Greek Comedy*. Oxford.
Orlov, A. (2007) 'Moses' heavenly counterpart in the Book of Jubilees and the *Exagoge* of Ezekiel the Tragedian', *Biblica* 88: 153–73.
  (2008) 'In the mirror of the divine face: the Henochic features of the *Exagoge* of Ezekiel the tragedian', in *The Significance of Sinai: Traditions about Sinai and Divine Revelation in Judaism and Christianity*, ed. G. J. Brooke, H. Najman and L. T. Stuckenbruck. Leiden: 183–200.
Ostwald, M. (1973) 'Was there a concept of *agraphos nomos* in classical Greece?', in *Exegesis and Argument: Studies in Greek Philosophy Presented to Gregory Vlastos*, ed. E. N. Lee and A. P. D. Mourelatos. Assen: 70–104.
O'Sullivan, L. (2009) *The Regime of Demetrius of Phalerum in Athens, 317–307 BCE: a Philosopher in Politics*. Leiden and Boston.
Page, D. L. (1934) *Actors' Interpolations in Greek Tragedy*. Oxford.
  (1941) *Select Papyri III: Literary Papyri, Poetry* (Loeb Classical Library). Cambridge, Mass.
  (1942) *Greek Literary Papyri* I (Loeb Classical Library). Cambridge, Mass.
  (1951) *A New Chapter in the History of Greek Tragedy*. Cambridge.
  (1981) *Further Greek Epigrams*. Cambridge.
Papadopoulou, T. (1998–1999) 'Literary theory and terminology in the Greek scholia: the case of πλάσμα', *BICS* 43: 203–10.
Papaioannou, S. (2013) *Michael Psellos: Rhetoric and Authorship in Byzantium*. Cambridge.
Papastamati-von Moock, C. (2007) 'Menander und die Tragikergruppe: neue Forschungen zu den Ehrenmonumenten im Dionysostheater von Athen', *MDAI(A)* 122: 273–327.
  (2014) 'The theatre of Dionysus Eleuthereus in Athens: new data and observations on its "Lycurgan" phase', in Csapo et al. (2014), 15–76.
Papathanasopoulos, Th. (1987) 'Το θέατρο του Διονύσου: η μορφή του κοίλου' ['The theatre of Dionysus: the form of the *koilon*'], *Αναστήλωση-Συντήρηση-Προστασία Μνημείων και Συνόλων* 2: 31–60.

Parker, P. (1983) *Miasma: Pollution and Purification in Early Greek Religion.* Oxford.
Parry, H. (1964) 'The approach of dawn in the *Rhesus*', *Phoenix* 18: 283–93.
Pasquato, O. (1976) *Gli spettacoli in S. Giovanni Crisostomo: Paganesimo e Cristianesimo ad Antiochia e Constantinopoli nel IV secolo.* Rome.
Pattoni, M. P. (2005) 'I *Pastoralia* di Longo e la contaminazione dei generi: alcune proposte interpretative', *MD* 53: 83–123.
Pavis, P. (1998) *Dictionary of the Theatre: Terms, Concepts, and Analysis*, transl. from the French by C. Schanz, preface by M. Carlson. Toronto.
Pavlock, B. (1985) 'Epic and tragedy in Vergil's Nisus and Euryalus episode', *TAPhA* 115: 207–24.
Pavlovskis, Z. (1977/1978) 'The voice of the actor in Greek tragedy', *CW* 71: 113–23.
Pearson, A. C. (1917) *The Fragments of Sophocles*, 3 vols. Cambridge.
  (1921) 'The *Rhesus*', *CR* 35: 52–61.
Pelling, C. B. R. (2002) *Plutarch and History.* London.
  (2005) 'Tragedy, rhetoric and performance culture', in *A Companion to Greek Tragedy*, ed. J. Gregory. Malden, Mass: 83–102.
Pelosi, F. (2010) *Plato on Music, Soul and Body.* Eng. tr. S. Henderson. Cambridge.
Pendrick, G. (1987) 'Once again Antiphon the Sophist and Antiphon of Rhamnus', *Hermes* 115: 47–60.
  (1993) 'The ancient tradition on Antiphon reconsidered', *GRBS* 34: 215–28.
  (2002) *Antiphon the Sophist: The Fragments.* Cambridge.
Perris, S. (2012) 'Stagecraft and the stage building in *Rhesus*', *G&R* 59: 151–64.
Perrone, S. (2009) 'Lost in tradition: papyrus commentaries on comedies and tragedies of unknown authorship', *TiC* 1: 203–40.
Perusino, F. (1993) *Anonimo (Michele Psello?): La Tragedia Greca.* Urbino.
Petrides, A. K. (2010) 'New Performance,' in Petrides and Papaioannou (2010), 79–124.
  (2013) 'Lucian's *On Dance* and the poetics of the pantomime mask', in Harrison and Liapis (2013), 433–50.
  (2014) *Menander, New Comedy and the Visual.* Cambridge.
  (2015) Review of Kotlińska-Toma (2015), *Eos* 102: 198–201.
Petrides, A. K. and Papaioannou, S. eds. (2010) *New Perspectives on Postclassical Comedy.* Newcastle upon Tyne.
Pfeiffer, R. (1949) *Callimachus, vol. I: Fragmenta.* Oxford.
  (1968) *History of Classical Scholarship from the Beginnings to the End of the Hellenistic Age.* Oxford.
Picard, G. Ch. (1994) 'Carthage from the battle at Himera to Agathocles' invasion (480–308 B.C.)', in *The Cambridge Ancient History*, 2nd edn., vol. IV: *The Fourth Century B.C.*, ed. D. M. Lewis et al. Cambridge: 361–80.
Pickard-Cambridge, A. W. (1946) *The Theatre of Dionysus in Athens.* Oxford.
  (1962) *Dithyramb Tragedy and Comedy.* 2nd edn. rev. T. B. L. Webster. Oxford.

(³1988) *The Dramatic Festivals of Athens*. 3rd edn. rev. J. Gould and D. M. Lewis. Oxford.
Pickering, P. E. (2000) 'Verbal repetition in *Prometheus* and Greek tragedy generally', *BICS* 44: 81–101.
(2003) 'Did the Greek ear detect "careless" verbal repetitions?', *CQ* 53: 490–9.
Pietruczuk, K. (2012) 'The prologue of *Iphigenia Aulidensis* reconsidered', *Mnemosyne* 65: 565–83.
Poe, J. P. (2003) 'Word and deed: on "stage-directions" in Greek tragedy', *Mnemosyne* 56.4: 420–48.
Pöhlmann, E. (2009) *Gegenwärtige Vergangenheit: ausgewählte Kleine Schriften*. Berlin.
Pöhlmann, E. and West, M. L. eds. (2001) *Documents of Ancient Greek Music*. Oxford.
Polacco, L. and Anti, C. (1981) *Il teatro antico di Siracusa*. Rimini.
Poli Palladini, L. (2001) 'Some reflections on Aeschylus' *Aetnae(ae)*', *RhM* 144: 287–325.
Porter, J. I. (1995) 'Οἱ κριτικοί: a reassessment', in *Greek Literary Theory after Aristotle*, ed. J. G. J. Abbenes, S. R. Slings and I. Sluiter. Amsterdam: 83–109.
(2005) 'Feeling classical: classicism and ancient literary criticism', in *Classical Pasts: The Classical Traditions of Greece and Rome*, ed. J. I. Porter. Princeton: 301–52.
Powell, J. U. (1925) *Collectanea Alexandrina*. Oxford.
Power, T. (2010) *The Culture of Kitharôidia*. Washington, DC.
Prauscello, L. (2006) *Singing Alexandria: Music between Practice and Textual Transmission*. Leiden.
Primavesi, O. (2004) 'Farbige Plastik in der antiken Literatur? Vorschläge für eine differenzierte Lesung', in *Bunte Götter: Die Farbigkeit antiker Skulptur: Ausstellungskatalog*, 2nd edn., ed. V. Brinkmann and R. Wünsche. Munich: 219–37.
Puchner, W. (2002) 'Acting in the Byzantine theatre: evidence and problems', in Easterling and Hall (2002), 304–24.
Pulleyn, S. (1997) *Prayer in Greek Religion*. Oxford.
Race, W. H. (1997) *Pindar: Nemean Odes, Isthmian Odes, Fragments*. Cambridge, Mass.
Ravenna, O. (1903) 'Di Moschione e di Teodette poeti tragici', *RSA* 7: 736–804.
Reeve, M. D. (1972–3) 'Interpolations in Greek Tragedy, I, II, III', *GRBS* 13: 247–65, 451–74; 14: 145–71.
(1996) 'Classical scholarship', in *The Cambridge Companion to Renaissance Humanism*, ed. J. Kraye. Cambridge: 20–46.
Revermann, M. (1999–2000) 'Euripides, tragedy and Macedon: some conditions of reception', in *Euripides and the Tragic Theatre in the Late Fifth Century*, ed. M. Cropp, K. Lee and D. Sansone. Champaign, IL: 451–67 (= *ICIS* 24/25).
(2005) 'The "Cleveland Medea" calyx crater and the iconography of ancient Greek theatre', *Theatre Research International* 30: 3–18.

(2006a) *Comic Business: Theatricality, Dramatic Technique, and Performance Contexts of Aristophanic Comedy*. Oxford.

(2006b) 'The competence of theatre audiences in fifth- and fourth-century Athens', *JHS* 126: 99–124.

(2010) 'Situating the gaze of the recipient(s): theatre-related vase paintings and their contexts of reception', in Gildenhard and Revermann (2010), 69–97.

(2013) 'Generalizing about props: Greek drama, comparator traditions, and the analysis of stage objects', in Harrison and Liapis (2013), 77–88.

Revermann, M. and Wilson, P. (2008) *Performance, Iconography, Reception: Studies in Honour of Oliver Taplin*. Oxford.

Reynolds, L. D. and Wilson, N. G. (2013) *Scribes and Scholars: A Guide to the Transmission of Greek and Latin Literature*, 3rd edn. Oxford.

Ribbeck, W. (1875) 'Über einige historische Dramen der Griechen', *RhM* 30: 144–61.

Richardson, N. J. (1993) 'Aristotle and Hellenistic scholarship', in Montanari (1993), 7–38.

Rigsby, K. J. (1996) *Asylia: Territorial Inviolability in the Hellenistic World*. Berkeley and Los Angeles.

Rijksbaron, A. (1976) 'How does a messenger begin his speech? Some observations on the opening-lines of Euripidean messenger-speeches', in *Miscellanea tragica*, ed. J. M. Bremer, S. L. Radt and C. J. Ruijgh. Amsterdam: 293–308.

(1994) *The Syntax and Semantics of the Verb in Classical Greek: An Introduction*. Amsterdam.

Ringer, M. (1998) *Electra and the Empty Urn: Metatheater and Role-playing in Sophocles*. Chapel Hill.

Ritchie, W. (1964) *The Authenticity of the Rhesus of Euripides*. Cambridge.

Robb, K. (1994) *Literacy and Paideia in Ancient Greece*. New York and Oxford.

Robert, C. (1915) *Oidipus: Geschichte eines poetischen Stoffs im griechischen Altertum*. Berlin.

Robert, L. (1936) 'Ἀρχαιολόγος', *RÉG* 49: 235–54, reprinted in Robert (1969–90) 1, 671–90.

(1966) *Monnaies antiques en Troade*. Geneva.

(1969–1990) *Opera minora selecta*. 7 vols. Amsterdam.

Roberts, C. H. and Skeat, T. C. (1983) *The Birth of the Codex*. London.

Robertson, R. G. (1985) 'Ezekiel the tragedian', in *The Old Testament Pseudepigrapha*, vol. 2, ed. J. H. Charlesworth. New York: 803–19.

Robinson, E. G. D. (2014) 'Greek theatre in non-Greek Apulia', in Csapo et al. (2014), 319–32.

Rode, J. (1971) 'Das Chorlied', in *Die Bauformen der griechischen Tragödie*, ed. W. Jens. *Beihefte zu Poetica* 6, 85–115.

Rohde, E. (1870) *De Julii Pollucis in apparatu scaenico enarrando fontibus*. Leipzig.

(1888) 'Γέγονε in den Biographica des Suidas: Beiträge zu einer Geschichte der litterarhistorischen Forschung der Griechen', *RhM* 33: 161–220, 638–9.

Roller, D. W. (2006) *The World of Juba II and Kleopatra Selene*. London.

Rooy, C. van (1965) *Studies in Classical Satire*. Leiden.

Rosato, C. (2005) *Euripide sulla scena latina arcaica: la* Medea *di Ennio e le* Baccanti *di Accio*. Lecce.
Roselli, D. K. (2005) 'Vegetable-hawking mom and fortunate son: Euripides, tragic style, and reception'. *Phoenix* 59.1: 1–49.
Rosen, R. M. (1999) 'Comedy and confusion in Callias' *Letter Tragedy*'. *CP* 94: 147–67.
  (2006) 'Aristophanes, fandom, and the classicizing of Greek tragedy', in *Playing Around Aristophanes: Essays in Celebration of the Completion of the Edition of the Comedies of Aristophanes by Alan Sommerstein*, ed. L. Kozak and J. Rich. Oxford: 27–47.
  (2012) 'Timocles fr. 6 K.-A. and the parody of Greek literary theory', in *No Laughing Matter: Studies in Athenian Comedy*, ed. C. W. Marshall and G. Kovacs. London: 177–86.
Rothwell, K. S. (1992) 'The continuity of the chorus in fourth-century Attic comedy', *GRBS* 33: 209–25.
  (1994) 'Was Carcinus I a tragic playwright?', *CPh* 89: 241–5.
Rotstein, A. (2012) '*Mousikoi Agones* and the conceptualization of genre in Ancient Greece', *CA* 31: 92–127.
Rouché, C. (1993) *Performers and Partisans at Aphrodisias in the Roman and Late Roman Period*. London.
Roux, G. (1967) 'Sur deux textes relatifs à Adonis', *RPh* 41: 259–64.
Royall, T. ed. (1993) *Japanese No Dramas*. Harmondsworth.
Rudd, N. (1989) *Horace Epistles Book II and Epistle to the Pisones ('Ars Poetica')*. Cambridge.
Ruffatto, K. J. (2006) 'Polemics with Enochic traditions in the *Exagoge* of Ezekiel the tragedian', *Journal for the Study of the Pseudepigrapha* 15: 195–210.
  (2008) 'Raguel as interpreter of Moses' throne vision: the transcendent identity of Raguel in the Exagoge of Ezekiel the tragedian', *Journal for the Study of the Pseudepigrapha*, 17.2: 121–39.
Ruijgh, C. J. (2001) 'Le *Spectacle des Lettres*, comédie de Callias (Athénée X 453c–455b), avec un *excursus* sur les rapports entre la mélodie du chant et les contours mélodiques du langage parlé', *Mnemosyne* 54: 257–335.
Ruiten, J. T. A. G. M. van (2006) 'A burning bush on the stage: the rewriting of Exodus 3:1–4:17 in Ezekiel tragicus, *Exagoge* 90–131', in *The Revelation of the Name of YHWH to Moses: Perspectives from Judaism, the Pagan Graeco-Roman World, and Early Christianity*, ed. G. H. van Kooten. Leiden: 71–88.
Russell, D. A. (1981) *Criticism in Antiquity*. London.
Russo, G. (2008) 'Due note a frammenti di tragici greci', *RFIC* 136: 129–36.
Rusten, J. (1982) 'Dicaearchus and the *Tales from Euripides*', *GRBS* 23: 357–67.
Rutherford, I. (2007) '*Theoria* and theatre at Samothrace: the *Dardanos* by Dymas of Iasos', in Wilson (2007a), 279–93.
  (2009) 'Aristodama and the Aitolians: an itinerant poetess and her agenda', in Hunter and Rutherford (2009), 237–48.
Rutherford, R. (2007) 'Tragedy and history', in *Companion to Greek and Roman Historiography*, ed. J. Marincola. Oxford: 504–14.

(2012) *Greek Tragic Style: Form, Language and Interpretation*. Cambridge.
Rzach, A. (1923) 'Sibyllen' and 'Sibyllinische Orakel', *RE* ii(1): 2074–83.
Sandys, J. E. (1903) *History of Classical Scholarship*, Vol. 1: *From the Sixth Century B.C. to the End of the Middle Ages*. Cambridge.
Sansone, D. (2013) Review of Liapis (2012), *BMCR* 2013.03.15 (http://bmcr.brynmawr.edu/2013/2013-03-15.html).
Saxonhouse, A. W. (2006) *Free Speech and Democracy in Ancient Athens*. New York.
Sayar, M. H. (1998) *Perinthos-Herakleia (Marmara Ereglisi) und Umgebung. Geschichte, Testimonien, griechische und lateinische Inschriften (Denkschr. Öst. Akad. Wiss. ph.-hist. Kl. 269)*. Vienna.
Sbordone, F. (1969) 'Il quarto libro del Περὶ ποιημάτων di Filodemo', *Ricerche sui papiri Ercolanesi* I: 289–367.
(1976) Φιλοδήμου Περὶ ποιημάτων. *Ricerche sui papyri ercolanesi* II. Naples.
Scafuro, A. C. (1997) *The Forensic Stage: Settling Disputes in Graeco-Roman New Comedy*. Cambridge.
Scaliger, J. J. (1600) *M. Manili Astronomicon*. Leiden.
Schachter, A. (1986) *Cults of Boiotia* (*BICS* Suppl. 38, 2 vols). London.
Schade, G. (1999) *Lykophron's 'Odyssee': Alexandra 648–819*. Berlin and New York.
Schauer, M., ed., (2012) *Tragicorum Romanorum Fragmenta*, Vol. 1: *Livius Andronicus; Naevius; Tragici minores; Fragmenta adespota*. Göttingen.
Scheer, E. (1881–1908) *Lycophronis Alexandra*, 2 vols. Berlin.
Scheer, T. (1993) *Mythische Vorväter: Zur Bedeutung griechischer Heroenmythen im Selbstverständnis kleinasiatischer Städte*. Munich.
Schein, S. L. (2013) *Sophocles: Philoctetes*. Cambridge.
Schenkeveld, D. M. (1993) 'Scholarship and grammar', in Montanari (1993), 263–306.
Schlapbach, K. (2008) 'Lucian's *On Dancing* and the models for a discourse on pantomime' in *New Directions in Ancient Pantomime*, ed. E. Hall and R. Wyles. Oxford: 314–37.
Schmid, W. (1940) *Geschichte der griechischen Literatur*, vol. I.3 (Handb. d. Altertumsw. 7/1/3). Munich.
Schmitz, T. (2010) 'A sophist's drama: Lucian and classical tragedy', in Gildenhard and Revermann (2010), 289–311.
Schneidewin, F. G. (1852) 'De hypothesibus tragoediarum graecarum Aristophani Byzantio vindicandis commentatio', *Abhandlungen der Gesellschaft der Wissenschaften zu Göttingen, philologisch-historische Klasse* 6: 1–38.
Schoch, R. (2012) 'Inventing the origins of theatre history: the modern uses of Juba II's *theatriké historia*', *Journal of Dramatic Theory and Criticism* 27: 5–23.
Schorn, S. (2004) *Satyros aus Kallatis: Sammlung der Fragmente mit Kommentar*. Basel.

Schramm, F. (1929) *Tragicorum Graecorum hellenisticae, quae dicitur, aetatis fragmenta (praeter Ezechielem) eorumque de vita atque poesi testimonia collecta et illustrata*, Diss. Münster.
Schütrumpf, E. (1970) *Die Bedeutung des Wortes ἦθος in der Poetik des Aristoteles*. Munich.
(1987) 'The meaning of ἦθος in the *Poetics*', *Hermes* 115: 175–81.
et al. (2008) *Heraclides of Pontus: Texts and Translations*. Piscataway, N.J.
Scodel, R. (2007) 'Lycurgus and the state text of tragedy', in *Politics of Orality*, ed. C. Cooper. Leiden and Boston: 129–54.
Scott Smith, R. and Trzaskoma, S. M. (2005) 'Apollodorus 1.9.7: Salmoneus' Thunder-Machine.' *Philologus* 149.2: 351–4.
Scullion, S. (2003) 'Euripides and Macedon, or the silence of the *Frogs*', *CQ* 53: 389–400.
(2006) 'The opening of Euripides' *Archelaus*', in *Dionysalexandros: Essays on Aeschylus and his Fellow Tragedians in Honour of Alexander F. Garvie*, ed. D. Cairns and V. J. Liapis. Swansea: 185–200.
Seaford, R. (2012) *Cosmology and the Polis: The Social Construction of Space and Time in the Tragedies of Aeschylus*. Cambridge.
Seeburg, A. (2002–3) 'Tragedy and archaeology, forty years after' *BICS* 46: 43–75.
Seeck, A. (1979) *Das griechische Drama*. Darmstadt.
Segal, C. (1982) *Dionysiac Poetics and Euripides' Bacchae*. Princeton.
Segre, M. ed. (1993) *Iscrizioni di Cos*. Rome.
Seidensticker, B. (2010) 'Dance in satyr play', in Taplin and Wyles (2010), 213–230.
Sells, D. (2012) 'Eleusis and the public status of comedy in Aristophanes' *Frogs*', in *No Laughing Matter: Studies in Athenian Comedy*, ed. C. W. Marshall and G. Kovacs. London: 83–99.
Sens, A. (2010) 'Hellenistic tragedy and Lycophron's *Alexandra*', in *A Companion to Hellenistic Literature*, ed. J. J. Clauss and M. Cuypers. Chichester: 297–313.
Shaw, C. A. (2014) *Satyric Play: The Evolution of Greek Comedy and Satyr Drama*. Oxford.
Shiloah, A. (1995) *Music in the World of Islam*. Detroit.
Sickinger, J. P. (1999) *Public Records and Archives in Athens*. Chapel Hill and London.
Sider, D. (1997) *The Epigrams of Philodemos: Introduction, Text and Commentary*, Oxford.
Sifakis, G. M. (1967) *Studies in the History of Hellenistic Drama*. London.
(1995) 'The one-actor rule in Greek tragedy', *BICS* 40: 13–24.
(2001) *Aristotle on Tragic Poetry*. Herakleion.
(2002) 'Looking for the actor's art in Aristotle', in Easterling and Hall (2002), 148–64.
(2007) Μελέτες για το αρχαίο θέατρο *[Studies on Ancient Theatre]*. Herakleion.

(2013) 'The misunderstanding of *opsis* in Aristotle's *Poetics*', in Harrison and Liapis (2013), 45–61.
Sistakou, E. (2008) *Reconstructing the Epic: Cross-readings of the Trojan Myth in Hellenistic Poetry*. Leuven and Dudley, Mass.
  (2012) *The Aesthetics of Darkness: A Study of Hellenistic Romanticism in Apollonius, Lycophron and Nicander*. Leuven, Paris and Walpole, Mass.
Slater, N. W. (1990) 'The idea of the actor,' in *Nothing to Do with Dionysos? Athenian Drama in its Social Context*, ed. J. J. Winkler and F. I. Zeitlin. Princeton: 385–96.
  (2002) 'Dancing the alphabet: performative literacy on the Attic stage', in *Epea and Grammata: Oral and Written Communication in Ancient Greece*, ed. I. Worthington and J. M. Foley. Leiden: 117–29.
Slater, W. J. (1986) *Aristophanis Byzantii fragmenta*. Berlin and New York.
  (1996) 'Inschriften von Magnesia 192 revisited', *GRBS* 37: 195–204.
  (2007) 'Deconstructing festivals', in Wilson (2007a), 21–47.
  (2010) 'Paying the pipers', in Le Guen (2010b), 249–81.
Small, J. P. (2003) *The Parallel Worlds of Classical Art and Text*. Cambridge.
  (2013) 'Skenographia in brief', in Harrison and Liapis (2013), 111–28.
Smith, D. G. (2012) 'Sicily and the identities of Xuthus: Stesichorus, Aeschylus' *Aetnaeae*, and Euripides' *Ion*', in Bosher (2012a), 112–36.
Snell, B. (1937) *Euripides Alexandros und andere Strassburger Papyri mit Fragmenten griechischer Dichter*. Berlin.
  (1964) *Scenes from Greek Drama*. Berkeley and Los Angeles.
  (1966) 'Die Iamben in Ezechiels Moses-Drama', *Glotta* 44: 25–32.
  (1971) *Szenen aus griechischen Dramen*. Berlin.
Solmsen, F. (1932) 'Zur Gestaltung des Intriguenmotivs in den Tragödien des Sophokles und Euripides', *Philologus* 87: 1–17.
Sommerstein, A. H. (1993) 'Kleophon and the restaging of the *Frogs*', in *Tragedy, Comedy, and the Polis*, ed. A. H. Sommerstein et al. Bari: 461–76.
  (1996) *Aristophanes: Frogs*. Warminster.
  (2003) 'The anger of Achilles, mark one: Sophocles' *Syndeipnoi*', in *Shards from Kolonos: Studies in Sophoclean Fragments*, ed. A. H. Sommerstein. Bari: 355–71.
  (2006) '*Syndeipnoi* (*The Diners*) or *Achaiōn Syllogos*', in *Sophocles: Selected Fragmentary Plays* (vol. I), ed. A. H. Sommerstein, D. Fitzpatrick and T. Talboy. Oxford: 84–140.
  (2010) *Aeschylean Tragedy*, 2nd edn. London.
Sourvinou-Inwood, C. (1995) *'Reading' Greek Death to the End of the Classical Period*. Oxford.
Stephanis, I. E. (1988) Διονυσιακοί τεχνῖται: Συμβολές στήν προσωπογραφία τοῦ θεάτρου καί τῆς μουσικῆς τῶν ἀρχαίων Ἑλλήνων [*Dionysiakoi Technitai: Contributions to the Prosopography of Ancient Greek Theatre and Music*]. Herakleion.
Stephanopoulos, Th. K. (1984) Review of Xanthakis-Karamanos (1980), *Hellenika* 35: 176–93.

(1988a) 'Tragica I', *ZPE* 73: 207–47.
(1988b) 'Tragica II', *ZPE* 75: 3–38.
(1995/1996) 'Der Tragiker Moschion: Erster Teil' *Archaiognosia* 9: 137–53.
(1997) 'Der Tragiker Moschion: Zweiter Teil', *Archaiognosia* 10: 51–63.
(2001) 'Χαιρήμων', in Ανθολογία Αρχαίας Ελληνικής Γραμματείας *[Anthology of Greek Literature]*, ed. Th. K. Stephanopoulos et al. Athens: 1. 404–7.
(2013) 'Marginalia Tragica I', *Logeion* 3: 66–70.
(2014) 'Marginalia Tragica II', *Logeion* 4: 193–200.
Stevens, P. T. (1945) 'Colloquial expressions in Aeschylus and Sophocles', *CQ* 39: 95–105.
(1965) Review of Ritchie (1964), *CR* n.s. 15: 268–71.
(1976) *Colloquial Expressions in Euripides*. Hermes Einzelschriften 38. Wiesbaden.
Stewart, E. (2017) *Greek Tragedy on the Move: The Birth of a Panhellenic Art form, c. 500–300 BC*. Oxford and New York.
Strasser, J.-Y. (2004) 'Inscriptions grecques et latines en l'honneur de pantomimes', *Tyche* 19: 175–212.
Strohm, H. (1959) 'Beobachtungen zum *Rhesos*', *Hermes* 87: 257–74.
Strugnell, J. (1967) 'Notes on the text and metre of Ezekiel the tragedian's *Exagôgê*', *Harvard Theological Review* 60: 449–57.
Suess, W. (1966) 'Der ältere Dionys als Tragiker', *RhM* 109: 299–318.
Susemihl, F. (1891–2) *Geschichte der griechischen Literatur in der Alexandrinerzeit*. 2 vols. Leipzig.
Sutton, D. F. (1980) *The Greek Satyr Play*. Meisenheim am Glan.
(1987a) 'The theatrical families of Athens', *AJP* 108: 9–26.
(1987b) *Papyrological Studies in Dionysiac Literature: P. Lit. Lond. 77, a postclassical satyr-play, and P. Ross. Georg. I. 11, a hymn to Dionysus*. Oak Park, Ill.
Swift, L. (2010) *The Hidden Chorus: Echoes of Genre in Tragic Lyric*. Oxford.
Taplin, O. (1971) 'Significant actions in Sophocles' *Philoctetes*', *GRBS* 12: 25–44.
(1976) 'XOPOY and the structure of post-classical tragedy', *LCM* 1: 47–50.
(1977a) *The Stagecraft of Aeschylus: The Dramatic Use of Exits and Entrances in Greek Tragedy*. Oxford.
(1977b) 'Did Greek dramatists write stage instructions?', *PCPhS* 203: 121–32.
(1987) 'Phallology, phlyakes, iconography and Aristophanes', *PCPhS* 33: 92–104.
(1993) *Comic Angels and Other Approaches to Greek Drama through Vase-painting*. Oxford.
(1997) 'The pictorial record', in Easterling (1997), 69–90.
(1999) 'Spreading the word through performance', in *Performance Culture and Athenian Democracy*, ed. S. Goldhill and R. Osborne. Cambridge: 33–57.
(2007) *Pots and Plays: Interactions between Tragedy and Greek Vase-Painting of the Fourth Century B.C.* Los Angeles.
(2009) 'Hector's helmet glinting in a fourth-century tragedy', in *Sophocles and the Greek Tragic Tradition*, ed. S. Goldhill and E. Hall. Cambridge 2009: 251–63.

(2012) 'How was Athenian tragedy played in the Greek West?', in Bosher (2012a), 226–50.
(2014) 'How pots and papyri might prompt a re-evaluation of fourth-century tragedy', in Csapo et al. (2014), 141–55.
Taplin, O. and Wyles, R. eds. (2010) *The Pronomos Vase*. Oxford.
Tarán, L. and Goutas, D. (2012) *Aristotle Poetics: Editio Maior of the Greek Text with Historical Introductions and Commentaries*. Leiden and Boston.
Tarn, W. W. (1913) *Antigonus Gonatas*. Oxford.
Tarrant, R. J. (1978) 'Senecan drama and its antecedents', *HSCPh* 82: 213–63.
Taylor, D. (2003) *The Archive and the Repertoire: Performing Cultural Memory in the Americas*. Durham, NC.
Tedeschi, G. (1998) *Luciano, Podagra: introduzione, traduzione e note*. Lecce.
(2002) 'Lo spettacolo in età ellenistica e tardo antica nella documentazione epigrafica e papiracea', *Papirologica Lupiensia* 11: ed. M. Capasso. Lecce: 87–187.
(2017) *Spettacoli e trattenimenti dal IV secolo a.C. all'età tardo-antica secondo i documenti epigrafici e papiracei*. Trieste.
Theocharidis, G. (1940) *Beiträge zur Geschichte des byzantinischen Profantheaters im IV und V Jahrhundert*. Thessaloniki.
Thum, T. (2005) 'Der *Rhesos* und die Tragödie des 4. Jahrhunderts', *Philologus* 149: 209–32.
Todd, S. C. (Tr.) (2000) *Lysias*. Austin.
(2007) *A Commentary on Lysias, Speeches 1–11*. Oxford.
Todisco, L. (2002) *Teatro e spettacolo in Magna Grecia e in Sicilia: Testi, Immagini, Architettura*. Milan.
(2012) 'Myth and tragedy: red-figure pottery and verbal communication in central and northern Apulia in the later fourth century BC', in Bosher (2012a), 251–71.
Tordoff, R. (2013) 'Actors' properties in ancient Greek drama: An overview', in Harrison and Liapis (2013), 89–110.
Torrance, I. (2010) 'Writing and self-conscious *mythopoiēsis* in Euripides', *CCJ* 56: 213–58.
(2013) *Metapoetry in Euripides*. Oxford.
Tracy, S. V. (2015) 'The dramatic festival inscriptions of Athens: the inscribers and phases of inscribing', *Hesperia* 84: 553–81.
Travis, R. (2000) 'The spectation of Gyges in *P. Oxy.* 2382 and Herodotus Book 1', *Classical Antiquity* 19: 330–49.
Trendall, A. D. (1959) *Phlyax Vases (BICS Supplement 8)*. London.
Trendall, A. D. and Webster, T. B. L. (1971) *Illustrations of Greek Drama*. London.
Trendelenburg, A. (1867) *Grammaticorum graecorum de arte tragica iudicorum reliquiae*. Bonn.
Tritle, L. A. (2009) 'Alexander and the Greeks: artists and soldiers, friends and enemies', in *Alexander the Great. A New History*, ed. W. Heckel and L. A. Tritle. Oxford: 121–40.

Tuilier, A. (1968) *Recherches critiques sur la tradition du texte d'Euripide*. Paris.
(1972) *Étude comparée du texte et des scholies d'Euripide*. Paris.
Turner, E. G. (1962) '2458. Euripides, *Cresphontes*', *P. Oxy.* 27: 73–81.
Tyrrell, W. B. and Bennett, L. J. (1998) *Recapturing Sophocles' Antigone*. Lanham.
Tzanetou, A. (2012) *City of Suppliants: Tragedy and the Athenian Empire*. Austin.
Utzschneider, H. (2010) 'Is there a universal genre of drama?', in *Literary Construction of Identity in the Ancient World*, ed. H. Liss and M. Oeming. Winona Lake: 63–79.
Vahtikari, V. (2014) *Tragedy Performances outside Athens in the Late Fifth and the Fourth Centuries BC*. Helsinki.
Valckenaer, L. C. (1767) *Diatribe in Euripidis perditorum dramatum reliquias*. Leiden.
Van de Water, R. (2001) 'Moses' exaltation: pre-Christian', *Journal for the Study of the Pseudepigrapha* 21: 59–69.
van Rossum-Steenbeek, M. (1998) *Greek Readers' Digests? Studies on a Selection of Sub-Literary Papyri*. Leiden.
van Wees, H. (2004) *Greek Warfare: Myths and Realities*. London.
Vassalo, S. (2012) 'The theater of Montagna dei Cavalli-Hippana', in Bosher (2012a), 208–25.
Verhasselt, G. (2015) 'The Hypotheses of Euripides and Sophocles by "Dicaearchus"', *GRBS* 55: 608–36.
Vernant, J.-P. and Vidal-Naquet, P. (1990) 'The historical moment of tragedy in Greece: some of the social and psychological conditions', in *Myth and Tragedy in Ancient Greece*, transl. J. Lloyd. New York: 23–8.
Vinegre, M. A. (2001) 'Tragedia griega del siglo IV A.C. y tragedia helenística', *Habis* 32: 81–95.
Völke, P. (2001) *Un théâtre de la marge: aspects figuratifs et configurationnels du drame satyrique dans l'Athènes classique*. Bari.
Wade, B. (1999) *Music in India: The Classical Traditions*. Rev. ed, New Delhi.
Walbank, F. W. (1938) 'Φίλιππος τραγῳδούμενος: a Polybian experiment', *JHS* 58: 55–68, reprinted in Walbank (1985), 210–23.
(1954) 'Fourth-century tragedy and the *Poetics*'. *Hermes* 82: 294–308.
(1955) 'Tragic history: a reconsideration'. *BICS* 2: 4–14.
(1960) 'History and tragedy', *Historia* 9: 216–34, reprinted in Walbank (1985), 224–41.
(1985) *Selected Papers*. Cambridge.
Walz, C. (1835) *Rhetores graeci* vol 8. Stuttgart.
Wankel, H. (1976) *Demosthenes: Rede für Ktesiphon über den Kranz*. 2 vols. Heidelberg.
Wartelle, A. (1971) *Histoire du texte d'Eschyle dans l'antiquité*. Paris.
Watson, L. C. (2003) *A Commentary on Horace's Epodes*. Oxford.
Webb, R. (1997) 'Salome's sisters: the rhetoric and realities of dance in late antiquity and Byzantium', in *Women, Music, and Eunuchs: Gender in Byzantium*, ed. L. James. London: 119–48.

(2007) 'Basil of Caesarea and Greek Tragedy', in *A Companion to Classical Receptions*, ed. C. Stray and L. Hardwick. Oxford: 62–71.
(2008) *Demons and Dancers: Performance in Late Antiquity*. Cambridge, Mass.
(2010) 'Between poetry and rhetoric: Libanios' use of Homeric subjects in his *Progymnasmata*', *QUCC* 95: 131–52.
(2013) 'Les *Images* de Philostrate: Une narration éclatée', in *La trame et le tableau: Poétiques et rhétoriques du récit et de la description*, ed. M. Briand. Rennes: 19–34.
Webster, T. B. L. (1954) 'Fourth-century tragedy and the *Poetics*', *Hermes* 82: 294–308.
(1956) *Art and Literature in Fourth Century Athens*. London.
(1960/ ²1969/ ³1978) *Monuments Illustrating Old and Middle Comedy*. London. (3rd edn., revised and enlarged by J. R. Green; supplements in *BICS* 27 [1980] 123–31.)
(1961/ ²1969/ ³1995) *Monuments Illustrating New Comedy*. London. (3rd edn., revised and enlarged by J. R. Green and A. Seeberg, 2 vols).
(1962/ ²1967) *Monuments Illustrating Tragedy and Satyr-Play*. London.
(1970) *Greek Theatre Production*, 2nd edn. London.
(1974) *An Introduction to Menander*. Manchester.
Wehrli, F. ed. (1967) *Die Schule des Aristoteles: Texte und Kommentare*, 3 vols, Basel.
Weiss, N. A. (2018) *The Music of Tragedy: Performance and Imagination in Euripidean Theater*. Berkeley and Los Angeles.
Welcker, F. G. (1841) *Die griechischen Tragödien mit Rücksicht auf den epischen Cyclus*, vol. 3. Bonn.
Wellenbach, M. C. (2015) 'The iconography of Dionysiac choroi: dithyramb, tragedy, and the Basel krater', *GRBS* 55: 72–103.
West, M. L. (1977) 'Notes on papyri', *ZPE* 26: 37–43.
(1979) 'The Prometheus trilogy', *JHS* 99: 130–48.
(1982) *Greek Metre*. Oxford.
(1983) 'Tragica VI', *BICS* 30: 63–82.
(1990) *Studies in Aeschylus*. Stuttgart.
(1992) *Ancient Greek Music*. Oxford.
(1999) 'Sophocles with music? Ptolemaic music fragments and remains of Sophocles' (Junior?) *Achilleus*', *ZPE* 126: 43–65.
(2000) '*Iliad* and *Aethiopis* on the stage: Aeschylus and son', *CQ* n.s. 50: 338–52.
(2007) 'A new musical papyrus: Carcinus, *Medea*', *ZPE* 161: 1–10.
(2013a) *Hellenica: Selected Papers on Greek Literature and Thought, Vol. II. Lyric and Drama*. Oxford.
(2013b) *Hellenica: Selected Papers on Greek Literature and Thought. Vol. III Philosophy, Music and Metre, Literary Byways, Varia*. Oxford.
(2013c) *The Epic Cycle. A Commentary on the Lost Troy Epics*. Oxford.
(2013d) 'The Greek poetess: her role and image', in West, M. L. (2013a), 315–40.
West, S. (1983) 'Notes on the text of Lycophron', *CQ* 33: 114–35.
(1984) 'Lycophron italicised', *JHS* 104: 127–51.

(2000) 'Lycophron's *Alexandra*: 'hindsight as foresight makes no sense'', in Depew and Obbink (2000), 153–66.
(2009) 'Herodotus in Lycophron', in Cusset and Prioux (2009), 80–93.
White, S. A. (1992) 'Aristotle's favorite tragedies', in *Essays on Aristotle's Poetics*, ed. A. O. Rorty. Princeton: 221–40.
(2007) 'Theophrastus and Callisthenes', in *Influences on Peripatetic Rhetoric: Essays in Honor of William W. Fortenbaugh*, ed. D. C. Mirhady. Leiden: 211–30.
Whitmarsh, T. (2013) *Beyond the Second Sophistic: Adventures in Greek Postclassicism*. Berkeley.
Wiemken, H. (1972) *Der griechische Mimus: Dokumente zur Geschichte des antiken Volkstheaters*. Bremen.
Wieneke, J. (1931) *Ezechielis Iudaei poetae Alexandrini fabulae quae inscribitur Exagōgē fragmenta*. Aschendorff.
Wilamowitz-Moellendorf, U. von (1883) *De Lycophronis Alexandra commentatiuncula*, Greifswald, reprinted in Wilamowitz (1935–72), 2. 12–29.
(1924) *Hellenistische Dichtung in der Zeit des Kallimachos*. 2 vols. Berlin.
(1935–72) *Kleine Schriften*. 6 vols. Berlin.
(1962) *Kleine Schriften*, vol. 4, ed. K. Laute. Berlin.
Wiles, D. (1991) *The Masks of Menander: Sign and Meaning in Greek and Roman Performance*. Cambridge.
(2007) *Mask and Performance in Greek Tragedy: From Ancient Festival to Modern Experimentation*. Cambridge.
Wilhelm, A. (1900) 'Nachlese zu griechischen Inschriften', *Jahreshefte des österreichischen archäologischen Institutes in Wien* 3: 54–7.
(1940) 'Beiblatt', *Wiener Jahreshefte* 32:61.
Wilkins, J. (1993) *Euripides: Heraclidae*. Oxford.
(2000) *The Boastful Chef: The Discourse of Food in Ancient Greek Comedy*. Oxford.
Wille, G. (1967) *Musica Romana*. Amsterdam.
Willink, C. W. (2002/2003) 'Studies in the *cantica* of Euripides' *Rhesus*', *ICIS* 27/28: 21–43.
Wilson, P. (1999) 'The *aulos* in Athens', in *Performance Culture and Athenian Democracy*, ed. S. Goldhill and R. Osborne. Cambridge: 58–95.
(2000) *The Athenian Institution of the Khoregia: The Chorus, the City and the Stage*. Cambridge.
(2007a) *The Greek Theatre and Festivals: Documentary Studies*. Oxford.
(2007b) 'Sicilian Choruses', in Wilson (2007a), 351–77.
(2007c) 'Pronomos and Potamon: Two pipers and two epigrams', *JHS* 127: 141–49.
Wilson, P. and Hartwig, A. (2009) '*IG* I 102 and the tradition of proclaiming honours at the tragic *agon* of the Athenian City Dionysia', *ZPE* 169: 17–27.
Wilson, W. T. (2005) *The Sentences of Pseudo-Phocylides*. Berlin.
Winkler, J. J. (1984) 'Aristotle's theory of the novel and the best tragedy'. Unpublished ms. based on a paper presented at the 1984 Annual Meeting of the APA.

Wiseman, T. P. (1988) 'Satyrs in Rome? The background to Horace's *Ars Poetica*', *JRS* 78: 1–13.
  (1998) *Roman Drama and Roman History*. Exeter.
Wörrle, M. (1988) *Stadt und Fest im kaiserzeitlichen Kleinasien: Studien zu einer agonistischen Stiftung aus Oenoanda*. Munich.
Wright, M. (2012) *The Comedian as Critic: Greek Old Comedy and poetics*. London.
  (2016) *The Lost Plays of Greek Tragedy*, vol. 1: *Neglected Authors*. London and New York.
Wyler, S. (2008) 'Faire peur pour rire? Le masque des Erotes', in *La Peur des images*, ed. L. Bachelot (*La Part de l'œil* 23): 105–21.
Xanthakis-Karamanos, G. (1979a) 'The influence of rhetoric on fourth-century tragedy'. *CQ* n.s. 29.1: 66–76.
  (1979b) 'Deviations from classical treatments in fourth-century tragedy'. *BICS* 26: 99–103.
  (1980) *Studies in Fourth-Century Tragedy*. Athens.
  (1996) 'The *Menedemos* of Lycophron', *Athena* 81: 339–65, reprinted in Xanthakis-Karamanos (2002), 330–57.
  (1997a) 'Echoes of earlier drama in Sositheus' *Daphnis* and Lycophron's *Menedemus*', *AC* 66: 121–43, reprinted in Xanthakis-Karamanos (2002), 359–83.
  (1997b) 'A survey of the main papyrus texts of post-classical tragedy', in *Akten des 21. Internationalen Papyrologenkongresses Berlin, 13.-19.8. 1995*, ed. B. Kramer, W. Luppe, H. Maehler and G. Poethke. Stuttgart 1997: 1034–48.
  (2002) *Dramatica: Studies in Classical and Post-Classical Poetry*. Athens.
Xella, P. (1969) 'Sull'introduzione del culto di Demetra e Kore a Cartagine', *SMSR* 40: 215–28.
Xenis, G. A. (2010a) *Scholia vetera in Sophoclis Electram*. Berlin.
  (2010b) *Scholia vetera in Sophoclis Trachinias*. Berlin.
Yunis, H. (2003) 'Writing for reading: Thucydides, Plato, and the emergence of the critical reader', in *Written Texts and the Rise of Literature Culture in Ancient Greece*, ed. H. Yunis. Cambridge: 189–212.
Zadorojniy, A. V. (1997) 'Tragedy and epic in Plutarch's "Crassus"', *Hermes* 125: 169–82.
Zanker, P. (1995) *The Mask of Socrates: The Image of the Intellectual in Antiquity*. trans. A. Shapiro. Berkeley and Los Angeles.
Zanobi, A. (2008) 'The influence of pantomime on Seneca's tragedies', in Hall and Wyles (2008), 227–57.
  (2014) *Seneca's Tragedies and the Aesthetics of Pantomime*. London.
Zarifi, Y. (2007) 'Chorus and dance in the ancient world', in *Cambridge Companion to Greek and Roman Theatre*, ed. M. McDonald and J. M. Walton. Cambridge: 227–46.
Ziegler, K. (1927) 'Lykophron der Tragiker und die Alexandrafrage', *RE* xiii: cols. 2316–81.

(1937) 'Tragoedia', *RE* vi(1): cols. 1889–2056.
Zimmermann, B. (2008) 'Seneca and pantomime', in Hall and Wyles (2008), 218–26.
Zuntz, G. (1955) *The Political Plays of Euripides*. Manchester.
  (1965) *An Inquiry into the Transmission of the Plays of Euripides*. Cambridge.
Zwierlein, O. (1966) *Die Rezitationsdramen Senecas*. Königstein/Ts.

# Index Locorum

AELIAN
*Varia Historia* 14.40: 40
AELIUS ARISTIDES
34.47: 317
AESCHYLUS
*Agamemnon*
281–316: 109
1300: 99
1389–90: 82
1583–1611: 46
*Choephori (Libation Bearers)*
423–28: 206
900–2: 78
*Eumenides*
214: 260
254–75: 75
275: 260
432: 260
*Myrmidons* fr. 132: 81
*Persians*
1–154: 81
618: 49
[*Prometheus Bound*]
425–30: 237
436–71: 102
609: 105
*Seven against Thebes*
1–77: 81
182–202: 279
203–63: 279
369–676: 279
375–676: 260
677–719: 279
961–1003: 237
1005–78: 83, 237
F 419: 46
AGATHON (*TrGF* I, 39)
*Aëropë* (F 1): 246
*Alcmeon* (F 2): 246
*Thyestes* (F 3): 246
*Telephus* (F 4): 54, 246, 262

ALEXANDER OF AETOLIA (*TrGF* I, 101)
*Astragalists* (F 1): 101
AMPHIS
*PCG* fr. 46 (K.–A.): 77
ANTHOLOGIA PALATINA
5.138: 106
7.707: 121
9.429: 106 (For Book 16 of *AP* see under ANTHOLOGIA PLANUDEA)
ANTHOLOGIA PLANUDEA
289: 302
ANTIPATER OF SIDON
*Epigr.* 59 (Gow and Page): 113
ANTIPHANES COMICUS
*Poiēsis (Poetry), PCG* fr. 189: 255, 330
ANTIPHON TRAGICUS (*TrGF* I, 55)
*Andromache* (F 1): 29, 268
*Meleager* (F 2): 29
ARISTOPHANES COMICUS
*Acharnians*
204–40: 75
280–327: 75
393–489: 340
*Assemblywomen (Eccleziazusae)* 729, 876: 200
*Clouds* 1265: 38
*Frogs*
89–95: 1
842: 339
962–3: 77
1044–364: 229
1264–77: 81
1298–328: 229
1309–63: 209
1501: 1
1502–3: 1
*Wealth*
83–5: 30
322, 626, 770, 801, 1096: 200
*Women at the Thesmophoria
(Thesmophoriazusae)* 39–268: 207

392

# Index Locorum 393

ARISTOPHANES OF BYZANTIUM
  *On Theatrical Masks* (F 373 Slater): 338
ARISTOTLE
  *Eudemian Ethics* 1239a37: 268
  *Nicomachean Ethics*
    1124b6–25a16: 199
    1150b6–10: 268
    1150b10: 41
    1159a27–33: 268
  *Poetics*
    1252a24–53a7: 289
    1447b20–3: 49
    1448a17–18: 339
    1449a4: 251
    1449a7–30: 272
    1449a15–18: 8
    1449b21–9: 212
    1449b24–8: 331
    1449b38–9: 277
    1450a15: 186
    1450a25: 276
    1450b4–8: 277, 280
    1450b7–8: 332
    1450b16–20: 212, 314
    1450b22–34: 75
    1450b23: 186
    1450b28: 186
    1451b1: 246
    1451b11: 186
    1451b19–23: 188
    1451b32–5: 75
    1452a27–9: 56
    1452a32–3: 332
    1452b34–53a12: 199
    1453a4: 186
    1453a17–22: 187, 274
    1453a23–30: 8
    1453b1–6: 94
    1453b7–11: 88
    1453b14: 273
    1453b26–31: 273
    1453b29–33: 8, 36, 56
    1454a37–b6: 255
    1455a26–9: 41
    1455a34–b1: 187–8
    1456a19–20: 186
    1456a25–31: 76, 200–1, 213, 244–5
    1456a25–7: 331–2
    1456a28–9: 273
    1456a34–b1: 277
    1458b17–24: 332
    1458a18: 197
    1459b34–60a2: 50
    1460b33–4: 8, 250
    1461b26–62a1: 195–6
    1461b26–62a17: 212
    1461b34–5: 197
  *Rhetoric*
    1399b29–31: 253
    1400a27–9: 253
    1400b9–15: 42, 253
    1403b23: 207
    1403b33: 7
    1404b18–25: 251
    1413b12: 48
    1417b18–20: 43–5
ARRIAN
  *Anabasis*
    3.1.4: 153
    3.5.2: 153
    7.14.10: 153
ASCLEPIADES OF TRAGILUS
  *FGrHist* 12 (F 5): 85–6
ASTYDAMAS JUNIOR (*TrGF* I, 60)
  *Alcmeon*
    F 1b: 8
    F 1b–c: 248
  *Antigone* (F 1e): 248
  *Hector*
    F 1h: 33, 246
    F 1i: 33–4, 254
    F 2: 34–5
    F 2a: 35
  *Herakles*
    F 4: 37–8, 88
    F 8: 37, 253, 281
ATHENAEUS
  *Deipnosophistae*
    351f: 40
    451e: 57
    586d: 153
    595d: 123
    595e: 153
    608b: 53
    608d: 49, 51–2
    608e: 49–50
    695a: 338
AUGUSTINE OF HIPPO (ST. AUGUSTINE)
  *Confessions* 36.4.2: 238

BASIL OF CAESAREA (ST. BASIL THE GREAT)
  *Letter to the Young Men on How to Profit from Greek Literature*
    4.8: 310
    6.6: 310

CALLIMACHUS
  *Iambus* 7, fr. 197 Pf.: 119
  *Hymn* 6: 116
CARCINUS JUNIOR (*TrGF* I, 70)
  *Achilles* (F 1d): 46
  *Ajax* (F 1a): 41
  *Orestes* (F 1g): 47
  *Semelē* (F 3): 47
  F 5 ('Sicilian fragment'): 45–7, 82–3, 256
  F 6: 39
  F 9: 47
CHAEREMON (*TrGF* I, 71)
  *Achilles Slaying Thersites* (Ἀχιλλεὺς Θερσιτοκτόνος) (F 2): 48
  *Alphesiboea* (F 1): 51–2
  *Bacchae*
    F 4: 49
    F 5: 49
    F 6: 49
    F 7: 49
  *The Centaur*
    F 10: 49–50
    F 11: 49–50
  *Io* (F 9): 49
  *Minyae* (F 10): 49
  *Odysseus* (F 13): 49
  *Oeneus* (F 14): 52–3, 64
  *Thyestes* (F 10): 49
  F 14b (from *The Centaur?*): 50–1
  F 17: 47, 49
CHAMAELEON
  *On Aeschylus* (fr. 39): 333
CHORICIUS OF GAZA
  *In Defence of the Mimes* 36–41 + 141: 320
CLEMENT OF ALEXANDRIA
  *Stromateis* 1.23.155: 126
COMMENTARIA IN ARISTOTELEM GRAECA
  XX, p. 437.2–6: 41, 269
CRATES OF THEBES (*TrGF* I, 90)
  F 1: 62

DEMOSTHENES
  2.24: 293
  6.31: 285
  9.2: 285
  9.3: 284
  18.180, 267: 182
  60.8: 291
DICAEARCHUS
  fr. 63 (Wehrli) = 62 (Mirhady): 335
  fr. 76 (Wehrli) = 100 (Mirhady): 348
  fr. 79 (Wehrli) = 113 (Mirhady): 335
  fr. 84 (Wehrli) = 104 (Mirhady): 335

fr. 80 (Wehrli) = 101 (Mirhady): 335
DICAEOGENES (*TrGF* I, 52)
  F 1b (*Medea?*): 28
DIO CHRYSOSTOM
  *Oration*
    2.2: 152
    7.119: 318
    7.120: 318
    13.20–1: 309
    15: 309
    17: 309
    17.8: 310
    18: 309
    18.7: 305
    19.4: 317
    19.5: 301–2, 315, 343
    52.3: 304, 314
    53.1: 331
    74: 313
DIODORUS SICULUS
  5.5.1: 46
  16.91: 152
  17.16.3: 152
  17.108: 122
  20.20: 112
  20.28: 112
DIOGENES OF SINOPĒ (*TrGF* I, 88)
  *Oedipus* (F 1f): 61
  *Medea* (F 1e): 61
  *Thyestes* (F 1d) 61
  F 1h: 61–2
  F 2: 62
DIONYSIUS I OF SYRACUSE (*TrGF* I, 76)
  *Adonis* (F 1): 60
  *Alcmene* (F 2): 60
  *Hector Ransomed* (Ἕκτορος λύτρα) (F 2a): 59, 88, 32
  *Leda* (F 3): 60
  F 4: 60
  F 5: 60
DIONYSIUS THRAX
  *Art of Grammar* 629b (Uhlig): 344
DURIS (*BNJ* 67)
  *On Tragedy* (fr. 28): 333
  *On Euripides and Sophocles* (fr. 29): 333

EPHIPPUS
  *PCG*
    fr. 9 (K.–A.): 48
    fr. 16 (K.–A.): 59
EPICHARMUS
  *PCG* fr. 206: 85
ERATOSTHENES
  *Catasterismi* 17: 266

# Index Locorum 395

EUBULUS
*PCG*
  fr. 25 (K.-A.): 59–60
  fr. 128 (K.-A.): 47, 49
EURIPIDES
*Aeolus* (F 20) (Kn.): 308
*Alcestis* 669–72: 99
*Andromache* 319–20: 281
*Andromeda*
  F 125 (Kn.): 263
  F 126 (Kn.): 264
  F 127 (Kn.): 264
  F 129 + 129a (Kn.): 264
  F 130 (Kn.): 265
  F 131 (Kn.): 265
  F 135 (Kn.): 265
  F 136 (Kn.): 266
  F 141 (Kn.): 267
  F 142 (Kn.): 267
  F 143 (Kn.): 267
*Bacchae*
  58–9: 27
  78–82: 27
  123–34: 27
  155–62: 257
  207–9: 53
  508: 49
  668–71: 284
  683–8: 53
  685–8: 53
  694: 53
  1078: 138
*Danae* (F 324 Kn.): 308
*Dictys* (F 336 Kn.): 37, 281
*Electra*
  37–8: 281
  253: 281
  367–72: 281
  380–5: 281
  383–4: 37
  404–5: 282
  527–44: 260
  842–3: 82
  1055–9: 284
*Hecuba*
  53: 76
  216–17: 82
  234–8: 284
*Helen*
  518: 83
  1301–68: 82, 245
  1301–52: 46
  1323–4: 46

*Heracles*
  158–64: 252
  476: 60
  815–73: 77
*Heraclidae* 181–3: 286
*Hippolytus*
  1–106: 237
  419–25: 284
  612: 310
  1423–7: 109
*Ion* 671–5: 284
*Iphigenia at Aulis*
  1: 76
  1–48: 81
  12: 76
  115–62: 81
  189–90: 76
  784–94: 230, 239
  1054–7: 257
  1499–509: 230
  1500–9: 239
*Iphigenia in Tauris* (*Iphigenia among the Taurians*) 495–512: 47
*Medea*
  230–1: 56, 193, 282
  465–519: 312
  1019–80: 113–14
*Melanippē Desmōtis* (*Captive Melanippē*)
  (F 495.40–3 Kn.): 37, 281
*Meleager* (F 530–1a Kn.): 29
*Oedipus* (F 540a.5–11 Kn.): 57
*Orestes*
  4–9: 45
  42: 53
  136–7: 258
  145–6: 258
  211–59: 313
  255–7: 315
  338–44: 230, 239
  496–525: 55
  544–50: 284
  866–956: 244
  890: 260
  899: 260
  903: 260
  960–1012: 244
  982–1012: 244
  1358–1602: 229
  1395–99: 206
  1425–30: 206
*Phaethon* fr. 773.19–42 (Kn.): 80
*Phoenician Women*
  103–92: 229
  301–54: 229

EURIPIDES (cont.)
  403: 308
  468–72: 252
  532: 310
  597: 47
  784–52: 260
  1104–40: 261
  1485–581: 229
  1581ff.: 237
  *Phrixus* (F 831 Kn.): 37
[*Rhesus*]
  1–564: 74
  1–526: 67
  1–51: 67, 69, 75
  5–6: 67
  19–22: 33
  34–40: 33
  41–8: 69
  52–148: 67, 69
  52–75: 70
  56–64: 73
  80: 33
  85–148: 67
  85–6: 82
  87–148: 70
  112: 46
  149–223: 67
  149–94: 69
  149–53: 78
  154–223: 67
  154–94: 70
  154: 78
  161–83: 86
  201–23: 69
  208–15: 71
  208–11: 74
  224–63: 67
  264–341: 67, 75
  284–316: 74
  301–8: 70, 77
  315–16: 73
  319–20: 73
  330–2: 73
  331: 73
  342–79: 70
  360–7: 81
  370–4: 73
  380–526: 67
  380–7: 67, 70
  383–4: 77
  388–526: 75
  388–454: 68, 74
  447–53: 71
  454–66: 68, 74
  460–2: 73

467–526: 68
498–509: 71
501–2: 71
502–7a: 71
507b–9: 71
521: 74
526: 78
527–64: 67–8, 80
565–996: 74
565–637: 67
565–94: 68, 74
573: 74
588: 74
595–674: 67, 75, 80
595–641: 68
600–4: 71, 73
608–10: 76
642–67: 67–8, 77
674–91: 67–9, 73, 75, 80
675–703: 210
692–727: 68
705: 71
709: 71
710–19: 71
728–881: 67
728–803: 75
728–55: 68, 211
736–7: 74
756–803: 68, 74, 77, 80
780–8: 74
790–1: 81
804–81: 75
806–992: 67
806–7: 78
808–19: 68
808: 78
820–32: 68, 74
833–81: 68, 74
882–982: 75
882–4: 73
885–982: 67
885–94: 68
886–8: 76
895–914: 68
915–49: 68
919ff.: 46
921–2: 72
938–49: 73
959–61: 68
962–73: 68, 72
970–3: 72, 85–6
970: 72
983–96: 68, 70
985: 67
989–91: 73

## Index Locorum

995–6: 73
*Suppliant Women*
  110: 53
  301–2: 288
  311: 288
  522–30: 291
  526–7: 288, 292
  561–3: 288
  671–2: 288
*Theseus* (F 382 Kn.): 54, 261
*Trojan Women*
  32–3: 76
  427–44: 115
  511–67: 206
  903–13: 284
F 666 (Kn.): 47
EZEKIEL (*Exagōgē*, *TrGF* 128)
  frr. 1–3: 131
  fr. 4: 131
  fr. 5: 131
  frr. 6–7: 131
  fr. 8: 131
  fr. 9: 131
  fr. 10: 132
  fr. 11: 132
  fr. 12: 132
  fr. 13: 132
  fr. 14: 132
  fr. 15: 132
  frr. 16–17: 132
  7–9: 143
  62: 142
  152–74: 144
  175–92: 144
  162–6: 144
  163: 142
  170–1: 144
  174: 142
  193–242: 135–6
  193–203: 138
  193: 136
  204–13: 138
  212–13: 138
  215: 137
  217: 138
  220–3: 138
  221: 137
  222: 137
  223: 137
  224–8: 138
  228–9: 138
  230–2: 138
  233: 142

  235: 137–8
  256–69: 130

FLAVIUS JOSEPHUS *See* JOSEPHUS

GALEN
  *In Hippocratis Epidemiarum* iii 17a.607.5–17 (Wenkelbach): 336
GORGIAS
  *Encomium of Helen* 9: 331
GREEK ANTHOLOGY *See* ANTHOLOGIA PALATINA
GREGORY OF NYSSA
  *Life of Makrina* 3: 311, 320
HERACLIDES OF PONTUS
  *On Euripides and Sophocles* (fr. 22.16): 333
  *On the Three Tragic Poets* (fr. 22.17): 181, 333
HERODOTUS
  1.8–12: 104, 140
  1.10.2: 104
  1.11.5: 105
  1.35.1: 101
  7.187.2: 112
HESIOD AND HESIODIC POETRY
  *Catalogues* fr. 43a (MW): 113
  *Ehoiai* fr. 129.2 (MW): 56
HOMER
  *Iliad*
    6.466–75: 34
    8.489–565: 66
    8.497–541: 70
    10: 66, 69
    10.1–179: 69
    10.11–13: 69
    10.251–3: 67
    10.299–337: 69
    10.299–302: 69
    10.333–5: 71
    10.416–20: 75
    10.435–41: 70
    10.435: 71
    10.484: 81
    10.523–4: 69
    11.1–2: 67
    11.56–66: 70
    22: 106
    22.226ff.: 140
    22.273–93: 35
    23.83–90: 101
    24.54: 102

HOMER (cont.)
*Odyssey*
  1.23–4: 58
  4.242–64: 71
HORACE
*Ars Poetica*
  123: 94
  185: 94
  220–39: 121
  287: 145
HYGINUS
*Fabula* 72: 36
HYPOTHESEIS, ANCIENT
  Hyp. to Euripides' *Alcestis*, 24 (Diggle): 339
  Hyp. to Euripides' *Hippolytus*, 25–7 (Diggle): 327
  Hyp. to Euripides' *Orestes*
    2 (Diggle) (Arg. 2c Mastronarde): 339
    35–40 (Diggle) (Arg. 2c Mastronarde): 338
    43–4 (Diggle) (Arg. 2d Mastronarde): 339
  Hyp. (b) to *Rhesus*
    430.23–431.44 (Diggle): 83
    430.26–431.29 (Diggle): 84
    431.23–44 (Diggle): 83
    431.30–44 (Diggle): 84
  Hyp. (c) to *Rhesus* 432.52–3 (Diggle): 85

INSCRIPTIONS
*CID*
  4, 87.32–3: 174
  4, 88.6–7: 174
*CIL*
  5, 5889: 302
  14, 4254: 302
*IAph* 11.21: 302
*ID* 1959: 168
*IG*
  ii² 2318: 182, 326
  ii² 2320: 181
  ii² 3092: 27
  vii 540: 219–20
  vii 1773.21–2, 24–7: 179
  xi, 105.16–18: 170
  xi 108.17–19: 170
  xi 2, 120.50: 168
  xi 4, 1043.14–16: 174
  xii 4, 2, 452A–B: 168
  xii 6, 253.11: 155
  xii 6, 1, 56: 177
  xii 6, 1, 154.31–2: 173
  xii 9, 207: 159, 162, 175
*IGUR* 223 + 229: 155
*I.Iasos* 153: 91
*IIsolMil* 18.25: 172

*IK*
  2.11: 174
  3 (Ilion), 2.41: 175
  5 (Kyme), 13.7: 174
  16.6 (Ephesos), 2070–1: 303.
  20 (Kalchedon), 1.70–1: 174
  28.1 (Iasos), 82.20–1: 174
  30 (Keramos), 9.10–11: 174
  47 (Heraclea Pontica), 9: 302
  152.27–8: 171
  152.12–13: 171
  152.16: 171
*IMT* 1437.11–12: 174
*IPriene*
  21.19: 174
  23.14: 174
  53 II.70: 174
  61.17: 174
*Milet*
  I 3, 152C.88: 173
  I 3, 153.24–5: 174
*OGIS*
  51: 165–6
  51.31–3: 93
*SEG*
  3, 334: 219
  9, 13.13–14: 155
  11, 52c: 238
  19, 335: 121, 219–20
  25, 501: 219–20
  34, 758.49–50: 174
  48, 2052.9–10: 155
*SIG*³
  424A: 220
  690: 220
  632.14–15: 110
  1080: 156
*TrGF* DID B 12 (cf. *ZPE* 163 (2007) 81–95): 156 (See also Tables 1, 2 and 3 on pp. 159–63)
ISOCRATES
  4.56–60: 291
  8.14: 285
IUBA II, KING OF MAURETANIA (*BNJ* 275)
  *Theatrical History* (frr. 15–19, 80–6): 342

JOSEPHUS
  *Jewish Antiquities* 2.344: 135–6
JUSTINIAN
  *Novella* 105.1: 301

'LETTER OF ARISTEAS'
  50: 126
  284: 129
  316: 129

## Index Locorum

LIBANIUS
  *Progymnasmata* 11.5–6: 311
LIFE OF AESCHYLUS
  Test. A1.15 (Radt): 348
LIFE OF EURIPIDES *See* SATYRUS OF
    KALLATIS
LIFE OF SOPHOCLES
  *TrGF* 4, T 1, 21–2: 207
LIVY
  23.1.5: 112
'LONGINUS'
  *On the Sublime*
    15.1: 314
    15.2–3: 343–4
    15.3: 315
    15.8: 316
LONGUS
  *Daphnis and Chloe* 1.20.2: 87
LUCIAN
  *Apologia* 5: 319
  *On the Dance* 27: 297–8, 317, 320
  *How to Write History* 1: 240–1
  *Lexiphanes* 22: 306
  *Podagra*
    1–2: 322
    332–5: 322
  *On Salaried Posts* 41: 320–1
  *Saturnalia* 28: 319–20
LYCOPHRON OF CHALCIS (*TrGF* I, 100)
  *Andromeda* (F 1c): 100
  *Cassandrians* (F 1h): 97, 99–100
  *Chrysippus* (F 9): 99
  *Elephenor* (F 1d): 100
  *Hippolytus* (F 1g): 99
  *Laius* (F 1i): 99
  *Marathonians* (F 1k): 101
  *Menedemos*
    F 2–4: 122–3
    F 2: 122–3
  *Nauplius* (F 4a): 100
  *Oedipus* 1 and 2 (F 4b): 99
  *Pelopids* (F 5): 99
'LYCOPHRON'
  *Alexandra*
    31–1460: 107
    31: 113
    34: 113
    44: 110, 118
    52: 113
    69–71: 113
    72–85: 92
    110–31: 118
    176: 110
    206–15: 101
    258–97: 112
    258–85: 106

314: 118
334: 115
347: 103
348–72: 107
365–6: 108
365: 115
384–6: 100
417–1282: 108
447: 110
450–68: 115
496: 118
621: 103
630: 110
576: 118
592–632: 108
623–4: 120
648–819: 108
720: 110
737: 112, 115
799: 110
801–2: 112
820–76: 108
836–41: 100
927–9: 110
930: 119
968: 113
1034–46: 100
1047–1133: 108
1051–2: 110
1066: 103
1093–8: 100
1099–1122: 115
1123–4: 110
1126–30: 110
1146–50: 113
1176: 115
1181–4: 110
1212–13: 110
1229: 108, 110, 115
1230: 113
1233: 108
1245–7: 101
1279–80: 113
1281–2: 108
1283–1450: 108
1292: 110
1294: 118
1362–8: 108
1391–6: 113
1413: 112
1446–50: 108
1447: 112
1454–60: 114
1460–1: 114
1464–5: 113
1474: 114

LYRICA ADESPOTA
Coll. Alex. no. 11 (Powell): 106
LYSIAS
  2.7–10: 291
  2.7–9: 291–2
  2.9: 292
  2.11–16: 291
  fr. 235 (Carey): 39

MENANDER
  Shield (Aspis)
    407–28: 40, 48
    428: 48
  The Shorn Girl (Perikeiromenē)
    271–91: 86
    295–6: 86
METAGENES
  Philothytēs (PCG fr. 15 K.–A.):
    37–8
MOSCHION (TrGF I, 97)
  F 4: 285
  F 5: 285
  F 6: 102–3, 286–90
  F 7: 102

OLD TESTAMENT
  Exodus
    3:21–2: 144
    14:6–8: 138
    14:9–10: 138
    14:10: 137
    14:11–14: 137
    14:15–18: 137
    14:18: 138
    14:19–20: 138
    14:19: 137–8
    14:21: 138
    14:22: 138
    14:23: 138
    14:24–5: 125
    14:28: 135
ORACULA SIBYLLINA
  3: 113–14
  3.311: 113
  3.356–64: 114
  3. 815–16: 114

PAPYRI
  P.Ashm. inv. 89B/31, 33:
    230
  P.Berol. 6870: 231,
    240
  P.Hib.
    2, 174: 202, 213–14
    2, 224: 50

  P.Louvre (Antiquités égyptiennes inv.
    E. 10534): 42
  P.Lugd. inv. 510: 239
  P.Mich. 2958.1–18: 231
  P. Oslo. 1413: 231
  P.Oxy.
    1176, fr. 39.7: 247
    2382: 103
    2458: 202
  PSI 1286: 334
  P.Sorb. 2252: 202, 237, 246
  P.Vind. 2315: 239
  P.Yale inv. 4510: 231
  P.Zenon 59533: 230
PARTHENIUS OF NICAEA
  Erotika Pathēmata 36:
    86–7
PAUSANIAS
  9.4.1: 6
PHILEMON COMICUS
  fr. 169 K.–A.: 180–1
PHILISCUS OF AEGINA (TrGF I, 89)
  Themistocles (T 5): 103
  F 1: 62
PHILO OF ALEXANDRIA
  De congressu eruditionis gratia 74:
    128
  De ebrietate 177: 128
  De vita Mosis 1.179: 135
  Quod omnis probus 141: 128
PHILODEMUS
  On Poems (PHerc. 994, col. xxv):
    40
PHILOSTRATUS, FLAVIUS
  Life of Apollonius of Tyana 5.9:
    321
  Lives of the Sophists
    513: 317
    607: 316
PLATO
  Gorgias 502c–d: 280
  Laws 659b: 152
  Menexenus 239b: 291
  Republic 395 C–D: 309
PLUTARCH (OR PSEUDO-PLUTARCH)
  Life of Alexander 72.1: 153
  Life of Cimon 8.7–8: 342–3
  Life of Crassus 33.1–7: 178,
    196
  Life of Demetrius 12: 343
  Life of Themistocles 32.6: 103
  Life of Theseus 32.5: 101
  Moralia
    3E–F: 309
    15D: 331

18C: 197
25B–28D: 308
27F–28D: 308
28C: 309
41D: 27
46B: 215
338B: 60
345E: 318
384C: 331
833C: 29
841f: 236, 328
POLYAENUS
Stratagems of War 6.53: 72
POLYBIUS
2.56.10: 94
2.56.13: 94
23.10.2: 94
23.10.12: 94
PORPHYRIO
In Horatii Artem Poeticam 1 (p. 162 Holder): 139

QUINTILIAN
Institutio oratoria 10.1.67: 344

SATYRUS OF KALLATIS
fr. 1 (Schorn): 26
SCHOLIA, ANCIENT
to Aeschylus, Eumenides 1: 136
to Euripides, Hecuba 342: 339
to Euripides, Orestes
176: 313
257: 313
643: 313
to Euripides, Phoenician Women 1539: 339
to Homer, Iliad 10.435: 70
to Sophocles, Ajax 864a: 313
to Sophocles, Oedipus at Colonus 900: 334
SEXTUS EMPIRICUS
Against the Grammarians
271: 308
280: 308
308 + 313: 307
SOPHOCLES
Ajax
1–133: 80
3–4: 76
167–71: 99
693–705: 258
866–78: 75
1185–1222: 81
1328–31: 284
1344–5: 282
Alētēs F 93–103: 248

Antigone
1–99: 278
18–19: 278
162–210: 278
249–77: 278
315–16: 284
407–40: 278
446–525: 278
446–55: 288
531–81: 278
631–765: 278
806–82: 278
998–1022: 278
1023–90: 278
1146–52: 258
1192–243: 278
1238–9: 82
1260–353: 278
*Chryses* F 726–30: 248
*Electra*
6–7: 74
552–7: 284
566–72: 46
660: 250
975–81: 252
1129: 259
1165–6: 259
*Ichneutai (Trackers)*
314.64–78: 75
314.100–23: 76
314.176–202: 76
*Oedipus Tyrannus*
543–4: 284
895–7: 257
*Philoctetes*
126–13: 258
128–29: 258
468–503: 57
662–70: 267
817–18: 267
895: 267
*Phrygians* (F 724–5): 59
*Shepherds (Poimenes)* (F 502–4): 81
*Thyestes in Sicyon* (F 247–69): 248
*Trachiniae (Women of Trachis)* 216–21: 257
*Tyro* (F 648–69): 247
SOSIPHANES OF SYRACUSE (*TrGF* I, 92)
*Meleager*
F 1: 62–3, 97
F 2: 63
F 3: 63
F 4: 63

SOSITHEUS (*TrGF* I, 99)
  *Daphnis or Lityerses* (F 2):
    121
STRABO
  14.5.15: 95
SUDA
  α 3406 Adler: 154
  δ 872 Adler: 342
  λ 821 Adler: 108
  ν 218 Adler: 154

TATIAN
  *To the Greeks* 24: 298, 320–1
TERTULLIAN
  *On the Spectacles* 30: 298
THEOCRITUS
  *Idyll*
    15: 97
    17.112–21: 93
THEODECTAS (*TrGF* I, 72)
  *Alcmeon*
    F 1a: 55–6, 282
    F 2: 55
  *Helen* (F 3): 56
  *Lynceus* (F 3a): 10, 56–7, 248
  *Oedipus* (F 4): 54, 57
  *Philoctetes* (F 5b): 57–8
  *Tydeus* (F 5a): 248
  F 6: 54, 262
  F 8 (from *Lynceus?*): 56–7
  F 9 (from *Thyestes?*): 58
  F 10 (from *Bellerophon?*): 58
  F 17: 58
  F 18: 54, 57
THEON
  *Progymnasmata*
    13: 317
    94, 7–33: 312

THUCYDIDES
  1.21.2: 111
  1.138.5: 103
  1.138.6: 103
  7.75.4: 94
TIMAEUS HISTORICUS (*FGrHist* 566)
  F 164: 46
TIMOCLES
  *Women at the Dionysia*, PCG fr. 6 (K.–A.): 330–1
TRAGICORUM ADESPOTA (*TrGF* 2)
  F 7: 53
  F 392: 62
  F 464: 308
  F 625: 54
  F 625.9: 246
  F 640b.28: 246
  F 649: 105–6, 140, 201
  F 664 ('Gyges fragment'): 10, 103–5, 140, 142, 188

XENOPHON
  *Anabasis* 4.8.25: 101

VERGIL
  *Aeneid*
    9.176–458: 87
    9.316–19: 87
    9.332–3: 87
    9.347–8: 87
    9.353–6: 87
    9.377–8: 87
VITA AESCHYLI *See* LIFE OF AESCHYLUS
VITA EURIPIDIS *See* SATYRUS OF KALLATIS
VITA SOPHOCLIS *See* LIFE OF SOPHOCLES

XENOCLES SENIOR (*TrGF* I, 33)
  *Likymnios* (F 2): 38

# General Index

Acarnania 193
Actium, Battle of 93; *see also* Augustus
actors/acting 8, 13, 15, 191–2, 195–7, 221,
  317–19, 326, 346
  and *asphaleia* 167
  and *asylia* 167
  Artists of Dionysus/Dionysiac Guilds
    (*Dionysiakoi Technitai*) 7, 93, 161, 163–7,
    171, 175, 178–9, 195, 217, 219, 221, 242
  *deuteragonistēs* 7, 67, 176
  *cantica* 215–16
  *epideixeis* 170
  *hypokritēs* 233
  *hypotragōidos* 240
  interpolations 83, 182, 198, 328
  *pantomimos* (pantomime actor) 233
  *protagonistēs* 7–8, 67, 153, 165–6, 171, 176
  *synagōnistai* 165
  *tragōidos* 207, 212, 216, 219–20, 233, 238,
    240–1, 300–1, 319–21, 323
  *tritagonistēs* 67, 176 *see also* Aristotle, actors/
    acting
actors, individual
  Aristocritus 153–4
  Aristodemus of Metapontum 191
  Aristomedes 155
  Athenodorus 153–4
  Hippasus of Ambracia 155
  Jason of Tralles 178
  Kallippides 196–7
  Kleandros 155
  Mynniskos of Chalcis 191
  Neoptolemus of Scyrus (-os) 152, 155, 182,
    191, 195–6, 198
  Nicostratus 238
  Parmenon, comic actor 197
  Pleisthenes 41
  Polus (-los) of Aegina 155, 177, 191, 195,
    317
  Theodorus 40, 195, 197
  Thessalus (-tt-) 153–4
  Timotheus of Zacynthus 155

Aegean, islands, *see also* Festivals
  Amorgos 159, 173 (Aigyalē)
  Andros 159, 173
  Cos 159, 168–9
  Delos 159, 162
  Ios 173
  Keos 159, 173 (Ioulis);, 173 (Karthaia)
  Lepsia 173
  Lesbos 159, 173 (Eresos), 223
  Naxos 159, 173
  Paros 160, 173
  Rhodes 155, 160
  Samos 160, 173
  Samothrace 91–2, 118
  Siphnos 160, 173
  Syros 160, 173
  Tenos 160, 173
Aeschines 182
Aeschylus
  *Agamemnon* 106
  and actors' interpolations 237
  and the *Alexandra* 97, 99, 109, 115
  and allusion in tragedy 261
  and the Cassandra tragedy (*P. Oxy.* 2746) 106
  and the 'death of tragedy' 1–2
  and the evolution of the tragic genre 273
  and Ezekiel's *Exagōgē* 17, 134, 136, 217
  and the Gyges fragment 11, 104–5
  and metre 251
  and music in tragedy 204, 229, 236, 238
  and naturalism 254
  and 'old tragedy' 178, 236; *see also* s.v.
  and 'political' as opposed to 'rhetorical' tragedy
    277, 279–80, 293
  and reperformances after his death 348
  and pseudo-Euripides' *Rhesus* 73, 75, 77–81,
    83–5
  and the scholia 345
  and tragedies with historical themes 111, 187
  and tragedy as reading material 304, 344
  and the tragic canon 2, 15, 180–5, 188–90,
    328, 332

Aeschylus (cont.)
   and the tragic chorus/choral song 209, 235
   and performances outside Athens 5, 150, 190, 272, 343
   and tragic plots of minimal incident 250
   and the treatise *On the Sublime* 344
   and the *Vitae* of the tragedians 348
   as linguistic model in late Antiquity 306
   *Choephori* (*Libation Bearers*) 255
   *Eumenides* 43, 255
   in relation to fourth-century tragic plays 9, 32, 43, 56, 58–9, 255–6, 259
   language 252, 332
   *Myrmidons* 32, 184
   *Nereids* 32, 184
   on a par with fourth-century dramatists 33, 40
   *Persians* 134, 136, 150, 250
   *Phrygians or Hector Ransomed* (Φρύγες ἢ "Εκτορος λύτρα, F 263–72) 32, 59, 184
   [*Prometheus Bound*] 77
   *Psychostasia* (*Weighing of the Souls*) 73
   *Seven against Thebes* 261
   treatise *On Aeschylus* by Theophrastus 333
   *Women of Aetna* (Αἰτναῖαι γνήσιοι, Αἰτναῖαι νόθοι) 84, 150
Agatharchus 324
Agathocles of Samos 97
*agōn hieros* 177
*agōn logōn* 2, 74, 249, 280, 285, 287, 293, 312
*agōn mousikos* 152–3, 162, 218
*agōn stephanitēs* 177
*agōnes nemētoi* 177
*agōnes skēnikoi* 153, 161, 163
*agōnothetēs* 170, 174, 217, 220; see also *chorēgos*
Aï-Khanoum, Agfhanistan 157
Alciphron 155
Alexander of Epirus 152
Alexander the Great 5, 16–17, 26, 91, 93, 100, 112, 121–2, 153–4, 158, 177, 191, 196
Alexander of Pherae 40, 102
Alexander of Pleuron (Aetolus) 95–6, 101, 335–7
Alexander Polyhistor 130; see also Ezekiel; Theodotus 130
*Alexandra* 12, 13, 92–3, 97, 100, 105, 107–20, 127, 210
   aetiology/allusions to cults in 109–10
   and Aeschylus 115
   and Antimachus 119
   and Callimachus 119
   and Catalogue poetry 109, 113
   and epic 109, 112, 119
   and the epinician hymn 119
   and Eratosthenes 119
   and Herodotus 109, 115
   and history/historiography 111–13, 119
   and the hymn 114
   and laments for the fall of cities 113
   and mythography 119
   and the 'Oracle of the Potter' 114
   and Philostephanus 119
   and Rome 108, 110, 116–20
   and the Sibylline Oracles 113–14
   and Stesichorus 119
   and Timaeus, the historian 115
   and tragedy 114–15, 119
   authorship and date 116–20
   connections with Hellenistic dynasties
      Attalids 118
      Ptolemies 118
      Seleucids 119
   'dark poem' 108
   female author of? 120
   Guard, character of 107
   'internal geometry' 115–16
   metamorphoses 110
   metre 108, 115
   'monodrama' 107
   *nostoi* 108, 115
   Tzetzes, commentary on 109
   vocabulary 109
   women as victims of male violence, in 113
Alexandria 17, 20, 84, 95–6, 116, 126–7, 164, 188, 210, 271, 324, 326, 336, 340–1
   Library of 333–41
   Mouseion (Museum) of 20, 127
Alexandria in the Troad 95
allusion, see self-consciousness, in tragedy
Amphipolis 72
Amyclae 110
Anaxagoras 324
Anios, king of Delos 118
Antigonids 118, 177
Antigonus Gonatas 100
Antigonus the One-Eyed 99
Antimachus of Colophon 119
Antioch 300
Antiochus III, Seleucid king 119, 170
Antipater of Sidon, epigrammatist 113
Antiphon of Rhamnous, orator 28
Antisthenes 61–2
'anti-tragedy' 3–6
Aphrodisias 299–300, 302
Aphrodite *Hilara* 165
Apollodorus Tragicus (*TrGF* I, 64)
   *Suppliant Women* 292
Apollodorus, tyrant of Cassandria 100
Apollonius of Rhodes 100, 119, 128
   *Ktiseis* 128
Archelaus, king of Macedon 152
Archinus, Decree of 328
Argos 162, 164, 171, 178, 191, 193, 218, 266–7
Ariarathes V of Cappadocia 162, 171

## General Index

Aristobulus 127
Aristodama of Smyrna 98
Aristophanes, comic poet, *see* playwrights (comedy)
    *Assemblywomen (Ecclesiazusae)* 213
    *Clouds* 1
    *Frogs* 1–2, 181, 235
    *Wealth (Plutus)* 213, 246
    *Women at the Thesmophoria* 76, 192
Aristophanes of Byzantium, scholar,
    *see also* scholars/scholarship
Aristotle *anagnorisis* 26, 28
    and actors/acting 7, 195–8, 348
    and Athenian dramatic festivals 326–7, 343
    and the 'death of tragedy' 2
    and the demarcation of history from poetry 111
    and fourth-century tragic plays/tragedians 29,
        40, 43, 45, 47, 50–1, 54–5, 185, 253,
        268
    and Plato's attitude to tragedy 280
    and 'poets nowadays' 270–6
    and the political function of tragedy 271–2
    and rhetoric in tragedy 279–80, 293, 332
    and scholarship on tragedy 20, 139, 329–33
    and theatrical machinery in fourth-century tragedy 255
    and the tragic canon 2, 8
    and the tragic chorus in the fourth century
        186, 200–2, 210, 213, 237, 244–6, 273,
        329; *see also embolima*
    and tragic diction 251
    and the tragic hero 199
    and the tragic plot 186–8, 247, 274, 330, 332;
        *see also* plots, tragic
    *dianoia* 277
    *Didascaliae* (non-extant) 327
    *ēthos* 277, 311, 339
    *hamartia* 132
    *katharsis* 331
    *melos*/music 212, 223; *see also* music, in tragedy
    *opsis* (spectacle) 212, 314, 344
    parts of tragedy 330
    *pathos* 311
    *peripeteia* 132
    *pistis* 311
    *Poetics* 329–30
    *Rhetoric* 332–3
    unities of time and place 17
    *Victories at the Dionysia* (non-extant) 327
    works on Athenian theatrical history 327
Armenia, cities of
    Seleucia on the Tigris 157
    Tigranocerta 157
Artawazd II, king of Armenia 178
Artemis, worship of 256

Artemisia, queen of Caria 154
Astydamas, *see* playwrights, tragedy (fourth century)/Astydamas II
Athenaeus 12, 52–3, 122, 261, 333, 338, 345
Athenocentrism 5–6
Attalid, dynasty 118
Attica
    Acharnae, deme of Attica 27
    Brauron 110
    Eleusis 43
    Oropos 163
Augustine of Hippo, St 238
Augustus 95, 121, 342
*aulētēs/aulos* 176, 205, 214–15, 218–23, 227, 233, 238, 240

Babylon 122, 153, 157
Bach, Johann Sebastian 232, 236
Basil of Caesarea
    *Letter to the Young Men on How to Profit from Greek Literature* 310–11
Boeotia, cities of
    Akraiphia 163, 171
    Coronea 92, 156
    Orchomenos 163
    Tanagra 163, 219
    Thebes 93, 110, 164, 172, 191, 193, 223, 250; *see also* festivals, Agrionia
    Thespiae 164, 191, 300; *see also* festivals, Mouseia

Callimachus 101, 114, 116, 119, 334
    *Hecale* 101
    *Pinakes* 335
Calydonian boar 29, 62, 261
Candaules 104–5; *see also* Gyges fragment, 'Potiphar's Wife'
Cannae, Battle of 112; *see also* Hannibal
Carcinus *see* playwrights, tragedy (fourth century)/Carcinus II
Carrhae 178; *see also* Crassus
'Cassandra tragedy' (*P. Oxy.* 2746) 140, 201
Cassandria 99
Catalogue poetry 109, 113
Caunus (Caria) 162
Chaeremon, *see* playwrights, tragedy (fourth century)
characters, tragic/mythical
    Abas 56, 248
    Achilles 32–5, 50–1, 59, 64, 67, 70, 73–4, 101, 106, 184, 230–1, 250, 253–4
    Adonis 60, 97
    Adrastus 101, 291
    Aegeus 263
    Aegisthus 82, 250, 252

characters, tragic/mythical (cont.)
    Aeneas 28, 67, 70, 82, 92, 108, 255
    Aëropē 40
    Aëthlius 98
    Agamemnon 46, 55, 69–70, 82, 110, 115,
        250, 254, 259, 269, 282, 284, 319
    Agave 178, 196
    Ajax, Locrian 107
    Ajax, Salaminian (Telamonian) 28, 41, 55, 74,
        115, 231, 240, 253, 274, 282, 311–12
    Alcmeon 36, 51–2, 55–6, 254, 274
    Alexandra, see Cassandra
    Alopē 41, 47, 248, 254, 268
    Alphesiboea 51–2, 55–6
    Amazons 109
    Amphiaraus 41–2
    Amphitryon 254
    Andromache 29, 59, 216, 230, 268, 339
    Andromeda 100, 241, 263–8
    Antigone 36, 229, 237, 248–9, 269, 278,
        288
    Aphrodite 68, 70, 77, 256, 259
    Apollo 254–5, 259
    Astyanax 34–5
    Atalanta 30, 261
    Athena 266
    Bellerophon 58
    Callirrhoē 55
    Cassandra (Alexandra) 99, 106–7, 140, 201,
        216
    Cercyon 41, 47, 254, 268–9
    Chiron 49–51
    Chrysothemis 250, 252
    Clytemnestra 55, 109, 250, 269, 284
    Creon, king of Thebes 36, 248–9, 278, 284–5,
        287, 319
    Danaus 56, 248
    Daphnis 121
    Dardanus 91–2
    Deiphobus 106
    Dictys 37
    Diomedes 55, 67–70, 73–5, 87, 108–9, 120,
        211, 253, 260
    Dolon 67–71, 73–5, 78, 86–7
    Electra 30, 229, 244, 250, 252, 258–60, 284,
        313, 338
    Elephenor 100
    Epeius 119
    Eriphyle 36, 42, 55, 248, 254
    Eteocles 249, 260, 279
    Eurystheus 291
    Furies (Erinyes) 75, 94, 223, 254–5, 260, 313,
        315–16, 343
    Haemon 36, 248, 278
    Hector 29, 32–5, 59, 66–71, 73–6, 78, 86,
        106, 110, 141, 250, 254–5

Hecuba 82, 110, 115, 284
Helen 309
Helenus 35
Hercules/Heracles 36, 112, 177, 248, 252,
    254, 257–8, 267, 320
Hermes 259
Hesione 113
Hippolytus 58, 99, 109, 310
Hypermestra 56, 248
Iolaus 285–6
Iphigenia 255
Iris 77, 255
Ismene 237, 249, 278
Jason 28, 42, 253, 312
Jocasta 43, 45, 257, 309
Laius 44, 63, 257, 274
Laodicē 118
Lycus 252, 254
Lynceus 56–7, 248
Lyssa 77, 255
Maeon 248
Medea 28, 42–3, 47, 61, 94, 109, 141, 185,
    253–4, 263, 273, 282, 311–12
Megara 36, 254
Meleager 27–9, 54, 274
Menelaus 108, 112, 115
Menoeceus 63, 316
Mestra 113
Muse 67–8, 70, 72–3, 76–7, 85–7, 187, 247,
    256
Nauplius 36–7, 100
Neoptolemus 57, 230–1, 258, 268
Odysseus 28, 41, 55, 67–71, 73–5, 77, 82,
    108–9, 112, 115, 211, 253, 258, 267–8,
    282, 284
Oedipus 36, 43–5, 57, 61, 249, 254, 256,
    259, 273–4, 284, 320, 322, 339
Oeneus 29, 52–4
Orestes 30, 37, 47, 78, 231, 250, 255, 258,
    260, 274, 281, 284, 313–16, 338–9
Palamedes 36, 100
Paris-Alexandros 67–8, 70, 77
Parthenopaeus 180, 261
Parthenopē 109, 112
Patroclus 33, 101
Pelasgus 60
Peleus 101, 257, 339
Pentheus 49, 178, 196, 250, 259
Phaedra 58, 263, 308
Philoctetes 41, 57, 109, 231, 267–8,
    322
Podalirius 110
Polyneices 249, 252, 278–9
Polyxena 59, 339
Poseidon 41, 259, 269
Priam 59, 106–7, 140, 201

Prometheus 287
Proteus 118
Pylades 78, 339
Rhesus 16, 66–88, 187, 255–6
Semelē 27
Talthybius 260
Tecmessa 231, 240
Telegonus 273
Telephus 101, 118, 274
Teucer 28
Theoclymenus 249, 255
Theseus 54, 60, 101, 249, 261–2, 292
Thetis 33, 257
Thoas 249, 255
Thyestes 40, 58, 61, 248, 274, 320
Tydeus 248
Xuthus 248
Chaeronea, Battle of 8, 189
*chorēgos/chorēgia* 14, 27, 90, 160, 168–70, 205–6, 217–18, 220, 234, 237, 326
*synchorēgia* 27
Chorikios of Gaza 320; see also mime
chorus/choral song
*choraulēs* 219
*chorodidaskaloi/hypodidaskaloi* 166, 174–5, 207
*choropsaltria* 169
*chorostatas (kho-)* 173
'*chorou*' (ΧΟΡΟΥ) in manuscripts 201–2, 213–14, 220, 237, 240, 246–7
'decline' of 18–19, 76, 149, 246
*embolima* 210, 237, 245–6; see also Agathon; Aristotle, and the tragic chorus
in *hypotheseis* 338
in Middle and New Comedy 214, 220, 246
in postclassical tragic plays/performances 18, 20, 33, 43, 67–71, 73–5, 80, 82, 85, 97, 104, 106, 108, 140–1, 155–7, 159, 167–9, 171–3, 175–7, 179, 197–8, 200–2, 208–20, 229, 245–7, 255, 302, 315, 317, 321–2
in Roman comedy 215
in Seneca 216
self-reference, choral, 257–8; see also self-consciousness, in tragedy
treatises on 232, 325; see also Aristotle, and the tragic chorus
Christians/Christianity
and the transmission of Ezekiel's *Exagōgē* 130
hostility towards theatre/tragedy 20, 298, 310
Cicero 93, 342
Cithaeron, Mt. 53, 284
citharode (*kitharistēs*)/citharodic performances 171, 209, 216, 219, 229, 238, 240
Stratonicus, citharist 40

Clement of Alexandria 126, 130–1
*Stromateis* 130
Cleoboulina (Kleoboulina) 120
cleruchs, Athenian 155
Cold War 3
Corcyra 161
Corinth 42–3, 113, 141, 254
Isthmus of 164, 172, 218
Corinthian War 8
cosmopolitanism 62
costume, tragedy 71, 206, 258–9, 297–8, 306, 318–21, 342–3
masks see separate entry
Crassus, Marcus Licinius 178, 196
Crates, Cynic philosopher, see playwrights, tragedy (fourth century)
Croesus 101
Cybele, cult of 27, 46, 256
'Cynic tragedies' 64
Cynoscephalae, Battle of 92, 116, 120
Cyprus 28, 164
Paphos 193
Salamis 177
Cyrene 155–7, 218

*dāmiergoi* 155
dance, in drama 18, 204–42, 342
choreography, tragic 205–7, 211, 221–2, 232–6, 240
*emmeleia* 206
*kordax* 206
*schēmata* 232
*sikinnis* 206 see also chorus/choral song
Dasii, Apulian family 120
'death of the polis' 4
declamation 193, 312, 316–17
Delphi 98, 162, 165–6, 170–2, 174–5, 178, 218, 220
Demeter and Korē, cult of 43, 45–6, 256
Demetrius, Jewish author 127
Demetrius the Besieger (Poliorketes) 162, 343
Democritus 324
Demosthenes 182, 194, 284–5
*deus ex machina*, see theatrical machinery, *mēchanē*
*didaskalos* 326
Didyma 161, 173
Dio Chrysostom, see scholars/scholarship
Diodorus of Sicily 122, 152–3, 155
Dion 164; see also festivals, Olympia
Dionysia festivals
Great or City D. 8, 25, 31–2, 36, 38, 121, 153–4, 167, 180–3, 195, 205, 217–18, 228, 236, 272, 276, 291, 326, 342–3

Dionysia festivals (cont.)
  outside Attica 155 (Rhodes), 155 (Samos),
    157–8, 159, 161, 168 (Delos), 169
    (Iasos), 169–71 (Cos), 169 (Cos),
    169–71 (Iasos), 172, 173 (Samos), 174
    (Priene), 175 (Euboea), 176–7, 179
  Rural D. (*kat' agrous*) 27, 218
Dionysism, 'monarchic' 154
Dionysius of Halicarnassus 111
*Dionysiakoi Technitai*, see Artists of Dionysus
Dionysus *Kathēgemōn* 165
Dioscorides 121
dithyramb/dithyrambic choruses/contests 27–8,
    59, 153, 156, 166, 168–9, 173–6, 179,
    206, 209, 215, 229, 257, 329
Dosiades 119
Dracontius of Sparta 101
Durham University, Living Poets project 349

Ecbatana 153
Egypt 56, 255
  actors' guild of 164
  cities of
    Alexandria *see separate entry*
    Leontopolis 128
    Memphis 118, 153–4
    Oxyrhynchus 105
    Ptolemais Hermiou 93, 164–5
    Schedia 128
  dramatic contest of 331 BC in 153
  exodus of Jews from, *see* Ezekiel
  purported absence from Lycophron's
    *Alexandra* 118
Ephesus 193
Epic Cycle 16, 64, 71, 99, 109, 119, 184
Epidaurus 162, 177, 272
*epimelētēs* 169; *see also chorēgos*
epiparodos 68
Eratosthenes 119
Erinna 120
Ethiopia/Ethiopians 58, 131, 263, 267
*ēthopoiia* 20, 311–12
Euboea 100, 176, 191, 193
  Chalcis 159, 162, 164, 175
  Eretria 159, 162, 175
  Karystos (Carystus) 159, 162, 175
  Kyme 174
  Oreos 159, 162, 175
Eubulus, Athenian statesman 9
Eumenes, king of Pergamum 340
Euphorion, Hellenistic poet 109, 119
Euripides
  *Andromache* 13
  *Andromeda* 196
  and actors' interpolations 83, 198, 237
  and actors' 'promptbooks' 202

  and actors' song 244–5
  and the *Alexandra* 99–100, 115
  and allusion in tragedy 260–3
  and ancient scholarship, *see* Aristotle; scholars/
    scholarship (sub-entries: Aristophanes of
    Byzantium; Dicaearchus; *hypotheseis*;
    Lives of tragic poets; scholia)
  and the chorus 235, 245–6, 257–8
  and dance 233
  and the 'death of tragedy' 1–2, 9, 243, 271
  and the edition of Lycurgus 236
  and the evolution of the tragic genre 15, 17, 19
  and Ezekiel's *Exagōgē* 17, 134–42, 217
  and the mime 303
  and the motifs of
    burial 287–8, 290
    ethical contingency 263–9
    *parrhēsia* 283–6
  and music 204, 209–10, 216, 222, 229–30, 232,
    238–9, 273; *see also* Agathon; 'New Music'
  and Nietzsche 2
  and 'old tragedy'/reperformance 177–8, 198,
    217, 233–41
  and performances in symposia, *see symposia*,
    and theatre
  and 'political' as opposed to 'rhetorical' tragedy
    276–83, 293
  and the *Rhesus* 12–13, 66, 73, 79–86, 88,
    187
  and rhetorical declamations 316
  and the Second Sophistic 307–11 (the utility
    of tragedy), 311–12 (tragedy and
    rhetoric), 313–15 (tragedy and *phantasia*)
  and tragedy as reading material 304, 325
  and the tragic canon 2, 8, 15, 54, 180–5,
    187–90, 328–9, 332
  and tragic performances outside Athens 152,
    190
  and tragic plots 19, 247–50
  and vase painting, *see separate entry*
  *Bacchae* 178, 196, 245, 250, 256, 259
  *Bellerophontēs* 58
  *Cresphontes* 247
  diction 251
  *gnōmai* 253, 305
  *Helen* 247–8, 255
  *Heracles* 255
  *Hippolytus* 58, 246
  *Ino* 248
  *Ion* 247–8
  in relation to fourth-century tragic plays/
    themes 9, 25, 27, 29, 35, 41–2, 46–7,
    49, 53–8, 62, 64, 203, 243; *see also*
    Aristotle, and 'poets nowadays'; *see also in
    the present entry* metatheatre; naturalism;
    and 'political' as opposed to 'rhetorical'

tragedy; and the motifs of (sub-entries: burial; ethical contingency; *parrhēsia*); and tragic plots
*Iphigenia at Aulis* 245, 254, 259
*Iphigenia in Tauris* (*Iphigenia among the Taurians*) 247–8, 255
metatheatre 258–60
metre 115, 142, 211, 251
naturalism 197, 250–6
never an actor 207
on a par with fourth-century tragedians 40, 48, 186, 213
*Orestes* 198, 245, 254–5
*Phaethon* 314–15
*Phoenician Women* 309
[*Rhesus*] 12, 32, 66–88, 187, 201, 210–11, 216, 246–7, 249, 255–6; see also Rhesus
*Stheneboea* 58
*Telephus* 193
Eusebius of Caesarea 130–1, 141
*Praeparatio Evangelica* 130
Eustathius of Antioch, pseudo- 130
*Excerpta Latina Barbari* 127
Ezekiel (-chi-), *Exagōgē* 14, 97, 188
and Aeschylus' *Persians* 17, 134
and the aetiology of religious traditions 140, 144
    Passover, institution of 132, 140, 143–5
    Unleavened Bread, Feast of 132, 144
and Christian apologists 129, 131
and *ekphrasis* 140
and Euripides 17, 134–42, 217
and *fabula praetexta* 145–6, 188
and genre
    'Buchdrama' 142
    'epic' plot 133, 140
    'Midrashic drama' 132
    tragedy? 17, 132–4, 140
and Hellenistic tragedy 139–42, 140 (Gyges tragedy, Cassandra tragedy)
and paradoxography 130
and the *Deuteronomy* 144
and the *Book of Exodus* 17, 140, 143–4
and the Masoretic Text 131
and the Midrashim 131
and the Targums 131
characters of
    Aaron 132
    Chum 131
    God 131, 133, 142
    Jacob 131
    Jethro 131
    Messenger (Pharaoh's soldier) 132, 135–8
    Moses 17, 130–2, 138, 140–1, 143–4

    Pharaoh, character of 131–2, 138
    Raguel 131
    Sepphora (Sephora) 131
chorus in 141
cultural and performance context of 17, 126, 129, 142
Elim, oasis of 132, 141
Madian 141
messenger speech 17, 132, 134–6, 142
metre 132, 140, 142
miraculous events in
    bird, marvelous (appearance of) 130, 132
    burning bush, miracle of 141–2
    cure of the leprous hand 132
    pillar of fire 137–8
    plagues of Egypt 132, 144
    Red Sea, splitting of 17, 132, 137, 139–40
    staff turned into a snake 132, 142
music (lack of) 217
transmission of ; see also Alexander Polyhistor; Clement of Alexandria; Christians/ Christianity; Eusebius of Caesarea; Pseudo-Eustathius of Antioch
unities of time, place and action violated 141–2

festivals with tragic performances (other than Dionysia)
Agrionia, at Thebes 165, 171
Alexandreia, various 160
Amphiaraia–Rhomaia, at Oropos 163, 171
Antigoneia, at Samos 162, 177
Aristonikeia, at Karystos 162
Asklepieia–Apollonia, at Epidaurus 162, 177
Athena Itonia, festival of 92, 156
Charitesia, at Orchomenos 163, 171
Demetrieia, various 162 (Karystos), 177 (Samos)
Heraia, various 162, 171 (Samos), 171 (Argos)
Homoloia, at Orchomenos 163, 171
Letoa-Rhomaia, at Caunus 162, 171
Mouseia, at Thespiae 162, 165, 171, 218
Naia, at Dodona 162, 171
Olympia, at Dion 152–3, 156
Panathenaia, at Athens 163, 218
Panathenaia, at Ilium (-on) 162
Ptolemaia, at Delos 162, 174
Pythia, at Delphi 165
Rhomaia, various 163, 171 (Magnesia on the Maeander)
Sarapieia, at Tanagra 163, 171, 219
Soteria, at Delphi 162, 170–1, 175–6
Soteria, various 163, 171 (Akraiphia)

Flamininus, Titus Quinctius 16, 112, 116; *see also* Lycophron/Alexandra; Cynoscephalae

Galen 336–7
George of Trebizond
    Latin translation of Eusebius' *Praeparatio Evangelica* 126
*gnōmai, see* maxims
Gorgias of Leontini 331
*grammatikē/grammatikoi, see also* scholars/ scholarship
Great or City Dionysia, *see* Dionysia
Gregory of Nyssa 320
Gyges fragment 10–11, 94, 103–6, 114, 140, 142, 188
gymnic contests 176

Hannibal/Hannibalic War 112, 120; *see also* Cannae, Punic Wars
Harpalus 121–2; *see also* Python
Hellanicus of Lesbos 111
Hellespont 165, 171
Hercules, son of Alexander the Great 112
Hermogenes 317
Herodotus 94, 101, 104–5, 109, 111, 115, 119, 140, 188
Hesiod 50, 56, 113, 119, 322
Hieron, tyrant of Syracuse 46, 150
Hieronymus of Cardia 119
'highlights' theory (performances of tragic excerpts) 196
Hipola (Seville) 321
Hippocrates 336
Homer 16, 32, 59, 64, 66, 72, 79–80, 85, 88, 101, 106, 112, 115, 119–20, 127–8, 183–4, 307–8, 310–11, 324, 331, 333, 336, 340–2, 344, 347
Homeric hymns 68, 114
Homeridae 7
Horace 93, 121
    *Ars Poetica* 93–4
Hydaspes, river 123
Hyginus 36, 154

Iasus (-os), Caria 91, 161, 169–70, 174
inscriptions, theatrical
    *Didaskaliai (-sca-)* 83–4, 218, 327
    *Fasti* 167, 218, 326–7
    'Victors' Lists' 218
Isocrates 54, 253
Israelites, *see* Ezekiel

John Chrysostom 300
Justinian, Emperor 301

*Khristos Paskhōn* 323
*kitharistēs, see* citharode

Lampsacus 103
Lenaea, festival of 31–2, 59, 85, 151, 154–5, 167, 218, 335
*Letter of Aristeas* 126–7, 129
Libanios 311–12
Libya 130–1
Lipari 200
Longinus 314–16, 319, 344
    *On the Sublime* 314–15
Longus 87–8
Lucian 240–1, 297–9, 302, 306, 317–22
    *Podagra* 306, 321–2
Lycophron of Chalcis (Pleiadist) 16–17, 95–6, 99, 118, 120–3, 177, 251, 336; *see also* Alexandra
    *Suppliants* 292
Lycurgus, Athenian statesman 9, 20, 182, 188–90, 327–8
Lysias 39, 291

Magna Greca (South Italy) 110, 152, 191–2
    Capua 112
    Daunia 109
    Locri 119, 193
    Metapontum 151, 193
    Rhegion 165
    Tarentum 124
    Thurii 151
Magnesia on the Maeander 103, 163
Makrina 311
Marathon, Battle of 101
Marathus 101
Marsyas of Philippi 72
masks 6, 150, 198–200, 206, 301, 318, 338, 346
Mausolus, satrap of Caria 54
maxims, in postclassical tragedy 20, 98, 305
Maximus of Tyre 320
Melinno, lyric poet 116
    *Hymn to Rome (Suppl. Hell.* 541) 116–17
Menander, *see* playwrights (comedy)
Menedemus of Eretria 121
Mesomedes 226
metatheatre, *see* self-consciousness, in tragedy
metics 169
metre, tragedy 208–9
    and the dating of the Gyges fragment 104
    *apolelumena* (free-flowing lyrics) 209
    colometry 234, 337
    in the *Alexandra* 108, 115

in Chaeremon's *Centaur* 49–51
in Ezekiel's *Exagōgē* 142
tendency to avoid resolution in Hellenistic tragedy 16
Miletus 161, 173, 223
Miltiades 188
mime 123, 298–301, 303–4, 312, 318, 320
*mimesis* 318, 320, 325, 331
Mimnermus 37
Moiro or Myro 98
Moschus, pseudo-
  *Megara* 128
motifs, in postclassical tragedy
  anthropophagy 61
  burial of the dead 103, 282, 284, 286–92
  ethical contingency 263–9
  *parrhēsia* 283–6
  'Potiphar's Wife' 58
Mozart, Wolfgang Amadeus 232
Mummius, Lycius (Roman general) 166
music, in tragedy
  *chrōma* (colouring) 225
  *genē* (scales) 225–6
  'Greater Perfect System' 227
  *harmoniai* (modes) 226–7
  *mousikē* 37, 333, 342
  musical instruments, see separate entry
  musical notation in papyri 229–32
  tetrachord 225
  *tonoi* (tunings) 224
musical instruments 342
  *auloi*, see *aulētēs/aulos*
  *kithara* 227; see also citharode
  *magadis* 27
  *pandoura* 228
  *pēktis* 27
  *rhombos* 27
  *syrinx* 205
  *tibia* 214–15; see also aulos
  *typanon* 27

Naples 112, 115
naturalism, in tragedy 250–6
Nemea 164, 172, 218
Neoptolemus of Parium 93, 139
Nero, Emperor 216
  *Antigone* 216
  *Oresteia* 216
New Comedy 141, 243, 247, 249; see also chorus/choral song; playwrights, comedy (Greek)
'New Music' 210, 229, 257–8
Nicander 119
Nietzsche, Friedrich 2

Nine Lyric Poets, the 96
Nossis of Locri 98

Oenoanda 299–300
Old Comedy 38, 121, 325; see also Aristophanes
Old Testament/Septuagint
  Daniel, book of 113
  Deuteronomy, book of 144
  Exodus, Book of 17, 134–40, 143–4
  Pentateuch/Torah 126, 131
'old' tragedy (*palaia tragōidia*) 8, 25, 167–73, 175, 177–8, 181, 183, 185, 188, 198, 207, 217, 220–1, 233–41
Olynthus 100
Opous 164
Oppian/Pseudo-Oppian 120
*orkhēsis*, see dance

Palladion, theft of 71; see also *Rhesus*
Pangaeum, Mt. 72; see also *Rhesus*
pantomime 233, 297–304, 312, 317–18, 320
paradoxography, see Ezekiel
Parian Marble 97–8; see also inscriptions/theatrical
Parthenius of Nicaea 86
Peace of Antalcidas 8
Peloponnesian War 6, 86, 189
Peloponnesian War, First 72
Pergamum 20, 118, 165, 340; see also Attalid, dynasty; scholars/scholarship (entry: Crates of Mallus); Eumenes
Peripatos (Lyceum) 333, 335; see also Aristotle; scholars/scholarship (entries: Aristoxenus, Chamaeleon, Dicaearchus, Heraclides, Praxiphanes)
Perseus, king of Macedon 118
Persian Wars 101, 103, 109
Phasēlis (Lycia) 54
Philip II, king of Macedon 8, 100, 152, 189, 196
Philip V, king of Macedon 92, 94, 170
Philo, Jewish poet
  *On Jerusalem* 127
Philo of Alexandria 127–8, 135
Philodemus of Gadara 40
Philostephanus 119
Philostratus, Junior 316–17, 321
Philoxenus, dithyrambic poet 59, 229
Phlegon of Tralles 116
Phocylides 128
Phrynis 257, see also 'New Music'
Phylarchus 94
Pindar 70–1, 73, 108, 347
Plato 54, 212, 223, 233, 256, 279–80, 306, 309, 318, 325, 329, 331
playwrights, comedy (Greek)

playwrights, comedy (Greek) (cont.)
Alexis 31
Antiochus, L. Marius of Corinth 219
Antiphanes 31
Aristophanes, 1–2, 30, 38, 75, 181, 192, 197, 200–1, 207, 209, 213, 229, 235, 246, 272, 275, 314, 325, 328–9, 335, 339, 343, 347–8; *see also* Old Comedy
Ephippus 47, 59, 185
Epicharmus 85, 215
Eubulus 185
Menander 5, 48, 86, 185, 200–2, 214, 220, 246–7, 249, 272, 298, 305; *see also* New Comedy
  *Shield* (*Aspis*) 185
Philemon 180
playwrights, comedy (Roman)
Plautus 141, 214–15; *see also* actors/acting, *cantica*
Terence 214
playwrights, satyr drama (post-fifth century)
Lycophron, *see* Lycophron of Chalcis
Python of Byzantium 17, 121–2, 153
  *Agēn* 122, 153
Sositheus of Alexandria in the Troad 17, 95–6, 98, 121, 140
  *Aëthlius* 98–9
  *Daphnis or Lityerses* 140
playwrights, tragedy (fifth century)
Achaeus of Eretria 35, 328
Aeschylus, *see separate entry*
Agathon 35, 54, 76, 152, 188, 200, 204, 207, 209, 245–6, 261–2, 273; *see also embolima*; plots, tragic/invented plots; riddles
Carcinus I 38
Choerilus 325
Euphorion, son of Aeschylus 77
Euripides, *see separate entry*
Ion of Chios 327–8
Iophon 1, 327
Morsimus 31
Neophron of Sicyon 335
Philocles I 31, 335
Phrynichus 97, 111, 187
Pratinas of Phlius 328
Sophocles *see separate entry*
Xenocles I 38
playwrights, tragedy (fourth century)
Antiphon 15, 28–30, 62, 64, 185; *see also* Antiphon of Rhamnous
Aphareus 183
Apollodorus of Tarsus 154
Archestratus 178
Astydamas I 31
Astydamas II 8–10, 15, 26, 30–9, 65, 73, 88, 106, 177, 180–1, 183–5, 188–9, 202–3, 214, 246–8, 250, 253–4, 273, 276, 281, 332–3
  *Achilles* 32
  *Alcmeon* 35–6, 254
  *Antigone* 36, 65, 180
  *Hector* 10, 32–5, 88, 106, 202, 247, 250
  *Parthenopaeus* 10, 30, 180
Carcinus II 15, 26, 31, 33, 38–47, 58, 64–5, 82, 184–5, 187, 213, 248, 251, 253–4, 268–9, 332–3
  *Aëropē* 40–1
  *Ajax* 41
  *Alopē* 41, 47, 248, 254, 268
  *Amphiaraus* 41–2
  *Medea* 40, 42–3, 47, 65, 185, 187, 253–4
  *Oedipus* 43–5
Chaeremon 15, 26, 40, 47–54, 58, 64, 178, 184–5, 213, 251, 332
  *Achilles/Achilles Slaying Thersites* (Ἀχιλλεὺς Θερσιτοκτόνος) 48, 178
  *The Centaur* 49–51, 64
Cleaenetus 40
Cleophon 197
Crates the Cynic 61–2
Dicaeogenes 15, 185, 201
  *Cyprians* 28, 201
Diogenes of Athens 15, 26–7, 64
  *Semelē* 26–7, 256
Diogenes of Sinope 15, 27, 60–2, 64, 155, 177, 201
Dionysius I, tyrant of Syracuse 15, 29, 32, 59–60, 64, 151
Evaretus 39
Patrocles of Thurii/Athens 15, 30
Philiscus of Aegina 26, 61–2, 103, 155
Philocles II 31
Sosiphanes of Syracuse 15, 62–3, 97
Theodectas of Phasēlis 10, 15, 26, 41, 54–8, 64, 129, 154, 184, 187, 213, 247, 251, 253, 268–9, 276, 332
  *Ajax* 55, 253
  *Alcmeon* 55–6, 64
  *Mausolus* 54, 154, 187
  *Philoctetes* 268
playwrights, tragedy (Hellenistic)
Aeantides 95–6
Diognetus 93
Dionysiades of Tarsus/Mallus 95–6
Dymas 91–2
Euphronius 96
Ezekiel, *see separate entry*
Herodes of Priene 92
Homerus of Byzantium 93, 95–6, 98
Lycophron of Chalcis, *see separate entry*
Moschion 39, 96–7, 100–3, 111, 118, 187, 201
  *Men of Pherae* 97, 102–3, 201, 282

## General Index

Telephus 99–100
Themistocles 97, 102–3, 187
Phaenippus 93
Philicus of Corcyra 96, 101
Sosiphanes of Syracuse II 95, 98
Zotion of Ephesus 92, 156
playwrights, tragedy (Roman)
  Accius 216
  Ennius 141–2, 215
    *Hectoris lytra* 141
    *Medea exul* 141
  Livius Andronicus 123, 215
  Naevius 215
  Pacuvius 216
  Seneca 216, 304
    *Agamemnon* 216
    *Trojan Women* 216
Pleiad 95–102, 140, 142; see also Lycophron of Chalcis; playwrights, tragedy (Hellenistic)
plots, tragic 247–50
  historical plays 16, 97, 99, 102, 187–8; see also Gyges fragment
  intrigue plays 247
  invented plots 188
  melodrama 5, 16, 19, 93, 273; see also 'anti-tragedy'
  'overstuffed' plays 247, 249
Plutarch 33, 40, 60, 103, 178, 196–7, 233, 235, 308–10, 317–18, 331, 333, 342–3
Plutarch, pseudo- 236, 328
Polybius 94
Polyperchon 112
Polyxenus, dithyrambic poet 215
Pontus, cities of
  Heraclea 193
  Olbia 193
Priene (Ionia) 161, 173–4, 193
Pronomos, aulos player 228; see also vase-painting, Pronomos vase
Ptolemy II Philadelphus 93, 101, 117, 140, 165, 325
Ptolemy III Euergetes 336–7
Ptolemy IV Philopator 96
  *Adonis* 96–7
Puccini, Giacomo 232
Punic (Carthaginian) Wars 112, 117, 120, 165

Quintilian 344

rhapsodes 219
*Rhesus* by pseudo-Euripides
  and Thrace/Thracian cult/lore 16, 66, 68–9, 71–2, 86
  authenticity and date 83–6

  characters, see characters, tragic (sub-entries: Aeneas, Athena, Diomedes, Dolon, Hector, Muse, Odysseus, Paris, Priam, Rhesus)
  cletic hymn, in 67, 70
  dramaturgy and stagecraft 75–8
  language and style 78–83
  metre and diction 79–80
  number of speaking roles 77
  reception in antiquity 86–8
  reliance on passages from earlier drama 80–3
  scene and setting 66
  sources 68–72 see also Aeschylus, Euripides, Sophocles
Rhianus 128
riddles 57, 262
Roman tragedy 216; see also playwrights, tragedy (Roman)
Romanticism 2

Salamis, island 173
Salmous 153
Sappho 37
Sardenia 117
satyr drama 13–17, 35, 37, 50–1, 53, 75, 80, 92, 97–8, 101, 117, 120–3, 153, 156, 163, 168, 206, 211, 215–16, 218–19, 274, 339; see also dance in drama, *sikinnis*; playwrights (satyr drama, post-fifth century); Polyxenus
Schlegel, brothers 2, 4, 6
scholars/scholarship, ancient and Byzantine (on tragedy) 324–49
  Andromachus 98
  Aristophanes of Byzantium 85, 234, 327, 337–42
  Aristoxenus of Tarentum 225–6, 232, 333–4
    *Comparisons (of Dances)* 232
    *On Tragic Dance* (frr. 103–12) 232, 333
    *On the Tragic Poets* (frr. 113–16) 333
  Asclepiades of Tragilus 85
  Chamaeleon of Heraclea Pontica 333
  Crates of Mallus 83, 340–1
  Demetrius Triclinius 347
  Dicaearchus of Messene 334–5
    *On the Competitions at the Dionysia* 334
    *Hypotheseis of the Plays of Euripides and Sophocles* 334
  Didymus Chalcenterus
    *On Comic Vocabulary* 341
    *On Tragic Vocabulary* 341
  Dio Chrysostom 299, 302, 304–5, 309–11, 313–15, 317–19, 323, 331, 343
  Dionysius Thrax 344
  Dionysodorus 83
  *diorthōsis* 336
  Duris of Samos 333–4

scholars/scholarship, ancient and Byzantine (on tragedy) (cont.)
  grammatikē/grammatikoi 331, 340, 344; see also Dionysius Thrax
  Heraclides of Pontus 333
  hypomnēmata 20, 337, 345
  hypotheseis, see also in the present entry Aristophanes of Byzantium; Dicaearchus of Messene
  Iuba II, King of Mauretania 342
  kritikē/kritikoi 331
  lexeis 345
  Lives (Bioi, Vitae) of tragic poets 21, 335, 348
  Manuel Chrysoloras 347
  Manuel Moschopoulos 347
  Maximus Planudes 347
  Parmeniscus 83
  philologoi 340
  Pollux, Julius (Polydeuces) 200, 342–3
    Onomasticon 200, 342
  Praxiphanes of Mytilene 334
  Psellos, Michael 347
  Satyrus 26, 247
    Life of Euripides 247, 348
  scholia 20–1, 197–8, 334–6, 338–41, 345–8
  Sextus Empiricus 307–8, 310
  syngrammata 345
  Thomas Magister 347
  'Tales from Euripides' 334; see also in the present entry Dicaearchus of Messene
  Tzetzes, John 109 see also Alexander of Pleuron (Aetolus); Alexandria; Aristotle; Lycurgus; Pergamum; see also in the present entry Aristophanes of Byzantium; Lives of tragic poets
Schönberg, Arnold 125
self-consciousness, in tragedy
  allusion 260–3
  choral self-reference 257–8
  metatheatre 258–60
Sicily 45–7, 82, 110, 117, 149–52, 190–2
  Acragas 151, 215
  Aetna, Mt. 45–6
  Catana 151, 193
  Gela 150, 157
  Morgantina 193
  Segesta 113, 215
  Syracuse 151, 165, 215, 218
Sicyon 164, 218
Smyrne (-na) 161, 173
Social War 9
Socrates 325, 331
Sophocles
  Ajax 73, 258
  and actors' interpolations 83, 237

  and the Alexandra 100, 115
  and allusion in tragedy 261
  and the chorus/choral song 245–6, 258, 325
  and the 'death of tragedy' 1–2, 243
  and the edition of Lycurgus 236
  and the evolution of the tragic genre 15, 19, 270–6
  and music/song 204, 216, 229, 238, 244–5
  and 'old tragedy'/reperformance 177–8
  and pantomime 302
  and the Rhesus 68, 73, 75, 78, 80–1, 85, 99
  and rhetoric/tragedy as a rhetorical form 252, 276–83, 293
  and rhetorical instruction/practice 304, 311
  and the tragic canon 54, 180–5, 188–90, 213, 328–9, 332
  as actor 207
  as linguistic model in Late Antiquity 306
  diction 251
  Electra 30, 245, 250, 258
  in relation to fourth-century tragedians 33, 333
  in relation to postclassical tragic plays 8, 30, 35–6, 44–5, 55, 57–9, 64, 102, 243, 247–8, 287
  Iobates 58
  metatheatre 258–60
  metre 115, 211 see also scholars/scholarship
  Oedipus at Colonus 245, 249, 254, 256, 259–60
  Oedipus Tyrannus 8, 44
  Phaedra 58
  Philoctetes 245, 267–8
Sosates, Jewish poet 127
Sparta 107, 110, 189
Sphinx 57, 63, 261
Stesichorus 111, 119
Stobaeus, John 11, 39, 98–9, 102, 253, 323
structuralism 3
Successors/Successor kingdoms 93, 112, 191
  Antipater 99
  Cassander 99
Sulla 163, 166
Susa 153–4
symposia, and theatre 123, 196

Tatian 298, 300, 320
Teos 161, 165, 173, 221
Tertullian 298, 300, 319
theatre buildings 6, 193–4
Theatre of Dionysus (Athens) 9, 30, 180, 182, 188–9, 194, 218, 328, 347
theatrical machinery 194–5
  ekkyklēma 346
  mēchanē 187, 255, 346
Themistocles 102–3, 188
Theocritus 93, 97

Theodectas (-ctes), *see* playwrights, tragedy (fourth century)
Theodotus, Jewish poet
 *On the Jews* 127
Theognis 37, 120
*Theoi Adelphoi/Epiphaneis* 164
Theon 312, 316–17
Thespis 325
Thessaly 193
Thrace/Thracians, *see Rhesus*
Thucydides 94, 108, 111, 275, 306
Timaeus of Tauromenium 46, 111, 115, 119
Timotheus of Miletus 100, 119, 229, 238, 257

Troezen 109
Tyre 154

vase-painting
 'Cleveland Medea' 192
 Pronomos Vase 206
 'Würzburg Telephus' 192
Vergil/Virgil 87, 120
Vitruvius 324

'wandering poets' 92
Wooden Horse 119

Xenophon 101